SALES ADMINISTRATION
Principles and Problems

SALES ADMINISTRATION

Principles and Problems

BY

BERTRAND R. CANFIELD

Sales Management, Babson Institute

REVISED EDITION

PRENTICE-HALL, INC.

NEW YORK   1947

Copyright, 1938, 1947, by

PRENTICE-HALL, INC.

70 FIFTH AVENUE, NEW YORK

First Printing.......July 1938
Second Printing....April 1939
Third Printing...October 1939
Fourth Printing...March 1941

REVISED EDITION

First Printing...January 1947
Second Printing....April 1947

PREFACE

Numerous books have been written describing fundamentals of sales management. Other works have effectively presented actual problems arising in the management of sales organizations in many lines of business. But no attempt has been made heretofore to bring together, in one volume, a complete description of principles correlated with actual sales management problems.

The purpose of this book is to give students of business, sales executives, and others a simple and concise description of the principles involved in the solution of the paramount problems of sales administration. The successful application of these fundamentals by many companies has been described throughout the text.

The unsolved issues presented by sales problems challenge the imagination. The susceptibility of sales problems to several solutions affords opportunities for group discussion and exchange of opinion, which stimulates creative thinking. The reality of actual problems dispels the impractical aspect of a purely theoretical approach to the study of sales administration. Problems call for definite action and develop a capacity for executive responsibility. They induce analytical thinking.

However, intelligent consideration of sales administrative problems presupposes a knowledge of the fundamentals or principles which affect decisions on management questions. Experienced sales executives have learned many of these principles through observation and trial. Students lacking business experience must refer to recorded principles found in texts on sales administration.

Following a description of the principles of each phase of sales management are several problems, illustrating the application of the fundamentals recorded in the text. These problems are based on the actual experiences of business organizations in various lines of industry. Each concern is discussed under an assumed name. Company location and minor details are occasionally fictitious.

v

To save the time of executives and students, much detailed description of circumstances remotely affecting each problem has been intentionally eliminated. The problems, of recent origin, have been collected by field research of the writer and from numerous other sources.

Each problem is followed by a list of questions to guide the student in arriving at a sound solution to the difficulties presented, to test his judgment, and to stimulate thought and group discussion on the problem.

In addition to a general bibliography, a list of reading references follows each chapter, to suggest to students sources of additional information bearing on the particular problems appended to each chapter.

Valuable assistance in the preparation of this book has been received from numerous sources. The publishers of *Printers' Ink, Sales Management,* and other business magazines; the Dartnell Corporation; the authors of authoritative books on sales and advertising; and individual sales executives have all contributed the experiences of successful sales organizations. References indicate my indebtedness to many of these sources.

BERTRAND R. CANFIELD

BABSON PARK, MASS.

TABLE OF CONTENTS

PART IV—SALES PROMOTION

PART V—SALES POLICIES

PART VI—SALES ABROAD

SALES ADMINISTRATION

CHAPTER ONE

THE FIELD OF SALES ADMINISTRATION

What Is Sales Administration?   Sales administration is the direction of those activities and functions involved in the distribution of products and services.   It embraces:

1. The conduct and control of personal selling.
2. Advertising and sales promotion.
3. Sales research and planning.
4. The recruiting, selecting, training, equipping, stimulating, compensating, transporting, and supervising of salesmen.
5. The establishment of sales territories and routes.
6. Sales costs and budgets.
7. The development of sales policies.
8. The coördination of sales, finance, and production.
9. The development of new products.

The number and scope of each of these functions varies widely according to the size and character of a business and the type of products sold.

The field includes both domestic and foreign sales, although in many companies the two operations are administered separately. Retail as well as wholesale distribution is involved, although retail sales management is a specialized activity not ordinarily included in a discussion of sales administration.   As usually considered, the term *sales management* is applied to the direction of sales of manufacturing, wholesaling, and service organizations distributing finished or semifinished commodities and services.

The subject of marketing, as ordinarily presented, is broader than sales management and includes, in addition to selling, the functions of financing, warehousing, grading, inspecting, and transporting, which are all closely related, but not ordinarily considered in the field of sales administration.

3

The Importance of Sales Management. The work of the sales manager has rapidly grown in importance with the rise of mass production. The need for improved methods of distribution to keep pace with our expanding productive capacity has made sales administration one of the most important functions of business.

Several other factors created by World War II have contributed to the growing importance of sales management:

(1) The excess productive capacity created by war needs has been responsible for a greatly increased volume of industrial and civilian goods. Technical and scientific developments have resulted in many new products and materials for which markets must be sought.

(2) To maintain the American standard of living, the highest in the world, sound sales management has to make sales at lower prices so that more people can enjoy more of the world's goods as a result of their labors.

(3) Government has exercised more control over the distribution of commodities, which calls for sales management able to adjust marketing methods and policies to federal and state regulations.

(4) The greatly increased per-capita income of consumers has created new markets and opportunities for the sales executive.

(5) Never before has there been a greater need for goods and services to rehabilitate devastated countries. Sales opportunities in foreign markets have broadened the scope of sales administration.

(6) Rapid advances in air transportation have opened new markets for manufactured products both at home and abroad.

(7) Shifts in population and buying power have altered channels of distribution and created new problems for sales executives.

The Scientific Approach to Sales Management. Sales management is characterized by lack of scientific standards and methods. Few principles and little data exist upon which to base decisions. Sales managers are guided mainly by personal experiences and observations. This lack of scientific method in sales administration may easily be accounted for by the fact that the sales manager is dealing specifically with the human element in controlling his organization as well as in developing the market.

The field of sales administration has been slow in development. During the Industrial Revolution that began more than a hundred years ago, management concentrated on the operation of machines rather than on the understanding of people. Frederick W. Taylor,

H. L. Gantt, and Frank and Lillian M. Gilbreth, who first applied scientific principles in production management, doubled the output of men and machines. The success of these scientists in the factory encouraged a few scientific-minded executives to apply the same principles of planning and control to the operation of salesmen.

The late John H. Patterson, when president of the National Cash Register Company, a quarter century ago, introduced the scientific approach to the management of salesmen when he proved by extensive experiments that the one best way to make a sales presentation could be standardized and taught so that the least experienced salesman could make the same effective sales talk as the successful man. Eventually the standardized sales talk was adopted by many progressive sales organizations.

In 1916 the Bureau of Salesmanship Research was organized by thirty important companies employing a large number of salesmen to experiment with the selection and the direction of salesmen. The staff was composed of several psychologists and the sales managers of the coöperating companies. The Bureau devised a practical application blank and the first rating scale for selecting new men and rating the performance of salesmen in service.

The success of these measures encouraged Henry Dennison of the Dennison Manufacturing Company and others to analyze sales methods and prove that measurement and scientific methods could be applied to selling with the same success as had been achieved in production management.

A small but growing number of companies are applying scientific methods to the management of salesmen. This trend is most pronounced in the experimentation with psychological tests in the selection and supervision of salesmen. It has been estimated that more than three hundred companies are now using scientific methods of selection with favorable results.

The scientific approach to sales administration strives to eliminate waste, increase efficiency, reduce costs, and improve service. It is based on the use of facts in determining a particular course of action. The scientific approach to any problem applies to sales management and involves the following steps:

1. Stating the problem.
2. Collecting information about it by observation, interrogation, records, interviews, and analysis.
3. Drawing conclusions.

A typical example of the scientific approach to the improvement of salesmen's results is described by W. H. Lough, sales training specialist. A large food product manufacturer, distributing its products to grocers through driver salesmen, wanted to determine the effect of specific sales methods on the salesmen's volume. A list of selling tactics was prepared, including such activities as installing displays, checking stock, discussing a "special" before the regular order is taken, and taking the initiative in suggesting the quantity to order. Observers were sent into the field with salesmen to observe and record their use of these tactics. The effectiveness of each selling method was compared with sales results.

The company found that salesmen who had displays in less than 40 per cent of the stores on their routes obtained average orders of $3.31; while those who had displays in 40 to 80 per cent of their customers' stores got average orders of $4.55, or 37 per cent more. The salesmen who made a physical check of stock secured an average order four times larger than that obtained by the men who did not check stock. The men who discussed the current "special" before taking the regular order increased the average size of their orders from $3.55 to $4.49, or about 23 per cent. Taking the initiative in suggesting the quantity a dealer should order produced an average order of $6.17, against an average order of $3.48 when the dealer specified the quantity.

This company had never required its salesmen to follow these resultful methods, yet they were simple and practical methods which any man could easily use. As a result of this investigation, a nine-point plan of sales procedure was adopted with greater sales effectiveness for every man in the organization.

Scientifically minded companies have made similar researches in interviewing and demonstrating methods, time spent in travel, waiting, interviewing, difficulties encountered, territory coverage, methods of approach, and standard presentations, and extensive investigation of simple selling sentences. Much of this research has been done by individual companies and is of little value to concerns in other industries or to those in the same industry on account of differences in products, policies, and sales methods.

Coöperative research of general sales problems has been undertaken successfully in a few progressive industries, and much valuable work may eventually be done by competitors coöperating in investigating marketing methods. The Life Insurance Sales Research Bureau, supported by more than a hundred life insurance companies, carried on excellent research in recruiting, selecting, training, and agency management, while the American Gas Association has sponsored investigations in the scientific selection and training of salesmen.

The techniques of personal selling, recruiting, selecting, training, control, and supervision of salesmen, which are described in detail in later chapters, are all susceptible to the scientific approach to the end that sound managerial judgments may be made on a basis of fact rather than guess. The scientific method of dealing with sales problems opens the way to improvements in sales administration paralleling those that have been achieved in production management.

The Sales Manager. The titles of sales managers are as diverse as their responsibilities and include such designations as director of sales, marketing manager, distribution manager, sales and advertising manager, vice-president-in-charge-of-sales, field sales manager, and sales promotion manager.

The personal qualifications of men doing successful sales management include sales experience, leadership, teaching ability, personality, industry, knowledge of people, courage, imagination, fairness, analytical ability, self-expression, ability to command respect, loyalty and coöperation, business judgment, resourcefulness, and initiative.

The sales executive's work requires that he be a student of economic conditions and political and social trends, since they affect the operation of his business. The growing influence of government in business requires him to be a close student of legislation, controls, and taxation.

Functions of Sales Managers. The functions of sales managers vary widely according to:

1. The type of product sold.
2. Method of distribution.
3. Size of organization.
4. The personal abilities and inclinations of the men themselves.

In general, the responsibilities of sales managers include:

1. Sales research of products, markets, and methods of distribution.
2. Sales operation, involving department organization, recruit-

ing, selecting, training, contracting, equipping, compensating, stimulating, and supervising salesmen.

3. Sales control, which embraces the establishment of sales territory, routing, expense control, transportation, quotas, costs, and budgets.
4. Sales promotion, including assisting salesmen and distributors with advertising.
5. Establishment of sales policy.
6. Administration of export sales.

These functions may be grouped into two phases: administrative, or planning; and executive, or operating. Certain sales managers, by experience and preference, are primarily executives or operating men concerned with personal sales production, field supervision of salesmen, and work with distributors and dealers. These men have usually been successful sales producers before they became managers. Frequently they are of the aggressive, inspiring, leader type, with wide acquaintance in the trade, great physical energy, drive, personal magnetism, and enthusiasm. Much of their time is spent in the field contacting their men and outlets. As a result of this field activity, they have a first-hand knowledge of the market, of competition, and of strengths and weaknesses of salesmen and distributors which is invaluable in meeting changing conditions and taking advantage of sales opportunities.

This type of sales executive, however, frequently neglects the equally important function of administration or planning for sales. The administrative functions of sales management include:

1. Research of markets.
2. Study of distribution trends.
3. Development of policies.
4. Investigation of sales methods.
5. Analysis of operations.
6. Creation of plans and programs.

The manager who is successful in performing these administrative functions is a different type from the executive primarily interested in field operations. The administrator type is a student of marketing trends, an analyst of sales methods, operations, and costs, and a researcher of selling tactics. He observes and records facts about the work of salesmen, gathers all available records of the results of sales activities, and measures the effectiveness of selling methods. He is objective in his investigations, frees himself from preconceived opinion or other bias, and uses the scientific approach, gathering facts upon which to base his judgments.

Thoroughly dissatisfied with past accomplishments, the true sales administrator tries to improve his methods. He supplants preachments with clearly defined instructions which are founded on facts instead of intuition. He is constantly experimenting and testing sales methods in an effort to raise the caliber of his sales management to a new high level of efficiency and results. Instead of fault-finding, he suggests practical, workable plans for getting more business.

This type of administrator, sometimes described as a desk sales manager, often lacks first-hand knowledge of market conditions and competition, the strengths and weaknesses of his salesmen and distributors, and trends secured through close contact with field operations. He is more interested in making plans and is satisfied to allow others to carry them out. The ability to inspire and win the loyalty of his organization may be lacking. Frequently he has little interest in personal sales contacts and has limited experience in selling.

The "ideal" sales manager combines the abilities and characteristics of these two types of men. He is a good executive, as well as a good administrator and planner. However, the abilities to analyze and plan, as well as carry out plans, are rarely combined in one individual. As a result, the executive type is often a poor planner and administrator, and the administrative type is frequently a poor executive.

To overcome this natural deficiency in human nature, responsibility for the functions of sales management is sometimes divided between two men. One, an administrator, is made responsible for the functions of sales research, analysis of operations, plans, and policies; while another, an executive, is put in charge of field operations, supervision, and dealer and customer relations. This division of responsibilities insures proper attention to the two important functions of sales management by men who are personally qualified for these two different types of work.

The person in charge of administration is usually in authority and carries the title of sales director. The executive responsible for seeing that the sales plans and policies are carried out is answerable to the sales director and has the title of field sales manager or division manager. Sometimes the work of these two men is coördinated by a third executive to whom both report. This higher official may have the title of vice-president-in-charge-of-sales, director of distribution, or manager of marketing.

When the size of an organization permits, assignment of these two important functions to two qualified men provides greater efficiency and secures a well-balanced operation. In many organizations, particularly small ones, the sales manager was formerly a successful sales producer, and his abilities and interests qualify him for the duties of operating executive rather than those of an administrator. Furthermore, the need for personal sales production in small companies puts the emphasis on field work rather than on administration, with resultant neglect of the planning and research functions.

Failure by top management to recognize these two fundamental functions of sales administration frequently results in misunderstanding of what is required of a sales manager as well as high turnover among sales executives, weakness in organization, and improper division of responsibilities.

Place of the Sales Manager in a Business Organization. The position of the sales administrator has grown in importance in many companies until today he occupies a place in business organizations comparable with the treasurer and the production manager. He usually is directly responsible to the president of the company and, in many concerns, is a member of the executive committee. The title of vice-president is commonly held by a sales director.

A survey of three hundred member companies of the Chicago Sales Executive Club showed that 48 per cent of the presidents of member companies arrived at the top executive position in their organizations through sales management. Many heads of successful corporations were formerly salesmen and sales executives.

The sales manager's position has grown rapidly in importance in the past decade as the emphasis has shifted from manufacturing to distribution. Not many years ago the development of production methods commanded first attention by top management. Production managers who could make a product of good quality at a low price found favor in the eyes of management and rapidly gained promotion and greater income.

The growing demand for many products in new and undeveloped markets brought sales increases with comparatively little effort or initiative on the part of the sales manager. As markets became saturated and competition more intense, however, sales managers, who formerly were not permitted to have access to sales figures and profit and loss statements, were taken into full confidence by management. Their views on policies concerning quality and type of product were invited, and they were given responsibility for the establishment of prices, policies, and other important marketing matters.

Slowly sales managers were given more opportunity by production-minded managements to utilize their specialized knowledge of marketing conditions to distribute at lower cost, thereby insuring a larger volume of production through lower prices to consumers.

The position of the sales executive has assumed the greatest importance in those companies manufacturing specialties which require creative sales effort, such as electric refrigerators, oil burners, office equipment, and intangible services, for example, life insurance, advertising, and investments which must be sold in large volume. In staple, necessity lines, where demand is automatic, the sales manager is still, in many companies, of minor importance.

The trend toward higher specialization in marketing operations, which earlier characterized manufacturing, has also broadened the scope of the sales administrator. In many concerns the director of sales has the assistance of a staff of specialists in sales promotion, planning, research, training, dealer development, and advertising. The work of these specialists must be supervised and coördinated, which increases the responsibilities of the sales executive.

While decentralization of sales operations has relieved sales managers of a great deal of routine control, at the same time their supervisory responsibilities over branch, district, division, regional, and product managers have increased.

As scientific method becomes used more generally in sales administration, the increased efficiency and measurable results secured will increase the prestige of sales executives and bring greater recognition for their work.

Reading References

Fundamentals of Sales Management, Doubman, Chapter I, F. S. Crofts & Co., New York, 1937.

Introduction To Sales Management, Tosdal, Chapter I, McGraw-Hill Book Co., New York, 1940.

Sales Management, Nolen & Maynard, Chapter I, Ronald Press Co., New York, 1940.

Sales Administration, Hayward, Chapter I, Harper & Bros., New York, 1926.

CHAPTER TWO

PRODUCT RESEARCH

What Is Product Research? Product research is a study of the physical characteristics, uses, appearance, container, name, and other factors relating to a product or to its production as these factors affect its market.

Why Product Research? Since a product or service is the basis of every manufacturer's sales effort, a thorough understanding of the characteristics of the goods to be sold is fundamental to sound sales administration. The nature of the product affects:

(1) The amount and character of demand, (2) the channels of distribution, (3) the operation and control of salesmen, (4) the advertising and sales promotion, and (5) such sales policies as prices, credits, and adjustments.

Product research is often the source of: (1) increased sales, (2) broader markets, (3) improved morale on the part of salesmen and dealers, (4) revived advertising, (5) stabilized prices, and (6) new outlets.

Classification of Products as Basis for Product Research. To determine the principal marketing characteristics of a product, first classify the product with each item in the following check list:

1. *Commodity Type.*
    a. Consumers' goods—durable, consumption, staple, specialty, novelty, necessity, or luxury.
    b. Industrial goods.
        (1) Raw materials—oil, iron ore, coal.
        (2) Installations—presses, boilers.
        (3) Accessory equipment—small motors, typewriters.
        (4) Operating supplies—brooms, pencils.
        (5) Fabricating materials—cloth, paint.

2. *Retail Distribution Channels.*

   a. Convenience goods—soap, cigarettes, razor blades.

   b. Shopping goods—millinery, women's coats and dresses.

   c. Specialty goods—radios, golf clubs.

3. *Relation to Other Products in Line.*

   a. Single product.

   b. Side line.

   c. By-product.

   d. Special product.

   e. To complete line.

4. *Uses or Applications.*

   a. Possible new uses.

   b. Special uses.

   c. Variety of uses.

   d. Most frequent uses.

5. *Brand Name.*

   a. Does it suggest nature of product or qualities?

   b. Is it easy to pronounce and spell?

   c. Does it aid in selling?

   d. Does it indicate origin?

6. *Relation to Production.*

   a. Labor required.

   b. Unit of production.

   c. Seasonal production.

   d. Standardization.

   e. Simplification.

7. *Design or Appearance.*

   a. Does it suggest quality?

   b. Size, shape, and color acceptable to buyer.

   c. Utility.

   d. Novelty or distinctiveness.

8. *Capital Requirements.*

   a. New equipment needed.

   b. Plant additions or changes.

   c. New tools.

   d. Additional sales personnel and advertising.

9. *Service Requirements.*

   a. Extent of service.

   b. By whom service is rendered.

   c. Parts.

      d. Service personnel.
      e. Effect on cost.
   10. *Physical Characteristics.*
      a. Perishability.
      b. Value and bulk.
      c. Shape, size, and nature.

Marketing Implications of Product Classification. The market-ing implications of these product factors are varied. Consumer commodities usually have broad markets; women predominate as buyers; units of sale are small; buyers have little technical knowl-edge of goods bought; and motives of purchase are instinctive and emotional. Consumer staples and necessities are bought on a price or a utility basis; distribution is broad; price is low; and profit is restricted. Consumer luxuries and specialties, however, subor-dinate price and emphasize quality; experience an irregular de-mand; enjoy individuality by a special process, patent right, or packaging; are usually branded; and have broader profit margins.

Industrial commodities usually have limited markets; are bought by trained buyers; men predominate as buyers; units of sale are often large; buying motives are rational and are based on such fac-tors as economy, durability, and dependability; service is consider-able; sales are direct from maker to user; and transportation is important.

Services have both broad and limited markets, as in the case of life insurance and social welfare services. Price is often subordi-nated, and choice is made on the basis of prestige or reputation.

Classified according to retail distribution channels, consumer goods of a convenience type demand broad distribution and promi-nent store display. They are usually sold in small units, through wholesalers; are often branded; are bought at frequent intervals; and are rarely sold through exclusive agencies.

Shopping goods are usually bought in department stores by women. They are sold direct to retailers; brands are unimportant; price is predominant; and distribution is limited to a few outlets.

Specialty goods are usually branded, widely advertised, and sold through exclusive agencies and direct from maker to dealer. The sales price is often high, and repeat purchases are infrequent.

The marketing significance of a single product is its more effective sale through specialized effort, lower warehousing and selling costs, simplified sales direction, and increased turnover. On the other hand, side lines and by-products give salesmen and dealers variety in meeting competition, broaden the market, increase the unit of sale, and decrease the unit cost of selling and advertising.

The uses or applications of a product broaden old and develop new markets, give salesmen and dealers talking points, form the basis for advertising campaigns, and increase turnover.

The effective naming of a product aids consumer identification, association with other products in a line, and makes for sound advertising.

A proper coördination of the production of a commodity with its sale is essential to the success of a sales program.   Factory operations vitally affect product costs and ultimate prices. Balanced production and stabilized factory employment depend on sustained sales efforts.   Large orders lower factory costs, while special orders increase costs and prices.

The design and appearance of a product may provide material for sales campaigns, facilitate convenience in use, suggest quality, create distinctiveness, and stimulate salesmen and dealers.

Plans for the development of a particular product should take into account the capital required for production, as well as the sale and advertising of improvements.   Increased expenditures are necessary for launching new models, products, and packages, as well as popularizing new uses and names, or developing new channels of distribution.   Estimates of costs are an important consideration in product research.

Any development in products that requires mechanical service demands careful consideration of the need for service and the possibility of extending the free-service period or reducing the cost of service.   Electric refrigerator manufacturers have made mechanical improvements that have brought about increasingly liberal service policies.

The physical characteristics of a product have an important bearing on marketing policies.   A perishable product must be sold direct or through outlets located conveniently for the ultimate consumer. A very heavy, bulky product may demand special transportation policies.

Check List for Analysis of New Consumer Product. A manufacturer planning to market a new consumer product will find it helpful to answer each of the following questions concerning consumers, channels of distribution, competition, price policy, sales program, and legal and related problems.   This list was prepared by the United States Department of Commerce to aid manufacturers in analyzing the various market factors affecting new consumer products.

I. *The Users of the Product.*

1. What type of consumers will use the product?
2. How many potential prospects are there?
3. Where do they live?
4. Will the price of your product meet their requirements?
5. Will your product's price compare with existing products and with similar products which may be introduced?
6. Is the market likely to expand or contract in the next 2, 5, or 10 years?
7. How often will consumers buy the product?
8. Will the product sell evenly throughout the year or seasonally?
9. What features of the product appeal most to consumers?
10. Are the products of this kind usually bought on time payments (on an installed basis) with the expectation of service?
11. If bought on an installed basis, will the price include cost of installation?

II. *Channels of Distribution.*

1. Where and how are consumers accustomed to buying products of this kind?
2. If you expect to get your product into consumers' hands in some other way than through the usual channels, are the reasons for this decision valid ones?
3. Assuming that you will distribute your product through retailers, what kind of retail stores will sell it?
4. How much do you know about the operations of this type of retailer?
5. What is the best and easiest method of selling to these retailers?
6. How many wholesalers, jobbers, etc., are there who can logically handle your product?
7. What is the best and easiest method of selling to them?
8. If products like yours are usually installed or have the expectation of a service guarantee, will you conform?

III. *Competition.*

1. What competition will your product face?
2. What is the reputation of competitive products?
3. Are manufacturers likely to enter the field with similar products?
4. Can any competitor bring out a seriously competitive item quickly?
5. Will marketing your new product cause competitors to give you additional or keener competition on your regular line?
6. How does your company stand with relation to competitors in the field to be served by the new product?
7. Will you use your company name on the new product, or will you build up a brand name for it?
8. Can your product compete favorably on a price basis with similar products already on the market?

IV. *Manufacturer's Price Policy.*

1. Do you know what your price policy will be?
2. Have you determined who will be entitled to discounts and allowances?

3. Have you set up a discount and allowance schedule for distributors, wholesalers, retailers, and others?
4. Have you decided on your f.o.b. net pricing point and policies affecting credit, collections, returned goods, consignment, order cancellation, and retail price maintenance?
5. Have you considered insurance and transportation costs in determining your price?

V. *The Sales Program.*

A. *The Sales Force.*

1. Can your existing sales setup handle the new product?
2. If so, will changes or additions be necessary?
3. If a separate sales force will be required, have you determined how to set it up, how many and what kind of men you will need, how to pay them, etc.?

B. *Advertising and Sales Promotion.*

1. Have you an existing promotion and advertising setup which can handle the new product?
2. Have you a satisfactory advertising agency connection, or are you planning one for the new product?
3. Have you decided on the details of the advertising program?
4. Are you familiar with sales promotion practices followed by distributors in this field?
5. Are you familiar with sales promotion and advertising practices of competitors?
6. Have you determined what type and how much sales promotion assistance to give your own salesmen?
7. Are you planning an organized publicity campaign (as distinguished from advertising)?
8. Will your promotion and advertising budget be based on: (a) cost of attaining a definite objective; (b) percentage of estimate sales; (c) an arbitrary sum; or (d) some other system?

VI. *Legal and Related Problems.*

1. Is the new product patentable?
2. Is its trade mark protected?
3. Are all claims to royalties or other indemnities settled?
4. Do royalties limit the market for the product?
5. Is there anything in the product, its labeling or advertising which may cause you to become involved in a possible violation of a federal, state, or local statute or ordinance?
6. Will codes, trade agreements, etc., restrict its sale in certain areas?
7. Is there anything in your pricing policies, trade practices, or selling setup that might involve a violation of federal or other statute or ordinance?
8. Have local tax and other problems been considered?
9. Have all transportation problems been considered?
10. Are there any special postwar regulations which affect your product?
11. Are there any labor or union regulations which might affect your product?
12. Are there any other problems, peculiar to your product, that should be considered?

When to Analyze Products. Products may be classified and analyzed for improvement according to commodity type, retail distribution channels, relation to other products in the line, uses or applications, brand name, relation to production, design, capital requirement, service requirements, and physical characteristics, as enumerated in preceding pages, when:

1. A new product is selected for manufacture.
2. A product has reached its peak and sales are declining.
3. Competition must be met.
4. Demand changes through new styles, customs, or designs.
5. New inventions threaten to replace old products.
6. Excess productive capacity must be utilized.
7. Rapid obsolescence creates repeat sales.
8. Price levels decline or increase to such an extent that product changes are necessary.
9. Broader markets are desired.
10. New features are to be added to present products.

Failure to make a thorough product investigation may result in:

1. Loss of reputation through poor products.
2. Failure of sales and advertising campaigns.
3. Overexpansion of production facilities.
4. Loss of competitive position.
5. Declining sales.

Results of Product Analyses. Product analysis by manufacturers has resulted chiefly in product changes of:

1. Style and design.
2. Simplification or diversification.
3. Rebranding.
4. Repackaging.
5. New uses and applications.

The most outstanding product changes have been in design. Typical of such changes are those made by the Aluminum Cooking Utensil Company, which altered its utensils by smoothing bottoms, rounding corners, doming covers, flattening beads, and improving fittings.

Simplification has been undertaken in numerous instances to cut production costs, reduce inventories, and lower warehouse and selling costs. The leading automobile tire manufacturers have discontinued all but their two best grades of tires and eliminated third-grade and substandard tires.

Diversification, on the other hand, has resulted in a multiplicity of products for concerns that seek variety to meet competition. The Spencerian Pen Company, which had made one-cent steel pens since 1860, turned to manufacturing fountain pens. The Strom-

1. OUR PRODUCT

No.	QUESTIONS	THE ANSWER OF TODAY Date	SUGGESTS THIS ACTION BE TAKEN Date	CHECK UP RESULTS TWO MONTHS HENCE Date
1	How do we know our product fully meets the customer's needs, tastes, or ideas?			
2	Have we recently checked with our customers whether or not our product is satisfactory to them?			
3	Is quality of our product the best possible for the purpose or service for which it is designed?			
4	Can we increase the utility of our product? Should we re-design?			
5	Can we develop new uses for our product?			
6	Can we improve the appearance of our product?			
7	What other improvements if any would be acceptable to our customers?			
8	Does our product meet nationally recognized standards and specifications for goods of its class or kind?			
9	Are products of some other industry displacing our products?			
10	Are there products for which buyers are waiting that we should be developing?			

FIGURE 1. Questionnaire, prepared by the Industrial Committee of the New England Council, to encourage manufacturers to analyze products and take steps for improvement.

berg-Carlson Telephone Manufacturing Company, which had made telephones for thirty-five years, introduced radio sets and exceeded telephone sales in six years.

Changing a brand name often results from product-name analysis. The Colorado Fuel and Iron Company sold coal for years under the brand name of Diavolo. When investigation showed that the name was a handicap to sales, the new name, C. F. & I. Coals, was adopted and popularized with advertising. Runkel Brothers, Inc. felt that their cocoa and malt product, named Runkomalt, lacked individuality and gave the impression that malt was the most important ingredient. Therefore they changed the name to Runko, with substantial sales increases.

Package improvement has been a striking result of sound product study. Confronted with the problem of relating the various items in its extensive line, the Russia Cement Company, makers of Le Page's Liquid Glue, completely redesigned its containers, giving them a simple, uniform design.

By product study, new uses have been developed by many manufacturers. The Lewis Manufacturing Company, division of The Kendall Company, discovered more than a hundred uses for its cheesecloth and substantially increased sales. Hinds Honey and Almond Cream has been used for the treatment of chapped hands since it was first made in 1875, but product research produced some fourteen other uses that served as the basis for a powerful advertising campaign.

Who Analyzes Products? Suggestions for product development usually come from one of these sources: (1) laboratory, (2) products-development departments, (3) sales department, (4) officials or staff, and (5) friends, customers, or trade papers.

Product improvements proceed in The Goodyear Tire and Rubber Company as follows:

1. Research to discover product.
2. Research to develop method of manufacture.
3. Patent search for conflicting art and applications to protect product and process.
4. Semi-plant development in order to:
   a. Establish method of production and uniformity and quality of product.
   b. Establish costs.
   c. Feel out market acceptance.
5. Patenting of coverage on applications of product.
6. Sales research to determine market.
7. Sales exploitation to get market or consumer acceptance.
8. Sales service and further product development to meet needs that arise.
9. Designing and estimating cost of equipment based on sales expectancy.
10. Budget approval.
11. Organization of sales force.
12. Advertising.

Product development in the Tire Division of the United States Rubber Company is organized under a director of development. Under him are five departments—Technical, Tire Engineering, Tire Quality, Tube Quality, and Personnel and Expense Analysis. The Technical Department, through field engineers, maintains outside contacts with vehicle manufacturers' engineering departments, sales divisions, and trade associations. The Tire Engineering Department finds better methods of construction by testing and studying

the product.   The Tire Quality Department preserves and improves the quality of the product, as does the Tube Quality Department for tubes, while the Personnel and Expense Analysis Department is concerned with the business side of the tire development.

Specialists in product design are frequently retained.   Norman Bel Geddes has styled metal furniture for Simmons Company and weighing scales for Toledo Scale Company; Walter D. Teague has improved cases for Eastman Kodak Company; and Gustav Jensen has styled for E. I. du Pont de Nemours & Company.   The Norge Corporation, as a result of its appeal to the public for ideas as to the design of an electric refrigerator, received more than a hundred thousand responses, which were turned over to a famous designer to interpret into a new cabinet design.   Sales increased beyond expectation.

Internal product research is normally supplemented by investigation without the company, usually through consumer committees.

General Foods Corporation has on file the names of a considerable number of interested consumers, who form a permanent consumer jury for General Foods products.   Whenever a new product is contemplated or an old product repackaged, one of the first steps is to send the innovation out to the jury for its opinion.

A large candy manufacturer has a "Taste Jury" of one hundred and twenty-five men and women in the United States and Canada, which renders judgment on new flavors.   The Seminole Paper Corporation, a division of the International Paper Company, offered, in each roll of toilet tissue, to pay one dollar for every new practical use submitted.   In nine months more than one million suggestions were received, resulting in four hundred practical product ideas.

The Customer Research Staff of General Motors Corporation invites more than a million motorists a year to pool their practical points of view with the technical skill of General Motors engineers, stylists, and research specialists in the improvement of General Motors cars.   This research is conducted largely by questionnaires asking for opinions on style, finish, speed, power, starting, and brakes.

Product developments may also arise from a study of possible accessories to an existing product, as in the case of the Hurley Machine Company, which developed a stand for an attachment ironer used in connection with Thor Washing Machines.   Or, an investigation of existing products may show their possibilities for special uses, as in the case of the Vick Chemical Company, which added nose drops and cough drops to its established Vapo-Rub.   Listerine

2

MARKET AND SALES INFORMATION

(Information to be furnished by Market Research and Sales Department)

NAME OF PERSON FILLING IN THE INFORMATION

Total market per year ________ or, ________ Per Business day (310 days)

Expect to sell per year ________ or, ________ Per Business Day (310 Days)

This product will compete with ________

At price per ________ of ________

Proposed selling price per ________ of ________

Can we market this product with present sales force? ________

If not, what additional costs or changes in plans are necessary?

How many customers may we hope to obtain for this product? ________

Is this product for present customers or new ones? ________

Will our marketing this product help or conflict with sales of our other products? (Explain fully) ________

Are sales seasonal or steady? ________

If seasonal, what is busy period? ________

How many units must we carry in inventory? ________

Can inventory be at mill or must it be localized? ________

If localized, where are best distribution points?

Name largest competitors who market this product

Are customers specifications or requirements on this product unreasonably rigid making this a difficult product to manufacture? (Explain fully) ________

Estimated cost to sell, per cent of sales dollar ________ %

Estimated quantity of samples required first year ________ Units

Other Information ________

REVIEWED AND INFORMATION APPROVED BY

____

3

MANUFACTURING INFORMATION

(Information to be furnished by Manufacturing Department)

NAME OF PERSON FILLING IN THE INFORMATION

PRODUCTION

Have we facilities to manufacture this product? ________

If so, where ________

Present equipment can produce ________ Units per ________

What additional expense or changes of plans are necessary to prepare present equipment to manufacture? (describe fully) ________

How many days are necessary to prepare equipment for production?

If we have no present facilities to manufacture this product, what is necessary to provide facilities and how much time will be required?

Do the specifications on measurements, quality, etc., make production control and manufacturing difficult?

Is experimental or research work necessary before production can be started? (Explain and state time and expense necessary)

Other information ________

SAMPLES

Can we produce samples at once? ________

If we can, how? ________

What will sample cost at present? ________ Per unit ________

How many days required to prepare for production of samples ________

Other information ________

REVIEWED AND INFORMATION APPROVED BY

____

FIGURE 2. Market, sales, and manufacturing information sections of a four-page new product survey form used in planning product improvements by a New England paper products manufacturer. Page four of this form is devoted to "Financial and Cost Information," which is also considered in arriving at a decision to develop a new product.

has done likewise in adding tooth paste and shaving cream to its original antiseptic.

The desire for new uses for existing raw materials caused Worcester Salt Company to develop a tooth paste with a salt base. Related lines are often the source of new products, as in the case of Cluett, Peabody & Company, which decided to make cravats after twenty-five years of shirt making. A study of market demand enabled Kenwood Mills to overcome a seasonal slump by making summer blankets.

Since products are never static in their relation to these factors, constant product research is necessary. Radio receivers that were a luxury a few years ago are a staple today, with changed demand, market, and distributing methods. Many sellers resist product changes because of the fear of losing product identity, the cost of making production changes, the desire for standardization, the indifference to market changes, and natural aversion to change.

Problem 1—Design Improvement

Home Appliance Manufacturing Company

The Home Appliance Manufacturing Company, St. Louis, Missouri, established in 1910, and capitalized at $900,000, manufactures a line of electrical appliances including electric fans, ventilators, small room heaters, and a kitchen mixer which is branded "Mix-Aid." The line is sold by five salesmen to electrical wholesalers and large retail outlets throughout the country.

The leader in the line is the Mix-Aid, retailing for $18, with eighteen attachments for freezing ice cream; making bread, cakes, and pies; extracting fruit juices; slicing vegetables; and performing many other functions in the preparation of foods.

Little attention has been paid to the design of the product. It weighs eighty-five pounds. Its height makes it hard to store in the average kitchen, and weight makes handling difficult. The mixer is of an irregular shape surmounted by a fractional-horsepower motor.

The product has been on the market seven years, but annual sales have declined from a peak of 3,500 to about 1,200 units. The management believes that the product does not conform to present-day kitchen styles, which demand color and modern streamlining. The advisability of redesigning for lighter weight and improved appearance is being considered. The influence of a new design in stimulating salesmen and distributors, meeting competition, and opening new outlets are other reasons for changing the appearance of the product.

Industrial engineers, however, warn of the cost of retooling and of the equipment necessary to produce a new design. It is also contended that the product does not depend for its success on the decorative, fashionable, or style element. A new model will make obsolete all dealers' present stocks and the machines in the hands of consumers. The cost of designers' services is another obstacle. The practicality of a design from a production standpoint involving possibly new materials, labor, and finishes, is also questioned.

Questions

1. Should the Home Appliance Manufacturing Company undertake the improvement in design of its Mix-Aid? Give your reasons for favoring or opposing this course.
2. If the company should redesign its product, what steps should be taken to improve the design?
3. What will be the effect of a new design for Mix-Aid on the other products in the line?

Problem 2—Expanding Product Line

Rawley-Larson Plating Company

The Rawley-Larson Plating Company, established in 1935 in a West-coast city, has seventy-five employees in its job shop, which specializes in metal plating and finishing. During the war it subcontracted the plating of metal parts. Additional equipment was bought and an addition was built to the plant. Personnel increased to three hundred.

To provide work for its employees and utilize its expanded facilities, the company employed an engineer from an aircraft plant. He decided that the high freight rates on steel to the West coast made it advisable to manufacture items that required little material and much labor. The company was too small to afford the services of highly paid research engineers, so it was decided to make metal products of extremely simple design; for example, can openers, graters, strainers, pancake turners, and other kitchen utensils.

The limited capital and marketing experience of the company caused the management to select mail order houses as a channel of distribution. An official of the company could contact the limited number of outlets of this type with little sales expense. Advertising would be unnecessary. The company could control its own distribution. Large-volume orders could be expected and there was little credit risk. Accordingly the engineer in charge of manufacturing procured the current catalogs of the leading mail order houses and studied the designs of small metal products pictured in them. Certain advertised items were purchased and their features were analyzed. Three designing engineers were employed and put to work making designs which would improve the catalog items. The sales appeal of each item was carefully studied with a view to making its size, weight, utility, and color more attractive to consumers. Details of production were planned which took into consideration the available equipment. Costs were analyzed. Patent attorneys were consulted in order to get patent protection on unique features.

In expanding its line in this way, however, the company was confronted with several questions which cast doubt on the advisability of these developments. The field under consideration was highly competitive. Large, experienced manufacturers of metal specialities with great volume could make and sell more cheaply. By confining its distribution to a few large mail order houses, the company would be seriously crippled by the loss of one or two customers.

Questions

1. Should the Rawley-Larson Company have expanded its line by taking the steps described in the problem? Give your reasons for favoring or opposing this course.

2. What other steps should have been taken, if any, to adjust the company's operations to postwar conditions?

Problem 3—Diversification

Clark Cereal Corporation

The Clark Cereal Corporation, established in Kansas City, Missouri, in 1896, produces and packages a full line of breakfast cereals which are nationally distributed and advertised to the amount of $800,000 annually. The trade name "Mary Martin," featured in all of the company's advertising, is widely and favorably known to housewives.

Early in World War II the company began the manufacture of naval ordnance in its machine shops, where for several years it produced a large part of the special processing and packaging machinery used in its own plants. Nearly two thousand workers were employed in this work. With the approach of peace the company was faced with the problem of utilizing this personnel and facilities, which were far in excess of the company's needs for peacetime machinery.

After a thorough analysis of the markets for products which could be economically produced with the equipment available, the company decided to manufacture small electrical appliances associated with food preparation. The coffee makers, mixers, toasters, and other appliances to be made by the company would be merchandised under the well-known trade name of "Mary Martin." They would also carry the name, Clark Appliances, to capitalize on the company name and reputation. More than a million dollars had been invested in advertising these names over a period of many years.

A survey was made of various methods of distribution of electric appliances, and the company elected to distribute through the customary wholesale-retail outlets represented by independent dealers, such as electric utilities, department stores, furniture, chain, hardware, and jewelry stores, 20 per cent of which do about 75 per cent of the business. These outlets are served by three thousand two hundred appliance distributors.

The company believed it advisable to establish a separate division and field sales organization for its appliances. Fourteen district territories were established, each in charge of a district manager, and manned by appliance salesmen to call on the retail and wholesale trade.

It was considered advisable to make the appliance division a decentralized, self-contained enterprise which would "stand on its own feet" and earn a profit. A policy of making only high-grade, high-priced products rather than poorly constructed, highly competitive, low-priced appliances was adopted.

The decision to add this line of appliances to the company's well-known line of packaged food products was opposed by part of the executives who maintained that, in view of the company's long and profitable activity in merchandising food products, it would be a mistake to make and sell appliances.

Other executives of the company favored as an alternate plan the manufacturing of private-brand appliances and selling them to a limited number of large-volume retailers, such as mail order houses, chain stores, and department store syndicates. This would limit the sales expense and insure a high volume of sales.

Questions

1. Should the Clark Cereal Corporation have diversified its products by manufacturing and distributing electrical appliances? Give reasons for your conclusions.

2. Should the company have made private-brand appliances for large retailers only?

Problem 4—New Product

Mid-Western Time Corporation

The Mid-Western Time Corporation, Chicago, Illinois, established in 1923, and capitalized at $300,000, manufacturer of electric clocks, sells through jobbers and thousands of retailers an annual volume of two hundred thousand clocks retailing under $5. Sales are made by company salesmen operating out of the home office and branches in the principal cities.

During the war the company developed a new type of radio alarm clock which could be set by the user upon retiring to tune in a desired station automatically at a given time. This new clock radio would be compactly designed for travel and office, and so simple that it could be operated by plugging into any electric outlet. It would be housed in a cabinet made of plastic in a variety of colors. It would be priced at $65, which would be high compared with the prices asked for alarm clocks at that time.

Instead of being sold through regular clock-jobbing channels, the new clock would be sold through exclusive shops and stores patronized by a wealthy clientele, such as high-class jewelry, leather goods, and gift shops.

To increase unit sales, the company planned to pack the product in dealer packages containing four clocks, each a different color. This idea was for introductory purposes only, but aimed also at securing a display.

In diversifying its line with a radio, the company was confronted with several problems that made such a change questionable. The ill will of old-line clock jobbers and retailers concerned in selling the mass market at low prices seemed likely. There would be the expense of developing new channels of distribution, many of which had never before handled alarm clocks. The old, low-priced line would be supplanted by high-priced clocks.

Questions

1. Should the Mid-Western Time Corporation have:
   a. Introduced the high-priced radio alarm clock in addition to the old line?
   b. Continued to make the old line of low-priced, electric clocks exclusively?
   c. Made the high-priced radio clock exclusively?
Give the advantages and disadvantages of the course you believe should be followed by the company.

2. Would the new clock be in competition with the old?

3. Classify the new radio clock according to the list of factors given previously in the text.

Problem 5—Simplification

General Lumber Corporation

The General Lumber Corporation, organized in 1885 in Chicago, Illinois, had extensive holdings of timber, operated its own mills in the

South and Northwest, and sold a large part of its own output direct to retail lumber dealers throughout the United States.

The corporation produced lumber in a wide variety of grades and lengths, each piece branded with its trade name, "Tru-Grain," on which several million dollars had been invested in national consumer and trade advertising.

Seeking to reduce its inventory and to cut storage and sales costs, the company considered the simplification and standardization of its line by producing exclusively a coördinated system of machined pieces so that 75 per cent of the lumber entering into all usual construction would be ready for a carpenter to put into place in conformity with any desired plan.

The new product, called "Ready Fit Fabricated Building Lumber," would be sold in 10 basic framing members, 9 lengths of square-end board stock, 6 lengths of diagonal-end sheathing, all cut and of only one grade. The production of all other grades and sizes would be discontinued by the corporation.

The new product costs less to put into a building, eliminates waste lumber and freight paid thereon, and provides economical yet good-grade lumber for the purpose.

In spite of these improvements, it is contended that many carpenters will refuse to purchase the simplified product, and sales will decline. There will be a demand for a variety of grades and sizes by dealers and consumers. The General Lumber Corporation will be unable to keep up with competitors who make a wide line of building lumber. The cost of introducing the new simplified lumber will be great, and education of the carpenter will be slow.

Questions

1. Should the company produce and market exclusively its Ready Fit Fabricated Building Lumber? Give reasons for your course of action.

2. Should the company produce the new product in addition to its old line of many shapes, sizes, and grades? Give reasons for your answer.

3. What would be the effect of the new line on the several thousand dealers now handling the company's product?

Reading References

Directing Sales, Bonney, pp. 21, 22, 23, 24, 26.
Management of an Enterprise, Balderston, Karabasz, Brecht, Chap. III.
Market Analysis, White, Chap. VIII.
Modern Sales Management, Frederick, Chaps. II, III.
Planned Marketing, Reed, Chap. VI.
Pricing for Profit, Churchill, Chap. IX.
Principles of Marketing, Clark, pp. 30–34, 456–474.

Principles of Merchandising, Copeland, pp. 11–16, 27–31.
Printer's Ink Monthly:
"Selling What the Consumer Wants," by Ben Nash, Nov., 1930, p. 36.
"How New Products Grow," by Powers, Mueller, Resek, Dinsmore, May, 1934, p. 40.
Printer's Ink Weekly:
"Freshen Up Your Product," by R. Dickinson, Feb. 6, 1930, p. 3.
"New Products," by editorial staff, Sept. 3, 1936, p. 53.
"New Uses—New Markets," by E. Peterson, Apr. 19, 1937, p. 17.
"New Products—A Cure for Saturated Markets," by W. W. Hay, Jan. 22, 1931, p. 81.
"Give Business New Products to Sell," by C. F. Kettering, June 25, 1931, pp. 92–97.
Sales Administration, Hayward, Chaps. II, III, IV, XXVII.
Scientific Sales Management Today, Hoyt, pp. 31, 43, 137.
Selling Policies, Converse, Chaps. I, II, VI, IX, pp. 142–149.

CHAPTER THREE

MARKET RESEARCH

What Is Market Research? Market research is the study of all problems relating to the transfer and sale of goods and services from producer to consumer. The two principal fields of market research are:

1. General research of consumption, standards of living, and purchasing power.
2. Individual research of specific marketing problems for formulation of policies and sales methods, solution of sales problems.

Typical objectives of market research are:

1. To discover and evaluate unexploited markets.
2. To secure a better knowledge of the types of consumers, their purchasing power, buying motives, and needs in present markets.
3. To supply facts for determining sales quotas and budgets.
4. To determine advertising appeals, appropriations, and desirable media.
5. To discover distributors' methods and points of view.
6. To establish sales territories or branches.
7. To determine business conditions as a guide to sales expansion.
8. To discover the nature and strength of competition.
9. To discover the real cause of sales resistance.
10. To determine price policies.

Conducting Market Research—Stating the Problem. In the beginning, the nature of the market research should be stated specifically, and its purpose and scope defined. The general objective of the research should first be determined. For example, the general research objective of a stove manufacturer may be to increase sales and profits. To attain this general objective, first determine the immediate objectives. An immediate objective may be an answer to the question, What are the reasons our salesmen are not selling more stoves? This question would involve an internal study, which would give rise to another question, namely, Why are consumers not buying our stoves? This question, in turn, calls for an external consumer survey.

What Information Is Needed? When the general and immediate purposes of the research have been determined, the next step is to determine what information is needed. The facts required are, of course, determined by the nature of the immediate objective. List the information needed in the form of questions; for example. Why are our customers not buying our stoves? What features do not appeal to them? Do they like the design? Are our stoves competitive in price, quality, size, style? Thorough study of the objective will suggest many such questions.

Where Is the Information to Be Secured? When the information required has been listed, the next step is to determine where it can be found. The two general sources of facts: within the organization and in the outside market.

Internal sources are financial records, sales reports, correspondence, and sales records, as well as the experiences and judgments of company executives and salesmen.

External sources of facts are: researches of government agencies, publications, trade associations, colleges, and advertising agencies relating to the characteristics of consumers, amount and trend of demand, competition, and purchasing power.

Who Should Be Questioned? Closely related to the method of securing the information is the question, Who should be questioned in the investigation? Two methods are commonly used in selecting respondents in market surveys:

1. The *random* method in which every person has an equal chance to be questioned.

2. The *controlled* method in which the persons to be questioned are selected in terms of age, sex, income, geographical location, race, and customers or noncustomers.

The random method is used in telephone and mail surveys when persons are selected at random for questioning. It is a suitable method when the number of respondents is neither very large nor very small. In making a mail survey by this method, question-

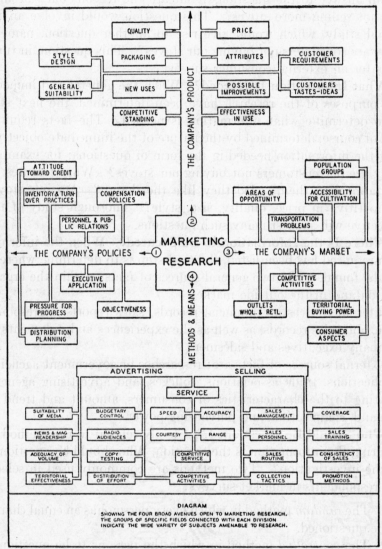

THE COMPANY'S PRODUCT

QUALITY   PRICE

STYLE DESIGN   PACKAGING   ATTRIBUTES   CUSTOMER REQUIREMENTS

GENERAL SUITABILITY   NEW USES   POSSIBLE IMPROVEMENTS   CUSTOMERS TASTES-IDEAS

COMPETITIVE STANDING   EFFECTIVENESS IN USE

ATTITUDE TOWARD CREDIT   POPULATION GROUPS

INVENTORY & TURN-OVER PRACTICES   COMPENSATION POLICIES   AREAS OF OPPORTUNITY   ACCESSIBILITY FOR CULTIVATION

PERSONNEL & PUBLIC RELATIONS   TRANSPORTATION PROBLEMS

②

MARKETING

THE COMPANY'S POLICIES ← ① RESEARCH ③ → THE COMPANY'S MARKET

④

METHODS & MEANS

EXECUTIVE APPLICATION   COMPETITIVE ACTIVITIES

PRESSURE FOR PROGRESS   OBJECTIVENESS   OUTLETS WHOL. & RETL.   TERRITORIAL BUYING POWER

DISTRIBUTION PLANNING   CONSUMER ASPECTS

ADVERTISING   SELLING

SERVICE

SUITABILITY OF MEDIA   BUDGETARY CONTROL   SPEED   ACCURACY   SALES MANAGEMENT   COVERAGE

NEWS & MAG READERSHIP   RADIO AUDIENCES   COURTESY   RANGE   SALES PERSONNEL   SALES TRAINING

ADEQUACY OF VOLUME   COPY TESTING   COMPETITIVE SERVICE   SALES ROUTINE   CONSISTENCY OF SALES

TERRITORIAL EFFECTIVENESS   DISTRIBUTION OF EFFORT   COMPETITIVE ACTIVITIES   COLLECTION TACTICS   PROMOTION METHODS

DIAGRAM
SHOWING THE FOUR BROAD AVENUES OPEN TO MARKETING RESEARCH.
THE GROUPS OF SPECIFIC FIELDS CONNECTED WITH EACH DIVISION
INDICATE THE WIDE VARIETY OF SUBJECTS AMENABLE TO RESEARCH.

Copyright by Ferdinand C. Wheeler

FIGURE 3. Marketing research involves a study not only of the individuals or concerns comprising a market, but also of the product, methods of distribution, sales policies, advertising, and personal selling.

naires may be mailed to every fifth, tenth, or twentieth person on the list.

The controlled method requires an exact definition of the types of persons or concerns to be questioned, data about the individuals selected, and determination of such factors as age, income, and sex, which are to be controlled. Sometimes data are not available on individuals or concerns, and the relationship between the information secured and the characteristics of the respondents is difficult to determine.

Only by using the controlled method, however, can researchers be sure in advance that the returns will come from the type of persons or concerns originally selected for questioning. This method is usually used with personal interviews. When the investigator is required to interview specific types of persons or concerns there is less opportunity for bias than there is when he selects respondents at random.

How Many Should Be Questioned? When the group to be surveyed is small and accessible, everyone can be questioned. When those to be questioned are too numerous to be interrogated individually, the large number may be divided into small, representative groups or "samples" for questioning. The size of the sample is an important consideration. The larger the sample the greater the possibility that the survey findings will be closer to the reaction of all individuals in the field. Usually an arbitrary number of individuals is selected for questioning.

Statisticians have prepared tables to determine scientifically the size of a sample. These tables are used in determining the number of responses required for a predetermined degree of accuracy. While they are statistically accurate, the value of these tables is questioned by certain market research authorities who believe that the many variables in marketing make them unreliable. Many other experts believe that statistical tables may be helpful in estimating the size of a sample.

Another statistical method of computing the size of a sample is to check the divergence in response by standard deviation and prepare a stabilization chart showing the gradual approach of the curve to a static position.

Drafting the Questionnaire. When the objectives of a market survey have been determined, the nature of the information desired and method of collecting the data decided upon, then the drafting of the questionnaire is the next step.

Phrasing the Questions. The phrasing of questions in a questionnaire is determined by such factors as the type of survey, the respondents, the length of the questionnaire, the subject of the survey, and type of interviewer. To secure reliable information, the questions should be worded so that they are clear, objective, concise and specific. They must not be misleading or embarrassing to

The Wrong Way	The Right Way
General Question: What do you think of advertised products?	*Specific Question:* Why did you last buy *x* product?
Embarrassing Question: How many baths do you take a week?	*Tactful Question:* A famous specialist says one should bathe daily. What do you think about it?
Ambiguous Question: What kind of hosiery do you buy?	*Clear Question:* What color of hosiery do you buy?
Leading Question: Isn't this a beautiful pattern?	*Nonleading Question:* Of these several patterns, which do you prefer?
Misleading Question: Would you buy this dress made of costlier materials?	*Straightforward Question:* Would you buy this dress?

Figure 4.

"FM" RADIO STUDY
CONSUMER SCHEDULE

(Questionnaire used by investigators in making a market survey of owners of Frequency Modulation radio receivers)

1. Have you a radio equipped with "FM" in your home? (If not owned, skip to Question 21.)
Yes .... No ....

IF YOU OWN AN "FM" SET, ANSWER THE FOLLOWING QUESTIONS:

2. What make (brand) is it? ....
3. What type set is it? ....
Phono Combination.... Console....
Table Set .... Translator ....

4. In buying this radio, *what three things* appealed to you most?
a. ....
b. ....
c. ....
    (Check most important)

5. Are you satisfied with the quality of reception you get on "FM"? (Please base your reply on the quality of reception *only* and *not* on the number of stations or the type of programs you are able to tune in.)
Yes .... No ....

6. IF NO:
In what way are you dissatisfied with it? ....
....

7. In your opinion, what are the advantages of "FM" reception?
1. ....
2. ....
3. ....
    (Check most important advantage)

8. In your opinion, how does the quality of "FM" reception compare with regular broadcast reception?
Great improvement ....
Somewhat of an improvement ......
No improvement ....
Comment ....
....

9. About how often is your radio played on "FM"?
Several times a day.. Once a day..
Several times a week... Seldom...
Comment ....
....

10. How many "FM" stations can you tune in? ....

11. How many of these "FM" stations come in? ....
Satisfactorily?.. Unsatisfactorily?..
Comment ....
....
....

12. Do you tune in "FM" stations with the tuning knob or with push buttons?
Tuning knob ....
Push buttons ....
Both ....
Explain why ....
....
....

13. Do you use a built-in or outside dipole aerial for receiving "FM" programs? ....
Built-in dipole... Outside dipole...

14. IF OUTSIDE: Did you purchase it: At the time you bought your set?....
Later? ....
Comment ....
....

15. IF BUILT-IN: Why don't you use an outside dipole? ....
....

16. How was "FM" first brought to your attention? ....
....
....

17. Where did you first hear an "FM" radio?
Dealer's store...... Home of friend or relative......... Other.........
(Specify)

18. Have any of your friends listened to "FM" on your radio?
Yes .... No ....

19. IF YES: What was their opinion of it? ....
....
....

20. Would you recommend a set equipped with "FM" to your friends?
Yes .... No ....
Comment ....
....
....

(Skip to Question 25)

NON-OWNERS:

21. Have you purchased a console or radio-phonograph combination within the past three years?
Yes .... No ....

22. IF YES:
a. What was the approximate (list) price of this set? $............
b. Did you consider the purchase of a set equipped with "FM" at the time you bought this set?
Yes .... No ....
c. Why did you decide to buy this set in preference to one equipped with "FM"?
....
....
....

23. Have you heard or read of this new type (FM) of radio broadcasting?
Yes .... No ....
a. IF NO: Interviewer should explain briefly the principal advantages of "FM" reception, present booklet and skip to Question 24.
b. IF YES: (1) In what way(s) was "FM" brought to your attention?
....
....
(2) Have you heard an "FM" radio?
Yes .... No ....
(3) IF YES: Where were you at the time?
Dealer's store ....
Home of friend or relative....
Other ....
(Specify)
(4) What did you think of it?....
....
....
....

24. What advantages of "FM" reception appeal to you?
Elimination of noise and static......
Improved quality (wider range) of tone ....
No station overlapping ....
No station fading ....
(Double check most important)

ASK ALL RESPONDENTS:

25. Have you heard the Frazier Hunt news broadcast on the Columbia network?

    Yes ....   No ....

    a. IF YES:
       (1) At what time does the broadcast come on? ...o'clock...M
       (2) What company or product does it advertise? ....

26. How many radios have you in your home and how old are they?

How Many?	*Makes*	*Age of Each*

Phono-combinations

Consoles

Table Sets

Portables

		Est. Inc. Group
Name		
Address		A(over 5-M)...
City & State		B(3-5M) ...
Date Interviewed		C(2-3M) ...
		D(1-2M) ...
Name of Interviewer ..		Man
		Woman

the person answering, and must be arranged in such order that answers to one question will not be influenced by the preceding queries.

The above examples (p. 34) of questions which violate these principles and the rephrasing of these questions illustrate the proper ways to word questions in a questionnaire.

Form of Questions. The general types of questions used in surveys are:

1. Yes-no questions: Do you fish?
2. Multiple-choice questions: Do you fish?
   a. A great deal?
   b. Occasionally?
   c. Rarely?
   d. Not at all?
3. Free-response question: How do you judge coffee?

The choice of type of question depends on the person to be interviewed, the survey method, and the number of persons questioned. Questions must be stated so that replies can be easily summarized.

The first questions should be interesting, simple, and designed to get the coöperation of the persons questioned. Also questions of special importance should be placed toward the beginning before the respondent tires. General attitudes should be determined first and specific preferences later in order to put respondents in the proper frame of mind to answer specifics. Questions which might be of little interest, embarrassing, or reflect on the respondents' pride or intelligence should be placed toward the end of the questionnaire. One question should lead to the next so that a train of thought is established.

"Reason Why" Questions. In order to measure a respondent's motives and opinions, the best current practice is to ask a series of related questions designed to uncover motives. Dr. Paul Lazarsfeld is author of this method which assumes that an action is induced by several reasons arising from the respondent's own purposes and attitudes; an advertisement or the attributes of the commodity, such as color, style, and price. Accordingly, specific questions are asked to reveal attitudes and influences which motivate action rather than a single query, for example, "Why do you buy?"

How General Motors Phrases Questionnaires. In phrasing questionnaires, the Customer Research Section of the General Motors Corporation gives the following instructions:

1. Design the question so that it cannot be misunderstood.
2. In dealing with technical features, emphasize effects.
3. Be good natured, avoid insincerity, and ballyhoo.
4. Employ words in common usage.
5. Since you are asking a favor, observe the principle of "give and get."
6. Questions on any series of items should all be asked the same way.
7. Guard against anything that will create bias in the mind of the buyer.
8. Arrangement of questions should facilitate flow of thought.
9. Ask questions in the same way in subsequent questionnaires.

Length of the Questionnaire. The number of questions in a questionnaire is determined by the survey method, the type of person questioned, and the time and place where the questioning takes place. The interest of the respondent in the information sought is an important factor in the length of the questionnaire. Photographers are so interested in cameras that a questionnaire on this subject to this group may be quite long. A questionnaire to housewives on the subject of washing dishes must be brief because of the limited interest in this task. In general, questionnaires should be as short as possible to secure the desired information and at the same time conserve the time of the interviewer and those questioned.

Testing the Questionnaire. To insure that a questionnaire is properly drafted and that questions are clear, objective, not leading, the right length, and phrased to secure the necessary information, it is desirable to test the questionnaire in a few personal interviews before it is used widely. Questionnaires are often revised eight or more times before they are put in final form. In addition to testing the questions, the research procedures, such as the method of collecting data, the type of respondents, nature of the sample, and instructions to investigators, may also be tested. Testing is often valuable in producing suggestions for additional subject matter, elimination of questions, and tabulation.

Collecting the Data—How Is the Information to Be Secured? Two general classes of market information are recorded and unrecorded information.

1. *Recorded data* are those which have been collected by concerns which make a business of collecting market facts such as Standard Statistics, Babson Reports, Inc., Brookmire, Moody, and Poors statistical services; government sources as the U. S. Department of Labor, Bureau of Foreign and Domestic Commerce, Bureau of Census, Federal Trade Commission, Department of Agriculture; advertising media as International Magazine Company, Curtis Publishing Company, Crowell Publications, *New York Times;* National and Columbia broadcasting companies; educational institutions including Harvard School of Business Administration, New York University; research foundations as National Industrial Conference Board, National Bureau of Economic Research and Brookings Institution; business associations as the Cotton Textile Institute, National Electric Manufacturers' Association, Copper and Brass Research Association, Life Insurance Sales Research Bureau, American Federation of Labor; advertising agencies as the J. Walter Thompson Company; business magazines as *Sales Management, Printer's Ink, Advertising and Selling,* and *Progressive Grocer.*

Recorded data may be obtained direct from these sources or their research reports may be found in business libraries in the principal cities.

Data may also be found in the records of the company for which the survey is being made. From this source, records of sales by products, seasons, territories, type of distributor, and similar classifications will provide essential information in certain types of surveys.

2. *Unrecorded data* are those which must be collected from original sources by mail, telephone, personal interview, or a combination of these methods.

Mail Surveys. The principal advantage of collecting data by mail questionnaire is its economy in reaching widely scattered concerns or individuals. This type of survey eliminates bias and anonymity. It permits individuals time to answer fully and secures responses from persons who would be difficult to reach in person. As a field staff is not required, the cost per interview is generally low. The disadvantages of a mail survey are that the responses may be superficial and not representative of the group to which the questionnaire has been mailed. Many will not trouble to answer a mail questionnaire, and therefore a low percentage of replies may be received. However, the majority of market investigators probably use this method. The General Motors Corporation has distributed more than a million questionnaires by mail annually to motorists to determine their preferences in automobiles.

Telephone Surveys. Information can be secured more rapidly by telephone than by any other survey methods. Persons otherwise difficult to reach may be interviewed readily and without difficulty. The cost per person interviewed is lower than it is by mail or personal inquiry. The type of person interviewed can be easily selected and the area controlled. When definite facts rather than opinions are desired, this method may be very effective.

Telephone interviews, on the other hand, must be limited in time and scope and are not practical when the questionnaire is lengthy or when an analysis of attitude, comments, and discussion is desired. The telephone cannot be used in rural areas. It is impossible to classify respondents by buying power, income, age, and nationality, but only persons in the higher income brackets are reached. In spite of these disadvantages, telephone interviews have been widely used, principally by the radio audience measurement services. If a few, brief, factual questions are asked, this method may be effective.

Personal Investigations. Personal investigations involve personal calls by selected and trained interviewers. This method is considered the most effective means of securing extensive information together with comments, attitudes, interpretation, and discussion from respondents. The types of persons interviewed can be closely controlled by age, income, standards of living, etc.

The high cost of a personal interview is the principal objection to this method. Other weaknesses of the personal interview are that the interviewer may bias the responses or select the wrong individuals to interview. This method also takes considerable time.

Personal investigations require proper organization and operation which involve the selection and training of personnel, routine for conducting the study, preliminary test of plan and personnel, supervision of field work, and editing of returns.

The research staff should be selected with respect to the characteristics of the persons to be interviewed, business experience, education, appearance, reliability, ability to contact people, and health. Investigators should be trained:

1. To avoid bias.
2. To record replies.
3. To be honest.
4. To follow instructions.
5. To have the proper attitude
6. To know the purpose of the survey and upon whom to call.

The method of conducting the survey should be determined in advance, and include:

1. The area to be covered.
2. The time when calls are to be made.
3. Method of coverage.
4. Instructions to investigators as to:
   a. Selection of respondents.
   b. Approach.
   c. Opening remarks.
   d. Method of questioning.
   e. Payment of investigators.
   f. Supervision.
   g. Editing.

Supervision of the investigators is important to insure effective interviewing, freedom from bias, proper coverage, and accuracy, and to be certain that the interviews reported have actually been conducted and that the information reported is that which was secured.

When completed, questionnaires should be turned in by the investigators and examined for completeness, contradictory or incorrect replies, and errors on the part of interviewers. At the same time answers may be classified or coded, and important comments recorded.

Combination Surveys. Two or more of the previously described methods may be combined when obtaining market data. Factual information may be secured from inaccessible respondents by telephone in cities; the mails may be used to reach large numbers of widely scattered persons; and personal interviews used when questions call for comment or discussion.

Organization of Data. After the information has been collected, it must be classified for summarization. Classification means organizing data having similar characteristics into one group so that they can be considered simultaneously. In a complex survey there are too many elements or statements to be considered individually so they must be classified or grouped. Classification is very difficult unless questions require only yes or no for answers. An excellent discussion of the psychological technique of classification may be found in Chapter Twelve, The Technique of Marketing Research.

After answers have been classified, they should then be tabulated by hand or machine. In machine tabulation, each response is numbered. The number is punched on a card. By running all cards through a sorting machine, a figure representing the total number of times each figure is punched is obtained. The final summary of figures is then converted into terms that serve as answers to the original questions.

Conclusions and Report. When the data are summarized, they are interpreted; conclusions are drawn; and results presented. Each item is weighed to determine its significance in the study. Tentative conclusions are reached, followed by final conclusions.

A report is prepared, in which the problem is stated, the survey method described, and the conclusions presented. These may be illustrated with graphs, charts, or maps.

Who Should Conduct Market Research? Market research may be undertaken by one of the following:

1. A market research department.
2. An outside research organization.
3. A trade association research department.
4. An advertising agency.
5. Government, educational, or consumer organizations.
6. Advertising media.
7. The sales organization.

The choice of facilities for market research depends upon the scope of the research problem and the funds available, but a growing number of concerns are providing for research within their own organizations. The market research department may be a part of the sales department or a separate division responsible to the general management. The advantages of the latter form of organization are that the findings of the department are free from bias, unhampered by the unsympathetic direction of a sales-minded executive; and all departments of a business may profit by its work.

Sales Analysis and Research Organization. A large manufacturer of plumbing supplies and equipment conducts market research through three people attached to the planning section in the executive offices and in the sales department. This group conducts internal research through analyses of salesmen's reports and product sales, and also forecasts sales. Under the direction of the sales department occasional field research is undertaken on selling problems.

A large radio manufacturer has organized a Sales Analyzation Department for internal sales research under the direction of a sales accountant. A large manufacturer of electrical equipment has organized its sales research activities into two sections: one called Market Analysis, whose responsibility is to determine the available business; and a second called Sales Direction, which develops plans and methods for securing the available business disclosed by the Market Analysis section. A manufacturer of textile specialties, with two operating divisions, has a sales research department for each division. Each has an executive head with from two to five assistants. The activities are fixed by the executive manager of each operating division.

Because a concern has access to its own sales records, sales analysis is usually undertaken within the organization, but frequently outside research organizations are employed for field research. As field research is often intermittent in character, it is usually more profitable to engage outside aid for this work. Outside research organizations have an unbiased viewpoint, broad research experience and experienced field men in the principal cities. One such organization claims to have more than fifteen hundred field investigators working out of thirty offices, rendering a nation-wide investigation service on a basis of from twenty-four to seventy-two hours.

Government agencies, particularly the Bureau of Foreign and Domestic Commerce of the United States Department of Commerce, have made extensive market surveys and collected valuable information on markets in the books entitled "Market Data

Handbook of the U. S.," "The Commercial Structure of New England," and "Atlas of Wholesale Grocery Territories."

The business departments of numerous colleges and universities, particularly Harvard School of Business Administration, New York University, and Ohio State University have conducted unbiased, scientific investigations of markets in various industries.

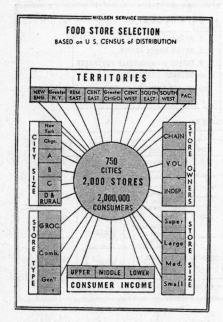

NIELSEN SERVICE

PRINCIPLES OF NIELSEN INDEX AUDITING
"BLANK" BRAND BAKING POWDER
IN JOHN DOE'S FOOD STORE

FOR DEC.-JAN. 1939

PURCHASES:	NO. OF ORDERS	PKGS.	VALUE
FROM MANUFACTURER	1	24	$7.00
FROM WHOLESALERS	10	62	19.10
TOTAL		86	$26.10

INVENTORY:	
JANUARY 1	114 Pkgs.
MARCH 1	93 "
CHANGE	21

CONSUMER SALES	
PACKAGES	107
PRICE, per Pkg.	$ .41
DOLLARS, total	$43.87

STORE PROMOTION	YES	NO
WINDOW DISPLAY	☒	☐
INSIDE ADVERTISING DISPLAY	☐	☒
INSIDE GOODS DISPLAY	☒	☐
LOCAL ADVERTISING, by Store	☒	☐
SPECIAL PRICE SALE	☒	☐
AT WHAT PRICE ?	$ .39	

FIGURE 5. Territories, cities, sizes and types of stores, and income levels surveyed every 60 days by the A. C. Nielsen Co. in preparing its drug, food, and liquor index. Used by manufacturers in making sales plans.

FIGURE 6. Information secured every 60 days by the A. C. Nielsen Co. about the purchases, inventory, sales, and promotion on a typical product in a typical food store. This information is supplied to subscribers to the Nielsen service.

Advertising mediums, such as the Columbia Broadcasting System, Curtis Publishing Company, Hearst Magazines, Inc., and Crowell Publishing Company, have made special industry surveys and analyses of subscription lists. An outstanding example of publication research has been done by Hearst Magazines, Inc., in the marketing study of the "Trading Area System of Sales Control." This is a classification of the retail trading areas of the country into six hundred and thirty-two primary places. It includes marketing maps for every state.

Limitations of Market Research. Market research has been severely criticized on the grounds that it is biased, inadequate, and misleading, and that it duplicates research by various agencies, and is technically imperfect.

According to the American Association of Advertising Agencies, through its committee on research, these questions should be considered in appraising a market research:

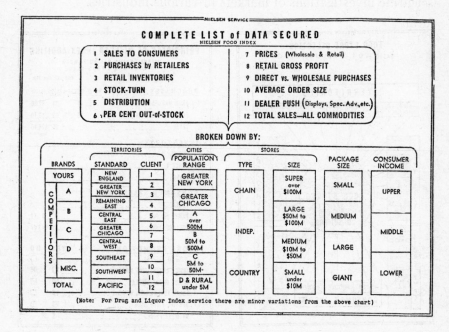

FIGURE 7. The twelve types of market information obtained by the A. C. Nielsen Co. in its surveys of retail food, drug, and liquor stores. This information is broken down into the useful marketing data shown at the lower part of the chart.

1. Who made the survey?

2. Does the title indicate exactly the scope of the survey?

3. Does the report contain all pertinent data as to how, when, and where the survey was made?

4. Is the sample ample?

5. Have data collected in one city or section been used to draw conclusions for the country as a whole?

6. Are percentages figured for groups or classes that contain too few instances?

7. Are percentages of increase estimated on ample bases?

8. Was information obtained by mailed questionnaires?

9. Is casual relationship attributed to any one single factor, when other contributing factors are present?

10. If questionnaires were used, were the questions such as to give fair and adequate answers?

11. Was the information gathered of such a nature that the memories of the people interviewed might have resulted in inaccuracies of fact?

12. Can the type of information obtained be relied on as accurate?

13. Have any original or unique statistical devices been employed?

14. Are charts misleading?

Problem 1—Sales Analysis

Hartman Paper Company

The Hartman Paper Company, established in Springfield, Massachusetts, with a capital of $200,000, manufactures in four mills a complete line of fine writing and book papers distributed through forty exclusive paper jobbers and an equal number of nonexclusive jobbers throughout the United States. A sales force of fifteen men contacts the jobbing trade and large direct buyers. The company invests $30,000 annually in direct advertising and sample books. Annual sales average $5,000,000. Five sales branches are maintained.

Following a change in the management of the company, a new sales manager advises the executive committee that a monthly analysis of the sales of the company should be made. This analysis would aid in controlling sales activities; help in sales direction by locating weak territories; show the various types of paper being sold by each salesman; determine which jobbers are pushing sales; help avoid excessive stocks; and aid in the establishment of sales policies.

It is proposed that the following sales analysis records be kept monthly:

1. Analysis showing sales by type of paper to each class of customer.
2. Comparison of exclusive jobber and general jobber business by geographical sales territories.
3. Analysis showing sales by grades to exclusive jobbers and summaries covering specific groups of exclusive jobbers.
4. Monthly analysis of sales billed by mills and grades.
5. Analysis of sales billed to customers by geographical sales territories, which are further subdivided into branch and salesmen's territories.
6. Analysis of sales by salesmen, branch, and general sales divisions.
7. Analysis of orders received each business day for each type of product set down in comparison with the same day of each month since the beginning of each year.

The sales manager proposes that a sales statistician be employed to be attached to the sales department and make the monthly analysis as outlined. A much simpler analysis of sales by lines has been made in the past by a clerk in the accounting department.

Opposition to the compilation of such a monthly analysis as proposed and to the employment of a sales statistician is based on the assumptions that such analysis will be an additional sales expense; that there is no current demand for much of the information secured; that much time and money were wasted in the past in making an analysis which served no practical purpose; and that such records are too voluminous and are unnecessary for proper supervision.

Questions

1. Should the company make a monthly sales analysis as proposed by the sales manager? Give your reasons for or against this course.

2. Describe in detail how each of the seven records suggested may be used in helping sales direction.

3. Is the proposal that a sales statistician be employed satisfactory? Give your reasons.

4. What other analysis might profitably be made of the company's sales? Of what use would this analysis be?

Problem 2—Industrial Market Survey

The Chase Chemical Corporation

The Chase Chemical Corporation, established in St. Louis, Missouri, in 1899, is a manufacturer of chemicals used in a wide variety of industries. Sales are made through an organization of forty men operating through ten district sales offices in the principal cities. Annual sales average $22,500,000.

Faced with a decline in sales following the war, the company considered the advisability of instituting a plant-by-plant survey of the chemical needs and buying habits of industry. The company considered that such a survey would be a sound defense against declining sales; would unearth new outlets; would disclose new uses; and would indicate needs for new products. In addition, the company hoped that such a survey would furnish the following:

1. Definite data on all prospects in each sales territory, evaluating real, potential, and worthless prospects.
2. Knowledge of chemical needs as a guide for further research.
3. Information on the competitive situation.
4. The location of business in order that it would serve as a step toward more effective and economical distribution.

The company believed that every possible prospect for its products should be visited and that lists of industries, from the largest corporations to the smallest filling stations, should be first compiled from accredited sources and augmented from such sources as chambers of commerce and telephone directories.

Whether this survey could be satisfactorily conducted by mail or through personal investigators was one of the first problems confronting the company. The advantages of low cost and broad coverage indicated the correspondence method. Yet the advantages of a larger percentage of replies, increased accuracy, and more comprehensive information pointed to personal research.

In the event that a personal survey was to be undertaken, the company had to decide whether it should be undertaken by an outside research organization or handled within the company.

It was suggested that the salesmen of the company would be ideal investigators, as such an arrangement would be rapid, take advantage of slack time in sales activity, increase the salesmen's prestige and improve their responsibility. The familiarity of the men with the market would also facilitate the gathering of the desired data.

Certain executives believed, however, that funds might be better spent in selling than in fact-finding. Unless expertly handled, it was believed that such a survey would be productive of little worthwhile information.

Questions

1. Should the Chase Chemical Corporation have undertaken the market survey under consideration? Give your reasons for or against the proposal.

2. Assuming that such a survey is to be undertaken, should it be conducted by correspondence or personal interview? Give reasons for your choice.

3. Assuming that the investigation is to be conducted by personal investigation, who should make the investigation? Give reasons to support your opinion.

4. Assuming that the investigation is to be carried out by correspondence, prepare a questionnaire to be mailed to industrial concerns.

5. Would bibliographical sources produce any information of value for such an investigation? What sources would you suggest?

Problem 3—Consumer Market Survey

Parsons Publishing Company

The Parsons Publishing Company, New York City, specializes in the publication of school textbooks in the field of history, chemistry, physics,

English, and geography. A staff of fifteen salesmen call on college professors and high school teachers to secure adoptions of the books and to see that bookstores are supplied. An annual volume of $6,000,000 worth of books is sold.

The company recently published a book on English Literature for high school seniors which has been adopted by a thousand high schools widely scattered throughout the country, including many in small towns and rural areas.

The first printing of the book is almost sold out. Before ordering a reprinting, the sales manager wants to know the reaction of high school teachers who have used the book. He is considering making a market survey by one or a combination of the following methods:

1. Using the company's salesmen to question teachers.
2. Employing experienced field investigators.
3. Using a mail survey.

Because schools that have adopted the book are widely scattered, and because high school teachers normally have classes when interviewers call, personal interviews are not considered feasible. Furthermore, the high cost of personal interviews is an important objection.

It is argued that the salesmen could be more profitably occupied closing sales than making a survey. They might also bias the answers.

The personal interview method, however, would provide more complete and reliable information than other methods, avoid misleading the respondents, and obtain a higher percentage of answers than the other methods.

A mail survey could be quickly made of teachers not accessible or readily available for personal interviews; outside investigators would not have to be employed; and the time of the salesmen would not be taken from their more important sales activities. The cost of each completed questionnaire would be less.

The mail survey, however, has a number of disadvantages arising from the fact that there is no control over the interview, and the respondent may or may not answer the questionnaire. If he does answer, he may do so any way and whenever he desires. The low proportion of returns received might not be adequate as a basis for sound judgment. A representative cross section of teachers would be difficult to obtain by mail. Follow-up letters would be necessary in order to get sufficient replies.

In view of the above facts, the sales manager was undecided which method to use in getting reactions from teachers concerning the English Literature textbook.

Questions

1. Should the Parsons Publishing Company undertake a market survey to determine the opinions of high school teachers on its English Literature textbook? Give reasons for favoring or opposing a survey.

2. Assuming that a market survey is to be undertaken, what method of securing the information should be used?

3. Prepare a questionnaire for use in the survey.

Reading References

Careers in Advertising, James, Chap. II.
Fundamentals of Industrial Marketing, Elder, Chap. V.
Handbook of Sales Management, Hall, Sec. V
Industrial Marketing, Frederick, Chaps. II, III.
Market Analysis, White.
Modern Sales Management, Frederick, p. 340.
New Psychology of Selling and Advertising, Link, Chaps. II–III.
Planned Marketing, Reed, Chap. VII.
Principles of Marketing, Holtzclaw, Chap. XIX.
Principles of Merchandising, Copeland, pp. 279–284.
Printer's Ink Monthly, "Market Research Uses," by Hovey, May, 1935, p. 21.
Sales Administration, Hayward, Chap. VII.
Sales Management Fundamentals, Hay, pp. 200–202.
Sales Quotas, White, Chap. IV.
Scientific Marketing Management, White, Chap. X.
Scientific Sales Management Today, Hoyt, Chaps. XI, XII.
Technique of Marketing Research, American Marketing Society, Chaps. V, VI, VII, VIII, IX, McGraw-Hill Book Co., New York, 1937.
The Consumer: His Nature and Changing Habits, Pitkin, p. 195.
"Time" Survey of Appleton, Wisconsin, Time, Inc., New York, 1932.
Watch Your Selling Dollar, Crossley, p. 260 (Race); pp. 262–273 (Sex); p. 90 (Climate).
What Makes People Buy, Laird, Chaps. I, II, III, IV, V, VI, X, XI.

CHAPTER FOUR

DISTRIBUTION RESEARCH

What Is Distribution Research? Distribution research is a study of the methods by which a product and its market may be brought together and of the various agencies engaged in the distributive process. It involves an investigation of the various types of distributors, their functions, and characteristics. The relative strength and weakness of distributing agencies, their relations with producers, and their ability to render efficient and profitable distributing services are considered. Such a consideration of the fitness of the distributing mechanism may raise such questions as:

1. Are distributors hostile to the manufacturer's brands?
2. Are they arbitrary in their demands for price concessions?
3. Do they give sales and advertising coöperation?
4. Do they cut prices on products to unprofitable levels?
5. Is their credit sound?
6. Do they give broad enough distribution?
7. Do they carry too many lines of competing products?
8. Do they buy in too small quantities to serve the trade?

These and many other questions motivate distribution research.

Why Undertake Distribution Research? The broad objective of investigations of distributing methods is to secure more efficient and economical service from existing agencies of distribution or to seek new channels of distribution which give promise of greater service to producer and consumer.

The need for distribution analysis has increased with changing conditions in recent years, particularly:

1. The growing resistance to rising costs of distribution.
2. The demand of ultimate consumers for more service and quick delivery.

3. The rapidly shifting consumer demand.
4. The improved transportation, especially the automobile, which has broadened trading areas.
5. The increasing pressure of competition.
6. The rise of new types of distributing agencies, such as the super-markets, rolling stores, and coöperatives.
7. The practice of many retailers of buying direct from manufacturers.

Changing buying habits of consumers and new social and economic conditions have not been met by many distributing agencies, with the result that many old and once successful channels of distribution are no longer effective. This has forced producers to examine their distributing methods and often seek new types of distributors who have kept pace with changing conditions.

What Constitutes Distribution Research? Distribution research involves a classification of existing distributive agencies and a consideration of their functions and effectiveness in relation to the distribution of a specific product. From the standpoint of a manufacturer, distributing agencies may be classified as: (1) internal, that is, operated by the company; and (2) external, that is, agencies operating independently without the company. And further, they may be classified as distributors of consumer commodities, or industrial commodities.

Internal distributing agencies are:

1. A personal sales force, the most common method of distributing consumer and industrial goods. This method is usually employed because it is flexible, direct, and individual. The sales force may be specialized according to function by creating special sales groups such as:

a. A missionary sales force to assist distributors with advertising, demonstrations, and such resale work as stock control and accounting.
b. A junior sales force to assist senior salesmen with prospecting, missionary work, analysis, or promotional work.
c. A specialty sales force to secure the introduction of new items or revive the sale of old items through distributors or direct to consumers as in the case of industrial commodities.
d. An engineering sales force to bring technical knowledge to the problems of customers in industrial selling.
e. An export sales force to sell in foreign markets.

2. Advertising ranks second in importance as an internal marketing agency and first in the case of mail-order concerns. While advertising is sometimes used alone, its most common use as a distributing aid is in conjunction with personal salesmen and other types of distributors. Its merit lies in its broad coverage, quick action, flexibility, and in a wide variety of applications in consumer and industrial distribution.

External distributing agencies in the sale of consumer goods are:

1. Retailers engaged in the distribution of goods to ultimate consumers, classified by the Bureau of the Census as follows:
   a. Merchandise carried:
      (1) Food group: grocery stores, combination food stores, meat and fish markets, candy and confectionery stores, and miscellaneous food stores.
      (2) Country general stores.
      (3) General merchandise group, including department stores, dry goods stores, general merchandise stores, and variety stores.
      (4) Automotive group, including motor vehicle dealers, filling stations, garages, tire and accessory stores.
      (5) Apparel group, including men's and boys' shops, women's and children's apparel and accessory stores, shoe stores, and family clothing and accessory stores.
      (6) Furniture and household group, including furniture stores, household appliance, and home furniture stores.
      (7) Restaurants and eating places, including lunchrooms, cafeterias, and refreshment stands.
      (8) Lumber and building group, including paint and glass, heating, plumbing, and electrical shops.
      (9) Other retail stores, including radio and music, hardware, farmers' supplies, cigar, drug, coal and wood, jewelry, book, and secondhand stores.
   b. Type of service rendered:
      (1) Cash and carry.
      (2) Credit and delivery.
      (3) Automatic, or coin-in-slot.
      (4) Mail order.
      (5) Home service, or rolling stores, pushcarts, and canvassers.
      (6) Self-service stores.
   c. Type of ownership:
      (1) Corporate chain, sectional, and national.
      (2) Voluntary chain of independent stores.
      (3) Independent store with partnership, corporation, or individual ownership.
      (4) Multi-unit independent store.
      (5) Company or industrial store.
      (6) Coöperative store.
2. Wholesalers engaged in the distribution of goods to retailers or large individual consumers. The terms "wholesaler" and "jobber" are used synonymously by many today in referring to merchant middlemen engaged in the quantity

buying of goods on their own account for resale to retailers. The designation "jobber" is sometimes applied to the buyer and seller of special lots of overstocks and unseasonable or damaged merchandise known as "job lots," or a small-lot purchaser who buys from wholesalers for resale to retailers. Wholesalers are classified by the Bureau of Census into 43 major groups as follows:

a. Merchandise carried:
    (1) Amusement and sporting goods.
    (2) Automobiles and automotive equipment.
    (3) Chemicals, drugs, and allied products.
    (4) Dry goods and apparel.
    (5) Electrical equipment and supplies.
    (6) Farm products.
    (7) Farm supplies, except machinery and equipment.
    (8) Food products.
    (9) Forest products, except lumber.
    (10) Furniture and house furnishings.
    (11) General merchandise.
    (12) Groceries and food specialties.
    (13) Hardware.
    (14) Iron and steel scrap and waste.
    (15) Jewelry and optical goods.
    (16) Leather and leather goods, except gloves and shoes.
    (17) Lumber and building materials.
    (18) Machinery—equipment and supplies.
    (19) Metals and minerals.
    (20) Paper and paper products.
    (21) Petroleum and petroleum products.
    (22) Plumbing and heating equipment and supplies.
    (23) Tobacco and tobacco products.
    (24) All other, including books, rubber goods, textiles, baskets, boats, feed, ice, and coal.

b. Type of service rendered:
    (1) Cash and carry.
    (2) Service, extending credit and delivery services.
    (3) Mail order.
    (4) Drop shippers.
    (5) Wagon distributors.

c. Type of ownership:
    (1) Independently owned.
    (2) Owned by parent manufacturing corporation.
    (3) Multi-unit independently owned.
    (4) Corporate chain.
    (5) Coöperative buying wholesalers.
    (6) Manufacturer's sales company.

d. Territory covered and type of lines carried:
    (1) National. (Six concerns in the dry goods field are in this group.)
    (2) Neighborhood or local.
    (3) District or territorial.
    (4) Private brand wholesalers.
    (5) Export and import wholesalers.
    (6) Specialty wholesalers dealing in a few related lines.
    (7) Manufacturing wholesaler.
    (8) Combination wholesaler and retailer.

3. Intermediaries, sometimes called "functional middlemen," who do not take title to merchandise, but whose principal duty is to bring producers, distributors, and large consumers together. They may be classified as follows:

    a. Brokers who negotiate sales on a commission basis for producers and often engage in wholesaling on their own account. They may be buying brokers engaged in the purchase of fruits, hardware, or dry goods, or selling brokers engaged in negotiating sales of foods, drugs, and hardware.

    b. Commission merchants who sell goods consigned to them by producers on a commission basis, largely in the grain, fruit, and vegetable trade.

    c. Agents, sometimes called "manufacturers' agents," representing several manufacturers in the sale of noncompeting goods. Another type of agent, known as a "selling agent," usually represents one producer exclusively and agrees to sell the entire output of a mill on a commission basis.

    d. Auction companies who dispose of large quantities of fruits, vegetables, tobacco, and furs for producers for a commission, at open sales. Nearly half of the California and Florida citrus fruit shipments are sold through auctions in thirteen principal markets.

    e. Export agents who represent domestic producers in foreign markets.

    f. Import agents who represent foreign producers in domestic markets.

Functions of Distributing Agencies. The functions of internal distributing agencies, personal salesmen, and advertising are:

1. To locate possible buyers.
2. To discover needs of consumers and dealers for a manufacturer's product.
3. To show and to tell how a product meets certain needs.
4. To create a desire for a product, to provide information and answer objections.
5. To aid customers in securing greater satisfaction or profit from the use or sale of a product.
6. To create good will for a product or firm.

The functions of external retail distributing agencies are:

1. To assemble merchandise from all parts of the world.
2. To extend credit to customers. This, however, is not a function of most chain and cash-and-carry retailers.
3. To assemble at retail stores and deliver to ultimate consumers.
4. To sell by trained sales people, window and store display, and advertising.
5. To warehouse within the store or in merchandise warehouses.
6. To finance sales and provide a store building, equipment, and merchandise to attract customers.
7. To take risks in style depreciation of merchandise, price decline, returns, damage, and theft.

8. To supply such service as reading rooms, restaurants, lectures, and postal, telegraph, and telephone services.

The functions of wholesale merchant distributing agencies are:

1. To assemble goods from many sources.
2. To warehouse merchandise until it is distributed to the retail trade.
3. To deliver to retailers, with the exception of cash-and-carry wholesalers.
4. To extend credit to retail merchants and occasionally to manufacturers.
5. To sell through a personal sales force and advertising.
6. To give merchandising assistance in the form of stock control, store arrangement, lighting, and advertising counsel to customers.
7. To store, grade, and package commodities bought in bulk for distribution to the retail trade.
8. To advise producers and retailers of market conditions and prices.
9. To take risks in theft, depreciation, price decline, returns, and adjustments.

The functions of intermediaries or functional middlemen of consumers' goods are mixed, but in general they are:

1. Selling through personal salesmen, usually on a commission basis. Orders taken by brokers are sent to principals, who usually ship, bill, and collect, although in many cases the last two functions are assumed by selling agents.
2. Furnishing market information—an important function which many intermediaries render to their principals.
3. Storage is provided by auction houses and commission men for their clients, although brokers usually render no storage service.
4. Credit is extended by certain auction houses to retail or jobber purchasers. Some brokers guarantee the credit of purchasers, although credit is not a normal brokerage function in the distribution of merchandise. Some brokers extend credit to their principals.
5. Sorting, grading and packing is sometimes undertaken by commission houses, although this is not a common function of intermediaries.

6. Customs service is a function of many import and export brokers who handle documents and other matters in connection with exports or imports.

Distributors and Their Functions in Industrial Markets. Distributing agencies in industrial markets are limited, since many industrial products are sold direct by producers to consumers. The following distributors handle industrial commodities:

1. Wholesalers sell direct to industrial and business consumers of operating supplies. Accessory equipment, such as office equipment and automotive and machine shop supplies, is often sold through wholesalers. Wholesalers also are active in the paper, iron and steel, waste, and materials markets. These distributors perform practically the same functions as wholesalers of consumers' goods—assembling, storing, extending credit, selling, and transporting.

2. Brokers are active in the distribution of staples and raw materials, such as cotton, wool, copper, crude oil, and grain. In the cotton cloth trade, particularly grey cloth, sales are made through brokers on a commission of 1 per cent. Brokers of industrial commodities are often employed in lines where the product is so standardized that the same grade can be obtained freely from several producers. Brokers in industrial lines function largely to bring buyer and seller together and do not extend credit, warehouse, or transportation services, or take title to the merchandise. Many brokers in raw materials operate on exchanges.

3. Selling agents, sometimes called commission houses, are active in the distribution of finished textiles, taking over all of the selling problems of small mills. Certain large agents offer their mills a large distribution throughout the country, with branch offices located in the principal cities, and abroad, through export departments. The proceeds of sales are guaranteed to the mills, eliminating the necessity for mills to maintain credit service. The agents frequently endorse the paper of mills for which they are agents. Selling agents are active in the sale of iron ore, anthracite coal, and some lumber.

4. Manufacturers' agents operate commonly in the field of accessory equipment, such as small motors, pumps, recorders, belts, and clocks, and confine their efforts to one market or locality with which they are familiar. They are employed on a commission basis by small companies making small unit-of-sale products, which

do not justify the operation of a manufacturer's sales organization. The agent represents several manufacturers of noncompeting products sold to the same industry, employs salesmen, but does not warehouse, advertise, or transport the product sold, only transmitting orders to his principal.

Merits and Limitations of Distributing Agencies. Retailers offer numerous advantages to manufacturers in the distribution of merchandise, six of which are:

1. An established trade and frequently a high reputation.
2. The ability to sell and extend credit on small purchases which would be unprofitable to a manufacturer.
3. Quick delivery service to consumers.
4. Prompt adjustments and mechanical service.
5. A knowledge of consumer preferences.
6. A wide variety of choices.

Manufacturers, on the other hand, cite the following disadvantages of distributing through retailers:

1. Poor sales service.
2. Lack of interest in advertised brands.
3. Poor management.
4. Competition from private brands of retailers.
5. Inadequate stocks of merchandise.
6. Absence of specialization in merchandise.
7. Poorly arranged stock.

Furthermore, retailers are charged with operating on insufficient capital, excessive overhead, poor location, and inferior credit and accounting methods.

Wholesale merchants offer many advantages to manufacturers as distributing agencies because they:

1. Purchase in large quantities.
2. Provide storage, credit, delivery, and sales services at low cost.
3. Handle small-unit purchases.
4. Possess an intimate knowledge of local markets, anticipating buyers' needs.
5. Make frequent contact with retailers.
6. Provide quick, widespread distribution on seasonal products.
7. Make quick fill-in deliveries to retailers.
8. Relieve manufacturers of much office effort and detail.

On the other hand, manufacturers find that the wholesale distributors:

1. Push their own private brands, to the neglect of manufacturers' brands.
2. Use poor sales methods, are simply order takers.
3. Have inadequate stocks to supply the retail trade, and employ hand-to-mouth buying.
4. Have inadequate delivery service.
5. Price-cut.
6. Overemphasize buying to the neglect of selling.
7. Have unsound credit extension.
8. Carry too many brands of one product.
9. Stock slow-moving, nonprofitable lines.
10. Lack knowledge of costs.
11. Have slow turnover.

Wholesalers, on the other hand, complain of such manufacturers for the following:

1. Direct selling to wholesalers' customers.
2. Preferential discounts to chains and direct buyers.
3. Tampering with wholesalers' salesmen.
4. Using specialty salesmen to force wholesalers to stock.
5. Poor selling coöperation.
6. Inadequate margins.

Within recent years, wholesalers have strengthened their position through:

1. Educating retailer customers.
2. Reducing costs.
3. Improving salesmanship.
4. Developing private brands.
5. Buying coöperatively.
6. Organizing voluntary chains of retailers.
7. Engaging in exclusive distributing arrangements with manufacturers.

The advantages to manufacturers in using intermediaries, such as brokers, selling agents, manufacturers' agents, and commission merchants, are:

1. The manufacturer and producer are relieved of the responsibility for sales.

2. Economical sales service is obtained for small manufacturers of limited capital.

3. An intimate knowledge of the market is obtained.

4. Financial assistance is given to the manufacturer in special cases.

5. Credit is guaranteed in certain cases.

The limitations of brokers' and agents' services are largely:

1. Lack of aggressive salesmanship.
2. Lack of interest in the affairs of principals.
3. Tendency to encourage speculation.
4. Interest in volume rather than in the manufacturer's profits.
5. Tendency to be overpaid in periods of high prices and underpaid in times of depression.
6. Failure to conform methods to modern requirements.
7. Opposition to advertised lines.

Prevailing Channels of Distribution. Certain channels of distribution are customarily used for the distribution of consumer as well as industrial commodities. These channels vary with the particular type of goods. Consumer commodities are usually distributed through the following channels of distribution:

1. Consumer goods—convenience type. The distribution of consumer goods of a convenience type such as foods, drugs, and hardware is usually through one or more distributive agencies in the following sequence:
    a. Manufacturer to broker to wholesaler to retailer to consumer.
    b. Manufacturer to wholesaler to retailer to consumer.
    c. Manufacturer to retailer to consumer.
    d. Manufacturer to consumer, house to house, or mail.
    e. Manufacturer to coöperative association to consumer.
    f. Manufacturer to retail store branches to consumer.
2. Consumer goods—shopping type.
    a. Manufacturer to broker or manufacturers' agent to retailer to consumer.
    b. Manufacturer to retailer to consumer.
    c. Manufacturer to wholesaler to retailer to consumer.
3. Consumer goods—specialty type.
    a. Manufacturer to broker or manufacturers' agent to retailer to consumer.

    b. Manufacturer to retail branch to consumer.

    c. Manufacturer to retailer to consumer.

    d. Manufacturer to consumer.

    e. Manufacturer to wholesaler to retailer to consumer.

  4. Industrial commodities are usually distributed through one or more of the following channels of distribution:

    a. Manufacturer to consumer.

    b. Manufacturer to selling agent to consumer.

    c. Manufacturer to wholesaler to consumer.

    d. Manufacturer to broker to consumer.

    e. Manufacturer to manufacturers' agent to wholesaler or consumer.

Factors Affecting Choice of Distributing Channels. A manufacturer has a choice of one or more channels of distribution for his merchandise. The channels chosen for a particular product will be determined to a large extent by the *type of goods* to be distributed, whether consumer convenience, specialty, shopping, or industrial installations, accessories, operating supplies, or fabricating materials. Each of these types of commodities follows customary channels of distribution as indicated previously.

The kind and amount of *service* required by the user of a product dictates the distributing channels for certain mechanical products. Where considerable service is involved in the use of a commodity, the maker frequently sells it through those of his own branches which are equipped to render service, or sales are made direct to distributors who have service facilities, for example, automobile dealers.

The nature of the *sales territory* is a factor in selecting channels of distribution. In a western territory with scattered dealers and limited population, wholesalers may be a satisfactory distributing channel; while in a thickly populated metropolitan district, direct sale to retailers may be advisable.

The *size of the sale* is a consideration in selecting types of distributors. A commodity selling for several hundred thousand dollars, such as a steam yacht, may be logically sold direct to the ultimate user, while a five-cent package of chewing gum is distributed through several middlemen.

The *amount of prevailing demand* for a product will affect the kind of distributor used. A new type of breakfast food of unknown merit to the trade and consumer will not be acceptable to retail

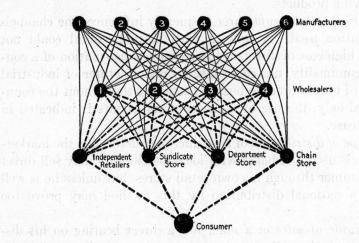

FIGURE 8. Chart of channels of distribution prevailing in the textile industry, illustrating how six competing manufacturers approach a prospective consumer. This chart was prepared by the Wholesale Dry Goods Institute.

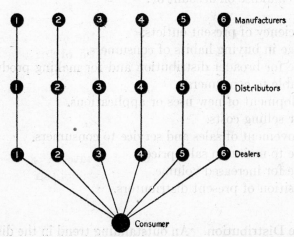

FIGURE 9. Chart of channels of distribution in the automobile industry, showing how six competing automobile manufacturers approach a prospective purchaser. This chart was prepared by the Wholesale Dry Goods Institute.

chains and large food retailers interested largely in the sale of quick-moving products.

The *capital of a manufacturer* frequently influences the channels of distribution used. A concern with limited capital could not afford the high cost of direct-to-the-consumer distribution of a convenience commodity, nor could a small manufacturer of industrial goods afford to sell direct to business concerns throughout the country; accordingly, the use of manufacturers' agents is indicated in the latter case.

The *scope of distribution* of a product may determine the marketing channels used. A baker with local distribution may sell direct to the consumer through his own retail stores, but unless he is well financed, a national distribution by this method may prove too costly.

The *volume of sales* of a seller has a direct bearing on his distributing methods. Direct sale to consumers may be possible for an established company with a strong demand for its products, while a new concern may employ various middlemen in the distribution of its product.

Reasons for Changing Channels of Distribution. A manufacturer is often confronted with the necessity for finding new outlets for his merchandise on account of:

1. Inefficiency of present outlets.
2. Change in buying habits of consumers.
3. Desire for broader distribution and for making products more available to consumers.
4. Development of new uses or applications.
5. Lower selling costs.
6. Improvement of sales and service to consumers.
7. Desire to maintain sales prices.
8. Desire for increased volume.
9. Opposition of present distributors.

Selective Distribution. An outstanding trend in the distribution of many commodities of the consumer, shopping, and specialty type is toward selective distribution, which is:

1. Exclusive sale to a limited number of wholesale or retail distributors located in strategic markets.
2. Limitation of sale to several wholesale or retail outlets in a

city or territory which are noncompetitive or which service different clientele.

3. Collaboration between a manufacturer and distributor serving a trade with a clearly defined and mutually agreed-upon basis.

One reason for selective distribution may be found in the 1935 retail census of distribution which shows that 2 per cent of all retail establishments did 33 per cent of all retail business, and 64 per cent of all stores did only 14 per cent of the total retail business.

The following reasons have led many manufacturers, in a wide variety of lines, to adopt some policy of selective distribution:

1. Lower production costs by stabilized distribution.
2. Lower selling costs through fewer distributor contacts.
3. Freedom from price-cutting and controlled sale makes it possible to maintain a fair price.
4. Simplified sales direction and control.
5. Better coöperation between manufacturer and distributors in sales efforts.

On the other hand, selective distribution presents numerous problems such as:

1. Restriction in volume through limited outlets.
2. Restriction in benefits of national advertising.
3. Limitation of distribution.
4. Distributors not behind an exclusive line.

Selective distribution is frequently employed in connection with consignment selling by which sales agents are appointed by manufacturers. Sometimes distributors make cash deposits with manufacturers and agree to act as selling agents in conformity with company policies. Such consignment contracts are made largely to secure price stabilization.

The passage of state fair-trade acts in 1936 and 1937, empowering manufacturers of trade-marked merchandise to fix its wholesale or retail resale price in intrastate commerce by contract with local distributors, also led to the signing of numerous contracts with selected distributors and furthered the trend toward selective distribution.

Selective selling has made greatest progress in the distribution of textile specialties, such as towels, sheets, and bedspreads, and in the marketing of drugs, perfumes, proprietary medicines, and electric lamps.

Process for Distribution Analysis. The steps that should be taken in considering types of distributors and channels of distribution for new products or old commodities are:

1. Review the advantages and disadvantages of prevailing channels of distribution for an old product or customary channels used in marketing similar products in case of a new commodity.

2. Consider the various factors previously listed which have a bearing on the choice of channels of distribution for a particular product.

3. Examine the methods of distribution of competitors.

4. Compare the experience of other manufacturers using similar channels of distribution.

Problem 1—Distribution Through Selling Agents

Morton Mills

The Morton Mills, established in Boston, Massachusetts, in 1903, with a capital stock of $600,000, manufactures for infants, children, and adults winter-weight knit underwear in several styles and a full line of sizes and weights. This underwear is sold through Larson and Wright, selling agents, with headquarters in New York City and branches in Philadelphia and Chicago.

The Morton Mills employs three hundred persons in its main mill at Boston and one fourth as many in a branch mill located in Providence, Rhode Island. The company formerly invested $24,000 annually in women's magazines, but in recent years it has eliminated such advertising. Sales of the company are highly seasonal, with about 80 per cent of the retail business on the line being done during the months of November, December, January, and February.

Larson and Wright handles the accounts of a number of small textile mills producing noncompeting textile specialities. It maintains a force of salesmen calling throughout the year on the wholesale and retail dry goods and department store trade all over the country. All of its retail accounts are guaranteed, and it maintains its own credit and collection department at its home office. Orders taken by Larson and Wright salesmen are transmitted through its offices to the mills of its principals. The agents remit to their principals the proceeds of all sales, less their commission of 5 per cent of net sales.

The Morton Mills has sold its line through its selling agents since its establishment for the reason that the company considers such a method economical for a seasonal business such as the company operates. Furthermore, the agents relieve the company of the details of selling and leave it free to devote its time to manufacturing problems.

The Morton Mills has also confined its distribution exclusively to wholesalers for these reasons: the product is seasonal; it requires widespread distribution; it is economical; volume is limited, making direct shipment expensive; fill-in deliveries through the wholesaler are quicker; and small retail inventories are possible when stock can be obtained through the wholesaler.

While the company is showing small profits, its sales volume is declining yearly, and only through economies in production are profits possible.

The company has been advised to eliminate its selling agents and employ its own salesmen in the dry goods trade. To overcome the seasonal nature of the business, a line of summer underwear has been recommended.

The policy of selling only through wholesalers has been criticized, since the dry goods wholesaler is suffering from the competition of direct-selling manufacturers, mail order houses, chain stores, and house-to-house canvassers.

Questions

1. Should the Morton Mills eliminate its present selling agents? Give reasons for your answer.

2. Should the Morton Mills have amended its policy of selling exclusively through dry goods wholesalers? Give your reasons.

3. Does the type of product affect the method of distribution in this case? How?

4. What other channels of distribution might be logically considered by the Morton Mills? Why?

Problem 2—Retail Distribution

Holcomb Heater Company

The Holcomb Heater Company, established in 1907 in Chicago, Illinois, for thirty years manufactured and distributed direct to consumers a line of heating and cooking stoves and furnaces. Sales were made entirely through the medium of mail order catalogs distributed to the rural market. Extensive advertising was done in the farm magazines.

A peak annual volume of $4,000,000 was secured by this method of distribution. However, by 1926 sales by mail had declined sharply in the face of keen mail order house competition and the trend to buying in trading centers encouraged by the increase in automobiles and good roads.

The company analyzed the market for furnaces and found an excellent opportunity to expand sales of this product. Accordingly, in 1927 it decided to open a retail store in a city of fifty thousand inhabitants near Chicago, which would distribute its own products exclusively. Salesmen were employed to sell furnaces direct to homeowners. This store was so successful that other stores were opened in cities under fifty thousand population throughout the Middle West, until in 1941 the company operated two hundred eighty-five company stores employing two thousand four hundred sales and merchandising people. Sales volume totaled approximately $8,000,000. These stores were closed during World War II, when the company was engaged exclusively in war work.

At the close of the war, the company announced plans to reopen its former stores and broaden its distribution by opening two hundred additional company stores. These stores would merchandise the company's own furnaces and stoves, and in addition products which it did not manufacture, including refrigerators, washing machines, stokers, oil burners, dryers, all made by well-known concerns.

The company also considered adding five hundred franchised dealer stores to sell its complete line as well as the retail lines of other manufacturers. These dealers would be given training at the factory. In addition, a Holcomb traveling staff would visit both company and franchised stores to conduct sales training and to standardize accounting and other operations. In the case of both company and franchised stores, architects and store-planning specialists would be retained to make the arrangement and equipment of both classes of stores identical. To secure distribution in the larger cities where the company did not have its own stores or franchised dealers, it planned to make merchandising arrangements with leading department stores to distribute its full line of stoves and furnaces.

These channels of distribution would be supported by an aggressive advertising campaign. Two hundred thousand dollars would be spent on advertisements placed in the leading farm, home, and women's magazines.

Although the company had been successful in the operation of its original two hundred eighty-five stores before the war, certain company executives believed that it was unwise to continue to expand the original chain and distribute the lines of other manufacturers. It was pointed out that the company was primarily a manufacturer of furnaces and should not further invest its capital in the highly competitive retail merchandising field.

The appointment of franchised dealers would involve the expense of training and controlling them, reducing the margin of profit on sales through this channel.

Since the company had developed its business in the small-town field, its entry into big-city markets was questioned. Its products had been designed to satisfy the demand in rural areas. Department stores were not considered aggressive merchandisers of the type of stoves made by the Holcomb Company.

Questions

1. Should the Holcomb Company enlarge its chain of company-owned stores? Give reasons for this expansion.

2. Should the company appoint franchised dealers and train them? Why?

3. Should the company distribute through big-city department stores? Give reasons for using this method of distribution.

4. Should the company have abandoned its original mail order business? Why was this channel of distribution eliminated?

Problem 3—Selecting Channels of Distribution

Martinson Milling Company

The Martinson Milling Company, Indianapolis, Indiana, established in 1897, is a flour-milling concern distributing cake, pastry, and bread flours through retail grocers and direct to bakeries. The company took over another firm which had developed and patented a method of packaging biscuits in dough form. The company was interested in developing the sale of the ready-prepared biscuits, as another outlet for its high-grade flour.

A separate division of the business was created to promote this new product and secure volume as quickly and economically as possible in order to provide a profitable flour outlet. In connection with the marketing of the new product, several problems arose. As the product was extremely perishable, it had to be kept under constant refrigeration, and quick turnover in the distributor's warehouse and store was necessary. Spoiled packages had to be removed from the stores. The retailer had to be educated in proper handling methods.

The question of proper channels of distribution offered a severe problem. After considering the possibilities of wholesale grocery distribution, the company decided to undertake its own wholesaling. Refrigerated trucks were put on the streets of six or eight cities, and driver salesmen were employed to call on the retail grocers.

The resulting volume of sales was gratifying, but the selling cost was high. Time limited the number of stops a salesman might make in a day, and since only one item was carried, his per-call sales did not yield sufficient volume to cover truck and overhead expenses. The company soon abolished this method of distribution.

Next, the company selected a number of truck distributors, specialty, or "wagon" wholesalers, operating their own trucks and distributing butter, cheese, mayonnaise, potato chips, dressings, and the like. A field organization was built to work with these distributors. This method, however, required time to make distributor connections and build a sales organization. Volume increased, but selling expense was still high. Sufficient territory was not being covered to consume any sizable volume of flour milled by the company.

Newspaper advertising had been used profitably in the cities where the product had been introduced.

Questions

1. What channels of distribution should be used by the Martinson Milling Company? Give reasons for your choices.
2. Should the company have continued with its own distributing organization to the retail trade? Give your reasons.
3. Should the company continue to distribute through independent "wagon" distributors? Why?

Problem 4—Wholesale Distribution

The Clayton Distributing Corporation

The Clayton Distributing Corporation, a coöperative organization of sixty electric appliance wholesalers, was established in 1945, with headquarters in New York City, to distribute home appliances under the brand name of "Clayton," to six thousand retail appliance dealers.

Members become stockholders through the purchase of a thousand shares of common stock at one dollar a share. They purchase appliances at regular prices but the additional margins above headquarters operating expense go to the members in quarterly dividends as additional profits in proportion to their purchases. A managing director, an experienced appliance sales manager, is employed to direct the affairs of the corporation. Members can be dropped from the organization only by a majority vote of members and with six-months' written notice.

The corporation first made arrangements with thirty manufacturers of appliances to supply Clayton appliances to the members. A jury of distributor members passes upon every product bought. The corporation will sell a complete line of Clayton appliances including air-conditioning units, heaters, refrigerators, toasters, ranges, cleaners, clocks, kitchen cabinets, percolators, coffee makers, home freezers, washers, radio and television sets, ironing boards, and steam irons.

Distributor members may handle other brands of appliances although preference will be given to all Clayton products. Only independent retailers will be sold the Clayton brand.

Each distributor has a sales quota of Clayton appliances based on the potentialities of his territory. Exclusive territories are assigned to each member and territories do not cross state lines. In Texas there are 4 members; in New York State, 4; in Florida, 1; and in North Carolina, 1. Similar distribution prevails in other states.

Among the advantages of membership in the corporation are economies in merchandising, advertising, and accounting. Members enjoy a high degree of security of franchise since they must be given six-months' notice before being dropped from the organization. Quantity purchases make possible lower prices. Competition among manufacturers for the corporation's business insures good service and quality products. A full line of products is provided the members.

The Clayton brand is nationally advertised in full-color pages in leading national magazines to create recognition for the brand name and sales for wholesalers and retailers.

Many home appliance distributors prefer to sell nationally advertised brands, such as General Electric, Frigidaire, Westinghouse, Zenith, and Philco, which carry a smaller margin of profit, but whose turnover is in greater volume. The quality of these brands is uniform and the service is superior. These manufacturers provide distributors and dealers with many merchandising aids and sales promotion materials. Their salesmen give sales assistance.

Questions

1. Is membership in the Clayton Distributing Corporation a profitable venture for an electric appliance wholesale distributor? Give advantages and disadvantages of this form of coöperative wholesaling.

2. Should the members distribute other brands of appliances in addition to the Clayton line?

3. What is your opinion of the policy of having a jury which passes on the purchases of products to be sold under the Clayton brand?

Reading References

Distribution Today, Rost, Chaps. III–X, inclusive.
Elements of Marketing, Converse, Chaps. XIV, XV, XVI, XVII, XVIII, XIX.
Essentials of Distribution, Converse, Chaps. VII, VIII, IX, X.
Marketing Principles, Organization, and Policies, Pyle, Chap. VII.
National Wholesale Conference, Chamber of Commerce of the U. S., Washington, D. C., Report of Committees on "Business Analyses" and "Wholesalers' Functions."
Outlines of Marketing, Agnew, Jenkins, and Drury, Chaps. III, IV, V.
Principles of Marketing, Holtzclaw, Chaps. IV, V, VI, VII, VIII.
Principles of Marketing, Maynard, Weidler, and Beckman, Chaps. XIV, XV, XVI.
Principles of Merchandising, Copeland, Chap. II.
Sales Administration, Hayward, Chaps. X, XII, XIII, XIV, p. 152.
Super-Market, Zimmerman, Chaps. I, II, III, IV.
Wholesaling, Beckman, Chaps. I, II, III, IV.

PART TWO

SALES OPERATION

CHAPTER FIVE

SALES DEPARTMENT ORGANIZATION

Why a Sales Organization? While some very small manufacturers operate profitably without a formal sales organization, a sales manager, or salesmen, the majority of concerns prefer to control their sales program through their own sales organization. Certain concerns dispose of their entire output to one consumer or distributor; others, primarily interested in producing, or possessing too limited capital to operate their own salesmen, have delegated their selling functions to selling agents, commission houses, brokers, or agents whose principal business is to bring sellers and buyers together. In a small company there is usually an executive, frequently the president, responsible for disposing of the output of the plant.

The large majority of concerns which have created formal sales organizations have done so in order to:

1. Relieve keymen of detail and give them time for proper planning and policy determination.
2. Divide and fix authority.
3. Prevent duplication or repetition of duties.
4. Allocate responsibility.
5. Eliminate friction and lost motion, and establish a routine.
6. Develop executives through fixing responsibilities.
7. Stimulate efforts of personnel.
8. Provide incentive for individual advancement in the organization through knowledge of opportunities ahead.
9. Insure proper supervision of individual salesmen.
10. Provide for proper policy formation, planning, and execution of plans.

Lack of proper organization in marketing usually arises from such causes as:

1. Time-worn practices in the industry.
2. Overconfidence of executives who established the business.
3. Reluctance of key executives to relinquish control.
4. Executives who are more concerned with production than with sales problems.
5. Sentiment toward relatives or old employees.
6. Absentee management.

Unsound organization results in a lack of planning; ineffective policies; improper execution of such policies through the lack of training, stimulation, and supervision of executive personnel; and improper coördination with the producing, financial, service, and other departments of a business.

When a business is small, the need for formal organization is not pressing; as sales increase, the sales promotion manager, sales research manager, and other executives are added—supposedly to take charge of the work these titles imply. Usually these titles are meaningless, as the heads of the business assume control of each so-called new department as it is created. The result is confusion, conflict of authority, and inefficiency.

In such cases organizations have grown around individuals rather than functions. Effective organizations are built around functions, rather than individuals, who not infrequently pass quickly from the industrial scene, leaving little behind. An organization that is established on basic functions, however, is more permanent.

The successive steps in the creation of an effective sales organization are:

1. Determination of the functions of the organization.
2. Logical grouping and dividing of functions.
3. Selection of personnel to perform the functions.
4. Charting the organization to illustrate relationships.
5. Preparing an organization manual specifying the scope and duties of each department, together with the duties of each individual department or division head.

Functions of Sales Organizations. While the functions of sales organizations vary with their size, products sold, methods of distribution, territory covered, and many other factors, they fall logically into two divisions, namely, sales planning functions and sales operating functions.

A. *Sales planning* is a most important function of marketing, which has been frequently neglected in the desire for sales activity.

Opportunism and impulse dictate too many sales activities. One reason for a lack of sales planning arises from the common practice of promoting successful salesmen to positions as managers. Such successful salesmen are primarily men of action, not temperamentally fitted for the analytical work of sales planning functions. Planning demands a man of contemplative, creative, and analytical ability. Only rarely does one find an individual who possesses these qualities, in addition to the drive, personal magnetism, and enthusiasm of a field salesman. The solution to the personnel problem of sales direction is to divide the duties of management between a "planning" manager, responsible for planning, and a "field" manager of the aggressive, inspiring, leader type, to carry out the policies developed by the planning manager. If a man with analytical ability is assigned to the planning end, he will be able to function more effectively, unencumbered with duties of field direction for which he would be temperamentally unfitted.

In some organizations sales planning is performed in a separate section of the sales division called a "sales planning department," "merchandise committee," or "sales engineering department." In smaller concerns a single individual, usually the sales manager, is responsible for planning policies and seeing that the field organization is inspired to carry out the plans.

Sales planning functions include:

1. Market analysis.
2. Product analysis.
3. Distribution research.
4. Coördination with other executives and departments in the business and outside distributive organization.
5. Policy development on price, credit, and service.
6. Sales statistics, budgets, and quota establishment.

B. *Sales operating* is a much more highly developed function of sales organization than sales planning for the reason that in many cases the abilities of sales executives are superior in this phase of management. The direction of sales operations may be best given to a man with energy, enthusiasm, and the ability to inspire maximum performance in men. The principal sales operating functions are:

1. Locating, selecting, and training salesmen.
2. Stimulating and supervising salesmen.
3. Paying salesmen.

4. Maintaining relations with distributors.
5. Controlling branch houses.
6. Coördinating sales and advertising when these functions are not performed by an advertising or sales promotion department.
7. Transporting, including warehousing.

Grouping or Dividing Sales Functions. The functions of a sales organization may be so grouped as to allocate control to one man or several individuals. These groupings are called line type, line and

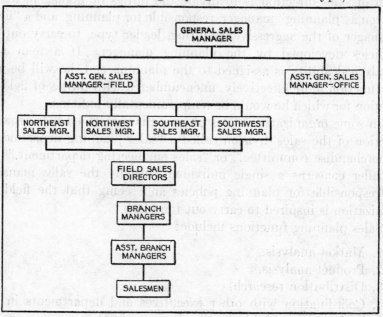

FIGURE 10. A typical straight-line type of sales organization of a national manufacturer and direct-to-the-consumer distributor of grocery products employing 1,200 house-to-house salesmen. The extensive field sales organization is typical of direct-to-consumer distribution. In this organization the general sales manager does not have the benefit of staff advice as in the case of a line-and-staff organization.

staff type, and committee type of organization. These types may be further divided into territorial sales, customer type, and product type of organization.

A. *The line type of organization* is one in which the responsibility centers in a sales manager or other sales executive, and authority flows in a straight line from him to the individual salesman. This type of organization is most commonly used by companies of limited size, covering small territories with one product or a small line of products.

The line type of organization has the following advantages:

1. Formulation or carrying out of sales plans is not delayed.
2. Authority is centralized.
3. Little opportunity is given to shift responsibility.
4. The tendency is to develop strong executives and give able men an opportunity to grow.

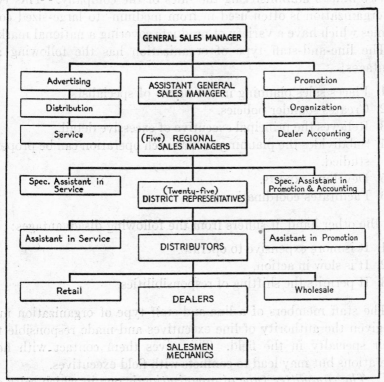

FIGURE 11. Sales organization chart of a large automobile manufacturing corporation selling four lines of cars. This chart illustrates a typical line-and-staff type of organization. The staff is composed of executives in charge of advertising, distribution, service, promotion, organization, and dealer accounting.

The line organization has the following limitations:

1. No specialization is possible.
2. Responsibilities may be too excessive for one man.
3. A highly capable man with planning ability as well as executive ability is required.
4. All subordinates tend to become "yes" men.
5. Business suffers with the loss of the top manager.
6. Subordinates have no opportunity to develop.

While the line type is often more theoretical than actual, it is probably the most commonly used and is a survival of the one-man management era in American business.

B. *The line-and-staff type of organization* is one in which the sales manager is given a staff of specialists in such sales fields as planning, research, statistics, engineering, promotion, and training, to advise him in administering the sales of the company. This type of organization is often used in from medium- to large-sized companies which have a variety of products covering a national market.

The line-and-staff type of organization has the following advantages:

1. Places sales planning in the hands of specialists.
2. Creates sounder policies.
3. Relieves the principal executive of excessive detail.
4. Subdivides the planning so that each operation can be properly studied.
5. Develops experts.
6. Facilitates coördination.

On the other hand, it suffers from the following disadvantages:

1. It is more expensive to operate.
2. It is slow in action.
3. It permits the shifting of responsibilities.

The staff members of a line-and-staff type of organization may be given the authority of line executives and made responsible for their specialty in the field. This gives them contact with field operations but may lead to conflicts with field executives.

C. *The committee type of organization* is one in which sales are usually planned by a sales committee, although the field execution may be delegated to a field sales manager, who may or may not be a member of the sales committee. The sales committee may be composed of president or general manager, treasurer, production manager, or advertising or sales research manager. This type of sales organization is usually employed in large corporations having extensive distribution and a wide variety of products. Frequently sales managers of subsidiaries of a large corporation serve on a sales committee which is responsible for the general sales policies and advertising of the group of associated companies.

The committee type of organization has the following advantages:

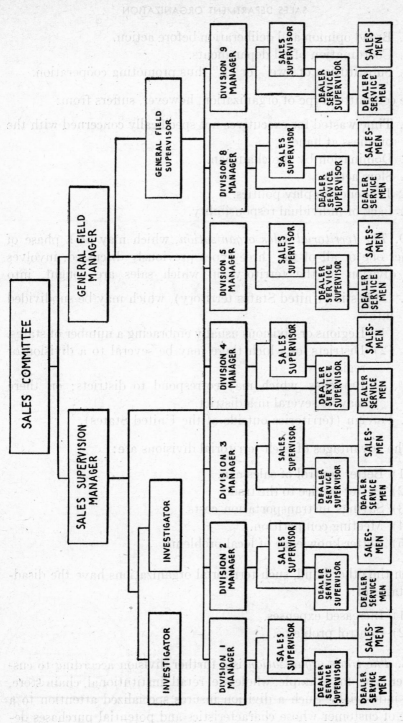

FIGURE 12. Sales organization chart of a large manufacturer selling to the food and drug trade, illustrating a committee type of organization. The committee is composed of executives in charge of sales, advertising, and research.

1. Broad opinion and deliberation before action.
2. Coördination of all departments.
3. Substitution of "we" for "I," thus promoting coöperation.

The committee type of organization, however, suffers from:

1. Time wasted for executives not specifically concerned with the business at hand.
2. Domination by the chairman.
3. Slow action.
4. Tendency to play politics.
5. Lack of individual responsibility.

D. *The territorial sales organization,* which may be a phase of either one or all of the three types previously discussed, involves the division of the territory, in which sales are sought, into

a. Domestic (United States territory), which may be subdivided into:
   (1) Regions or divisions usually embracing a number of states.
   (2) Districts, of which there may be several to a division or region.
   (3) Branches, which may correspond to districts; or, there may be several in a district.
b. Foreign (territories outside of the United States).

The advantages of such territorial divisions are:

(1) Better control of salesmen.
(2) Better service to the trade.
(3) Savings in transportation costs.
(4) Meeting competition.
(5) Better knowledge of local problems.

On the other hand, such territorial organizations have the disadvantages of:

(1) Increased expenses.
(2) Control problems.

E. *The trade organization* is a further division according to customer type, for example, wholesale, retail, institutional, chain store, and industrial. Such a division insures specialized attention to a type of customer whose characteristics and potential purchases demand the services of a special kind of salesman and organization.

F. *The product organization* is found particularly in companies which sell a wide variety of products of varying characteristics. For example, a national manufacturer of chemical and pharmaceutical products divides its sales organization into advertised products, chemical and pharmaceutical products, and professional products, with a separate group of salesmen assigned to each line.

Factors Determining Structure of Sales Organization. The type of sales organization best adapted to the distribution of a particular product depends upon a number of factors. Six of these are discussed below.

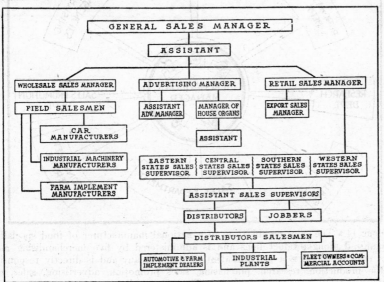

FIGURE 13. Sales organization chart of the lubricating oil marketing division of an oil company. Note the division of organization functions according to types of distributors, wholesalers, and retailers.

1. *The nature of the products sold* may affect the type of organization. A repeat, essential product demanding broad distribution will require a more complex type of organization than a luxury that has no repeat market and is sold through a limited number of outlets. A perishable product demanding frequent distribution may call for a large sales force, constant supervision, and a complex type of organization with division managers, district managers, and specialized sales groups for certain classes of the trade. The number of products sold also affects the organization, since a wide variety may require specialization of the organization along product lines.

2. *The abilities of executives* in an organization may influence the distribution of authority and the complexity of the organiza-

tion. An organization under an able executive might function effectively as a line type, but a less able man may have to surround himself with a staff to secure effective operation.

3. *The size of a company* may affect the type of organization required. A small company may operate successfully with a line type, while a large concern with a highly functionalized organization may use a committee to advantage.

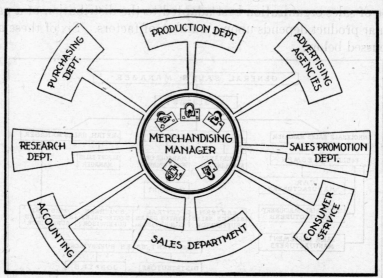

Figure 14. The sales organization of a national manufacturer of food specialties is organized along product lines and is administered by five merchandising managers, each of whom is a vice-president of the company and is directly responsible for the production, research, purchasing, sales promotion, advertising, sales, and profits of a related group of products. The merchandise managers are responsible to the president of the company.

4. *The methods of distribution* of a product have a bearing on the organization. A repeat product sold direct to consumers by house-to-house canvassers calls for a complex type of organization to provide adequate supervision and control, while an industrial specialty may be sold direct to a limited market through a simple line type of organization.

5. *The financial status of a company* may indicate the type of organization. A manufacturer with limited capital may delegate his selling to a manufacturers' agent and require no sales organization.

6. *The selling policies of a company* may have a direct bearing on its organization setup. Certain aggressive concerns emphasize sales supervision which requires a complex field organization. An-

other company may favor extensive research, in which case it will organize with a research staff to advise the general sales manager, thereby creating a line-and-staff type of organization.

Relation of Sales Department to Other Departments. A number of departments in a business organization have a bearing on the operations of the sales department, and these departments must be coördinated with the sales department.

The production department has a direct relation to sales in determining the type of merchandise to produce; the quantity, design, and packaging of the product; the balancing of production to demand; and many other factors. The production manager may be a member of a sales or merchandising committee. Or, coördination may be effected through personal contact of the heads of the two departments.

The advertising department is sometimes a section of the sales department; in other instances advertising is separated from sales and placed under a vice-president or director of distribution, who is responsible for both sales and advertising and whose function is to coördinate these two forces. Otherwise the two executive heads coördinate by personal contact or through an executive committee.

Occasionally the sales research department is a section of a general commercial research department responsible to the president or general manager; in other cases sales research is a staff function of the sales organization.

The credit, treasury, and accounting departments have a direct relation to sales, for their responsibilities are not considered as complete until buyers have been billed and collections made. These departments are usually separate from the sales department, since credit executives are not influenced in extensions of credit by a direct desire to increase sales. Sales cost accounting is sometimes performed in the sales department, but for general purposes the accounting department performs all accounting functions for the sales department. Coördination with the credit and accounting department is ordinarily done through an executive committee or through personal contact between the heads of the departments.

In some organizations the traffic department is included in the sales department since its functions are the physical phase of distribution; in other concerns traffic is a function of the manufacturing department. In certain concerns traffic is a separate function and is coördinated with the sales and manufacturing divisions through an executive or management committee.

Separate Sales Corporations. Many corporations which manufacture consumer products for national distribution have organized subsidiary sales corporations. The principal reason for the organization of such corporations is to effect savings in state taxation of foreign corporations. Most states levy an annual tax on both domestic and foreign corporations based on some form of valuation of capital stock. In the case of foreign corporations, that is, those incorporated in a state other than the one in which they are doing business, a state corporation tax is usually based on capital stock allocated to the state in which the foreign corporation is operating or on capital employed within the state levying the tax. A separate sales corporation which would require a much smaller capital than that of its parent manufacturing corporation would consequently be subjected to a much smaller tax by the states in which it does business than would the parent corporation if it were doing business in those states. The sales corporation would be taxed in all of the states in which it does business, but since these taxes would be based on the smaller capitalization of the sales corporation, there would be a saving in the amount of taxes paid. In certain states annual taxes are levied on net income, in which case the same opportunity to effect savings through a separate sales corporation would not exist.

The other advantages of separate sales corporations lie in the direction of simplified expense control in the allocation of marketing expenses; the clarifying of the organization procedure by elimination of confusion as to responsibility through the separation of sales and production; the identification of the function of the sales corporation; a marketing-minded administration in sympathy with sales objectives, which makes for more efficient operation; and possible side-line expansion without involving the parent company. By incorporating in each state which has a local corporation law entitling the sales organization to the protection of state courts with the least inconvenience and expense a legal advantage is gained.

On the other hand, the disadvantages of such a separate corporation may be: additional record-keeping and accounting; additional cost of creating and maintaining a corporate entity; lack of coördination between the parent and subsidiary corporation; and little marketing advantage inherent in such an arrangement.

Separate sales corporations are found in the distribution of foods, office appliances, chemical specialties, farm machinery, soap, motorcars, and underwear. In export selling the prevalence of the separate sales corporation is more pronounced than it is in domestic selling.

Types of Sales Organizations in Various Industries. The types of sales organizations employed in the distribution of various types of commodities illustrate the lack of standardization in organization procedure. The sales organization of a manufacturer of waxes and polishes with national and foreign distribution is headed by a president and general manager, assisted by a sales manager who has responsibility for nineteen branch managers located in key cities here and abroad. Under the branch managers, one hundred ten salesmen operate, each of whom calls on jobbers and retailers and is responsible to his branch manager. Demonstrators are employed by branch managers for retail store service. The advertising department of the company, under the supervision of an advertising manager, is under the immediate direction of the president and the general manager. The line type of organization of this manufacturer is consistent with the relative simplicity in number and variety of its products and the method of distribution of the company.

A manufacturer of oil burners and electric refrigerators with large domestic and foreign distribution divides its sales organization along product lines—one for refrigeration and another for oil burners, both of which function independent of each other and distribute their products through different channels.

The oil burner sales division is headed by the president, assisted by a general manager, who is, in turn, assisted by four section managers. The organization here is divided into four sections representing four geographical divisions of the United States. Each of the four sections is again divided into districts, of which there are forty-two in the country. The districts are under the supervision of district sales representatives, who are responsible to the four section managers. Each of the district sales representatives contacts from thirty-five to forty dealers monthly and is responsible for the merchandising, sales training, and advertising of the dealer organizations.

The refrigerator division is also headed by the president, assisted by a sales manager and an assistant sales manager, who is, in turn, responsible for a field sales force of eight district sales representatives and four sales engineers, who contact wholesale distributors. Distributor sales organizations sell local retailers.

The form of organization of this company illustrates the simplification of organization functions in the sale of a secondary product, in this case a refrigerator. The importance of the product, as well as its technical nature, has a bearing on the type of organization used here.

A manufacturer of greases and lubricating equipment with broad distribution divides the functions of its sales organization by types of customers. The sales organization is headed by a general sales manager, who is assisted by a wholesale sales manager, retail sales manager, and advertising manager. The wholesale sales manager supervises a field organization which contacts automobile, industrial machinery, and farm implement manufacturers. The retail sales manager supervises sales to distributors and jobbers. He is assisted by four regional sales supervisors, who are aided by assistant supervisors calling on distributors and jobbers, and who aid their salesmen. The retail sales manager is also assisted by an export sales manager responsible for foreign sales. The advertising manager occupies a position on a par with the wholesale and retail managers, and like them is directly responsible to the general manager of sales.

One of the largest manufacturers of electrical equipment in the world has organized its electrical-appliance sales department along product lines with five product sections as follows:

1. Domestic heating section, responsible for table and heating appliances.
2. Fan and vacuum cleaner section.
3. Commercial cooking section, responsible for the sale of heavy-duty cooking equipment, such as bake ovens, commercial toasters, waffle irons, and the like, which are sold to hotels, ships, and institutions.
4. Water heater section, responsible for the sale of electric water heaters of various types.
5. Range section, responsible for the sale of electric ranges.

Each of these sections is under the supervision of a sales manager, who is responsible for sales of apparatus in his section, the engineering and designing of new devices, and the setting of prices, discounts, and policies.

A general sales manager of the appliance division and an assistant supervise the five product sales managers and determine department sales policies.

A sales promotion manager, who is responsible for sales promotion plans for all sections, reports to the general sales manager. An advertising section operated by the advertising agency of the company reports to the general sales manager.

The field-selling organization is divided geographically into seven districts: northeast, mid-Atlantic, southeastern, central, northwestern, southwestern, and Pacific Coast. Each district is in charge of a domestic appliance district sales manager, who reports to the general sales manager. The districts are further subdivided into territories covered by individual salesmen.

Problem 1—Organization Decentralization

Murton Beverage Corporation

The Murton Beverage Corporation, established in Chicago, Illinois, in 1895, manufactures carbonated beverages, including ginger ale and orange, lime, and lemon sodas. This corporation maintains its own bottling plants in Chicago, Boston, Atlanta, and Los Angeles, and distributes its products nationally in annual volume of $9,000,000 to the drug, confectionery, and grocery wholesale trade through a sales force of twenty wholesale salesmen who work under the direction of a sales manager, who, in turn, makes sales plans, supervises product developments, creates sales policies, and is generally responsible for the success of the sales of the corporation. He is assisted by an assistant sales manager, who is responsible for the field operations and the execution of plans developed by the sales manager. He spends his time largely in contacting the salesmen of the company who operate out of the local bottling plants.

Sales of Murton products showed steady increases since the establishment of the corporation; however, a survey of business conditions disclosed that the economic situation for the future was unfavorable, with a probable lessening in consumer demand and a decline in orders from jobbers. With this possibility in view, the management believed that sales effort should be expended on the retail trade to maintain a flow of orders through jobbers.

To undertake sales to retailers, the company believed that adjustments in its sales organization would have to be made. The possibility of decentralizing the organization was considered. This change would mean that the country would be divided into regional sales divisions, with regional headquarters in the largest cities in the various regions. It was thought that five regions would be adequate.

Each regional headquarters would be a complete unit under the supervision of a regional sales manager, supervised by the assistant sales manager and responsible to the sales manager of the company. Each of the five regional managers would be given full authority in his territory to employ salesmen, develop local sales plans, and create sales policies subject to the approval of the sales manager. He would be required to answer to the home office for sales volume, and would sell at prices established by the sales manager.

The sales force would be increased to one hundred twenty men, of which number twenty would be the original wholesale force and would continue to sell only to jobbers; the one hundred new men would sell exclusively to the retail trade. The men would be divided among the five regions in proportion to the potential demand.

The creation of a decentralized organization was opposed on the grounds that expenses would be increased, control of the management weakened, personnel problems created, and the stimulation of the general management would be missing.

Questions

1. Should the Murton Corporation have decentralized its sales organization as described in the problem? Give your reasons for or against this proposal.

2. Should the former centralized organization be maintained? Give reasons for or against this course.

3. What type of sales organization should be created with decentralization? Would an extension of the home office organization be necessary?

4. Make an organization chart of the revised organization which should be created.

Problem 2—Organization by Product Specialization

Walker Textile Mills

The Walker Textile Mills, Philadelphia, Pennsylvania, established in 1905, is a unit of an organization of seven textile mills with annual sales of about $20,000,000. This company manufactures three lines of textile products: gauze and surgical bandages, curtain material and cheesecloth, and industrial and converting textiles. These are distributed through a sales organization of forty-five men through six sales branches located in the principal markets of the country. Each line is of approximately equal importance from the standpoint of sales volume and profit.

The sales organization is headed by a general sales manager who is assisted by an assistant sales manager in charge of sales to hospitals and the dry goods trade, and another assistant sales manager in charge of industrial and converting sales. These assistants contact the six branch managers, who, in turn, direct the forty-five salesmen.

The sales manager coördinates the functions of the organization by means of a merchandising committee, composed of himself and his two assistants.

Half of the salesmen in the organization, approximately twenty-two, sell all three product lines, calling on hospitals, dry goods stores, and industrial concerns. The balance are assigned to the specific product lines in large centers: some sell exclusively to hospitals; some call only on the retail dry goods trade; and others deal with industrial concerns.

The criticism has been made that such specialization of the sales organization simply adds to operating expenses and does not increase the effectiveness of the salesmen.

The sales manager, however, contends that the division of the organization along product lines enables him to assign specialized tasks to home office executives and field representatives who are specialized by training and experience to understand the needs of the trade and serve retailers and consumers more satisfactorily.

Further objection is made to the organization because half of the organization sells all three lines while the remainder of the force is specialized. The management defends this division on the grounds that in certain territories the demand is not sufficient to justify specialists on each line of products.

Questions

1. Is the present form of the Walker Mills sales organization satisfactory, or should changes be made in the division of functions? Give reasons for your answer.

2. Of what value is the merchandising committee? Should it be retained? Give reasons for your decision.

3. What is the present type of sales organization in this problem?

4. Should the six branch managers be in charge of the three types of special salesmen, or should separate branch managers be employed to manage these specialists?

Problem 3—Separate Sales Corporation

Watkins & Sharp Company

The Watkins & Sharp Company, established in Providence, Rhode Island, in 1909, capitalized at $200,000, manufactures a complete line of children's underclothing and sleeping garments. This underclothing is sold throughout the country to department stores and dry goods stores by a sales force of twenty men, who are directly responsible to the general manager in charge of sales. Many of the company's salesmen who covered sparsely populated territories where sales volume was limited and traveling expenses high had difficulty in selling a profitable volume of the company's products to meet expenses.

Rather than curtail its organization or consolidate territories, the company considered the advisability of supplying its sales organization with noncompeting products of a similar nature made by other manufacturers. Officials were reluctant, however, to detract from the prestige of the Watkins & Sharp name and line by distributing the products of other concerns. The addition of quality products would enable the salesmen in low-volume territories to fill out their lines and cut their costs of selling. A number of products for use by children, for example, hosiery, shorts, and waists could be sold along with Watkins & Sharp underclothing. The company could make a substantial profit on these related products.

One method whereby other lines might be added without detracting from the manufacturer's long-established reputation was through the formation of a separate sales corporation. Such an organization, to be called the Children's Sales Company, would serve as selling agents of the Watkins & Sharp Company, as well as other noncompeting manufacturers. Officials believed that such a separate sales company would be better able to concentrate on sales problems, be more flexible than the parent company, and more capable of serving the trade. The attorneys of Watkins & Sharp indicated that tax savings on foreign corporations in a number of states in which the company was selling would be affected by such an organization. The capital of the sales company would not be in excess of $20,000.

When the prospect of creating a separate sales organization was made known, the company received offers, from manufacturers whose lines would be carried, to coöperate in a joint direct-mail advertising campaign to the trade. This advertising would be developed by the advertising manager of the sales corporation. By sharing in the cost of this advertising, all companies would be able to advertise to the trade more profitably than before.

The parent company would control all of the stock in the separate sales company, which would be housed in the same offices with the parent company. It would be staffed by the present sales officials of the parent company and would employ the same salesmen.

Objections to the creation of a separate company were made on the grounds that the expenses of incorporation were considerable and that the prestige of the manufacturing company would be affected by carrying side lines. On the other hand, manufacturers of other lines objected to their products being sold by Watkins & Sharp salesmen under that name.

Questions

1. Should Watkins & Sharp have incorporated a separate sales corporation? Give reasons for your decision.

2. What type of sales organization should be adopted in the event that the company should incorporate a separate sales organization?

3. What would be the position of the advertising manager in charge of the coöperative advertising of the sales corporation in the event of its formation?

Reading References

Business Organization and Management, Dutton, Chap. IV.
Handbook of Sales Management, Hall, Sect. I, p. 10.
Intensive Sales Management, Aspley, Chap. II.
Modern Sales Management, Frederick, p. 38.
Sales Administration, Hayward, Chap. XXVIII.
Sales Management Today, Doubman, Chap. II.
Salesmen in Marketing Strategy, Lyon, Chap. XIII.
Scientific Marketing Management, White, Chaps. IV–XI.
Selling Policies, Converse, pp. 413–415.

CHAPTER SIX

RECRUITING SALESMEN

Why Recruit Salesmen? The procurement of salesmen is important not only in the formation of a new sales force, but also in the successful operation of an established organization. Continuous recruiting is necessary in order to:

(1) make replacements because of resignation, disability, and death, as well as inefficiency; and

(2) offset declining sales of a sales organization over a period of years.

Spasmodic recruiting is often necessary when a decision has been made to:

(1) introduce new products or revive sales of old products;

(2) exploit new markets;

(3) undertake promotion work;

(4) educate distributors.

The importance of recruiting varies widely with the type of product or service sold, type of customer served, capital available, volume of business, range of distribution, methods of distribution, and other factors. Commodities that are broadly distributed and have a large volume of consumption demand extensive sales organizations which have a continuous recruiting problem. On the other hand, many industrial products with limited markets, produced by concerns of small capital, require small sales organizations. These, accordingly, have little difficulty in securing salesmen.

The sales-recruiting problem is growing in importance with the increasing pressure of competition, the tendency toward direct sales contact, the rapid turnover in many sales organizations, the changing channels of distribution, the close cultivation of retail outlets, and the increasingly large investments in the development of salesmen.

What Type of Salesman Is Wanted? The first step in procuring salesmen is to get a definite picture of the type of man desired, in other words, to set up a standard or ideal-man type for the particular sales job to be performed. Such a type of individual will differ with the product, class of buyer, demand for the product, and nature of the sales job.

Types of individuals may be defined by such personal characteristics as age, sex, race, religion, height, weight, complexion, and appearance. Income, whether married or single, ability to save money, number of dependents, and many other factors should also be considered. Those personal characteristics which should be considered in the selection of a salesman for a specific product depend largely on the nature of the sales work to be performed. Accordingly, the type of man required may be determined by:

1. *Job analysis.* This method of determining the personal characteristics necessary for success in a specific sales job is frequently used informally by employers through their own knowledge of the nature of a sales job. Less frequently, but more desirably, a survey is made from analyses of the following:

a. *The duties performed by salesmen.* In this analysis the activities of the salesmen in the organization are described in detail either by observing them on the job or by asking each salesman to list his duties. When a complete list of duties is obtained, a very clear picture of the job results.

b. *The difficulties encountered by the salesmen* in the performance of their work. This analysis may be made by observing the salesmen or by asking them to list their principal problems. When the list of difficulties is complete, the problems arising from the job are definitely apparent.

Such a job analysis, composed of duty and difficulty analyses, automatically discloses the qualifications needed with respect to personal characteristics, experience, and abilities to perform the specific duties and surmount the specific difficulties.

A job analysis made by a large soap manufacturer revealed one hundred sixty-five major difficulties encountered by its salesmen, disclosing the need for personal characteristics, such as knowledge, tact, resourcefulness, imagination, and other personal qualities vital to the solution of such difficulties. In a duty analysis, the same organization listed more than one hundred separate duties of its salesmen, for example, driving a company automobile, calling on dealers, making collections, erecting window displays, demonstrating, and other duties calling for specific abilities.

A specific list of qualifications based on the job may be readily secured by paralleling sales duties and difficulties with the obvious personal qualities needed.

c. *Character of the product.* While an analysis of the sales job will disclose the many personal traits necessary in a salesman, a further examination of the character of the product will suggest other necessary characteristics. A highly technical product may require a salesman with technical education or experience, while a style product may call for a salesman with a knowledge of color, design, or appreciation of art.

d. *Type of buyer.* If a product is sold largely to professional buyers, the salesman may need experience in dealing with this type of trade. If a product is sold exclusively to women who have no knowledge of its intrinsic value, a salesman whose appearance is good and who has social grace may be more successful than one whose chief characteristic is his knowledge of the product.

e. *Demand for the product.* A product which is little in demand will call for salesmen with greater selling ability and more sales experience than will a product for which the demand is so great that the sale is practically automatic and little sales ability is required.

2. *An analysis of the personal history records of the present salesmen in the sales organization.* This is another way of determining the desirable personal traits for salesmen of a specific product, and establishing the particular type of salesman that should be recruited.

How to Analyze Personal History Records of Salesmen. An analysis of history records of salesmen is made as follows:

1. Select from your files the completed application blanks of all present and former salesmen.

2. Ask several of your sales supervisors or executives who are familiar with the work of these salesmen to serve as a rating committee to rate each salesman either "good" or "poor" according to individual sales records and after taking into consideration one or more of the following factors:

    a. Dollar volume of sales produced.

    b. New accounts secured.

    c. Missionary services rendered.

    d. Profit on sales produced.

    e. Low expense ratio.

Each man should be rated by several members of the rating committee as "good" or "poor"; and the final rating assigned is the average of the several ratings. Sometimes salesmen are classified as excellent, good, fair, or poor. If desired, failures can also be classified, but a breakdown carried this far will increase the statistical work, and is not necessary.

3. Analyze the personal history factors that appear on each application blank, selecting one item at a time, for example, "previous sales experience" may be considered first.

a. The first step is to find the range of years of previous sales experience of the entire group. The range may extend from less than one year to twenty years. By examining all good and poor applications, find the shortest and longest range of experience, and arbitrarily establish experience divisions by breaking the range into previous sales experience divisions, as follows:

(1) Less than one year.
(2) One to two years.
(3) Three to five years.
(4) Six to ten years.
(5) Eleven to fifteen years.
(6) Sixteen to twenty years.
(7) Over twenty years.

b. The next step is to examine the application blanks and list the number of men in each division according to whether they are good or poor as follows:

PREVIOUS SELLING EXPERIENCE

Number of Years	Number of "Good" Men	Number of "Poor" Men	Total	Percentage of "Good" Men
Less than 1	10	20	30	33⅓
1 to 2	20	10	30	66⅔
3 to 5	25	5	30	83

Follow this same procedure with each of the personal history items on the application form—age, education, marital status, number of previous jobs, membership in organizations, and any other items for which information is available.

c. Next determine the proportion of successful men in each division of each item to the total number of men, as is shown in the last column of the preceding table.

d. In selection of new men the divisions of the items studied on the application blanks, which show the greatest percentage of successful men, are the significant factors to be considered. The preceding table shows that 83 per cent of the good salesmen had from three to five years of previous sales experience when they were employed.

e. Prepare a description of an "ideal" applicant by selecting the division of each personal history item having the highest percentage of successful men. The description of an ideal applicant is a composite of the most successful personal history items of the most successful salesmen.

Such a description of an ideal salesman, while helpful in selecting new men, can rarely be paralleled in practice. It provides, however, a guide for the employer in determining the qualifications to be sought in an applicant. If the sales executive goes no further in his approach to scientific selection, he will be fortifying his judgment with additional information which should prove helpful in selection.

A description of an ideal retail salesman for a leading electric refrigerator follows:

1. He is between thirty-five and thirty-seven years of age.
2. He has from two to four years of high school education; is married and has two dependents; belongs to a civic club or lodge; has earned from $300 to $350 a month in his previous occupation; has savings or investments; is buying or owns his home and enjoys watching outdoor sports.

Establishing a Score for the "Ideal" Salesman. Some sales executives believe that a further step should be taken in establishing a score, or numerical value, for each personal history factor so that the difference between the ideal man and actual applicants can be expressed statistically. This is done by converting the highest percentage of successful men of each personal history factor to points. The previous table shows, under "Number of Years" of previous selling experience, that the highest successful group has from three to five years of experience, representing 83 per cent of all good salesmen. This percentage is converted to "points," or, in this example, 83 points.

A point table can be developed in this way, which is based on the highest percentages of successful men for each personal history factor. From this point table the score for the ideal refrigerator salesman described previously was established as follows:

1. Age (35 to 37 years)—63 points.
2. Education (1 to 4 years of high school)—57 points.
3. Marital status (married)—53 points.
4. Dependents (2)—62 points.
5. Club membership (civic club and lodge)—73 points.
6. Previous earnings (from $300 to $350 a month)—84 points. .
7. Savings and investments—76 points.
8. Home ownership—69 points.
9. Sport attendance—70 points.
10. Previous selling experience (3–5 years)—83 points.

Total point score for "ideal" salesman, 690 points.

Point scores can also be developed by using as a base the percentages of unsuccessful men for each personal history factor.

Establish a Score for a Good Salesman. So far the point rating for the ideal salesman has been described and established. But since we cannot expect to select ideal men, it is logical to prepare a point table for the good man by establishing a *weighted* average of the scores earned by all men in the good group. Because the number of good men in each division of each personal history item is different, it is necessary to weight the score of each division by multiplying the number of points by the number of good men in each division. For example, under "Number of Years" of previous selling experience, the method of weighting each division is as follows:

Number of Years	Number of Good Men	Points	Weighted Points
Less than 1	10	33	$10 \times 33 = 330$
1 to 2	20	66	$20 \times 66 = 1,320$
3 to 5	25	83	$25 \times 83 = 2,075$
Total	55	182	

Total points score of all good men divided by total number of good men in group equals the average previous experience score for good men, or

$$3,752 \div 55 = 67 \text{ points.}$$

This same method is used in securing the weighted average score of each personal history item of the good men as well as the poor men.

Final Selection Tables. From the points earned on various items by good men and poor men, as computed by the weighted average method described previously, final selection tables for predicting the success of an applicant can be set up as follows:

Qualification	Good Men	Poor Men
Age	55	40
Education	50	35
Marital Status	45	30
Dependents	56	40
Club Memberships	65	20
Previous Earnings	70	48
Savings & Investments	65	51
Home Ownership	60	20
Sport Attendance	60	30
Total Score	526	314
Average Score	58	35

When the personal history factors of an applicant are scored and compared with the average scores of good and poor men, as shown above, the potential success or failure of the applicant is indicated. At least a potentially poor salesman can be clearly discovered among the applicants.

Value of Weighted Personal History Scores in Selection. The value of weighted personal history scores in selecting salesmen has not been proved conclusively for a sufficient number of cases to establish its scientific worth. The factors considered have only a superficial relationship to the personal characteristics that distinguish the good from the poor salesman. For example, they do not reveal a man's willingness nor the abilities needed to succeed in selling. This method fails to consider such intangible personality traits as tact, determination, attitude, temperament, and persistence, which are so essential to sales accomplishment. Many of the factors are interrelated. For example, age has a bearing on marital status, and previous selling experience and previous earnings are related to savings and investments. For this reason these factors should be considered together rather than independently. Furthermore, there are often extenuating circumstances, such as economic conditions, family situations, and the type of product previously sold, which affect a man's productiveness.

The completeness and reliability of the personal history information provided on the application form is often questionable and makes the analysis faulty. For these reasons, certain sales executives believe that from the point of view of scientific accuracy, the weighted personal history is an inaccurate method of selecting salesmen. Others consider it misleading, saying that it blinds the employer to human factors which are important.

The Guardian Life Insurance Company, Phoenix Mutual Life Insurance Company, The American Gas Association, and other companies have developed personal history rating systems with which to select salesmen. The personal history items, weights, or scores developed by these companies do not, of course, have any significance for other employers, including direct competitors. The company interested in incorporating a weighted personal history blank with selection program will have to develop its own.

An analysis of the personal histories of successful and unsuccessful salesmen should be made, however, by every sales manager interested in experimenting with better selection methods. The principal danger in using a weighted personal history system of selection is the tendency to overemphasize this statistical approach to the fundamentally human problem of selection.

A simpler and more practical approach to improving selection is to analyze the application blanks of your successful and unsuccessful salesmen to determine the factors —of age, experience, education, etc.—which are characteristic of successful men without attempting to weight their personal history factors.

```
┌─────────────────────────────────────┐
│                                     │
│   PERSONAL HISTORY SCORE            │
│         Ages 30-39                  │
│                                     │
│  Name_____Agency_____     │
│                                     │
│   ITEM          APPLICANT  SCORE    │
│  Marital Status    ____     ____    │
│  Education         ____     ____    │
│  Previous Income   ____     ____    │
│  Insurance Owned   ____     ____    │
│  Occupation        ____     ____    │
│  Selling Experience ____    ____    │
│  Living Expenses   ____     ____    │
│  Length of Residence ____   ____    │
│  Present Organizations____  ____    │
│  Length of                          │
│  Negotiations      ____     ____    │
│   TOTAL SCORE                       │
│                                     │
│  LOW    BORDERLINE   HIGH           │
│  0-45     46-57     58 & over       │
│                                     │
│   Y13c  8 37 1                      │
│                                     │
└─────────────────────────────────────┘
```

FIGURE 15. Personal history factors, about which information is secured from the candidate's application form, are listed on the personal history score form used in rating applicants by the Phoenix Mutual Life Insurance Company. A different scoring slip is used for each age group.

How Large Life Insurance Companies Analyze Personal Histories

Beginning in 1916 the Phoenix Mutual Life Insurance Company has continuously analyzed the records of a large number of successful and unsuccessful agents. The relation of success in life insurance selling to various personal history items was studied and tested by statistical methods. From the many personal history items studied the following ten were selected in 1937:

1. Marital status and dependents.
2. Previous income.

3. Previous occupation.
4. Selling experience.
5. Insurance owned.
6. Education.
7. Minimum living expenses.
8. Organizations of which applicant is at present a member.
9. Length of residence in the community.
10. Length of time of negotiations.

Each of the ten items was subdivided and scored as follows:

1. *Marital Status and Dependents*—Single 2; single with dependents 3; married, no other dependents 6; married, wife and one other dependent 7; married, wife and two or three other dependents 8; married, wife and four or more other dependents 6; widowed, separated or divorced, with dependents 3.

2. *Education*—Grammar or high school education 4; college, one to three years 5; college graduate 8.

3. *Previous Income*—Student or no income 0; Under $100 per month 1; $100–$149 per month 2; $150–$174 per month 3; $175–$199 per month 4; $200–$249 per month 5; $250–$399 per month 7; 400 or more per month 9.

4. *Life Insurance Owned*—Never owned more than $2,999 life insurance, score 0; now owns $3,000–$4,999 score 3; now owns $5,000–$7,999 score 5; now owns $8,000–$14,999 score 7; now owns $15,000 or more score 9; owned $10,000 or more—lapsed score 4; owned $5,000–$9,999—lapsed score 2; owned under $5,000—lapsed score 0.

5. *Previous Occupation*—Executive 9; salesman of intangibles 6; salesman of tangibles 4; retail business-tradesman 8; retail business-miscellaneous 5; office worker—semi-executive type 6; office worker—clerical type 3; engineer 4; professional 3; manual work 2; other 4.

6. *Selling Experience*—None 5; less than one year 3; one year–four years eleven months 6; five years–six years eleven months 8; seven years–nine years eleven months 7; ten years or more 6.

7. *Minimum Living Expenses*—Under $100 per month 0; $100 to $124 per month 1; $125–$149 per month 3; $150–$174 per month 5; $175–$199 per month 7; $200–$399 per month 9; $400 or more per month 8.

8. *Length of Residence in Community*—Stranger 4; less than one year 2; from one to three years 4; from three to five years 5; five years or more 6; previous extensive residence—returned within past three months 5; previous extensive residence—returned from three to fifteen months ago 2; occasional residence over period of years 4.

9. *Present Membership in Organizations*—None score 0; one organization 4; two organizations 5; three organizations 6; four organizations 7; five organizations 8; six organizations 9; seven or more organizations 8.

10. *Length of Time of Negotiations*—Less than three months 5; from three to six months 6; from six to twelve months 7; twelve months or more 8.

Each sales applicant is scored in the same way on each of the ten items regardless of age, but his score is interpreted according to his age. Critical scores obtained from actual production records and persistency of salesmen with the company vary for each age group as follows:

	Low	Borderland	High
Ages 20–24	0–33	34–39	40 and over
Ages 25–29	0–38	39–47	48 and over
Ages 30–39	0–45	46–57	58 and over
Ages 40–44	0–50	51–62	63 and over
Ages 45 and over	0–56	57–65	66 and over

To determine the total score for any sales applicant, his score for each of the ten items is noted on a "Personal History Scoring Slip." The total of the ten figures is an applicant's score. For example, an applicant, thirty-five years of age scores 64, a high score when compared with the critical average, when he possesses the following qualifications:

Qualification	Score
Marital status and dependents—Mar., wife, & 1 ch.	7
Education—High school grad.	4
Previous income—$325 a mo.	7
Life insurance owned—$6,000	5
Previous occupation—Floor salesman	8
Selling experience—9 years	7
Min. living expenses—$250 a mo.	9
Length of residence—5 yrs. or more	6
Membership in organizations—3 org.	6
Length of negotiations—Less than 3 mos.	5
Total score	64

The company believes that no scoring system has as yet been devised which will predict absolute success or failure at the time of application. Careful judgment by managers will always be needed, and there will always be exceptions. If applicants who fall in the low-score groups are eliminated, however, the likelihood of losing a potential success is almost nil, according to the Phoenix Mutual Life Insurance Company, with whose permission this method is described.

Scoring of personal history factors is superior to the general-impression method of interviewing and can be developed by any firm that has a sufficient number of cases, by setting a range of values for the items on its application form. In determining the score for each personal history factor, sufficient items should be used and an adequate number of cases studied.

Life Insurance Sales Research Bureau Analysis of Personal Histories. A scoring system for selecting life insurance agents based on the personal history records of more than ten thousand life underwriters has been developed by the Life Insurance Sales Research Bureau. The Bureau gathered and analyzed twenty-four personal history items and devised a scoring system so as to give a satisfactory prediction of success, for example: when a score of two points is assigned a man who owns $2,500 of life insurance, and a score of four points is assigned to a man who owns $5,000 of life

PERSONAL RATING CHART
Qualifications for Life Insurance Selling Name_____

RATING SCALE							PENALTY POINT TABLE		
1	2	3	4	5		6	7		8
Factors	Qualifications for Standard Rating	Maximum Points	Penalties	Net Points					Penalty Points
Age	25 to 40 Years, inclusive	3				Age	Under age 25		2
							Ages 41-50 inclusive		2
							Over 50 years		3
Education	College Graduate	3				Education	Less than College Graduate, but at least High School Graduate		1
							Less than High School Graduate, but at least 1 year High School		2
							Less than 1 Year High School		3
Marital Status	Married / Single, if under age 25	5				Marital Status	Single (Ages 25-40)		1
							Single (Ages 41 and over)		2
							Separated, Divorced, Widower		3
Previous Experience	1 Year or more Outside Selling (see Penalty Table for exceptions)	4				Previous Experience	Life or General Insurance Selling		1
	Retail Store Proprietors						Two Years or more Financial Selling		2
	Executives						Less than 1 Year Outside Selling (less than 6 months—take prior occupation)		2
	Insurance Clerks						Inside (Store) Selling		2
	Sales Promotion or Management						Student, Teacher, Clergy, Social Service		2
							Clerical Workers (other than insurance)		2
							Bankers, Doctors, Lawyers, Scientists		3
							Non-Selling Occupations not Mentioned		3
FINANCIAL STATUS — Life Ins. Owned	Under Age 25—$1,000 or more / Ages 25-29—$3,000 or more / Ages 30 and over—$5,000 or more	1				FINANCIAL STATUS — Life Ins. Owned	Under Age 25—less than $1,000 / Ages 25-29—less than $3,000 / Ages 30 and over—less than $5,000		1
Savings (including Life Ins. C.V.)	Under Age 25—$250 or more / Ages 25-29—$500 or more / Ages 30 and over—$1,000 or more	1				Savings (including Life Ins. C.V.)	Under Age 25—less than $250 / Ages 25-29—less than $500 / Ages 30 and over—less than $1,000		1
Years in Community	2 Years or more	3				Years in Community	Less than 2 Years but more than 1 Year		1
							Less than 1 Year but more than 3 Months		2
							Less than 3 Months		3
Employed	Employed	2				Employed	Unemployed 3 to 6 Months		1
							Unemployed 6 Months or More		2
	Total	20							

Pub. 326-37 The Guardian Life Insurance Company of America. See Reverse for Instructions.

FIGURE 16. Personal rating chart used by The Guardian Life Insurance Company of America in rating the qualifications of sales applicants. If an individual's qualifications are as set forth in column 2, "Qualifications for Standard Rating," he is given the maximum points allocated for each factor, "Maximum Points," column 3. If his qualifications are as set forth in column 7, the "Penalty Point Table," he is penalized according to column 8, "Penalty Points." The points penalized are noted in column 4, "Penalties," and subtracted from "Maximum Points," column 3, the difference being noted in column 5, "Net Points." The rating is obtained by adding up the points given in column 5, "Net Points."

insurance, it is done not because someone merely thinks that a man should own a large amount of life insurance to be a successful life underwriter, but because the actual records showed that the man who owned the larger amount tended to remain in the business longer and to sell more insurance than the one who owned only $2,500 of life insurance.

After determining the relative importance of twenty-four items, the ten items in the scoring system selected as the ones giving the best prediction of success were:

1. Dependents.
2. Occupation.
3. Employment status.
4. Time with present employer.
5. Present membership in organizations.
6. Officer in how many organizations.
7. Net worth.
8. Minimum current living expenses.
9. Amount of life insurance owned.
10. Length of negotiations.

The scores on the item "dependents" were as follows: no dependents, 3; one dependent, 4; two dependents, 6; three dependents, 8; four dependents, 8; five dependents, 7; and six or more dependents, 4. If the prospective agent has two dependents he receives a score of six.

To obtain a prospective agent's total numerical score, each of the ten selected items on his application blank is scored by referring to the Bureau's scoring system developed by its analysis of personal history factors. The scores are then totaled. The next step is to interpret this score in terms of probable success or failure.

The first interpretation takes into consideration the age of the prospective agent. Since older men tend to receive higher scores than do younger men, an age adjustment table is included in the plan. The applicant's score is classified in the table as poor, fair, good, very good, or excellent. Prospective agents who are rated excellent are those who tend to produce much more business and may be expected to remain in the business longer than those with lower ratings. Those with good ratings who survive one year in the business produce one and one-half times as much as the agents with poor ratings according to the experience of the Bureau.

The Bureau warns that no rating plan has ever been devised that will predict absolute success or failure at the time a prospective agent makes application. No plan can be substituted for good judgment. It is still necessary to follow other established selection procedures, such as obtaining inspection reports, checking references, evaluating personal characteristics, and checking a man's physical condition.

The establishment of standard personal qualifications. After a job analysis has been made and the personal history records of present successful and unsuccessful salesmen have been analyzed, the two will form the basis for a standard of personal qualifications. The qualifications of the applicant may be readily compared with the standard established to determine the applicant's fitness for the job.

A standard of qualifications will vary with each sales organization, depending on the nature of the sales job, type of product, class of trade, and other factors previously mentioned.

Standard Qualifications for Salesmen of a Paper Products Manufacturer. A specialty paper products manufacturer, whose line consists of approximately ten thousand items—tags, labels, and crepe paper, and the like—and who sells direct to retail stationery and office supply distributors, as well as to large consumers, established the following standard of qualifications for his salesmen:

Age: The ideal starting age is between 23 and 27. Generally men of this age are more easily taught and adapt themselves more readily to new conditions than men of older years, yet they have the maturity of judgment and stability that younger men do not possess. These ages are not arbitrary limits, as the qualities mentioned may be possessed by older or younger men.

Health: A sound physical condition is most essential. New salesmen should be physically fit and have good resistance to disease and fatigue.

Education: A high school training or its equivalent is the minimum educational qualification desirable. An applicant who possesses to a high degree all other qualifications may be employed, provided he has the ability and willingness to remove his educational deficiency by proper courses of study.

Experience: Previous selling experience is not essential, although experience in high-grade retail and wholesale establishments, particularly in stationers' and jewelers' stores, has been found of value in learning to sell the line.

Personal Appearance: Neatness and cleanliness are necessary, as well as good taste in style and color of clothing. A courteous, dignified, and clean-cut bearing is desirable for creating a favorable first impression on prospects and customers.

Character: There should be no doubt as to the honesty and integrity of the man, and his manner of living should be free from conditions and habits harmful to his social and physical welfare.

Personality: Among the many factors that make up this qualification, cheerfulness, industry, resourcefulness, tact, coöperativeness, and a sense of humor are the most essential.

Cheerfulness: This quality, combined with a sense of humor, enables a man to maintain a healthy mental attitude toward his work regardless of its difficulties.

Industry: This quality keeps a man going voluntarily without letdown throughout the day, week, or year. It includes the elements of stick-to-itiveness and persistence, as well as those of thoroughness and attention to detail.

Resourcefulness: This quality, which overcomes seemingly serious obstacles or objections, largely by use of a good imagination, enables a man to visualize a new condition or state of affairs, for example, a new use for an article, or a new way of accomplishing a result. A resourceful and imaginative man does not become or remain an imitator or a routine worker.

Tactfulness: The ability to work harmoniously with others. The ability for teamwork is a necessary attribute for success in selling our line.

Attention to Detail: A certain attention to and mastery of ᴅ
for our salesmen. A man to whom many details are irksome aɪ
not as a rule be successful. On the other hand, the type of m
and exacting in details usually lacks imagination. It is wise tᴏ
salesmen from either class.

Functional Types of Salesmen. In the past, sale
consisted largely of making sales. While the primaɪy purpose oɪ
salesmen is still the procurement of orders, they now perform a
great many nonselling activities brought about by the demands of
customers for service and the realization on the part of sellers that
lasting success depends on the satisfaction of their customers. Not
only have wholesale salesmen been called upon to dress windows,
make collections, educate dealers, and many other promotional activities, but industrial buyers have demanded highly specialized
product knowledge not possessed by the average industrial salesmen. Furthermore, the pressure of competition has made it necessary for salesmen to perform various service duties to cope successfully with competitors.

Specialized types of salesmen and sales groups have developed to
meet these changed conditions affecting salesmen's operations.
These salesmen fall into the following six separate categories:

1. *Specialty salesmen* employed by manufacturers specialize exclusively in the introduction of a new product or the revival of sales
of an old product. They call on retailers to secure introductory
distribution or to broaden the distribution of an established line,
particularly in the food, drug, hardware, and dry goods lines.

Their need arose from the increasing difficulty experienced by
manufacturers in the face of keen competition in securing adequate
distribution through retail outlets and in the reluctance of wholesalers to introduce new items. Specialty men usually take small
orders from retailers. These orders are turned over to wholesalers
specified by retailers. Wholesalers deliver, bill, and collect for the
merchandise sold by the manufacturer's specialty salesmen.

Specialty salesmen may travel with wholesalers' salesmen, sometimes paying the expense of transportation, but usually specialty
men operate individually or in crews. Sometimes specialty men
are employed for a limited period until distribution is secured, while
in other cases permanent specialty crews are maintained which
travel from market to market.

Limitations of specialty salesmen from the standpoint of the
manufacturer are their high cost, since they usually take small or-

ders; the antagonism of the trade through overselling; and the large volume of rejected orders by wholesalers for reasons concerning credit, or by retailers upon delivery by wholesalers. Wholesalers object to specialty salesmen who consume the limited credit of retailers; they oppose the sale of products for which they have no regular demand; and they resent the specialty salesman's taking the time of their salesmen when they work the trade together.

In spite of these objections, manufacturers of drugs, foods, and hardwares consider that specialty men are necessary to secure distribution, since they are aggressive and experienced.

2. *Junior salesmen* are employed to save the time of regular senior salesmen in the performance of nonselling activities. They are usually used in the sale of specialties, such as office appliances, home appliances, and other types of selling involving much preliminary prospecting for customers, planning of sales, or following up of customers. Juniors may be used for obtaining information about prospects, making demonstrations, or doing anything required by the senior salesmen except selling the product.

A typewriter company used junior salesmen to increase the sales call efficiency of regular salesmen by placing typewriters on trial with prospective buyers. Juniors located key prospects and secured information leading to later sales interviews by senior salesmen.

A large vacuum cleaner organization that sells to housewives call their junior salesmen "planters," for their duty is to plant machines in homes for trial use. They are followed by "closers," who follow up the trials arranged by the planters or junior salesmen.

Under another plan junior salesmen attempt to complete sales and perform the full functions of a senior salesman but are subject to the orders of senior salesmen. Many concerns employ young men as juniors largely for the purpose of training them for full-function sales jobs when territories are available.

3. *Missionary salesmen* are employed to assist retail and wholesale distributors in the resale of manufacturers' lines. While junior salesmen often do missionary work, in certain instances a missionary sales crew or a missionary salesman is employed purely for promotional or instructional purposes. Frequently regular senior salesmen may engage in missionary work, which consists of retail clerk education, stock arrangement, window and store advertising displays, special sales drives, and sales work on consumers.

The California Fruit Growers Exchange maintains a missionary sales force which works with wholesale and retail fruit distributors in the display and advertising of Sunkist oranges.

Sometimes the designation of "missionary" is applied to specialty salesmen who introduce new items or revive the sale of old products. The representatives of the Coca-Cola Company function somewhat as missionary men doing merchandising work with retailers in the proper dispensing and advertising of their product.

4. *Senior salesmen* sell the full line of their company's products and spend their time largely seeking orders and in direct-sales activity rather than in locating prospects, servicing, promoting, and introducing new items. Their clientele is usually established, and they ordinarily call on dealers on a regular schedule, or, if selling to consumers, they perform all selling functions unless aided by juniors.

5. *Sales engineers* are engaged in the sale of technical products, such as rubber belting, motors, electrical equipment, and pumps. Sales are usually made to trained buyers who demand technical information.

The Goodyear Tire and Rubber Company employs and advertises the services of its GTM, or Goodyear Technical Man, a sales engineer specializing in the sale of rubber belting for industrial use.

A sales engineer may make lengthy analyses of needs or applications of his product in industrial concerns; follow up such surveys with definite sales engineering proposals; and close sales on the basis of his knowledge of engineering problems. In certain concerns sales engineers close no sales but merely serve as advisers to the regular senior salesmen of the company.

6. *Export salesmen* represent domestic organizations in foreign markets, calling on foreign distributors. They are frequently promoted from the domestic sales force. Export salesmen must have a knowledge of foreign exchange, tariffs, and shipping regulations; of political and market conditions in the countries in which they are operating; and of their company's product and policies. As they operate far from headquarters, they are usually given considerable responsibility in quoting prices and interpreting policies.

Standard Characteristics of Each Functional Type of Salesman. Separate standards of qualifications should be set up for each functional type of salesman employed, on account of the widely different duties, types of customers, and demand conditions experienced by each salesman. A junior salesman may well be a young man with limited experience and product knowledge, but an export sales-man should have age, broad experience, and an intimate knowledge of company products and policies.

Sources of Salesmen. When the question, What type of sales-man is wanted? has been answered by job analysis and analysis of personal history factors of present men, and when standard personal qualifications have been established, the next question is, Where may such a salesman be found? In the following discussion the various sources will be considered separately.

Sources From Which Present Salesmen Were Secured. Knowledge of the sources where present successful salesmen were obtained offers one convenient and logical answer to the question, Where may good salesmen be obtained? With adequate records, particularly application blanks of present salesmen, it is not difficult to determine the sources of present successful and unsuccessful salesmen.

The Life Insurance Sales Research Bureau made an analysis of the sources of four hundred thirty-five life insurance agents, good and poor, in fifty-three agencies, representing twenty companies. This survey revealed that agents known to managers and their assistants, and presumably brought into the business by them, are more successful than agents recruited from other sources; while agents recommended by influential persons are usually good sales-men, as are also voluntary applicants.

A manufacturer of men's wear analyzed its sources of salesmen and found that about 47 per cent were added through the company's own salesmen; 21 per cent were obtained by advertising; 12 per cent were voluntary personal applicants; 10 per cent applied by mail; and the balance were developed within the organization.

A manufacturer of toilet preparations, with a sales force of nineteen men, obtained its organization from the following sources: 63 per cent through company salesmen; 21 per cent by advertising; 11 per cent by personal application; and the remainder were devel-oped within the organization.

The Previous Occupations of Present Salesmen. Previous oc-cupation gives a clue to likely sources of new salesmen. Applica-tion blanks readily provide information for this analysis. In the study made of life insurance agents, mentioned previously, it was found that agents who were formerly specialty salesmen, engineers, proprietors, executives, and clerks were decidedly higher producers than teachers, lawyers, and inside salesmen. When each occupational group was considered as a whole, however, the engineers, proprietors, and executives were less successful than specialty salesmen, investment men, bankers, and clerks.

Other Sources. Numerous other sources of salesmen are available and in the absence of proved sources offer an opportunity to test their value for a particular type of man desired. These sources include:

Present salesmen. This is one of the best sources of new sales recruits for the following reasons: they are in frequent contact with and know the ability of other salesmen; they are aware of salesmen who are seeking to make new connections; they like to choose their own associates; and they prefer to have good men selling with them rather than against them.

Salesmen are frequently given a bonus for introducing new salesmen to the organization, as in the case of a cash register company which paid its regular salesmen a bonus of $50 for recommending a salesman who made good. Old salesmen were required to write letters of recommendation to division managers, and when new men so recommended reached their regular sales quota for two months in succession, the old salesman making the recommendation received his bonus.

Objections to this method are that salesmen may recommend personal friends of inferior ability and may resent the management's refusal to accept them; in commission organizations salesmen may be reluctant to bring in new men to sell in competition.

Present salesmen may be encouraged to suggest new salesmen by means of sales meetings, letters and bulletins, and personal contacts. Salesmen may be given a list of desirable qualifications for new salesmen and asked to prepare a list of customers, neighbors, friends, and acquaintances for discussion with the sales manager.

Present customers. This furnishes a good source, since customers are usually favorably disposed, know the seller's product, and are generally acquainted with salesmen who are seeking new connections.

A large investment house seeks salesmen through its clients by means of the following letter:

Dear Sir:

A short time ago we opened our Boston office to take care of our rapidly increasing business throughout New England. We are now looking for two or three high grade men to fill positions in our new organization. As one of our customers, you realize the worth of our investments and the benefits to be derived from same, and we thought you might appreciate the opportunity of recommending someone who is looking for a permanent and dignified connection with a business that offers many possibilities, even to executive positions. If you will send us the names in the enclosed envelope of any you think worthy of this opportunity, we would greatly appreciate it.

Advertising. There are several methods of advertising for salesmen, such as classified or display in daily newspapers, direct mail advertising to selected lists, and business paper advertising. There is considerable difference of opinion as to the value of each type of advertising for salesmen.

FIGURE 17. Several types of newspaper advertisements for salesmen. A large display advertisement is illustrated. The classified advertisements for salesmen illustrate the "blind" newspaper box address and the office address without company name.

1. *Newspaper advertising.* Organizations with a large turnover in men find newspaper advertising a prolific source of men, although they are sometimes of questionable ability. Unless an advertisement is highly selective, hundreds of men may respond, creating an expensive problem of interviewing and selecting, with a tend-

ency to mass recruiting and an ultimate breakdown in the selection procedure.

Newspaper advertisements may be *blind* or *open;* open advertisements identify the advertiser, while blind advertisements carry only a key or telephone number or street address. Organizations having difficulty in inducing men to consider their type of selling usually use blind advertisements. These often arouse antagonism on the part of applicants, who feel that they have been tricked into responding. The response from open advertisements is usually considerably smaller but higher in quality.

Advertisements which are selective usually state definitely the qualifications of the man sought and describe the job as difficult and the remuneration moderate. The response is usually small, but the grade of applicant is higher, and the process of interviewing consumes much less time and money.

The attitude of many sales executives toward newspaper advertising is expressed in a bulletin sent to branch managers by a national food manufacturer who distributes direct to consumers.

While we do not want to encourage advertising for men in newspapers, we sometimes find it necessary to use this medium. *Help Wanted* ads in newspapers should be used as a last resort. In placing ads in papers the following factors should be considered: (a) The circulation of the paper and its popularity as a want ad medium. (b) Evening and Sunday papers are extensively and thoroughly read by a large number of people and we believe that they are the best for our purpose. (c) The ad must be set up to attract attention. A white margin of about one-fourth inch at top, bottom, and sides is desirable. (d) It is usually best to run an ad for two days.

An example of results from classified newspaper advertising by a large company over a period of three years and seven months is significant: [1]

Numbers of advertisements run	888
Responses received	11,988
Appointments made	5,527
Appointments kept	3,951
Men hired	521
Men going into field	255
Men failing	168
Men succeeding	87

Display advertisements for salesmen, which are placed on financial or sport pages rather than on classified pages, are usually read by men who have jobs rather than by those looking for work.

[1] O. R. Johnson in *Administration*.

The value of newspaper advertising as a source of salesmen should be tested in individual cases by keeping records of the number of inquiries; number of men interviewed; number hired; type of paper used, such as morning, evening, or Sunday; frequency of appearance; and quality of inquiries.

2. *Direct mail advertising.* Direct mail advertising is sometimes used successfully to reach groups of men who may be likely candidates for a sales force. Such men may be in occupational groups, which analysis shows constitute a good source of salesmen. They may be men who are unusually ambitious, such as those subscribing to study courses, attending night or summer schools, or belonging to self-improvement organizations. Other men who may be circularized are those who think they are in blind-alley jobs, who dislike their present work or are economically disturbed. To reach these possibilities a mailing list must be procured and letters prepared and mailed.

3. *Business paper advertising.* In every industry reliable magazines or trade papers serve as a medium for advertising for salesmen. Salesmen who are progressive and may be seeking new opportunities can be readily reached through classified or display advertisements in the trade press. The circulation of such papers is limited and the volume of inquiries may be small, but the quality is usually higher on account of the selective nature of the medium.

Schools. Sales candidates from schools and colleges, while lacking in practical background and experience, have the advantage of being adaptable and easily trained. The Northwestern Mutual Life Insurance Company studied the five-year sales records of one hundred sixty college graduate agents averaging twenty-two years of age and found that their average sales showed steady increases each year as follows:

	Average Production
First year	$44,737
Second year	51,984
Third year	80,151
Fourth year	88,627
Fifth year	99,885

One objection to college graduates as salesmen is that they do not stay long enough to become effective. The Northwestern survey showed that 70 per cent of college graduates contracted remained until the end of the first year; 45.6 per cent remained until the end of the second year; 42.5 per cent, the third; 39.4 per cent, the fourth; and 34.4 per cent, the fifth. Compared with the insurance business as a whole, the percentages indicated here are distinctly favorable.

Certain sales organizations recruit from colleges for summer selling. One organization selling direct to consumers employed seven hundred students and teachers during one summer. Many colleges with business courses or schools of business administration today provide young men with a knowledge of business fundamentals, which equips them for earlier sales production than was possible in the past among college graduates.

Own organization. Every concern has within its own factory or office possible candidates for sales work who are familiar with company policies and products, and who are possessed with loyalty developed over a period of years. It is possible for an employer to observe such men closely and judge their abilities accurately. The selection of company employees for sales work also serves as an incentive to employees and as a form of promotion. The disadvantage of this plan, however, is that such men may lack sales ability.

Salesmen from competitors. Salesmen employed from competitors are trained in selling, know the trade and product, and in some instances expect to bring new customers with them. On the other hand, such men often demand more compensation as an inducement to join a new organization; they may be set in the ways of competitors; and they may be arbitrary or independent in their attitude. The employment of the salesmen of competitors may create antagonism in the trade, and there is no assurance that a salesman hired from a competitor will be as successful with his new as with his old organization. Many companies have a definite policy against hiring salesmen from competitors.

The attitude of many companies toward hiring the salesmen of competitors is expressed in the instructions of a large food products company to its branch managers:

Loyalty cannot be bought. It comes through respect for and confidence in one's employers and through ambition and happiness in one's work. This company will not resort to any unfair practices in order to acquire the services of any individual. The company's employees are not allowed to interfere with the employees of competitors nor attempt to dissatisfy such employees with their present connections, nor to solicit or suggest that such employees apply to this company for employment. We do not refuse to employ men who have previously worked for competitors; many of our most loyal and efficient employees have had such training. But we do refuse to permit members of our organization to engage in efforts to dissatisfy, disorganize, and deplete the present personnel of companies competing with us.

Salesmen from related lines. Salesmen who sell related but non-competing lines often have experience with the same class of trade and perhaps have established contacts and good will. Yet their success in a similar line may be no indication of their ability to sell another product.

Employment services. While employment bureaus generally specialize in clerical workers, occasionally employment services are familiar with sales procurement problems and list competent salaried salesmen. Agencies are rarely interested in placing salesmen on commission. Such sales employment agencies may suggest a variety of applicants, saving the employer's time in interviewing candidates. Sales executives sometimes assume that a salesman who cannot sell his own services to a prospective employer but must rely upon an agency to place him is lacking in the initiative and sales ability to qualify him for sales work. Others believe that only floaters, failures, and undesirable candidates seek placement through agencies. This assumption is not generally true, and it is sometimes advisable that specifications for sales jobs to be filled be left with employment agencies who specialize in sales personnel.

Purchasing agents. Professional buyers are constantly subjected to sales solicitations and are in daily contact with salesmen who are seeking new connections. Purchasing agents know the abilities of salesmen and are in an excellent position to recommend able men. A purchasing agent often takes a personal interest in the success of a salesman whom he has recommended.

Influential people. People with many contacts, such as secretaries of chambers of commerce, church officials, secretaries of civic clubs, city and state officials, and bankers, are usually acquainted with salesmen seeking connections and are often a source of sales personnel. In interviewing such persons, explain briefly why a salesman is being sought, tell of the success of present salesmen, describe the type of man wanted, and discuss training so that the influential person will be better able to assist in locating a desirable man.

Sales managers in other lines. Many concerns that employ salesmen have a file of voluntary applicants who cannot be absorbed into their businesses. These files are an excellent source of sales recruits if the coöperation of the sales manager can be secured. Also, related lines of business may employ part-time salesmen who require an additional account or two. Sales managers in these lines may be willing to exchange names of their part-time salesmen.

Preliminary training school. A training course is often a sound source of desirable salesmen. Men who are employed, but who may be considering a change, can enroll for training after working hours. A training school enables such men to continue their own occupation and to receive their usual income while learning a new business. The school gives the employer an opportunity to discover a candidate's fitness for selling.

Voluntary applicants. Salesmen who voluntarily apply for a sales connection reveal a high degree of interest and probably some knowledge of the employer. In periods of prosperity such applicants are usually few in number. Although a limited source, this type of recruit is worthy of consideration.

Miscellaneous sources. Salesmen may be recruited also from the "Situations Wanted" advertisements; by observing salesmen in other lines; by advertising in college papers; by contacting salesmen who call to sell other goods; by contacting retail dealers' salesmen; and by utilizing fraternal and club affiliations.

Problem 1—Sources of Salesmen

Barbour Life Insurance Agency

The Barbour Life Insurance Agency, located in a city of fifty thousand population in the Middle West, and serving a rich rural area, has an annual production of $5,000,000 worth of life insurance through twenty full-time and ten part-time agents, all of whom receive their compensation in the form of commissions. The greatest source of production is the city in which the agency is located, but the manager decided that additional agents must be secured in the rural and small-town districts.

The method planned by the manager for securing such agents was:

1. To canvass the company's present policyholders in the rural towns in which agents are to be sought.

2. To write and canvass prominent citizens of the rural towns, explaining that the company was looking for agents.

3. To insert a display advertisement in a weekly newspaper circulating in the locality. This advertisement, listing the desirable qualifications of the agents wanted, was to be run in two issues. The name of the company was to be signed to the advertisement. Replies were to be sent to the manager.

Associates of the manager of the Barbour Agency, with whom he discussed this plan, objected to it for the following reasons:

1. Policyholders do not want to be bothered by requests for names of possible agents.

2. Prominent citizens have neither the incentive nor the ability to suggest likely agents.

3. Nominators will believe that it is an attempt to sell them life insurance and will resent such a patent subterfuge.

4. The local newspaper advertisement will attract only floaters who are out of jobs.

5. Letters to nominators may in many cases land in wastebaskets.

In view of these objections, the manager was undecided whether to go ahead with his plans or to attempt some other method of recruiting sales agents.

Questions

1. Was the manager's plan for securing agents sound? Give your reasons for or against the plan.

2. What other sources of agents might be used?

3. What procedure should the manager follow to insure the most likely sources of agents?

Problem 2—Types of Salesmen

Eastern Insurance Company

The Eastern Insurance Company with assets of $150,000,000 was established in 1923 in Philadelphia. It specializes in automobile, public liability, workman's compensation, fire, fidelity, burglary, plate glass, personal accident, and health insurance. It is represented by one thousand two hundred salaried salesmen who operate out of ninety branch offices in the principal cities of the country. The company sells direct to the insured rather than through brokers and agents, as is usually the custom.

The two types of salesmen in the automobile sales department are new business salesmen and service salesmen. The duties of the new business salesmen consist of the solicitation and sale of all types of automobile insurance and affiliated lines, and coverages to owners of individual automobiles and owners of fleets of cars and trucks. Three hundred new businessmen are in the automobile department.

The service salesmen are responsible for service to and regular contact with current automobile insurance policyholders. Personal calls are made upon them for the purpose of reviewing their insurance needs; of recommending additional coverages and securing the names of friends and acquaintances who own automobiles, as prospects for the new businessmen. The service salesman requires sales ability in his service work, since he is expected to produce a quota of new accounts in addition to his service duties. Both types of salesmen concentrate their efforts in metropolitan areas where the company's offices are located. They are subject to transfer to any branch office as sales conditions and policy may require.

Different qualifications are required for each of the two types of salesmen. The new businessman must have considerable initiative, courage, drive, and energy needed in making new contacts and securing new customers. He should be optimistic in temperament and not easily discouraged. The service salesman must have a helpful attitude, resourcefulness, be able to get along well with people, wear well, and have the maturity and manner to command respect so that customers will act on his recommendations.

Both types of salesmen should be between twenty-four and thirty years of age, and preferably unmarried. They should have at least a high school education, and it is to their advantage if they are college graduates. Previous business experience is desirable but it need not necessarily be sales experience. The company is interested in men who have earned at least part of their college expenses.

Good appearance is an important consideration. Men should use good English, and have an agreeable speaking voice and a friendly manner. Imagination, intelligence, character, and ability to think quickly are important characteristics.

The advantages of having two types of salesmen are the more aggressive, skillful development of new business as well as the conservation of existing business which insures steady company growth and the building of good will. Salesmen who are especially successful in opening new accounts often lack interest in following up their customers to sell additional coverages or types of insurance. Other salesmen become discouraged when trying to secure new accounts and devote their efforts to cultivating old customers.

The use of two types of salesmen has been questioned because of the added expense of employing two salesmen to do the normal work of one. Customers may resent having to do business with two salesmen. Confusion and misunderstandings may result. Service salesmen lose the stimulus of securing new business. Additional clerical and administrative work is involved. New business salesmen may create ill will by high-pressure methods.

Questions

1. Considering the nature of this business, do you believe that the company should employ new business and service types of salesmen? Give definite reasons in addition to those mentioned in the problem.

2. How should each type of salesman be recruited?

3. Could other functional types of salesmen be advantageously employed by this company? What types would you suggest?

Problem 3—Recruiting Salesmen to Retailers

Robertson & Walker Company

The Robertson & Walker Company, New York City, pack a coffee branded "R & W," in one-pound canisters. It is sold in an annual volume of approximately $10,000,000 through wholesale grocers in all parts of the country. A considerable amount of money is invested in advertising in national women's magazines. On account of keen competition and declining sales, the company is considering the use of retail specialty men, who will secure distribution in territories where no distribution now exists and in other areas where competition is seriously affecting R & W volume.

A number of large competitors of the company employ specialty salesmen, who call on retail grocers, taking orders for coffee and turning them over to wholesale grocers for delivery and billing. Heretofore, the company has employed no specialty salesmen to call on retail food outlets. A force of twenty salesmen calls on wholesalers, coöperatives, and a few chain store systems.

The president of the company opposes the use of specialty men for only one product and that a staple. He believes that consumption of the company's coffee cannot be increased rapidly and that money spent for specialty salesmen should be used for advertising. (This form of publicity, of course, would keep the name of the product before consumers and remind them to buy the product when they see it displayed in retail stores.) The president also feels that specialty men are not approved by wholesalers and are disliked by many retailers.

Furthermore, the president believes that many specialty orders are rejected by jobbers for poor credit, or that when such orders are actually delivered by the wholesaler, the retailer refuses to accept them. In his opinion, the growing number of chain stores and voluntary groups which purchase through a central buying office limits the field of specialty men.

The sales manager of the company, on the other hand, maintains that retail food merchants will not stock R & W coffee on the strength of the company's advertising or the demand of consumers; that the wholesaler's salesmen will not push the product or introduce it in new retail outlets; and that many wholesalers are antagonistic toward advertised brands although the quality and margin of profit on R & W coffee is equal to other well-known brands on the market. If the decline in sales is to be halted, the sales manager believes that the only way to secure new distributors or revive sales in territories where volume is falling is by means of specialty men.

When distribution has been secured and volume has increased, the sales manager favors reducing the number of specialty men and permitting the advertising to continue its work of developing consumer preference through the retail outlets.

Questions

1. Should the company add specialty salesmen to secure retail distribution? Give reasons for your decision.

2. If the employment of specialty salesmen is not advisable, how can the company secure distribution in territories where its product is not now sold?

3. Is the sales manager's suggestion that specialty men be temporarily employed a sound idea?

4. Could other functional types of salesmen be profitably employed by this company?

Problem 4—Sources of Sales Engineers

Larson Regulator Company

The Larson Regulator Company, Chicago, Illinois, manufactures a full line of high-grade automatic regulating and control devices for the oil and gas industry, equipment which is highly technical and is used by engineers. Annual sales approximate $2,400,000 and are made direct to oil refineries and gasoline plants through a sales force of five salesmen.

None of the company's salesmen has technical training, all are employed for their ability as salesmen rather than because they are engineers. For several years the sales of the company have shown a steady increase.

Officials of the company, observing the rapidly changing processes in the oil industry, believe, however, that a general technical education on the part of salesmen is becoming increasingly necessary. Since the products of the company had been built and developed by engineers widely experienced in refining processes, officials of the company assumed that men of similar training should be recruited for the sales organization.

If a decision were made to employ men of engineering training, the officials believed that such men, with actual plant and design experience, might be found in the employment of oil and gasoline refiners, who are present customers of the Larson Regulator Company.

Several objections arose to the employment of such men:

(1) The present organization was functioning successfully without technically trained salesmen.

(2) If new men were secured from present customers, such men would have no sales experience, and ill will in the sales force might be created.

(3) The company would be faced with the problem of making salesmen out of engineers.

(4) Competitors employed salesmen with or without engineering training.

The company believed that young men of technical training could be sought by means of advertisements in the technical magazines circulated in the refining industry. The officials believed that technically trained men would be better able to take the responsibility of making the proper choice of equipment for buyers and sell a result rather than a product.

In the past experience of the company, the success of the company's regulating equipment depended largely upon the efficient operation of the rest of a customer's plant equipment. A salesman who understood only controlling devices was sometimes limited by the fact that he did not understand enough about the operation of a plant to defend his own devices by pointing out that the source of trouble in the equipment lay elsewhere.

Questions

1. Should the Larson Company have sought technically experienced and trained men for its sales organization? Give your reasons.

2. Was the contemplated source of such men satisfactory? Give your reasons. If not a satisfactory source, where might such men be secured?

3. What functional type of salesman is now employed by the company? What functional type is being considered?

Reading References

Developing and Managing Salesmen, Giles, Chap. I.
Handbook of Sales Management, Hall, Chap. VII.
Intensive Sales Management, Aspley, pp. 63–68.
Management of the Sales Organization, Russell, pp. 26–33.
Principles of Personal Selling, Tosdal, pp. 480–486.
Sales Administration, Hayward, p. 260.
Sales Management Today, Doubman, Chap. V.
Salesmen in Marketing Strategy, Lyon, Chap. IV.
Selection and Training of Salesmen, Kenagy and Yoakum, Chap IX.

CHAPTER SEVEN

SELECTING SALESMEN

Importance of Selecting Salesmen. A sales manager's success depends upon the organization he builds; his value is increased or decreased in proportion to the number of successful or unsuccessful salesmen in his organization. Proper selection is the foundation of a successful sales organization, and no job in a business is more important or more difficult.

The penalties of poor selection are high turnover of salesmen, expensive recruiting, and a mediocre sales force. The turnover in many organizations is due largely to faulty selection. In life insurance, automobile, investment, home appliance, and many forms of specialty selling, the turnover has been estimated to run from 30 to 50 per cent a year. The average length of service of all life insurance agents is probably not in excess of three years. It has been estimated that the turnover of insurance agents is from sixty to one hundred thousand annually.

The cost of recruiting and training salesmen is high. An analysis by several life insurance agencies showed an average cost of $404 for each new agent. The lowest cost given by any of the agencies was $102 and the highest $692, covering a recruiting and training period of three months, according to the Life Insurance Sales Research Bureau. Broken down, the induction cost in an average urban insurance agency is as follows:

Recruiting Costs per Man:
Advertising and circularizing	$ 5.10
Postage, travel, and miscellaneous	7.10
License and bond	2.10
Time of manager and assistants	93.70
Total	$108.00

Training Costs:

Office space and rent	43.47
Supplies and equipment	8.70
Telephone	7.85
Postage and stationery	3.10
Stenographic service—direct mail	10.90
Time of instructors	222.00
Total	$296.02
Total cost, recruiting and training	$404.02

Mediocre selling is another consequence of poor selection. Figures supplied by fifty-one life insurance companies indicate that only 8 per cent of the agents paid for more than $100,000 of business. In one large company, 21 per cent of the full-time agents paid for 75 per cent of the business received from all agents.

That sound methods of selection make for increased production and lower turnover of salesmen is illustrated by the Phoenix Mutual Life Insurance Company, which, after adoption of an improved method of selection, reported that five hundred salesmen sell more than three times as much life insurance as one thousand seven hundred sold before the careful selection of salesmen was inaugurated. Turnover of salesmen was reduced 34 per cent in ten years, and the compensation of salesmen, despite a lower commission rate, averages among the highest in the country.

Process of Selection of Salesmen. The process of selection naturally divides itself into two parts:

1. The establishment of standard qualifications for the various functional types of salesmen to be employed, which has been explained in detail previously.
2. The establishment of a system for measuring applicants with the predetermined standard. Just as a yardstick or tape is used for comparing objects with the standard linear yard, so measuring devices must be adopted to compare sales applicants with standard qualifications of salesmen.

Several measuring sticks are in general use for comparing the qualifications of sales candidates with a preconceived standard, such as:

1. Application forms.
2. Letters of reference from previous employers.
3. Patterned personal interviews.

4. Sales aptitude testing.
5. Physical examinations.
6. Termination records.
7. Field observations.
8. Miscellaneous methods.

Adopting one or more of these various devices, sales managers set up a system of selection of sales applicants. In many organizations personal interviews are the only selection device employed, while in others all of the methods listed are used.

Application Blanks. The first step in sound selection is to secure information about the applicant. While this may be done in various ways, the most common method is to have the prospective salesman fill out an application blank. There are wide differences in the contents and arrangement of application blanks used by different sales organizations. Some blanks are simple single-sheet forms listing a dozen or more questions, while others consist of eight pages, listing more than a hundred questions. Some application forms ask few direct questions, but simply request an applicant to write a letter listing his qualifications. Attempts have been made to standardize application forms, but the most satisfactory form is one which has been prepared for an individual business. This should contain questions which would reveal qualifications needed by a salesman engaged in the sale of a particular product or service.

The usual information sought on an application form is: name; address; date and place of birth; lineage; physical characteristics, such as height, weight, and complexion; schooling; past business experience; references; investments; home ownership; religion; dependents; health; recreations; and citizenship.

Questions should be included which will bring out an applicant's desirability for a particular sales job. A sales "job analysis" should indicate questions to be asked on the application form. A question, for example, "Have you done special study at a night school or business college?" may be asked to get an idea of the initiative and industry of an applicant. The question, "Can you furnish a fidelity bond, if required, and at our expense?" is asked by a company which does not require a salesman to be bonded, but seeks information to test the honesty of an applicant through his willingness to furnish a bond. Another concern, in an effort to determine whether the applicant was industrious or spent his summers in recreation, asks, "What did you do during your school vacations?"

Often an applicant is given a brief interview before being asked to fill out an application blank. One manufacturer requests sales

(Important: This application must be kept with salesman's papers in cashier's file.)

Salesman's Letter
TO VICE-PRESIDENT IN CHARGE OF SALES—MILLS NOVELTY COMPANY, CHICAGO

NAME--- DATE-------------------

ADDRESS--- AGE--------

PERMANENT ADDRESS--

(Write a letter here. Give all facts about your education, experience, earnings, etc. Say why you think you will succeed with us.)

(OVER)

FIGURE 18. Page one of a salesman's application blank used by the Mills Novelty Company. The applicant is asked to write a letter stating his qualifications to the prospective employer.

applicants to take the application blank away so that they may have time to consider their answers carefully and have an opportunity to verify facts about which they may be uncertain.

Some concerns use a preliminary application blank, a short form to save the applicant's time.

Letter of Reference. The value of references from previous employers is much debated; some may be as valuable for what is unsaid as for what is said. A natural desire to help the unemployed, irrespective of their ability, accounts for the letters of recommendation given to salesmen who have been discharged. While the usual letter of reference is not of great value in judging

Your Employment for Last 6 Years
START WITH PRESENT EMPLOYER

FROM	TO	POSITION	FIRM NAME	ADDRESS	BUSINESS

DO NOT WRITE IN SPACE BELOW

Progress Account

SALESMAN'S NAME ·

DATE	SALES IN $	COMMISSIONS PAID	LEADS FURNISHED

124-2 4-26-32 1M

FIGURE 19. Page two of the Mills Novelty Company salesman's application form. A detailed account of the applicant's previous employment is requested here. At the bottom of the page, space is provided for a record of the salesman's progress with the Mills Company.

the character of an applicant, it is well to determine fundamental facts of a candidate's previous employment. Radical disagreement between the applicant's statements and those of his former employer usually indicates an applicant's inaccuracy and in certain cases dishonesty.

.... Branch Office

CONFIDENTIAL PERSONAL HISTORY RECORD

Please give some answer to every question below. You are considering a change of considerable importance. You do not want to make a mistake in taking this step. The fullest information in answer to the questions below will enable us to assist you in making sure you are taking a step which will lead to your success. If any question does not apply to you write "No" or "None" after it.

1. Name.. 2. Date ....

3. Address ....

4. Date of birth.. 5. Where born........................

6. Nationality of parents (American, English, Scotch, Irish, French, Hebrew, etc.):........................

7. Height.............. Weight..... ....lbs. 8. No. of dependents: Wife..............Children..............Others..............

9. Single ☐ Married ☐ Widowed ☐ Divorced ☐ or Separated ☐

10.

Schooling:	Name of School	Check last year completed	Did you Graduate?	Year
Grammar School		5☐ 6☐ 7☐ 8☐ 9☐		
High or Preparatory School		1☐ 2☐ 3☐ 4☐		
College or Technical School		1☐ 2☐ 3☐ 4☐		
Special Study	Subject Studied	How long in course?		
Correspondence Courses				
Business College or Trade School				
Night School				

11. Number of years since leaving school?........................

12. What did you do during the vacation following each year you attended High School?

Vacation after freshman year?........................

Vacation after sophomore year?........................

Vacation after junior year?........................

Vacation after senior year?........................

13. What did you do during your college vacations (if any)?

After freshman year?........................

After sophomore year?........................

After junior year?........................

Y10. (4.31.6)   (OVER)

FIGURE 20. First page of a confidential personal history record form typical of salesmen's application blanks used by many sales organizations. This form is filled out by all sales applicants of a large life insurance company.

A large manufacturer of paper products sends the following letter to an applicant's previous employer:

John Doe & Company
New York City
Gentlemen:

Mr. William Blank of 329 South Street, Ourtown, New York, has applied for a position as salesman with us. He states that he was in your employ from January 1, 1936 to December 1, 1937, as a district representative.

May we ask if his statements agree with your records and also for what reason he left your employ.

A stamped envelope is enclosed for your reply.

Yours very truly,
Sales Manager
Void Manufacturing Company

Personal interviews or telephone conversations with previous employers of applicants often enable a sales manager to get at facts and impressions never clearly expressed in letters.

A large life insurance company considers a prospective agent's previous education and background a very important factor in his selection. This company writes to previous employers a letter of four pages, with perforations at the fold. The third and fourth pages contain a questionnaire blank for the former employer to fill in, tear off, and mail back to the company considering the applicant.

On the first page of the four-page letter is an individually typed letter which reads:

Dear Sir:

Mr. William Blank of 990 West St., Oldtown, Ohio, is applying to us for a selling position and refers us to you as a previous employer. It will assist him in getting properly placed if you will kindly answer the questions on the attached sheet. An addressed envelope is enclosed for your reply.

You realize, we are sure, that you will be of real service to Mr. Blank, if you will aid him to secure, not necessarily this position, but the position for which he is best fitted.

Every effort is being made by us to select only the highest type of representative, and when we have found such a man, we endeavor to start him off with the best possible chance for success. We require a thorough course of training and offer him full coöperation.

In order that Mr. Blank may have every consideration, we trust that you will give these questions your prompt and thoughtful attention.

References may be secured from an applicant's previous employers by telephone. This is a rapid method of verifying the applicant's period of service, wage, reason for leaving, ability, and such personal qualifications as habits, industry, health, aggressiveness, and popularity. Employers often object, however, to giving an unknown inquirer information over the telephone, particularly when the record of the previous employee was not satisfactory.

A sales applicant may also be investigated through a professional investigating agency, which calls upon employers and friends of the applicant.   This method is expensive, however, and it may not be

1. Mr.. states that he was
   in your employ as..from
   ....19.......to... 19........
   Does this correspond to your record? Yes (   ). No (   ).

2. He states that he left because...

   Is this an adequate statement? Yes (   ). No (   ).

3. He states that he received $............................... (in salary or commissions)
   Is this correct? Yes (   ). No (   ).
   If not correct, how much did he receive? $...............................

4. Were you personally acquainted with him and his work?
   Yes (   ). No (   ).

5. How do you rate him on the following points?

	Bad	Poor	Fair	Good	Excellent
Promptness in meeting financial obligations					
Personal habits and conduct . .					
Industry and determination . .					
Ability to manage his own time .					
Ability to convince others . . .					
Aggressiveness					
Popularity with fellow workers .					
Health and endurance					

Would you be willing to re-employ him? Yes (   ). No (   ).

Signature...

Any additional information that would assist us in judging the applicant's fitness for the position would be appreciated. The reverse page is left blank for your record of such facts.

76.(11.30.-4.)   (OVER)

FIGURE 21. A questionnaire sent to previous employers of a sales applicant by a life insurance company to ascertain the correctness of statements made by the applicant on his application form.

so productive of worth-while information as a direct request for information.

The character of an applicant's reference should be considered in evaluating its worth. A reference from a reliable concern and a sales executive of high reputation is obviously worth more than a recommendation from an unknown source.

Personal Interviews. The personal interview is the most common method of selecting salesmen and the most important step in the selection process. Many experienced sales executives pride themselves on their ability to select salesmen solely by means of a personal interview. However, many tests have been made which demonstrate that personal judgment alone is a poor guide in selecting salesmen. Judgments differ so widely among apparently able interviewers that they are of little value, indicating but slightly what sales performance may be expected of a sales applicant. Estimates of interviewers are usually subjective and colored by personal experiences. Some employers believe that all fat men are lazy, blonds are unstable, and redheads are energetic. Many pseudo-scientific theories for interviewing salesmen have been advanced ranging from character analysis to astrology, but these schemes have little to recommend them as a sound basis of selection.

One promoter has prepared a series of photographs of "sales types" to be used in interviewing sales candidates, which are reported to have been widely sold to gullible sales executives who were seeking a solution to the difficult problem of selecting salesmen. One sales executive is known to consult a book of horoscopes in selecting salesmen. Such unscientific schemes indicate the general admission of inability to judge sales ability in the course of personal interviews. Nevertheless, interviews constitute at this time one of the fundamental methods of selection, and continuous experiment is making them more reliable.

Interviews with prospective salesmen have a dual purpose:

1. To determine the candidates' fitness for the sales job and
2. To present the job to applicants.

Various methods have been devised to improve the quality of interviews from the standpoint of determining a candidate's fitness for a job. One method is to use a patterned interview to aid interviewers in recording and analyzing their impressions.

The Patterned Employment Interview. Many employment interviews are often little more than mechanical question-and-answer processes or mental fencing duels between interviewers and applicants. In an effort to improve the quality of employment interviewing, certain companies have developed the "patterned interview" which is a standard interviewing procedure designed to insure that a well-rounded, planned interview is conducted. The standard interview process includes: (1) routine for interviewing sales applicants; (2) interviewing guide and rating sheet; and (3) composite interviewing rating sheet.

Routine for Interviewing Sales Applicants. The art of employment interviewing has been largely neglected. The interviewer should be qualified to interview applicants. He should have a knowledge of the sales job and the personal qualifications required. A job description and qualifications are helpful. He should know people and recognize his own prejudices, likes, and dislikes, and not let them prejudice his judgment of the applicant.

A clearly defined routine for conducting interviews with applicants provides a track on which the interview can run. The following steps should be taken:

1. *Get acquainted* by general discussion of matters of common knowledge, mutual friends, and subjects not related directly to the job.

2. *Describe the sales job,* duties, responsibilities, difficulties, income, and advancement possibilities, the company and organization. Do not oversell the job.

3. *Get the applicant to talk* by asking questions which will reveal his personal characteristics and qualifications for the sales job.

Certain companies have prepared an interview guide, listing the questions which the applicants should be asked. Typical interview questions appearing on the interview guide, of a large producer of electrical appliances, grouped according to personal characteristics are:

Experience:
How did you get your last job?
What did you do?
How did you get along?
What did you like to do most?
Were you ever criticized for the work you did?
Industry:
Did you work nights on your last sales job?
How do you like to canvass?
What did you do during vacations when you were in school?
What was the source of your spending money when you were in school?

Sociability:
    What do you do in your spare time?
    To what extent do you and your wife entertain?
    Do you belong to any social organizations?
    Did you belong to the Boy Scouts when you were a boy?

These and other questions, not asked on the application blank, are suggested to interviewers to reveal the characteristics of applicants and to encourage them to talk about themselves and their work. The interviewer at once makes notes on the interview guide of the applicant's responses to these questions. Similar questions can be prepared to reveal the qualifications for any sales job.

4. *Control the interview* by not permitting the interview to get sidetracked. Do not allow the applicant to talk on any one subject long, or to discuss unrelated subjects. The interviewer should not embarrass the applicant nor increase his strain. The interview should not be hurried, but when the interviewer has all the information he wants, the interview should be closed and not allowed to drag on.

5. *Record impressions* after the interview. The interviewer should not attempt to make an extensive record of his impressions during the interview as this slows up the procedure. He may make brief notes of his impressions or check his Interview Rating Sheet.

Interview Guide and Rating Sheet. The interview guide and rating sheet is a valuable tool for aiding the interviewer in evaluating the applicant. It is useful in recording impressions as they are made so that they may be reviewed and appraised at leisure. It also provides a list of the characteristics to observe. The guide should be based on an analysis of the sales job for which the applicant is being considered. The personal qualities essential for successful performance of the work, as determined by the job analysis, should be listed on the sheet.

Appearance:	dress	skin	breath	teeth	cleanliness
	weight	height	bearing	neatness	
Voice:	pleasing	strong	weak	unpleasant	harsh
Speech:	fast	deliberate	accent	choice of words	
Manner:	confident	nervous	aggressive	timid	sincere
	easy	affected	critical	enthusiastic	
Apparent					
health:	good	fair	poor	questionable	
Alertness:	slow thinker	grasps ideas quickly		vague	

A leading electric appliance manufacturing plant has analyzed its sales job and looks for the above personal characteristics in sales applicants, which are listed on its interview guide. Each characteristic in the preceding table is checked affirmatively or negatively by the interviewer during the interview.

INTERVIEW RATING FORM

BETTER PACKAGES, INC., Shelton, Conn.

SCORE

Applicant .... Territory ....

INSTRUCTIONS—READ CAREFULLY

This rating sheet provides a practical method through which the acceptability of the individual can be judged with a reasonable degree of accuracy and uniformity. Indicate your opinion of this applicant by placing an "X" on the phrase in the block which seems best to fit the applicant. If you can't make up your mind between two phrases, place your "X" in the narrow space between two blocks. Please follow instructions carefully.

1. Disregard your general impression of the applicant and concentrate on one factor at a time. Make your rating with the utmost care and thought.

2. After you have rated the applicant on all factors, write on the bottom of the sheet any additional information about the applicant which you feel has not been covered by the rating report, but which is essential to a fair appraisal.

PERSONAL APPEARANCE	UNTIDY	TRIFLE CARELESS	FAIRLY WELL-GROOMED	NEAT	GOOD TASTE	DISTINGUISHED
POISE	EXTREMELY ILL AT EASE	SOMEWHAT SELF-CONSCIOUS	CALM	GOOD POISE	WELL BALANCED	PERFECT SELF-CONTROL
PHYSICAL ENERGY	PEPLESS	SHOWS LITTLE	FAIRLY ENERGETIC	VITAL	VIGOROUS	DYNAMIC
ENTHUSIASM	UTTERLY LACKING	SHOWS LITTLE	SOME SPARK	DISTINCT ENTHUSIASM	VERY ENTHUSIASTIC	OUTSTANDING
PERSONALITY	DISAGREEABLE	COLORLESS	PASSABLE	PLEASING	VERY LIKEABLE	EXTREMELY LIKEABLE
ALERTNESS	DULL	BARELY AWAKE	AVERAGE ALERTNESS	INTELLIGENT RESPONSE	ON HIS TOES	ONE JUMP AHEAD
MECHANICAL APTITUDE	NONE	LIMITED APTITUDE	SOME APTITUDE	HAS A KNACK	SKILLFUL	EXCEPTIONAL APTITUDE
AGGRESSIVENESS	SUBMISSIVE TYPE	SLIGHTLY TIMID	SOME AGGRESSIVENESS	A PUSHER	VERY PERSUASIVE	INDOMITABLE
SALES EXPERIENCE	NONE	VERY LITTLE	ADEQUATE EXPERIENCE	GOOD BACKGROUND	VERY GOOD BACKGROUND	EXCELLENT BACKGROUND
KNOWLEDGE OF PACKAGING	NONE	VERY LITTLE	SOME	ABOVE AVERAGE	THOROUGH KNOWLEDGE	EXCEPTIONAL KNOWLEDGE

Additional Information Helpful or Essential to a Fair Appraisal

....

....

....

....

DATE ....

Signature of Rater

FIGURE 22. Interview rating form used in judging applicants for sales positions with Better Packages, Inc. This form enables comparison of the opinions of several interviewers.

Items usually listed on an interview guide are: physical, mental, personality, speech, and ideas. It is futile to list such qualities as industry, loyalty, dependability, and honesty as these cannot be determined in a personal interview.

In the interview guide or judgment blank used in interviewing prospective agents for a large life insurance company, each personal characteristic is qualified by several descriptive statements, one of which is to be checked by the interviewer to indicate his judgment of each trait.

JUDGMENT BLANK

For Recording Interview with the Prospective Life Insurance Representative

Prospective Representative..Date of Interview..................................

Branch Office..Interviewer..

Type of contract considered..

How many interviews have you had with the applicant?..

The total length of the interviews has been about......................Hours...Min.

Directions: The following questions ask for your judgment of the prospective representative on a number of different points. Before attempting to record your opinion on any item **read and consider carefully** all the descriptive statements under the line to the right of each question. In making each decision take into account your entire knowledge of the man, based on the interview, study of his personal history, and recommendations of others.

Indicate your opinion on each quality by making a cross (X) on the line, just where you think it ought to be. For example, if in Question 2 you think the prospective representative is a little lower than indicated by the statement "usually creates confidence", but not quite low enough to be recorded "no impression" then put the cross on the line somewhere between these two points.

1. What is your opinion of his **character** and **integrity**?	Absolutely trustworthy	High character	Good as general average	Somewhat doubtful	Unreliable
2. How does applicant impress you as to his **sincerity**?	Insincere	Some doubt as to sincerity	No impression	Usually creates confidence	Absolutely sincere
3. Is he **sold on life insurance** as a profession?	Dubious as to advantages of this work		No definite attitude		Believes in it as profession
4. Does he look ahead? Does he possess **enthusiasm, imagination and ambition**?	Keen interest in the world and in his own future	Some enthusiasm and ambition		Vague interest in life and in his own future	Apathetic
5. Does he possess **self-confidence and determination** and can he **stand punishment**?	Self-confidence in the face of difficulties	Shows grit		Somewhat easily discouraged and apt to lean on others	Gives up in the face of difficulties
6. Does he give evidence of **industry**?	May loaf on the job	Will tend to take things easily	Will be fair worker	Will work systematically	Will be consistent hard worker
7. Does he possess the **ability to convince others**?	Very convincing	Frequently able to bring others to his point of view	Clear but not persuasive	Fails to put his ideas across	Tends to be swayed rather than to sway others
8. Is he **intelligent** and is he familiar with current history and modern business?	Quick to grasp situations and use knowledge		Limited grasp of facts and situations		Unable to understand and absorb information
9. Has he a good **command of English**?	Makes obvious mistakes	Does not express himself well	Unnoticed	Fair command of English	Speaks well and forcefully
10. Was he **successful** in his last job?	Failure	Poor	Fair	Somewhat successful	Successful
11. Has he **social instincts**? Does he like meeting people?	Really enjoys meeting people	Meets people easily		Some strain in meeting people	Dislikes meeting people
12. Does he have a pleasing **personality** and are his general appearance and bearing good?	Pleasing personality and favorable first impression	Satisfactory appearance	Colorless	Somewhat unfavorable impression	Unpleasant personality or poor appearance
13. Is his **health** good and has he **physical endurance**?	Poor health or little endurance	Health only fair or not much endurance	Average health and endurance	Good	Excellent

Vote.......................... Remarks..
(Yes or No)

FIGURE 23. Judgment blank used by interviewers of the Phoenix Mutual Life Insurance Company in recording their impressions of sales candidates. This form enables comparison of the opinions of several interviewers.

Certain companies combine an interview guide with a rating form. The form is designed to secure a numerical rating on each applicant. The various traits listed on the form are given a numerical value, or weight, according to their significance for success in the particular sales job, for example, personality may be weighted 30, appearance 40, health 20, and speech 10, and the applicant rated on this basis. The personal characteristics of successful and unsuccessful salesmen in the organization must be carefully analyzed in determining the weight of each trait.

The process of analyzing personal characteristics of salesmen and establishing proper weights requires skill and experience not available in many sales organizations. It is more desirable to use an unweighted rating form than to attempt to weight the various characteristics without accurate analysis.

Composite Rating Sheet. In order to compare the reactions or ratings of several interviewers, a composite rating sheet may be used. The ratings of individual interviewers are posted on the composite form to facilitate comparison of the several judgments which should be made on every applicant. A large paper products company uses a composite rating form on which space is provided to record the judgments of five interviewers.

Number of and Place for Interviews. Salesmen are usually selected on the basis of several interviews. The interviewing of an applicant by several executives at different places and times, and under varying conditions, gives a clearer impression of his characteristics.

A large food product manufacturer and distributor favors three interviews: one at the company office, another on the job, and the third in the applicant's home or in the presence of his wife.

Another manufacturing concern selling to retail stationers and through its own retail stores requires that sales applicants be interviewed by a senior salesman, a district manager, and a store manager. Visiting company executives as well as good customers are also asked to interview the candidate. This company holds interviews in its district offices, and applicants are taken to luncheon at a club or hotel where they may be observed and judged in a social setting.

Many employers believe that applicants should be interviewed by several individuals, although tests have often shown that the combined judgments of a group are often no better than that of one member of the group.

The Phoenix Mutual Life Insurance Company has made a study of the number of interviews which a manager should conduct in order to select salesmen properly. It has found that there is a decided relation between the number of interviews with a sales applicant and his future success in the business. Several interviews enable a manager to make a better selection and put a prospective salesman in a better position to decide whether or not he wishes to enter the life insurance business.

The first interview. The first interview with an applicant is largely for the purpose of getting acquainted and preparing for more thorough interviews later. The interviewer should aim to make the applicant feel at ease and to secure his confidence so that he will not feel that he is being grilled. The interviewer should keep an open mind and not be influenced by first impressions until all information about the prospect has been obtained. The first interview should probably not exceed thirty minutes in length. The personal appearance and bearing of the applicant should be noted, and he may be questioned about his age, education, and experience. Usually he is asked why he would like to sell the employer's line.

Presenting the job. An important purpose of the first interview is to present facts about the job and company to the applicant. The applicant is just as much concerned with the opportunities in the prospective job as the employer is concerned with the possibilities in the candidate.

The applicant should be given a brief description of the company, its products, the market, the training, and the possible future for its salesmen. To shorten the time of the interviewer in giving this information, a number of companies have published booklets describing: the sales job; history, growth, reputation, and financial strength of the company; its policies and plan of merchandising; opportunities for promotion; favorable working conditions; employee benefits; earnings of present salesmen; stability of employment; qualities of the product. The disadvantages of the job are also emphasized, for example: long hours, heavy samples, keen competition, other obstacles.

An excellent example of selling the sales job to the applicant is the booklet published by the Life Insurance Sales Research Bureau, Hartford, Connecticut, for use by the life insurance companies who are members of the Bureau, in recruiting and selecting agents. This sixty-three-page booklet entitled, "Career Underwriting—A

Life Work," gives an outline of the opportunities for life insurance agents, and the information which will enable a man to decide whether or not he should undertake life underwriting as a career. The booklet contains the following chapters:

1. The Characteristics of an Ideal Job.
2. A Career as Well as a Job.
3. Adequate Opportunity and Financial Security.
4. The Market for Life Insurance.
5. An Honorable and Socially Beneficial Calling.

The booklet is used by agency managers to interest qualified men in life underwriting as a career and is given to applicants for agent contracts.

A similar booklet, written by a vocational psychologist, and entitled, "Your Career—Shall It Be in Creative Selling?" has been published by The Todd Company, Inc., Rochester, New York, for use in recruiting salesmen to sell check-writers and related products. This seventeen-page booklet discusses such topics as:

1. The Value of a Definite Ambition.
2. The Real Values of Selling.
3. Emotional Experiences That Make Selling Important.
4. A Good Salesman Is Skilled in the Social Arts.
5. Types of Salesmen.
6. The Creative Salesman Is Problem-Minded.

A unique feature of this booklet is its vocational interest test containing fifty-seven questions which may be answered by the applicant to enable him to determine whether or not he has the aptitude for creative specialty selling. A key to answers of typical salesmen is included so the applicant can score his answers and compute his aptitude for this type of sales work. He is invited to take additional tests of a similar nature used by the company in selecting salesmen for its organization.

Other companies including the Jewel Tea Company, The Mills Novelty Company, Equitable Life Insurance Society, the General Foods Sales Corporation, and the General Electric Company, Appliance and Merchandise Department have published similar booklets describing their organizations and the duties and opportunities of their salesmen.

Sound slide films picturing the opportunities in selling, product features, market potential, and earnings of successful salesmen have been used by other companies in presenting their sales work to applicants.

All of these booklets and films serve to eliminate applicants who do not have sufficient interest to warrant further consideration.

The second interview.   With the general facts about an applicant secured at the opening interview, and the job presented, there is a second interview, which is largely for the purpose of getting a more intimate knowledge of the personality of the candidate.   After the ice has been broken in the opening interview, the applicant should be more at ease and reveal more clearly his abilities.   If he is interested, he should have intelligent questions to ask about the company or the job.   Some sales executives show the applicant samples of the products sold by the company and watch his reactions. Sometimes the candidate is referred to another executive for interviewing or sent out with a salesman.   Other devices for testing the applicant's fitness are introduced at this time.

Subsequent interviews.   In subsequent interviews confirmations of previous judgments are sought.   These interviews may be held in a nonbusiness setting, such as the salesman's home, a club, or a restaurant, to secure impressions of the social attitudes of the applicant.   When an applicant has been rated in previous interviews, any doubts raised by these ratings should be dispelled in subsequent interviews.   A clear understanding of all the details of the work should be given the applicant.

Sales Aptitude Testing.   One of the most controversial subjects in sales administration is aptitude testing for selecting salesmen. The unfavorable experiences of sales executives who do not know how to use or apply tests properly have made them skeptical of the value of testing.   Aptitude tests have produced certain significant results for companies which have experimented extensively with them by matching test scores with the productiveness of present salesmen and using this information in testing and selecting new salesmen.   The benefits of sales aptitude tests are that they improve selection by screening out those who are likely to fail, and serve as a check on the prejudices of interviewers.   They are not, however, predictive of sales success.   Companies sometimes find them helpful in the supervision of men in that they reveal traits and attitudes, strengths and weaknesses.   They are also sometimes used to indicate potential talent for promotion.

The limitations of aptitude tests, however, must be recognized. They are still in a state of experimental development and cannot be considered scientific. After an extensive study of sales aptitude tests, one of the largest corporations reported to its distributors:

Good sales aptitude tests are a valuable aid in selecting salesmen. They are not infallible and should be used as a supplement to, rather than a substitute for, the personal interview and other established methods for employing salesmen.

A survey of five hundred sales executives was made by J. R. Hilgert, of Pennsylvania State College, in 1945 to determine the use of sales aptitude tests. Of those replying, 85 per cent did not use tests; 5 per cent were in the process of experimenting with them; and 10 per cent used tests in selecting salesmen. A small number of those not using tests reported that they had tried them but found them worthless. Certain of these concerns bought a number of standard tests and gave them without professional advice; others used tests mentioned in trade journals; one used a part of the Life Insurance Sales Research Bureau Aptitude Index; several hired amateur psychologists.

Such unscientific approaches to sales aptitude testing are largely responsible for disappointing results. Many executives fail to realize that aptitude testing is a complex, technical task calling for specialized experience. The best testing results were reported by Hilgert from forty companies which employed a professional testing service.

A survey of one thousand eight hundred sales executives and psychologists by the Dartnell Corporation lead to the following conclusions:

There has not yet been developed any one standard "salesmanship" test dependable for all companies and it is improbable that such a test can be developed. No psychological tests or test have yet been devised that can be safely administered and interpreted by the sales manager. Aptitude tests can be valuable if they are used only as an aid to other selection methods, if they are interpreted with special reference to the needs of the particular company involved and if they are interpreted by a psychologist experienced in the use of such tests for salesmen. Only a few in the country are so experienced.

Not more than three hundred companies have even experimented with sales aptitude testing, which indicates that selection of salesmen by this method is still in its infancy. And of this small number, probably less than a dozen organizations have made a serious effort to develop a scientific sales-testing program.

Those who have experimented with sales aptitude testing have followed one or more of the following courses:

1. Purchased standard aptitude and psychological tests and administered them without professional guidance.
2. Retained professional psychologists, usually identified with leading universities, to develop testing programs for the specific needs of the individual company.
3. Employed professional aptitude-testing services which supply a series or battery of standard psychological tests and evaluate the answers, rendering a report and recommendation to the client.

One professional sales-testing service, typical of several in the field, operates as follows:

1. The client selects a group of sales applicants.
2. The testing service sends the client a battery of five standard tests developed by well-known psychologists to test:
   a. Mental ability.
   b. Personality.
   c. Sales aptitude.
   d. Vocational interest.
   e. Analytical ability.

One battery is supplied for each person in the group.

3. Each person tested fills out each of the five test forms which together require from three to five hours to complete. No supervision is necessary and the tests may be taken anywhere.

4. The completed tests are then sent to the testing service for analysis by its psychologists who submit to the client a report and recommendations on each person tested.

5. The sales manager compares the report and recommendations with his own conclusions and determines whether or not the applicant should be employed.

For this service the testing organization charges a fee of $25 per person and claims that it is highly accurate in predicting the failure or success of new salesmen.

Reliable psychological testing services use a battery of standard tests, usually five or six in number, including such well-known tests as:

1. The Otis Form A test of mental ability.
2. The Bernreuter Personality Inventory.
3. The Canfield Sales Sense test.

4. Strong Vocational Interest test.

5. Moss Social Intelligence test.

One testing service has experimented with a battery of tests by giving the tests to representative groups of "superior" and "poor" salesmen of various types, such as house-to-house salesmen, salesmen selling to retailers, industrial salesmen, and insurance agents. Scores for superior and poor men of each type were secured for each test in the series or battery. These scores were weighted by the number of men making each score and an average score for the superior and the poor men was determined.

In testing tests, ranges of scores are next determined from the average scores of the superior and poor groups. Individual scores vary considerably within the range of each group. If salesmen in the superior group made scores from 30 to 68, the range of superior scores would be from 30 to 68.

In order that scores on the various tests may be compared, the actual test scores are converted to percentile scores. A percentile score is determined by dividing the entire group of salesmen into one hundred groups, each of which includes 1 per cent of the men tested. A man whose test score is in the 60 percentile is superior to 60 per cent and inferior to 40 per cent of all who took the test.

Next, a profile or pattern is drawn on a percentile scale which shows graphically the range of scores of superior salesmen for each test in the battery. The ranges for poor and passable salesmen are likewise drawn on the profile. These profiles make it easy to compare individual scores with the scores of superior or passable men by plotting the scores of individuals on the profile. The accompanying illustration shows a typical profile established as a result of experiments which determined the percentile scores of superior office equipment salesmen. Similar profiles were established for salesmen engaged in various types of selling, such as insurance, house-to-house, dealer, industrial, office equipment, and driver salesmen, as a result of experimental tests of salesmen engaged in these types of selling.

The test scores of each salesman are plotted on the profiles of men doing a similar type of selling. In this way the test scores of applicants are compared with those of salesmen in similar work.

The office specialty salesmen charted in the accompanying illustration were tested for mental ability and other traits, but there were no significant differences between the better and the poorer men in this organization on these qualities; therefore their scores were not charted for comparison.

In another sales organization, the factors that differentiate the best and the poorest salesmen would probably be different because of variables in the job, type of customer served, product, and policies. No single set of characteristics would differentiate the best from the poorest salesmen in general.

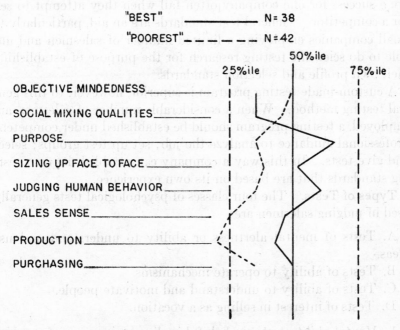

FIGURE 24. A profile of psychological test scores used by a sales aptitude-testing counsel in comparing the scores made by salesmen of an office specialty concern and the scores of eight hundred ninety-three salesmen representing ninety-six companies selected from more than twelve thousand salesmen tested.

The unbroken perpendicular line, headed "50%ile," represents the average score made by the eight hundred ninety-three salesmen. The two perpendicular broken lines on either side of the 50 percentile represent the limits between which 50 per cent of these men fall on their test scores. Twenty-five per cent of the men score above the seventy-fifth percentile line; while 25 per cent score below the twenty-fifth percentile line.

The unbroken, zigzag line represents the median score made by thirty-eight of the "best" salesmen of the office specialty company. The broken zigzag line represents the median score made by forty-two of the so-called poorest salesmen of the same organization.

This profile shows the significant differences between the best and the poorest salesmen of this company, compared with salesmen generally. The profile shows that the better salesmen are not as inclined toward mixing socially. They rate higher in purpose; are better able to judge human behavior; have wider knowledge of sales techniques; are more interested in production processes, which contributes to better presentations of the superior construction of their product; have a greater interest in purchasing and therefore can deal more effectively with purchasing agents.

The standard test scores established by testing services fail to take into consideration the specific duties and characteristics of successful salesmen of a particular company. Salesmen's duties often vary widely, and traits which make a successful salesman in one company are not necessarily those of successful salesmen in a competing line. This difference in the qualifications of successful salesmen of similar products is illustrated by the fact that men who are a success for one company often fail when they attempt to sell for a competitor. General test standards are an aid, particularly to small companies employing a limited number of salesmen and unable to do scientific testing research for the purpose of establishing their own profile and selection standards.

A custom-made testing program is superior, however, to this general testing method. When a considerable number of salesmen are employed, a testing program should be established under competent professional guidance to analyze the job; set up test groups; select and give tests. In this way a company can establish its own testing standards that are based on its own experience.

Types of Tests. The four classes of psychological tests generally used in judging salesmen are:

A. Tests of mental alertness or ability to understand and use ideas.

B. Tests of ability to operate mechanisms.

C. Tests of ability to understand and motivate people.

D. Tests of interest in selling as a vocation.

1. *Mental ability tests* are helpful in discovering men of superior intelligence required for selling complex products to purchasing agents or executives. They are also useful in eliminating highly intelligent men for sales work where unusual mental alertness is not required, such as in food, liquor, tobacco, and house-to-house selling. Outstanding tests of mental ability are the Higher Examination Form A Otis Self-Administering Test of Mental Ability which takes thirty minutes to administer; Bureau Test VI, Test of Mental Alertness; and American Council on Education Psychological Examination.

2. *Mechanical aptitude tests* are helpful in selecting sales engineers or salesmen of mechanical products. Tests of this type are: the Hazlehurst Primary Mechanical Ability Test, the MacQuarrie Test for Mechanical Ability, and O'Rourke Mechanical Aptitude Test.

3. *Tests of ability to understand and deal with people* include personality, extroversion, dominance, social intelligence, sales aptitude, aggressiveness, and temperament tests which apply particularly to salesmen. Outstanding tests of this type are: Personality Inventory, by Robert G. Bernreuter, which is a single questionnaire con-

---

BETTER PACKAGES INC.

SALES QUESTIONNAIRE

NAME..
              Last   First   Initial

DATE..
                      Print name and date above

INSTRUCTIONS

Read these instructions carefully

On the following pages are 60 problems in information, vocabulary, arithmetic, etc. Do not turn this page until you are told to do so. You will have ____ minutes to work on the problems. You will be told when to start and when to stop. You may not be able to finish all the problems in the time allowed, but work as rapidly and accurately as you can. Try each problem, but if you realize you cannot do it, pass on to the next one. Do any necessary figuring in the margins.

The following examples will show you how to answer the problems:

1. The number of inches in a yard is
    A (3) B (12) C (16) D (36)...A   B   C   (D)
Four possible answers are given, but only one is correct; that is 36. Do not write 36, therefore, D has been circled at the right, after the problem. DO NOT WRITE 36; draw a circle around the letter which indicates the correct answer.

2. 8 times 4 =
    A (2) B (24) C (32) D (84)...A   B   (C)   D
The correct answer is 32, therefore, C has been circled at the right.

3. CLUMSY means about the same as
    A (graceful) B (awkward) C (fall) D (dizzy)...A   (B)   C   D
The correct answer is "awkward" so B is the response.

4. FINGER is to HAND as TOE is to
    A (foot) B (head) C (arm) D (heel)..(A)   B   C   D
A FINGER has the same relationship to the HAND as a TOE has to the FOOT. The correct response is "foot"; therefore A has been encircled.

If you have any questions, ask them NOW. No questions will be answered once the signal to start has been given.

DO NOT TURN THIS PAGE UNTIL YOU ARE TOLD TO DO SO

TIME START...   TIME FINISH...

FIGURE 25. Page one of a four page multiple choice sales aptitude test of sixty questions given to sales applicants by Better Packages, Inc. In addition to this test, applicants are given an occupational interest and interest analysis test.

sisting of six tests, four of which deal with characteristics of salesmen—extroversion, dominance, self-confidence, and social independence. It is published by the Stanford University Press, Stanford, California.

The Thurstone Personality Schedule, designed to test neurotic tendencies, is distributed by the Psychological Corporation of New York City.

The Allport A-S Reaction Study tests ascendance-submission in personality. The attitude of a salesman is important. He may take an aggressive, dominant attitude or an attitude of submission or hesitancy. This test measures the degree to which a prospective salesman may take either of these courses.

The Moss Social Intelligence Test measures understanding of human nature, ability to deal with others, and social judgment essential to successful selling.

The Humm-Wadsworth Temperament Scale is designed to measure emotions, attitudes, and sentiments, important factors in sales work.

The A. R. Root extraversion-introversion test distinguishes the objective, outspoken extravert from the introspective, sensitive, unimaginative introvert type of personality.

Other tests of ability to deal with people, which have been used in testing salesmen, are: the Social Intelligence Test by F. A. Moss, T. Hunt, and K. T. Omwake, and Washburn's Social Adjustment Inventory.

Several attempts have been made to develop a test of sales aptitude. No general sales aptitude test has been devised, however, up to this time to measure scientifically an individual's fitness for sales work. The author has devised a test of knowledge of sales terms and situations, entitled "How Perfect Is Your Sales Sense," which has been used by many companies as one of a battery of mental and personality tests with reported good results. This test should not be considered alone as a scientific test of aptitude for selling.

A test of sales management and supervisory knowledge has been developed by the author to measure the knowledge of sales executives. This test, which has been used by more than one hundred companies, should not be considered an absolute measure of sales supervisory aptitude. When used with other tests, however, it may reveal significant qualifications for sales supervision.

4. *Vocational interest tests* are designed to measure the interest

of a sales candidate in sales work. The various activities connected with selling appeal to certain persons as stimulating, interesting, and a source of satisfaction, while others consider sales work as a humiliating, discouraging, distasteful task.

Test of Sales Management and Supervisory Knowledge and Aptitude

Copyright—1944 By Bertrand R. Canfield—Second Edition

How to take this Test

For each of the questions listed, several possible answers are given. You are to select the one or more correct answers as indicated in Column 2 of the form and write its number or their numbers in Column 3 on the accompanying "Answer Form". Be sure to put the answer numbers that you believe are correct in Column 3 headed "Correct Answer Numbers"

For example: Question O. Which two of the following

sales management positions ranks first and second in authority and responsibility in most sales organizations? (1) Branch sales manager. (2) Sales supervisor. (3) General sales manager. (4) Division Sales manager. (5) District sales manager. (6) Product sales manager. (7) Vice-President in charge of sales.

The correct answers have been recorded on the answer form opposite question "O" in column 3 as 7-3.

Time started..................... Time finished.................

---

1. A salesman employed for ten years by a wholesale hardware concern has consistently ranked tenth in sales volume in an organization of forty men. During the last year he has fallen to 35th place in sales. Reports from customers indicate that he has been drinking excessively with a few of his customers. Which two of the following courses should be taken in his case?
(1) Warn him if his drinking does not stop and sales do not increase he will be discharged. (2) Discharge him after a hearing which confirms reports. (3) Transfer him to another territory. (4) Discuss the matter with customers with whom he has been drinking and get their co-operation. (5) Get his pledge to stop drinking and increase sales efforts. (6) Offer him an extra bonus if he regains his old place in the organization.

2. The two most effective methods of training new men without previous selling experience in selling home appliances to dealers are: (1) Listening to lectures by sales manager. (2) Trip through the factory. (3) Watching a successful salesman sell. (4) Selling under observation and correction of trainer. (5) By correspondence. (6) Group discussion of sales problems.

3. In recruiting salesmen for selling technical specialties to industry, the two most likely sources to produce good men are: (1) Newspaper advertising. (2) Recommendation of purchasing agents. (3) Technical magazine advertising. (4) Suggestions of present salesmen. (5) Employment agencies. (6) Colleges.

4. Which four of the following sales training tools would be most useful in training a retail dealer organization of 500 dealers and their 1,000 consumer specialty salesmen at a series of division training meetings? (1) Charts and graphs. (2) Visual portfolios. (3) Sound moving picture films. (4) Sales playlets. (5) Slide films. (6) Sales training books.

5. In selecting ten salesmen to call on automotive dealers for a wholesale auto accessory house, which four of the following selection methods would be most likely to reveal their qualifications: (1) Letters of recommendation from previous employers. (2) Physical examination. (3) Psychological and aptitude tests. (4) Personal interviews by sales executives. (5) Credit agency investigation. (6) Comparison of personal history factors with those of present salesmen. (7) References.

6. The two best places to interview an applicant for city salesman of office appliances, with annual earnings of $6,000: (1) At a hotel. (2) In the salesman's house. (3) At the local branch office. (4) At a social club. (5) In the manager's home. (6) On the golf course. (7) At employment agency.

7. A house-to-house salesman of home appliances should have a predominance of which four of the following personal characteristics: (1) Good appearance. (2) Initiative. (3) Imagination. (4) Sincerity. (5) Persistence. (6) Cheerfulness. (7) Confidence. (8) Originality. (9) Sympathy. (10) Generosity. (11) Aggressiveness. (12) Charm.

8. The two most effective ways to stimulate a drug specialty manufacturer's sales organization calling on retail drug outlets are by: (1) A bonus. (2) Merchandise awards. (3) Free trip to the factory. (4) Silver trophy. (5) Additional territory.

9. A salesman representing a poultry feed mill, selling to rural feed dealers, in order to get an order for $350 from a new customer promised the customer a 10% advertising allowance. The mill has a firm policy against advertising allowances to dealers. Upon receiving this

---

FIGURE 26. The first page of the Canfield four-page fifty-question test of sales supervisory knowledge used in qualifying men for sales executive positions.

Vocational interest tests have demonstrated practical values in selecting salesmen, particularly The Strong Vocational Interest Blank by Dr. Edward K. Strong, Jr., of Stanford University, who has employed this test extensively in measuring interest for selling life insurance, real estate, and vacuum cleaners. Another well-known interest test is the Preference Record by G. Frederic Kuder,

order conditioned upon payment of the allowance, the sales manager should take which one of the following steps: (1) Return the order to the customer with a letter explaining the company's policy. (2) Accept the order this time on the condition that there will be no further allowances. (3) Accept the order without question. (4) Require the salesman to explain the policy to the customer and get an unconditional order. (5) Revise the policy in fairness to all customers, paying all an advertising allowance.

10. A large railroad equipment manufacturer pays its 30 sales engineers for actual expenses incurred in selling when away from their headquarters city. The men submit itemized statements weekly, and from these the company has established an average for each salesman which is considered reasonable. One of the leading salesmen has been exceeding his allowance for six weeks. Which two of the following courses should the sales manager follow: (1) Call it to the salesman's attention and ask his co-operation in reducing expenses. (2) Ask salesman for detailed explanation of the overage. (3) Refuse to pay the excessive expense claims. (4) Change the method of expense control. (5) Include expenses as a part of salesmen's salary. (6) Overlook the overage and maintain morale of salesman.

11. The sales manager of a soap manufacturer selling direct to retailers found that many orders taken by salesmen from retailers were rejected by the credit department under the treasurer as poor credit risks. Which two of the following actions should be taken by the sales manager? (1) Appeal to the president to require the credit manager to pass more orders. (2) Educate salesmen to sell dealers with better credit standing. (3) Persuade the credit manager to be more liberal in extending credit. (4) Co-operate with credit manager by gathering credit information. (5) Subscribe to mercantile credit reports on dealers.

12. To aid branch managers in selecting wholesale district salesmen for a manufacturer of electrical home equipment, sold through regional distributors, the branch manager should be provided with which two of the following: (1) A job description of the duties of the salesmen. (2) Statement of selection routine or system. (3) Photographs of "sales types" usually successful in selling. (4) Sales talk about company to use in selling the applicant on the opportunity. (5) Earnings records of most successful salesmen. (6) Testimonial letters from customers.

13. The two best methods of transportation for 50 city salesmen calling on retail druggists for a drug specialty manufacturer in cities in excess of 50,000 population are: (1) Personal automobiles. (2) Taxi cabs. (3) Street cars. (4) Company-owned cars. (5) Drive-yourself rented cars.

14. Which two of the following measures should a sales manager of a candy manufacturer take with a salesman of average sales ability who, after repeated warnings, does not begin calling on his trade until after ten o'clock in the morning? (1) Discharge him. (2) Assign a supervisor to accompany the man. (3) Require him to report at the office at 8:30. (4) Have him 'phone the office each morning from a customer's store. (5) Ignore his tardiness. (6) Install a meter in his car to record starting time. (7) Offer a bonus for starting on time.

15. A life insurance agency manager will find it most advantageous to his personal sales production to take which two of the following courses: (1) Join a civic club. (2) Sing in a church choir. (3) Captain a charity drive. (4) Play golf. (5) Take a course in insurance selling. (6) Subscribe to insurance magazine.

16. Which two of the following duties are most important in the work of a sales engineer of heavy industrial equipment? (1) Closing sales. (2) Reporting activities. (3) Demonstrating. (4) Locating prospective customers. (5) Following-up old customers. (6) Adjusting claims. (7) Analyzing needs. (8) Making collections.

17. An organization engaged in nationwide selling to wholesale and retail outlets of a line of established and new individually packaged food specialties in annual volume of $500,000 requires which four of the following functional types of salesmen? (1) Sales engineers. (2) Export salesmen. (3) Missionary salesmen. (4) Specialty salesmen. (5) Senior salesmen. (6) Junior salesmen. (7) City salesmen. (8) Country salesmen. (9) Service salesmen.

18. A salesman 60 years old has served a meat packer for 25 years in charge of a city territory and is widely and favorably known, producing an average volume of business which has declined in recent years so that his work is no longer profitable. The management is undecided as to which two of the following steps should be taken in this case: (1) Pension him. (2) Give him inside sales work. (3) Transfer him to another territory. (4) Warn him to increase sales or he will be discharged. (5) Reduce size of his territory. (6) Give him more territory. (7) Take no action.

19. Which two of the following discount policies would be most effective in stimulating sales of a new drug specialty sold direct to independent neighborhood drug gists? (1) Quantity discount. (2) Trade discount. (3) Cash discount. (4) Introductory discount. (5) Term discount. (6) Geographical discount.

20. In setting the price to the ultimate consumer on a new brand of tooth powder, the manufacturer should consider which four of the following factors are most important? (1) Current economic conditions. (2) Trend of retail prices. (3) Prices of competing products. (4) Cost of manufacture. (5) Demand for tooth powder. (6) Return on capital invested. (7) Cost of distribution and promotion. (8) Cost of research and development.

FIGURE 27. The second page of the Canfield test of sales supervisory knowledge.

available from the Science Research Associates, Chicago. Other interest tests are: Interest Inventory for Sales People, published by the Personnel Institute, Chicago, and Aptitude Index by the Life Insurance Sales Research Bureau.

Steps in a Testing Program. The practice commonly employed by companies in developing a testing program for selecting salesmen, includes the following steps:

1. A sales job analysis is made to determine the duties and related personal qualifications needed to do the job. These qualifications usually include intelligence, interest, personality, sales aptitude, etc., in varying amounts according to the complexity and nature of the job. This analysis determines the type of tests required in selection.

2. An experimental group of representative salesmen is selected to be tested. One half of this group should be composed of outstanding men and one half of poor salesmen. The criterion for classifying the men as good and poor should be their individual sales records as determined by their dollar volume, number of new distributors secured, and profitable operation.

3. The tests are given to the experimental group in a body under the same conditions. The entire battery should be given at one time, and specific instructions for taking the tests should be given.

4. The tests are scored and the results tabulated on a master sheet.

5. A range of scores for each test is established for the good class and the poor class.

6. The weighted average scores are found for each group by multiplying each test score by the number of men who make that score. All of these totals are added and the product is divided by the total number of men in each class to provide a weighted average score for each test for each class.

In order that all test scores may be comparable, the actual test scores are converted to percentiles according to tables accompanying the scoring keys. When several tests are used, a score of 80 on one may be the equivalent to a score of 60 on another. However, if these scores are converted to percentiles they may be readily compared.

7. Standards for selection of applicants are established. A percentile range from average to high for the good salesmen is established as a standard for selection for each test used. The percentile

scores of applicants are compared with this standard. A pattern or profile showing graphically the standard percentile scores of good men on each test may be drawn. For ready comparison the profiles of applicants' percentile scores may be drawn on the same pattern.

Physical Examinations. Good health is one of the primary qualifications of salesmen, since it has a direct bearing upon personal appearance, mental attitude, and energy. Physical examinations are frequently used in the selection of salesmen by many com-

62 Rev. 5 6-1-30 10M SP

ORGANIZATION CHANGE

LOCAL OFFICE / SALES AGENCY .... DISTRICT .... DATE ....

NAME ....

ADDRESS ....

POSITION .... DATE COMPENSATION { COMMENCES / CHANGES / ENDS ....

ENGAGEMENT
PREVIOUSLY EMPLOYED BY US { YES / NO .... IF SO WHERE .... HOW LONG .... POSITION ....
SALARY RECOMMENDED $ .... PER MONTH .... % COMMISSION
AMOUNT OF ADVANCE OR DRAWING ACCOUNT RECOMMENDED $ .... PER MONTH
MONTHLY QUOTA { $ .... / POINTS .... SALESMAN'S EQUIPMENT { Sales Training Course No. .... / Price Book No. .... / Portfolio No. ....

TERRITORY
ASSIGNED ....
WITHDRAWN ....
CURRENT ASSIGNMENT ....

TRANSFER
FROM OFFICE .... POSITION ....
TO OFFICE .... POSITION ....
(If any compensation change indicate below)

CHANGE IN COMPENSATION
DATE EMPLOYED .... LAST CHANGE IN COMPENSATION, DATE .... FROM $ .... TO $ ....
CHANGE NOW RECOMMENDED .... FROM $ .... TO $ ....
REASONS FOR CHANGE ....

TERMINATION OF EMPLOYMENT
DISMISSED OR LEFT VOLUNTARILY .... WOULD YOU RE-EMPLOY? ....
ABILITY ....
CAUSE OF LEAVING? (Give complete reasons) ....

REMARKS

APPROVALS
BRANCH MANAGER .... DATE ....
DISTRICT MANAGER .... DATE ....
GENERAL OFFICE .... DATE ....

Issue in quadruplicate.
Mail original and two copies to the District Manager.
Retain fourth copy.
If approved, District Manager will mail two copies to the General Sales Dept., New York, if for Sales Personnel; to the Service Dept., Harrisburg, if for Service Personnel.
Third copy is to be retained by District Manager.

FIGURE 28. Changes in a salesman's territory and compensation as well as his termination record are incorporated in this form used by the sales personnel division of a large manufacturer of specialties.

panies. Particularly where the sales job demands many calls and the carrying of heavy sample cases, the physical fitness of applicants should be carefully considered.

Termination Records. A number of companies keep termination records of their salesmen. These are useful in selection, for they may point out causes of failures and suggest personal qualities which should be considered in the employment of salesmen. Such a record may be in the form of a judgment blank to record the personal weaknesses of the departing salesman. An analysis of termi-

REPORT OF SALESMAN LEAVING EMPLOY OF COMPANY

TO BE FILLED IN BY BRANCH MANAGER

DATE..........

SALESMAN'S NAME.......... OFFICE..........

DID THE SALESMAN HAVE THE PROPER QUALIFICATIONS?..........

WHO SELECTED HIM?.......... WHO TRAINED HIM?..........

IF THE SALESMAN WAS UNSUCCESSFUL WHAT IN YOUR JUDGMENT WAS THE REAL REASON FOR HIS FAILURE?..........

....

IF THE SALESMAN WAS SUCCESSFUL WHAT IN YOUR JUDGMENT WAS THE REAL REASON FOR HIS LEAVING?..........

....

PREVIOUS RECORD (Check or fill in squares:)

PERSONAL: AGE ☐ MARRIED ☐ SINGLE ☐ NO. OF DEPENDENTS ☐

EDUCATION: GRAMMAR SCHOOL ☐ HIGH SCHOOL ☐ COLLEGE ☐

SELLING EXPERIENCE: SPECIALTY SALESMAN ☐ COMMERCIAL SALESMAN ☐

OFFICE EXPERIENCE: GENERAL ☐ BOOKKEEPING ☐ ACCOUNTANT ☐ C.P.A. ☐

NO PREVIOUS BUSINESS EXPERIENCE ☐

REMARKS:..........

....

....

APPROVED: BRANCH MANAGER.......... DATE..........

DISTRICT MANAGER.......... DATE..........

TO BE FILLED IN BY GENERAL OFFICE

Date Employed or Basis Changed	Basis	SALES MADE BY MONTHS DURING EMPLOYMENT												TOTAL SALES	Average Monthly Sales	Average Monthly Earnings at 15% Commission
		Jan.	Feb.	Mar.	Apr.	May	June	July	Aug.	Sept.	Oct.	Nov.	Dec.			

DATE RESIGNED / DISMISSED..........

MONTHLY QUOTA DURING LAST YEAR.......... % SALES TO QUOTA LAST YEAR.......... THIS YEAR TO DATE..........

REMARKS..........

....

....

SIGNED.......... DATE..........

Printed in U. S. A.

FIGURE 29. A termination record form, showing the reasons for dismissal of a salesman, provides valuable information for selecting salesmen and establishing standard salesmen's qualifications. The termination record illustrated is used by a large office equipment corporation.

nation records is helpful in determining standards of qualifications for salesmen.

The Phoenix Life Insurance Company considers that one of the most important studies which it has made in connection with the selection of agents is an analysis of terminations. At the time an agent's contract is cancelled, the man's record is analyzed, and information is secured from the agency manager so that the causes of failure may be determined. The company believes that a large proportion of these failures are traceable to selection. It has found that important factors causing failure are: age; attitude of a man's wife; type not sufficiently aggressive or too analytical; financial condition; laziness; lack of organized effort; and evidence that a man was not sufficiently sold on the business when he was selected.

Field Observation. Some companies require a sales candidate to spend a short time on the job with one or more good salesmen to get a better understanding of the work. At the same time, the company representative observes the applicant and reports his impressions to the employing sales executive. Before a final decision is made to employ an applicant, the sales manager may spend a few hours in the field with the candidate. This should be done where a difference of opinion exists about the qualifications of an applicant, or where there is doubt in the employer's mind as to whether the man is fitted for the work. Good customers may be asked for their opinion of the man, and in this way the buyer's viewpoint can be taken into consideration.

Miscellaneous Methods. There are numerous theories of character analysis occasionally applied in the selection of salesmen. One is the theory of pigmentation, or that buyers prefer blonds to brunettes. An exponent of this theory says:

The normal blond has positive, dynamic, driving, aggressive, active, and quick characteristics; while the normal brunette has negative, static, conservative, submissive, cautious, plodding, slow, and deliberate characteristics.

A study of one hundred and fifty-two highly successful salesmen found that eighty-two were designated brunettes, while only seventy were listed as blonds by their employers.

Other theories of selection are based on facial characteristics, complexion, stature, walk, and voice. Some sales executives believe in astrology, while others maintain that phrenology is helpful in selecting salesmen. However, there is no scientific foundation for the validity of these theories.

Testing Techniques of Selection. The consensus among sales executives who seriously seek a sounder method of selecting salesmen is that the establishment of standard qualifications and a system for measuring applicants with the standard, as described in detail, is fundamentally of great assistance; however, it is incomplete and may always be so.

Employers of salesmen should continuously test their methods of selection in the light of experience. Rating scales for evaluating personal qualifications may be revised on the basis of performance records. Personal qualification standards may become valueless with changes in the job, methods of distribution, character of the product, and so forth. The findings on mental and aptitude tests should be compared with the performance of salesmen, selected on the basis of such tests. Through continuous research on various phases of selection, improved techniques will be evolved.

Problem 1—Selection by Personal History Scores

Harwood Food Corporation

The Harwood Food Corporation, located in Philadelphia, Pennsylvania, operates eighty branch offices and warehouses throughout the United States, out of which operate some 1,200 salaried driver salesmen, calling direct on 800,000 home owners with a complete line of packaged food specialties.

The company seeks salesmen through its present organization, influential businessmen, schools, clergymen, chambers of commerce, newspaper advertising, and employment bureaus.

An analysis has been made of the personal history records of the present salesmen of the company, and bar charts have been prepared scoring various personal history items, such as: age, 21 to 23 inclusive, score 22; 24 to 28 inclusive, score 50; 29 to 35 inclusive, score 20; and above 35, score 8. Scorings for the number of positions held in the past five years are: one, score 20; two, score 30; 3 to 5, score 28; and 6 or more, score 9. Scorings for previous experience are: one time over direct selling, score 14; service direct selling, score 38; other sales experience, score 8; and no sales experience, score 20. The scores for education for high-volume salesmen are: grammar school, score 16; one to two years of high school, score 24; more than two years of high school, score 22; and grammar school and at least six-months' outside study, score 18. Scores for dependents are: single, score 10; married and not more than two children, score 19; and married and more than two children, score 16. Scores for investments are: home ownership, score 13; savings and investments, score 11; and no savings and investments, score 6.

Candidates for the sales force fill out an application blank calling for the above personal history information, which is rated according to the scores established. If a candidate's qualifications exceed the basic score of 120, he is considered favorably for employment, and if his score is less than the base of 120, he must be sufficiently outstanding in personal qualities to offset the deficiency in his personal history score.

Following the scoring of the applicant's personal history, he is given three interviews by a branch manager, who also interviews the former employer or examines the reference given by the candidate.

Although the scores of personal history factors were developed after a careful study of the records of a hundred successful and unsuccessful salesmen, the objection has arisen that possibly an insufficient number of records were considered in establishing the scores, and that a few exceptional cases would create a serious margin of error in determining the various values. Furthermore, the scoring plan is criticized for establishing an inflexible standard for measuring variable personal characteristics. Tact, initiative, energy, and personality are not measured at all by the scoring system.

Certain advocates of the rating plan contend that the scores should be interpreted more literally, not merely to serve as a guide in checking the impressions gained in personal interviews. The basic score of 120 should be the absolute minimum. In the opinion of these persons, candidates scoring below 120 should not be considered for employment.

At present, the company does not favor aptitude tests for sales candidates, although the Strong Vocational Interest Test and the Bernreuter Personality Inventory have been recommended as desirable measurements of sales characteristics. The Allport A-S Reaction Study has been suggested also, but the company has never considered these tests.

Questions

1. Should the personal history record scoring plan used in the selection of salesmen by the Harwood Food Corporation be continued as it is used at present? Give reasons for your decision.

2. Should the personal history score be considered more seriously and the base of 120 be set as an absolute minimum? Candidates scoring below 120 would not be accepted on any consideration. Give reasons for your decision.

3. Should the vocational interest tests be included in the selection procedure of the company? Give reasons for your decision.

4. Should the company's selection procedure be changed in any way to make it more effective?

Problem 2—Selection Method

Martinson Insurance Agency

The Martinson Insurance Agency, established in a large city in Massachusetts, has contracted 16 full-time commission agents, of which 10 are seniors and 6 are juniors, with a total annual production of $1,500,000. The agency manager gives new agents an intensive course of training, but a great many of the men contracted have failed after a few weeks or months in the field. This high turnover of agents has been attributed by the agency manager to poor selection methods, rather than to any deficiency in the training program.

The selection methods of the agency have consisted of two personal interviews with each applicant, one by the agency manager and one by a supervisor. A check is made on references from previous employers of the prospective agent. A candidate is required to take the state examination for life underwriters, and if he passes this test, he is given a contract by the agency manager.

The manager determined to change his selection procedure to some extent in the hope of improving the caliber of agents selected. He decided, in addition to present methods, to give candidates a psychological test to determine their intelligence, since he believed that the complexities of an insurance contract demanded agents of above-average mental ability.

He also determined to contract no agents under thirty-five years of age, in the belief that younger men do not have the maturity essential to life insurance selling. The manager believed that prospects for insurance were prejudiced against young men as agents, and were unwilling to take very seriously the recommendations of a youngster.

The supervisor of the agency maintained, however, that young men were more ambitious, had more energy, and were more adaptable to the training program of the agency.

The manager also believed that candidates should be tested for sales ability before being contracted. He proposed that each candidate be required to obtain, from friends, neighbors, or acquaintances, the names of ten possible prospects for life insurance and prepare logical plans for presenting insurance to these prospects. The candidate would be given assistance in preparing the plans and told how and where to locate the prospects.

The supervisor was skeptical as to whether or not candidates would be willing to invest the time and study necessary to secure the names of prospects or to plan sales to them before receiving contracts. Furthermore, he believed that the time of the manager and supervisor was too valuable to devote to helping prospective agents in this way.

Questions

1. Are the present methods of selection of the Martinson Insurance Agency sound? Give reasons for your opinion.

2. Are the proposed selection methods of the manager sound? Give your reasons.

3. If you do not favor either the present or proposed methods of selecting agents, how would you select the agents for the Martinson Agency?

Problem 3—Selecting by Interview

Speedwell Motor Corporation

The Speedwell Motor Corporation, Detroit, Michigan, manufactures six- and eight-cylinder passenger cars, in annual volume of more than one million units, sold through more than ten thousand dealers throughout the country. The company employs a large force of wholesale representatives to call on its dealers. These men travel out of the company's branches located in the principal cities of the country.

In selecting company salesmen the general sales manager insists on three qualifications. The predominating requisite is enthusiasm and aptitude for selling, that is, the applicant must want to sell more than anything else. The second qualification is that the salesman must express his thoughts in a convincing and intelligent manner. Third, he must know the meaning of industry.

The sales manager believes that one can easily detect these qualifications in an initial interview with an applicant, and that the selling presentation of an applicant, on his first contact for a job, is the best proof of his ability. If he is successful in convincing the interviewer that he is the man for the job, it is obvious that he can be trained to present the merchandise in the same intelligent and convincing manner.

The sales manager feels that the various theoretical and scientific methods of qualifying salesmen are beneficial only in a limited degree, perhaps in detecting minor qualifications which, in the final analysis, are not of great consequence.

The applicant's previous connections are investigated, not for the purpose of determining whether or not he was successful, but rather for verification of his integrity, loyalty, and personal habits.

Having selected several hundred sales representatives, the sales manager attributes the low turnover of salesmen in the company largely to the type of training rather than to the qualifications applicants may have possessed at the time they were employed.

The sales manager's views of selection have been questioned on the ground that they are based upon mere chance accumulation of experience and are little better than guesses. In the judgment of the critics, such a method is too subjective, and the interview situation is too unnatural to enable an applicant to sell himself capably to an interviewer.

Questions

1. Is the sales manager's method of selecting salesmen for the Speedwell Motor Corporation sound? Give reasons for your decision.

2. What method of selection should be used by the company in selecting salesmen?

Reading References

Developing and Managing Salesmen, Giles, Chap. II.
Directing Sales, Bonney, Chap. V.
Handbook of Sales Management, Hall, Sec. VII.
How to Select Better Salesmen, Rados, Chaps. 18, 19.
Intensive Sales Management, Aspley, Chap. IV.
Management of the Sales Organization, Russell, pp. 38–55.
Modern Sales Management, Frederick, Chap. XII.
Principles of Personal Selling, Tosdal, pp. 486–515.
Psychology of Selecting Men, Laird, Chaps. V, VI, IX, XI.
Sales Administration, Hayward, pp. 262, 263, 264.
Sales Management Fundamentals, Hay, pp. 9–15.
Sales Management Today, Doubman, Chap. V.
Scientific Sales Management Today, Hoyt, Chap. VI.
Selection and Training of Salesmen, Kenagy and Yoakum, Chaps. X, XI, XII, XIII

CHAPTER EIGHT

CONTRACTING SALESMEN

Why Contract Salesmen? There is considerable difference of opinion among sales executives as to the value of written agreements with salesmen. Those who favor contracts with salesmen give the following advantages of formal agreements:

1. Prevents misunderstandings.
2. Protects the employer against third parties by limiting the authority of the salesmen.
3. Safeguards investment in salesmen's equipment.
4. Psychological reasons.
5. Prevents the introduction of new considerations in arrangements between employer and salesmen.
6. Controls the activities of commission salesmen.
7. Prevents competition by former salesmen.
8. Provides for handling of "split commissions."
9. Protects the employer's interest in product improvements made by salesmen.
10. Makes definite provision for termination of a salesman's services.
11. Affords opportunity to outline clearly and completely various types of bonus and profit-sharing plans.
12. Prevents territory encroachments.

The principal disadvantages of salesmen's agreements are:

1. They tie the hands of both employer and employee by fixed provisions which might require modification or reinterpretation in the light of future conditions.
2. Contracts are not enforceable.
3. Contracts hamper the employer in discharging incompetent salesmen.

4. Contracts hinder close personal relationships.

Contracts are used universally by life insurance companies to show the duties of agents, their authority and limitations as well as the scale of commissions paid. The same is true in most specialty product concerns where salesmen are paid on a straight commission basis.

The National Cash Register Company has used formal written contracts with its commission sales agents to avoid misunderstandings, provide for compensation arrangements, describe sales territories, and regulate split commissions. The Todd Sales Company, manufacturers of check-protecting devices, check forms, and bankers' supplies, made agreements with all of its commission salesmen in the form of formal contracts.

What a Salesman's Contract Should Cover. A good salesman's contract should generally include the following essential elements:

1. Proper identification of the contracting parties, full names, and addresses.
2. Definite explanation as to why contract is being made.
3. Detailed outline of territory assigned.
4. Compensation arrangements, quotas, split commissions, reserves, and the like.
5. Obligations of the salesman.
6. Obligations of the employer.
7. Joint agreements of both parties.
8. Description of consideration.
9. Time of performance—definite beginning and end of contract.
10. Conditions of performance.
11. Specific arrangement for termination of contract.
12. Definite mention of the law which is to govern the contract.
13. Acknowledgment.
14. Special orders such as house orders, trial orders, and government orders.
15. Collection expenses.
16. Travel expenses.
17. Trade-ins.

The specific items which should be included in a salesman's contract depend upon the nature of the job, the type of products sold, and the method of compensation and control of salesmen.

Compensation Arrangements. The compensation paid salesmen is one of the principal elements in sales contracts and agreements, because often compensation plans are so complex that misunderstandings easily arise between the management and the salesmen.   There is a real need for agreements, particularly where salesmen are paid on a straight commission basis.   The amount of

Form R-183-B 7500 Sets 1-30

ORIGINAL

SALESMAN'S AGREEMENT

This agreement made in triplicate this.......................day of..19......,

between .... COMPANY, a corporation duly organized and existing under the laws of the State

of Ohio, and having a place of business in the City of..............................., State of...................... as

party of the first part, hereinafter called "the Company," and...of the

City of................................, State of...................., as party of the second part, hereinafter called "the Salesman."

WITNESSETH: That in consideration of the covenants herein contained, the Company agrees to consign ____ ____ of its manufacture to the Salesman and the Salesman agrees to diligently endeavor to dispose of said _____ by sale at retail to household consumers only, in accordance with the terms and conditions of this agreement.

First.—The Salesman shall give such guarantee or bond as shall be satisfactory to the Company for the full and faithful performance of all the terms and conditions of this agreement.

Second.—The Salesman shall personally pay all expense incurred in or arising out of the transaction of said business consummated by him, including the cost of delivery and return of machines, and if such _____ __ or accessories thereto are damaged or lost, to pay for the repair or replacement of the same. To also pay all personal, town, county, city, or state soliciting license fees.

Third.—The Salesman shall report in writing semi-monthly on the 15th and last days of each month, or as directed from time to time by the Company, on forms furnished by the Company, giving a full and complete account of all business transacted by him, and to deliver and remit to the Company all monies collected by him in connection with such business, and the Salesman expressly agrees that he will keep safe and not mingle Company funds with his own personal funds, and that he shall not be entitled to withhold on account of any alleged claim for compensation due him, or for any purpose whatsoever, any portion of any money or monies collected or received by him under this agreement, and to refrain from dealing with persons under the age of twenty-one (21) years.

Fourth.—The Salesman shall return when and as requested, and without expense to the Company, either before or at the termination of this agreement all _____ ____ and other property (including canvas covers) to the Company at such place or places as it may direct.

Fifth.—The Salesman shall have no authority or power to pledge the credit of, or to incur bills in the name of the Company in any way, nor to permit or bring any suit in the name of the Company, or cause the arrest of any person.

Sixth.—The Salesman agrees to sell _____ consigned to him at the prices and terms established by the Company through the medium of its current price schedules to the extent and amount disclosed by said schedules, subject to all the terms and provisions herein stated.

Seventh.—The Salesman agrees that the Company in its uncontrolled discretion may accept or reject any sale consummated by the Salesman, and if rejected the Salesman agrees to promptly pick up and deliver to the Company without expense the ____ _____ ____ the sale of which has been rejected by the Company.

Eighth.—The Salesman agrees, that on accounts or sales which the Company lists as uncollectible or against which the _____ are repossessed on accounts or sales consummated by the Salesman, to forfeit all unpaid commissions on said account or sale, and to pay the Company $3.00, plus a refund in cash of all the commissions advanced to him by the Company on said sale or account, less Fifty (50%) Per cent of the money paid by the customer, excluding the first payment if any, and authorizes the Company to deduct this amount, or any other money owing by the Salesman to the Company from any commissions accrued or to become due him, or from any other money due him or to become due him by the Company.

Ninth.—The Salesman agrees to refrain from making any assignment of any commissions that may be due, or become due him under the terms of this agreement. To repossess and deliver to the Company any ____ _____ which he has sold, when directed, without additional compensation, and in default of so doing, hereby authorizes the Company to apply the expense of repossessing the same to any commission or monies which may become due him.

Tenth.—All machines traded in by the Salesman from new sales consummated by him shall be immediately delivered to the Company together with a bill of sale signed by the customer, and the Salesman shall warrant that the title thereto is good and free from all incumbrances or payments owing thereon.

Eleventh.—The Salesman agrees to furnish his own equipment and automobile for carrying out the terms of this contract, and to pay all expense connected with the maintenance thereof, and to hold the Company harmless from any and all liability including all costs and attorney fees from any and all injuries and damages to persons or property, caused in any manner by the use of said equipment or automobile maintained by the Salesman during the life of this agreement.

Twelfth.—The Salesman agrees that no back commissions shall become due or payable in the event of the termination of this contract until twelve months after the date of said termination, and further agrees not to interfere in any manner before or after the termination of this agreement with the sales of _____ made by the Salesman, or by any other of the Company's representatives, and if such interference is made, he agrees to pay to the Company One Hundred ($100.00) Dollars stipulated damages, and authorizes the Company to deduct such amount from any commission or commissions due to become due him under this agreement.

FIGURE 30. First page of a contract signed with commission salesmen by a manufacturer of household appliances.

commission for each item in a line should be stated. It should be made clear in the agreement that commissions are paid only on net sales and do not include payment of commission on freight, cartage, installation, or other unprofitable items entering into the transaction.

The Company agrees—

Thirteenth.—That whenever the Salesman shall dispose of any one of its _____ _____ in accordance with its current prices, as disclosed by its price schedule, and when such sale is accepted by the Company, he shall be entitled to a credit on such sale so accepted, subject to all the provisions of this agreement, a sum equal to the amount of money the customer has agreed to pay for such _____ _____ exclusive of any old _____ allowance, and/or discount, over and above the price of the particular _____ and the class of sale as is shown in the attached schedule, or subsequent schedules that may be issued from time to time by the Company, payable as follows:

A. On all _____ sold for cash, the compensation shall be paid when the total proceeds received from the sale thereof are turned over to the Company

B. On all installment sales accepted by the Company, the Salesman shall be entitled to a commission equal to the first payment made by the customer plus a cash advance as determined by the schedule hereunto annexed, provided, however, that in all cases the Salesman agrees to allow an unaccrued commission of not less than $10.00 to remain on each time sale consummated by him (except on sales where the customer agrees to pay for said _____ within a period of four months and/or sixty days, in which event the Salesman agrees to allow an unaccrued commission of not less than $12.50 and $13.00 respectively on each such sale so consummated by him, and if the customer fails to pay within the contract period, agrees that such additional commission shall be forfeited by him), and agrees that the amount of cash commission paid is to be regulated in accordance with the terms of this provision.

C. The Company further agrees to pay the Salesman a collecting commission of 15% on all monies collected and remitted to the Company in regular manner by said Salesman, on regular ____ _____ installment accounts placed in his hands for attention by the manager. It is specifically understood and agreed that no collection commission shall be paid however, on cash sales, first payments, refunds or any discount allowed the customer.

D. The unaccrued commissions referred to in paragraph 13-B hereof shall accrue and be payable to the Salesman only after this contract shall be in continuous operation for a period of four months from date, and then at the rate of 50% of each regular monthly installment paid by the customer in accordance with the customer's contract, but if the customer's installments are not made regularly, or are not in an amount as specified by contract, or if for any reason the Company deems it advisable to accept a lesser monthly payment than contracted for, then the unaccrued commission shall not accrue or be payable until after the Company has received Forty ($40.00) Dollars in cash on account of such sale, excluding the first or down payment. Such back commissions when and as payable are to be accounted for and paid to the Salesman on the 15th day of each month, after deducting from said back commissions any refunds due, or other obligations due the Company here or at any other place.

Fourteenth.—It is mutually agreed that if any _____ ___ sold by the Salesman shall be removed by the purchaser thereof beyond the territory controlled by the Company's branch office at ...., the Salesman waives all claim for commission that may be unpaid on said account on the date of said removal, and agrees to permit the Company to forfeit the same on its books.

Fifteenth.—It is further understood and agreed that in case of any controversy between the Company and the Salesman arising out of this agreement that all entries or statements contained on the records or books of the Company shall be binding on both of the parties hereto under this agreement, and shall be admissible in evidence in any proceedings at law or in equity, as prima facie evidence of the truth of such entries or statements, and the Company shall have the right to proceed in a civil action against the Salesman for the stipulated damages herein provided, or for any amount overdrawn on Salesman's commission or for any money due the Company for refunds on account of repossessions, and for the collection of any or all of said claims, the Company shall not be limited or bound to first apply the Salesman's commissions, if any.

Sixteenth.—This agreement shall remain in full force until superseded by a new one duly executed in writing, except that this agreement or any subsequent agreement may be terminated at the pleasure of either party.

Seventeenth.—It is further mutually understood and agreed that the price schedule annexed hereto signed by the Salesman constitutes a part of this contract in the same manner as if it were set forth in full in the body of this agreement.

WITNESS our hands and seals this day and year first above mentioned.

_____ _____ _____ COMPANY.

WITNESSES:

.... By..

.... Manager.

.... Salesman.

Duplicate copy is to be retained at the branch office for ready reference and filing.

FIGURE 31. Second page of the contract signed with commission salesmen by a manufacturer of household appliances.

"Acceptable orders" should be defined in the agreement when it is stipulated that salesmen shall receive a commission on all orders accepted. Orders may not be accepted because of poor credit of the buyer, or the buyer may refuse delivery, or the seller may refuse to ship because the order was not taken in accordance with the house rules or terms of sale. Sales contracts accordingly frequently state: "Commissions are payable only on orders accepted by the selling firm, shipped to the purchaser, and accepted and paid for by the purchaser."

The time when commissions shall be paid is an important stipulation in contracts with commission salesmen. When the full purchase price is collected with the order, commissions are usually paid when the order and money are received by the company. When less than the full purchase price accompanies an order, commissions are usually paid when the purchase price has been paid in full. Provision should also be made for the payment of commissions on past sales made by a salesman who has severed his connection with the employer.

Stipulation is usually made for the payment of "advance commissions" and the establishment of "commission reserves" against which advance commissions, paid on merchandise returned for credit, or on uncollectible accounts, may be charged.

A policy of disposing of split commissions is usually included in the sales contract. The need for a split-commission provision arises when merchandise is sold in one territory for delivery in another. There are various methods of making a division of the commission, the most common being on a fifty-fifty basis. Half of the commission goes to the man who secured the original order, and half to the man in whose territory the merchandise is shipped. A large heating equipment manufacturer splits commissions on a thirds basis. One third goes to the man in whose territory the order is secured, one third to the man in whose area the contractor is located, and one third to the man in whose district the product is to be installed.

Quotas and bonus provisions are usually incorporated in salesmen's contracts by concerns using such methods of compensation. The amount of the quota is stated in units and in dollars and cents, for each product in a line, or by class of customer. The amount of bonus which shall be paid for whatever fractions of the quota are attained is also specified.

As commission, quota, bonus, and salary arrangements are

changed from time to time, some organizations append these as separate provisions to their salesmen's contracts.

Territorial Boundaries. Since salesmen are usually given exclusive territories in which to operate, misunderstandings frequently arise when the size of the territory is decreased, when the salesman is transferred, or when another salesman encroaches upon an exclusive territory. To prevent such misunderstandings, sales contracts with commission salesmen ordinarily define the territory rights of the salesman.

Sometimes a map outlining the territory of a salesman is attached to the sales contract, and the definite boundaries are stipulated by states, counties, trading areas, and cities. A penalty clause for territory violation has been written into sales contracts. One such reads:

Salesmen shall not solicit or make sales in a territory other than that mentioned in this contract, without special permission from the company. Should you make a sale in another territory, other than the one specified in this contract, you will receive one-third of your commission only. Should any salesman from an adjoining territory make any sales in your territory, you will receive two-thirds of the commission. In case a jobber should sell retail in your territory, the company will request said jobber to pay you a commission of .... % of the selling price.

Termination. An important clause in a salesman's contract is that covering problems arising when a salesman is discharged or voluntarily leaves the employment of a company. The salesman usually has valuable and sometimes confidential company property in the form of samples, price lists, and equipment. Frequently the salesman is entitled to a commission reserve account or a settlement on a bonus.

A large manufacturer of office equipment includes the following termination clause in its salesmen's contracts:

Upon termination of this contract, the salesman shall immediately make proper accounting for and return to the company all property belonging to it of every description, including machines, unused order blanks, sales manuals, scrap books, advertising matter, stationery, etc., then in his possession.

Upon cancellation of this contract by either party, all rights and interest in this contract, which it is expressly agreed is not assignable, on the part of the salesman shall immediately cease and he shall not be entitled to any commission or remuneration thereafter of any kind except for unpaid commissions upon the basis of the schedule then in force upon orders theretofore actually received, accepted, and filled by the company.

Duration. Closely related to the termination of a sales contract is the question of duration. The employer of salesmen must be free to dispense with the services of a salesman within a reasonable time, and at the same time a salesman must be given sufficient tenure to maintain his morale. The length of time for which salesmen's contracts are written varies widely, but few companies contract men for longer than one year. The period for which notice of termination may be given by either party is also variable and ranges from immediate termination to thirty days.

Certain contracts specify acts which may constitute grounds for termination of contracts with salesmen. Such a clause in the sales contract of an office equipment manufacturer reads:

> The company shall have the right to terminate this agreement if in the sole judgment of the company or its authorized representatives, the salesman has been guilty of a breach of trust in the conduct of the business, or of neglect of the company's business, or an act detrimental to the company's interest, in which event the termination of this agreement may take effect immediately and without thirty days' notice, by the depositing of a letter addressed to the salesman or delivered in person by a representative of the company, or the sending of a telegram containing such notice of termination.

An office appliance company has a clause in its agent's contract to the effect that it may be terminated at any time by either party by a written notice to that effect.

A large wire rope manufacturer's sales contract provides for termination by either party upon two-weeks' notice in writing. A manufacturer of material handling equipment provides for termination of its salesman's contract by written notice of either party, thirty days in advance.

Price Quotations. Definite provisions are incorporated in many sales contracts concerning the obligation of the salesmen to sell only at the prices and terms designated by the company. Commission salesmen are sometimes tempted to offer price reductions, rebates, concessions, or to accept trade-ins of old equipment without the authority of their employers.

To forestall such concessions a Chicago manufacturer of industrial operating equipment includes a unique clause in its salesman's contract:

> Any allowance such as a price cut, quantity discount, trade-in of old equipment, and the like, will be split fifty-fifty between the salesmen and the company.

The company believes that such a clause gives the salesman sufficient latitude to act without first writing to the home office for permission and at the same time makes salesmen more conservative in granting allowances to customers.

The Todd Sales Company, however, has the following definite clause in its salesman's contract prohibiting such allowances:

> The salesman agrees that he will sell the products of the company at the prices and in accordance with the terms as set forth in the schedule issued by the company from time to time. He shall not allow, directly or indirectly, any rebate or concession from his commissions, nor accept from customers notes, due bills, or I.O.U.'s in lieu of cash. Second-hand or traded-in machines may be resold in the name of the company only when issued by the company for resale.

Traveling Expenses. The subject of traveling expenses is so often the source of controversy in sales organizations that many salesmen's contracts include a clause stating the obligations of the company and of the salesman on this point. A large wire rope manufacturer covers the subject of expenses by stating:

> The company employs the second party as salesman at a salary of $.... per month and his legitimate traveling expenses when absent from his home and engaged upon the business of the company.

An office appliance manufacturer in its contracts with salesmen states:

> The salesman agrees that he will pay all of his own expenses of every kind and nature and shall have absolutely no authority to bind the company for any of his expenses or for any indebtedness of any kind or nature whatsoever.

The expense clause may also list the various classes of expenses which a salesman is allowed to incur, such as meals, lodging, travel, telegrams, and telephone.

Agreements by Salesmen. The salesman's employment contract usually specifies that the salesman is not authorized to make binding contracts without confirmation by his firm. Salesmen may be given authority to make agreements with customers, but usually such contracts are acknowledged by an authorized agent of the employing concern to indicate to the buyer that it is satisfied to accept contracts containing guaranties made by its salesmen. A selling organization is not bound by any contract made by its salesmen, unless it is evident that an authorized agent of the company led the buyer to believe that the salesman had such authority.

One large sales organization provides for agreements by salesmen in its sales contract as follows:

It is expressly agreed that the salesman has no authority to bind the Company to any agreement and that any sales made by him on its behalf are subject to its approval and acceptance.

Salesmen in Competition.

Companies such as laundries, bakeries, and cleaners, whose salesmen have frequent and close contact with customers, often seek protection by contract against salesmen who may leave and go into competition with them. Such protection is usually sought for a period of six months to one year. A typical clause covering this problem is the following, taken from a salesman's contract of a food manufacturer who distributes his products from house to house:

The salesman further agrees that he will not at any time, either while in the employ of the company or after leaving its service, or upon the termination of this contract, for any cause, exhibit or make known to any person or persons not connected with the company any of its business methods, forms, names of customers, or any information relating to the company's business; and the salesman further agrees and covenants that he will not at any time while he is in the employ of the company nor within the period of one year (subject to proviso below) after leaving its service nor within the period of one year (subject to proviso below) after the termination of this contract, with or without cause, either:

1. For himself or any other person, firm or corporation, directly or indirectly engage in the business of selling teas, coffees, baking powders, extracts, spices, or other like merchandise in any of the aforesaid territory which shall have been assigned or entrusted to him by the company, or in any territory in which he has solicited or taken orders or reorders for or sold or delivered any merchandise for the company; or

2. For himself or any other person, firm or corporation, directly or indirectly solicit or take orders or reorders for or sell or deliver any such merchandise in such territory; or

3. In any way directly or indirectly solicit, divert, take away, or interfere with any of the custom, trade, business, or patronage of the Company in such territory; or

4. Render any services, as an employee or in any other capacity in the counties of .... and state of .... to any person, firm or corporation engaged in the business of buying, selling, and dealing in teas, coffees, baking powders, spices, extracts, and other like merchandise.

Proviso: Where the statutes of the state governing this contract prohibit such limitation, the period of limitation herein is hereby amended to agree with the maximum period of limitation permitted by such statutes.

Subagencies.

Salesmen's contracts sometimes contain a clause which prohibits a salesman from appointing a subagent to do the majority of the selling work in his territory. Such clauses usually permit the employment of junior salesmen, but require that the senior salesmen be actively engaged in selling and provide the necessary supervision for juniors.

Rights to Discoveries and Improvements. Salesmen with inventive minds who are engaged in the sale of mechanical appliances often suggest desirable improvements or invent betterments in the products which they are selling. In such cases the employing company is interested in securing the exclusive rights to the discoveries and inventions of the salesmen. Typical provisions for obtaining title to improvements made by salesmen are illustrated in a clause from the contract of a check protector manufacturer:

The salesman agrees that he will, and he does hereby sell, assign, transfer, and set over to the company, its successors or assigns, all right, title, and interest in and to any and all inventions, discoveries and improvements relating to machines, devices, methods or products for protecting commercial documents of any kind from alterations, which he has made or may make while in the employ of the company; and that he will at any and all times fully disclose to the company, or any person or persons designated by it, any and all such inventions, discoveries and improvements; and that he will, whenever required to do so by the company, execute and deliver all such further papers and documents, including application for letters patent, and assignments of any patents that may be granted which the company may deem necessary in order to carry the provisions of this agreement into full effect and to secure to it the exclusive right and benefit of such inventions, discoveries, and improvements.

Informal Agreements with Salesmen. Rather than execute formal contracts, many firms prefer to use simple memorandums or statements of conditions under which a salesman is employed. Arrangements are often outlined in detail by correspondence. A valid written contract need not be in the form of a single instrument, but may comprise several letters or telegrams written over a period of time. Such memorandums or confirming letters may be adequate for employing many types of salesmen when the compensation plan is simple and the job is not complex.

Verbal Agreements. Verbal agreements with salesmen are equally as effective as written contracts. An employer instituting suit on a verbal contract must, however, introduce convincing proof of the nature of the verbal promises made. Cases may be cited where verbal agreements have not proved effective to alter the contents of a written contract.

Salesmen's Bonds. Many companies whose salesmen handle funds or make collections require them to be bonded by professional bonding firms, or to furnish real estate bond or personal surety guaranty. When legal action is required on a professional bonding company's bond, the full information concerning the salesman's violation is simply referred to the bonding company, which handles the prosecution of the case. When the salesman's bond is signed by an individual surety, the employing company is compelled to sue the surety to obtain settlement when the salesman violates the provisions of his bond. The employer should satisfy itself that the salesman's bondsman is financially responsible, since sales executives have been held personally liable for deficiencies of salesmen when due care was not exercised in investigating the surety of the salesmen.

Problem 1—Contract with Salesmen

Oakland Writing Machine Company

The Oakland Writing Machine Company, New York City, manufactures and distributes typewriters through its own sales force of more than two hundred salesmen. The salesmen are paid a straight commission on net sales, graduated according to the type of machine sold. The men operate out of thirty branch offices established in the principal cities of the country.

Salesmen have always been employed on the basis of a verbal agreement between the branch managers and the salesmen. This has not always proved satisfactory, and misunderstandings have at times arisen between the branch managers and the salesmen over the questions of commissions due, commission reserves, price concessions, and other compensation matters. In a western territory a salesman left the company, taking with him the business of a large organization which had been developed at the expense of the Oakland Company, and the company was powerless to prevent the loss.

For these reasons the sales officials of the Oakland Company believed that a contract should be signed with all salesmen employed. Accordingly, the following contract was prepared by the legal department of the Oakland Company in collaboration with the sales department:

SALESMEN'S CONTRACT OF THE OAKLAND WRITING MACHINE COMPANY

THIS AGREEMENT, made this ... day of ...., 19.., between OAKLAND WRITING MACHINE COMPANY, INC., of New York, New York, U. S. A., party of the first part, sometimes hereinafter called the "Company" and .... of ...., party of the second part, sometimes hereinafter called the "Salesman," WITNESSETH:

In consideration of the mutual covenants hereinafter contained, it is hereby mutually agreed as follows:

The party of the first part hereby appoints the party of the second part Salesman for the sale of the writing machines which the OAKLAND WRITING MACHINE COMPANY may from time to time manufacture and sell, in such territory as the party of the first part may from time to time designate, and the party of the second part accepts said appointment upon the following terms and conditions:

DURATION. This contract may be terminated at any time by written notice given by either party to the other.

GENERAL OBLIGATIONS OF THE SALESMAN. The Salesman agrees:

(1) To devote his entire time and attention and his best endeavors to the successful prosecution of the business of the Company, in the territory which from time to time may be assigned to him, and to conform strictly with the rules, regulations and instructions of the Company, which, from time to time, may be in force.

(2) The Salesman expressly agrees, as a condition of this contract, that by reason of the execution of this contract, he will be able to learn the details of the business of the Company and the methods, plans, organizations, forms and literature employed by the Company in the operation of its business and in the sale of its merchandise, and that he will become acquainted with the lists of customers and prospective customers of the Company. By reason and in consideration of such facts, he expressly and particularly agrees that, for the period of time covered by this contract and for a period of two years after its termination, he will not, directly or indirectly, either in his own name or as the agent or employee of anyone, other than of the Company, anywhere within the territory which may have been assigned to him from time to time or in which he may have been at any time engaged with the Company, engage in manufacturing, buying, selling, or dealing in typewriters of any kind whatsoever, or any other kind of merchandise which the Company may have manufactured or dealt in during the time that this contract is in force. And he further agrees that any information obtained by him in any manner regarding the Company's customers, property, business, affairs, plans and policies will be treated by him as confidential information and that he will not, in whole or in part, now, or at any time hereafter, disclose such information, nor use such information in any way, except as a salesman to further the business of the Company.

(3) That he will, and he does hereby, sell, assign, transfer and set over to the Company, its successors or assigns, all right, title and interest in and to any and all inventions, discoveries and improvements relating to machines, devices, methods or products for writing which he has made or may make while in the employ of the Company; and that he will at any and all times fully disclose to the Company, or any person or persons designated by it, any and all such inventions, discoveries and improvements; and that he will, whenever required to do so by the Company, execute and deliver all such further papers and documents, including application for letters patent and assignments of any patents that may be granted which the Company may deem necessary in order to carry the provisions of this agreement into full effect and to secure to it the exclusive right and benefit of all such inventions, discoveries and improvements.

(4) That he will pay all of his own expenses of every kind and nature and shall have absolutely no authority to bind the Company for any of his expenses or for any indebtedness of any kind or nature whatsoever.

(5) All machines, merchandise, books and materials furnished the Salesman shall remain the property of the Company. All moneys collected by said Salesman from customers upon sales of merchandise shall be the sole property of the Company, and the identical moneys and funds so received shall, without deduction of any kind for any purpose whatever, be delivered without delay to the Company.

(6) That he will sell the products of the Company at the prices and in accordance with terms as set forth in the schedule issued by the Company from time to time. He shall not allow, directly or indirectly, any rebate or concession from his commissions, nor accept from customers notes, due bills, or I.O.U.'s

in lieu of cash. Second-hand or traded-in machines may be resold in the name of the Company only when issued by the Company for resale.

(7) That he shall receive commissions according to the Company's schedule in force at the time of the sale. No commissions shall be received by him for sales made outside of the territory assigned him, except in accordance with the Company's special rules governing such out of territory sales. Commissions on sales where the full purchase price is collected with the order shall be paid, with the exception of deductions for reserve, as soon as practicable after the order and all moneys collected thereon are received by the Company; commissions on sales where less than the full purchase price is collected at time of sale shall not become due and payable until such purchase price shall have been paid in full. Should the Company see fit to advance any part or the whole of any commission before payment in full by the customer, then in case the amount of actual cash finally received upon the sale (after deducting fees and expenses of local attorneys and collection agencies, if any) is less than the full amount of the account against the customer, such portions of the loss as may be specified shall be charged back upon the reserve or commission accounts of the Salesman, in accordance with the provisions of the commission schedule in force at the time of the sale. The Company reserves the right to accept the return of any merchandise sold and to refund to the customer any payment which may have been made thereon, in which case no commission shall be paid and any commission advanced on the sale shall be charged back to the Salesman. It is further agreed that in no case shall the Company be liable for failure to collect any account even though such failure be due to the negligence of the Company or its agents.

(8) The Company reserves the right to withhold the Salesman's reserve fund and, if advisable, all commissions that accrue after a Salesman severs his connection with the Company until such time as all of his sales have been paid up in full.

(9) That he will, on demand, furnish to the Company, if requested, complete reports on all sales of writing machines or other products made by the Company and sold by him in his territory.

(10) It is expressly agreed that the Salesman has no authority to bind the Company to any agreement, and that any sales made by him on its behalf are subject to its approval and acceptance.

(11) It is understood that under this agreement, the status of the Salesman is that of an independent operator, operating on a commission basis.

TERMINATION. Upon the termination of this contract the Salesman shall immediately make proper accounting for and return to the Company all property belonging to it of every description, including machines, unused order blanks, sales manuals, scrap books, advertising matter, stationery, etc., then in his possession.

Upon the cancellation of this contract by either party all rights and interest in this contract (which it is expressly agreed is not assignable) on the part of the Salesman shall immediately cease and he shall not be entitled to any commission or remuneration thereafter of any kind except for unpaid commissions upon the basis of the schedule then in force upon orders theretofore actually received, accepted, and filled by the Company.

INTERPRETATION. If any question arises as to the validity, construction or performance of this contract in any City, County, or State court or court of the United States or foreign country, it is agreed that the laws of the State of New York shall govern without reference to the place of execution or performance of the same.

IN WITNESS WHEREOF, we have hereunto set our hands and seal the ..... day

of ...., in the year one thousand nine hundred and ....
Witness to signature of Salesman THE OAKLAND WRITING MACHINE Co.
.... By ....
Director of Sales

....
Salesman

Questions

1. Should the Oakland Writing Machine Company have adopted the contract as drawn? Give reasons for your decision.

2. Is the contract as drawn fair to the salesmen as well as the company? How would you change it?

Problem 2—Contract with Life Insurance Agents

World Life Insurance Company

The World Life Insurance Company of New York, one of the largest life insurance companies in the country, adopted in 1944 a new contract for its agents incorporating, among other features, a new method of compensation designed to provide the following:

1. Adequate opportunity for the underwriter to earn a satisfactory income selling life insurance.
2. Larger compensation for business of good persistency and for steady and conscientious service to policyholders.
3. A commission schedule to smooth out fluctuations in income.
4. Compensation for service rendered policyholders after age has reduced the underwriter's capabilities for new production.

The following compensation features are incorporated in the contract:

1. New policy commissions on first year cash premiums graded as to type of policy and duration of premium payments starting with 45 per cent for ordinary life to 20 per cent for five to nine payment life policies.
2. Renewal commissions payable on second and third policy years varying as to type of policy but averaging 15 per cent for the second year and 10 per cent the third year.
3. Service fees providing compensation for satisfactory service to policyholders payable beginning the fourth policy year upon evidence of service for the duration of the premium-paying period. The service fees are: fourth policy year, 5 per cent; fifth policy year, 10 per cent; and sixth and subsequent years, 3 per cent.

The new underwriter's contract follows:

The World Life Insurance Company
New York, N. Y.

....

....

.... 19....

....

You are hereby appointed an agent of the undersigned General Agent of the World Life Insurance Company under the following conditions:

Purpose of Appointment. (1) The purpose of this appointment is to authorize you to solicit applications for insurance and annuities in the World Life Insurance Company in .... in the territory assigned General Agent.

Commissions. (2) (a) You shall receive as compensation for your services commissions based upon percentages of first-year premiums on policies written and placed in force by you when paid in Cash to Company or General Agent, and, subject to the fulfillment of the production requirement prescribed by subsection (b) of this section, further commissions based upon second and third policy years cash premiums, all at the rates set forth in the following schedules.

Insurance

Type of Policy	Commission First Policy Year	Commission Second Policy Year	Commission Third Policy Year
Ordinary Life	45%	15%	10%
30 Payment Life and over	45%	15%	10%
20 to 29 Payment Life	40%	15%	10%
19 Payment Life	37½%	15%	10%
14 to 18 Payment Life	35%	15%	10%
10 to 13 Payment Life	30%	15%	10%
5 to 9 Payment Life	20%	10%	5%
Regular Endowments			
Endowment Period			
35 and over	40%	15%	10%
34	39%	15%	10%
33	39%	15%	10%
32	38%	15%	10%
31	38%	15%	10%
30	37%	15%	10%
29	37%	15%	10%
28	36%	15%	10%
27	36%	15%	10%
26	35%	15%	10%
25	35%	15%	10%
24	34%	15%	10%
23	33%	15%	10%
22	32%	15%	10%
21	31%	15%	10%
20	30%	15%	10%
19	28%	10%	5%
18	26%	10%	5%
17	24%	10%	5%

Type of Policy	Commission First Policy Year	Commission Second Policy Year	Commission Third Policy Year
16	22%	10%	5%
15	20%	10%	5%
14	19%	10%	5%
13	18%	10%	5%
12	17%	10%	5%
11	16%	10%	5%
10	15%	10%	5%
9	14%	7½%	5%
8	13%	7½%	5%
7	12%	7½%	5%
6	11%	7½%	5%
5	10%	7½%	5%

Retirement Income Endowments
Endowment Period

35 and over	40%	15%	10%
34	39%	15%	10%
33	38%	15%	10%
32	37%	15%	10%
31	36%	15%	10%
30	35%	15%	10%
29	34%	15%	10%
28	33%	15%	10%
27	32%	15%	10%
26	31%	15%	10%
25	30%	15%	10%
24	29%	15%	10%
23	28%	15%	10%
22	27%	15%	10%
21	26%	15%	10%
20	25%	15%	10%
19	23%	10%	5%
18	21%	10%	5%
17	19%	10%	5%
16	17%	10%	5%
15	15%	10%	5%
14	14%	7½%	5%
13	13%	7½%	5%
12	12%	7½%	5%
11	11%	7½%	5%
10	10%	7½%	5%

Limited Payment Endowments
20 Payment Endowment
Endowment Period

40	33%	15%	10%
35	33%	15%	10%
30	32%	15%	10%
25	31%	15%	10%

Limited Payment Endowments
15 Payment Endowment
Endowment Period

40	29%	10%	5%
35	28%	10%	5%
30	26%	10%	5%
25	24%	10%	5%
20	22%	10%	5%

Type of Policy	Commission First Policy Year	Commission Second Policy Year	Commission Third Policy Year
Limited Payment Endowments			
10 Payment Endowment			
Endowment Period			
40	25%	10%	5%
35	24%	10%	5%
30	23%	10%	5%
25	21%	10%	5%
20	19%	10%	5%
15	17%	10%	5%
Term, Joint Life, Etc.			
10, 15 and 20 Year Optional Term...	25%	10%	5%
Term, Automatic Conversion			
1 year	25%	—	—
2	25%	5%	—
3	25%	5%	5%
4	25%	7½%	5%
5	25%	7½%	5%
Yearly Renewable Term	25%	5%	5%
Preliminary Term	25%	—	—
Convertible Income Rider and Term			
Portion of Balanced Protection	25%	10%	5%
Continuous Income or Deferred Survivorship Annuity Rider			
(a) If attached at issue	Same % as policy to which it is attached.		
(b) If attached after issue	17½%	3%	3%
Child's Protection Agreement	Same % as policy to which it is attached.		
Joint Life	Same % as corresponding plan for single life. Use age of older life if commission depends on age.		
Single Premium Life	2%	—	—

Annuities

Single Premium			
Life Annuities	2%	—	—
Refund Annuities	2%	—	—
Joint and Survivorship Annuities	2%	—	—
Annual Premiums			
Optional Deferred Income			
Ages at issue up to 34	22½%	3%	3%
35 " 44	17½%	3%	3%
45 " 54	15%	3%	3%
55 and over	12½%	3%	3%
Deferred Survivorship Annuity	17½%	3%	3%

Number of Commissions After First Year. (b) You shall be entitled to receive commissions on cash premiums for the second and third policy years (at the rate provided in subsection (a) of this section) under new policies written and placed in force by you *only* in calendar years in which the paid for volume represented $50,000 or more of life insurance. In determining whether you have qualified for second and third policy year commissions, life insurance credit shall be allowed on annuities to the extent provided by the Company's "annuity equivalent basis" in effect when the annuities are placed in force.

The question of whether you have qualified for second and third policy year commissions on policies written and placed in force by you during the calendar year in which this contract became effective or during the calendar year in which this contract shall be terminated shall be determined by assuming the contract to have been in force for the entire calendar year, and by computing the amount of insurance written and placed in force by you during such full year as if the average daily rate of your paid business for the portion of such year during which your contract was in force had been maintained for the entire calendar year.

Service Fees. (c) In addition to all other compensation which you are entitled to receive in accordance with the foregoing provisions of this contract, you shall be paid service fees at the rates provided in the schedule set forth below (at end of this subsection 2 (c)), based upon all fourth and subsequent policy year premiums paid in cash to continue in force policies written and placed in force by you with Company, so long as this contract remains in force, *provided* that you present to General Agent satisfactory evidence that service has been rendered by you. And you hereby agree that General Agent and/or Company shall determine what shall constitute satisfactory evidence of service in each case. In the absence of such satisfactory evidence of service, no service fee shall be payable to you.

The rates of service fees as to all forms of policies with the exception of those listed below under "Exceptions" shall be as follows:

Fourth Policy Year	5%
Fifth Policy Year	10%
Sixth and All Subsequent Policy Years	3%

Exceptions

5 to 9 Payment Life		Years	3%
Fourth Policy Year	5%	**10 to 19 Year Endowment**	
Fifth Policy Year	5%	**15 to 19 Year Retirement Income Policies**	
Sixth and All Subsequent Policy		**10, 15 and 20 Year Optional Term**	
Years	3%	**Yearly Renewable Term**	
5 Year Endowment		**Convertible Income Rider and the Term**	
Fourth Policy Year	3%	**Portion of Balanced Protection Policies**	
Fifth Policy Year	3%	Fourth Policy Year	3%
6 to 9 Year Endowment		Fifth Policy Year	5%
10 to 14 Year Retirement Income Policies		Sixth and All Subsequent Policy	
Optional Deferred Income Policies		Years	3%
Survivorship Annuity Rider if attached		**5 Year Term Automatic Conversion**	
after issue		Fourth Policy Year	3%
Fourth Policy Year	3%	Fifth Policy Year	5%
Fifth Policy Year	3%	**4 Year Term Automatic Conversion**	
Sixth and All Subsequent Policy		Fourth Policy Year	3%

(On Joint Life, Survivorship Annuity Rider, and the Child's Protection agreement, the rate of service fee shall be the same percentage as allowed on policy to which it is attached at issue.)

Compensation on Conversions and Rewrites. (d) When any policy is converted or rewritten by you, commissions and service fees shall be payable on the new policy at the rates effective for such policy. The interest of the agent who placed the original policy in force shall be preserved in accordance with the Company's rules and regulations, and commissions and service fees payable to him shall be deducted from compensation otherwise payable to you on the new policy.

Compensation on Waived Premiums. (*e*) No commissions or service fees shall be payable on renewal premiums that are waived by Company in accordance with the provisions of a policy contract.

Change in Compensation. (*f*) In event of any increase or decrease in the rate of first year commissions and in the number and rate of subsequent commissions or service fees allowed General Agent by Company, General Agent, upon written notice to you, may correspondingly increase or decrease the first commissions and the number and rate of subsequent commissions or service fees payable on policies placed in force by you after such notice.

Termination. (3) This contract shall terminate automatically:

(*a*) Upon the death or mental incapacity of either General Agent or Agent.

(*b*) Upon withdrawal of Company from the territory in which General Agent has jurisdiction.

(*c*) Upon termination of contract of the World Life Insurance Company with General Agent. (If contract terminates for this reason, Company agrees to continue its provisions until either a successor to General Agent is appointed or Company notifies Agent in writing of termination of its provisions.)

And this contract may be terminated at any time voluntarily:

(*d*) By either General Agent or Agent furnishing notice of termination in writing to the other.

Commissions upon Termination. (4) (*a*) Termination of this contract in accordance with any one of subsections (*a*), (*b*), and (*c*) of section 3 shall not affect your established rights to first and subsequent policy year commissions.

(*b*) If this contract should be terminated within two years from its effective date in accordance with section 3 (*d*), no further renewal commissions shall be payable thereafter.

(*c*) If this contract should be terminated by General Agent by notice in writing because of the intentional withholding by you of funds of Company or General Agent, or because of your failure to account properly for any such funds, or because of any other misconduct on your part, no commissions shall be payable thereafter, regardless of the number of years it has been in effect.

Responsibility. (5) All funds received and collected by you for Company and General Agent shall be received by you in trust and shall not be used by you for any purpose whatsoever, but shall be remitted at once to General Agent with a full and detailed statement. You hereby agree to furnish a bond satisfactory to General Agent and Company for the proper accounting of such funds, and you further agree that all books of accounts, documents, vouchers, and other books and papers of any nature whatsoever connected with the business of General Agent shall be the property of Company and subject at any and all times to examination by it and its authorized representatives.

Exclusive Representation. (6) All of your time shall be devoted to soliciting applications for insurance and annuities in the World Life Insurance Company, and you agree to submit to General Agent all applications secured by you.

Rebating. (7) You will not pay or allow, or offer to pay or allow, directly or indirectly, any rebate of your commissions or service fees on any policy issued by Company, and you will not accept business from, or pay commissions or remuneration to, any person who is not licensed to represent Company. Failure to comply with this section shall be deemed sufficient cause for immediate termination of this contract.

Rules and Regulations. (8) The rules and regulations of Company (as now set forth in its Field Manual) of which you now take notice, and such other rules and regulations as may from time to time be issued by Company, whether by way of amendment of present rules and regulations, substitution therefor, or in addition thereto, shall be binding upon you and shall form a part of this contract as if set forth herein.

Medical Fees and Term Charges. (9) When a policy is issued in accordance with the application and is returned undelivered, you will pay the medical fee and/or any term insurance costs charged by Company. You also agree to pay any term insurance and/or medical fee charged by Company on premiums settled for by a note which is not paid when due.

Recalled Policies. (10) If Company recalls any policy and returns the premiums paid thereon, you agree to refund any commissions previously paid to you.

Authorization. (11) Company is authorized and empowered, in event of termination of its contract with General Agent for any reason whatsoever, to pay you, your heirs, executors, administrators or assigns, all commissions payable under this contract in accordance with its conditions.

Indebtedness. (12) Company and General Agent may offset against any claim for commissions or service fees hereunder any debt or debts now due or which may become due at any time hereafter from you to them, or either of them, whether arising under this contract or otherwise, which debt or debts shall be a first lien against commissions and service fees payable under this contract.

Waiver. (13) Failure of General Agent and Company to insist upon strict compliance with any of the conditions of this contract and the rules and regulations of Company and General Agent shall not be construed as a waiver of any of the conditions and rules and regulations but the same shall remain in full force and effect.

Release. (14) This contract supersedes any contract heretofore existing between you and General Agent in writing or otherwise, except that any obligations of you and General Agent under any prior contract, resulting from the termination thereof, shall not be affected.

Effective Date. (15) The effective date of this contract is ...., provided your license to solicit has been approved by the proper State Department.

....
General Agent

I hereby accept the above appointment in accordance with its conditions this .... day of ...., 19.., and agree to perform faithfully the duties incident to the appointment in conformity to the general rules and regulations of Company and General Agent, and such instructions as I may receive from the Officers of Company and General Agent.

....
Signature of Person Appointed

THE WORLD LIFE INSURANCE COMPANY approves the above contract and guarantees the payment of commissions and service fees subject to all the conditions therein.

....
Assistant to the Vice-President

This contract as adopted was criticized by some of the Company's executives who objected to the payment of service fees to agents for rendering service to policyholders. They believed that it would be practically impossible for the company to secure satisfactory evidence of service rendered and that fees would be paid to agents who had not earned them. This feature would lead to misunderstandings between the management and the men.

The Company proposed to define service and indicate several ways in which service could be given to policyholders for which the agent would receive credit. A certificate form signed by the insured, certifying that service requirements had been met would be required in all cases before payment for service was made.

Questions

1. Analyze each clause of the World Life Insurance Company agent's contract carefully and describe desirable changes or additions to make it more satisfactory to the company and the representative.

2. Is the payment of service fee provision in the contract desirable? Describe the advantages of this feature as well as its disadvantages.

3. Why are commission rates varied according to the type of insurance policy?

Reading References

Dartnell Corporation, "Salesmen's Contracts and Agreements," Chicago, Illinois, Report No. 352.

Printer's Ink Weekly, "What a Salesman's Contract Should Include," by Edwin J. Heimer, Jan. 30, 1930, p. 10.

Sales Management and Advertisers Weekly, "Legal Pitfalls in Hiring Salesmen," by L. T. Parker, Aug. 25, 1928, p. 421.

Sales Management, "Does Your Contract with Salesmen Invite Law Suits?" by L. T. Parker, Feb. 19, 1927.

CHAPTER NINE

TRAINING SALESMEN

Why Train Salesmen? Coincident with selection, training of salesmen is one of the most important problems of sales administration. Some of the many reasons why salesmen should be trained are:

1. To increase sales.
2. To reduce selling costs.
3. To attract the better type of salesman to the organization.
4. To unify all selling effort.
5. To reduce the turnover of salesmen by making them more productive.
6. To shorten the time necessary to place a new salesman on a profitable basis.
7. To make supervision simpler and more satisfactory.
8. To insure proper representation by preventing intangible losses created by the mistakes of untrained men.
9. To safeguard the investment in new salesmen.
10. To reduce the number of salesmen by multiplying the ability of the force.
11. To meet the demands of trained buyers for intelligent understanding of their problems.
12. To meet increasing competition and growing sales resistance.
13. To reveal ability of new salesmen.
14. To stimulate new selling methods by exchange of opinions.
15. To stimulate salesmen to increased production.

In view of these many advantages arising from an effective sales training program, it might be assumed that sales training is universally employed. On the contrary, n any concerns employing salesmen do no training worthy of the name. The most common objections to training salesmen are:

1. "Salesmen are born, not made."

2. The sales job presents such a variety of conditions that no two prospects are alike, therefore, there can be no one best way of selling.

3. Some sales executives believe that they do not have the time to train salesmen—other duties are more important.

4. Training is too expensive for the indefinite results secured.

5. Training is too slow.

6. Salesmen who are trained are usually hired by competitors at a loss to the company doing the training.

7. Training is a fad; it is theoretical and not practical for use by salesmen.

8. No worth-while practical training material is available with which to train men.

9. The business is "different," and training is not practical.

Evidence of definite results secured through sound training of salesmen is offered by sales executives of concerns in various lines. The director of education of a large company states:

The turnover of salesmen trained has been less than a third as high as it was among salesmen who were not given the benefit of training. The first one hundred graduates of our training course increased their sales volume, and consequently their earnings, 50 per cent over the average of 250 others who had not yet received training. One salesman who had been with the company for two years was falling below 50 per cent of his quota and upon completing the course he began producing at quota speed. Four months later he had made such a record that he was made a district sales manager.

The vice-president-in-charge-of-sales of a large automobile manufacturer says:

Our training activities constitute the most constructive work of our sales department. Over 5,000 of some 7,500 retail salesmen enrolled in our course, paying their own money for the privilege.

The director of sales training of a large soap manufacturer reports:

Our figures show that the experienced, untrained salesmen trail the experienced, trained men on an average of more than three per cent. Many of the trained men, after three to six months' experience, were well ahead of the record established by salesmen in the same section the preceding year.

The experience of the Equitable Life Assurance Society, with forty-four regular agents graduated from its school of life insurance salesmanship, showed that seven graduates with more than a year's previous experience increased their average monthly paid premiums 91 per cent; twenty agents with less than a year's previous experience increased their monthly paid premiums 47 per cent; and the remaining seventeen graduates without previous experience showed an increase of more than 30 per cent in monthly paid premiums over experienced agents.

Specific Sales Training Objectives. The first step in initiating a sales training program is to select from the many possible objectives a few specific aims and state them in simple terms. Although the ultimate objective of training is to make a profit, the immediate aims come first and should be clearly defined.

A statement of training objectives clarifies the trainer's understanding of what he is doing; it helps show the management what is to be accomplished; it keeps the training program on the right track; shows supervisors what the training is intended to do; and gives the salesmen a definite understanding of how the training will be helpful to them.

Some of the specific training objectives are: increasing the unit of sale; improving the merchandising methods of dealers; selling more higher-priced units; doing better missionary work; making better sales presentations; making more and better product demonstrations; selling larger orders; getting more and better dealers; increasing service sales; getting improved advertising coöperation.

These and similar aims should be established and made a matter of record for each phase of the training program. They should be communicated to supervisors, salesmen, distributors, and company executives. An objective chart should be prepared to show each objective and its related training activity for use in presenting the training program to the sales organization and dealers.

Who Should Be Trained? The problem of training salesmen must take into account three classifications of men: beginners, seniors, and supervisors. In each case the training methods used vary to some degree.

Beginner salesmen. Irrespective of previous experience, it is generally conceded that salesmen who are beginning work with a sales organization should receive some form of training before they can carry out their new duties. Furthermore, it is much easier to train new salesmen than men already in the organization. New men are more receptive to training: they recognize that there are many things about their new work which they do not know. Ac-

cordingly, the majority of training programs begin with the beginner salesman, and unfortunately most of them stop there.

Senior salesmen. There is a growing recognition of the importance of training salesmen who have been in the organization for
some time. In many organizations it has been assumed that because a salesman has sold a product for a period of time he knows
all that should be known about his job. This assumption, coupled
with the difficulty of "teaching an old dog new tricks," has caused
many concerns to ignore the experienced salesman entirely in their
training program. Furthermore, an experienced salesman is often
antagonistic toward training because he is too proud to admit that
he may lack knowledge, and he resents "going to school." However, experienced salesmen, as well as new men in the sales organization, frequently need a broader viewpoint of their work, selling
ideas, inspiration, and information. Such training enables experienced men to develop into executive positions, increases their effectiveness and income, and helps them to become better trainers of
distributors' salesmen.

While the problem of training experienced salesmen is admittedly
more difficult, if it is approached tactfully by demonstrating the
value of training with new men and avoiding impractical material
and academic methods, senior salesmen can be induced to support
and participate in a development program.

Sales supervisors. In many organizations, particularly those with
large sales forces, the key to the sales training problem is the sales
supervisor or branch manager. Life insurance companies are spending much time and money in training agency managers to develop
their agents and supervisors through numerous agency managers'
schools.

In initiating its sales training program, Procter & Gamble Company established a school at headquarters for training sales instructors, each of whom, in turn, was responsible for training twenty
salesmen in the field. These instructors were given three-weeks'
training for the twofold purpose of mastering the training course
and learning how to train other men.

The necessity for training field managers or supervisors arises
from the fact that sales training, to be completely effective, must
be carried on continuously in the field. Much headquarters training material cannot be applied by a salesman in the field without
local instruction. Problems of selling vary with the locality. To
develop skill in using the training material provided by the home

office, a salesman must be trained on the job by a sales instructor, supervisor, or branch manager.

Some sales executives object to assigning training responsibility to branch managers for the reason that many branch managers and supervisors lack the ability to train others. If a training program is to be effective, however, the coöperation, if not the active participation of branch executives, is necessary. One large corporation is rating its branch managers in terms of their ability to develop men and emphasizing the fact that their advancement in the company depends on their attitude toward training. When branch managers cannot be developed into trainers, sales instructors from headquarters may be utilized.

Distributors' salesmen. The sales training activities of many large companies are directed, not only toward the training of their own salesmen, but the salesmen of distributors. The major sales training problem of automobile manufacturers is the training of retail automobile salesmen, numbering in the thousands.

The Frigidaire Sales Corporation has an extensive training program for the salesmen of retail refrigerator dealers.

What to Teach Salesmen. The subject matter of a sales training course depends first upon the nature of the sales job and, second, upon the difficulties encountered by the salesmen. A training course should be custom-made for the individual business. The nature of the job in some industries, like meat packing, may demand emphasis on product training, while in others, like soap manufacturing, little product knowledge is required. The main difficulty in marketing a drug specialty may be price competition, while in the sale of a technical product the principal problem of the salesman may be lack of technical knowledge.

1. *Job analysis* to determine subject matter and provide training material is fundamental to a well-constructed training plan. By means of job analysis, job specifications should be developed. These, as defined by the American Council on Education, are: "A series of statements which define the essential things that should be accomplished in performing efficiently the duties of a given assignment."

Job specifications may be secured by requiring the salesmen to list the things which they believe should be done to perform their work efficiently. A study of salesmen's daily reports may reveal duties performed by the salesmen. An observer accompanying several salesmen and noting their various activities can secure a list of duties.

A job analysis will reveal activities from which may be drawn subjects for training. If the job requires that salesmen compute resale prices for dealers based on varying mark-ups, the arithmetic of figuring mark-ups may be a logical subject for training the salesmen. If the duties of salesmen include the maintenance of a company motorcar, the training may logically include a section on the care of automobiles.

2. *Difficulty analysis* is also required to secure sales training subject material. Since selling involves many variable situations and nonrepetitive duties, a job analysis alone is inadequate to disclose all phases of a sales situation. In analyzing the difficulties encountered in selling, attention is called to those duties the mastering of which gives the greatest trouble. These should receive preference in a training program. The difference between the successful salesman and the poor salesman is really nothing more than the number of difficulties which each is able to overcome. A tabulation of difficulties, with the best solutions for each, automatically gives sound subject material for a training course.

When the American Radiator Company prepared its original sales training course under the direction of Dr. W. W. Charters, two hundred and sixty-five difficulties encountered by salesmen were listed, together with their solutions. The Procter & Gamble Company discovered one hundred and sixty-five major difficulties in its search for sales training material.

Difficulties found in selling may be logically grouped under the following headings:

1. Personality difficulties, arising from lack of confidence, tactlessness, poor appearance, nonattentiveness, tardiness, discourtesy, ill health, laziness, indifference, and poor voice.
2. Knowledge difficulties, created by ignorance of product features and applications, advertising, price, adjustment policies, and competition.
3. System difficulties, resulting from poor time control, routing, record-keeping, and paper work.
4. Selling technique difficulties, created by lack of preliminary plan for interview, information conce. ning prospect, anticipation of objections, proper approach, and knowledge of needs. This classification includes also faulty demonstrations, in-

ability to meet objections, and failure to offer convincing proof
of value and secure action.

5. Trade difficulties, arising out of competition between distributors, price-cutting, preferential treatment, and so forth.

6. Product difficulties, encountered by the salesmen in such matters as packaging, construction, and operation of the product.

A few typical difficulties, of each classification given above, which
were discovered by difficulty analysis of the work of heating equipment salesmen were:

1. *Personality difficulties:* Is too aggressive; is discouraged; has
family troubles; lacks physical strength for the work; is in a rut;
is afraid of pushing sale for fear of offending customer; lacks convincing voice and manner.

2. *Knowledge difficulties:* Does not know how to estimate radia-
tion; does not know how to size the pipe on a heating job; does not
understand the sales promotion of the company; and does not know
the type of equipment needed for a job.

3. *System difficulties:* Has too many accounts to call upon; fails
to keep catalogs, price lists, and advertising material in good order;
has no standard forms for estimating; has no system for remembering back calls, promises to customers, and special jobs; and has not
learned to route his territory economically.

4. *Selling technique difficulties:* Does not fit sales talk to customer's particular tastes and peculiarities; cannot get back into interview when once interrupted; has no method for selling customer
whose store is crowded; awkward in opening interview; gets into
argument; and discusses competition too freely.

Method of Obtaining List of Difficulties. There are several
methods of securing a list of salesmen's difficulties, all of which may
be used effectively. The most common method is to interview
good, fair, and poor salesmen in sufficient numbers to bring out all
difficulties. In interviewing salesmen of the Studebaker Corporation, a preliminary outline of general duties was prepared which was
used in questioning salesmen. Under the heading, "Selling New
Dealers," the question was asked, "What difficulties do you encoun-
ter in selling a franchise to a new dealer?" Coincident with securing a list of difficulties, interviewers seek to find solutions to the
problems revealed by asking the question, "How do you meet this
objection?" The skill of the interviewer and his knowledge of the

work are important factors in determining the success of the interview.

To save time and expense, questionnaires to salesmen are also used to ascertain difficulties and their solutions. A large heating equipment company once used this method, phrasing the difficulties in the form of forty-four questions, which were sent to the sales force. Twenty prizes totaling $1,000 were offered for the best answers. One hundred and eighty-four men submitted answers. A typical question-and-answer given by one salesman follows:

Question: How do you work out an interview in advance of the call?

Answer: In working out an interview in advance of the call, I first review and analyze all correspondence and other information available concerning the matter to be discussed. Next, I determine what objects I wish to accomplish in making the call; these I fix firmly in mind so that they can be introduced at the proper time. Last, I try to put myself in the place of the person I am about to call upon, and imagine what arguments or objections he may interpose and how these may best be met and overcome.

Observation of salesmen at work is another effective method of determining difficulties and their solutions. Many salesmen are not conscious of their principal difficulties, and only by watching them at work are these problems revealed. Certain situations may become unnatural in the presence of an observer and may call for ingenuity on his part, but these difficulties may be readily overcome. The Research Bureau for Retail Training, University of Pittsburgh, sent an observer into department stores for a period of six weeks to watch sales people and observe their difficulties. As a result, sixty-seven difficulties were obtained.

Sales meetings are sometimes used to secure difficulties and solutions. One large company called together its eight leading salesmen for a one-day Sales Clinic, at which their principal difficulties were discussed and solutions suggested.

Information secured by difficulty and job analysis constitutes the subject matter of the sales training program. This material may be arranged under the following headings:

1. The product.
2. The market.
3. The company—history and organization.
4. Policies on credit, service, delivery, adjustments, and prices.
5. The salesman's job—a description of duties.
6. Advertising and sales promotion.

7. Salesman's technique, including locating buyers, planning interviews, conducting interviews, meeting objections, demonstrating, and closing sales.
8. Work records.
9. Cultivating customers.
10. Salesmen's equipment.
11. Competition.

Arranging Training Material. After the subject matter has been collected by job or duty, and difficulty analysis, the material must be arranged in convenient form to impart to the salesmen.

Manuals. Manuals are the most common form of presenting training material. The Procter & Gamble Company originally arranged its training materials in thirteen manuals, with such titles as:

1. "The Salesman's Job—What and Why."
2. "Selling Company Policies and Terms."
3. "Appealing to Buying Motives."

The Waters-Genter Company, manufacturer of Toastmaster and electrical appliances, has produced six manuals of appliance salesmanship for training retail sales persons, with such titles as:

1. "Understanding the Customer's Viewpoint."
2. "Using Facts to Win Decisions."
3. "Fitting the Customer's Needs."
4. "Demonstrating to Win Decisions."
5. "Overcoming Sales Difficulties."
6. "Helping the Customer to Buy."

Other types of manuals used in sales training are rule books, standard procedure manuals, handbooks, and product and engineering manuals.

Films. The most advanced method of presenting training material is by means of films, of which there are several types: moving, still, silent, and sound. The most common type film used in training is the talking slide film, which is a strip of 35-mm. width motion picture film with pictures and text. This film is projected by a special slide film projector equipped with a turntable to revolve a disk that carries conversation, sound effects, and music synchronized with the film. The film is moved manually.

The advantages of training slide films are that they appeal simultaneously to eye and ear, deliver their message in a darkened room free from distractions, and put personality and drama into the presentation.

Slide films are used for training by the Coca-Cola Company, the

FIGURE 32. Sales training manuals used by leading sales organizations in instructing salesmen in product features, product applications, company history, sales technique, and sales policies. These manuals are used for individual and group teaching and to supplement field training.

Metropolitan Life Insurance Company, Frigidaire Sales Corporation, Ford Motor Company, General Electric Company, Studebaker Corporation, and many others.

FIGURE 33. A portable Illustravox sound slide film projector which plays twelve and sixteen inch records running from nine to fifteen minutes per side and projects still pictures on a screen to illustrate the story. The recorded message is synchronized with the illustration on the screen. This projector is used in training manufacturers', wholesalers' and retailers' salesmen and in introducing new products to consumers.

Motion pictures, both sound and silent, are being used in great number for training factory and dealer salesmen. A large tire company has produced a sound motion picture for training dealers and their salesmen. It was shown to more than 12,000 salesmen at 989 meetings. A fruit growers' organization showed a four-reel talking picture to more than 39,000 retailers, jobbers, and their employees. The Frigidaire Sales Corporation, Shell Oil Company, Remington Arms Company, Bates Mfg. Company, and many others use moving pictures extensively in training salesmen.

Charts. Charts are frequently used in sales training to show the sequence of steps in a sale, or to illustrate product features or the divisions of an organization for group instruction.

Cases or problems. To make sales instruction more concrete, cases or problems are growing in popularity as training tools.

Cases may be used to illustrate selling principles and difficulties; to serve as a basis for a series of round-table discussions of sales problems; or in connection with sales demonstrations.

Sales cases should be natural; written, at least in part, in dialogue form; graphic; sufficiently complex to arouse interest and discussion; and should illustrate one or two points clearly, rather than describe every point with equal emphasis.

Cases may be readily collected in the course of making a difficulty analysis. They should be carefully edited.

Miscellaneous training material. Other forms in which training material may be presented are question-and-answer sheets, training cards, stock cards, job sheets, playlets, employee magazines or bulletins, and lecture outlines.

Sales Training Methods. After the training material to be given to the salesmen has been arranged in teaching form, the next prob-

FIGURE 34. Latest model S.V.E. projector used for selling and sales training which accommodates both slide films and two inch by two inch colored slides. This equipment is not bulky and expensive. It can be more easily carried and used with less effort than a motion picture projector.

lem is to adopt a sound procedure for presenting the facts to the salesmen.

Group methods. These are the most common because they are economical; more salesmen can be reached by this type of training; and it is most suitable for presenting certain types of material. Group training is most effective for training on:

1. The product, its features, and applications.
2. The policies of the company on credits, collections, adjustments, and so forth.
3. The company history and organization.
4. Advertising and sales promotion.
5. Routine duties.
6. Preliminary sales technique.

Group training may be of the formal type with full-time instruc-

FIGURE 35. Sixteen millimeter Bell & Howell sound-on-film projector used for projecting sound sales and training motion pictures. One case contains the speaker and the other the projector and amplifying unit. It has a capacity of 2,000 feet of film.

tors, formal programs, study and recitation periods, and examinations. The International Business Machines Corporation and the National Cash Register Company have specially constructed school buildings for training salesmen and servicemen. Other group training may consist of meetings held at regular or irregular intervals.

Types of Group Sales Training Meetings. A good group sales training meeting uses one or more of the following five basic methods:

1. *The lecture or telling method,* which is the quickest and easiest way to impart information about products, policies, and new developments, does not show salesmen how to apply their knowledge, but is ideal for making announcements and in imparting purely factual information.

2. *The demonstration method,* which is used to show how prod-

FIGURE 36. Soundscriber electronic recorder used in making records of salesmen's presentations and demonstrations for study and analysis in sales training courses. Permanent, unbreakable seven inch disks of plastic make thirty-minute recordings which may be played back for discussion. Sales training lectures are recorded and filed for re-use by salesmen and instructors. One organization has furnished its salesmen with this equipment for reporting their calls and interviews and for dictating letters.

ucts operate or how to sell or use knowledge of the product, advertising, company, service, and policies, is the first step in preparing salesmen to sell. It is also used to illustrate how to approach prospects, meet objections, and to discuss products and policies.

3. *The discussion method* or conference of experienced salesmen is employed to interchange ideas, pool experiences, and work out solutions to common problems in such a way as to develop ability to analyze sales situations and think clearly and constructively. This method is effective in training senior salesmen although inexperienced men may profit by listening to the discussion.

4. *In the dramatization method or practice presentation* two salesmen take the parts of salesman and prospect or customer for the purpose of illustrating selling technique or method of presentation of product, policies, and advertising. Criticism or comment by the trainer or members of the group usually follows the dramatization. This method is very similar to field training.

5. *The panel method* of presenting the methods or points of view of several specialists, experts, or salesmen on sales techniques, product features, manufacturing processes, policies, etc., offers an opportunity to exchange ideas and pool the experiences of successful men. Interest may be aroused by conducting this type of meeting similarly to the popular radio programs, for example, "Information, Please."

Variety can be secured by using one or more of the above methods in each group training meeting.

Group Discussion Method For Training Experienced Men. Group discussion, which has been successfully used for many years in training and upgrading supervisors in industrial plants, has only had limited use in training experienced salesmen and supervisors. This method of training is effective in developing experienced salesmen and supervisors because it is practical and realistic. The subjects discussed are usually actual problems or sales experiences from the work of salesmen or supervisors. The conference does not have the traditional going-to-school aspect of lectures distasteful to many experienced men. It gives each man the opportunity to be heard and to participate in the discussion. It provides for a valuable interchange of ideas and pooling of experiences. The men learn to think clearly and constructively about their problems. Solutions to perplexing problems may actually be achieved.

Subjects for discussion by salesmen are selected by the sales manager or trainer, and usually include such current problems encountered by the salesmen in the field as meeting price competition, handling claims and adjustments, selling to the prospect who is satisfied with his sources of supply, the salesman's job, and presenting technical features.

In order that the salesmen can be prepared to participate in the discussion, actual cases, taken from the experiences of the men, are distributed in advance of the discussion meeting. Or the group may assemble for impromptu discussion.

Discussion Leadership. Leadership of group discussions calls for skill and experience. The leader must be able to stimulate a flow of experiences from the group, guide the discussion, and summarize the results. An effective technique for conducting conferences has been developed, based on experience in this method of training. It includes the following steps:

1. *Introducing the subject* for discussion in clear, simple language so that all grasp the problem without confusion.

2. *Open the discussion* by asking a "starter" question to provoke expressions of opinion from the group. An example of a starter question on the subject of price competition is: What do you do when a prospect says, "Your competitor's price is lower"?

3. *Start a blackboard chart* on which the ideas of the salesmen may be listed and organized under appropriate headings as they are contributed by the group members. Chart headings are written on the board. For example, a chart heading on price competition may be:

Handling Price Competition

Possible Course of Action	Reasons for	Reasons against

Other chart headings which may be used for other topics are:

Advantages	Disadvantages	
Situation	Positive Results	Negative Results
What's Wrong	Causes for Condition	Remedies

As each point is brought out in the discussion, it is posted by the leader on the board chart under the appropriate heading.

4. *Stimulate discussion* of each point by following these suggestions:

a. Refer questions back to the group or an individual. (The leader should not answer the questions himself.)

b. To provoke thought start your leading questions with "how" or "why."

c. Use specific cases or problems that illustrate the idea to provoke discussion.

d. Allow the group time to think things out—do not hurry the thinking.

e. At times keep quiet and let the group members do the talking.

f. Distribute discussion among the members—do not allow a few individuals to monopolize it.

g. Avoid sidetracks, that is, keep discussion on the subject.

h. Catch every comment no matter how timidly or crudely expressed, and aid the individual in rephrasing it.

i. Maintain direction of the group thinking by exercising active, intellectual leadership.

j. Direct questions to individuals who have had little or no part in the discussion.

k. Do not permit members to indulge in discussing personalities, carry on side discussions, discuss irrelevant matters, or monopolize the discussion.

5. *Summarize discussion* when a general agreement has been reached or the topic has been exhausted. If the group's interest in the topic has died, it should be dropped, or in case the discussion has not been adequate, the topic should be rephrased in order to revive interest in it. In summarizing the discussion, the leader may say: "On the basis of the discussion so far, it would seem that the group believes . . . and . . . is the case."

Planning Group Discussions. Group discussions should be thoroughly planned to insure their success. It is usually advisable to admit only experienced salesmen and limit the size of the group to twenty-five. An average of about twenty men is satisfactory. The less pressure brought to bear to force attendance, the better the reaction of the salesmen. The number of meetings will depend largely on the nature of the topics to be discussed, although a continuous program should be adopted with meetings spaced at intervals so that the program will not become burdensome. The length of each meeting will be determined by the scope of the topic discussed. Meetings of an hour or less are usually too short, while those lasting more than two hours are exhausting and destructive of interest. The ideal length is apparently one and one-half to two hours with a five-minute recess period.

The following suggestions may prove helpful:

1. Set a day and time of day most convenient for salesmen to meet.

2. Start and conclude each meeting at the appointed time.

3. Keep a record of attendance at each meeting.

4. Provide a comfortable, well-ventilated and lighted meeting room, removed from noise and disturbance, and large enough so that the men will not be crowded. Arrange for a blackboard or a large paper chart. Chairs with wide side arms on which notes can be taken should be provided. Also provide racks for hats and coats.

5. Adopt a "No Smoking" rule. Post "No Smoking" signs in the room and sell the salesmen on coöperating. Try a fine for smokers. At a two-hour meeting, ban smoking during the first hour and permit it during the second.

Individual Methods.   These should be used to supplement group training.   There are three common methods of training salesmen individually: by personal conferences and discussions with sales executives, by training on the job, and by correspondence.

1. *The personal conference* method of training is an excellent supplement to other training methods. In individual meetings, the trainer discusses with each salesman his record, difficulties, territory conditions, and customer relations. A rating scale is sometimes used in checking the progress of the salesman, and he is advised on how to improve his technique.

2. *Training on the job* is an important method of training both new and experienced salesmen. This method is rarely done effectively, however, since it is expensive, and often difficult to obtain good trainers. "Breaking in" a new salesman is not effectively done on the job. Selling skill cannot be acquired by observing another salesman any more than skill in playing the piano can be obtained by watching a competent pianist play. Practical instruction in selling technique can be gained only in a natural setting. While preliminary discussions of technique may be advisable in group conferences, individual training in technique on the job is the only sound method.

The following six steps in training on the job were developed by Dr. W. W. Charters:

1. Analysis by the salesman of the method of performing the job.
2. Demonstration by the trainer who may say, "You watch me while I do it."
3. Explanation by the trainer, after the sale has been completed, giving reasons for performing each step.
4. Trial by the salesman. When a man tries to do a thing himself, he really begins to learn, and several trials may be necessary before the job is learned.
5. Correction by the trainer after the trial sale has been completed to show the salesman where he was wrong.
6. Supervision by the trainer to insure that the man performs as trained.

An objection which sometimes arises to this method of field training is that the presence of two men at a sales interview arouses the resentment of the prospect. If the situation is handled tactfully and the trainer remains in the background and does not participate in the interview, little difficulty should be experienced.

Individual field training is universally used in life insurance selling, and by numerous sales organizations employing route salesmen.

Using War Training Methods in Training Salesmen. During World War II the Training Within Industry service of the War Manpower Commission developed a job instruction training program for new workers in industrial plants which has been successfully used by sales executives in training new salesmen.

The two parts of the job instruction training plan applied to "breaking-in" new salesmen are entitled: "How to Get Ready to Instruct" and "How to Instruct."

How to Get Ready to Instruct. If the training on the job is to be satisfactory, a little time in advance of the actual training is required for preparation. Hours and days of time will be saved later and the mistakes and failures so discouraging to new salesmen will be prevented if this time is given to preparation.

The three get-ready points to be followed in preparing to train on the job are:

1. *Have a time table.* A definite date should be set at which time the initial field training should be completed and a predetermined standard of performance attained. When faced with "breaking-in" a new salesman it is a mistake to say, "It takes time," or "He just has to learn." Instead the trainer should say, "Jones should be able to sell five units a week by January first." The names of the new men should be listed, with the date when each

should have completed his initial field training and have sold a certain amount.

2. *Break down the job.* There is one best way to sell every product or service, and there are a few "key points" in every sales presentation that may make or break the sale. If these key points are made correctly, the sale is successful; if any of them is omitted, the sale may not be closed. These key points must be impressed upon the new salesman, if he is to succeed.

The key points should be listed on a sales job breakdown sheet. Doing this takes only a few minutes. The sheet is a valuable aid to the trainer in instructing the new salesman. A job breakdown sheet must be prepared for each sales job. For example, a sheet for an appliance specialty salesman may list the following key points in making a sales presentation:

    a. *The approach.*

    Locate prospect's needs, ask questions, use portfolio.

    b. *Present advantages.*

    c. *Prove benefits.*

    Demonstration, testimonials, references.

    d. *Get commitments.*

    Get prospect's agreement on benefits.

    e. *Close the sale.*

3. *Have everything ready.* The salesman's portfolio, advertising, demonstrating equipment, samples, price list, and photographs should be in order and ready for use in training the new man. The trainer sets the correct example for the trainee.

How to Instruct. When the trainer has prepared to instruct by observing the three "get ready" points, the following four-step method is used to "break-in" a new man or correct the faulty methods of an experienced salesman.

Step I. Prepare the salesman to receive the instruction by putting him at ease. He should not feel embarrassed. Describe the job in detail using a job analysis. Find out what he already knows about the work. If he is an experienced salesman who has sold a similar product or service, he may have considerable knowledge to begin with so you will not need to tell him the things he already knows. Start where his knowledge ends. Get him interested in learning the methods used by successful salesmen in performing the job.

Step II. Present the method of selling. Tell, show, and illustrate, one at a time, each of the "key points" of making a sales presentation from the job breakdown sheet. The new salesman cannot comprehend all of the five or six "key points" at one time. Take up the "approach" first and tell, show, and illustrate how that step should be done before presenting the next. Make each key point clear. Be patient; repeat the explanation; go slowly and give the new man no more information than he can master. He must understand each step in the sale clearly and not be confused. This step may be taken at the local office before the man begins his work.

Step III. Try out his performance. After the salesman understands clearly the method of selling, next have him make several sales presentations using the method he has been taught. These may be made to the trainer at the sales office before the new man goes into the field. Watch these practice presentations closely. Have the new man repeat them and explain to the trainer what he is doing and the reasons for doing it. Many men merely go through the motions without really understanding what they are doing. Explain the key points and make sure that the salesman understands them clearly. Correct his mistakes, but do not be too critical or imply that he is not intelligent. Continue this process until you know that he understands.

After the man has proved in these practice presentations that he can sell, try out his performance in the field by accompanying him on several calls on prospects. Let him sell and watch him. After each call correct his errors and continue to do so until he is proficient.

Step IV. Follow-up. Put the new salesman to work early, allowing him to call on prospects to get the "feel" of the job by doing it himself. Tell him to consult you or some other salesman you designate if he needs help. The wrong salesman might misinform him. To observe his methods make calls with him frequently, perhaps once a day at the start, or once a week later on. Be on the lookout for any incorrect or unnecessary tactics. Do not sell for him or take over a presentation during an interview, but after the call, point out his mistakes and show him the correct method. Get him to look for the key points as he progresses. Taper off this coaching on the job until he is able to work under normal supervision.

When sales supervisors and trainers use the four steps in job instruction, salesmen get into production sooner, break-in time is reduced, and interest and enthusiasm on the part of the men are increased. It is far more effective than the usual practice of start-

ing instruction or correcting salesmen without thought or plan.
Many supervisors are poor trainers because they know the work so
well that they have forgotten the things that are new to the learner
and fail to pick out the key points that make the sales presentation
successful.   The present plan overcomes these weaknesses and provides an easy, practical program for sales instruction.

4. *Training by correspondence* is a common individual method
of training.   It is usually less expensive than other training methods and may be very useful in imparting knowledge about the company, product, policies, and other subjects usually covered in group
training.   Skill cannot be acquired by mail, however, and it is impossible to insure that lessons sent by mail will be studied or even
read.   It is very difficult for many men to apply information received in a correspondence course without discussion, demonstration, or elaboration.

Manufacturers distributing specialties through many wholesale
and retail outlets have used correspondence courses to train thousands of salesmen of their distributors and dealers.   These courses
are often prepared by service organizations specializing in the
preparation of sales training.

Such companies as the General Electric Company, Imperial Oil
Limited of Canada, Packard Motor Car Company, Iron Fireman
Manufacturing Company, Loyalty Group Insurance Company,
Chrysler Sales Corporation, Cities Service Company, The Standard Oil Company of Ohio, and the Shell Petroleum Corporation
have from time to time contracted with a large correspondence
school to prepare specialized training for their salesmen and
dealers.

The correspondence school carries on research of the product and
sales methods and writes a series of training manuals, which are
subject to the approval of the sponsoring sales organization.   These
manuals are published by the school under its own name and that
of the company sponsoring the course, and are distributed by the
school direct to salesmen who are enrolled in the course by the sponsoring company.   Each textbook is accompanied by a series of
practice problems which are answered by the salesman and returned
to the school for grading and comment by its instructors.   A
diploma is issued by the school to all salesmen completing the
course.   Manuals are also prepared for leaders of group discussions
of the material in each text.

This plan relieves the sponsoring company of the research and preparation of training material as well as the distribution of texts and the servicing of the courses. The sponsoring company, through its sales organization, secures enrollments from its distributor and dealer salesmen.

A typical example of correspondence courses of this type are those sponsored by the Lamp Department, General Electric Company, for salesmen of lamp distributors and dealers.

General Electric Lamp Department, in coöperation with a large correspondence school has published four separate correspondence courses:

1. Home-lighting sales training.
2. Industrial-lighting sales training.
3. Office- and school-lighting sales training.
4. Store-lighting sales training.

The home-lighting sales training course consists of five textbooks on the fundamentals of light, seeing, home-lighting equipment, and lighting salesmanship.

These texts are mailed to salesmen who are enrolled and employed by public utilities. Group meetings to demonstrate and discuss the principles presented in each textbook are held at frequent intervals by local sales trainers and lighting specialists, who use a group leader's manual prepared by the correspondence school.

The course in store-lighting sales training also consists of five texts, two of which deal with fundamentals of store lighting and selling and the remainder with specific store-illuminating methods. The office-, school- and industrial-lighting sales training courses each consist of four books, two fundamental and two specialized texts. Group leaders' manuals, which are built around each text, are furnished dealers and distributors for use in conducting discussions and demonstrating the principles to their salesmen.

Sales managers and trainers representing General Electric lamp dealers and distributors are trained in conducting their tie-in training through training courses of from two to three days, held at General Electric Lighting Institute, Nela Park, Cleveland, Ohio. In addition, the correspondence and group training are supplemented with General Electric traveling field clinics and sound motion pictures to demonstrate the fundamentals of lamps, lighting, and selling, which are discussed in the various textbooks. The enrollment for these correspondence courses is in the neighborhood of six thousand salesmen, more than 75 per cent of whom will complete the training.

Where Training Should Be Done. There is much difference of opinion concerning the question of the best place to conduct sales training. Some sales executives favor centralized or home office training; others prefer decentralized or branch office training; while still other concerns prefer a combination of centralized and decentralized training.

Centralized training is usually employed by small companies which operate no branches and can train a small number of men conveniently at home offices. Many large organizations manufacturing technical products also find centralized training most effective. Concerns manufacturing goods with a large unit of sale can justify the cost of bringing salesmen into headquarters for training.

The International Business Machines Corporation trains its salesmen of tabulating machines and time recorders at its headquarters at Endicott, New York, with incidental training at branches.

The advantages of centralized sales training are:

1. Complete equipment and facilities exist at headquarters for training.
2. Experienced personnel is usually available, and home office executives may assist in the training.
3. Production facilities enable salesmen to see manufacture at first hand, or to participate in production.
4. The student receives a strong impression of the resources and personnel of the company.
5. Uniformity of training is possible, and economical.

Objections to centralized training are:

1. It is costly to pay the transportation of students to the factory and expenses while they are in training.
2. Salesmen who are given factory training may not produce when they go into the field.
3. Salesmen receive no training in developing skill by conducting actual sales interviews.
4. The field organization has no responsibility for training.

Manufacturers of small unit-of-sale, nontechnical products sold through many salesmen direct to consumers usually employ decentralized or branch office training. The Fuller Brush Company,

Real Silk Hosiery Mills, and the Hoover Company, train through branches exclusively. Much of the training on these products concerns sales technique, skill in which can be developed most effectively through field training.

A large food product manufacturer who sells through retail grocers places the responsibility for training its one thousand two hundred salesmen on branch managers and its district representatives.

Manufacturers of technical products and life insurance companies often supplement branch training with advanced training at headquarters for salesmen who have proved their ability in the field. A large life insurance company trains its agents, first, in the territory under the supervision of the agency manager; second, at district schools directed by the educational director of the company; and third, at an advanced school held at the home office under the supervision of the educational director.

Initial Sales Training. There are two prevailing methods of training new salesmen in an organization. One method aims to get the new man into production at the earliest possible time with enough information to enable him to close sales. This is often accomplished by the use of a standardized sales talk which can be learned in a few hours. The other plan of initial training is founded on the principle that a salesman should be very thoroughly trained, able to diagnose a prospect's needs, understand his product completely, and know all company policies before calling on prospects.

A large office equipment manufacturer formerly started each new salesman's training with from six to eight weeks' study of the product and its applications. During this period, the salesman received no contact with field work, and his earnings suffered. Because of unsatisfactory earnings, his interest and enthusiasm dwindled, and he often sought a salaried job. Now, new salesmen memorize a standardized "approach" of four points:

1. Interview the official with the power to authorize the adoption of the equipment.

2. Obtain his permission to study the office records and routine.

3. Secure his commitment to purchase, if proof can be established that the results to be secured will warrant the investment.

4. Maintain contact with this official.

The new salesman learns to execute this approach without any product knowledge, which makes it possible for him to engage in

field work within three to six days. Whenever he succeeds in gaining the four objectives of the approach, the branch manager carries
on for him and in his presence. Life insurance companies usually
train in a similar way to enable new men to become producers at the
earliest possible time by means of standard sales talks developed for
certain needs.

The more lengthy training method is exemplified by the Westinghouse Electric and Manufacturing Company, which employs graduates from technical schools and gives them thirteen-months' training, and two-weeks' sales school and headquarter's sales office
training before assignment to a district office territory.

In many companies the expense of training, the uncertainty of
the performance of the new man, and the demand for sales volume
demand a limited initial training period.

Continuation or Follow-Up Training. The initial training of
new salesmen comprises the entire sales training program of many
companies. More foresighted sales organizations, however, recognize the necessity for an extended follow-up training program designed (1) to provide more detailed information regarding the product or service, policies, and sales methods, and (2) to develop each
salesman to the maximum of his abilities.

Sales training should be continuous. Salesmen need regular
reeducation. Products are continually improved, new features introduced, new applications are being discovered, new competition
is entering the market, and new selling methods are developed.
Continuous training is needed to keep salesmen informed and
skillful in meeting these new conditions.

When a salesman has completed his initial training and has had
a certain amount of success selling, he often stops using the good
information and tested selling methods learned in his earlier training. About this time he encounters difficulties and his sales decline.
Follow-up training is needed to correct these weaknesses, to restore
his effectiveness, and to help him to continuous improvement.

The following methods of continuation training have been used
effectively to follow-up initial training:

1. Weekly sales training meetings for group discussion of current
sales problems are held at local or branch offices and lead by supervisors who have been trained in group leadership. When these
meetings are well planned and regularly scheduled, they are an
effective follow-up of initial training.

2. Periodic regional district schools are held by home office executives and trainers to review plans and methods and to introduce more advanced techniques, new product features, and policies

3. "Postgraduate" schools are held at the home office for experienced salesmen to train them in specialized applications of the product or service, technical features, and more advanced selling methods.

4. Continuous field retraining is carried on by field supervisors or trainers to redrill salesmen in work methods, in meeting difficulties, and to observe their methods, to correct, and to help them solve their problems.

5. Correspondence training is carried on by means of bulletins, house organs, and films, and is an excellent means of retraining in tested sales methods and of informing men about new products and policies.

6. Indirect training by courses in selling or mechanical, electrical, or chemical engineering offered by local evening schools and colleges.

7. Individual development can be encouraged by the management subscribing for sales and industry magazines or new books on salesmanship for the salesmen.

Salesmen should be kept continuously interested in the training and what it means to them in personal progress in the organization. The sales records of men who have been trained may be compared with those who lack training to show the worth of the training. Appropriate recognition may be given for completion of each portion of the program. Older salesmen may be consulted in developing the training material and be given a part in the instruction to win their coöperation. Certain companies have organized training clubs with eligibility for membership and ratings based on training progress. Special awards have been made for proficiency in the training course. Friendly rivalry may be developed between trainees through contests which are built around the training program.

Typical Sales-Training Programs. The following examples of sales training programs of successful companies illustrate the various types of training described previously.

Group training. A group sales training program is operated by Celanese-Celluloid Corporation, manufacturer and distributor of plastics. Schools for salesmen are held in each branch or district office at which home office sales and technical experts lecture and demonstrate each product in the line. Groups are limited to six to twelve salesmen.

Following the demonstrations, group discussions serve to develop an exchange of experience on selling methods and product applications among the salesmen. The leader questions the group on methods of selling specific products.

Individual training. A practical field training program is used to instruct new salesmen of General Foods Sales Corporation, distributing food specialties to retail grocers. This four-step plan is similar to the job-instructor training used during the war by the War Manpower Commission.

When a new General Foods district representative is employed, he reports to one of the company's twenty-four district sales offices. The district manager trains him on company policies and employee relations, and turns him over to the assistant district manager who gives the new man the retail sales manual to study and shows him slide films which describe sales methods. The new salesman then prepares to take an examination on the subject matter in the manual. At the end of his first week of initial training he should have a good basic knowledge of the job and how to do it.

Field training on the job. When he has completed his basic training at the district office, the new man goes into the field. The first two days he calls on grocers with a definite product assignment, accompanied by a trainer who does all the selling while the new man watches. This demonstration of selling methods, or showing step is the first phase of training on the job.

In the second step (practice) the new man calls on the trade and does the selling while the trainer observes and corrects him. Each call is discussed. When a satisfactory degree of proficiency is attained, the new man is ready for the third step.

The third step is the follow-up. The trainer devotes a full day to each man at least once a month. The trainer observes and then checks the man's performance on a form which lists all of the elements of the job. The trainer calls on the new salesman's trade the day after he has made a coverage to evaluate the salesman's work objectively.

Continuation training. The B. F. Goodrich Company uses a continuation plan for training experienced salesmen who are selected by field executives for an advanced course at the home office. This four-week's course covers organization, background knowledge of the rubber industry, discussions by department managers, lectures on distribution methods, markets, service, inventory control, field operations, advertising, sales promotion, and retail merchandising. Slide films, motion pictures, and factory and laboratory trips are used during the training. Men are tested by oral and written examinations.

The home office training is continued with an average of eighteen meetings held annually in company stores throughout the country. This group training reviews the home office instruction and provides new material to keep the men informed about new developments. Sales manuals are restudied and men are given examinations on their contents. Moving pictures, slide films, and demonstrations are used in this follow-up training.

Dealer training. A unique training program for the sons of dealers who intend to carry on their fathers' businesses is the Chevrolet Postgraduate School of Modern Merchandising and Management, established by the Chevrolet Division of General Motors Corporation. The purpose of the school is to provide a practical, well-rounded training in the fundamentals of management and profitable operation of a dealership.

Students are selected by dealers on merit and potential possibilities. They must be between twenty-one and thirty years of age and either sons, sons-in-law, younger brothers, or some other close relative of a dealer. Each of the nine Chevrolet sales regions is limited to a maximum of three students a term.

Each term is eight weeks in length and there are four terms a year. The cost to the dealer is $400 per student a term. Classes are held in the General Motors building in Detroit. The method of instruction includes trips through manufacturing and assembly plants, proving grounds, and laboratories where engineers explain the various operations. In a two-day service school men are taught the mechanical features of the car. In the classroom, department heads, their assistants, leading executives of the corporation, and selected dealers explain all phases of the operation of a dealership. The subjects which are discussed include: retail automobile selling as a vocation, the automobile industry, General Motors Corporation, the Chevrolet market, organization of territory, the franchise, the product, principles of new-car operation, Chevrolet trucks, principles of used-car operation, retail and wholesale financing, and other related subjects.

The Training Program Plan. In establishing a sales training program, the program of training should be put in writing. Objectives should be clearly stated, material obtained, and course subjects selected, as previously described.

The duration of the training, that is, the schedule in days and hours, should be determined. The methods to be used and the

FIGURE 37. A record of each student salesman's progress in the sales training course is kept on this form by the sales training department of a manufacturer of office equipment.

personnel involved should be designated. The number of salesmen to be instructed, whether new or old men, is a fundamental decision to be made in preparing the training plan.

Evaluating the Training Program. There are numerous ways of determining the effectiveness of a sales training program. A training progress report, listing the various functions of the salesmen who are being trained, with ratings on each function by sales instructors or supervisors, is a useful device for appraising the effectiveness of the training of the individual. A record of sales volume, sales per call, number of calls, interviews, and amount per sale before and after training for each salesman trained may be significant if no conflicting factors disturbed the situation during the training period. Written tests may indicate progress achieved by training. Conference check-ups made by a conference leader are useful.

Organization for Training. The size and nature of the training organization is largely determined by the size of the sales force, type of product sold, and aims of the training program. Rather than set up an expensive training organization, it is better to organize the training so that it may be conducted by the line or supervising sales executives, as a part of their regular duties. Branch managers are often responsible for group training of men who operate out of branch sales offices. Field supervisors are best situated to conduct individual field training.

To assign sales training to a general sales manager, already over-burdened with responsibilities, can only result in indifferent train-ing. Many sales executives are not fitted by temperament or teach-ing ability to assume training duties. The executive in charge of sales training should have sales experience, patience, and tact, coupled with the ability to conduct research for training material and create a logical training program.

The sales training director of a large automobile manufacturer was a former university professor, personnel director of a large de-partment store, and director of the bureau of research of a large university.

When Procter & Gamble Company originated its sales training program in 1923 for six hundred men, three men were employed for the sales training department, two of whom had little sales experi-ence but were trained investigators. The third, who had long sales experience and analytical ability, was the training director. The training program of a large heating equipment company was initi-ated by one man with the aid of a sales training consultant, who advised on the collection and organization of training material.

Training is usually a staff function administered by the general sales manager. It may also be a function of a sales personnel or sales promotion department.

Problem 1—Centralized Sales Training versus Decentralized Training

Great Eastern Life Insurance Company

The Great Eastern Life Insurance Company, established in New York City in 1905, is represented by one thousand two hundred commission agents operating out of one hundred agency offices in the principal cities of the country.

The company established in 1908 a home office training department and placed in charge a successful agent formerly connected with a large university. He was assisted by two former agents of the company who had successful records before coming to the home office.

The training manager and his two assistants offered a two-weeks' course in training at the home office for new agents, who paid their own expenses while attending the course. The training consisted of showing the new agents the many reasons why people buy life insurance; the various Great Eastern contracts available; and the rates, regulations, and procedure. Practice was offered in reviewing life situations and the ap-propriate policies.

Practical methods of selling life insurance were discussed and demonstrated by the trainers. Methods of prospecting were described and illustrated. The best ways to plan and systemize sales activities were described. Actual cases taken from the field sales experience of the company were analyzed by the instructors. Standardized sales presentations for the principal life insurance needs were given to the new agents, and they were coached in delivering them.

The home office schools were attended by from 35 to 50 per cent of the new agents contracted by the company, and in the opinion of the general agents were a great aid in putting new men into production within a short time. In the opinion of the superintendent of agencies, however, the turnover of company agents, which was 60 per cent annually, indicated a deficiency in the training program.

The superintendent of agencies of the company believed, moreover, that training would be more effective if conducted by the agency managers at the agencies. He believed that the real job of training was scarcely touched by the home office, which could not do joint selling with new men. Furthermore, the problem of prospecting varies materially with the location. In the opinion of the superintendent, the home office was not developing skill, but simply imparting information; the new men were not being taught habits of work.

The superintendent of agencies advocated the complete training of new agents at the agency offices by the following system:

1. Coaching the new man on the retirement income plan, giving him a standardized sales talk, and requiring him to use it exclusively.

2. Having the new man accompany the agency manager, who solicits prospects by means of the retirement income sales talk, the same sales talk the new man is to use.

3. After two mornings of demonstration by the agency manager, the new man solicits prospects by means of the retirement income sales talk for two mornings, while the manager listens and corrects the mistakes of the new man.

4. Thereafter, the new agent spends from fifteen to twenty minutes daily between 8:30 and 9:00 A. M. with the manager, discussing plans for the day.

5. The new agent spends from thirty to sixty minutes each afternoon with the manager, going over and analyzing his interviews.

6. The new man keeps track of his time and turns in a report to the manager weekly.

7. The new man begins in a week or two to go to his friends for names of their friends to solicit.

8. After the new man has succeeded in closing several contracts by using the retirement income sales talk, he is given another standardized sales talk on another need, and so on, until he gradually acquires knowl-

edge of various insurance applications and the ability to present them to prospects.

The agency superintendent believes that such a plan will be productive because the new agent is given practical ideas of interviewing from the manager's demonstrations. He respects the manager's ability as he sees the manager demonstrating. He also sees the manager fail and does not become so discouraged when he fails. Furthermore, the manager is given a better idea of the ability of the agent from seeing him in action. Actual field work helps to keep the manager's feet on the ground, and stimulates his imagination with regard to sales plans.

The home office sales training manager opposes the agency training plan, as he believes that few agency managers can train new men satisfactorily. It will be impossible to give uniform training through one hundred agencies, and managers will not take the time for training.

Questions

1. Should the company adopt the training plans of the superintendent of agencies? Give reasons for your decision.

2. If the decentralized plan of training were adopted, should the home office training department be abolished? Give reasons for discontinuing it, or indicate its activities under the new plan.

3. If you object to any feature of either plan as described in the problem, what changes would you make?

Problem 2—Initial Sales Training

Watson Paint Company

The Watson Paint Company, established in Chicago, Illinois, in 1907, makes varnish, enamel, and lacquers which are distributed by thirty salesmen direct to wholesale and retail paint dealers in all parts of the country. The company invests $100,000 annually in national advertising. It has branch plants in St. Louis, Cincinnati, and New York City, out of which salesmen operate. Salesmen, compensated by a straight salary, have usually three to four years' sales experience in other nonrelated lines before they are employed.

Experienced paint salesmen are hired at the branches and sent immediately to the home office of the company in Chicago for a week's or ten-days' intensive training. This training includes a thorough trip through the plant and laboratories; and morning, afternoon, and, frequently, evening sessions which cover a study of the various products made by the company and their application. The training is done by the general sales manager, assisted by other officials of the company. Extensive technical knowledge of paint is not required.

Advertising policies and methods are studied thoroughly so that new salesmen will have a full understanding of the company's publicity. The organization of the company and its history are also studied to give the new salesman a knowledge of the company's background. No attempt is made to train the men in sales technique at the home office. Upon completion of the school course, the new men are given a written examination.

When the new salesmen leave Chicago, they are sent to the branch through which they are to work, and there the details of their territories are given to them by the branch manager. The new men then start out on their territories, where their work is carefully watched and supervised by the branch manager.

Occasional bulletins describing new products or improvements are mailed to all salesmen from the home office by the general sales manager as a part of the sales training program. Company officials believe, however, that salesmen often neglect to study these bulletins.

Supplementing this training, sales meetings are held every six months at each branch, where experienced as well as new salesmen are given information about new products, and selling problems are discussed. These meetings are usually informal.

The general manager of the company believes that the initial period of a week or ten days at the home office is inadequate and should be lengthened or discontinued. Since he feels that the time is too short to give adequate training, and that many subjects which should be discussed are ignored on account of limited time, he advocates a six-weeks' training program at the home office during which time training in sales technique should also be given.

Another official of the company maintains that lengthy training at the home office is an unnecessary expense, and that new salesmen should be trained by going immediately into the field to observe an experienced salesman. He believes that new men learn more readily in an actual selling situation.

Questions

1. Should the company extend or limit the period of initial training for new salesmen? Give reasons for your answer.

2. Are the subjects of the training program of the company satisfactory? If you agree, give your reasons. If you believe the program should be changed, suggest desirable changes.

3. Is the organization for training correct? Give reasons for your opinion.

4. How can the company secure new training material for the extension of its sales technique training program?

Problem 3—Conference Sales Training

Wainwright Rubber Company

The Wainwright Rubber Company, established in 1892 in Akron, Ohio, has fifteen plants located in various parts of the country, and manufactures and distributes an annual volume of $300,000,000 worth of several thousand types of rubber specialties and sundries including tires and tubes. The tire division of the company employs three hundred salesmen who call on tire distributors and dealers from coast to coast.

For several years the company has trained its experienced salesmen by means of the conventional type of group sales training meetings held at its branch offices in the principal cities. The training at these meetings consisted of prepared lectures by managers of sales, merchandising, service, advertising, and sales promotion, who have used the usual charts, graphs, blackboard demonstrations and a series of printed booklets. Occasionally slide films have been used to train the salesmen in company policies, products, and procedures of these departments.

Because it was dissatisfied with this method of training, the company at the close of World War II, reviewed its training program and established a new training objective and plan. The new training was intended to train the company's salesmen so that they could train distributors in the fundamentals of sound, aggressive merchandising, and business management, thereby equipping them to move a profitable volume of tires and tubes into retail channels.

In seeking a new and more effective method of training, the various methods used by the company in training production workers during the war were considered. The conference-discussion method of training was favored by some of the company's sales executives, who contended that each salesman had considerable experience and ability which would be useful to other salesmen if each man's information, methods, and thinking could be shared with other members of the organization through conference discussions.

This method of training would consist of holding meetings of groups of from fifteen to twenty salesmen to discuss a series of problems commonly experienced by company salesmen in the field. Each conference would be in charge of a conference leader who would be chosen from among the salesmen. He would be a salesman who had successful sales experience. The objective of the leader would be to establish a common ground at the conference table so that each man would feel free to contribute to the discussion, and thereby bring about the fullest participation. The leader would not dominate the discussion but simply direct and control it so as to encourage a free exchange of opinion and experience. To do this he would have to be thoroughly prepared on the topic to be discussed by drawing up in advance leading questions to provoke discussion. He would use a blackboard in the meeting on which the question to be discussed would be written and the answers of the salesmen listed. Only one topic would be discussed at each meeting.

Assuming the topic discussed at a meeting was to be, "How to Select Distributors," the leader would open the discussion with the question, "What kind of a man would make a good distributor?" In reply, the group would be expected to suggest from twenty to thirty characteristics, each of which would be thoroughly discussed. At the close of each conference, the leader would summarize the discussion and a transcript of the comments would be prepared and distributed to each man present. This would be used later by each man in holding training conferences for his distriburors' salesmen.

After an indoctrination five-days' training course, during which time company, policies, history, background, production, procedure, and products would be discussed, new salesmen would join experienced salesmen in this conference-discussion training. The training would be continuous with meetings held quarterly at principal branch offices.

This type of training was opposed by certain executives who believed that it would lack direction and control; that the discussion would wander and get sidetracked by the relating of anecdotes and reminiscences; that important aspects of the subject would be overlooked; that salesmen are not teachers and do not have training or experience in conference leadership; that no systematic plan for the conferences would be developed in advance, and that the meetings would fail to arrive at sound conclusions.

Those who favored this method of training believed that it would stimulate thinking and the exchange of good experience; the academic atmosphere always resented by salesmen would be dispelled; the arguments would sustain interest; the intelligence of the men would be complimented and their self-importance increased by being given an opportunity to contribute from their knowledge and experience.

Questions

1. Should the Wainwright Rubber Company adopt the conference discussion method of training described in the problem? Give reasons for favoring or for opposing this method of training.

2. If you favor this method of training how can the instruction as planned be improved to make it more effective? Describe in detail a comprehensive program of conference training.

3. If you oppose this method of training, what other type of instruction would you suggest for these salesmen?

4. Is the training of new salesmen satisfactory? If this training can be improved, describe how you would make it more effective.

Problem 4—Training Distributors' Salesmen

Grayson Motor Company

The Grayson Motor Company, Detroit, Michigan, manufactures more than a million six- and eight-cylinder passenger cars and trucks annually, which are distributed through several thousand dealers from coast to coast. The products are widely advertised and sell for less than $1,000. The company maintains branches in thirty cities.

With increasing competition in the low-priced field, the company is considering the inauguration of a sales training program for its distributors' salesmen. The company plans to appoint a district sales instructor in each of its thirty sales districts and give each instructor special training at the factory under the direction of the general sales department of the company. Meetings will be held with company officials, and district instructors will be given an opportunity to study and assimilate the background of the company. Trips will be made through the company's plants, and sales methods will be studied.

After two-weeks' training at the factory, the district instructors will return to their respective districts and open sales training classes for all Grayson retail salesmen in each district. District sales training schools will be conducted in branch establishments, where salesmen will come regularly to attend classes, or district schools may travel from city to city to hold classes with salesmen from the surrounding territory.

Instructors in sales training would be provided by the company with the most modern sales training equipment, including slide film sound projectors and films and recordings illustrating and describing the product, company, and sales methods and practices. Cutaway models of Grayson passenger cars and trucks, advertising literature, photographs, and specially prepared textbooks would be used by the instructors in the course of study.

The cost of the training program has been estimated at approximately $100,000 for the first year, with additional expense for revising the program and equipment each succeeding year.

The training program would be sold to the company's dealers by company salesmen, supported by a direct advertising campaign to dealers describing the training in such terms as:

After months of painstaking preparation, exhaustive analyses of selling points, detailed study of the most successful ways of presenting them, and employment of the best talent, Grayson is able to announce its Sight-Sound System of training for all Grayson salesmen. This training will show in pictures and tell in words how the best Grayson salesmen approach prospects, present their case, overcome objections, and close sales.

The general sales manager believed that the training program would revive interest of retail salesmen and dealers in the Grayson cars and trucks; induce better selling methods; and increase the volume and profits of the dealers and the company. He cited examples of poor salesmanship by Grayson salesmen as disclosed by a national investigation. He believed that dealers would welcome such a training program.

Other executives of the company felt that the training would be very expensive and that no tangible results would be secured. They pointed out that training at its best is a slow development process; many salesmen resent going to school; they do not want to take the time from their sales work; and that the company can not compel attendance as the salesmen are all paid on a commission basis. They believed, furthermore, that salesmen can not be taught selling skill in classrooms, and that salesmen lack confidence in sales trainers who are not outstanding salesmen.

Questions

1. Should the Grayson Motor Company have adopted the sales training program as planned? Give reasons for your decision.

2. If you object to the training program as outlined, what methods of training would you use, if any? Describe.

Reading References

American Management Association, Marketing Executive Series:
  The Sales Supervisor's Part in Training, by Jay Ream, No. 35, 1926.
  Training the Sales Supervisor to Train, by Folger and Field, No. 59, 1928.
  Training of Salesmen, by Hoffman, Lovett, McDonald, Symonds, No. 60, 1928.
Developing and Managing Salesmen, Giles, Chap. III.
Directing Sales, Bonney, Chap. VII.
Handbook of Sales Management, Hall, Secs. VIII–IX.
Intensive Sales Management, Aspley, Chap. VI.
Principles of Personal Selling, Tosdal, Chap. XIX.
Printer's Ink Monthly, "Teaching the Salesman to Handle His Job," by H. G. Kenagy, Apr., 1927, p. 31.
Printer's Ink Weekly, "Sales Training Today," by R. W. Palmer, Dec. 6, 1934.
Sales Administration, Hayward, p. 265.
Sales Management Fundamentals, Hay, pp. 15–57.
Sales Management Magazine:
  "How American Radiator Analyzes a Sales Difficulty," by Richard C. Hay, Nov. 26, 1927, p. 919.
  "Why Every National Cash Man Must Learn a Standard Sales Talk," by G. E. Irving, Feb. 23, 1929, p. 427.
Sales Management Today, Doubman, Chap. VI.
Salesmen in Marketing Strategy, Lyon, Chap. VII.
Scientific Marketing Management, White, Chap. XII.

Scientific Sales Management Today, Hoyt, Chap. VII.
Selection and Training of Salesmen, Kenagy and Yoakum, Chaps. XIV–XV.
Training Driver-Salesmen, Policyholders' Service Bureau, Metropolitan Life Insurance Co., New York.

CHAPTER TEN

EQUIPPING SALESMEN

Why Equip Salesmen? A salesman must be provided not only with mental equipment, as discussed in the preceding chapter on sales training, but also with physical equipment to display his product, demonstrate its merits, and prove its value to prospective customers. Just as the work of a carpenter can be no better than the quality of his tools, so the efforts of a salesman are directly affected by the character of his selling equipment.

A few of the many reasons for providing salesmen with good physical equipment are:

1. Saving the salesman's time.
2. Gaining the attention of the buyer.
3. Standardizing the presentation of all salesmen in the organization.
4. Appealing not only to the hearing, but also to the sight, touch, or taste of the buyer.
5. Keeping the salesman and prospect on a direct line of thought.
6. Avoiding distractions during a sales interview.
7. Providing salesmen with an abundance of selling points.
8. Presenting the complete story.
9. Increasing the confidence of the salesman.
10. Reducing time of training salesmen.
11. Dramatizing the sales presentation.
12. Saving the buyer's time.

On the other hand, certain sales executives object to giving their salesmen physical equipment for the following reasons:

1. Physical equipment carried by a salesman arouses the resist-

ance of a prospect, since the equipment is a contant reminder that something is going to be sold.

2. Prospects may become so interested in a salesman's equipment that his remarks may fall on deaf ears.

3. Elaborate equipment may give a prospect the impression that a strange salesman is going to make a long call.

4. Some salesmen believe that it is undignified to carry physical equipment.

5. Equipment encourages lengthy conversations by reminding a salesman of something additional to talk about.

6. Equipment tempts a salesman to fall into a mechanized sales talk.

7. Equipment is not needed on many interviews.

8. The carrying of heavy equipment dissipates the energy of the salesman.

Sales Equipment Used. The type of physical equipment required by salesmen depends upon the nature of the product sold, type of buyer, method of travel, number of salesmen employed, and custom in the trade. A salesman of steam shovels who obviously cannot carry his product in a sample case must resort to some type of illustrative material to describe its operation. If the steam shovels are bought by technically trained purchasing agents, some engineering data and mechanical performance figures are a logical part of the salesman's equipment. Should the shovel salesmen travel by automobile, their equipment must be adapted in size and quantity to the space available in an automobile.

Salesmen's equipment may be generally classified as:

(1) interviewing equipment,
(2) informative equipment,
(3) operating equipment.

Interviewing Equipment. The most important classification is interviewing equipment, which includes samples, sample cases, models, portfolios, projectors, demonstrating devices, charts, diagrams, and sales kits.

The product itself, or a sample. If a product is easily portable, it may of itself be the one essential piece of a salesman's equipment. The use of an actual product as equipment is especially important in the sale of new products or those which cannot be readily described to buyers. Products in which a style element enters to a large

FIGURE 38. Loose tray sales sample case of an electrical specialty manufacturer. Each wood-frame, cloth-covered tray slides in and out independently and is readily accessible from the drop front of the case.

FIGURE 39. Salesmen of a large paint manufacturer carry this cowhide, three-shelf sales case with drop front for effective display.

FIGURE 40. Drop-front salesman's sample case fitted with partitions and a shelf to display effectively a line of pickles in jars.

FIGURE 41. A loose two-tray candy and biscuit salesman's case with space in bottom for boxes. Each tray slides in and out independently.

Courtesy Knickerbocker Case Company, Chicago, Illinois

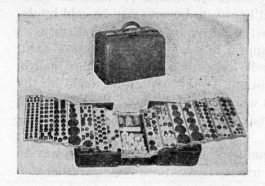

FIGURE 42. Gladstone type confectionery salesman's case fitted with fourteen aluminum trays. This case may be equipped with a container for wet or dry ice to refrigerate the contents.

FIGURE 43. Extension tray sales case opened on a metal folding stand especially made for displaying samples carried in this type of case.

FIGURE 44. A line of packaged waxes and polishes is sold to retail merchants from this cowhide, drop-front, extension tray sales case.

FIGURE 45. Extension tray sales sample case affording full or partial display of food, drug, or hardware items.

FIGURE 46. Combined salesman's brief and sample case fitted with two removable self-covered trays divided into partitions to carry a line of bottled goods conveniently and compactly.

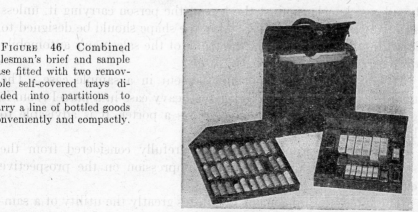

Courtesy Knickerbocker Case Company, Chicago, Illinois

extent are usually carried by salesmen. Staple products, the characteristics of which are well known to buyers, may be sold by description and are not included in the equipment of the salesmen.

The product itself may appeal to any of the five senses—sight, touch, taste, hearing, or smell—depending upon its nature, and in this way contribute substantially to the impression made by the salesman. Demonstrations which show and prove the merits of a product are facilitated by making the product a part of the salesman's equipment.

Getting a prospect to examine a product is an excellent way to secure sales interviews, as curiosity makes prospects interested who would otherwise refuse to listen.

Product or sample cases. While a salesman may carry the actual product or a sample openly in his hand, for convenience in carrying and for protection, products and samples are usually housed in carrying cases.

Careful attention should be given to designing the sample case in order to:

1. Insure that its quality and appearance is in keeping with the quality of the product.
2. Make it fit in with the salesman's selling talk.
3. Provide for a convenient arrangement of samples therein.
4. Insure an attractive display.
5. Protect the samples.
6. Keep the cost consistent with quality.

The shape of a sample case is important from the standpoint of convenience in carrying by the salesman and storing in transit. A broad case knocks against the legs of the person carrying it, unless swung away from the body. Also, the shape should be designed to fit with other equipment in the trunk of the salesman's automobile or to carry in a Pullman coach.

Weight is another important element in a sample case. The temptation to a salesman to leave a heavy case in a parcel room is great, and unless a salesman employs a porter, it is advisable to keep the case light.

External appearance should be carefully considered from the standpoint of making a favorable impression on the prospective customer.

The internal arrangement facilitates greatly the utility of a sample case. There are various methods of arranging cases with telescoping trays made of aluminum or wood with transparent or open tops. The trays may be divided into individual sections. Or, a case may be divided into sections for holding glass jars or vials. Refrigerated cases are made possible by carrying dry ice in airtight trays. Interiors may be lined with aluminum or washable cloth for cleanliness.

Many sales organizations have cases made to order by concerns specializing in the manufacture of salesmen's sample cases, or standard cases may be purchased to fit the equipment needs of many concerns. A periodic review of salesmen's cases to insure their good condition and completeness is advisable. Likewise, the freshness and cleanliness of samples should be checked at regular intervals.

A large food packer has given much thought to the development of salesmen's cases. Vacuum bottles are used to keep products hot. Opened duplicates of regular packages of various items are used for sampling purposes. Other equipment in the case includes: silver spoon, fork, knife, scissors, can opener, paper napkins, tea towels, polishing cloth, dummy soup tins, dummy bean tins, individual paper cups, paper plates, paper spoons, pickle tray, and tack hammer.

Bakers and confectionery manufacturers generally equip their salesmen with telescoping-tray sample cases filled with actual cakes and candies.

The Multibestos Company has created an ingenious sample case to display its brake linings and let the prospect see and feel the linings which the salesman is discussing. The several varieties of the product are displayed on a specially constructed metal base, which is readily removed from a substantial carrying case.

A vacuum cleaner company created a case for its house-to-house salesmen based on requirements of low cost, compactness, lightness, and good appearance. The case is 3½ inches deep, 13½ inches long, and 9¼ inches wide, and complete weighs five pounds. It is finished in imitation leather and holds eight cans. These cans contain baking soda, kapok, rice, sand, cracker crumbs, confetti, string, and toothpicks, each of which is used in demonstrating the product. In addition, the case contains advertising matter and a small screw driver. The salesman carries the demonstration kit and a vacuum cleaner on his calls. Contents are inspected regularly. A charge of $3 made to the salesman for the case and contents is applied to commission accounts.

When companies charge salesmen for sales sample cases and contents, such charges or deposits are usually refunded to the men when the samples are returned.   This practice is particularly true in organizations of commission specialty men.

The proper use and maintenance of sample cases by salesmen is a training problem in sales organizations.   Unless salesmen are convinced of the value of using samples in selling and are instructed in the use of sample cases, most of the investment in this type of equipment will be wasted.   Periodic inspection of cases and supervision of their use are imperative.

Models.   In many industries where products are too large to be carried, miniature models have been used effectively as salesmen's equipment.   Such miniatures secure the attention of prospects, enable salesmen to make actual demonstrations, and capitalize on the universal interest in mechanical toys.

There are various types of miniature models used as salesmen's equipment, such as working models, non-operating models, cross-section models, and toy models.

The disadvantages incident to using models are the high cost of designing and preparing special miniature parts; the quick obsolescence of models due to a change in design of the product; and the problem of keeping models in good operating condition.

Working models in miniature are sometimes impractical in operation, although for several years a furnace manufacturer has successfully used a working model of a hot-air furnace, equipped with a fan and an electric heating unit which is plugged into a convenient light socket.   This model is used in selling to home owners and simulates the actual operation of a hot-air furnace.

An electric motor manufacturer provides each salesman and distributor with a complete set of portable models of all of the company's motors.   Salesmen set up on desks of prospects exact models of motors in which they are interested, plug them into the nearest light socket, and present a complete demonstration of the company's method of direct power application.   The models serve to secure interviews and break down sales resistance so successfully that many sales have been traced to a working demonstration of a model motor.

A manufacturer of fire extinguishers has produced a miniature model of a fire extinguisher.   The company's salesman starts a small fire in an ash tray on the desk of a prospect, fills the miniature extinguisher with chemical liquids, inverts the model, and foam issues from the nozzle, blanketing and smothering the fire on the prospect's desk. The miniature extinguisher is packed in an attractive case with the bottles of chemicals and a cleaning cloth to remove the residue after the demonstration.

A maker of conveying equipment provides salesmen with a miniature model of a portable elevator used in piling boxes and barrels which are placed on the miniature lift and elevated by turning a crank on the model. Prospects show keen interest in using the model by raising and lowering the miniature barrels and boxes.

Many companies use nonoperating miniature models of their products as salesmen's equipment. A plumbing equipment manufacturer makes porcelain-enameled plumbing fixtures, which are too heavy and bulky to be carried by salesmen, yet possess unique, noncompetitive features. To show these features the company has made complete miniature models of its regular fixtures, including an enamel kitchen sink, which is carried by the company's salesmen.

A large electric ventilating company provides its salesmen with miniature houses to demonstrate movements of air and the necessity for ventilating equipment.

Cross-section miniature models are sometimes given to salesmen to illustrate the internal construction of mechanical products or parts. Full-sized cross-sections are also used in the case of small machines or mechanical parts. A manufacturer of fire extinguishers supplies its salesmen with cross-section or cutaway models of its hand extinguisher. Salesmen use the models in demonstrating the internal construction features of the product.

A manufacturer of valves and fittings cannot require its salesmen to carry bronze valves in making calls on prospects. So the company has created a twelve-inch cardboard cut-out of a valve, which in one piece presents exterior and interior construction features with explanation. Salesmen carry these paper cross-section models on sales calls with good effect.

A spark plug manufacturer's salesmen are equipped with cutaway spark plugs to show features of their products' internal construction. A tire manufacturer supplies its retail distributors' salesmen with cross sections of the carcass of automobile tire casings to show the cord construction and thickness of tread of the product.

Toy models have been used to excellent advantage by several companies as sales equipment. A washing machine manufacturer supplied salesmen with inexpensive miniature washing machines and ironers bearing the company's name, to arouse interest of prospects.

Portfolios. The term portfolio has a variety of meanings when applied to salesmen's equipment. In certain organizations it is a carrying case used for loose papers; in others, a book of advertising proofs; and in still others, a book of pictures used to illustrate selling points in a sales interview.

The commonly accepted use of the term portfolio is a standardized sales presentation in picture and story, bound in book form. Such an interview portfolio arranges sales points in logical sequence; develops one idea at a time; and uses illustrations profusely, including charts, photographs, and cartoons. In the portfolio may be found testimonial letters, illustrations of product installations, names of users, clippings, diagrams of construction features, advertising, and swatches. The material must be specially prepared for the individual organization and revised as changes are made in the sales program.

The value of an interview portfolio as a piece of salesman's equipment lies in its ability to:

1. Focus the prospect's attention.
2. Locate the prospect's needs.
3. Emphasize all selling points.
4. Keep the sales interview on the right track.
5. Appeal to sight as well as hearing.
6. Save time.

Interview portfolios are used by salesmen selling direct to consumers, by salesmen selling to retail dealers, by salesmen selling to wholesalers, and by salesmen of industrial products. The content of the portfolios used for these types of selling varies with the product sold and the nature of the sales job.

In using sales portfolios, salesmen connect their sales talk with the pages of the portfolio as they turn them in the presence of the buyer. Certain manufacturers provide a standard sales talk to accompany each page in the interview portfolio. The salesman should so familiarize himself with the contents of the portfolio and sequence of pages that he can refer quickly to any particular page or subject. To avoid mechanized use of the portfolio, the salesman introduces it into the interview casually, and does not necessarily attempt to go through it from cover to cover.

A manufacturer and distributor of soda fountains has had unusual sales results by equipping its salesmen with a visual interview portfolio. Investigators were sent into the field to observe selling methods and found, upon analysis of a soda fountain sales presentation, that there were thirty-four major points in the discussion, which fell into three groups:

(1) The general desirability of having a soda fountain in the store.
(2) The requirements of a good soda fountain.
(3) The particular merits of the maker's soda fountains.

Illustrations were prepared with captions to illustrate the thirty-four selling points. The illustrations were bound in leather-covered books, costing, complete with research, about $120 each. Using the portfolio, salesman reduced time spent with each prospect from seven to two hours. Sales volume in a twelve-month period, after the adoption of portfolio, increased 43 per cent without increasing the number of salesmen needed.

A popular form of portfolio is an easel or pyramid display type of binder made completely graphic. Several portfolios of this type are used in merchandising the various units of a stove maker's line from small, pocket-sized portfolios to large, "jumbo" portfolios. The portfolios are used to aid the memory of salesmen in giving standardized presentations, preventing outside interruptions, and helping the customer to concentrate.

A rubber company uses two visual interview portfolios: one for factory salesmen in interviewing prospective dealers, and another for use by dealers in selling to ultimate consumers. The factory salesmen find the portfolios valuable in conducting interviews with filling-station operators, who are frequently interrupted by customers.

The Northwestern National Life Insurance Co. has developed a complete loose-leaf interview portfolio for its agents. The book features the outstanding needs for life insurance and the company's contracts to meet those needs.

A well-known maker of refrigerators equipped salesmen with a pocket-sized interview portfolio of the accordion-fold type, illustrating the principal selling points and different models of the product. The convenience of this small portfolio made it a popular selling tool.

Physical types of salesmen's portfolios. There are several commonly used physical types of salesmen's portfolios. The 10 by 11½ inch, three-ring binder is most generally used. A popular type is the loose-leaf, pyramid-easel portfolio which presents material at eye level and enables concentration on one point at a time without any distracting material in sight. This type enables the salesman to control easily the use of the book as it is placed on a table or desk before both prospect and salesman. The pyramid portfolios may be obtained in a wide variety of sizes.

Another recent type of sales portfolio is the ring-binder easel, which is a standard, loose-leaf, ring binder with the addition of an automatic easel device to the back cover. This portfolio may be given eye-level display value by standing the binder on a desk and pulling out the easel back.

Sales portfolios are also produced in accordion-fold binder type, upon the leaves of which illustrations may be mounted. This type of portfolio enables several pages to be viewed at one time. Salesmen sometimes prefer this type, which can be spread out to obscure the distracting papers on a prospect's desk.

Zipper sales portfolios have the advantage of keeping their contents protected against soil and damage, and at the same time are convenient to carry and present a dignified appearance. The zipper fastener runs around the outside edge of the binder and can be provided with a lock to make the portfolio "theft proof."

1. Advertising portfolios. While interview portfolios used in selling to distributors usually include proofs of advertisements running in current publications, direct mail pieces, radio network programs, and other media, the volume of advertising done by many companies demands that a separate portfolio for advertising be supplied to salesmen.

Advertising portfolios contain, not only proofs of advertisements of various media used, but also schedules of insertions, circulation coverage, testimonials of effectiveness, and records of response from previous advertising.

Companies doing a large volume of advertising issue advertising portfolios for salesmen, containing proofs of current advertisements and schedules with suggestions for dealer tie-ups.

2. Miniature sales portfolios. To facilitate the use of sales interview portfolios by salesmen, they are sometimes issued in pocket size so as not to arouse resistance by prospects. A washing machine manufacturer produced for retail salesmen a pocket-size portfolio which was 8½ by 12½ inches when open and 5½ by 8½ inches when folded. The portfolio had an imitation leather cover and was fastened with snap buttons. The first page illustrated the

company's products and the features of their construction; subsequent pages discussed personal safety, saving washing and drying time, saving ironing time and labor, saving mending time and labor, washing and damp drying, and various features of the company's products.

Picture projectors. Consistent with the improvement in industrial picture production, more salesmen are being equipped with moving and still picture films and projectors for use in conducting sales interviews. Films are particularly effective as salesmen's equipment in:

(1) Handling group-selling to best advantage.
(2) Demonstrating heavy equipment in a prospect's office.
(3) Dramatizing a product or service through the introduction of a human-interest plot.
(4) Creating good will through showings to clubs and civic groups.
(5) Showroom selling.
(6) Saving of selling time.

1. Slide films. There are several types of films for use by salesmen, the most common being the slide film, which is a standard strip of motion picture film, 35-mm. wide, carrying from sixty to two hundred "frames" or individual pictures. This film is projected in a special slide film projector, which is plugged into a convenient light socket. Each picture or frame is advanced manually by the operator.

Sound slide film equipment consists of a 200-watt electric lamp which will project a picture 8 by 12 feet at a distance of 50 feet, together with an amplifier and electro-dynamic loud-speaker incorporated in the unit. Sound records 10, 12, and 16 inches in size are revolved on a turntable which is a part of the single unit. This type of equipment is illustrated on page 187.

The advantages of sound slide film projection are:

(1) It insures uniformity of the message, making every salesman an effective public speaker.
(2) It makes possible complete concentration of eye and ear during a sales presentation.
(3) It permits voice presentation in any language, making it helpful in export selling.

(4) It makes a sales presentation the way a star salesman would make it.

2. Sound moving pictures. Sound motion pictures create the utmost realism in visual selling equipment by reaching the ear as well as the eye. Sound pictures not only show action but with spoken words tell the selling story so that it is absorbed without effort. Thus a more permanent impression is made on the mind of the prospect.

The latest sound-on-film 16-mm. equipment is in two units, weighing about fifty pounds. With sound-on-film, the sound is photographed on the margin of the film at the time the exposure occurs. The projector throws a beam of light through the margin of the film where the sound is recorded, which beam is transmitted back into sound waves by a photoelectric cell and then amplified by a loud-speaker in a separate unit. The "Filmosound," produced by Bell & Howell Company is typical of sound-on-film 16-mm. equipment and is illustrated in Figure 35.

The cost of producing a sales moving picture depends upon the type of picture required. Single 400-foot reels, taking about twelve minutes to show, may range in price from $3,000 to $15,000.

Demonstrating devices. Many companies equip their salesmen with unique demonstrating devices to enable them to present outstanding features of their products in dramatic and novel ways. Such devices get the attention of prospects, enable prospects to participate in the sales demonstration, and avoid interruptions.

Several companies supply their salesmen with collections of miscellaneous unrelated objects useful in demonstrating selling points. The Iron Fireman Manufacturing Co. provided its salesmen with a kit containing:

1. A small food grinder to show the conveyor principle of the product.
2. A ratchet wrench for demonstrating the ratchet feed.
3. A pressed-steel frying pan and a cast-iron frying pan to break and show the relative strength of cast iron when compared with pressed steel.

Other equipment in the kit included a carpenter's bit, plumber's wax candle, machinist's hammer, fruit jar, and automobile carburetor.

A paint manufacturing company equips salesmen with a hammer, piece of zinc coated with enamel, bottle of muriatic acid, brush, and cans of the product to prove the merit of its automobile enamel finishes.

An insulating board manufacturer provides salesmen with a test outfit to demonstrate the value of a new insulating wallboard. The outfit consists of a pasteboard box about five inches square, one inside surface of which is painted black, a fast conductor of heat; another surface is plain, untreated; and a third inside surface is covered with aluminum foil, the material used on the new insulating wallboard. A round hole is cut in the fourth side of the box for the insertion of an electric light bulb. A small candle is supplied for dropping a bit of wax in a circle on the outside of each of the three surfaces, to be tested for heat conduction. With the electric light inserted in the box, the drops of wax on the outside soon begin to melt on the surfaces which are not insulated, proving the insulating value of the aluminum-foil-insulated surface, typical of the company's insulating board.

Charts and diagrams. Charts and diagrams are a highly valuable form of graphic presentation for equipping salesmen. Several useful forms of diagrams are:

1. Graphs to show fluctuations in activity of sales, business conditions, or prices for products or territories.
2. Bar charts to compare by length of bars relative values, costs, volume, prices, and the like.
3. Pie charts to indicate by circles divided into segments the relation of certain parts, such as costs and volume, to the whole.
4. Figure charts to show by outline drawings of figures of various sizes the relative importance of certain facts, for example, sales of women's apparel might be compared by picturing a small figure of a woman with a large figure of a woman, indicating small sales compared with large sales.
5. Maps to indicate geographical distribution of readers of an advertising campaign.
6. Cube charts to show with different-sized cubes comparative sales volume.

Charts and diagrams are used chiefly as sales interviewing equipment for illustrating sales points or product features. Particularly in the sale of intangibles, diagrams serve to show benefits which would not otherwise be apparent. Most life insurance companies provide salesmen with charts of insurance values.

Advance cards and business cards. Traveling salesmen of many companies are equipped with "advance cards" to mail to prospects or customers in advance of their calls. These are usually postcards illustrating the factory, products in the line, or distinctive features of products, and carrying a simple message, such as: "I expect to call on you on . . . . (*date*) with a complete line of . . . . products." The card is signed by the salesman.

Many salesmen object to using business cards in securing interviews, while others use cards in practically every sales interview. Business cards are a standard piece of salesmen's equipment and are often printed in novel shapes to attract attention and advertise the business or product sold. Salesmen's cards often have a utility value through the printing of measuring or statistical information on the reverse side.

Advertising materials. Copies of current advertising booklets, folders, broadsides, and publication advertisements run by the company on each product in the line and not included in an advertising portfolio should be a part of the salesmen's equipment. Not only should these advertising pieces be used in conducting interviews, but they should be left by the salesmen with prospects and customers to be read after the interview. They serve to emphasize selling points and in the case of dealer selling are an important factor in the sales interview.

Sales kits. To protect the numerous items of salesmen's equipment previously mentioned and provide a convenient way for transporting them, carrying cases, usually called sales kits, are provided.

Courtesy Knickerbocker Case Company, Chicago, Illinois

Figure 47. Zipper closure-type leather sales kit with expansion pockets for advertising, catalogs and order book.

These kits are made to order to carry the various pieces of salesmen's equipment, and should embody the features of good appearance, arrangement, weight, and size mentioned above in connection with sample cases. Frequently the sample case and sales kit are combined in a single unit.

A maker of linoleum has developed a sales kit for dealers of floor coverings. An attractive, black imitation-leather case is divided on the inside into sections for samples, advertising, catalogs, cross-section models, photographs, order blanks, price lists, and other things.

Informing Equipment. In addition to equipment used in interviewing, salesmen are provided with such informative materials as sales manuals, policy books, catalogs, price lists, and service and engineering manuals instructing the salesmen in company policies, prices, and product features.

Sales manuals. Sales manuals are often used in sales training, as well as serving as books of reference for salesmen in the field, in which case they become a part of the salesmen's equipment and are given a place in the sales kit. They serve salesmen as source books of general information on company organization, policies, and products.

The principal purposes of a sales manual are: to improve the knowledge of salesmen and the effectiveness of their sales presentation; to organize selling material so that it may be readily utilized by salesmen before and during sales interviews; and to provide new data about products and policies.

Manuals usually contain the following information.

1. The history of the company and organization.
2. The product—its features and applications.
3. Information concerning the product, installations, and large customers.
4. Selling technique.
5. Answers to common objections.
6. Company policies on prices, service, trade-ins, credit, allowances, returned goods, spoilage, and advertising.
7. Instructions to salesmen concerning reports, order forms, and equipment to be carried.
8. Testimonial letters from satisfied users.
9. The advertising program.
10. Manufacturing processes and policies.

The most common difficulties in the use and preparation of sales manuals are:

1. The manual is not used by the salesmen.
2. The manual is poorly arranged and written—too wordy, theoretical, and involved.
3. The physical form of the manual is not conducive to use.
4. The manual is out of date and contains much obsolete material.
5. The manual is not adapted to the various types of salesmen in the organization.

The problem of getting the salesmen to use the manual has been approached in some companies by sending salesmen questionnaires covering each section, and rewarding salesmen who return all questionnaires properly answered.

An industrial-product manufacturer succeeded in interesting salesmen in the sales manual by inviting them to contribute their best sales ideas for a new edition of the manual. Thereafter salesmen considered the manual a book of their own making and used it effectively.

Another company held a series of lectures for salesmen at which material from the manual was presented and the interest of the men revived.

Another method of maintaining interest and use of a sales manual is to send frequent additions to salesmen for insertion in loose-leaf binders, or to require outstanding manuals to be returned to the home office for correction.

The physical form and size of a sales manual depend upon the amount and kind of material, conditions of use, and frequency of revision contemplated. The leather-bound, three-ring, loose-leaf manual, 9¾ by 11½ inches, carrying a standard 8½ by 11 inch, letter-sized sheet of paper, is the most common size and type used. Such a binder permits frequent changes in material and is not too large to carry conveniently in a sales kit. Pocket-sized manuals are sometimes used for convenience in carrying in a salesman's pocket.

Some companies prefer permanently bound manuals to the loose-leaf type for the reason that the contents cannot be removed and lost. Furthermore, such manuals usually present a more attractive appearance.

Unless the material in a sales manual is up to date, it soon loses its effectiveness, and for this reason certain companies revise their manuals annually; others publish new manuals every six months. The majority supply new material regularly in loose-leaf form.

Separate sales manuals may be prepared by a single company selling to different markets through several types of sales forces, in which case a manual would be provided for sales engineers selling to industry; an institutional sales manual for salesmen selling to institutions; and a retail sales manual for salesmen selling to retailers.

There are numerous sources of material for sales manuals, such as:

1. Job analysis by a difficulty and duty analysis of the activities of salesmen.
2. Questionnaires sent to salesmen to secure material on difficulties, duties, and selling methods.
3. Contributions by branch managers.
4. Interviews with successful salesmen.
5. Interviews with leading distributors.
6. Company home office executives.
7. Correspondence with salesmen.

The arrangement and writing of the sales manual may be delegated to the advertising department under the supervision of the sales executives.

Service and engineering manuals. Separate manuals are usually prepared which describe the technical features of a product for use by salesmen in making installations or performing service duties. Technical-product manuals carry extensive technical descriptions. The engineering manual carried by salesmen for a manufacturer of commercial refrigeration contains technical information on the theory of refrigeration, refrigerants, heat transfer, insulation, air circulation, cooling solutions, pressure and vacuum gauges, thermometer conversion tables, and pressure and temperature data.

Other informative equipment. Salesmen are usually provided with catalogs for use in describing and illustrating each type or model in the line. Catalogs are used frequently in sales interviews and often left with prospects.

When a line of products is subjected to price changes, special price lists are prepared and become a part of the salesmen's regular equipment. Prices are not usually quoted in catalogs, since it is much more economical to revise price lists than to change the catalogs. Prices are usually quoted at list in price sheets, and salesmen offer discounts according to the type of customer and quantity purchased.

Companies sometimes issue policy books for salesmen, listing the various policies maintained by the company on prices, discounts, allowances, credits, and returned goods.

Operating Equipment. To facilitate the operation and control of salesmen, they are provided with various forms for reporting new orders, lost orders, missionary functions, credits, expenses incurred, demonstrations conducted, and other activities. Special order books and pads of printed forms for reporting on these operations are an important part of the salesmen's equipment, and provision should be made in the kit for these forms. A description of the use of these forms will be found in a later chapter dealing with control of salesmen.

Problem 1—Sales Manuals

Baxter, Loose Mfg. Company

The Baxter, Loose Mfg. Company, established in 1890 at Attleboro, Massachusetts, manufactures six distinct groups of silver-plated and novelty wares, including silver-plated hollowware, flatware, copperware, and novelties sold by twelve salesmen direct to jewelry, department store, gift shop, stores for resale, and to hotels, hospitals, drug and confectionery stores, restaurants, and cafeterias. They also sell to wholesalers of restaurant equipment, drug sundries, hardware, and groceries.

Since its establishment, the company had supplied its salesmen with information about its products and policies through the medium of occasional bulletins or letters issued by the sales manager. These were often misplaced or lost by salesmen, who frequently wrote the sales manager for information which had been previously distributed. To solve this problem, the sales manager proposed the preparation of a sales manual for distribution to all salesmen.

Since this was a small company, however, with a relatively small office force that had neither the time nor talent to write a good sales manual, the sales manager was doubtful that a worthwhile manual could be prepared in view of the great diversity of products and outlets sold.

One of the company salesmen who had previous experience in writing advertising was called into the home office to develop the manual. He first prepared an outline of contents, which included:

1. History of the company.
2. Personnel of the company and its organization.
3. The advertising program.
4. Answers to objections.

5. Description of company policies.
6. Testimonial letters from product users.
7. Instructions concerning the filling out of orders and report forms.
8. A list of the products sold by the company and their prices.

This material was written up by the salesman, approved by the sales manager, printed and inserted into a loose-leaf, imitation-leather-bound, pocket-size book, 6 by 9 inches, with one hundred and twenty-five pages.

The sales manual was first shown and discussed in the presence of all the salesmen of the company at an annual sales convention at the home office. Following the discussions, an examination was given all salesmen on the principal items in the manual, and the examination papers were gone over by the sales manager with each salesman.

The salesmen were also supplied with a sales kit containing photographs of the principal products made by the company, a catalog illustrating and pricing all items in the line, and a sample case with actual samples of the products of the company.

At the sales convention salesmen asked numerous questions concerning subjects which had not been mentioned in the sales manual, particularly about credit terms and discounts, which had recently been revised to each class of trade. The management replied that such confidential information was not included in the sales manual for fear that it would fall into the hands of competitors, and that if terms were later changed, this would necessitate a change in the manual.

A check by the management several months after the new manuals had been issued showed that few salesmen were carrying the manual, and that none was using it for reference.

Questions

1. Should the Baxter, Loose Mfg. Company have prepared a sales manual for its salesmen? Give reasons for your decision.

2. If the company was wise in giving the salesmen a manual, could its preparation have been improved? Describe how you would have prepared the manual.

3. Did the company properly insure the use of the sales manual by the salesmen? If not, what should have been done to insure the use of the manual?

4. Were the contents of the manual satisfactory? If not, what other information should have been included?

5. Was the physical form of the manual satisfactory? If not, what form should have been used?

Problem 2—Salesmen's Equipment

Style-Fit Shoe Company

The Style-Fit Shoe Company established in 1880 in Lynn, Massachusetts, employs five thousand men and women. The company daily manufactures twelve thousand pairs of men's and women's shoes with annual sales of $12,000,000. Forty salesmen call on several thousand retail shoe distributors throughout the country.

For several years the company's salesmen have carried the following equipment:

1. One or more cases of actual samples of shoes made by the company.
2. A sample case of shoe findings such as laces and accessories.
3. A catalog of stock shoes.
4. A catalog of findings.
5. An advertising portfolio illustrating national magazine advertisements, local newspaper advertising cuts, window display advertising pieces, direct mail advertising folders and blotters, and outdoor advertising signs.
6. An order book for specially made shoes.
7. A regular stock order book.
8. A findings order book.
9. A sales and expense report book.
10. A prospect report book.
11. A lost-order report book.
12. A new account report book.
13. A route list report book.
14. An expense money requisition book.
15. Advance cards.
16. Correspondence paper and envelopes.
17. Credit rating books.
18. A weekly and monthly auto expense report.

All salesmen travel by automobile.

This equipment was housed in a leather carrying case, with the exception of the shoe samples, which were packed in trunks especially made to accommodate them. Salesmen were required to check over samples before leaving the sales office on a selling trip.

The sales manager believed that the salesmen were required to carry too much reporting equipment and too little equipment, aside from samples, for use in conducting interviews. The expense of salesmen's sample cases was considerable, and a substantial amount of the salesmen's time was taken up in packing and handling baggage. However, the custom in the shoe trade to buy from samples is long established, and the sales manager doubted that the use of sample cases could be eliminated.

A large competitor of the Style-Fit Company recently produced a talking moving picture featuring the arch construction of its men's shoes. This film was shown to dealers and their salesmen in specially arranged sales meetings in dealers' stores by the factory salesmen of the competitor. According to reports received by the Style-Fit Company, the pictures aroused much interest on the part of shoe dealers and their sales personnel, and resulted in increased sales in stores where they were shown. The projector and film was routed by prearranged schedule from dealer to dealer and operated by the factory salesmen.

The sales manager of the Style-Fit Company believed that a similar film could be used to advantage by the company's salesmen. The Style-Fit shoe for women had special arch construction which could be featured in a film. Another executive favored the use of talking slide films for this purpose.

Questions

1. Should the Style-Fit Company make any change in the present equipment of its salesmen? Give reasons for your decision.

2. If you believe the equipment of the salesmen should be changed, describe in detail what changes should be made.

3. Should the company consider equipping its salesmen with moving picture projectors for conducting dealer meetings, or for any other purpose?

4. Should the suggestion that slide films be used be adopted? Give reasons for your answer.

Problem 3—Sales Models

The Martin Oil Burner Corporation

The Martin Oil Burner Corporation, established in 1915 in Newark, New Jersey, manufactures oil burners for domestic and industrial heating. It sold an annual volume of $2,000,000 to an exclusive-dealer organization which distributed throughout the New England, Middle Atlantic, and Central States. The company employs ten wholesale salesmen on a straight-salary basis.

Salesmen selling to dealers are equipped with a fifty-page, loose-leaf interview portfolio containing: illustrations of the various models made by the company and diagrams showing the many superior mechanical features of the three types of oil burners on the market; photographs of installations; illustrations in which comparisons of untidy basements, equipped with old-fashioned furnaces, are made with clean basements in which oil burners have been installed; and testimonial letters from distributors and users of the product.

In addition to the visual interview portfolio, salesmen are supplied with a sales manual containing the company's history and policies, answers to objections, and helpful aids in performing their duties. Various reporting forms are also included, and the whole is packed in a leather-bound, zipper-type sales kit.

A salesman of the company has suggested to the sales manager that the company provide salesmen with miniature non-working models of the oil burner, constructed of light metal, 5 by 5 by 4 inches in size, for demonstration to prospective dealers. In his opinion this model will attract attention, arouse the dealer's interest, and aid other salesmen in conveying a better impression of the physical characteristics of the product. The sales manager was receptive to the suggestion but thought that possibly the cross-sectional, nonworking parts of the burner in actual size would better serve to illustrate the principal constructional features of the product. These parts would be produced in light metal and packed in a specially built carrying case for the salesman's use.

Another executive thought that dealers were not so much concerned with the physical appearance and constructional features of the product as they were with the sales and turnover possibilities. He advocated some type of equipment which would aid the salesmen in discussing the resale possibilities of the product.

Questions

1. Should the salesman's suggestion for a non-working miniature model burner be adopted? Give reasons for your decision.

2. Should the sales manager's suggestion for several sectional models of parts be adopted? Give reasons for your decision.

3. Should the suggestions for models be rejected and equipment be produced for demonstrating resale values? If so, what equipment should be used?

4. Is the present equipment of the salesmen satisfactory? If not, what changes should be made?

Reading References

Management of the Sales Organization, Russell, Chap. IV.
Modern Sales Management, Frederick, p. 275.
Printed Salesmanship Magazine, "Strategy in Planning an Advertising Portfolio,"
    by George W. Hopkins, Mar., 1932, p. 42.
Printer's Ink Weekly:
    "Guiding the Presentation," by M. L. Harter, Sept. 5, 1935, p. 91.
    "Pictorial Selling," by C. G. Carter, Jan. 21, 1937, p. 53.
    "Selling Goes Visual," by H. Simmons, June 17, 1937, p. 17.
Sales Administration, Hayward, Chap. XVIII.
Sales Management Today, Doubman, Chap. VIII.
Salesmen in Marketing Strategy, Lyon, Chap. VIII.

CHAPTER ELEVEN

SALESMEN'S COMPENSATION

Purposes of Compensation Plan. A sound method of compensating salesmen involves more than the payment of an amount of money adequate to provide for a reasonable standard of living for salesmen. A good system of compensation should also provide for the following:

1. An incentive to salesmen to do more business.
2. Flexibility to enable salesmen to increase their earnings as they become more efficient.
3. A reasonable stabilization of earnings in periods of prosperity and depression.
4. The loyalty of salesmen.
5. The directing of salesmen's efforts to the sale of such products at such times and places as desired by the management.
6. The retirement of salesmen too old to sell efficiently.
7. The keeping of the unit cost of sales expense consistent with the income from the area served.
8. The promotion of coöperative action among salesmen for the development of sales.
9. The securing of salesmen's confidence in the compensation plan through a clear, simple, and understandable explanation of its operation.
10. The prevention of salesmen from overstocking customers and creating ill will by pressing for immediate orders.
11. Insuring to the employer a reasonable return on the salesmen's services.
12. Reducing turnover of salesmen and stabilizing employment.
13. Relieving salesmen of anxiety regarding regularity of earnings.
14. The control of the salesmen's activities by the management.

239

15. The payment of a subsistence income to beginning salesmen
until such time as they are able to produce in sufficient volume to earn a living wage.

Factors Affecting Method of Payment. There are numerous
factors which have a direct bearing on the type of compensation for
salesmen, such as the following:

1. The job to be done dictates in a large measure the nature of
the payment plan. If the product is in wide demand, heavily advertised, competition limited, the market unsaturated, and selling
automatic, there is little creative selling effort demanded of the
salesman, and his compensation may be justifiably low. If, on the
other hand, a product is in little demand, the price high, and the
competition keen, the salesman's job is more difficult and he must
be compensated accordingly. If a selling job requires considerable
missionary or nonselling work such as assisting dealers in reselling
to consumers, salesmen must be compensated for this indirectly productive activity. A sales engineering job requires technically
trained men, who must be paid in proportion to their ability.

2. The type of product influences to a great extent the payment
plan. There is a marked difference in sales ability required in selling an electric dynamo and selling copper wire, although both are
sold to purchasing agents for electric power plants. Staple products
ordinarily require less sales ability than specialties. High-priced
products are harder to sell than low-priced products. Products
with repeat possibilities offer salesmen greater income opportunities
than single sales commodities. A salesman carrying a line of ten
products ordinarily has better chances of increasing his income than
a man selling one product of equal price and demand.

3. The market for a product affects the method of paying salesmen. A product which may be consumed by every man, woman,
and child offers such broad sales possibilities that the compensation
per unit sold may be low. On the other hand, salesmen of steam
yachts, which are sold to a limited market, may receive high
remuneration per unit. In some markets competition is keen and
a higher grade of sales ability is demanded, which calls for higher
pay.

4. The method of distribution may have an important bearing on
the choice of salesmen's compensation. Sales through wholesale
and retail outlets may be automatic, since these distributors exist
largely for filling demand, while sales made to ultimate consumers

may require a higher grade of sales ability and a different method of compensation. A man selling to large distributing outlets, such as chain stores, department stores, and mail order houses, would require a different method of compensation than one soliciting, for example, one twelfth of every dozen orders from retail druggists.

5. The amount of advertising used to promote a product will have a bearing on the salesmen's payment plan. A company which makes a very heavy investment in printed selling usually makes a proportionately lower investment in personal selling. With a large amount of advertising behind a product, the degree of personal sales ability necessary to sell the product is less and compensation is lower. Salesmen of unadvertised products must be paid for the greater effort and ability demanded in selling such commodities.

6. The ability of the salesmen influences the payment plan, as many salesmen of outstanding accomplishment require a commission which pays them in direct proportion to their ability to make sales. A salesman of mediocre ability would be reluctant to work on a straight-commission basis, much preferring a straight salary. The very able salesman requires a different type of compensation from the order-taking type of salesman if both types are to work with maximum efficiency. The temperament of the individual salesman, his need for incentive, ability to save, and standard of living should all be taken into consideration in arriving at a payment plan.

Methods of Paying Salesmen. Since the successful sales compensation plan depends upon a number of factors described previously, it is obvious that no one system of payment can be effective for all types of business or even all companies in a single industry. Sound payment plans cannot be developed except by experiment, and only through trial and error can be found the solution to the problem of paying salesmen in an individual business. There is no perfect plan for paying salesmen, and the best method is one which provides: (1) incentive; (2) control; and (3) stability of earnings for the salesmen.

There are two basic methods of paying salesmen—salary and commission—but there are many variations of these methods, all of which seek to secure: (1) the highest volume of sales, (2) the sale of the most profitable merchandise, and (3) the lowest expense for selling.

Salary compensation. The most common method of paying

salesmen is by straight salary. Advantages and disadvantages of this method, from the standpoint of the employer and the salesman may be given as follows:

1. *Advantages of salary method to company:*
   a. Allows management to exercise full control of the time of salesmen.
   b. Encourages salesmen to do missionary work.
   c. Makes salesmen loyal to company.
   d. Allows salesmen to make more accurate reports of their work.
   e. Is easy to compute and requires little accounting.
   f. Allows salesmen to coöperate more readily in making joint sales.
   g. Allows salesmen to be transferred readily without adjustments in compensation.
   h. Allows salesmen to be more contented, since they have an assured, regular income.

2. *Disadvantages of salary method to company:*
   a. Salesmen become dissatisfied unless salaries are increased from time to time.
   b. It is difficult to fix salaries or grant increases commensurate with the real ability of the salesmen.
   c. Once fixed, it is hard to adjust salaries downward in periods of falling sales.
   d. Salaries make salesmen order takers, satisfied to secure just enough business to keep their jobs.
   e. The company takes the risk in paying a salary to a new man whose ability has not been proved.
   f. Salaries offer no incentive to salesmen to increase their sales.
   g. Salaries place a responsibility on the management to make good selection of new salesmen.

3. *Advantages of salary payment to salesmen:*
   a. Provides a regular, insured income to cover living expenses.
   b. Compensates for missionary work which may not directly result in sales.
   c. Provides for the pioneering work necessary in a new job or territory before sales may be made.
   d. Permits the management to accept the risk for time invested in selling.

4. *Disadvantages of salary method to salesmen:*

a. There is no incentive for a man to develop himself.

b. Increases in salary are often difficult to secure.

c. Salary income is not flexible to changes in business conditions and does not keep pace with better business.

The amount of salary paid salesmen depends upon a number of factors, such as: length of service, past experience, personality, knowledge of the company's products, policies and competition, and bargaining ability of the salesman. The amount of salary payable under some plans is fixed automatically each year by the ability of the salesman to accomplish certain objectives.

Applications of salary method. The straight salary method of paying salesmen is generally used in the sale of staple commodities, such as food, hardware, and drugs through wholesale and retail outlets when considerable missionary work is necessary. Where, in the sale of technical products through sales engineers much indirect sales work is undertaken, salaries are commonly paid. Also, in companies where sales are frequently made through the joint efforts of several salesmen, a salary plan is satisfactory. Sales executives are usually paid straight salaries.

Commission Compensation. Next to the straight salary, the straight commission method is the most common device for paying salesmen. The commission graduates compensation on a percentage basis according to volume of net sales. Numerous benefits as well as disadvantages arise from this method for both the management and the employees:

1. *Advantages of commission method to company:*

   a. Salesmen are paid only on results and accordingly work harder.

   b. The company takes no risk, since salesmen are guaranteed nothing.

   c. The company with limited capital is enabled to secure the services of salesmen which would otherwise be impossible.

   d. Since earnings are unlimited, a commission provides incentive to a salesman to increase his sales.

   e. A commission plan often attracts able salesmen to an organization.

2. *Disadvantages of commission method to company:*

   a. The relationship between the company and the salesman is more distant.

  b. Pressure is exerted on a salesman to make sales at a sacrifice of good will.

  c. The control exercised by the company over the salesman is weak.

  d. Coöperative effort with other salesmen is not promoted.

  e. Effort is placed on those items in the line which are easiest to sell and often least profitable.

  f. Salesmen may be inclined to accept large allowances on trade-ins.

  g. Salesmen earn little during periods of depression, and their morale is affected.

3. *Advantages of commission method to salesmen:*

  a. Great independence of operation is allowed, since the salesmen work for themselves.

  b. Earnings depend on individual efforts rather than on arbitrary decisions of management to increase compensation.

  c. Producers do not indirectly pay compensation of nonproducers as in the case of a salary plan.

  d. No coöperation of salesmen is necessary in the organization.

4. *Disadvantages of commission method to salesmen:*

  a. Income is often irregular.

  b. Commissions decline rapidly in periods of bad business.

  c. The salesman takes all the risk of securing business.

  d. The management gives salesman little assistance.

Applications of commission method. The straight commission method of paying salesmen is universally used in the sale of specialties of fairly high price and broad market such as automobiles, office equipment, oil burners, life insurance, and securities. When maximum incentive is necessary and the sale is reasonably difficult to make, a commission is the usual method of payment. This method is commonly used in paying direct-to-the-consumer or house-to-house salesmen. It is also used by small companies which have a broad market for their product.

A few variations of the straight commission plan are: the sliding commission, the group commission, and the individual item commission.

Sliding commission. By this plan a salesman is paid a certain percentage of net sales up to a certain amount, after which the rate of commission increases or declines as higher sales volumes are reached.

The advantage of a sliding commission to the company is that the salesman is given an incentive to increase his sales volume under a step-up rate plan, while the selling expense of the company is reduced under a step-down rate plan.

Group commission. By this plan the various products sold by the salesmen are arranged in groups, and a different rate of commission is paid upon each group. The commission rates are varied according to the profit value or the desirability of selling the various groups. The advantage of this plan is that it induces the salesmen to push the most profitable items by fixing higher rates of commission on these lines.

Individual item commission. By this plan the individual items sold by the salesmen carry different rates of commission. The advantage is the same as with the group commission plan with the exception that it is somewhat more complicated.

To overcome the disadvantages previously indicated in the salary and commission plans individually, various combinations have been made of the two basic plans, as outlined below.

Salary and Commission. Under the salary and commission plan a salesman usually is paid a small salary and a straight, or other type of, commission on net sales. This method has the merit of combining the advantages of control over the salesmen with the stimulation to increased sales afforded by the commission. The degree of stimulation or control may be regulated by adjusting the amount of salary and commission. The salesman is assured a regular income, paid for missionary work, and assisted during the breaking-in period and in times of depression.

The disadvantages of this plan are: the objections to the straight commission plan, such as:

1. Overselling, selling the items that are easiest to sell, and not coöperating with fellow salesmen, are still present.
2. The salesman who is content with a small salary will not try to increase his efforts to earn the extra commission.
3. The commission may mean little to salesmen in a period of depression.

The salary and commission method is used in the sale of many staple products with specialty characteristics which have a higher price than staples and keen competition. Also, when salesmen must do missionary work and at the same time need stimulation to increase sales, this method is effective. Many companies desiring some measure of control over salesmen are using this method. A few life insurance companies are trying out this method of compensating new agents.

Drawing Account and Commission. Closely related to the salary and commission plan, but leaning toward the commission, is the drawing account and commission compensation. The drawing account is an advance loan on a salesman's anticipated commissions, which is paid regularly each week like a straight salary. If a salesman fails to earn sufficient commissions to cover his drawing account, he is expected ultimately to reimburse his drawing account before receiving additional commission. For example, a salesman is paid a commission of 10 per cent and given a drawing account of $50 weekly. If his sales are only $300 the first week, his earned commissions are 10 per cent of $300, or $30. Nevertheless, he receives a compensation check for $50, the amount of his drawing account, and incurs a deficit of $20. If his sales are $700 the second week, he earns 10 per cent of $700, or $70, which covers his drawing account of $50 and replaces the deficit of $20 incurred the previous week. The salesman is now even with the house.

Unless a contract has been drawn between the employer and the salesman to provide for the reimbursement of the company for overdrawn drawing accounts, the salesman is only morally liable for his deficits, and in the event he leaves the company it is practically impossible to collect such deficits from the salesman.

1. *Advantages of a drawing account and commission plan:*
    a. The beginning salesman is relieved of financial worries during his breaking-in period.
    b. The drawing account enables the management to exercise some control over the activities of the salesman.
    c. It enables better selection of men.
    d. Maximum incentive is given through the commission.
2. *Disadvantages of a drawing account and commission:*
    a. Salesmen leave after incurring deficits on drawing accounts.
    b. They encourage indifference on the part of the salesmen.
    c. They put the salesman in the embarrassing position of a debtor to his employer.
    d. They do not give the control of a salary payment.
    e. They involve considerable bookkeeping.
    f. They create controversy and misunderstanding between management and salesmen.

To prevent deficits in drawing accounts the following methods are being used:

1. A maximum amount is set on drawing accounts to curb losses.

2. The amount of the drawing account is decreased weekly until, at the end of the tenth week, nothing is paid the salesmen except earned commissions.

3. Salesmen are required to sign notes, payable a year from date, for the amount of their drawing account.

4. A drawing account is paid only if certain tasks are performed, as: names of prospects handed in, daily reports of calls, demonstrations conducted, etc.

5. Salesmen are required to borrow money at their banks, and the employer endorses their notes.

6. Monthly or quarterly settlements are made with salesmen.

The drawing account and commission method is used generally with the straight commission plan in the sale of specialties, such as pianos, automobiles, securities, and office appliances. Dissatisfied with heavy losses on drawing accounts, many companies are resorting to small straight salaries plus commissions for beginning salesmen, or the payment of larger commissions, in lieu of drawing accounts.

Salary, Expenses, and Commission. This plan is another variation of the salary and commission plan with the exception that, in addition, the expenses of the salesmen are advanced by the management. In some cases the salary and expense allowance is later deducted from the total amount of commissions earned by the salesmen. In other companies the salary and expenses are paid outright to the salesmen, who are paid a small commission in addition on all of their net sales.

Where the expenses of the salesmen are considerable, as in traveling in a country territory, it is sometimes necessary for the management to defray the salesman's travel costs, to insure a thorough coverage of the territory.

Administering commission methods. In administering commission methods of paying salesmen, a commission reserve account is usually established. The purpose of a reserve account is to provide for reimbursement of the company in cases where commissions have been advanced to salesmen on unearned drawing accounts, uncollected accounts, and where purchases are returned by customers for credit. Such a reserve fund usually pays the salesman a legal rate of interest and is turned over to the man when he leaves the company. The amount of the fund varies with different employers.

The problem of dividing commissions among several salesmen participating in a sale arises in connection with the straight commission method. An arbitrary policy is usually established for dividing the commissions on a fifty-fifty basis, although other methods of division are practiced, such as a three-way split when three salesmen enter into the transaction.

Bonus Methods. A bonus is an amount paid as a reward for effort resulting in sales volume, profit, or reduced expenses beyond a certain predetermined amount. That is, if the management sets a sales volume goal or quota for a salesman at $10,000 a month, and he sells $15,000, he has exceeded his quota by $5,000, on which amount he receives a bonus of a predetermined percentage, say, 2 per cent, or $100, for his extra effort. Sometimes a bonus is based on the achievement of a certain percentage of the quota set. A bonus of a certain amount may be paid for passing 60 per cent of quota, an additional bonus for 70 per cent of quota, and so on.

Bonus methods are not a sole method of compensation; they are always used in conjunction with other types of compensation plans. A bonus is nothing more than an extra commission paid on net sales after a predetermined volume has been reached.

An important factor in a bonus plan is the quota, which may be expressed in dollars or units. A dollar quota may be more easily reached when the price level is rising than when prices are falling. If the prices of a commodity fluctuate widely, a dollar quota may not be satisfactory. A quota expressed in units will avoid price fluctuations.

Quotas are also established for various time periods such as:

1. Annual quotas, which are the most common and have the advantages of reducing the turnover of the organization by keeping salesmen for yearly periods and providing larger bonus payments, which may be invested by the salesmen.
2. Semiannual quotas, which place the incentive closer to the man and frequently provide greater stimulation.
3. Quarterly quotas, which provide still closer incentive and flexibility.
4. Monthly or weekly quotas, which require more accounting and do not provide so large a bonus as for longer periods.

A sound method of establishing the quota is vital to the success of a bonus plan. Unless the quotas are fairly set, the salesmen will either make their quotas without difficulty and the bonus will provide little incentive, or they will consider the quota impossible of attainment and make no efforts to reach it. Methods of establishing quotas are discussed in another chapter.

Types of bonuses. Bonuses are useful in stimulating salesmen to accomplish definite objectives in their work. There are several types of bonus plans, such as the following:

1. A bonus based on *volume of sales* has the advantage of securing volume for a plant with high overhead or excess capacity, but it may cause salesmen to ignore the higher-priced, high-profit items, and push the low-priced, low-profit, easily sold items. It is the most common bonus basis and is easy to apply.

2. A bonus based on *increased sales* has the advantage of stimulating salesmen to increase their sales volume over previous figures. A bonus percentage is set for attaining various percentage increases.

3. A bonus based on *individual product sales* is established for the purpose of pushing slow-moving or highly profitable products and introducing new items. It is paid to a salesman who has exceeded a certain predetermined volume of sales established for the product to be pushed.

4. A bonus based on *lower selling costs* is for the purpose of encouraging salesmen to reduce their traveling expenses. It has the disadvantage of automatically reducing sales activities and frequently sales volume. The bonus is paid for reducing expenses below a certain predetermined percentage of expense to sales volume.

5. A bonus based on *company profits* gives salesmen an opportunity to share in the profits of the company in proportion to their ability as measured by length of service, volume of sales, and other factors. The individual salesman's percentage is usually fixed by the management at the beginning of the year.

The advantages of a profit-sharing bonus are: the salesmen are actuated by the owner motive; they are profit-conscious rather than volume-conscious; turnover of salesmen is reduced; and a spirit of coöperation is developed.

The disadvantages of profit-sharing bonus plans are:

a. Profits made by the company are often not within the control of the salesman.

b. Few salesmen have any information about the financial structure of their company.

c. In periods of depression when there are no profits, salesmen will become dissatisfied with such a plan.

d. Suspicions may be aroused as to the fairness of the plan.

e. Such plans are often complicated to operate.

f. The poor salesmen will benefit from the work of the able men.

6. A bonus based on *branch sales* is given to all salesmen operating out of a branch, provided that a predetermined volume or profit is secured by the branch. Each salesman receives a certain predetermined share of the group bonus.

7. A bonus based on *sales activities* is paid for exceeding a predetermined number of interviews; dressing a certain number of windows; calling on a quota of new prospects; or selling a maximum number of new accounts.

A bonus plan may fall into one of two classifications—individual bonuses or group bonuses.

The individual bonus is paid to individual salesmen on the basis of their own achievement rather than the performance of the group. It is the most common type, and is an effective stimulant from the standpoint of the direct relation between the salesman's individual accomplishment and his own income. In the sale of consumer goods where one salesman contributes very little to the success of another, the individual bonus is most effective.

A group bonus is paid to individual salesmen on the basis of performance of all salesmen in the organization. The objective of this bonus is to encourage coöperativeness between salesmen and districts. It considers that perfect teamwork in selling is more important than maximum individual performance, and that there are many services expected from salesmen indirectly affecting their individual sales.

In the sale of industrial goods involving the joint efforts of salesmen in selling to architects, engineers, owners, and contractors often located in different territories, a group bonus is most effective.

On the other hand, a group bonus plan may cause the mediocre salesman to depend upon the good salesman to carry his bonus for him; and it may thwart the initiative of the abler men who realize that they cannot capitalize to the fullest extent upon their own abilities. In many organizations there are salesmen who lack ambition and energy to the extent that they work merely to hold their jobs. Such men would penalize the efficient man under a group bonus plan.

The advantages of bonus plans in general are:

1. To develop a spirit of coöperation.
2. To induce the performance of desirable sales activities.
3. To reduce the turnover of the sales organization.
4. To stimulate salesmen to increased activity.
5. To induce saving by salesmen.
6. To provide incentive without encouraging overselling.

The disadvantages of bonus plans in general are:

1. Quotas are unfair.
2. Involve complications so that frequently they are distrusted by salesmen.
3. Provide payments at end of year, leaving too long a time between payments, during which salesmen lose interest.
4. Provide a weak form of incentive.

Salary and bonus. The most common use of a bonus is in connection with a straight salary method of compensation. By this plan, salesmen are controlled and paid for missionary work through the medium of the salary and given an incentive through a bonus payment. The incentive is not so strong as with a commission on all sales, but neither is the salesman inclined so much to oversell or to strive for volume as when he is paid a commission. This plan is also easy to apply and administer, and is widely used in the payment of salesmen of industrial products who must do much missionary work and at the same time need an incentive to increase their sales. Likewise, salesmen for wholesalers and retailers who perform many nonselling duties are frequently paid bonuses in order to stimulate their sales.

Salary, bonus, and commission. In this plan there is one controlling factor, the salary, and two incentive factors, the bonus and commission. The bonus may be paid for specific sales activities, individual product sales, or group performance; while the commission may be paid for volume of net sales. In this way the efforts of the salesmen may be directed to definite tasks, and at the same time volume may be encouraged. If, however, both bonus and commission are paid for volume alone, little is gained by the double incentives, and a single bonus or higher commission would achieve the same results with fewer complications.

Point Systems. A point system is based on the payment of salesmen for the performance of specific sales tasks for which they are credited a certain number of points. A value is fixed for each point, for example, two cents, and the accumulation of two thousand points in one week would entitle a salesman to $40. The number of points is fixed for each task.

A typical point system provides credit for selling a desirable product of one point per dollar sale. Other credits are given as follows:

Easy-selling, advertised product	one point
Product offering double profit	two points
Product offering triple profit	three points
Products hard to sell	two points
Products with high repeat sales	two points
Products being closed out	two points

The schedule may also include credits for securing particularly desirable business and coöperating with the credit, advertising, and sales departments. Penalty points may also be assessed for complaints from customers, returned goods, and misrepresentation of facts.

A point system is applied by various methods. Some companies base the salesman's compensation entirely upon the points earned each week. Others pay for points in the form of a bonus in addition to a straight salary. The plan may also be used independently of compensation as a device for rating the activities of salesmen. The advantages of a point system are:

1. It provides a direct reward for a well-rounded selling job.
2. It maintains close control over the salesmen by management.
3. It is highly flexible and adaptable to any selling situation.
4. It serves as an inducement to desirable missionary work.

Certain disadvantages of this method are:

1. Salesmen question the application of the system.
2. Many details are involved in its administration.
3. There is an overemphasis on minor sales duties.
4. There is an incorrect evaluation of the point and penalty scores.

Salesmen's Security Plans. The growing interest in social security, hospitalization, accident and health, and retirement plans for workers is reflected in the adoption by progressive companies of security plans for their sales representatives.

The first over-all security plan for salesmen was announced by the Penn Mutual Life Insurance Company in 1945, covering more than a thousand agents and their dependents. This comprehensive plan provides:

1. Group life insurance.
2. Weekly accident and sickness benefits.
3. Hospitalization, including surgical and hospital expense.
4. Hospital expense benefits for dependents.

Agents who have completed one year or more of service and whose annual earnings are a thousand dollars or more are eligible to participate. Participating agents contribute to the cost in proportion to their annual commission earnings while the company pays a substantial part of the cost. For example, an agent earning from $4,000 to $5,000 in annual commissions, with dependents including wife and unmarried children, contributes $5.19 a month. He receives group life insurance protection in the amount of $4,000; weekly accident and sickness benefit of $40; daily hospital benefit $5 and dependents $4; maximum surgical fee reimbursement $150. No medical examination is required.

In announcing the plan, the president of the company stated,

This plan is an expression of the company's responsibility to its field force and of its appreciation of the important contribution which the sales organization has made to the development of the company. We believe it will help our men to become better salesmen.

The Penn Mutual Life Insurance Company initiated a retirement income plan for its full-time agents in 1941. This plan provides a retirement annuity beginning at the age of sixty-five for all representatives under the age of sixty-one who have been under contract for at least one year and earning $600 or more in commissions in the preceding year. Each man contributes 3 per cent of his commission earnings providing they are not less that $600 or more than $4,800 and the company contributes a like amount.

With the consent of the company, a man may retire between the ages of fifty-five and sixty-four, provided he has completed not less than fifteen years under the plan. In the event of a representative's death prior to the commencement of his retirement income, his beneficiary will receive an amount equal to his contributions with 3 per cent compound interest. If he leaves the service of the company before retirement, he receives the amount of his contributions without interest. If a man becomes disabled before retirement age, he may receive all contributions made by him and, in addition, 3 per cent compound interest, or a paid-up deferred annuity commencing at age sixty-five, purchased by his own and the company's contributions. For example, a salesman who begins contributions at the age of thirty and earns an average yearly income of $4,800 receives an annual retirement income payable in monthly portions, beginning at age sixty-five, of $1,763, or about $150 a month.

A similar retirement plan was started by the Equitable Life Insurance Company of Iowa in 1938 for its sales representatives. Agents whose total first-year premiums equal $1,000 and not less than $1,500 in subsequent years can qualify for the plan. An agent contributes 3 per cent of his total annual first-year and renewal commission income, and the company contributes an equal amount, giving the man the benefit of total contributions of 6 per cent of his earnings. The retirement age is sixty-five years. An agent contributing to the plan twenty years and earning an average of $5,000 annually during that period may expect to receive at the age of sixty-five a retirement income of $68.10 a month for life.

Prevailing Compensation Plans. An analysis of salesmen's compensation plans of one hundred and eighty-three small- and medium-sized Pacific Coast concerns, by the Sales Manager's Bureau of the Los Angeles Chamber of Commerce, showed that 100 paid straight salaries; 78 paid commission, of which 67 advanced drawing accounts regularly, 3 occasionally, and 8 gave no drawing accounts whatever. Five firms used a profit-sharing plan.

An analysis by the American Management Association of 177 salesmen's payment plans of large companies showed straight salary, 34; straight commission, 55; salary and commission, 30; salary and bonus, 46; and commission and bonus, 12.

Problem 1—Group Bonus Compensation

The Galeton Instrument Company

The Galeton Instrument Company, established at Providence, Rhode Island, in 1902, manufactures electrical measuring instruments, pyrometers, and automatic combustion control systems serving forty industries. The company maintains four branches in the principal industrial centers, from which travel forty-nine sales engineers who analyze needs of industrial concerns for instruments and prepare recommendations based on these surveys.

Since its establishment the company has paid its sales engineers straight salaries ranging from $5,500 to $1,200 annually, plus expenses. The increasing expense ratio of the company has, however, caused the management to consider a plan for reducing salesmen's expenses.

The sales manager suggests that the salesmen be given an annual group bonus to be effected by a reduction of sales expenses. Under this plan the sales department would be allowed a maximum expense of 20 per cent of annual net sales, and if actual sales expense amounted to only 16 per cent, the remaining 4 per cent would be divided equally between the sales bonus fund and company profits. At the beginning of the fiscal year, this group bonus fund would be estimated and proportioned individually on a percentage basis among those salesmen who have had at least two years' service. The individual portions would be determined by the sales executives, who would be guided, not only by individual sales volume, but by the judgment, coöperativeness, experience, length of service, and executive ability of the individual salesman.

The general manager of the company, however, favored another plan, a group bonus, which would be determined not on the basis of expenses but company profits. This plan would give the salesmen, not only a salary as before, but also an opportunity to participate in the profits earned by the company instead of sharing in possible reductions in sales expense as in the former plan.

After all tax and dividend obligations were met, inclusive of a 6 per cent common stock dividend, the remaining profits would be divided between the common stock and a main sales bonus fund. The sales bonus fund would be distributed on a percentage basis among the individual members of the sales force, as the previous bonus fund would be distributed, at the beginning of the fiscal year when probable sales volume and anticipated profits for the year are estimated. The bonus fund would be likewise proportioned, as in the previous plan, among the individual members of the sales force with an appraisal by the sales executives of the value of each individual to the company.

The forty-nine salesmen compensated by the plan would be informed by monthly profit and loss statements how their annual bonus prospects were developing. When profits under this plan corresponded to a 12 per cent common dividend, a high-grade senior salesman would receive, as his share of the sales bonus, an amount equal to about 50 per cent of his total annual salary. Individual shares of the sales bonus might range from zero during a depression to 100 per cent of salaries during periods of prosperity.

The chief advantage of this method, according to the general manager of the company, is the superiority of the group sales bonus divided annually among the salesmen on the basis of intangible services, as well as volume of sales. Since many services indirectly affecting individual sales are expected from the salesmen, and team work is considered more important than maximum individual performance by the company, the group bonus is preferred to individual incentives.

Questions

1. Should the company adopt the group bonus based on reducing expenses? Give reasons for your decision.

2. Should the company adopt the group bonus based on company profits? Justify your answer.

3. Should the company base a bonus on direct, individual accomplishment rather than group effort?

4. Is the method of determining the percentage of the bonus fund sound? Give reasons for your conclusion.

5. Should the company adopt an entirely different method of paying salesmen than that suggested in this case?

6. If a bonus plan should be adopted, when should the bonus be paid?

Problem 2—Plan for Stabilizing Salesmen's Compensation

Ruxton Electrical Manufacturing Company

The Ruxton Electrical Manufacturing Company, established in Buffalo, New York, in 1917, manufactures a wide line of electrical equipment for intercommunicating purposes, telephones, loud speakers, and radio receiving sets. The radio sets are nationally advertised. The company has for many years paid its thirty salesmen on a straight salary basis ranging from $60 to $80 weekly. They sell direct to large industrial concerns and electrical wholesalers for distribution to the retail trade.

The company was faced with growing competition and sought a method of stimulating its salesmen and at the same time stabilizing their earnings so that they would not fluctuate widely in good times and depressions. The company had experienced trouble in the past in adjusting the salesmen's salaries consistent with their performance and hoped to find some way to overcome this difficulty.

The sales manager of the company proposed the following new plan of compensation. The salesmen and line sales executives of the organization would actually set their own basic salaries. Uniform annual quotas would be set by the management on:

1. Sales volume.
2. Desired profit on sales.
3. Maximum selling expense.

If the salesmen and executives succeeded in reaching 100 per cent of their quotas, they would be entitled to a basic salary set by the management of $60 weekly in the case of salesmen, and variable in the case of executives. If the salesmen or executives fell short of their quotas, their compensation would be reduced accordingly.

In determining the salesmen's compensation on the basis of profit-and-sales expense, as well as volume of sales, the management maintained that salesmen's compensation should not be based on volume alone because a salesman can easily increase his volume of sales by selling the lower profit, easy-to-sell commodities in the line. Accordingly, in determining the salary which the salesmen should earn according to actual performance, ability to sell in volume was rated at only 40 per cent of the basic salary rate.

The company also considered the profit on sales a very important factor in determining the compensation of its salesmen, and accordingly rated it 30 per cent of the basic salary objective. Salesmen would have to sell merchandise which carried at least a 20 per cent profit if they wished the sale to be included in their compensation. Each salesman was to be given a list showing the approximate profit on each class of merchandise in the line.

With generally increasing costs of traveling salesmen, the company based the earnings of its salesmen on a consideration of their ability to sell at low expense. From its past experience the company considered that younger salesmen, particularly, were inclined to ignore the item of expense, whereas the older salesmen saved on expense. Under the new plan the extravagant salesmen would be penalized by receiving a lower salary, while the savers would benefit from their ability to economize by receiving a higher salary rate. The amount of the salesman's expense quota would be $3\frac{1}{2}$ per cent of net sales, which would be rated as 30 per cent of his basic salary in computing his earned salary.

Each salesman's weekly salary would be determined at the close of each year for the succeeding year by measuring the salesman's performance on volume, profit, and expense for the closing year against his quota on each of these three factors. In determining each salesman's salary for the succeeding year, his volume for the year closed would be weighted at 40 per cent; his profit on sales, 30 per cent; and his sales expense, 30 per cent of the salesman's basic salary quota of $60 a week.

A typical case of how Ruxton salesmen would set their own salaries illustrates the method of compensation. At the close of 1945 a salesman's weekly salary rate for 1946 is determined by comparing his showing on volume, profit, and expense for 1945 with the standard quota for these factors.

The salesman sells a total volume of $70,000 during 1945. The average profit on his sales for 1938 was 25 per cent. His 1945 expense amounted to $3,500.

To arrive at this salesman's weekly salary rate for 1946 his ability to sell in volume in 1945 is compared with the annual volume quota set by the management, or $100,000. Since his total 1945 sales were $70,000 and his volume quota was $100,000, obviously he made 70 per cent of his volume quota in 1945. As sales volume would be valued by the company at 40 per cent in computing the weekly salary of the salesman for 1946, his volume value will be 70 per cent of the 40 per cent par value factor, or 28 per cent.

Next, the salesman's ability to sell at a profit during 1945 as compared with his profit quota of 20 per cent is considered. Since his 1945 average profit on sales was 25 per cent compared with his profit quota of 20 per cent, his ability to sell at a profit during 1945 was 125 per cent of his profit quota. Accordingly, his profit value for 1945 will be 125 per cent of the 30 per cent profit value factor, or 37.5 per cent.

Now the salesman's ability to sell at low expense during 1945 as compared with his expense quota of 3½ per cent is considered. As his 1945 sales expense was $3,500, and his expense quota was $2,450, or 3½ per cent of his net sales of $70,000, his expense value will be $2,450 divided by $3,500, or 70 per cent of the 30 per cent par value factor, or 21 per cent.

Adding the value of the salesman's services during 1945, which amounted to 28 per cent for volume, 21 per cent for expense, and 37.5 per cent for profit, the total worth of the 1945 activities of the man amounts to about 86 per cent. As the salesman's par weekly salary rate set by the management is $60, and his value for 1945 equalled 86 per cent, his salary rate to be paid him weekly during 1946 will be 86 per cent of $60, or $51.90. Beginning January 1, 1946, the salesman will be paid $51.90 weekly for the 52 weeks in the year. Then at the close of 1946, his salary for the succeeding year will be calculated again on the basis of his 1946 showing on volume, profit, and expense.

However, it might happen that the salesman may make such a good record during 1946, exceeding his volume, profit, and expense quotas, that he will be worth more than the $51.90 weekly wage set on January 1, 1946, and paid him weekly throughout the year. Accordingly, at the close of 1946 when the salesman's ability for the past year 1946 is measured, it may be found, for example, that the salesman's 1946 activities were 96 per cent of quota, or 10 per cent more than the 86 per cent of 1945 quota on which his salary of $51.90 weekly received during 1946 was set. Therefore, his earnings of 10 per cent, averaging $5.19 in excess of his 1946 basic weekly salary of $51.90, are paid him in a lump sum or bonus amounting to $266.24 about March 1, 1947.

The salesmen of the organization would not be permitted to earn a bonus of more than 20 per cent above their weekly salaries set on the first of each year. Accordingly, salesmen's incomes would never be excessive and would be stabilized when periods of depression came.

If the 20 per cent added to the annual weekly salary rate of the salesman does not equal the basic salary quota of $60 a week, the salesman would be allowed to earn up to the $60-a-week quota. If, for example, a salesman received a weekly salary of $45, the limitation of 20 per cent maximum bonus would restrict his earnings to average $54 a week. However, with the maximum set at $60 a week, the salesman's extra earnings or bonus may average up to that amount weekly.

The policy of limiting the bonus or extra earnings of the salesmen to 20 per cent, in addition to their basic weekly salaries, would stabilize the salesmen's incomes and prevent the violent fluctuations or inequalities which occurred when the income of the salesmen was not limited by the management.

New salesmen in the company would start at an arbitrary weekly salary rate as low as $35, and if they made progress at the end of their first year, might earn as much as $60 a week. At the end of his first year, a new weekly salary rate would be established by the salesman, and any earnings which he may have made above his old weekly rate are paid him in a lump sum.

In exceptional cases, salesmen of extraordinary ability might earn a salary rate in excess of the weekly basic salary quota of $60, plus earnings up to 20 per cent above that amount. However, as the salesman's salary rate advanced, owing to his ability to sell in high volume at good profit and with minimum sales expense, it naturally would become more difficult for him to earn additional compensation; whereas a new salesman receiving a small weekly salary would soon, if he had ability, earn up to the maximum.

· To participate in extra earnings in excess of their weekly salaries, sales representatives would be required to remain in the employment of the company for an entire calendar year. Statements of earnings would be mailed salesmen monthly.

Questions

1. Should the company have adopted the plan prepared by the sales manager? Give reasons for your decision.

2. If you consider another plan of compensating salesmen superior to the one suggested, outline such a plan in detail.

Problem 3—Paying Specialty Salesmen

Allen-Johnson Motor Sales Company

The Allen-Johnson Motor Sales Company, established at Baltimore, Maryland, in 1909, is a wholesale distributor that sells at retail the eight-

and twelve-cylinder passenger cars made by a large Detroit automobile manufacturer. The cars retail in excess of $2,000. The company employs twenty salesmen, who are paid a straight commission of 6 per cent of the net sales value of the car and receive drawing accounts of $75 a week, which are applied against their commissions.

A commission reserve of 10 per cent of the total commissions earned by the salesmen is maintained by the company for the purpose of protecting it against the cancellation of orders by customers, poor credits, and overdrafts by salesmen. When the fund has been built up to several hundred dollars, each salesman is paid his full commissions. The salesmen are paid interest on the reserve while it is in the possession of the company.

The company salesmen sell both new and used cars. The average earnings of salesmen are approximately $6,000 yearly, and the best earnings in good times are from $10,000 to $12,000.

Upon reviewing the drawing account status of the salesmen, the sales manager found that ten of the twenty men were not earning their drawing accounts. These ten men make an average earning of $50 a week or less. Six of these salesmen were in arrears as much as $3,000, and others in lesser amounts. Eight men earn an average drawing account of $75 a week.

The sales manager decided that losses on drawing accounts must stop and gave the salesmen in arrears the following notice:

I have decided to handle the drawing accounts of our salesmen with debit balances on a new basis. I propose to set the old accounts aside temporarily and treat the old debit balance as a separate proposition until further notice. Beginning the first of next month, I will start a new account for you. Any commissions that you make in excess of your drawing account will be credited, half to your new drawing account and half against your old debit balance. This will give you an opportunity to receive something extra, and you can take care of your debit balance gradually. However, from now on you will have to make your drawing account or we will not be justified in sending it to you. We are giving you three weeks' notice.

We will send your regular drawing account for the next three weeks. On the fourth week we will determine whether you have done enough business to entitle you to your drawing account. If the amount of your commissions is less than your drawing account, we will send only the amount of your commissions. From then on we will send you weekly only the commissions earned by you for that week.

Questions

1. Was the sales manager's solution to the drawing account deficits sound? Give reasons for your opinion.

2. Should the company have adopted another method of paying its salesmen? Explain in detail.

3. If you consider that the sales manager should have adopted another method of handling the drawing account deficits, explain such a method.

Problem 4—Salary-Bonus-Commission Plan

The Carson Chemical Company

The Carson Chemical Company, established at Pittsburgh, Pennsylvania, in 1906, with a capital of $350,000, manufactures and distributes through forty salesmen a line of druggists' products prescribed by the medical and dental professions and sold by the drug trade. Included in the line are laxatives, ointments, tooth paste, and similar products, several of which are heavily advertised in national magazines and radio broadcasts.

Sixty per cent of the company's sales are through drug wholesalers. Salesmen spend 35 per cent of their time selling, and the balance is spent in missionary work with the dental and medical professions and drug trade.

Salesmen are paid a basic salary, which ranges from $1,800 to $4,000 a year, depending on the salesman's length of service with the company and his selling ability. In addition to this salary, all of the expenses of the salesmen are paid by the company. Salary and expense payments are carried separately, the salary is paid on the fifteenth and thirtieth of the month. Expenses are settled separately on the same dates.

In addition to a basic salary, salesmen are paid a bonus and commission. A bonus is paid every three months and is based on quotas established for each of the products sold and for each of the twelve sales districts in the country. District quota figures are then subdivided into product quotas for each of the states in a district. These individual product quotas are determined by considering past sales, potential sales, and the judgment of the sales executives.

A bonus is paid quarterly for all sales of each product over quota, with a deduction of a like amount on all sales under quota. The amount of the bonus varies with the product, just as the amount of the quota varies with the product. For example, the steadiest selling product in line *A* carries a bonus at the rate of 2 per cent on all sales over quota, with a deduction of 2 per cent on all sales under quota. If the quarterly quota of a salesman in Idaho on product *A* is $6,000, and the salesman sells $7,000 worth of the item, he receives a bonus of 2 per cent on $1,000, or $20 for the quarter. However, if the salesman sold only $5,000 worth of product *A*, he would be charged with 2 per cent of $1,000, or $20 deduction from bonus.

On some items which are in a development stage, the company pays a bonus of 2 per cent on all sales over quota, without any loss to the salesman for bonus deduction for sales under quota as on old items.

In addition to the quarterly bonus paid on the sale of individual items, as explained previously, the company pays a quarterly commission on certain items. For example, on product B, the fastest selling item in the line, and the one which the company desires to develop, a straight commission of 1 per cent is paid on all sales irrespective of quota, and a bonus of $2\frac{1}{2}$ per cent is paid on all sales over quota, with a deduction of only $1\frac{1}{4}$ per cent for all sales short of quota. If the quarterly quota of a salesman in Idaho on product B is $10,000, and he sells $12,000 worth, he receives a commission of 1 per cent, or $120, plus a bonus of $2\frac{1}{2}$ per cent on $2,000 sales over quota, or $50, making total earnings of $170 in addition to his regular salary.

On slow-moving items, the company pays a straight commission of 2 per cent of sales and no bonus.

While this plan has been operating several years, a decline in business conditions has reduced sharply the earnings of the salesmen, several of whom object to the penalty features of the payment plan. The management, however, believes that commissions and bonuses are so liberal in combination with the straight salary paid the salesmen that there should be no objection on the part of the salesmen to deductions for failure to make quotas.

In view of this criticism of the compensation plan, the management has agreed to review the plan and consider desirable changes.

Questions

1. Should the company continue with the plan as now operating? Give reasons for your decision.

2. Should the plan be amended in any way? Describe what changes you would make, if any.

3. If you think the plan should be abolished, what plan of payment would you use?

Reading References

American Management Association, "Compensation of Industrial Salesmen," by C. R. Cary, Industrial Marketing Series No. 7, 1930.
Directing Sales, Bonney, Chap. VI.
Handbook of Sales Management, Hall, Sec. XI.
Intensive Sales Management, Aspley, Chap. V.
Management of the Sales Organization, Russell, Chap. VI.
Modern Sales Management, Frederick, Chap. XIII.
Principles of Personal Selling, Tosdal, Chap. XX.
Printer's Ink Weekly, "How Should We Pay Our Salesmen?" a series, by C. K. Woodbridge, Aug. 7, 1930, p. 3; Aug. 14, 1930, p. 81; Aug. 21, 1930, p. 50; Aug. 28, 1930, p. 103.

Sales Administration, Hayward, Chap. XIX.
Sales Management Fundamentals, Hay, pp. 118–131.
Sales Management Magazine, "300 Compensation Plans for Salesmen and How They Work," Jan. 19, 1929, p. 125.
Sales Management Today, Doubman, Chap. IX.
Salesmen in Marketing Strategy, Lyon, Chap. XI, pp. 309–323.
Scientific Sales Management Today, Hoyt, Chap. XIII.

CHAPTER TWELVE

STIMULATING SALESMEN

Why Stimulate Salesmen?   Salesmen are continuously subjected to severe mental pressure, the sales resistance of buyers, and the opposition of aggressive competitors.   Disappointments are often keen.   Refusals are many times more numerous than orders. Salesmen are frequently far removed from the assistance and advice of their employers.   The physical demands of selling are great —long hours spent walking and talking to antagonistic or noncommittal prospects are wearing on the nerves and physique.   The combined mental and physical strain of selling demands the constant stimulation of salesmen if a high measure of efficiency is to be attained.

One of the greatest problems of sales executives is the human relations problem.   The salesman whose wife is seriously ill usually suffers a serious relapse in sales volume; an unwanted mother-in-law may ruin not only a salesman's home life, but his sales performance; and an overdrawn bank account may cause more worry to a salesman than an aggressive competitor.   Coping with these personal difficulties calls for a keen understanding of human nature, tact, and initiative on the part of sales executives.

Usually of an emotional nature, a salesman requires sincere encouragement, inspiration, and coöperation.   A spirit of friendly, hustling coöperation must pervade the organization.   Loyalty of all men on the force must be developed.   Pride in the company and its progress should be encouraged.   To accomplish these objectives, a sales manager must have a definite plan of stimulation.

In the past, many sales executives have often relied entirely upon stimulating measures to obtain sales volume.   However, the pepletter-type of sales executive has been largely replaced by the sales manager who recognizes that motivation is an important, but not the sole, method of increasing sales and profits.   Sales contests and conventions are no substitute for sound training, and enthusiastic platitudes can never take the place of a good product, properly priced, as a tool for building sales volume.

How to Stimulate Salesmen. There are numerous methods of stimulating salesmen, some of which are:

1. Compensation plans.
2. Sales contests.
3. Sales conventions.
4. Salesmen's magazines and bulletins.
5. Individual correspondence with salesmen.
6. Personal conferences with salesmen.
7. Promotions.

Compensation for Stimulation. Various compensation plans to stimulate sales have been discussed in detail in the preceding chapter. A compensation plan is often one of the strongest incentives to salesmen because it gives a desirable and tangible reward for accomplishment. Several compensation devices which may be very effective stimulants, are commissions, bonuses, profit-sharing plans, point systems, and combinations of these methods.

Sales Contests. While some salesmen respond to compensation incentives, other salesmen are motivated more effectively by other types of stimulation, for example, as contests. Sales competitions are often effective because they have a strong appeal to the competitive instinct, which is particularly marked in salesmen, and the play instinct, which may cause a man to prefer walking miles around a golf course to mowing his lawn.

Objectives of contests. Sales contests have various objectives, some of which are:

1. To maintain sales volume in slack times.
2. To bring salesmen out of mental depression.
3. To stimulate sales of a particular product or line.
4. To stimulate coöperation between salesmen.
5. To relieve the monotony of routine selling.
6. To secure the coöperation of wives of salesmen.
7. To develop company spirit, group consciousness.
8. To create rivalry between salesmen and between branches.
9. To introduce new products.
10. To secure new customers.
11. To sell large accounts.
12. To increase percentage of exchanges.
13. To improve collections.

Objections to Contests. Several disadvantages arise in connection with sales contests. The most common of these are:

1. Salesmen create ill will by overselling.
2. Interest subsides and sales decline after a contest.
3. Contests create jealousy and antagonism between salesmen.
4. Salesmen may withhold orders preceding a contest.
5. Salesmen resort to "charity" appeals to win.
6. Salesmen who lose are disappointed, and the morale of the force suffers.
7. Men do not always have equal opportunity; handicapping is difficult.
8. Contests are only a temporary stimulant.
9. They encourage sales of volume, low-price, and low-profit items.
10. Contests do not improve the character of salesmen.
11. Missionary sales activities are neglected.
12. Older salesmen consider contests childish.

Types of Sales Contests. To arouse the interest of salesmen by appealing to their competitive and play instincts, a contest is usually built around a group competitive sport, such as baseball and football, and air, boat, automobile, and bicycle races.

A large appliance manufacturer staged a salesmen's football contest with a series of three games running from October 6 to December 27, with competition between seven sales districts and fifty-four regions. Each region constituted a conference, and each district represented a team.

A large rubber company staged a similar football contest with salesmen organized into two teams, which elected their own captains and sold toward predetermined quotas.

A golf game was played by the three thousand salesmen of a large office equipment company. One hundred per cent of quota meant eighteen holes, which made par for each hole 5½ per cent of each man's monthly quota. After finishing the eighteen holes, those salesmen making 100 per cent of quota moved to the driving green, where they matched sales qualifying for special prizes. Salesmen were given such instructions as: "No caddies allowed, carry your own bag"; or "Beware of water and bunkers on the fairways."

Air races are a popular theme for salesmen's contests. One company operated a transcontinental air derby for a three-month period. A company airplane was sent to the territories of salesmen who were winners in the contest.

A poker game contest was run by a typewriter manufacturing company. A separate deck of playing cards was maintained for each salesman. When a sale was made, cards were drawn from the salesman's deck at the home office and mailed to him. The sixth and subsequent cards drawn from the deck were redeemed by the company at the end of the contest at the rate of two dollars per card. Extra cards were issued for each twenty-five demonstrations. At the end of the three-month period, salesmen made up their best poker hand of five cards and returned it to the company to compete for merchandise prizes.

Prosperity contests. Contest themes are also based on "prosperity" or "good times." One corporation operated a "War on Hard Times" contest, dividing the salesmen into two armies, officered by salesmen with such titles as "General Depression" and "Colonel Can't." A contest publication was used to promote interest in the affair.

An office equipment corporation staged a "Put Men to Work" sales campaign, publishing pictures of men put to work each week and awarding "Scrolls of Accomplishment" to quota-breaking salesmen.

An adding machine company ran a "Prosperity" sales contest for a twelve-weeks' period, setting a certain number of points for each product sold and awarding merchandise prizes to all salesmen exceeding a quota.

Military subjects. War games are popular contest subjects. A large utility company staged a war to capture "Fort de la Quota" and to sell an increased volume of electric ranges. Five divisions of the company were divided into the Army, Navy, Marine Corps, Air Service, and Coast Guard. A large fort was constructed of wallboard. Superimposed over the surface was a coating of thin, individual wooden blocks resembling armor plate. Salesmen were permitted to take shots at the fort for each range sold by removing one of the blocks. Before the contest closed, all of the blocks had been removed, revealing a picture of destruction.

A life insurance company staged a contest attack on "Chateau Lacy," named in honor of one of the executives of the company. Agents were divided into three attacking companies under the direction of a captain. The chateau was surrounded by a series of three trenches, sections of which were assigned to each man. As the trenches were captured, they were blocked in with colored chalk on a large illustrative map of the battlefield in the agency office.

Apparel contests. Sales contests involving wearing apparel have been widely used. A "Straw Hat" contest, in which the prizes are straw hats awarded to salesmen who reach quotas, is a popular springtime sales stimulator. The refrigerator division of an electric appliance company staged a "Necktie Party" contest. Four colors of neckties were used to indicate the salesman's progress in the contest. All salesmen wore black neckties until two refrigerators were sold, green neckties until five refrigerators were sold, and blue neckties until nine refrigerators were sold. When a salesman's quota was reached, he was presented with a gold necktie.

A progressive life insurance agency staged a "Nudist" contest. Posted around the salesmen's room were cardboard manikins of each man, the head of which bore an actual photograph of the agent it represented. As each man produced business, he was presented with pieces of paper clothing to be pasted on the manikin so that the manikin would be completely dressed at the end of the contest. The agency staged a nudist banquet at the end of the contest. The men were dressed just as their manikins were clothed at the end of the campaign.

Hunting contests. There are numerous types of "Hunting" sales contests, including treasure hunts, wild game hunts, and gold rushes. The Studebaker Corporation, Frigidaire Corporation, and Chevrolet Motor Company have used this type of contest successfully with retail salesmen. Salesmen are divided into district camps, such as "El Dorado Camp," "Klondike Camp," and "Bonanza Camp," for a gold rush, and each one has a "claim" to work.

Building construction contests. Competitions which relate to the construction of new buildings tie up the building of sales by salesmen with the physical construction of the company. The National Cash Register Company conducted a "New Building" contest coincident with the erection of a new administration building. This contest was followed immediately by a "New Building Equipment" contest, which compared the inspirational equipment of salesmen with the furnishing of the new building.

Another company related an addition to its factory with a sales contest. The country was divided into six sales districts, and each district was assigned a pyramid of bricks. Every dollar's worth of business counted as one brick. Each salesman was sent a supply of paper bricks to be attached to each order.

The choice of contest subjects depends upon the timeliness of the theme. The type of salesmen in the organization may have an effect upon the theme selected. A force of older, serious-minded salesmen would not react to a nudist contest like a group of youngsters. The type of product sold may determine the contest subject. Sales of high-priced products may not occur frequently enough to make a race contest interesting.

Promoting sales contests. To be effective, contests must be dramatized and promoted to the sales force to arouse interest in the competition. Numerous devices have been used for stimulating the enthusiasm of salesmen in contests, for example, bulletins, letters, novelties, score boards, salesmen's magazines, and sales meetings.

When an electric refrigerator company staged a circus sales contest among seventeen thousand retail salesmen, an elaborate promotion plan was devised. Writers were sent to interview circus stars and executives to get colorful material. The contest was announced before a convention of distributors with a brass band, circus tent, posters, ticket takers, and ballyhoo men to create a circus atmosphere.

Individual distributors took the circus atmosphere to their territories. One erected a large circus tent, hired a circus band, dressed it in red, yellow, and blue uniforms, and assembled in the tent two hundred and sixty salesmen, who listened to sales supervisors dressed as barkers present the circus contest. Another distributor staged a circus parade through the streets of his city to open the contest. Another hired a hotel ballroom, erected a tent, and brought in circus actors to perform for salesmen.

An elaborate weekly mail campaign to salesmen followed, with such pieces as a large circus poster announcement, colorful illustrated circus letterheads carrying stimulating letters, a prize portfolio, a souvenir program, a trick die-cut mailing piece, a real souvenir elephant book, and a special house organ called *The Barker*.

A large business machine manufacturer employs an extensive promotion campaign in connection with each of its sales contests. The company's salesmen's publication is the basis of contest promotion. This is mailed frequently to salesmen and posted in sales offices. Special letterheads are designed for each contest. Upon this stationery, letters are written to individual salesmen, over the sales manager's signature, encouraging them to greater efforts. On intercompany stationery, letters are written to district sales managers, giving them instructions for stimulating their salesmen. These include an opening talk by the manager, display of contest material, inspirational talk, special prizes, and quota cards.

Special letters on the contest are sent to all office men and servicemen employed in the various branch offices of the company, urging them to aid salesmen in their office to win the contest.

Letters are written by the sales manager to the wives of all salesmen, urging them to encourage their husbands to win the contest. An elaborate book of merchandise prizes is sent to salesmen's wives.

A large central scoreboard is a feature of most sales contests. In the general sales manager's office of an equipment company is a large scoreboard upon which are posted the report cards sent in by salesmen who succeed in reaching their quotas. Cards of various colors are used to signify certain standards of accomplishment.

In a sharpshooter sales contest, an automobile manufacturer furnished dealers with large targets, on the circles of which appeared the number of points established for salesmen's quotas. Salesmen placed sharp-pointed metal arrows at the various scores shown on the target to indicate their progress.

Other contest promotional devices employed are: published photographs of the leaders, reproductions of telegrams and letters from winning salesmen, publication of lists of salesmen giving their comparative standings, and illustrations of prizes. This material is often produced by the sales promotion or advertising department, or an outside organization specializing in the development of sales contests may be retained to plan and promote a contest.

Final promotion is an important part of contest operation. A meeting for awarding prizes to the winners is often arranged; the names and pictures of winners are published in the company magazine; publicity is sent to local newspapers in the territories where the successful salesmen are located; and personal letters are written to the winners by the president of the company.

Contest awards. The five principal types of prizes awarded to winners of sales contests are: (1) money, (2) merchandise, (3) combination cash and merchandise, (4) honor, (5) vacations.

1. *Money prizes* offer several advantages: they are universally desirable and easy to award, and represent the most tangible value. However, they are transient. A large maker of business machines uses cash prizes in numerous sales contests. In one contest salesmen on winning teams who achieved 150 per cent of quota received

$45; those who made 125 per cent of quota received $35; while members of losing teams received $35 for 150 per cent of quota and $25 for 125 per cent of quota.

In a football contest, a pharmaceutical house awarded salesmen cash prizes totaling $8,190, comprising 457 individual awards. This company sets a maximum of $200 and a minimum of $10 for its sales contest prizes.

A variation of money prizes is the awarding of listed common stocks of national concerns, such as General Motors and Pennsylvania Railroad. Such prizes encourage salesmen to save.

2. *Merchandise prizes* have the advantage of interesting a salesman's wife and other members of his family; of frequently appearing larger in value than cash; and of serving as a constant reminder of achievement. Another advantage is that these prizes may be bought in quantities at wholesale prices.

An analysis of merchandise prizes given in many sales contests of a large sales organization shows the following preference: prizes useful to men, 76; prizes for women, 90; prizes to be used in the home, 251; prizes for children, 10; prizes for outdoor or camp use, 13; and prizes for the automobile, 9.

Large users of merchandise sales contest prizes usually publish a catalog of the prizes offered. One business equipment maker published a prize catalog of forty-seven pages, listing more than two hundred pieces of merchandise—from a sailboat to a toy electric train. These prizes were offered for achieving 110 per cent, 125 per cent, 150 per cent, 175 per cent, 200 per cent, or better, of a four-months' quota.

Distributors of premium merchandise provide sales organizations with catalogs at cost and cuts of merchandise, and handle the shipping of prizes direct to winning salesmen, relieving the employer of the necessity of stocking prize merchandise.

A large Chicago packer staged a canned meat sales contest for its branch house employees and salesmen, offering $5,000 in prizes, including a sedan, electric refrigerator, radios, outboard motor, and hundreds of smaller prizes for men and women.

A large cash register company ran a four-months' contest for junior salesmen, offering a set of golf clubs as the grand prize in the contest. It also conducted a personal progress sales contest offering merchandise prizes such as davenports, lounging chairs, desks, lamps, clocks, golf clubs, and silverware.

3. *Combination cash and merchandise awards* are made by many

companies. By the use of both types of awards, the desires of salesmen for either type of prize are satisfied, and the interest of the family of the salesman is stimulated.

4. *An honor award* for winning a sales contest is often a greater incentive than money or merchandise. The fundamental emotion of pride in achievement is strong in most salesmen, who will strive for recognition more than they will for compensation. Honor awards are usually in the form of a physical emblem, such as a watch, cup, plaque, banner, certificate, medal, ring, pin, or button.

A penalty for failure may be as effective in spurring salesmen to greater effort as a reward for achievement. A general agency of a large life insurance company awarded an ash tray in the form of a nymph to the agent who made the best showing each month, and a miniature figure of a white goat to the agent who reported the smallest sales. Agents were required to keep these awards on their desks for a thirty-day period.

The president of a large food manufacturing company annually awards a golden trophy to the winning sales district in each division in an annual "president's" sales contest. Merchandise prizes are also awarded to winning salesmen.

A refrigerator manufacturer awarded a "vice-president's" trophy of a football player poised on a pedestal to each of the eleven highest ranking salesmen in a "football' contest. The high men in each region received football ash trays, and fourteen hundred men who made their quotas received bronze pocket pieces.

Outstanding salesmen of a printing corporation are awarded lapel buttons signifying each year's attainment, in addition to being given watches engraved with data concerning their accomplishments.

Membership in an honorary organization gives further recognition to able salesmen. A large life insurance company has organized for outstanding salesmen a club named after the president of the company. Another company maintains a "Hundred Point Club" for salesmen who have secured 100 per cent of their annual quotas. Salesmen have been elected to this club as many as twenty times for achievement for as many years.

5. *Vacation awards* in the form of a trip to the home office or a sales convention are often an ideal reward for salesmen who rarely have an opportunity to get away from their home territories. One business machines company staged a "gangplank" contest for salesmen to qualify for a trip to Europe. A large Chicago packer gave sixteen free trips to Chicago to the salesmen selling the most canned

meats during a thirty-day period. Another company rewards salesmen who exceed 100 per cent of their quotas by giving them a trip,
with all expenses paid, to the home office.

Duration of contests. The length of a sales contest is an important factor in its success. Enthusiasm cannot be maintained continuously at high pitch; salesmen who are unsuccessful soon lose
interest, and competition eventually loses its novelty even to winners. The average contest runs for a period of from thirty to ninety
days, although a contest to build a gradual increase in sales may
extend over a longer period.

A food specialty manufacturer has a "president's" annual sales
contest which lasts four months during the fall and involves the sale
of a long list of products, a large sales organization, and a national
market. It would not be practical to run a shorter contest effectively in this case.

A pharmaceutical manufacturer runs two sales contests a year:
one, which lasts six weeks, in the spring; and one, which lasts
eight weeks, in the fall. The company has found that enthusiasm
cannot be maintained as long in the spring as in the fall.

A leading maker of office equipment runs a series of sales contests
for varying periods of time. While a four-months' merchandise
prize contest is being conducted, a special cash prize contest may be
in progress as well as an annual convention trip contest.

Contests are usually run for specific products in the active business months of the spring and fall, or in active selling seasons.

Scoring of contests. To be successful, sales contests must be arranged so that every salesman may have a fair chance to win something. The conditions must be equitable. To set unattainable
goals is the surest way to kill the value of a contest. Handicaps
must be used, if necessary, to equalize opportunity.

There are three common bases for scoring contests:

1. *Volume of production* is the simplest, but the least equitable
basis, unless all salesmen have an equal chance of winning, which is
rarely the case. This basis also induces overselling.

2. *Percentage of increase* over the same period the previous year
is another basis that gives new salesmen an opportunity to win,
but also favors the salesman who did not work hard the previous
year.

3. *A point system* is a very practical method of scoring because

its flexibility enables it to be easily applied and it places emphasis on the specific sales jobs that the management wants accomplished. A variable number of points may be set for a sale to a new customer, a sale to an old customer, a sale to an exclusive dealer, highest trade-in values, largest number of calls, largest number of continuous days of selling, and other sales activities.

4. *A quota system* based on volume of sales is another basis of scoring. By this method quotas are fixed for each salesman, based on a system of quota setting which may involve past sales, business conditions, competition, available market, and other factors as they affect each salesman's opportunity to sell. Quota setting is difficult, and unless properly done will result in unfairness to salesmen and inequality of contest opportunities. A quota is an excellent device to handicap salesmen with better territories and opportunities.

Handicaps are sometimes arranged for sales contests by classifying salesmen arbitrarily according to types of dealers, size of dealer, old salesmen, new salesmen, city salesmen, country salesmen, and so forth.

The scoring of salesmen of an office equipment maker is done on the quota basis and takes into account territorial possibilities. Awards are made for achieving from 125 per cent to 150 per cent of volume quota. A chemical company also ran sales contests on the basis of sales volume quotas, making awards for excess percentage over quotas. A large Chicago packer staging a sales contest for canned meats operated on the point basis given below:

Corned beef:
No. 1 tins .... 40 points per case
No. 2 tins .... 80 points per case
No. 6 tins .... 120 points per case
Roast beef:
No. 1 tins .... 50 points per case
No. 2 tins .... 90 points per case
No. 6 tins .... 135 points per case

Nine other lines of canned meats were given an allotted number of points on a case basis, depending upon the size of the can.

In a "sharpshooter" sales contest on old and new cars, a motor car manufacturer fixed a basis of 600 points for new cars and 300 points for used cars, with a minimum of 3,600 points.

Group sales competitions. Sales contests may be staged to encourage competition between individual salesmen in an organization, but group competitions are an additional stimulant. Large companies using contests operate competitions between regions, districts, divisions, and branches, as well as between individual salesmen. The largest manufacturer of one type of office equipment runs interdivisional competitions in its various contests between its Pacific, Central, Southeastern, Southern, Northeastern, Northern, and Canadian divisions.

In sales contests branches may be teamed in pairs, and one branch pitted against another. A prize of 1 per cent of the winning branch's sales for the month may be divided between the manager and salesmen in the winning branch.

Principles for planning contests. In summary, the following principles should be observed in planning sales contests:

1. Plan far enough ahead.
2. Give every salesman a fair chance to win something.
3. Sell the contest to salesmen.
4. Reach the mediocre as well as the good salesmen.
5. Adopt a sound contest theme.
6. Select good cash, merchandise, or honor awards.
7. Provide for the postcontest slump.
8. Set up a fair system of scoring.

Sales Conventions. A very common sales-stimulating device is a sales meeting, or convention, which may be held for three general purposes: to inspire salesmen, to train salesmen, and to combine inspiration and training. Sales conventions are held for the manufacturer's salesmen, wholesale distributor salesmen, retail dealers, and retail salesmen.

Advantages. The principal benefits of sales conventions in general are:

1. Stimulate sales and maintain the morale of the salesmen.
2. Inspire salesmen.
3. Unify a sales organization.
4. Correct faults of salesmen.
5. Initiate new products and policies effectively.
6. Impress salesmen with resources of the company.
7. Impress salesmen dramatically with product features.
8. Acquaint salesmen with officials of the company.

Disadvantages. The general objections to many sales conventions are:

1. Salesmen are taken from their work.
2. The expense of staging conventions is considerable.
3. The activities of the company are disrupted.
4. Program is poorly planned.
5. Salesmen compare grievances.
6. Individuals receive little aid on personal problems.
7. Salesmen consider conventions a vacation.
8. The expense of bringing salesmen to meetings is considerable.

Types. There are numerous types of sales conventions, such as:

1. National conventions at headquarters.
2. Sectional conventions in districts.
3. Local sales meetings at branches.
4. Convention by telephone.
5. Convention by radio.
6. Convention by mail.
7. Traveling sales convention.
8. Conventions for distributors and their salesmen.

The national convention at headquarters is usually held annually, although in some companies it is held every two or three years. The national convention has these advantages:

1. It gives salesmen an opportunity to become acquainted with home office executives and others who have coöperated with them in their work.
2. It enables salesmen to absorb the enthusiasm of the company officials and carry it back with them into the field.
3. It keeps up the morale of the force.
4. It gives salesmen new talking points and confidence.
5. It clears up grievances and doubtful policies.

However, many sales executives are opposed to national conventions for the reasons that they are difficult to plan and direct; entail great expense; permit the possibility of playing politics; disrupt company routine; and place emphasis on general rather than specific problems.

Annual national conventions are held by many large life insurance companies, such as the Massachusetts Mutual Life Insurance Company, Provident Mutual Life Insurance Company, and Berkshire Life Insurance Company. Attendance is largely limited to leading producers.

A leading business equipment manufacturer holds annual conventions at its headquarters which last from three days to one week and are attended by salesmen who have made 100 per cent of their annual quotas. A large-scale company also brings in to its home office all of its salesmen who have qualified for the 100 per cent club by reaching their quotas. The expenses of all salesmen are usually paid during these conventions.

Instead of holding conventions once a year, certain organizations prefer to hold them every two or three years, during which time more information can be accumulated and greater enthusiasm generated because of the less frequent occurrence.

In the sale of style commodities, more than one convention may be held a year. A shoe manufacturer holds two conventions a year, at the beginning of the fall and spring seasons.

In some large companies it is impractical to bring all salesmen together at headquarters for an annual convention, so a selected group of salesmen who exceed their quotas are invited to annual meetings with all expenses paid. The balance of the salesmen, who fail to qualify for the annual convention, are frequently reached through local or district meetings.

Branch, district, division managers, and supervisors, however, are usually brought to the home office of large companies at least once a year for management meetings with all expenses paid.

Sectional conventions are growing in popularity, not only with large companies, but with smaller organizations, for the following reasons:

1. They are less expensive from the standpoint of paying the expenses of salesmen to the meetings and the loss of business while in attendance.

2. They are more serious, and less like a vacation.

3. They are informative to home office executives, who are brought into contact with field conditions.

4. They specialize in the problems of the district in which they are held.

5. They afford better opportunity for personal contacts.

6. They meet competition by keeping salesmen closer to the field.

On the other hand, it is maintained by some sales managers that district meetings fail to produce the enthusiasm of large group gatherings; they take valuable time of executives in the field; and if several meetings are held, they cost as much as one large meeting costs.

A cartridge company gave up annual conventions in favor of district meetings, at which the district sales manager and his men met with executives from the home office for the detailed consideration of particular sales problems from each territory. A shoe manufacturer holds sectional meetings for salesmen, each attended by from twelve to twenty salesmen, whose expenses are paid. A building material producer holds sectional sales meetings at which all salesmen can be assembled for a one-, two-, or three-day meeting.

Local sales meetings at branches are held frequently, sometimes once a day, once a week, or at least every month, and are attended by all salesmen in the branch. The purpose of such meetings is to inspire and inform the men and to aid them in coping with current problems. The program for such meetings includes such topics as:

1. Review of current results.
2. Discussion of interesting sales by salesmen.
3. Discussion of difficulties encountered and solutions proposed.
4. Actual demonstrations of sales technique between salesmen and manager.
5. Round-table evaluation of demonstrations.
6. An inspirational windup by the manager.

Such meetings are usually not over one hour in length and should be carefully prepared by the manager. Sometimes visual sales-training material is used, or an outside speaker is introduced.

Conventions by telephone are a novelty which have been used by a few sales organizations to stimulate the interest of their salesmen. A Mid-western manufacturer who was initiating a new merchandising program at the start of the fall season arranged for a long-distance, two-way telephone hook-up with its twelve salesmen located in twelve cities in different parts of the country. The salesmen were sent copies of a new advertising portfolio and display stand, and were asked to listen in on their own telephones at eight o'clock on the evening of the day appointed for the meeting.

The meeting was opened from the company's headquarters by the sales manager, who described the company's sales program; he was followed by the vice-president in charge of production, who told about the product's features. The advertising agent of the company was next introduced. He described the advertising program;

the manager of the Chicago branch next spoke; and finally the individual salesmen told of their own work. The program lasted thirty minutes.

An enterprising life insurance agency uses the same plan for occasional meetings with ten outside agents, some of whom are as far away from the agency office as one hundred and fifty miles. The meetings last three minutes, during which time the manager makes a short talk, presents an idea for special effort, asks for comments, and offers encouragement. The meetings cost only $10.50 for the three minutes. Inside agents listen in on the meeting also.

Convention by radio is a new plan, which was initiated by a large motor car manufacturer, who held an international meeting of salesmen and dealers by means of a ninety-minute broadcast over the Columbia network. The meeting was held in two parts: one hour, from 1 until 2 P. M., was devoted to a dramatized presentation depicting the evolution of a new model car; the second half, from 2:45 until 3:15 P.M., was devoted to answers to questions telegraphed in by salesmen during the intermission. Speakers on the program included, in addition to the president, the chairman of the board, the vice-president-in-charge-of-engineering, and the general sales manager. The first insurance policy ever taken out for a radio program insured the success of the radio convention to the extent of $500,000.

A large specialty appliance sales organization staged a spring sales meeting for fifteen thousand salesmen, which was called the "Hour of Ours" broadcast. The broadcast lasted one hour, from 11 A.M. until 12 noon, and included talks by the president of the company, the head of research, the vice-president-in-charge-of-sales, and the general sales manager. In addition, there were entertainment features by well-known radio artists. The program was part of a day's sales meeting of dealers from all parts of the country. One distributor's meeting was attended by three hundred and fifty salesmen.

Conventions by mail. Many companies have conducted sales conventions by mail on account of the expense of staging large conventions and paying the traveling and living expenses of salesmen. It is frequently impossible to bring all of the salesmen in a large organization to a convention, with the result that the men who have the greatest need for the inspiration and instruction do not receive it. No time is lost at mail conventions, and salesmen do not return to their territories exhausted. Poor public speakers are no handicap, and the mail convention can last as long as is desirable. A mail convention lacks, of course, the stimulation of personal contact with major executives and other salesmen.

The mail convention, which usually extends over a period of several weeks, consists of a series of mailings, which includes: an address by the president, a trip through the factory, a speech by the production manager, a talk on advertising by the advertising manager, a speech by the advertising agent, and talks by branch managers. One convention opened with addresses of welcome by the governor of the state and the mayor of the city from which the mail convention emanated.

A packing company ran an airmail convention for six hundred salesmen, located from coast to coast. The convention lasted five days and featured speeches by the president, sales director, advertising director, advertising agent, and well-known users of the products.

Another company used a mail conference plan as an economy measure. A series of mimeographed bulletins was prepared and mailed to all salesmen to give them a résumé of the advertising and merchandising plans of the company.

Traveling sales conventions. When a company has more salesmen and dealers than can be conveniently housed and entertained at its home office, it may take its convention to the field. A large drug manufacturer chartered a twelve-car, streamlined, million-dollar train to take a sales convention to forty thousand salesmen and ten thousand dealers of its products. Two convention hall cars were used for some one hundred and fifty sales meetings, and meals were served in dining cars. The train carried a dance car, where the company's own orchestra played for salesmen and their wives or friends. Several cars carried elaborate exhibits of the company's products.

A leading printing equipment maker equipped a train to carry its sales story to hundreds of salesmen and customers in the printing trade.

Conventions for distributors and their salesmen. To inspire and inform dealers, many companies hold district sales meetings annually. These meetings are usually held at the opening of the active selling season and feature new models, and advertising and promotion plans. They are common in the sale of mechanical specialties, such as automobiles, refrigerators, oil burners, and radios.

One of the best-planned conventions of this type is held annually by a large appliance manufacturer. The company annually appoints a special convention committee, which is aided by an advisory committee of sales executives. Men experienced in arranging convention programs are put to work; skits and presentations are planned; convention talks are outlined; a moving picture studio is set up to produce sound pictures; and advance men working with convention chairmen of every distributor plan preliminary details in every convention city. Every available man in the home office sales department is assigned to writing scripts and talks and preparing charts and materials. Four crews, each consisting of about ten home office sales executives, are assembled, and parts assigned and coached for several months. Then the four crews, each accompanied by a baggage car loaded with scenery and necessary equipment, leave the factory to present the spring convention in thirty-six district headquarters cities. Each convention is staged in the leading hotel for one day, and repeated on a second day, depending on the number of dealers attending. Attendance on some days has exceeded a thousand dealers and retail salesmen.

Each session is preceded by orchestra music and called to order by the district manager and the crew leader. A home office executive also speaks briefly. The morning session is devoted to demonstration and discussion of new models by means of playlets, pantomimes, talking moving pictures, and brief speeches by members of the crew. A brief recess is held in the middle of the morning program. The morning session is followed by luncheon at the hotel for all dealers and salesmen at the expense of the company. The afternoon session is devoted to sales and merchandising, with the following typical program:

1. "Sales Leaders," a brief address by the crew manager.
2. "Fifty Words," a sales playlet enacted in a dealer's showroom.
3. A sound moving picture, featuring a special product.
4. "Commercial Presentation," illustrating sales to commercial prospects.
5. Recess.
6. "Puddle-Fishin'," a sales playlet in four scenes, with a cast of eight.
7. "Salesmanship in Print," a dramatization and illustration of the company's advertising program.
8. "Shoot the Works," an inspirational address.
9. "The Final Element," a closing exhortation by the crew manager.

Convention programs. The program for convention meetings is a vital factor in their success. The nature of the program is determined largely by the objective of the meeting. A convention for the purpose of training salesmen will favor a serious program.

while a meeting for stimulation will call for enthusiasm and bally-hoo.

There are several methods of presenting serious material at a sales convention: speeches, discussions, questions and answers, and demonstrations. The poor quality of many public speeches has led many organizations to resort to open forum discussions led by experts, with subsequent discussion from the floor. This method secures the participation of a large number and brings out interesting information.

One life insurance company held a "Speechless Convention" at which sales demonstrations were given by successful agents and seminars were conducted for small groups of agents with similar interests.

Round-table discussion by a large group is another effective convention device. Panel discussions, in which several leaders discuss sales methods informally before the convention, are productive of considerable interest.

Conventions are usually opened with brief remarks by the president of the company, who states the objective of the meeting. Next, the products are demonstrated; new features discussed; advertising is illustrated and the advertising program explained in detail; the credit manager talks on credit and sales; the service manager discusses service; suggestions from salesmen are invited; the sales manager discusses quotas and selling technique; and successful salesmen explain their methods.

Conventions of a serious purpose call for some form of entertainment. Professional entertainers may be employed; the salesmen and their wives may be taken to a theatre; a supper dance may be held at a country club; or the force may be taken to a ball game or race meet.

The details of a sales convention should be put into the hands of a convention committee. The place of meeting should be given serious consideration. Many companies hold sales meetings at hotels which offer convenient facilities for housing, feeding, and entertaining the men. Companies sometimes prefer to hold sales meetings at the factory or general offices, where the salesmen can become acquainted with the personnel and observe the factory operations. Sales meetings are sometimes held at camps or country clubs to avoid the distractions of other meeting places.

An advertising campaign for stimulating interest in the convention must be planned. Letters, broadsides, and booklets may be used to illustrate the convention city, entertainments, and program, and encourage attendance. A daily news bulletin may be published during the meeting.

The time for holding a convention is also an important consideration. Meetings are usually planned to initiate spring or fall selling drives. Some companies hold conventions during "off" periods when salesmen are not busy.

A record of the proceedings of each meeting should be sent to the salesmen following the convention. Provision should also be made for the salesmen to take notes during the meetings.

One of the most effective methods of inspiring, entertaining, and instructing salesmen at a sales convention is by means of dramatizations. Few effective conventions are held which do not feature one or more playlets. One-act plays, properly staged, secure the attention of the audience of salesmen through their novelty; serious business is eased into the consciousness of salesmen by way of entertainment; and plays move and inspire through the humorous, the dramatic, and the spectacular. Sales plays may serve a wide variety of purposes, including instruction of salesmen in locating prospects, answering objections, meeting competition, and advantages and uses of a product.

FIGURE 48. Sales plays are a very effective method of stimulating as well as training salesmen. This scene is from a sales play staged by company representatives at a sales convention of a large electric refrigerator manufacturing corporation.

A large life insurance company has used sales playlets extensively at its sales conventions. The company staged a mock trial, entitled "The People vs. John Doe," to instruct salesmen in time control. "A Voice from Nowhere" featured methods of conducting sales interviews. Another playlet, entitled "How to Become a Successful Agent in Three Easy Lessons," and "Men Buy Because . . . ." instructed in sales technique. Two to seven actors were used in each playlet, which was written by company sales executives and sent out to branch offices for production. Before the convention met a professional dramatic coach visited each branch for rehearsals.

An oil burner manufacturer staged a playlet, entitled "On Trial," at a national sales convention to give dealers and their salesmen facts with which to meet sales objections. The president, officials of the company, and dealers took part in the presentation.

A large electric appliance maker stages numerous playlets in its annual sales conventions, which are carried to the thirty-six sales districts of the company by four crews.

A leading tire company presented "The Play Without a Name" to company salesmen in the principal cities of the country and offered a prize for the best suggestion for a name. It was then put on the road for seven weeks as a part of one-day dealer conferences in twenty-one cities.

When a building material company held a sales convention, workmen brought in sand, brick, and metal lath and used the company's products in constructing a wall before the salesmen, while an executive explained the advantages of each product.

Salesmen's Magazines and Bulletins. To provide continuous stimulation for sales organizations, many companies resort to weekly bulletins or monthly salesmen's magazines. These publications are designed to inform the salesmen of new products, new advertising, new company policies, and to inspire salesmen by reporting promotions, successful sales, and the work of outstanding men in the organization. The form of these publications may be a single, letter-sized, mimeographed sheet, or a twenty-four page magazine printed in colors on enamel paper and profusely illustrated.

A large soap maker publishes monthly a salesmen's magazine which illustrates effective window displays installed by salesmen; describes current radio programs; quotes testimonials from enthusiastic customers; tells of transfers and promotions of salesmen; and lists desirable books for salesmen to read.

A food manufacturer publishes a twenty-one page monthly, describing for the twelve hundred company salesmen the success of current advertising drives; illustrating effective local newspaper and

FIGURE 49. Salesmen's magazines are an excellent medium for stimulating salesmen. Illustrated are *Smith-Corona Star Record* and *Typogram*, published by L. C. Smith & Corona Typewriters, Inc.; *The Kodak Salesman*, published by Eastman Kodak Co.; *Moonbeams*, published by the Procter & Gamble Co.; *Salesgrams*, published by General Foods Sales Co., Inc.; and *Salesman's Bulletin*, published by the Specialty Appliance Sales Division, General Electric Co.

handbill advertising tie-ups; and telling of unusual sales performances and productive store sales.

Individual Correspondence with Salesmen. Correspondence between sales executives and individual salesmen is one of the most effective methods of stimulating salesmen. It deals with the personal problems of individual salesmen, which are often the source of indifferent or effective sales operations. Personal letters give a sales manager an opportunity to approach the difficulties of his salesmen in a friendly, human way, and to gain their confidence and win their coöperation.

Much ineffective correspondence between sales executives and their men is carried on under the guise of form "pep letters," which are nothing more than shallow, insincere admonitions to get more business. Good letters to salesmen should have a positive, optimistic tone; they should be definite; they should show a knowledge of the salesman's problems; they should mix news, gossip, and inspiration in proper proportions; they should offer practical suggestions and worth-while ideas; and they should be sympathetic and just.

Letters may be useful in encouraging salesmen and also serve as an excellent medium of sales training to give technical information, product facts, and promotion methods to the sales organization.

Personal Conferences with Salesmen. Personal conferences between sales executives and supervisors and individual salesmen are an excellent method of stimulation. When provided with concrete evidence from sales records concerning the operations of a salesman, a sales executive can go into a conference with a definite knowledge of the causes of difficulties in a territory and can offer a salesman constructive suggestions. Conferences with salesmen which rely upon table-pounding and exhortation are rarely effective. By taking a sympathetic, helpful attitude toward a salesman in difficulty, a sales executive can inspire and lead a man on to increased efforts and better results. Personal conferences may be held in a salesman's home or in a social setting, as in a club or restaurant, to put the interview on a more personal, intimate basis. The inclusion of a salesman's wife in the interview is sometimes desirable. Sales executives frequently plan a regular schedule of contacts with all salesmen in their charge for a frank discussion of the salesmen's problems.

Promotions. Opportunities for promotion in a sales organization provide a strong stimulus to increased effort and interest on the part of the salesmen. Impartiality in making promotions,

promotions made from within the organization, and the publicizing of advancements—all serve as inducements to the members of the organization. Certain companies publish the pictures and describe the achievements of salesmen who merit promotion. Other companies have a definite advancement program which cuts down turnover and increases activity on the part of the sales force.

Problem 1—Headquarters Sales Conventions

Industrial Equipment Company

The Industrial Equipment Company, established in Toledo, Ohio, in 1928, manufactures lift trucks, portable elevators, and steel storage racks which are sold direct to industrial concerns, warehouses, and factories by a force of one hundred salesmen. Business magazine advertising to the extent of $30,000 is run annually. The salesmen are paid on a straight commission basis and operate from their own homes. The average salesman earns from $2,000 to $3,500 annually and pays his own expenses. Total sales of the company average $3,500,000.

The company, confronted with the problem of unifying its organization and stimulating its salesmen to increased production, has been holding national conventions at its headquarters only once every two or three years, because of the expense involved in paying the transportation and living expenses of salesmen to and from the home office. Such infrequent meetings, however, were not conducive to satisfactory results, since the salesmen lost contact with the company in the years when no conventions were held.

Several suggestions for stimulating the salesmen were made by the officials of the company. One believed that a successful convention could be conducted by mail, by sending each salesman twice a week brief addresses by officials of the company concerned with credit, service, shipments, adjustments, and advertising in conjunction with inspirational messages. The effectiveness of this plan could be tested by sending each salesman a series of questions to be answered on the question sheet and returned to the home office for grading. The questions would be designed to compel the men to refer to the convention mailings. Weekly prizes in cash would be awarded to all who received a grade of 100 per cent on these tests.

The sales manager of the company did not believe that the salesmen would be interested in the mail convention. He favored an annual, three-day convention at the home office for all of the salesmen, with all expenses paid. The convention would serve to demonstrate the superiority of the company's products and instruct the men in figuring prices, analyzing applications, and specifying equipment. Problems would be distributed to the men for discussion. No formal speeches would be made. One day would be devoted to product discussion, one to the discussion of sales problems, one to answers to objections, and so forth. The morning of the third day would be spent in the factory, with the afternoon spent at a baseball game. The sales manager believed that this convention would not cost the company in excess of $20,000.

The general manager favored a convention at the home office, but believed that it should be confined to a more intensive, one-day meeting, and that the salesmen should pay half of their expenses in traveling to and from, and during their one-day stay at, the home office. In this way the cost to the company would be reduced, and the salesmen would take more interest in the meeting by reason of their contribution to the cost.

The sales manager did not believe that many of the salesmen would be willing to pay half of the expenses of attending the meeting. As an additional concession, the general manager agreed to pay half of the expenses of such of the wives of the salesmen as wished to come to Toledo for the convention.

Questions

1. Should the company have adopted the plan for holding a convention for its salesmen by correspondence? Give reasons for your decision.

2. Should the company have adopted an annual convention plan, paying all expenses of its salesmen for a three-day meeting at the home office? Justify your answer.

3. Should the company have adopted an annual, one-day convention plan, dividing the cost with the salesmen and their wives? State reasons.

4. Outline a convention program for whichever type of convention plan you prefer.

5. If you do not favor any of the plans stated in the problem, what method of stimulating salesmen would you suggest?

Problem 2—District Conventions

The Taylor Vacuum Cleaner Company

The Taylor Vacuum Cleaner Company, established in Chicago, Illinois, in 1919, manufactures and distributes its product, retailing for $60, direct to housewives through eight thousand salesmen, who are paid a straight commission. Wholesale sales are also made to department stores and central stations. The sales force is controlled by forty division managers, one hundred district managers, and eight field sales managers. For several years the company held national conventions of its division, district, and field sales managers at the home office in Chicago, for the purpose of exchanging ideas between the factory executives and field managers. The eight thousand line salesmen were not included in these meetings.

So long as the organization was of medium size this plan was satisfactory, but the management believed that the organization had reached such a size that convention decentralization was necessary. Accordingly, it was proposed to break up the annual meeting into five parts, holding sectional meetings for division and district managers at New York City, Chicago, Detroit, St. Louis, and Washington. The eight field managers were to meet at the home office as before to plan the district meetings.

This proposal met opposition on the ground that the number of men involved did not justify sectional meetings, which would be more expensive than a single national convention. It was contended, also, that the salesmen should be included in the convention, since they needed the instruction and stimulation more than the field managers.

The company operated a "High Hat Club" for salesmen who annually exceeded their sales quotas. It was suggested that members of this club be rewarded by having their expenses paid to an annual convention at the factory. The cost of bringing the salesmen into the home office was estimated at a minimum of $200 a man.

The program for the district, division, and field managers' meetings heretofore included such subjects as the following: the advertising program; field training, and supervision of new salesmen; group and individual employment methods; instruction of present men in demonstrations and closing tactics; management methods; operating expenses; trade-ins; collections; and repossessions.

The company had no experience in staging conventions for salesmen, and those who opposed this plan believed that such conventions required expert management to be successful.

Questions

1. Should the company have decentralized its national convention for district and division managers? Give reasons for your decision.

2. Should the company have initiated an annual convention for salesmen members of the "High Hat Club" at the factory? Give reasons for your answer.

3. Should the company have staged sectional meetings of all salesmen in the organization? Why?

4. Was the program for the managers' meetings satisfactory?

Problem 3—Sales Contest

Midland Steel Products Company

The Midland Steel Products Company, established in 1904 in Chicago, Illinois, makes and distributes through a force of five hundred salesmen a complete line of metal office equipment, including filing cabinets, counters, desks, and steel shelving, direct to business concerns, city and government offices, libraries, and other users. Salesmen are paid a commission and a bonus for exceeding quota and operate out of thirty branch offices located in the principal cities.

Faced with a decline in sales brought about by a general business depression, the company decided that steps must be taken to stimulate the salesmen to increase their contacts and sales volume.

The sales manager advocated a sales contest for cash prizes and a trip to the company's headquarters at Chicago. The contest would be called a "Gold Rush." The thirty branches of the company would function as "trading posts," with the branch managers as "assayers." Prospects were "claims" to be staked. An order was a "nugget." The salesmen would be divided into four groups according to their quotas. Within each group there were six progressive ranks to which one could attain: "tenderfeet," "prospectors," "diggers," "panners," "sluicers," and "old timers." Each step represented a certain percentage of quota, 70, 80, 90, 100, 125, and 150 per cent, respectively.

Cash prizes would be awarded for attainment of each of the successive steps of quota. The contest would run ninety days, and the quotas would be the regular sales quotas established for that period. A salesman exceeding his quota 125 per cent had an opportunity to win $200 and a trip to the factory, with all expenses paid. The top man in each of the four groups would be awarded the factory trip.

To encourage competition between the thirty branches, salesmen working out of the winning branch would each be given a share of a branch prize of $200.

The contest would be promoted with a mail campaign, to each salesman in the organization, consisting of semiweekly bulletins written in the language and spirit of a gold rush, announcing the standing of the individual salesmen and branches in the contest. Special contest letterheads would be prepared upon which inspirational letters would be sent to each man over the sales manager's signature. Various officials of the company would address the men through the contest bulletins. Meetings would be held daily at each branch, where large scoreboards depicting a gold rush would be erected. Upon these boards the standing of each salesman would be posted daily.

The contest would start September 1, the beginning of the active fall selling season, and run through to December 1, during which time the men would have the best opportunity to reach their quotas.

The general manager of the company objected to the sales contest on the grounds that it would create antagonism between the salesmen, result in overselling, and cost the company considerable money for prizes and promotion. The company had no previous experience in conducting a sales contest.

The sales manager estimated that the total cost of the sales contest would be in the neighborhood of $30,000 and that the anticipated increased sales and better morale of the salesmen would justify this expenditure.

Questions

1. Should the Midland Company have adopted the sales manager's suggestion for a "Gold Rush" sales contest? Give reasons for your decision.

2. Assuming that the contest would be used, give brief answers to the following:

    a. Is the theme satisfactory?
    b. Is the method of scoring the contest satisfactory?
    c. Are the rewards in the contest satisfactory?
    d. Is the length of the contest proper?
    e. Does the method of promoting the contest promise to be effective?
    f. Is the time for holding the contest satisfactory?

3. Should some other method of stimulating the salesmen be used, aside from the sales contest?

Problem 4—Salesmen's Honor Clubs

Wadman Novelty Company

The Wadman Novelty Company, Milwaukee, Wisconsin, makes an extensive line of advertising novelties including calendars, blotters, rulers, buttons, and pencils, which are sold direct to advertisers by the company's sales organization of one hundred and fifteen salesmen operating out of eighteen district offices in the principal cities of the country. The typical Wadman salesman is forty-eight years old and earns an average of $5,600 annually on a straight commission basis.

To stimulate its salesmen to increased production, the company is considering the organization of salesmen's honor clubs for men attaining a specified volume of sales within a certain period and performing certain tasks. Various clubs are under consideration.

The "Star Salesmen's Club" is to be composed of the ten leading salesmen in the organization at the close of each calendar year. Membership is to be determined on a point basis with points awarded for sales volume and missionary work. For example, 10 credit points will be given for each dollar of sales; 2 points for each dollar collected on overdue accounts; 2 points for collection in full at the time that the order is signed; 50 points for each weekly sales report; 5 points for each new customer, and other point awards for similar missionary work. The nonselling credit points must not exceed 50 per cent of the points earned by sales volume. The club members are awarded a prize of a free vacation trip on the Great Lakes.

The "Monthly High Five Club" would be operated on the same point basis as the "Star Salesmen's Club," with awards to the five salesmen who earn the highest number of points each month in the year. A new High Five Club would be elected every month and each man qualifying would receive a bonus of 3 per cent of his net sales for the month. A man may become a member of the High Five Club as many months in the year as he is able. This club sets the incentive closer to the men, provides a different type of reward, and makes it possible for more men to participate in extra earnings.

The "Freshman Club" would be composed of any number of salesmen who have been with the company one year or less, and who qualify by selling a specified volume of business their first year, based on the potential of their individual territories, past sales in each territory, and current business conditions. Men who qualify for the Freshman Club would be automatically disqualified for the Monthly High Five and the Star Salesmen's Club. A bonus of 2 per cent of their annual sales would be awarded members of this club in addition to a trip to the home office with all expenses paid for one week.

The "Openers Club" would be composed of all salesmen who open the greatest number of new accounts every quarter. The amount of the initial order would not be taken into consideration when qualifying men for this club. Merchandise awards would be made every three months to the wives, sweethearts, or mothers of men who qualified. A choice of awards consisting of home appliances, housewares, and small furnishings would be given the winners. Wives would be sent a form letter the first week of every quarter urging them to get behind their husbands and encourage them to open new accounts.

The sales promotion manager, who favors the establishment of these honor clubs, believes that they will reduce turnover of salesmen, stimulate increased sales, improve morale, and increase the earnings of the men, with resulting greater sales and profits for the company.

The sales manager, however, thinks that the salesmen will resent the plan as undignified and juvenile; that it will arouse jealousies and hard feelings on the part of men who do not qualify for the clubs; the amount of detail involved will require much clerical work, and the expense of rewards and bonuses will be considerable.

Questions

1. Should the Wadman Novelty Company adopt the honor salesmen's clubs plan? Give reasons, in addition to those mentioned in the problem, for favoring or rejecting this method of stimulation.

2. In your opinion what better method of stimulating salesmen could be used by this company? Describe the method in detail.

Reading References

Developing and Managing Salesmen, Giles, Chap. VI.
Directing Sales, Bonney, pp. 72–93.
Handbook of Sales Management, Hall, Chaps. XIII–XIV.
How to Run Better Sales Contests, Kaufman, Chaps. I, II, VII.
Management of the Sales Organization, Russell, Chap. VII.
Modern Sales Management, Frederick, Chap. XIV.
Principles of Personal Selling, Tosdal, Chap. XXIII.
Printer's Ink Weekly, "National Conventions or Local," July 17, 1930, p. 133.
Sales Administration, Hayward, Chap. XIX.
Sales Management Today, Doubman, Chap. X.
Salesmen in Marketing Strategy, Lyon, Chaps. IX, X, XII, XIII.
Sales Strategy of John H. Patterson, Founder of the National Cash Register Company, Johnson and Lynch, Chaps. XIV, XLVIII, XLIX.
Scientific Sales Management Today, Hoyt, Chap. XIV.
Selection and Training of Salesmen, Kenagy and Yoakum, Chap. XVI.

CHAPTER THIRTEEN

SUPERVISING SALESMEN

What Is Sales Supervision? Sales supervision may be divided into two phases: supervision of a salesman's *methods* of performing his duties, and supervision of the *man* himself, or his personality and attitude.

Supervision of a salesman's working methods is merely a continuation of his initial instruction. When a new salesman goes into the field alone to meet prospects and customers, his initial instruction is at an end, and supervision begins. During the preliminary instruction period a salesman is told how to perform the simplest and most fundamental requirements of selling. But it is not enough merely to *tell* a salesman how to do his job; he must also be *shown* how to do it and then required *to do it over and over again*, with helpful suggestions, until he can do it skillfully. Supervision does not consist in giving a salesman information; its purpose is to aid him in acquiring *skill*. We often fail to distinguish between knowing *what* to do and knowing *how* to do it.

Many salesmen have the fundamental knowledge about their companies, products, and policies, but fail utterly in applying this information to the solution of their customers' and prospects' problems and in the closing of sales. It is with the application of knowledge and the acquisition of skill by the salesman that supervision is concerned. This is a much slower and more difficult process than imparting facts to salesmen, but it is the key to the whole problem of building a successful sales force.

Supervision also means a continuous checkup on the effectiveness of initial instruction and the discovery of such weaknesses of the salesman as need to be corrected.

Development of a salesman's personality and attitude is an equally important phase of supervision. Personal effectiveness is fundamental to success in any type of selling, and salesmen want,

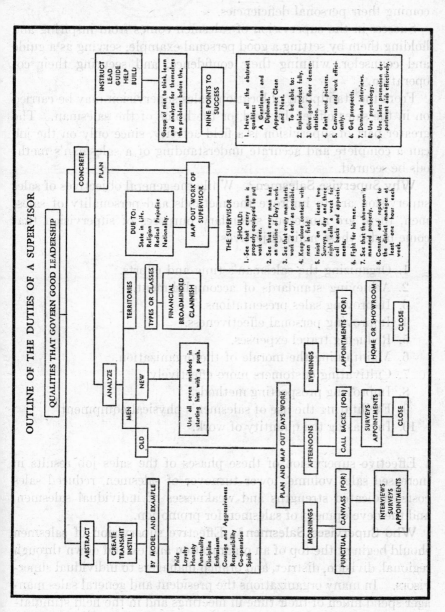

Figure 50. The duties of a sales supervisor of a household appliance; chart prepared by Pittsburgh Water Heater Corporation to improve the quality of supervision.

and need, assistance from an understanding management in overcoming their personal deficiencies.

Success in the supervision of salesmen comes from inspiring and
holding them by setting a good personal example, serving as a guide
and counselor, winning their confidence, and securing their co-
operation.

From the standpoint of location, sales supervision may be carried
on in the sales office, the field, or the home of the salesman. The
greater part of supervision is a field activity, since only on the job
can a complete and accurate understanding of a salesman's methods be secured.

Why Supervise Salesmen?   While the general objectives of sales
supervision are to improve the methods and personality of salesmen, there are numerous secondary purposes of supervision that
come under these main objectives:

1. Organizing the salesman's time and efforts.
2. Achieving standards of accomplishment.
3. Improving sales presentations.
4. Improving personal effectiveness.
5. Reducing travel expenses.
6. Maintaining the morale of the organization.
7. Cultivating customers more effectively.
8. Improving prospecting methods.
9. Facilitating the use of salesmen's physical equipment.
10. Increasing the quantity of work.

Effective supervision of these phases of the sales job results in
increased sales volume, lower turnover of salesmen, reduced sales
costs, indicated strengths and weaknesses of individual salesmen,
and the development of salesmen for promotion.

Who Supervises Salesmen?   Effective supervision of salesmen
should begin at the top of an organization and extend down through
regional, division, district, and branch managers to individual supervisors.   In many organizations the president and general sales manager spend much of their time in meetings and in the field stimulating and supervising the work of the salesmen in the organization.

The founder and chairman of the board of a large home appliance
manufacturing concern spends 80 per cent of his time contacting
salesmen in the field.   The vice-president and general manager
and general sales manager of a large paint company spend much
of their time in field and office supervision of salesmen.   In small

companies the sales manager or another company official is often the sole supervisor of salesmen. In large organizations, however, the immediate supervision of salesmen is usually the responsibility of branch managers under whom work individual supervisors.

The average number of salesmen to a supervisor varies from seven to ten. A large tobacco company has one supervisor to every five salesmen. The supervisors of a large packing company, known as "general salesmen," have from five to seven salesmen under their direction.

The field supervisors of a leading food products manufacturer, called "district representatives," supervise an average of four to five retail salesmen. The district representatives are in turn supervised by district sales managers, each of whom has an average of five representatives in his charge.

Field supervisors are variously called "sales instructors," "field trainers," "crew managers," and "senior salesmen," which titles signify the nature of their duties. In many companies supervisors do no personal selling, but spend their entire time stimulating and training salesmen in their charge. They are usually compensated by a straight salary plus expenses, although in some companies they receive a percentage of sales made by salesmen under their direction. In many specialty lines where salesmen are paid straight commissions, supervisors are given only an "override," or commission on the sales of the men in their charge. However, unless a supervisor is adequately paid for the indirectly productive time spent in supervision, he will neglect his supervisory work and spend most of his time selling for his own account.

1. *Supervision by branch managers.* Supervision by branch managers or district sales executives is usually effective, since these men have earned their positions by showing that they have the experience and ability to supervise salesmen. Branch managers are active in the supervision of salesmen of specialties and in the sale of life insurance. Branch or agency managers spend much of their time in field and office work with agents.

In many companies, however, branch office executives are so burdened with administrative duties that they cannot find time for adequate supervision. In some cases, branch office managers are appointed to relieve the branch sales managers of the work of handling warehousing, deliveries, credits, and collections. But all too often supervision is neglected for routine office details.

Effective sales supervision by branch managers requires regular and systematic effort by the manager in the field as well as the office. Some managers have definite office hours, such as eight to nine in the morning, and five to six in the evening, devoted especially to individual meetings with salesmen. Regular days are set aside for field work with individual salesmen.

The branch managers of a large cheese company are responsible for supervising the salesmen of their distributors through office and field contacts.

2. *Supervision by field supervisors.* Field supervisors are frequently employed to assist branch and district managers when the number of salesmen operating out of a branch office is too great to be supervised effectively by the branch manager.

Successful supervisors are usually reasonably successful salesmen. They have proved their ability to manage their own time and personal affairs. Leadership and teaching ability, energy, ambition, patience, and sympathetic understanding of sales problems—are all desirable qualifications for sales supervisory work.

The most common source of sales supervisors is from within a sales organization. This source gives a branch manager an opportunity to study his men, observe their qualifications, and select the man who has shown that he can teach and inspire his associates. However, a man from within an organization may not have as much prestige with his fellow salesmen as a supervisor secured from another company in the same field. A salesman experienced in another line may make a good supervisor, although first he has to be trained in the new line.

Those companies that have been most successful in developing good field supervisors have given them intensive training in supervision before permitting them to supervise men. Branch managers in these companies consider themselves as supervisors of supervisors and by regular conferences lay down definite objectives, analyze the work of their supervisors, and insure proper development of their salesmen.

Field Supervision. Field supervision is the most important phase of sales supervisory activities, for it is concerned with the methods of the salesmen in locating prospects, securing and conducting interviews, meeting objections, and closing sales.

The duties of a field supervisor of a large manufacturer of electrical appliances, as outlined in its *Supervisor's Standard Procedure*, illustrate the field responsibilities of a supervisor:

1. Conduct morning checkup meetings.
2. Give regular, frequent, close supervision to each man in the group.
3. Enforce a complete activity program for each man.
4. See that each man knows and uses the standard plan and understands how to demonstrate.
5. Concentrate activity of men on best prospects.
6. Canvass with a new man until he has demonstrated his ability to get inside interviews.
7. Meet at noon with entire crew to review morning accomplishments and arrange a definite program for afternoon and evening.
8. Divide time equally among men according to their needs.
9. Aid wherever possible in the closing of sales.
10. Follow up and cover every important piece of work, whether successful or not, by a check-up talk.
11. Visit the new man at his home and sell his wife on the job.
12. Be prepared to promote and make replacements in group by knowing where to get another good man.
13. See that all new products and sales information released by the company are explained to each salesman.
14. Read over carefully with each salesman each piece of new literature.
15. Support and execute all national, district, or special sales campaigns.
16. Constantly train salesmen in the simple fundamentals of good salesmanship.
17. Reëmphasize continually the opportunities offered by the product for the successful salesman.
18. Know the family and domestic conditions of each salesman.
19. Take a personal responsibility for the earnings of men working for you.
20. Insist on daily reports from each salesman.
21. Analyze these reports and correct any weaknesses.
22. Keep an up-to-date supervisory control sheet on each man and a group summary sheet on the whole group and check by means of these sheets the work being done by each man.

In field work, supervisors are required to:

1. Take all men out to territory together.
2. Assign starting point and streets to canvass for each man and see that each man starts to canvass.
3. Keep men from scattering.
4. Work with each man each day during canvass activity.
5. Assign men call-backs and user calls.
6. Assign themselves for afternoon work to a man who needs them most.
7. Work at night with the man who needs most help.

Supervising sales interviews. The most effective method of improving sales presentations is to have the supervisor coach on the job. Such coaching does not consist in helping a salesman to close difficult sales, in impressing the salesman who is being supervised with the ability of the supervisor, or in taking a salesman on a tour of buyers while the supervisor does all the work. Sound supervision on the job follows the formula of Dr. W. W. Charters, which is:

1. *Analysis* by the supervisor who studies the salesman's method of selling.

2. *Demonstration* by the supervisor who, when starting to coach a salesman, says, "You watch me while I do it." The supervisor conducts one or more sales to show the salesman how the interview should be conducted.

3. *Trial* by the salesman after the supervisor has made several demonstrations. The supervisor says, "Now you try one, while I watch." This step is important, for when the salesman tries to do the job himself he really begins to learn. Numerous trials may be necessary before the salesman overcomes his difficulties.

4. *Correction* of the salesman by the supervisor. When the salesman is conducting interviews, the supervisor watches him carefully to see where he goes wrong. The salesman finishes the trial interview, and the supervisor then corrects his mistakes.

5. *Follow-up or supervision* by the supervisor. When the salesman can conduct sales interviews acceptably, he is left to himself for several days. The supervisor returns later and coaches him by the same process.

The checkup talk method of supervision. Supervisors of a large manufacturer of electrical specialties sold direct to consumers use the checkup method of supervising presentations. Supervisors are provided with a series of outlines, in the form of questions, concerning the manner in which a salesman handles the various phases of the company's standard sales procedure.

Supervisors accompany and observe salesmen conducting interviews. Following each interview, the supervisor conducts checkup talks based on actual observation of the salesmen in action. The outlines or questionnaires are referred to by the supervisor in checking up on the interviewing technique of the salesmen. For example, the check-up questionnaire used in a check-up talk by a supervisor in criticizing a salesman's handling of price follows:

1. Did the salesman avoid discussion of price until he had convinced the prospect of the need, economy, convenience, and worth of the product?

2. If the prospect makes direct inquiry about price, did the salesman side-track it with suggested questions such as, "Do you think this model will be large enough for your needs?"

3. Did the salesman quote down payments and monthly payments unless convinced that prospect was a cash customer?

4. Did the salesman break price figures down to a weekly or daily basis?

5. Did the salesman compare daily cost with the expenditures that the prospect is accustomed to make, such as bus fare, cigarettes, gasoline, newspaper, etc.?

6. Was the salesman unafraid to quote price, being prepared to meet the prospect's objections with a story of quality?

If the supervisor who observed the sale could answer "yes" to these questions, the salesman's method of closing was considered satisfactory. Other steps in the sales interview would be checked in a similar way with the questionnaires, and the defects of the salesman noted for correction.

Joint sales work. Another method of supervising salesmen is through joint sales work in which the salesman involved arranges for interviews, secures appointments, introduces the supervisor or branch manager to the prospect, and steps aside to permit the supervisor to conduct the interview. The salesman maintains an attentive interest in the interview, a friendly attitude toward the prospect, but does not interrupt the presentation of the supervisor, who may bring the salesman into the interview with occasional questions.

After the interview, the supervisor analyzes the various steps in the sales presentation, and, in the event that the salesman has selected a poor prospect, points out why the individual interviewed was not a potential buyer. Subsequent interviews may be conducted by the salesman with the supervisor as an observer and critic.

When the supervisor does most of the joint selling, the salesman does not get an opportunity to correct his mistakes and practice for improvement. However, joint selling bolsters the morale of an unsuccessful salesman, shows the supervisor the type of prospect being cultivated, and demonstrates to a poor salesman the correct way to make a sales presentation.

In undertaking joint sales work, the supervisor must have a definite understanding with the salesman concerning the credit or commissions paid on joint sales in cases where the supervisor shares in the compensation or engages in selling on his own account. A schedule of joint sales work should also be prepared by the supervisor to proportion his time properly among the most deserving salesmen.

System of Field Supervision. An organized routine for salesmen in daily contact with their sales office is used by progressive organizations to insure continued effectiveness in carrying out sales plans in the field.

The daily program followed by city salesmen, representing a successful home appliance retailer, is typical of this type of supervisory control. Each day's routine operates on schedule. The office opens at 8:45 and men must report promptly. For twenty-five minutes they handle routine details. The morning sales meeting begins promptly at 9:10 and lasts twenty minutes. From 9:30 to 12:30 each salesman calls on a minimum of twenty-five new prospects previously listed for the day's work. Experience shows that these calls result in 39 per cent away from home; 25 per cent do not answer the bell; 10 per cent own a similar product; 15 per cent are poor prospects, and 25 per cent are good interviews. One or two evening appointments are secured, about 60 per cent of which result in sales. Salesmen lunch from 12:30 to 1:30. During the afternoon twelve call-backs are made on prospects to secure evening appointments. At 4:30 the salesman reports to his office on his calls and telephones prospects who were out during the morning. By 7:15 the salesman starts on appointments for evening calls, and at 9:30 telephones his report to the branch manager who is at the office to receive each salesman's report.

This program gives each salesman a definite daily job to do. He knows whom he is going to see and what he is going to see them about. He accomplishes twice as much as the man who works without a plan. The law of averages insures his success.

Principles of successful field supervision. The following principles of successful field supervision are set down by a large home appliance manufacturer for the instruction of supervisors. They apply equally well to the work of a sales supervisor in any line.

1. A salesman must see clearly the purpose of training and how it will get him what he wants.

2. A salesman's understanding is limited to the extent of his experiences, so keep within them.

3. The supervisor must clearly define the "why" of each subject.

4. All new ideas and experiences tend to fade unless anchored by repetition and drill.

5. Ideas and practices fixed by repetition and drill must be *used* to be retained.

6. Impress upon new salesmen the importance of being punctual by setting the right example yourself.

7. The new salesman should be given an opportunity to express his opinions and ideas.

8. You should take the initiative in every phase of field work, but this does not mean doing all the work yourself.

9. Keep the day's program moving, avoid lulls, be definite and aggressive, and eliminate lost motion and nonessentials.

10. Do not leave a man feeling that it can't be done.

11. Do not finish any day's work in the field without permitting a salesman to test his ability.

SALESMAN'S PROGRESS REPORT

Salesman..   Time of Training: from...................to...................incl.
                                                                                    (Date)   (Date)
District......................Unit and Section..................   Breaking in ☐   Other period ☐   Supervisor follow-up ☐

Section Headquarters...   (Enter the dates and check period you have just completed)

Check (✓) how man Functions					List Outstanding Weak Points for Supervisor to Follow-Up
Poor	Fair	Good	Sup.		
—	—	—	—	The Call Book	
—	—	—	—	The Sample Case	
—	—	—	—	Planning	
—	—	—	—	Approach	
—	—	—	—	The Presentation	
—	—	—	—	Reasons for Buying	
—	—	—	—	Resale	
—	—	—	—	Building Good-Will	
—	—	—	—	Collections	
—	—	—	—	Records and Reports	
—	—	—	—	Sales Talks	
—	—	—	—	Equipment	
—	—	—	—	Aggressiveness	
—	—	—	—	Dependability	
—	—	—	—	Judgment	
—	—	—	—	Resourcefulness	
—	—	—	—	Attitude	

State the specific points on which you trained him:

List his outstanding strong points:

Remarks, making sure to express your opinion of the salesman's value to the Company.

Signature

FIGURE 51. A salesman's progress report used by field sales trainers of a large soap manufacturer in rating the work of retail merchant salesmen. This form is used by supervisors in following up the trainers and in strengthening the weak points of individual salesmen.

Field supervision records. If field supervision is to be effective, the observations and analyses made by the supervisor of the salesmen's selling and working methods must be a matter of record. Supervision records will indicate progress made by each salesman, show training needs, and take the place of inaccurate memory. Only those records that aid in developing the salesman should be kept.

A soap manufacturer, employing twelve hundred salesmen, requires sales trainers or supervisors to fill out a salesman's progress report, rating each salesman on sixteen points, including: aggressiveness, specific knowledge, understanding of human nature, planning ability, judgment, sales instinct, enthusiasm, coöperativeness, initiative, industry, tact, personal appeal, leadership, dependability, health, and appearance. In addition, the salesman is rated on the use of his call book, presentation, records and reports, approach, collections, selling company policies, building good will, and resale work.

This report is reviewed by the management and used in further supervision of the salesman. A comparison of several such reports of a salesman indicates his progress in correcting difficulties of personality and sales methods.

The manager of a large life insurance agency requires each supervisor to make a weekly report of supervisory activities called a "Weekly Check List of Personal Supervision," listing the kind of assistance given individual agents. The manager summarizes these reports monthly, and insures that agents requiring supervision are receiving attention and that all phases of supervisory work are being handled.

Office Supervision and Stimulation. While field supervision is concerned chiefly with training on the job to insure satisfactory selling methods, office supervision deals with the personal development of the salesman, the stimulation of his morale, and the organization of his time and efforts to accomplish definite objectives.

In large sales organizations, office supervision is usually a responsibility of branch managers, assisted by field supervisors, while in small concerns sales managers are responsible for supervision. Office supervision should be a continuous process, definitely planned.

Setting standards of accomplishment. The most effective devices for supervising and stimulating salesmen are definite objectives, expressed in daily, weekly, or monthly goals. Salesmen will work harder and accomplish more if given definite assignments. Accordingly, specific objectives should be set based on:

1. Volume of sales.
2. Number of calls and interviews.
3. Number of orders.

SALESMAN RATING FORM

__________ SCORE

BETTER PACKAGES, INC., Shelton, Conn.

Salesman__________ Territory__________

INSTRUCTIONS—READ CAREFULLY

This rating sheet provides a practical method through which the ability of the individual can be judged with a reasonable degree of accuracy and uniformity. Indicate your opinion of this employee by placing an "X" on the phrase in the block which seems best to fit the employee. If you can't make up your mind between two phrases, place your "X" in the narrow space between two blocks. Please follow instructions carefully.

1. Use your own independent judgment.
2. Disregard your general impression of the employee and concentrate on one factor at a time.
3. When rating an employee, call to mind instances that are typical of his work and way of acting. Do not be influenced by UNUSUAL SITUATIONS which are not typical.
4. Make your rating with the utmost care and thought, be sure it represents a fair and square opinion. DO NOT ALLOW PERSONAL FEELING TO GOVERN YOUR RATING.
5. After you have rated the employee on all factors, write on the bottom of the sheet any additional information about the employee which you feel has not been covered by the rating report, but which is essential to a fair appraisal.

KNOWLEDGE OF ALL MACHINES	VERY POOR	LIMITED	AVERAGE	ABOVE AVERAGE	THOROUGH KNOWLEDGE	EXCEPTIONAL KNOWLEDGE
ENTHUSIASM	UTTERLY LACKING	SHOWS LITTLE	SOME SPARK	MORE THAN MOST	VERY ENTHUSIASTIC	OUTSTANDING
DEPENDABILITY	UNRELIABLE	FREQUENTLY UNRELIABLE	OCCASIONALLY UNRELIABLE	USUALLY RELIABLE	VERY RELIABLE	ALWAYS RELIABLE
CANVASSING	NEVER	ONLY WHEN PUSHED	IRREGULARLY	CONSISTENTLY WITH FAIR RESULTS	CONSISTENTLY WITH GOOD RESULTS	CONTINUALLY ABOVE REQUIREMENTS
ANALYTICAL ABILITY	INCAPABLE	TRIES TO ANALYZE	OCCASIONALLY ANALYZES	USUALLY ANALYZES	VERY GOOD ANALYSIS	UNUSUAL ABILITY
RESOURSEFULNESS ALERTNESS	NONE	MISSES OPPORTUNITIES	DISPLAYS SOME INITIATIVE	INTELLIGENT APPLICATIONS	VERY CLEVER	CAPITALIZES ALL OPPORTUNITIES
PHYSICAL ENERGY	PEPLESS	TIRES EASILY	JUST ENOUGH	SOME RESERVE	USUALLY HAS SURPLUS	UNUSUAL ENERGY AND ENDURANCE
SALES PERFORMANCE	VERY POOR	BELOW AVERAGE	AVERAGE	SLIGHTLY ABOVE AVERAGE	VERY GOOD	EXCELLENT
COOPERATION	CONSISTENTLY UNCOOPERATIVE	RELUCTANT TO COOPERATE	SOMETIMES UNCOOPERATIVE	USUALLY COOPERATES	ALWAYS COOPERATES	ENTHUSIASTIC COOPERATION
PERSONALITY	DISAGREEABLE	COLORLESS	PASSABLE	FAIRLY POPULAR	WELL LIKED	EXTREMELY POPULAR

Additional Information Helpful or Essential to a Fair Appraisal

____

____

DATE__________ __________ Signature of Rater

FIGURE 52. Form used by sales supervisors of Better Packages, Inc., in rating the effectiveness of salesmen.

4. Number of new customers.
5. Number and amount of collections made.
6. Number of prospects secured.
7. Number of demonstrations conducted.
8. Amount of advertising distributed.
9. Number of windows dressed.
10. Number of repeat sales.

Certain companies require salesmen to make their own analysis of past work records and establish their own objectives in terms of daily calls, interviews, prospects, sales volume, new customers, and the like. This has the effect of putting a salesman on record as approving of his objectives and establishing them as his minimum program. It facilitates supervision since it provides a measuring stick of the progress of a salesman.

Many life insurance agents have an objective of one application a week, and all seek to make a minimum of six calls a day, which is the average maintained by successful agents.

A successful life insurance agency has established a weekly objective for all agents of twenty-four contacts or prospects actually interviewed; five interviews at which an attempt was made to close a sale; and ten new prospects and one application.

Supervising time employment. Much can be done in the sales office to supervise salesmen's time employment. Not only should salesmen who work out of a sales office be required to arrive promptly in the morning, but they should not be permitted to remain for long periods in the office during the day.

Time employment in the field is supervised by printed forms filled in by the salesman showing the number of hours worked, number of interviews conducted, number of calls made, average time spent selling, and results of interviews. These reports may be required daily or weekly and are reviewed by the branch manager and supervisor, who make suggestions and check performance against standards established previously for each item.

Supervisory Meetings. Well-planned and well-conducted morning meetings are an excellent medium for supervising salesmen who are in daily contact with their sales office. They are used largely in supervising salesmen of home appliances, office equipment, life insurance, automobiles and other types of specialties.

Supervisory meetings each morning give a definite starting point for the day's work, provide a full program of work for each man's day and a close checkup of his work. They give the salesman the benefit of all new ideas and profitable experiences and show him how to make effective use of promotion materials and advertising. They are a continuous sales training program. In addition, morning meetings serve to inspire and stimulate salesmen to greater accomplishment and create a high morale and coöperating organization. These meetings provide an opportunity to eliminate the loafer and uncoöperative salesman.

Morning meetings must be properly planned and conducted if they are to be effective. Many organizations have tried supervisory meetings and abandoned them because they were not well planned nor intelligently directed. One executive, the branch manager, his assistant or supervisor should have the responsibility and give the necessary time to preparing for morning meetings. There should be a definite objective for the meetings, to help the salesmen do a more effective and profitable job of selling.

The program should be planned several weeks in advance. The methods of group training described previously in the chapter on sales training may be used. Demonstrations of product features, practice sales presentations, discussions of sales policies and problems, motion pictures and slide films may be a part of the program. Lectures, criticism, banal inspirational messages or exhortations are seldom effective.

Suitable subjects for morning meetings are: presentation of mechanical and construction features; discussion of new product uses and applications; panel discussion of using selling time and effort effectively; presentation of features of competitive products; promotional problems; using visual material in sales presentations.

A typical program for a morning meeting of an automobile sales organization follows:

1. Roll Call—8:30–8:33.
2. Checking quota board—8:33 to 8:38.
3. Discussion of appraisals—8:38 to 8:50.
4. Arrangements for demonstrations—8:50 to 8:55.
5. Arrangements for deliveries—8:55 to 9:00.
6. Reports of salesmen—9:00 to 9:10.
7. Arrangements for personal interviews with the sales manager— 9:10 to 9:13.
8. Slide film—9:13 to 9:30.
9. Passing out daily work sheets—9:30 to 9:33.

To insure the success of morning meetings, rules of order should be adopted providing for attendance and punctuality at meetings, discipline of the meeting and participation in the discussions.

Life insurance agency managers frequently hold breakfast meetings at a hotel, where enthusiasm and optimism are generated by favorable progress reports, descriptions of successful sales, and stimulating, brief addresses by well-known personalities in the community.

Saturday morning is a favorite time for office meetings. Difficulties of salesmen are discussed, demonstrations of sales methods are conducted, promotion plans described, roundtable discussion is held, and brief talks are made.

Evening meetings are held by some companies so that salesmen may spend the daytime hours in the field. These evening meetings are held chiefly for stimulation, although instructive material is often presented. A large house-to-house sales organization holds two evening sales clinics a week.

Understanding Salesmen. An important and often neglected function of a sales manager is the development of a better understanding of his salesmen. The sales manager who gets the best results from the men working with him is the one who understands them best, and understanding comes from close personal relations.

A salesman's effectiveness is directly related to his interest in his job. The degree to which a sales supervisor knows this interest and sustains it depends upon his knowledge of the wants of each salesman in terms of pay, ambition, pride, self-respect and security. The nonfinancial interests of many salesmen are more important than their pay. By understanding his men, a supervisor can appeal to those factors of greatest interest to them and get better results.

Through close personal contact, a sales executive learns the motives, strengths, and weaknesses of his men, and is able to arouse their loyalty and coöperative spirit, and build good morale which is essential to a strong organization.

Understanding New Salesmen. Understanding a salesman begins when he is first employed. A new salesman should be contacted more frequently during the first days of his employment than later when he has become settled in his work. The first impressions of a new man are often lasting, and failure properly to introduce a new salesman to his duties, responsibilities, relationships and company policies may dull the interest and initiative of an ambitious man.

To insure an effective contact with a new salesman, a standard induction process should be established and carried out by means of a personal interview as follows:

1. Give the new salesman confidence in the company by a brief description of the company history, organization, products, and policies.

2. Inform the new salesman about his duties with a job description and territory analysis; let him talk with other salesmen; introduce him to others in the organization.

3. Review the terms of service, features of the contract, compensation, retirement, promotion, insurance, and leaves.

Understanding interviews should be arranged with all salesmen at which time each salesman is invited to an informal "sit-down chat" in the sales manager's or supervisor's office. These interviews have several advantages. They give a salesman a feeling that he is being considered as an individual who merits personal attention. They also reveal his capacities and mental attitude. They indicate those factors which determine his interest in his work and disclose his grievances. These interviews also produce worthwhile suggestions for work improvement and provide an excellent opportunity for constructive morale building in the organization.

For several years there has been a growing recognition on the part of enlightened management of the viewpoint of workers. This development was initiated by personnel executives and has found expression in labor-management committees, employee counseling, systems for handling grievances, employee attitude studies, suggestion systems and similar efforts to develop better relationships between management and workers. These industrial relations activities apply equally well to the management of salesmen and point the way to a new, more effective approach to sales supervision.

The management of one of the largest and most progressive sales organizations in the country, employing more than a thousand salesmen, has for several years considered the viewpoints and interests of its salesmen by following a policy of "consultative supervision" which it describes as follows:

Because it places emphasis upon respect for the personality and human dignity of each individual and allows maximum development of his natural capacity, the management believes that the most enduring and in the long run most satisfactory relations will be attained by means of consultation and explanation. This means that:

1. Salesmen should be encouraged to express their views on matters affecting their jobs and interests.

2. Consideration should be given to their views before reaching decisions materially affecting their jobs and interests.

3. All those who direct others should see to it that no one is ignored on those things about which he thinks he has a right to be consulted.

4. All matters affecting a salesman should be fully and freely explained.

5. Supervisors should try to remove promptly sources of dissatisfaction.

Interviews concerning suggestions, grievances and better understanding of salesmen's attitudes should be conducted on the theory that, if salesmen are placed in a position to talk freely, they will reveal a true situation not so much by the exact thing discussed or complained about as by the supervisor's ability to interpret what is said in terms of basic causes. If a salesman is given an opportunity to discuss a personal problem or sales situation he will usually recognize the logical solution and act accordingly. Basic causes of the problem, such as home conditions, financial worries, moral problems, emotional complexes and antagonistic attitudes, will usually be revealed so that steps may be taken to solve the difficulty.

The effectiveness of a sales executive's understanding of his salesmen depends largely upon his skill as an interviewer. While interviewing is an art, the following are fundamental principles which, if observed, make interviews more productive:

1. Make it easy for salesmen to approach you. Many sales executives unconsciously assume a manner that does not invite suggestions or comments from salesmen. Personal interest in men and sympathetic curiosity invites confidences.

2. Put the salesman at ease with an informal attitude of sincere, friendly interest; assure him that his remarks will be regarded as confidential.

3. Encourage him to talk freely, and listen attentively until he is talked out. Never interrupt him while he is talking.

4. Discuss the matter, but do not argue.

5. Try to discover how the salesman thinks and feels and why.

Consider all of his views but look for the background factors that may color his opinions such as his home life, physical condition or financial worries.

Using War Training Methods in Supervising Salesmen. The Training Within Industry service of the War Manpower Commission developed during World War II a job relations training program for instructing supervisors in war plants in the most effective methods of dealing with production workers. This program, based on the best supervisory practices in industry, is equally effective in improving relations with salesmen.

Several progressive companies have used the job relations training program in sales supervision. The basic principles of the T. W. I. job relations program as applied to salesmen are:

1. *Let each salesman know how he is getting along.* Keep salesmen posted on how they are measuring up with what is expected of them from the standpoint of volume, expense, missionary work, and other features of their work. The attitude that "everything is all right unless I tell you so" is not good supervision. The man who is doing well should be told so. It is more important to check the man who is just beginning to weaken. It is a mistake to say, "You've been slipping for quite awhile." A salesman should be told as soon as he begins to skid. Know what you expect of each man. If he does not meet your expectations, point out ways he can improve.

2. *Give credit when credit is due.* Each salesman deserves to know when his efforts contribute to good results. Look for extra or unusual performance and recognize it promptly. Recognition of good work or faithful performance makes it easier to get extra effort again.

3. *Tell salesmen in advance about changes that will affect them.* It is not always practical to tell a salesman in advance about work changes that will affect him, but he should be given an opportunity to express himself about a new situation whenever possible. He should know why the change is being made before it takes place. It is human nature to resist change. He will accept new conditions more readily, and you will avoid many misunderstandings, if you will consult with him before changes are made. If he resists the change get him to accept the new situation by pointing out the benefits that he will enjoy under the new condition.

4. *Make the best use of each man's special ability.* Take advantage of each man's special interests, skill, and ability, and give him as much of this particular work as he can handle. One man may be interested in arranging displays, another in making collections, or another may be skilled in following-up customers. Whatever a man's special ability, he should be given an opportunity to use it. Look for abilities not now being used.

Solving Sales Personnel Problems. Supervisors who apply these four principles in their relations with salesmen will prevent many misunderstandings, but when problems arise, a supervisor must be able to deal with them effectively. Use the four basic steps of job relations in handling sales personnel problems:

1. *Get the facts.* When a salesman makes a serious mistake, violates a policy, or has a misunderstanding, get all of the facts about the man, review his application, personal history, test scores, performance record, and length of service. Get full information about the situation in which he is involved. Review the policies which apply. Talk with the men concerned. Consider external factors which may affect the man's attitude or the problem, such as home life, health, and background. Before you take action get the whole story.

2. *Weigh and consider.* Do not jump at conclusions. When all of the facts have been assembled, they should be fitted together and their relationship to each other considered. They will suggest possible courses of action which must be weighed in respect to your objective and the effect on the individual, the organization, and sales volume. When you act without evaluating the whole situation, more difficult related problems may arise later.

3. *Take action.* When a decision has been reached after full consideration of the facts, take prompt action. If the problem is one which it is your responsibility to handle, action should not be delayed. However, in certain cases a supervisor may need help or the matter must be referred to the sales manager, who has the authority to act. In taking action timing must be considered. Choose the most favorable time to act for best results.

4. *Check results.* Every action should be followed up within a reasonable time to determine its effect. If the action did not solve the problem, all of the facts should be reconsidered to determine what was overlooked. Watch for an increase in sales, better attitude, and improved relationships.

Sales supervisors who apply these principles acquire a better understanding of their salesmen and deal with them more effectively. These fundamentals may serve as the foundation of a practical supervisory training course.

Handling Salesmen's Grievances. Management as well as labor has generally recognized the value of a systematic grievance procedure for bringing about a better understanding between employees and management. From management's point of view, a grievance procedure provides a communications system for bringing employees' complaints to the attention of management so that causes may be corrected. Few sales managers, however, have taken advantage of grievance procedures in improving personal relations with salesmen. A salesman with an unsettled grievance, real or imaginary, expressed or unexpressed, is a source of trouble. The hidden grievance grows and soon arouses an emotional attitude that is completely out of proportion to the original complaint. It may be a matter of a disputed expense account, a split commission, or an unpaid bonus which so unsettles a salesman that his effectiveness is seriously impaired. To ignore these grievances or fail to provide a method by which they will be given serious consideration creates poor morale. Frequently the only outlet salesmen have for their grievances is at a sales meeting which is the worst possible place to discuss grievances from the standpoint of the salesmen as well as the morale of the organization.

Sales management should establish a procedure understood by all salesmen for dealing with grievances. The salesman's immediate supervisor is the first person to receive and act upon a grievance. If he can handle the complaint satisfactorily, opportunity is given to develop a closer relationship between him and his men. Union contracts usually require grievances to be written out on special forms. Answers are promised within a specified time. The supervisor's authority is sometimes limited in certain types of grievance cases. A record may be kept of grievances submitted.

Grievance interviews are more effective if the following principles are observed:

1. Listen to all grievances with an open mind toward the grievance and the man who presents it. Give careful consideration to the arguments of the salesman and listen to his story without interruption. Make a real effort to see his point of view.

2. Get all of the facts. Consult available records bearing on the grievance.

3. Keep the discussion on a friendly basis. Avoid personal issues.

4. Avoid snap judgment or hasty decisions. Weigh carefully the value of each point.

5. Give a definite answer. Be diplomatic in refusals, admit your errors, do not evade responsibility for the decision.

6. Follow through on your decision promptly.

Determining Salesmen's Attitudes. Every sales manager and supervisor has opportunities to observe the attitudes or morale of salesmen during frequent contacts with them. These observations, however, cannot be accurate unless the force is small and the executive makes a conscious effort to observe and record salesmen's attitudes, dissatisfactions, and wants. Furthermore, many executives are not sensitive to morale situations.

For these reasons sales managers often fail to satisfy the nonfinancial needs of their salesmen, one of the principal causes of dissatisfaction and lack of confidence in management. The sales manager who does not know what his men think about the company, their work, company policies, and their supervisors is working in the dark. The salesman who thinks his company is treating him fairly and who believes his manager is just, is usually a happy and successful producer.

In a small organization, the sales manager can frame a series of questions designed to reveal a salesman's attitude. This list of questions may be written, and the sales executive may make notations as a salesman is interviewed; or the questions may be merely kept in mind and asked spontaneously as the interview proceeds. The success of this method of determining salesmen's attitudes depends on the skill of the sales executive in securing answers and his objectivity in evaluating the results of the interview.

The sales executive must, of course, have the confidence of his men to the extent that they will have no reluctance in expressing their opinions candidly. If the salesmen have cause to fear that they will be discharged or suffer reprisals for honesty in answering questions, they cannot be expected to answer honestly. Strict confidence must be guaranteed the salesman in reference to anything he may say. Even though the executive may not be told the whole truth, he will learn enough to be able to discern the salesman's attitude and understand his individual problems.

In a large sales organization attitudes may be determined by questionnaires which are answered anonymously. By assuring the men that their identities will not be revealed they will be more honest in matters that may be unfavorable.

The multiple choice or yes-and-no type of question is most effective as salesmen are not required to write their answers or reveal their identities by their handwriting. These questions permit considerable shading of meaning, are much quicker to answer and can be readily measured by statistical methods. Typical questions of this type are:

1. Are there other companies in this industry that treat their salesmen better than we do?
( ) All others are better.
( ) Most of the others are better.
( ) About the same.
( ) Our company is better than most others.
( ) Our company is best of all.

2. If you could work for a competitor at the same compensation you are earning with us, what would you do?
( ) Work anywhere else than here.
( ) There are one or two companies I'd rather work for.
( ) I'd just as soon work here as elsewhere.
( ) I'd rather work here than for any other company.

3. Is our method of salesmen's expense control fair?
( ) Very unfair   ( ) Usually fair   ( ) Always fair
( ) Frequently unfair   ( ) Almost always fair

4. If you were to make a good suggestion in connection with your territory, advertising, or company policies how likely would you be to get credit for it?
( ) I would never get any credit.
( ) I probably would not get credit.
( ) I probably would get credit.
( ) I would be sure to get credit.

If the questions relate specifically to company problems, policies, and practices, they should provide information upon which to formulate policies. A survey of this kind may reveal:

1. Supervision is satisfactory.
2. Compensation is adequate.
3. Training is not thorough.
4. Promotions are not made on merit.
5. Other aspects of supervision which are vital to effective sales management.

Suggestions from Salesmen. Many progressive companies have increased production, reduced costs and stimulated morale of factory and office employees with suggestion systems. The same idea may be adapted to the sales organization for the improvement of sales methods, policies, and controls.

The first step is to appoint a sales executive, who shall be responsible for developing a practical suggestion plan. He shall also put it into action, and carry out the promotion and administration. The plan must answer such questions as:

1. What kind of suggestions should be invited?
2. How will the suggestions be paid for?
3. Who will judge the value of suggestions?
4. How will they be submitted?
5. How will rewards be publicized?
6. How can interest be stimulated?

A committee of salesmen may be selected to consider suggestions submitted. This method serves to maintain interest and makes the salesmen a party to the plan, and helps to avoid the danger of the idea deteriorating into another organization routine. The decisions of the committee may be made subject to final approval by the sales manager.

Salesman-Management Committees. The value of coöperation through conferences between management and workers was demonstrated during World War II when more than two thousand employee-management committees were organized to create a better understanding and to improve efficiency in production.

Well-operated committees have brought about greater good will and understanding, better morale, reduced turnover, higher grade personnel, improvement in training, and better workmanship. These benefits in the plant and office may also be enjoyed in the sales organization with the establishment of a salesman management committee.

McCormick and Company, Baltimore, spice packers, have had for several years a sales board composed of a group of the best representatives of the company's salesmen who come in once a year for a week's meeting when sales and advertising methods and policies are considered. The factory's problems and the policies of the entire business are also discussed.

Austin Nichols and Company, New York, food and beverage distributors, have a salesman-management committee composed of six salesmen elected by the salesmen themselves which meets periodically with the sales manager. This committee deals with such sales problems as:

1. Better inventory control.
2. Accumulation of nonsalable goods.
3. Estimates of actual and potential demand.
4. Market conditions.
5. Competition.
6. Salesmen's compensation.

7. Sales quotas.

Four major policies guide the operation of this committee:

1. No major executive shall control the meetings. One executive serves with one of the salesmen's elected representatives as cochairman of each meeting.

2. The salesmen are represented by not more than six of their number, as too large a group is not effective.

3. All questions raised at each meeting are discussed frankly and completely.

4. Decisions must be reached within a reasonable time and followed up sincerely by both management and salesmen.

A sales executive of the company says:

One of the most valuable contributions the plan provides is better understanding between salesmen and management about the problems of each. It makes for better business and human relations to bring them into the open. It works particularly well in an organization which has branches, cooperating distributors or sub-jobbers. It improves morale all down the line.

Leadership of Salesmen. The ability to lead salesmen successfully is often the factor that determines the success of a sales manager. Leadership is skill in judging the abilities and personalities of subordinates and, on the basis of this judgment, assigning tasks to them fitted to their personalities and skill. Successful leadership of a sales organization depends on skillful human management, the ability to use the best in your men. The sales manager must analyze the personalities of his salesmen and be able to cope with them. Good salesmen may have odd and irritating personalities, but these annoying characteristics are often traits that are invaluable in sales work. A stubborn man may by his very persistence and determination make a successful salesman. The tactless person with a driving, forceful character is often an outstanding sales producer.

It is useless to try to change the personalities of men. Accept them as they are and use them to the best advantage. Men must be taken as nature made them. Skillful leadership plans to use men in accordance with their personalities. If an important prospect must be sold by dash, initiative and enthusiasm, a man with those characteristics should be assigned to the job. The customer who is slow in action may best be sold by the plodding, persistent person.

When he has selected the right man for a particular job, the good sales leader does not rely upon his authority to give orders and enforce them with his discipline. He secures performance through good will and respect. Instead of commanding his men to "go and do this," he briefly explains the reason for doing the job or points out the benefits. He suggests rather than commands. The old boss said, "Go!"; the modern sales supervisor says, "Let's go."

Problem 1—Field or Office Supervision

The Home Cleaning Appliance Corporation

The Home Cleaning Appliance Corporation, St. Louis, Missouri, manufactures vacuum cleaners sold direct to consumers by the company's field organization of three thousand commission salesmen, who operate out of two hundred company sales offices located in the principal cities of the country. The product is extensively advertised in national women's magazines. Each branch office is supervised by a branch manager, who has under him an average of two supervisors, each of whom has an average of seven to eight men in his charge.

Supervisors sell their own accounts as well as supervise. They are paid a commission, or "override," on all sales made by men under them. The supervisors work with the various men in their groups as they need assistance, checking their methods and helping them close sales. Many of the supervisors, however, spent a large part of their time attempting to close sales for their own account since they were paid a higher commission on their own sales than on sales made by men under their supervision. This resulted in many mediocre salesmen receiving little field supervision.

The vice-president-in-charge-of-sales of the company favored the abolishment of field supervision, the elimination of the override, and the retention of the former supervisors as field salesmen, working entirely for their own accounts. He proposed greater supervision by the branch office manager. Each salesman would be required to telephone the branch office manager at noon and again at half-past five in the evening to report on calls, interviews and sales. The expense of the calls would be paid by the company. The phone calls would indicate that the salesmen were working in the territory assigned.

In addition, the branch manager would hold a meeting each morning from eight to half-past eight o'clock. At this time enthusiasm would be aroused by stories of sales successes on the previous day, demonstrations of the proper way to conduct sales interviews, optimistic reports of the sales progress of the branch, and by showing sales training films. Thus the men would be sent into their territories encouraged for the day's work.

Each salesman would be expected to keep a record of his activity on a Daily Check Sheet furnished by the company. Listed on this form would be spaces for recording the number of calls, the time spent in the field, the number of interviews secured, and the results of each call of each salesman every day. These daily reports would be turned into the branch manager each morning for the preceding day. An analysis of these reports would furnish a basis for individual conferences between the branch manager and those salesmen whose work was not satisfactory.

Questions

1. Should the present method of field supervision be supplanted by the sales manager's plan for office supervision of the salesmen? Give reasons for your decision.

2. If you believe that field supervision should be continued, how would you overcome the problem of inadequate supervision under the present method?

3. Assuming that field supervision should be continued, how many salesmen should be under the direction of each supervisor?

Problem 2—Individual Supervision

Longdale Food Corporation

The Longdale Food Corporation, Long Island City, New York, manufactures and sells to food wholesalers and chain stores an annual volume of $3,000,000 worth of a ten-cent packaged dessert specialty through a wholesale sales force of ten men. A specialty sales force of eight men works individual retail stores in the principal cities, taking orders for filling and delivery by wholesalers. The product is advertised in national women's magazines to the extent of $100,000 annually.

Both wholesale and retail specialty sales groups report directly to the sales manager of the company, who spends about 20 per cent of his time in the field contacting salesmen and customers. The salesmen make weekly sales reports to the home office stating the number of calls made each week, the number of calls sold, and the volume and number of sales.

One of the eight specialty salesmen, whom we shall call Mr. A, employed for six years, was not maintaining his previous year's average sales of $500 a week, and the sales manager decided to call him into the home office from his territory in Philadelphia, and discuss his difficulties in order to determine the reason for his declining sales. Preceding the salesman's visit, the sales manager had prepared a summary of Mr. A's daily work records for the past six months, which showed the following average performance:

Calls per Week	Per Cent Calls Sold	No. of Sales	Average Sale
80	66⅔	53	$7.00

The sales manager also prepared an average performance record of the other seven men on the sales force:

Calls per Week	Per Cent Calls Sold	No. of Sales	Average Sale
100	75	75	$9.00

The sales manager showed Mr. A his record and compared it with the average performance of the other specialty salesmen in the organization. The comparison revealed that Mr. A was below the standard of the organization on calls, sales, and volume of sales.

The manager next broke down the standard performance of the organization by daily units, on a five-day-week basis, and established the following objectives for Mr. A to strive for in his territory. These standard objectives were as follows:

Calls per Day	Per Cent Calls Sold	No. of Sales Daily	Average Sale
20	75	15	$9.00

The sales manager discussed with Mr. A the probable reasons for his failure to make the same number of calls as other members of the sales force, and it was revealed that Mr. A frequently did not make his first call each day until nine-thirty o'clock. His reason for this late start was that many grocers were busy filling orders in the early morning and could not be readily contacted until after nine o'clock. Furthermore, calls were scattered, and much time was taken up in traveling through the territory.

The inability of Mr. A to equal the average of the organization in percentage of calls sold was discussed, and the salesman maintained that business conditions were not good in the area in which he had been working. Many grocers were going out of business, and others were doing very little buying.

Mr. A stated that there were many small grocery and food stores in his area that bought in small quantities, and this fact largely accounted for his low average sale.

The sales manager assured Mr. A that he had confidence in his ability and that if he would make every effort to accomplish the three-point daily objective which had been established, his sales volume would undoubtedly increase.

Questions

1. Did the sales manager supervise the salesman, Mr. A, properly? If his supervision could be improved, state definitely what should be done. In what ways was the supervision satisfactory? In what way was the supervision faulty?

2. Was the sales manager's method of spending 20 per cent of his time in the field sound supervision?

Problem 3—Field Group Supervision

Marshall Specialty Company

The Marshall Specialty Company, Milwaukee, Wisconsin, manufactures oil burners, oil-burning boilers, and hot-water heaters sold direct to home owners, contractors, and builders through thirty branch offices located in the principal cities of the country. The company has a sales organization of six hundred salesmen, who are paid a straight commission and operate out of the branch offices.

The salesmen in each branch are directed by the branch manager, who is assisted by an average of three supervisors on commission, who in turn are responsible for from ten to thirty salesmen. The principal problem of the branch managers and supervisors is to get the salesmen to canvass or "prospect" for possible buyers. Few of the salesmen have any organized method of locating prospects, and all object to "cold canvassing," or searching for prospects by house-to-house calls.

To secure a greater number of prospects for salesmen, the company is considering the adoption of organized group canvassing. The best sections of each city would be selected for intensive work. Three groups of six salesmen each, each group in the charge of a supervisor, would leave the branch office by automobile each morning at eight-thirty for an appointed place in the section to be worked. Arriving in the section, the three groups would separate, each taking four square blocks for canvassing. Each salesman would be assigned by his supervisor to canvass a side of a street. The accompanying diagram indicates how the groups would work.

Supervisors would accompany their men while canvassing and show them how to approach prospects. Their knowledge of the product and their sales methods would be supervised. The salesmen would contact twenty homes before noon by this method, securing a minimum of two prospects. In the afternoon, salesmen would be left to their own devices to follow up old prospects, old customers, and to keep appointments with new prospects.

Salesmen would turn in to the management each morning at an eight o'clock meeting a report of the number of prospects secured the previous day, the number of interviews conducted, and the sales closed.

The home office sales executives believe that the group canvassing method would break down the common prejudice against cold canvassing, since salesmen would not work alone but would gain courage through contact with other members of the group engaged in the same effort.

Some of the branch managers did not favor the group-prospecting plan for the reason that the number of prospects secured by group canvassing was not sufficient to repay the men for time spent in this way. Commission salesmen would resent such organized direction of their efforts since they preferred to manage their own time.

Questions

1. Should the company have adopted the group-prospecting plan as described in the problem to secure prospects for salesmen? Give reasons for your decision.

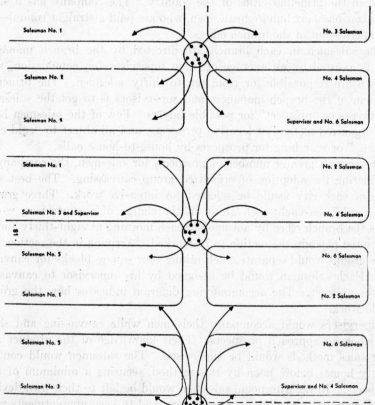

FIGURE 53. This diagram shows how salesmen would operate under an organized group canvassing plan.

2. If you do not favor the group-prospecting plan, what method of supervision do you suggest to solve the company's problem?

3. Is the early morning meeting a good supervisory device? The daily sales report?

Reading References

A Basis for Supervision of Industrial Sales Personnel, G. R. Salisbury, U. S. Dept. of Commerce, Domestic Commerce Series, No. 62.
Directing Sales, Bonney, pp. 86–88.
Handbook of Sales Management, Hall, Sect. X.
Modern Sales Management, Frederick, Chap. XVII.
Principles of Personal Selling, Tosdal, Chap. XXII.
Sales Administration, Hayward, p. 310.
Sales Management Fundamentals, Hay, p. 220.
Sales Management Today, Doubman, pp. 274–275.
Scientific Marketing Management, White, p. 132.
Scientific Sales Management Today, (1929 edition), Hoyt, pp. 25, 37, 40, 209.
Selection and Training of Salesmen, Kenagy and Yoakum, Chap. XV.
Selling Policies, Converse, pp. 433–436.

CHAPTER FOURTEEN

EVALUATING SALESMEN'S PERFORMANCE

The sales manager is constantly confronted with the problem of evaluating his salesmen's performance:

1. To determine their progress.
2. To consider them for promotion, transfer, or demotion.
3. To arrive at a fair basis of compensation.
4. To understand their attitudes, discover their strengths, and weaknesses.
5. To make his conferences with them more effective.

The objective and subjective judgment are used as general bases for judging a salesman's performance. Both objective and subjective judgments should be taken into consideration in appraising a salesman's worth.

Objective Judgments of Salesmen. The usual basis for judging a salesman's work is an objective or impersonal consideration of the following three principal factors: (1) volume of sales, (2) profitable sales, and (3) sales expense. These primary factors are sometimes supplemented by others, such as:

1. New customers secured.
2. Advertising secured.
3. Demonstrations.
4. Missionary work.
5. Collections.
6. Ratio of sales to calls.
7. Night calls.
8. User contacts.
9. Adjustments.
10. Service calls.
11. Selling full line.
12. Trade-ins.

Psychological tests are also used to form objective judgments of men.

Volume of Sales. Many sales managers judge salesmen entirely by their volume of sales expressed in units or dollars and cents. While this is the simplest and most convenient index of a salesman's performance, it is often a poor indication of either good or poor salesmanship.

Volume is many times affected by factors unrelated to the ability of a salesman so that it is dangerous to judge a man's showing by volume alone. Economic conditions and market factors often create a demand for products totally unrelated to a salesman's ability. Effective advertising or a unique product feature may be largely responsible for volume. It is much easier to sell staples in volume than specialties or luxuries. Sometimes volume is secured by price concessions, rebates, freight allowances, special discounts, or reciprocity rather than by the efforts of the salesman. For these reasons, volume is not always a conclusive index of a salesman's effectiveness. Volume is so essential, however, to certain companies, particularly those with high overhead and large productive capacity, that a man's ability to sell in large volume may indicate successful performance. When volume is considered as a factor of performance, it should be analyzed critically in relation to the current market, advertising, price, character of product, and cost of selling, in order to determine whether these factors or the salesman's ability account for the performance.

Profitable Sales. Volume of sales alone is not a sound basis for judging a salesman's performance. A salesman usually can increase his volume by selling the lower profit, easy-to-sell items in his line. The wholesale grocery salesman who sells a high volume of sugar at a gross profit of 2 or 3 per cent may not be as good as the man who sells a lower volume of fancy packaged specialties at a gross profit of 40 per cent.

Gross profit on sales is an important factor in judging a salesman's performance. The man who sells the high gross profit items may be a better salesman than the representative who pushes the low gross staples. However, keeping records of the gross profit on each item sold and the profit performance of a salesman consumes time and increases clerical expense. Although this expense is justified in many cases, certain concerns do not compute salesmen's gross profit performance for this reason.

Sales managers are beginning to recognize the necessity for determining sales costs. Considerable cost information exists in books of account and can be readily made available for judging the profitable performance of individual salesmen.

Sales Expense. Ability to sell high gross profit items is an important factor in evaluating a man's performance, but in the last analysis the net profit on a salesman's operations indicates his real worth from a financial point of view. Net profit is determined by deducting from gross profit the distribution costs of:

1. Direct selling, including salaries, travel expense, sales office expense.
2. Advertising and sales promotion expenses, transportation, warehousing, storage.
3. Credit and collection expense.
4. Financial expenses and pro-rated general administrative and branch supervision costs.

Of these various items of sales cost, salesmen's travel expense is a large factor usually exceeded only by compensation. Expense is more or less under the control of the salesman, and his ability to operate at low cost is a factor in evaluating his performance.

A salesman who can cover his territory at an annual expense of 2.5 per cent of net sales may be considered a better man from the standpoint of sales expense than a man who spends 4 per cent of net sales. The nature of the territory, however, must be considered as well as the market conditions and demand for the product. A man covering the Rocky Mountain territory would naturally incur greater sales expense than a man working in the New York metropolitan area.

Certain companies have found that younger men spend more in covering their territories than older men. When competition is on a service basis, and price and quality are more or less uniform, sales expense may be high.

Because direct sales expense may be easily determined for individual salesmen, it is often used as a factor in judging a man's work. Sometimes it is included in a sales compensation plan or extra compensation is paid for reducing sales expenses.

It must be remembered that a man with an excessively low sales expense ratio to net sales may not be developing his territory to the fullest, and may be criticized as much as the man who has an excessively high expense ratio.

Other Objective Measurements. Secondary factors employed as a basis of objective judgments of salesmen's performance are largely determined by the objectives of individual sales organizations and the specific nature of their sales jobs. A concern interested in expanding its distribution may establish as a criterion of salesmen's performance the number of new retail and wholesale outlets established. The man who sells the greatest number of new distributors is credited with the best performance.

A national advertiser that adopted a new policy of coöperative advertising with its distributors announced to its organization that salesmen's performance would be judged according to the number of distributor advertising agreements secured. A large food manufacturer evaluates the retail representatives' performance on their ability to get preferred position for their products on merchants' shelves and in counter and window displays. A public utility appliance sales organization judges its salesmen's effectiveness by the number of night calls they make at the homes of prospects. Records are kept of these calls and these are compared with volume of sales in rating sales performance.

Similar bases for judgment are:

1. New prospects secured.
2. Number of repeat sales.
3. Claims adjusted.
4. Windows dressed.
5. Trial demonstrations made.
6. Ratio of sales to quota, or customers lost.

Usually these objective judgments are combined with one or more of the primary bases—volume, profit, and expense—in arriving at a comprehensive evaluation of a salesman's work.

Test Measurements. Intelligence and aptitude tests are being used by an increasing number of companies when evaluating salesmen who are being considered for promotion, transfer to new territories, or new types of sales work. The various types of tests available are described previously in the discussion of psychological testing methods.

Tests also may be used in appraising men who are having difficulty in maintaining their work standards, or present problems of getting along with others, or show physical or personality difficulties which may affect their performance.

Subjective Judgments of Salesmen. To supplement objective measurements of salesmen, progressive sales managers are adopting methods to improve the quality of their subjective judgments. A subjective judgment is one based entirely on the personal opinion, bias, and emotional background of the individual who is passing judgment. While many sales executives pride themselves on their ability to judge men, only a few with long experience in dealing with salesmen are able to appraise attitudes and abilities with reasonable accuracy. Most subjective judgments are so colored by prejudice and bias, often unconsciously, that they are unfair or of little value in appraising sales performance. Each executive has his own standards of judgment so that it is difficult to compare his opinions with those of others and arrive at a useful composite opinion of a man's performance.

In small sales organizations, where the sales manager is in frequent contact with his men, he has a better opportunity to observe their abilities. In large organizations, however, where it is impossible for the management to keep in close touch with all salesmen, the appraisal of a man's performance is much more difficult.

Many supervisors are reluctant to give a man a low rating, or they are so superficial in their judgments that their opinions are of little value. The salesman who pushes himself forward, is the most vocal, or is the best self-promotor, is often adjudged a superior salesman; while the less aggressive but more capable man may be unrecognized. Recognizing these weaknesses of subjective judgments, personnel and sales executives have long been interested in finding a better way to formulate opinions of a man's attitude, cooperativeness, enthusiasm, and quality of work, and expressing and recording them so that they can be compared with judgments of others.

Rating Scale. One method of improving judgments of salesmen is the use of the rating scale, which has been widely employed in appraising factory and office workers, and by the War Department in rating commissioned officers. Its use by sales executives has been limited although it offers many opportunities to minimize the undesirable features of subjective judgments.

The advantages of using a rating scale are that the same characteristics are considered in appraising all salesmen; prejudice and bias is minimized, and the judgments of several executives may be compared and reduced to numerical value if desired. Furthermore, the scale provides for an organized, comprehensive consideration of each salesman's characteristics which are fundamental to successful performance of the job.

The weaknesses of the rating scale method are:

1. Ratings are often superficial and routine.
2. The terms descriptive of characteristics are not clearly understood.
3. Raters dislike to rate down.
4. The terms do not convey the same meaning to all raters.
5. Scales are too general.
6. Prejudice and bias affect ratings.
7. Raters have limited experience in judging men.

Many rating plans have been abandoned for lack of conscientious, competent administration, and proper instruction of the raters.

Preparing a Salesman's Rating Scale. The following steps should be taken in developing a practical salesman's rating program:

1. State the objectives of the ratings: for example, evaluating salesmen for promotion, increased compensation, transfer, discovery and correction of weaknesses. The purpose of the rating program should be stated specifically so that the rating scale can be developed to serve these objectives.

2. Analyze the sales job, duties, and responsibilities to determine the personal characteristics essential to the performance of the work. Salesmen, supervisors and executives may be asked to describe the job in detail and name the personal characteristics considered essential in the work. Typical characteristics to be considered are: dependability, sociability, industry, loyalty, coöperativeness, appearance, voice, intelligence, initiative, imagination, leadership, business judgment, experience, self-confidence, courage, and health.

3. Select the first five or six characteristics considered most important and define each with descriptive phrases so that the raters will think of each characteristic in the same specific terms. Each trait should be defined objectively in terms of the sales job. For example, "industry" may be defined as follows: "Starts early, quits late, never takes time off, makes many calls, does night work, never has to be prodded to make more calls, works Saturdays, and in bad weather, etc."

4. Prepare a rating scale using one or more of the several rating systems:

    a. The letter system—A-B-C-D.
    b. The adjective system—excellent, good, fair, poor.

    c. The ranking system—first, second, third.

    d. The percentage system—5, 10, 20, 30, 40 per cent.

    e. The linear scale, at one end of which a trait is named and described, and which has short, descriptive phrases at intervals beneath the scale line, each with a numerical value. The rater checks the scale at the point most descriptive of the salesman being rated.

    5. Score or weight each characteristic. Numerical scores make for precise judgments and make possible comparisons of the ratings of several salesmen and the judgments of several raters. The traits rated are not of equal importance in performance of the sales job, and each must be given its proper weight in relation to all of the characteristics considered.

    6. Prepare instructions for rating. To secure comparable ratings and considered, conscientious judgments, it is essential to instruct the raters and sell them on the value of the rating program. Each salesman who is to be rated should also be sold on the objectives of the plan.

    The following statement, used by a large company, illustrates one way to present the plan to salesmen: "The salesman being rated is assured of a deliberate analysis of his special abilities. He does not have to push himself forward to obtain recognition. It does away with unintentional injustice to the capable but unspectacular salesman. His abilities, as well as those of the more aggressive man, are known, and his promotions and increases depend upon them. He is assured of a fair rating because he is rated by several superiors, not just one."

    When ratings are well sold, salesmen like to be rated and give full coöperation to any rating plan they consider equitable. If the men are made a party to the development of the rating program, their coöperation is secured more readily.

    The rating sheet should carry the following brief instructions to raters:

    a. Use your own independent judgment.

    b. Disregard your general impressions of the salesman and concentrate on one factor at a time.

    c. Study carefully the definitions given for each factor and the specifications for each degree.

    d. When rating a salesman, call to mind instances that are typical of his work and way of acting.

e. Do not be influenced by unusual happenings which are not typical.

f. Make your ratings with the utmost care and thought.

g. Be sure that it represents a fair opinion.

h. Do not allow personal feelings to govern your rating.

In addition, one or more conferences in which all details of the rating system are discussed should be held for the raters. Special literature may be provided for those doing the rating.

7. Test the scale for reliability with a small group of salesmen before attempting to rate all of the men in the organization. In this way, the weaknesses in the plan can be eliminated.

Utilizing Salesmen's Rating. Salesmen's ratings should be utilized to the fullest in interviews with salesmen who are weak in their work or being considered for discharge, promotion or transfer. If improvements in ratings are brought to the attention of the men themselves and their supervisors, morale is stimulated.

The ratings should be used in reviewing requests for salary increases and salesmen informed that their ratings are considered in making increases.

When a salesman is transferred to another territory his ratings should accompany him and be reviewed by his new supervisors.

An annual or semi-annual report may be prepared, showing the changes in salesmen's ratings, so that managers and supervisors may be kept informed of men who have improved their ratings.

Ratings serve to point out weaknesses in a salesman's performance which may be corrected by the proper training. They indicate subjects for training, and are a guide in determining the type of training required.

Sales executives and supervisors should discuss each salesman's rating with him in a helpful way so that he will have confidence in the program and understand that the management is interested in helping him improve his performance.

Frequency of Ratings. If ratings are to be useful and comparable, they should be made at regular intervals. Semi-annual ratings are adequate for most companies. When ratings are made more frequently they become routine, and raters do not give them serious consideration.

Problem 1—Salesman Rating

Mormac Packing Corporation

The Mormac Packing Corporation, Chicago, Illinois, established in 1882, produced a complete line of beef and pork products and related specialties sold direct through 600 salesmen to meat retailers, chain stores, wholesalers, restaurants, and institutions.

The company maintained forty distributing branches in the principal cities of the country, out of each of which traveled an average of twelve to eighteen salesmen under the direction of a branch manager, who was also responsible for all of the operations of a branch. Some of the larger branches employed as many as forty salesmen and maintained large warehouses and distributing facilities.

The company exercised unusual care in the selection and training of its salesmen. However, the branch managers, particularly in the larger branches, could not keep in sufficiently close touch with their salesmen to be constantly aware of their weak and strong points and selling effectiveness. The intimacy required to appraise salesmen and to hold them to high standards of performance was lacking. The branch managers, being at a loss to know how well individual salesmen met the requirements of their jobs, could not make sound decisions regarding promotion, salary determination, transfer, or discharge.

To provide branch managers with a means of measuring the effectiveness of their salesmen, a rating program was proposed. A committee was appointed to develop the rating plan, including preparing a rating sheet, deciding upon the characteristics to be rated, determining the rating procedure, and informing branch managers and salesmen regarding the plan.

The rating sheet illustrated with this problem was prepared, calling for ratings of "outstanding," "above average," "average," "below average," and "weak" on each of the following ten characteristics: 1. Capacity for growth. 2. General sales ability. 3. Personality and appearance. 4. Character. 5. Dependability. 6. Mentality. 7. Analytical sense. 8. Enthusiasm and force. 9. Originality, imagination, resourcefulness. 10. Expression.

A scale of values was established to enable the completed ratings to be reduced to numerical values for useful comparisons. This scale, shown in the accompanying illustration, gives each characteristic its proper significance in relation to the sales job.

Branch managers would rate their salesmen every six months, and their ratings would be reviewed by the district managers and compared with previous ratings. Each salesman would be given a report on his rating by the branch manager and an opportunity to defend himself if he felt that he had been treated unfairly.

Salesman's Rating

Salesman _____

Branch _____

Symbols {
5—Outstanding
4—Above Average
3—Average
2—Below Average
1—Weak
}

Date: _____

Rated by: _____

	SYMBOL	VALUE

NOTE: The definitions following each of the points below are explanatory only. They are given for the purpose of uniform interpretation of the various qualities to be considered. They are not intended to restrict you in your considerations.

1. CAPACITY FOR GROWTH: Is he intelligently ambitious? Does he have good business judgment? Does he appear to have executive ability? Can he develop to the point where he can assume greater responsibility?

2. GENERAL SALES ABILITY·
   (a) Results consciousness   (c) Responsiveness to special tasks   (e) Merchandising ability
   (b) Distribution of product (d) Knowledge of our products and policies (f) Prestige with big buyers
                                                                           (g) Detail work

3. PERSONALITY AND APPEARANCE: Popularity with organization and trade, tact, courtesy, physique, health, vitality, neatness, cleanliness.

4. CHARACTER Loyalty, integrity, temperance, moral conduct, handling of personal affairs.

5. DEPENDABILITY. Does he follow instructions? Will he do what you expect him to do and do it conscientiously and thoroughly?

6. MENTALITY Intelligence, mental alertness, judgment.

7 ANALYTICAL SENSE Natural inclination to analyze situations and reports. Ability to reach conclusions and make decisions based on the facts.

8. ENTHUSIASM AND FORCE. Ability to generate enthusiasm and to convince others; energy, aggressiveness, and consistency of purpose.

9. ORIGINALITY, IMAGINATION, RESOURCEFULNESS: Alertness for development of new and better ways of doing things; initiative in putting them into effect.

10. EXPRESSION: Voice; clarity, both verbally and in writing.

(See reverse side for Numerical Key of Values)

FO Form C 259

Printed in U. S. A.

Numerical Key of Values
for Salesman's Rating Symbols

	5 (Outstanding)	4 (Above Average)	3 (Average)	2 (Below Average)	1 (Weak)
1	12 0	10 8	9.6	8.4	7.2
2	12 0	10 8	9.6	8.4	7.2
3	12 0	10 8	9.6	8.4	7.2
4	12 0	10.8	9.6	8.4	7.2
5	10 0	9 0	8.0	7.0	6.0
6	10 0	9 0	8.0	7 0	6.0
7	8 0	7.2	6 4	5 6	4.8
8	8 0	7 2	6 4	5.6	4.8
9	8 0	7 2	6 4	5.6	4.8
10	8 0	7 2	6 4	5.6	4.8

The total value, i.e., by addition of the values on each of the 10 points, establishes the rating as follows:

100="Outstanding" i.e., No. 5
90="Above Average" i.e., No. 4
80="Average" i.e., No. 3
70="Below Average" i.e., No. 2
60="Weak" i.e., No. 1

Advocates of this rating program maintain that it will minimize prejudice, bias, and guesswork in judging salesmen, and will also provide a complete picture of a man's performance, assuring a fair appraisal of his worth to the company.

Opponents of the program believe that branch managers would rate superficially simply as a matter of routine, without due consideration of each man's characteristics. Judgments would often be influenced by prejudice, and raters would hesitate to rate-down men.

Questions

1. Should the Mormac Packing Corporation adopt the salesman rating program? Give reasons for your decision.

2. Is the rating form prepared by the committee satisfactory? Criticize favorably or otherwise the choice of characteristics to be rated and the scale of values.

3. What steps should be taken in the preparation of a rating system?

Problem 2—Objective Evaluation of Salesmen

Rockwell Agency, Atlantic Life Insurance Company

The Rockwell Agency of the Atlantic Life Insurance Company was established in Boston in 1921 by Charles A. Rockwell, a former agent of the Atlantic Life Insurance Company, one of the ten largest life companies in the country. The agency has contracted thirty full-time underwriters and fifteen part-time agents, who together produce an annual volume of eight million dollars worth of insurance.

In order better to evaluate the performance of the agents and to supervise them more effectively, the agency manager proposed that each underwriter keep on a special form a daily record of: 1. The number of hours spent in the field. 2. The number of sales contacts made. 3. The number of contacts resulting in progress. 4. The number of new prospects secured. 5. The number of first interviews. 6. The number of second interviews. 7. The number of third interviews. 8. The total number of interviews. 9. The number of present policyholders seen.

A form was prepared on which could be recorded daily the nine types of sales activities listed above. Two agents volunteered to complete the form daily and turn it over to the agency manager who would analyze the activities of the men and point out to them their strengths and weaknesses.

This evaluation plan had been tested for a year by two of the full-time underwriters in the agency, and the following summary of sales activities resulted:

SUMMARY OF SALES ACTIVITIES OF SALESMEN *A* AND *B*

| | Salesman A | | Salesman B | |
Average Time and Effort Expended	Daily	Weekly	Daily	Weekly
Hours spent in field	4.4	26.3	6.7	40.2
Number of sales contacts	2.5	15.1	5.9	35.5
Contacts resulting in progress	1.7	10.5	5.0	30.1
New prospects secured	.5	3.2	4.1	25.0
Number of first interviews	.5	3.2	1.8	11.0
Number of second interviews	.2	1.3	.4	2.3
Number of third and subsequent interviews	.6	3.8	.2	1.5
Total number of interviews	1.3	8.2	2.9	17.4
Customers contacted	.05	.33	.6	3.7

The comparative sales accomplishment of the two salesmen who kept a record of their activities showed that salesman *A* sold an average of $7,627 worth of insurance monthly, while salesman *B* averaged $15,332 in sales each month. In number of contracts closed, salesman *A* averaged 1.6 monthly, compared with 6.5 contracts closed by salesman *B*.

The agency manager believed that this objective record of sales activities clearly indicated the relation of effective working methods to sales accomplishment and the importance of each agent keeping records of his activities to enable the management to evaluate his performance continuously and discover his strengths and weaknesses.

Some agents objected to keeping records of their daily activities, claiming that it was time consuming and expensive, and they resented the routine and detail involved. They believed that the information would be used by the agency manager to find fault with their work. Furthermore, they contended that the reports could easily be falsified and that a man could not be judged fairly by such activities, which often had little relation to his sales accomplishment.

The agency manager proposed to have each agent's work record analyzed weekly. In this way he could keep closely in touch with the agent's progress and be able to assist him in improving his sales and earnings. Weekly reports would be given to each underwriter, and in personal conferences with the agency manager the activities of each salesman would be discussed.

Questions

1. Should the agency manager adopt this method of evaluating his salesmen's performances? Give reasons for your decision.

2. What other performance factors should also be taken into consideration in judging the work of the agents?

3. What other methods of judging the accomplishment of these agents should be used?

Problem 3—Salesman Evaluation

The Parkinson Rubber Company

The Parkinson Rubber Company, Akron, Ohio, is one of the world's largest producers and distributors of rubber footwear, including tennis and basketball shoes, overshoes, and boots. The line, which is nationally advertised, is sold through thirty-thousand wholesale and retail chain and independent stores and mail order houses in urban and rural districts in all parts of the country.

The company maintains fifteen sales and distributing branches in the principal cities, out of which travel one hundred fifty salaried wholesale salesmen who are assigned exclusive territories and sell the full line.

The accounts sold are classified as "salesmen's accounts," which are handled entirely by the individual salesmen, and "house accounts," including larger customers, which are sold directly by the branch manager.

The branch management, as well as the general sales manager, is faced with the problem of evaluating the work of the individual salesmen as an aid in supervision and in determining quotas, compensation, promotions, or discharges.

In the present method of appraising the work of a salesman, each branch manager considers the work of each of his men on the basis of his annual sales volume, attitude, coöperativeness, and standing with the trade. This method has been criticized by both management and men as inadequate and sometimes unfair to individual salesmen. Men who work in rural territories believe that it is unjust to compare their sales volume with that of city salesmen. Men who sell low-volume but high-profit items feel that they should not be appraised on volume alone but have credit for selling profitable goods. Those who travel economically believe that their low expense record should be considered.

One branch manager suggested that the only fair way to evaluate the salesmen's performance was on a basis of their direct selling costs, which would include salary and travel expenses. Each man's salary would be determined as a per cent of his gross sales to arrive at his compensation cost. Each salesman's travel expenses would be determined as a per cent of his gross sales to find his travel cost. The combined salary and travel expenses would be computed as a per cent of gross sales to give total sales cost for each man. The total number of calls of each salesman would be considered in relation to his total expense to find his cost per call.

The branch manager believed that this method of appraising the worth of each salesman would eliminate the prejudice and bias of subjective judgments and the inequalities of judging a man on the basis of sales volume alone. This plan would insure that a salesman would be considered fairly according to his ability to produce sales at the lowest cost.

The branch manager had the following analysis made of the costs of the eleven salesmen under his direction for a period of one year to illustrate how the men could be evaluated and compared on the basis of cost:

PARKINSON RUBBER CO.
SALESMEN'S COST—BRANCH C
Jan. 1, 1945, to Dec. 31, 1945

Salesmen	Gross Sales	Salaries	% Gross Sales	Travel	% Gross Sales	Total %	No. Calls	Cost per Call
#1	$61,836	$5,000	8.10	$2,221	3.61	11.71	584	*$15.45
#2	76,947	2,600	3.38	815	1.06	4.44	2,120	1.60
#3	18,322	1,800	9.85	Paid out of salary		9.85	....	....
#4	48,318	2,700	5.14	657	1.37	6.51	1,261	2.66
#5	67,995	2,500	3.68	900	1.33	5.01	1,352	2.51
#6	65,494	2,400	3.68	1,361	2.08	5.76	1,116	3.37
#7	66,511	2,700	4.06	1,778	2.68	6.74	1,151	3.89
#8	896	51	5.70	....	....	5.70	Special	
#9	198,055	5,267	2.65	114	.06	2.71	960	5.61
#10	21,611	1,650	7.64	709	3.28	11.92	Territory transferred	
#11	3,126	197	6.32	....	....	6.32	Territory transferred	
Total	$629,111	$26,865	4.26	$8,555	1.36	5.62		
House	400,178							
Grand Total	$1,029,289							

* Includes cost of both Salesmen #1 and #3.

Some executives of the company objected to the branch manager's plan to appraise salesmen on a basis of cost. They maintained that a man's gross sales were often determined by local preferences, advertising, quality of distributing outlets, or favorable business conditions, rather than by a salesman's ability. Furthermore, a man's travel expense was largely affected by the extent of his territory. The man who traveled at low cost might be covering his territory inadequately. The cost method of appraisal does not take into consideration the interest and attitude of the individual.

The management was undecided as to what action to take on the branch manager's suggestion and planned to submit his proposal for discussion by all branch managers at their next meeting at the home office.

Questions

1. Should the Parkinson Rubber Co. adopt the branch manager's plan for evaluating salesmen on the basis of direct selling costs? Give reasons for your decision.

2. What other method or methods of evaluation might have been used by the company? What are the advantages of these methods?

3. Analyze the cost analysis of salesmen of Branch C and rate the eleven salesmen in order of merit on the basis of their cost performance.

4. On the basis of this cost analysis, what use may be made of this information in the supervision of these salesmen?

Problem 4—Sales Performance Standards

Occidental Refining Company

The Occidental Refining Company, Philadelphia, Pa., refines and markets gasoline, oil and a full line of petroleum specialties in Pennsylvania, New Jersey, Delaware, and Maryland. The company owns or leases two hundred retail outlets and maintains tank and pump investment in several hundred others throughout its territory.

The company's salesmen may be considered general sales managers in their assigned territories responsible for sales volume and with many other duties in addition to the solicitation of business. The salesmen must be market analysts, real estate men, and maintenance engineers in addition to salesmen of a variety of products. They must understand the different lines of business that represent the principal markets for those products.

For several years each man's performance and compensation were determined by annual ratings made by his supervisor. The qualities and characteristics rated emphasized appearance, poise, character, attitude, and education rather than sales performance. This rating system tended to depreciate achievement in the opinion of some executives.

The sales manager believes that new sales performance standards should be established which are based on a definable and measurable set of conditions that would represent satisfactory performance in a salesman's territory.

Accordingly eight salesmen were called into the home office to confer with the management on performance standards to insure that executive judgment would be conditioned by field thinking. At an informal discussion of performance standards, the salesmen were given an opportunity to express their views in an atmosphere completely free from influence and pressure by management. The salesmen recommended that their performance should be judged on a basis of measurable standards, only after their district manager had personally reviewed their accomplishment, compared it with the standards, and given them an opportunity to discuss their achievements. As the eight salesmen consulted could not agree as to the kind and number of standards of performance, the management appointed a committee representing both salesmen and management to coordinate the various viewpoints so that a standard could be developed that would meet the approval of management and the salesmen.

The sales performance standards committee did not believe that the salesmen should be judged on a basis of personal characteristics but on definite measurements of quantity and quality of work. It was a difficult task, however, to determine these measurements. Some standards were immeasurable, others required so many statistics and paper work that the work load was prohibitive, while some were administratively ponderous.

Four major standards were selected by the committeee and approved by the management:

1. Sales Volume.
2. Acquisition and Retention of Sales Outlets.
3. Sales Realization or Profit on Sales.
4. Selling Expense.

Each standard was clearly and simply stated in measurable terms. For example, the standard on acquisition and retention of outlets was stated as follows:

The salesman's performance is up to standard when:
1. He holds all selected accounts.
2. He secures competitive selected accounts when competitive contractual relationships expire.
3. He secures all new selected accounts as they become available.
4. He furnishes accurate information to keep his records up to date.

The standard description of sales volume read:

The performance of the salesman is up to standard when he has equalled or exceeded the sales volume objectives for all products as jointly agreed upon by the district sales manager and the salesman.

The standard description of sales expense was:

All loans which have been approved as a result of recommendations by the salesman must be repaid in accordance with the terms of the original agreement with the customer and the salesman's operating expenses must be within the budget established and agreed upon by the district sales manager and the salesman.

The standard description on sales realization read:

The sales realization of the salesman is up to standard when the average gross profit on products which he sells equals or exceeds the agreed gross profit objectives for all products jointly agreed upon by the district sales manager and the salesman.

Each sales district would be permitted to break down these general standards into substandards to aid in their administration, but no departure from the basic plan would be permitted. The performance of a salesman would not be determined for each standard on a mathematical basis, but as a result of discussion between the district manager and each salesman on the basis of statistics on sales volume, sales outlets, gross profit, and selling expense at their disposal.

Performance reviews would be held semiannually at which time the district manager would measure each salesman's performance against the established standards and make it clear to the man what would be expected of him and the methods for accomplishing that objective. The district manager would point out the salesman's weaknesses, give him whatever help or information is needed to correct them, and fix a date when the weaknesses must be corrected.

In the opinion of the management, these semiannual reviews would improve the character of supervision of the district managers by bringing them in closer touch with their men, and thus enabling them to understand better the salesmen's problems, and to help them when they need it.

The effect of performance standards on the salesman would be desirable by giving them a voice in establishing the objectives so that they would be more inclined to accept them sincerely. They would take more interest in their work and become more productive because they would know that they would be judged on the basis of their performance against these objectives, and would be paid accordingly.

On the other hand, it was contended that such factors as economic and market conditions, competition, and the calibre of dealers in each salesman's territory were not definitely measurable and would affect the man's ability to perform according to standard. While these factors might be considered by the district manager, in setting annual objectives for each salesman, their determination would be largely a matter of personal judgment. Differences of opinion on the part of the district manager and salesmen concerning these factors might lead to misunderstanding and ill will.

Furthermore, the relative importance of each of the four basic standards was not considered. Some district managers might give more weight to acquisition and retention of outlets; others might consider sales volume or profit more important. In certain cases the high volume man might get more credit than he deserved.

Some company executives believed that it was not practical to establish standards of performance that would be fair and workable for all salesmen.

Questions

1. Should the company have adopted the four performance standards described in this case? Give reasons for your answer.

2. Was the method of determining performance standards sound? Why?

3. Should the personal characteristics of the salesmen, such as attitude, interest, coöperativeness, be considered in judging their work? Give reasons for your conclusion.

Reading References

Introduction to Sales Management, Tosdal, pp. 418–426.
Manpower in Marketing, Benge, Chap. XVII.
Personnel Management, Scott, Clothier, Mathewson, Spriegel, Chaps. XIII, XIV, XIX.
Personnel Management and Industrial Relations, Yoder, Chap. XII.
Personnel Relations, Walters, Chap. VII.
Sales Managers Handbook, Aspley, Third Revised Edition, Section 20.
Sales Management, Nolan, Maynard, Chap. 20.
Supervising People, Halsey, Chap. XII.

PART THREE

SALES CONTROL

CHAPTER FIFTEEN

SALES TERRITORIES

What Is a Sales Territory? A sales territory is commonly understood to be a geographical area to which a salesman is assigned. In some cases geographical areas are ignored, and salesmen are assigned to certain classes of buyers, such as retailers, wholesalers, institutions, and industries, although these buyers are usually grouped and assigned to salesmen along geographical lines. Assignments of salesmen may also be made according to types of products, but here again the salesmen usually confine their efforts to definite geographical areas as well as classes of buyers.

In the sale of some products or services, salesmen are not assigned by either geographical areas or types of buyers, but are free to roam at will wherever their fancy may lead them. Frequently no territories are assigned for the introduction of new products when the market has been undeveloped, or in the case of highly competitive lines such as life insurance and automobiles. Commission salesmen are often reluctant to be confined to definite territories where their efforts may be restricted.

However, when salesmen are not restricted in their efforts to definite territories, they are often given "protection" in certain geographical areas by being given all inquiries or "leads" that may come from the areas to which they have been assigned.

Why Establish Sales Territories? Sales territories are established for the following reasons:

1. To assure thorough coverage of the potential market.
2. To meet competition more effectively.
3. To make comparisons between the accomplishments of different salesmen.
4. To avoid conflicts between salesmen and overlapping of effort.
5. To equalize the opportunities for all salesmen in the organization.

6. To facilitate control and operation of salesmen.
7. To cut travel expenses.
8. To eliminate backtracking of salesmen.
9. To select and train salesmen to handle a certain type of buyer in a certain geographical area.
10. To provide salesmen with sufficient prospects to consume their full time and at the same time not give them more than they can do effectively.
11. To save the salesmen's time.
12. To insure proper service to customers.
13. To give salesmen responsibility.

Sales territories are not established by some companies because:

1. It takes time and is expensive to allocate territories fairly.
2. Territories create disagreements and dissatisfaction among the salesmen.
3. Salesmen operate more effectively when not confined to a definite area or class of trade.
4. Salesmen resent territory reductions.

How to Establish Sales Territories. There are numerous ways to determine the geographical area of a sales territory. It is often done arbitrarily, in the case of new companies with broad markets, by giving salesmen a certain number of states or sections of the country irrespective of the potentiality of these areas. In such cases territories are so poorly established that revision must sooner or later be undertaken, with consequent aggravating problems of adjustment.

On the other hand, many progressive concerns have established, and others are now organizing, sales territories on more scientific bases. Territories are scientifically determined by considering the following factors:

1. Market potentialities.
2. Transportation, or the method of travel.
3. Competition.
4. Demand for the product.
5. Extent and policy of sales development.
6. Volume of business necessary to cover a territory.
7. Method of distribution.
8. Economic conditions.
9. Type of product.

10. The ability of the salesman.
11. Miscellaneous factors affecting allocation of sales territories.

Market potentialities. To insure equal opportunities to all salesmen and distribute sales and advertising energy uniformly, territories should be as identical from the point of view of possibilities as it is practical to make them. Steps in the basic division of a national market into sales territories are:

A. Select a market index or indexes of the potential market for the product.

Indexes of the potential market for life insurance which are used in establishing territories for life insurance agencies, are:

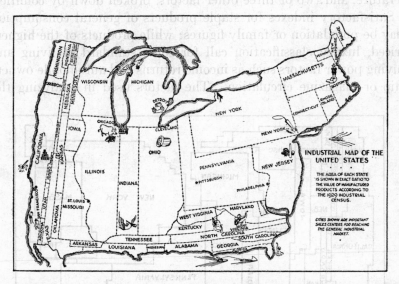

FIGURE 54. An industrial sales territory map of the United States, prepared by Russell T. Gray, Inc., showing the area of each state determined by the index of value of manufactured products according to the 1929 Industrial Census.

1. Number of personal income tax returns, insurable population.
2. Total bank deposits.
3. Combined circulation of six national magazines.
4. Value added by manufacture.
5. Estimated yearly agricultural income.

Indexes of industrial market potential used in establishing industrial sales territories are:

1. Number of manufacturing establishments.
2. Wage earners in manufacturing establishments.

3. Cost of materials, containers, fuel, and purchase of electric energy in manufacturing establishments.
4. Value of manufactured products.
5. Value added by manufacture.
6. Rated capacity of power equipment.

Index factors of market potential used in establishing sales territories may be obtained from the Bureau of the Census, U. S. Department of Commerce, Hearst Magazines, Inc., and other sources.

A large manufacturer of automotive products uses the following factors in establishing sales territories: population, income tax returns, automobile registrations, magazine circulation, winter temperature, and two or three other factors, broken down by counties.

Satisfactory indexes for staple products of general consumption may be population or family figures; while products of the higher-priced, luxury classification call for some standard of living and buying power factors such as income returns and automobile ownership or magazine circulation. The factors used in analyzing the

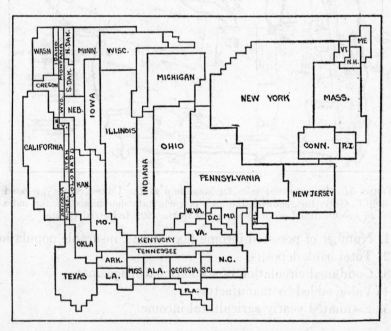

FIGURE 55. This map shows how the various states in the United States would look to a life insurance sales executive if the area of each state were determined on a basis of life insurance buying power. This map, prepared by the Life Insurance Sales Research Bureau, is based on the indexes of insurable population, number of income tax returns, total bank deposits, combined circulation of six magazines, value added by manufacture, and estimated yearly agricultural income.

market potentiality will depend upon the type of product, its sale price, and distribution.

B. Next distribute the market index or indexes selected, by county, city, state, or trading areas on a percentage basis of the national total, for example: a state breakdown of the three index factors—total population, wired homes, and total retail outlets—in the states of Maine, New Hampshire, and Vermont would show the following percentages of the national totals:

	Total Population	Wired Homes	Retail Outlets	Combined Average
Maine	.65%	.77%	.75%	.723%
New Hampshire	.38	.51	.42	.436
Vermont	.29	.32	.32	.31

Combined average total for three state......1.469%, or ⅟₆₈ of the United States potential based on these three factors.

Here the three factors are given equal weighting. If the wired homes factor is twice as important as the two other factors of population and retail outlets, its value may be doubled. The various factors selected can be readily weighted according to their relative importance.

This process of taking the percentages of any potential factor or index, or a combination of several factors, should be completed for the entire country on a county, state, or trading area basis.

C. Combine the index percentages into sales areas of equal potential. The size and number of sales areas depend upon the number of salesmen available, frequency of coverage wanted, extent of market development, and intensity of competition.

For example, to divide the national market into sixty-eight potentially equal territories, for sixty-eight salesmen, use the state percentage figures on population, wired homes, and retail outlets in the preceding example. The total average percentage of the three factors for Maine, New Hampshire, and Vermont is 1.469 per cent. There are sixty-eight salesmen. To make each man's territory potentially equal, his share of the national market would be 1.469 per cent. Therefore, one of the sixty-eight salesmen should be given a territory comprising Maine, New Hampshire, and Vermont.

By this method sales territories can be equitably distributed according to the potentiality of the market. While other factors should be taken into consideration in determining the extent of areas assigned to individual salesmen, the market potential is a basic consideration in arriving at a sound territory allocation.

In establishing sales territories, a decision must be made as to the type of the geographical unit on which territories shall be based. Four common bases for territories are: (1) the county unit, (2) the state unit, (3) the trading area unit, and (4) the city unit.

The *county unit* has long been the basis for fixing many sales territories. The United States Bureau of the Census collects and publishes statistical data according to counties.

The *state unit* of territory allocation is satisfactory for companies cultivating the national market extensively, operating with a limited number of salesmen calling infrequently on buyers. The state unit of allocation is ordinarily too large a territorial division of the market for any intensive sales development and control. Statistical analysis by states is much less frequently practiced than by counties.

The *trading area unit* has several advantages. It reduces to a minimum the amount of detail in determining territories. This unit is based on the actual flow of retail trade while county units are established primarily for political purposes. County statistics can be readily converted into trading area figures, thus making obsolete the county system of control.

Wholesale trading areas have been established by the United States Department of Commerce in its *Atlas of Wholesale Grocery Territories.*

In determining territories *The Market Data Handbook of the United States* [1] is likewise valuable. Included in this handbook are three maps of the United States, helpful in establishing territories:

1. A wholesale grocery territory map.
2. A consumer trading area map.
3. A retail shopping area map.

The Hearst Magazines, Inc., marketing department has spent many years in the development of the study *Trading Area System of Sales Control.* The J. Walter Thompson Company has published *Population and Its Distribution,* which is very useful in fixing territories.

The *city unit* basis for allocating territories is made possible by the publication of census figures by communities. The trading

---

[1] Domestic Commerce Series No. 30.

area system also organizes these figures for all communities of two thousand five hundred population and over.

An example of territory allocation by market analysis is the case of a drug product manufacturer, which originally established sales territories arbitrarily along county and state lines, and then decided to revise its territory allocation on the basis of trading areas established by measurement of market potentialities. The company then decided that its new territories must be based on authentic market research. A buying power index, based upon twenty-two unweighted factors including population, retail volume of sales, passenger car registrations, and income tax returns, was used. This index showed a high degree of correlation with retail drug sales and drug outlets through which the products of the company were distributed. By using this index, the company equalized the market potential of all its salesmen.

Since the company distributed through drug jobbers, it combined retail trading areas with wholesale trading areas to enable the salesmen to work more closely with wholesalers and benefit from retail business in their territories.

Other factors considered in determining the territories were accessibility for coverage and immediate sales volume to justify the cost which is involved in the full-time coverage of a salesman. A maximum average ratio of direct selling expense to estimated sales was established as a guide in limiting the size of each salesman's territory.

The territories, based on buying power, were adjusted with respect to wholesale territories, frequency of coverage, and immediate sales volume. It was found that the adjusted sales areas did not vary more than 12 per cent from the size of the territories originally determined by the buying power index.

Transportation, or the method of travel. An important factor to be considered in establishing the geographical area of a sales territory is available transportation. The increased use of automobiles by salesmen and the greater number of good roads have made it possible to cover larger territories than heretofore. Territories should be laid out along highway lines to facilitate coverage by salesmen.

When customers are widely separated, railroad transportation is often the most economical, in which case the location of rail lines must be taken into consideration in arriving at territory areas.

Airplanes are enabling salesmen to cover more territory than before. If the salesmen travel by air, air lines must be taken into consideration in determining sales territories.

Bus lines are opening many heretofore remote sections of sales territories to traveling salesmen. Thus the influence of bus routes on the allocation of sales areas is considerable.

A complete set of maps showing the lines of train, trolley, airplane, bus, and boat transportation, as well as automobile roads, should be used in the establishment of sales territories for economy and efficiency of coverage.

Competition. This is a vital factor in determining extent of the area to be assigned to a salesman. If competition is keen, a territory must be covered more frequently to secure a portion of the available business, and for this reason the size of the area should be restricted. When there is little competition, buyers may be contacted less frequently, and the salesman can cover a larger area.

On the other hand, competition may be so firmly entrenched that a salesman cannot secure enough business to justify the expense of covering a certain territory. In this event he may be given a territory in which he can secure sufficient sales volume to justify his expense.

Demand for the product. The factor of demand has a bearing on the size of a territory. Where a product is little known and a salesman must take time for lengthy explanations to buyers, his selling progress is slow. If good distribution is desired, a limited territory is advisable. If the demand for a product is infrequent or the repeat sales are slow, a larger territory may be necessary to enable a man to secure a profitable volume of sales. The usual practice in introducing new products for which there is little demand is to "skim the cream," or sell a few desirable buyers and work a larger territory rather than strive for thorough distribution.

Extent and policy of sales development. Some companies introducing a new product adopt the policy of getting broad, but thin, national distribution rather than intensive local distribution. Broad distribution, spread thinly, calls for large sales territories. A policy of intensive sectional development demands small sales territories. New territories intensively covered demand more effort than many older areas and may therefore be smaller in size.

Volume of business necessary to cover a territory profitably. Certain companies establish a maximum ratio of direct selling expense to expected sales as a guide in limiting the size of a sales territory. For example, a company determines that salesmen's travel expenses must not exceed 4 per cent of net sales in any territory. The expected sales in territory *A* are $100,000, and the cost of covering the territory is $5,000. This cost is $1,000, or 1 per cent, in excess of the maximum ratio of selling expense to net sales. In this case the size of the territory is reduced to curtail sales expenses, or the area is increased to the extent of increasing the volume of sales without increasing the expense ratio proportionately.

Some companies will not create new sales territories from established areas unless the new territories produce sufficient immediate sales volume to justify the cost involved in the full-time coverage.

Method of distribution. The channels through which a product is distributed affect the size of the salesmen's territories. If a product is sold through wholesalers and chains exclusively, the territories of the salesmen will usually be large in area. If a product is sold direct to the consumer and salesmen are given exclusive territories, such areas are often small in geographical size. Salesmen calling on grocery retailers may have smaller territories than salesmen calling on gift shops, since there are a larger number of grocery outlets.

Economic conditions. One of the principal sales operation problems in a period of depression is the reduction of salesmen's territories to a point where expenses are not out of proportion to sales volume. When business declines, owing to adverse business conditions, many companies realign sales territories.

Local economic conditions resulting in greatly increased opportunities for sales likewise demand a curtailment of territory area to insure maximum sales effort in the area of highest opportunity. Strikes, floods, and droughts which more or less permanently affect the business of a territory call for a realignment of territory. Industrial activity may affect demand and create a need for territorial changes.

Type of product. The nature of a product will influence allocation of territories. The degree of repeat sale will determine the frequency of call. Thus small sales territories are required for repeat products and large territories for non-repeat products. The amount of service a product requires, if such service is rendered by the salesman, will determine the amount of area covered.

Ability of the salesman. In the last analysis, the ability of the salesman in the territory should have a considerable influence on the size of the area assigned. A very able man can cover more territory effectively than a mediocre salesman.

Miscellaneous factors affecting allocation of sales territories. There are numerous considerations which influence the determination of territories:

1. Limiting the size of territories to permit salesmen to spend their week ends at home.
2. Limiting territories to permit salesmen to live at home.
3. Limiting territories to areas served by branch warehouses.

These factors should all be taken into consideration in the setting up of sales areas. Since many of these conditions are changing constantly, periodic changes of territories are necessary to maintain a reasonable expense to sales ratio and secure the desirable volume of sales.

Many territories are poorly allocated because only one or two of these factors have been considered. Many companies use no further guide than transportation facilities—highways or railroad lines—to determine their salesmen's working districts. Little attempt is made to apportion the sales opportunities equally among all salesmen, and frequently one man has too much territory, with the result that buyers are being neglected and competitors are getting more than their share of the available business. In many instances salesmen are still being confined to territories that were established many years ago under vastly different market conditions.

If sales territories for consumer merchandise are allocated along trading area lines, the problem of determining their boundaries is solved by following the trading area boundaries established in the *Atlas of Wholesale Grocery Territories,* United States Department of Commerce; *Trading Area System of Sales Control,* Hearst Magazines, Inc.; *Population and Its Distribution,* J. Walter Thompson Company, and *The Market Data Handbook of the United States,* and *Market Data Handbook of New England,* United States Department of Commerce.

If, on the other hand, territories for consumer goods have been set up arbitrarily on a county basis, the boundaries are often mistakenly determined by state or county lines because they are conveniently found on any map; they are easy to determine; and market statistics are usually compiled in state and county units. Sales do not stop at county and state lines but are determined by buying habits that take no cognizance whatever of political boundaries. The buyer goes where transportation facilities will most conveniently carry him to sources of supply for the merchandise that he wishes to buy.

Many sales managers of products that are sold through retail and wholesale outlets are arbitrarily limiting territories to state boundaries, with resulting high sales costs. The best illustrations of the inadequacy of state boundaries are provided by the many twin cities in the country which are in the same trading area but located in different states. St. Louis, Missouri, and East St. Louis, Illinois, are separated only by the bridged Mississippi River. A St. Louis, Missouri, salesman should logically cover East St. Louis, Illinois. When sales territories are established on state and county lines, an Illinois salesman must incur additional travel expense and consume time to reach East St. Louis. The same conflict is found between New York City and Newark, New Jersey; Philadelphia, Pennsylvania, and Camden, New Jersey; Kansas City, Missouri, and Kansas City, Kansas; Omaha, Nebraska, and Council Bluffs, Iowa; Huntington, West Virginia, and Ashland, Kentucky.

Numerous cities in the country draw their retail trade from three or more states. Merchants of Wilmington, Delaware, for example, serve buyers in Marcus Hook, Pennsylvania; Penns Grove, New Jersey; Elkton, Maryland; and many Delaware towns. Joplin, Missouri, draws trade from Galena, Kansas; Picher, Oklahoma; Harrison, Arkansas; and many Missouri towns. These two trading centers illustrate the fallacy of establishing sales territories on state and county boundary lines.

From the sources previously mentioned, it is very easy for a sales manager to fix boundaries for sales territories along logical lines of trade rather than meaningless political boundaries. County records may be easily converted into trading area records by consulting *County Composition of Trading Areas*, published by the Hearst Magazines, Inc.

In the State of Ohio the marketing division of the Hearst Magazines, Inc., has established 54 retail trading areas. These are designated as 41 urban areas and 13 rural areas. These trading areas were established on a basis of 33 statistical factors, and their boundaries defined by the range of store deliveries, newspaper circulation, topographical obstacles, and character of transportation facilities, supplemented by direct questionnaires and magazine circulation figures.

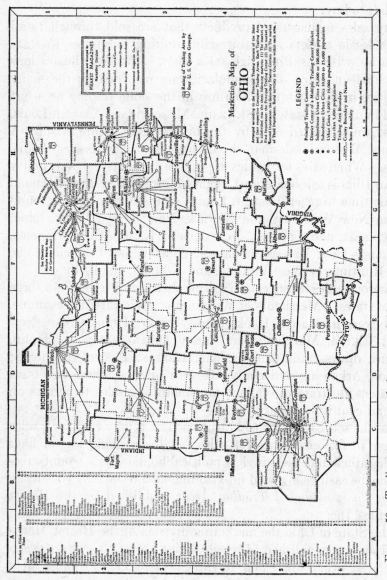

FIGURE 56. Trading area map of the state of Ohio, prepared by the marketing division of Hearst Magazines, Inc., showing the principal trading centers and their respective consumer trading areas. Each trading area is subdivided into markets of first, second, and third importance.

In setting up territories for salesmen selling to wholesalers, wholesale trading areas as outlined in the *Atlas of Wholesale Grocery Territories* provide logical boundaries. These areas are useful not only in the distribution of food products but for consumer commodities, the distribution of which is affected by transportation facilities and competition from near-by jobbing points.

In the case of industrial products, sales of which are not affected by retail trading areas, territory boundaries may be logically established along county lines. Industrial markets are heavily concentrated in a few states in the North and East. The Department of Commerce publication *A Basis for Establishing Industrial Sales Territories* ranks each county in the country on a basis of industrial market potentiality and illustrates with marketing maps the concentration of industrial sales opportunities. This information is invaluable in the allocation of sales territories for industrial goods. There are various types of products and services, not distributed through wholesale and retail outlets, which cannot use the trading area to advantage in territory allocation. Life insurance sales are little affected by consumer buying habits, and the county basis of territory allocation has been found most desirable. The establishment of territories for investment and security salesmen on a trading area basis is not practical. Security buyers are not in the habit of coming into a trading center to purchase.

Adjusting the Size of Sales Territories. After a territory has been established, it is frequently necessary to adjust the size of the area for various reasons mentioned previously:

1. To meet increasing competition.
2. To give more opportunity to a salesman of ability.
3. To secure a reasonable ratio of expense to sales volume.

Salesmen usually resent a reduction in the size of their territories as a restriction on their opportunities to increase sales and income. The problem of getting a salesman to accept a reduction in territory is facilitated by a careful analysis of territorial potentials. Records of sales volume, calls, and the expense of covering a territory provide a sales manager with the facts to convince a salesman that an adjustment in the area of his territory is warranted. Sometimes a salesman is guaranteed as large an income from his adjusted territory as he made in his old territory.

Many sales territories are not covered so intensively as they might be, and salesmen are inclined to overlook many sales opportunities in a desire to cover a large area. Frequently a reduction in the size of a territory provides for more intensive cultivation, with resulting increased sales and reduced expense.

Sales managers are sometimes obsessed with a desire for national coverage and prestige. Large territories are established, with the result that freight costs climb, salesmen's traveling expenses increase, and advertising expenditures mount. Large territories are often a costly concession to ambition, and salesmen are sent all over the country to sell factory output that could be easily consumed within a five-hundred-mile radius of the plant.

Maps showing the location and boundaries of each territory should be prepared for ready reference by sales executives. Individual territorial maps may be prepared and housed in special cabinets in the sales office, or a large national map may be used, upon the surface of which the boundaries of each sales area may be drawn.

Salesmen should be given maps outlining their sales territories, so that they may confine their efforts to their own particular areas and become familiar with the district for which they will be held responsible.

Despite all the assistance provided by government and private research in the allocation of sales territories, it is impossible for a sales executive to sit at his desk and lay out sales areas that would be completely satisfactory. There are so many factors influencing the size and shape of a territory that the process of allocation is still largely one of trial and error. However, with the advice of a salesman who is familiar with local conditions, plus the available statistics, sales territories can be eventually established that will be satisfactory to both management and salesmen. The result will be more effective coverage and lower selling costs.

Problem 1—Establishing Sales Territories

Baker Shoe Company

The Baker Shoe Company, located in Brockton, Massachusetts, manufactures and sells men's and women's shoes direct to shoe dealers and dry goods and department stores throughout the country, with a sales force of sixty men operating out of six branch offices located in the principal cities. Since its establishment in 1919, the company has arbitrarily assigned sales territories along state and county lines, varying the size of the territory according to the amount of available business that the management believed a salesman could secure on a maximum expense ratio of 5 per cent of net sales. The salesmen were paid a small salary and commission. When business conditions were unfavorable for any extended period, the company was often obliged to curtail the size of sales territories and thus reduce traveling expenses when sales volume declined. This aroused resentment on the part of the salesmen, who claimed that additional territory was required by them in periods of business depression to maintain their previous volume and earn their customary commissions.

A new plan for allocating sales territories was suggested by the sales manager, who favored allowing each salesman five points for every town in his territory with a population of 25,000 or over, three points for every town from 10,000 to 25,000 population, one and one-half points for each town of 5,000 to 10,000 population, and one-half point for each town of 2,500 to 5,000 population. Totaling up the points, based on the population of urban places in a territory, gave a salesman his territory rating. The maximum number of points allowed a salesman would be ten. In other words, a man with two cities, each with 25,000 population or over, in his territory would be rated ten, equivalent to a single territory.

The company considered how the plan would apply in the state of Iowa, which has eight cities of 25,000 or over, totaling 40 points; eleven cities of 10,000 to 25,000 population, totaling 33 points; fourteen towns of 5,000 to 10,000 population, totaling 21 points; and forty-six towns of 2,500 to 5,000, totaling 23 points. The total number of points in Iowa would be 117. Additional towns in adjoining states would have to be included in the territory to bring the total number of points to 120, representing twelve salesmen needed to cover the state under the sales manager's plan. The state of Iowa was covered by two salesmen.

The sales manager believed that the additional number of salesmen required under his plan was justified, because the territory would be cultivated more intensively and much business now going to competitors would be secured by the company's salesmen. He conceded that the number of points to constitute a territory could be increased from ten to twenty or thirty, if necessary, depending on conditions in the territory.

Questions

1. Is the sales manager's plan for basing salesmen's territories on the population of the towns and cities sound? Give reasons for your decision.

2. Should the company have reduced the size of salesmen's territories in periods of business depression?

3. Is the present allocation of territories along state and county boundaries satisfactory?

4. If you believe another method of territory allocation would be more desirable, explain your plan in detail.

Problem 2—Open Territories versus Protected Territories

The Walker Weatherstrip Company

The Walker Weatherstrip Company, Minneapolis, Minnesota, sells weatherstrip direct to home owners, through a straight commission organization of four thousand salesmen, operating in urban places out of one hundred branch offices located in the principal cities of the country. The installation of the product is handled by mechanics, and salesmen spend all of their time selling.

For ten years the company followed the policy of giving each of its representatives an exclusive territory, arbitrarily bounded by county and state lines. Each man was protected against encroachment by other company representatives. This policy appealed to many men who objected to working up prospects, only to have them sold by another salesman, for the same company, who received the commission. In the opinion of the management, it was easier to obtain commission salesmen on a closed territory basis. One of the principal problems of the company was securing salesmen.

Analysis of numerous closed territories, however, disclosed that many salesmen were not working them to the fullest advantage. Some salesmen spent their time working only on wealthy prospects; others could not sell wealthy prospects and worked on middle-class prospects. This inability of salesmen to adapt themselves to the requirements of their territories left hundreds of potential orders unwritten, thus encouraging activity by competitors.

While the management realized that it was impossible to secure all of the available business in a territory, it believed that many of its salesmen were not doing their best. Furthermore, many territories were inactive, and salesmen were not earning enough to maintain their morale. In some sections home owners were away for a greater part of the summer, and sales were at a low ebb. Salesmen in such territories demanded new areas where there were better sales opportunities.

For these reasons the management considered the advisability of abolishing all protected territories and permitting salesmen to work where they wished. With open territories, salesmen could sell many of their friends who lived in other territories and exert their efforts in sections where they would get the best results. Men capable of selling wealthy buyers would have many more opportunities than existed heretofore in their protected areas. If a salesman became ill or suffered an accident, his territory was not covered under the closed-territory plan, whereas under an open-territory plan a new salesman could be assigned to the area.

All advertising inquiries and leads received by the company would be distributed in rotation to all salesmen, and coöperation would be extended to all men.

Questions

1. Should the Walker Company have abandoned its exclusive-territory plan of assigning salesmen in favor of the open-territory plan? Give reasons for your decision.

2. Could any other method of territory allocation be used in this case? Describe in detail.

Problem 3—Basing Territories on Market Potential

Norton Scale Company

The Norton Scale Company, Albany, New York, manufactures and sells two lines of scales. The principal line is sold to retail meat dealers, grocers, confectioners, and drug stores by a force of retail salesmen. The secondary line consists of portable scales sold to manufacturers for weighing materials used in production processes. Plant engineers, production managers, and purchasing agents are prospects for this type of scale. A separate force of industrial salesmen sells to manufacturers.

The territories of retail salesmen, who are paid their expenses and work on a straight commission, have been assigned arbitrarily on a state and county line basis. A new plan has been proposed to allocate on the basis of the minimum population necessary to produce a certain volume of business. The company would analyze each section of the country to determine the number of retail outlets, purchasing power per capita, number of automobiles in relation to the population, incomes over $2,000 a year, and percentage of foreign-born population. According to these factors, different sections of the country would be classified into four groups: Group A, with an expectation of $100 of annual sales for each thousand population; Group B, with $90 for each thousand population; Group C, with $80; and Group D, with $70. Each salesman's territory would have a potential volume of $40,000 a year. For example, in a Class A section of the country, a salesman would be assigned a territory of 400,000 population to enable him to secure $40,000 worth of business on a basis of $100 per thousand population. In a Class C section of the country, a salesman would be assigned a territory of 500,000 population to enable him to secure $40,000 worth of business on the basis of $80 per thousand population.

This method of territory allocation was favored by several executives of the company for the reason that it would equalize the opportunities of all salesmen and simplify the work of assigning areas to men. It was opposed on the grounds that it failed to take into consideration many local factors having a great influence on the possibilities of an area, such as competition, business conditions, the cost of covering the area, and other factors.

The industrial salesmen, who heretofore had been assigned territories on a state and county line basis, would not be assigned any definite geographical area, but would be assigned classifications of customers, such as automotive manufacturers, metal products manufacturers, drug manufacturers, manufacturing chemists, and the like. This method promised to give better service to customers by salesmen especially trained and experienced in the problems of each type of manufacturer. In the opinion of several company officials, the technical problems involved in the use of scales in certain industries demanded the services of a sales specialist.

On the other hand, this method of assignment promised to be more expensive from the standpoint of travel cost, since much time of the salesmen would be spent traveling to and from customers.

Questions

1. Is the proposed plan of territory allocation for retail scale salesmen sound? Give reasons for your decision.

2. Should the industrial scale salesmen be assigned classifications of customers? Give reasons for your answer.

Problem 4—Basing Territories on Trading Areas

The Gallatin Corporation

The Gallatin Corporation, Trenton, New Jersey, manufactures and distributes composition floor coverings sold through wholesale floor-covering dealers, who in turn resell to department and furniture stores throughout the country. The fifteen salesmen of the company are assigned sales areas that have been established on the basis of their accessibility to train and bus transportation lines. The territories are bounded by state and county lines, which are laid out for the most convenient coverage. The salesmen are paid a straight salary and, in addition, their expenses when on the road. They travel out of their homes, which are located in the territories.

The company plans to revise its territories to provide for expansion and to add two salesmen to the organization. The sales manager favors the establishment of territories on the basis of wholesale trading areas. The *Market Data Handbook of the United States* would be used, in which publication trading areas for budgetary control purposes and wholesale grocery territories are outlined on maps. The areas shown on these maps would conform with the territories served by the wholesale customers of the company.

After the territories of distributors had been determined in this way, each salesman would be assigned to such wholesale areas as, on account of his location, he could cover most effectively. When a distributor had several branch offices, the territories that these offices served would be included in the salesman's territory.

When each salesman's territory had been tentatively outlined by this method, statistics appearing in the *Market Data Handbook of the United States* would be used to measure the potential market. Such factors as population, income tax returns, magazine circulation, competition, and others would be used to determine the potential business of each territory and assure that all territories were approximately equal. The territory potentiality would be checked against the company's past sales in the territory and the salesman's salary and expenses, to determine whether or not the territory as outlined would be profitable to work.

If the territory as outlined promised an adequate volume of sales at a justifiable expense, it would be adopted, and a salesman assigned to work it.

This method of establishing sales territories was opposed for the reasons that it would require considerable detail work and disorganize the present territories, with resulting dissatisfaction to the company's salesmen.

The sales manager believed that this method was more scientific than the establishment of territories on an arbitrary basis and would result in more equal opportunities for the salesmen and better service to the customers of the company.

Questions

1. Do you consider as sound the plan for establishing sales areas on wholesale grocery territories adjusted by market analysis? Give reasons for your answer.

2. Would any other method of territory allocation be more effective? Describe in detail.

Reading References

Handbook of Sales Management, Hall, pp. 263–265.
Management of the Sales Organization, Russell, Chap. V.
Modern Sales Management, Frederick, Chap. XI.
Sales Administration, Hayward, p. 303.
Sales Management Fundamentals, Hay, p. 84.
Salesmen in Marketing Strategy, Lyon, pp. 244–267.
Scientific Sales Management Today, Hoyt, pp. 136–158.

CHAPTER SIXTEEN

ROUTING SALESMEN

Why Route Salesmen? Time is a salesman's capital. Since about 40 per cent of the average salesman's time is spent in traveling, it is important to plan where and how he should spend his time. Traveling hours are not productive hours, and many salesmen lacking self-direction skip and jump through a territory, start late, quit early, take long lunch hours, and in many other ways dissipate their time and energy.

A survey of the time employment of a group of twenty-eight city and forty-eight country salesmen of tires, machinery, and groceries showed that city men in an average day spend two hours traveling, waste three hours, and have three hours of productive time. Country salesmen spend three and one-half hours traveling, waste two and one-half hours, and have two hours of productive time in an average day.

The Dennison Manufacturing Company found that its salesmen spent 40 per cent of their time in traveling and 15 to 20 per cent in waiting to see prospects.

This high percentage of time spent in traveling and waiting indicates the necessity for a plan of travel regulation for salesmen. One sales manager has prepared a Wasted Time Table to show his salesmen the value of time lost in terms of income:

Yearly Income	Value of Half Hour	Half Hour a Day for a Year	Hour a Day for a Year
$2,000	$ .43	$123.00	$246.00
3,000	.63	189.00	378.00
4,000	.83	249.00	498.00
5,000	1.04	312.00	624.00
7,500	1.56	468.00	936.00

Increasing selling time an hour a day is equivalent to increasing sales pressure by more than 10 per cent, and making an average of one more call a day is equal to adding a month to the selling year. Much of this can be accomplished by planned routing.

There are advantages other than saving valuable selling time arising from proper routing of salesmen. A definite route insures a thorough coverage of a territory by providing for calls upon all of the desirable prospects. It is not uncommon for salesmen to travel several hundred miles to see a favorite customer, passing on the way hundreds of worth-while prospects located in many desirable markets. While these good prospects are being overlooked, a competitor salesman secures their business.

A typical example of how salesmen overlook opportunities is told by L. J. McCarthy, Director of Market Research, Hearst Magazines, Inc. A retail salesman was selling to drug stores in the eastern part of the state of Iowa. During the course of seven weeks, this man visited eighty-nine places, but fifty-six of them were towns having less than two thousand five hundred population, in which his previous annual sales had been less than $50. Davenport, the most important market, was visited once. Four dealers were seen. Waterloo, another important market, was also visited once, and Dubuque, the fourth largest market, was not visited at all during the seven weeks' period. On the other hand, there were six trips made to Iowa City without sound business reason. In the four principal trading centers of the area the salesman limited his calls to two each, although there were over one hundred prospects in them, and they furnished 25 per cent of the previous year's business. During the seven weeks, 66 per cent of the salesman's time was spent in small towns which produced only 20 per cent of his sales.

A good route provides a salesman with a definite rather than indefinite task. Given a definite goal to reach, a quota of calls, and a minimum number of prospects to interview, a salesman will accomplish more work than a man who goes out without a fixed objective. The same benefits that come from the establishment of sales volume quotas can be secured by setting sales call quotas.

Routing is an important factor in reducing the traveling expenses of a salesman. Long jumps, backtracking, and profitless calls, all creating high travel expense, are largely avoided if the salesman's route is laid out in advance to take advantage of the most economical transportation facilities. When an automobile route is predetermined, allegations by the salesman of excessive mileage are out of the question, since the sales manager can readily recognize unfair charges. When the route is planned, train transportation can often be used more effectively, with savings in cost over automobile travel.

When it is necessary to get in touch with a salesman in the field, a predetermined route greatly facilitates the problem of locating him. When price changes, inquiries from customers or prospects, credit reports, or other information must be communicated to a salesman, a duplicate route list in the hands of the home or branch office executives tells exactly where the salesman may be reached.

On the other hand, there are numerous problems arising in connection with the establishment of salesmen's routes that cause many organizations to allow salesmen to route themselves. A survey of one hundred and ten concerns by the Dartnell Corporation disclosed that four times as many concerns allow salesmen to route themselves as require salesmen to follow a routing laid out by the sales office.

Many concerns employing salesmen on commission find that these men usually prefer to work their territories without interference from the management and resent dictation of route or territory coverage. It is practically impossible for employers to require commission salesmen to follow a fixed route. Since commission men often pay their own expenses, sales managers have not been so much concerned with the cost factor as with the lack of thoroughness in coverage of a territory in the hands of commission men who often have no plan of travel.

Some sales managers believe that routing by the management destroys the initiative of the salesmen. They contend that salesmen should not be restricted in their activities but should be allowed full freedom to develop their territories as they see fit.

In the sale of highly specialized lines and technical equipment when salesmen must do considerable engineering or nonselling missionary work, the irregular character of their work makes it very difficult to confine them to exact routes and schedules. When salesmen must make special trips to investigate complaints, make adjustments, or supervise installations, it is difficult to route them closely.

Other sales managers contend that a salesman knows more about his territory than the management and is in a better position to route himself. They assume that a salesman's knowledge of detours, general road conditions, train or bus schedules, and all of the other factors to be considered in a territory is better than the home office sales executive's information, and for this reason the sales manager should not attempt to influence the travel plans of the salesmen.

Some sales managers prefer to let their salesmen route themselves. The expense involved in analyzing each salesman's territory and in preparing route plans is considerable. Route plans must be revised as travel conditions change in each territory, thus adding to the expense.

Preparing Salesmen's Routes. The preparation of salesmen's routes involves four fundamental steps. Each of these will be considered separately in the following discussion.

1. *Analysis of present coverage of each territory.* This step should precede the development of a routing plan. A complete picture should be obtained of:

The number of present customers.
The number of logical prospects.
The frequency of coverage.
The cost per call.
The towns visited.
The average time spent in each town.
The average time spent with each customer.

These facts, covering a period of a year or more, may usually be obtained from sales records and may form the basis for any sound adjustment in territory coverage.

A large paint manufacturer made such an analysis of a salesman's territory and found: that the average cost per call was $18.70; that a town in which no sales were made had been visited seven times at an expense of $131; that one dealer was visited once and sold $18.20 worth of paint at a cost of $18.70; that another dealer was called on once and bought $1,850 worth of paint; and that a dealer buying $208 worth of paint a year was not called on at all.

A large manufacturer of rubber footwear analyzed the coverage of its salesmen and found their cost per call varied from $1.61 to $5.61. One salesman made forty-one calls on a customer buying $19,358 worth of shoes a year and eighty-two calls on another customer buying $17,044 worth a year. Another salesman sold 63 per cent of his annual volume in his home town, where he made twenty-five to thirty calls a year on customers; while other customers one hundred and fifty miles away were seen only six or seven times a

year. This company was securing 51 per cent of its volume from
1 per cent of its customers.

In a similar territory analysis, a camera manufacturer found
that 90 per cent of its volume came from cities of one hundred thousand population, and 81 per cent of the sales volume was obtained
from two hundred dealers in those cities.

Such significant facts as these, disclosed by an analysis of a territory, reveal the necessity for more effective time employment of
salesmen and indicate where changes must be made in the methods
of covering sales territories, in order to cut costs and increase volume.

These facts do not imply that a salesman should necessarily
avoid certain classes of towns or dealers, but indicate the advisability of carefully scrutinizing towns and dealers from the standpoint of past sales and future sales possibilities. The fact that a
dealer will buy $500 worth a year on one call, while another dealer
buys only $200 after twenty calls, is no indication that all dealers
should receive fewer calls. However, a planned route enables a
salesman to make more frequent calls on big-volume accounts and
fewer contacts on low-volume accounts.

2. *Determining call frequencies.* With each territory analyzed,
the next step is to multiply the individual outlets in each territory
by the frequency with which they are to be contacted. The first
step in determining the frequency of contact is to make a classification of the total number of accounts and prospective buyers. This
grouping may be made on the basis of potential volume, size and
credit position.

A manufacturer of engineering products sold to manufacturers
determined the call frequency of salesmen by classifying customers
and prospects into eight groups as follows:

Class *A*—Very large customers and prospects in industries where the product
        is the principal equipment purchased.

Class *B*—Large customers and prospects and mill supply houses serving in-
        dustries requiring less of the product.

Class *C*—All other large industrial concerns, including municipalities, supply
        houses, architects, and contractors.

Class *D*—Smaller industrial customers and prospects, including large office
        buildings.

Class *E*—All public works departments and all normally active industrial cus-
        tomers and prospects.

Class *F*—Industrial prospects and customers using very little equipment.

Class *G*—Customers and prospects having seasonal demand only.

Class *H*—Customers and prospects having rare demand.

Call frequencies were then established for each of these classes as follows: Class *A*, once a week; Class *B*, once in two weeks; Class *C*, once a month; Class *D*, once in two months; Class *E*, once in four months; Class *F*, once in six months; Class *G* and Class *H*, no calls.

A large paint manufacturer classified his three hundred seventy-nine accounts and prospects, in one territory, into four groups:

1. Large accounts and prospects.
2. Small accounts and prospects with good development possibilities.
3. Large accounts and prospects requiring only occasional calls.
4. Small-volume prospects and customers.

Call frequencies were established for each of these classes as follows: Group 1, once a month; Group 2, every forty-five days; Group 3, every two months; and Group 4, every ninety days. Multiplying the number of customers and prospects in the territory, three hundred seventy-nine, by these frequencies gave a total figure of three thousand two hundred sixteen calls a year in the territory. This averaged eleven calls a day.

The frequency of calls of a salesman depends on several factors, such as the type of customer, type of product, amount of demand, nature of the selling job, advertising volume, and others, all of which help to answer the question, "How often must prospects and customers be visited to get the maximum amount of sales consistent with reasonable cost?" This question must be answered for each individual prospect and customer in a territory if routing is to be effective.

Large customers buying frequently in good volume demand more of the time of a salesman and should be seen more frequently. On the other hand, small buyers with limited volume possibilities should be seen less often.

Certain types of products such as frequent repeaters, perishables, and large-volume commodities call for frequent contact by salesmen with buyers. Heavy industrial installation equipment, on the other hand, is bought infrequently, and salesmen may call only once or twice a year.

The nature of the sales job affects call frequency. Salesmen doing missionary work with dealers, such as dressing windows, training clerks, or reselling to consumers, cannot cover so much territory or make so many calls as specialty salesmen introducing new products to dealers.

The average number of daily calls made by salesmen and the frequency of contact in various lines is shown in the following table:

Product	Sold To	Calls Per Day	Frequency of Contact
Wooden boxes	Manufacturers	10	
Dictating machines	Offices	6	90 days
Adding machines	Bus. offices	6	90 days
Hardware	Wholesalers	3–5	60 days
Candy	Wholesalers	15	60 days
Air compressors	Wholesalers	4	30 days
Cheese	Retailers	20–40	5 days
Insurance	Public	8–10	
Soap	Wholesalers	15	30–60–90 days
Bakers' machines	Users	12	Semiannually
Vacuum cleaners	Users	40	
Stationery	Retailers	7	Variable

In establishing call frequency for individual customers and prospects, the management should consult with the salesman in the territory for his opinion as to call frequency for each account. He should take into consideration previous sales records of each customer as well as future possibilities for sales. In the case of unknown prospects, published credit ratings may be a guide in classifying them for contact.

The call frequency in many lines sold through wholesale and retail outlets has been increased in recent years through the growing practice of hand-to-mouth buying to secure increased turnover of inventories. Retailers who formerly purchased their season's requirements at one time today buy only a seven to ten days' supply, and salesmen are obliged to call frequently to secure their share of the available business.

3. *Considering transportation methods.* The next step in route planning is a consideration of transportation facilities. A selection must be made from various methods of travel, including train, airplane, bus, trolley, or automobile, as they are available in each territory. The rapid development of transportation has made possible a quick and economical coverage of sales territories not heretofore possible. In many territories it is possible to use a combination of several modes of travel with a saving in time, expense, and energy of the salesman. Train travel costs have been reduced and speed increased to a point where many large territories in which customers are widely scattered can be covered more economically

by this method. Although automobiles are very effective for covering densely settled areas, their value decreases in city selling, where traffic congestion makes surface and subway electric lines more rapid and economical. By careful study of the travel facilities of each territory, with the aid of highway maps, train time tables, and bus schedules, an efficient route can be prepared.

An examination of salesmen's itemized expenses or automobile reports will reveal the actual costs of travel in a territory and prove useful in pointing out to the salesman the advisability of utilizing more economical transportation methods.

4. *Other considerations in routing.* Aside from the determination of call frequency and transportation facilities, there are other factors having a bearing on the route of a salesman. The location of the salesman's branch headquarters or home city in relation to other cities in the territory will affect the layout of routes. If the branch headquarters are centrally located, it may be possible to bring a salesman back to his home over week ends, thus saving hotel expenses and improving the morale of the man. However, if a territory headquarters or branch is located in one corner of the area to be covered, longer routes, which will keep the salesman out for several weeks, may be necessary.

The average length of time spent by a salesman with a prospect or customer must be considered in scheduling and routing. If a salesman spends an average of thirty minutes traveling to, waiting for, and talking with, each prospect and customer, and there are sixteen calls to be made in a city, the total time spent in the place will be eight hours. While the time spent in contacting must be approximated and additional time must be allowed to provide for emergencies, a general estimate of this time is necessary if a working schedule is to be prepared and a route determined.

The travel time between cities and towns should also be considered in routing. This time can be accurately estimated for train, bus, and airplane travel and can be approximated for automobile travel. This factor is influenced largely by the size of the territory, the traffic congestion, and the method of travel. Traveling can be done in nonselling hours, at night, on Saturday afternoon, or Sunday in many cases, thus saving valuable selling hours for contacts with buyers.

Not only should each prospect and customer be evaluated for routing, but also each town or city in a territory should be assayed before it is put on a route list. Many small towns do not contain enough worth-while prospects and customers to justify the time and expense necessary to reach them. Each place in a territory should be considered from the standpoint of potential sales. One company ranks in numerical order every place of two thousand five hundred population and over in a sales territory in order of its value as a source of business, eliminating low-ranking places from salesmen's routes.

Routes may be affected by climatic conditions, seasonal demand, or the economic situation. A national manufacturer of sunburn remedies adjusts its salesmen's routes to intensify coverage in vacation areas during the summer season. Many salesmen's routes in the northern states are curtailed in the winter on account of traveling conditions. A city that is affected by a strike is dropped from a route until business returns to normal.

Types of Sales Routes. Routing may be undertaken in great detail, to effect close control of a salesman's activities, or very loosely, with the men practically doing their own routing. Four varying degrees of route control are illustrated in the paragraphs below.

1. *Initial routing for new salesmen.* Many companies lay out a route for new salesmen, listing the towns and cities to be visited in the most convenient and economical order. This route is discussed with the new man, and if he is familiar with the territory to be covered, his suggestions are invited. He is urged to follow the route as closely as possible, deviating from it only whenever local conditions justify changes. This is a loose method of route control that may operate satisfactorily in the sale of technical products and specialties, or when the selling job is not of a routine nature and territories require flexible coverage. Salesmen of ability may control their own time satisfactorily by this method. However, many salesmen require more control than initial routing affords.

2. *Routing by salesmen.* Many companies leave the routing problem entirely in the hands of their salesmen, making no attempt to influence the method of covering a territory. Lacking knowledge of territorial conditions, traveling facilities, and prospects, many sales managers believe that their men are in the best position to route themselves. This method of handling routing is followed largely in the sale of consumer goods by house-to-house canvassing, or office specialties through commission salesmen.

The successful life insurance agent daily routes his calls in a restricted area, arranging them by location to save time in going from one call to another. He makes up a daily route list and also an emergency list of prospects to take the place of those who cannot be seen.

FORM 54-34 REV.5.

PLAN YOUR WORK

List below Calls you propose to make today.

WORK YOUR PLAN

Remember, Lost Order Reports aid the management and you.

Date ______ Salesman ______

TO DO TODAY

	PROPOSAL	STUDY	DEMONSTRATE	FIRM	ADDRESS OR DEPT.	PARTY TO SEE	SALES TOOLS NEEDED	NEXT CALL DATE	AMOUNT SOLD
1									
2									
3									
4									
5									
6									
7									
8									
9									
10									
11									
12									
13									
14									

ADDITIONAL CALLS - NOT PLANNED

1									
2									
3									
4									
5									
6									
7									

REMARKS	NO. CALLS	RECORD FORM ITEMS SOLD		NO. OF INSPECTIONS				PROSPECTS DEVELOPED								DISPOSITION				
	TO-DAY	STOCK	SPL.	VIS.	VER.	L.L.	S.C.	FIL.	LED.	SAL.	STK.	FURN.	SER.	R.AS.	TOTAL	SOLD	LOST	DROPT	DEF.	TOTAL

Turn into office each night with day's prospect follow-up, and inspection slips attached.

FIGURE 57. Salesmen of an office equipment manufacturer plan their own calls daily on this form. Space is also provided for calls on prospects not originally listed and for summarizing the day's activities.

3. *Routing by salesmen approved by management.* In some cases the salesmen and the company jointly plan the route for a week or a month in advance. This plan, followed by a certain box company, requires salesmen to submit on Saturday of each week a list of concerns to be called upon for the coming week. The day on which each concern is to be seen is determined. City salesmen go over the weekly list in person with the branch managers. Road salesmen mail the route lists on Saturday, and branch managers review them on Monday morning. Suggestions or changes are mailed or wired to the men in the field. When the occasion warrants it, salesmen put their route plans aside and go to some distant part of their territories to handle an inquiry or complaint that cannot be delayed.

A refrigerator company follows the same method, and route lists are mailed to the home office by salesmen with their expense reports, which are not considered complete unless a route list is attached.

By this method the management exercises a loose control over salesmen's routes, but the men mainly determine where they shall spend their time.

4. *Routing entirely by management.* The routes of salesmen of staple products, who call regularly on the same dealers, are often planned in considerable detail by their management. The routine

SALESMAN PLAN SHEET			
FOR WEEK BEGINNING_____SALESMAN_____			
	NAME	ADDRESS	CHARACTER OF CALL
DAY:	1		
	2		
	3		
ADDRESS:	4		
TOWN:	5		
	6		
HOTEL:	7		
	8		
	9		
	10		
DAY	1		
	2		
	3		
ADDRESS:	4		
TOWN:	5		
	6		
HOTEL:	7		
	8		
	9		
	10		
DAY:	1		
	2		
	3		
ADDRESS:	4		
TOWN:	5		
	6		
HOTEL:	7		
	8		
	9		
	10		

FIGURE 58. A Salesman's Route Plan Sheet used by representatives of a Mid-Western box manufacturer. The salesmen route themselves, completing this form and mailing it each week end to their branch managers, who are thus posted on the plans of each salesman for the coming week. Corrections in routing are telephoned or wired each salesman, when necessary, by the branch managers.

nature of wholesale and retail food, drug, and hardware selling lends itself ideally to detailed routing plans. From the standpoint of time, the management may establish one-week, two-week, seasonal, or occasional routes. Many route plans are simple statements of the places to be visited by the salesmen, their order of coverage, and the approximate time allowed. No attempt is made to designate specific prospects or customers to be called upon, or the time of arrival or departure from the different places visited.

A few companies have prepared detailed route plans for their salesmen such as the following:

1. *Skip-stop route plan.* By this plan accounts and prospects are first classified according to potential sales, and next a call frequency is set for each class of account and prospect. The Class *A* accounts, for example, are seen every thirty days; the Class *B*, every sixty days. Towns and cities may also be classified according to the number and class of accounts and prospects located therein. Thirty-day trips are laid out to bring salesmen in contact with all Class *A* customers and prospects every thirty days, on which trips all Class *B* buyers are "skipped." Every sixty days trips are planned to cover both Class *A* and *B* buyers. One company uses this plan based on a "town record" for each town in each territory. This record has one column classifying the accounts in each town as *A, B,* and *C,* according to their value to the company. Other columns are provided for the name and address of the account, credit limit, and estimated volume of business. The various accounts in each town are listed in accordance with the classifications. The town record is used in making up routes in each territory on a skip-stop basis.

This plan has the advantages of lowering sales costs by reducing the amount of time spent with small, unprofitable accounts and enabling the salesman to spend more time in developing profitable buyers. Thoroughness and intensiveness are sacrificed to concentration on the most fertile spots. Mileage covered by the skip-stop plan is often less than the distance covered when all accounts are contacted on every trip. One company found a saving of two thousand miles annually in one territory, or $164 in automobile expense.

This plan is not so effective in territories where there are long distances between accounts. In such areas it may be advisable to visit several classes of accounts on each trip to save travel expense. Furthermore, the plan must be kept flexible, and accounts reclassified as the potentiality of the accounts changes.

2. *The sector routing plan.* The sector plan is the routing of towns or accounts to insure logical, economical, and efficient sales coverage of retail stores in an area, group of towns, a town, or any group of stores. It is based on topography, roads, proximity of places, and distances.

A salesman's territory is divided into several sectors, and each sector is further divided into several routes or trips. A typical example of how the sector plan is operated by a large manufacturer of grocery specialties, whose twelve hundred salesmen call on retail grocers, follows:

TERRITORY 66

Sector No. 1—Sector Point: Shawnee, Oklahoma

Trip 1	*Trip 2*	*Trip 3*
Shawnee	Tecumseh	Seminole
	Pink	Bowlegs
	Macomb	Maud RFD #2
	Pearson	Snomac
	Shawnee RFD #2	
	Little Keokuk Falls	
	Prague	

Trip 4	*Trip 5*
St. Louis	Wewoka
Maud	Cromwell
Earlsboro	Okemah RFD #2
Earlsboro RFD #2	Schoolton
Meeker	New Lima
McLoud	
Dale	

Sector No. 2—Sector Point: Cushing, Oklahoma

Trip 1	*Trip 2*	
Cushing	Ripley	Vinco
Yale	Mehan	Merrick
Davenport	Signet	Fallis
Avery	Glencoe	Wellston
Tryon	Morrison	Warwick
Gano	Stillwater	Chandler
Stroud	Perkins	Sparks
Kendrick	Carney	
Agra		

In this territory there are five sectors with a total of twenty-one trips. The stores in the territory are classified into *A, B,* and *C* groups as follows:

	A Stores	B Stores	C Stores	Miscellaneous	Total
Sector #1	85	200	507	390	1,182
Sector #2	26	59	132	88	305
Sector #3	14	28	86	59	187
Sector #4	24	49	107	62	242
Sector #5	26	71	158	78	333
Total	175	407	990	677	2,249

Retail salesmen are assigned to cover definite sectors and trips by district representatives, who make the assignment on "assignment confirmation" forms. When a salesman has covered the trips assigned, he reports his activities on an "assignment report" form, which is used to measure the success of the retail salesman and the management ability of the district representative in assigning salesmen.

3. *Daily route plan.* In the case of city salesmen of office appliances, automobiles, and other specialties, the management frequently plans daily routes for each salesman. A certain number of prospects to be called upon during the day is selected, concentrated in one part of the city, and arranged in the most economical order of coverage. These prospects may be divided among new prospects, old prospects, and customers, to insure well-balanced work. The salesman is required to report on these calls each day and is given only as many names of prospects as may be covered by the salesman in one day.

4. *Time control route plan.* To insure that salesmen spend sufficient time with prospects and customers, and at the same time do not delay in covering their territories, some companies compute average selling time and actual travel time, based on train, bus, and air time tables. Time schedules are prepared showing the time of arrival and departure of the salesman from each town and city in his territory. This plan is effective for salesmen who do not use their time to the best advantage. It is effective and practical only in routine selling in which a certain number of dealers are called upon regularly. It has the additional advantage of acquainting buyers with the approximate time of a salesman's call so that they may save orders for him. The management also knows where a salesman may be reached in the territory at any particular time.

Insuring Territory Coverage as Planned. The most effective routing plan is worthless unless salesmen follow the routes as designed. Not only should the management plan how and where salesmen must spend their time, but it must be assured that all customers and prospects are being seen in accordance with the predetermined system.

The most common and practical method of checking activity of a salesman is by means of the daily call report form, which is filled in by each salesman daily, listing the names of prospects and customers called upon, date of the call, the result of the call, person

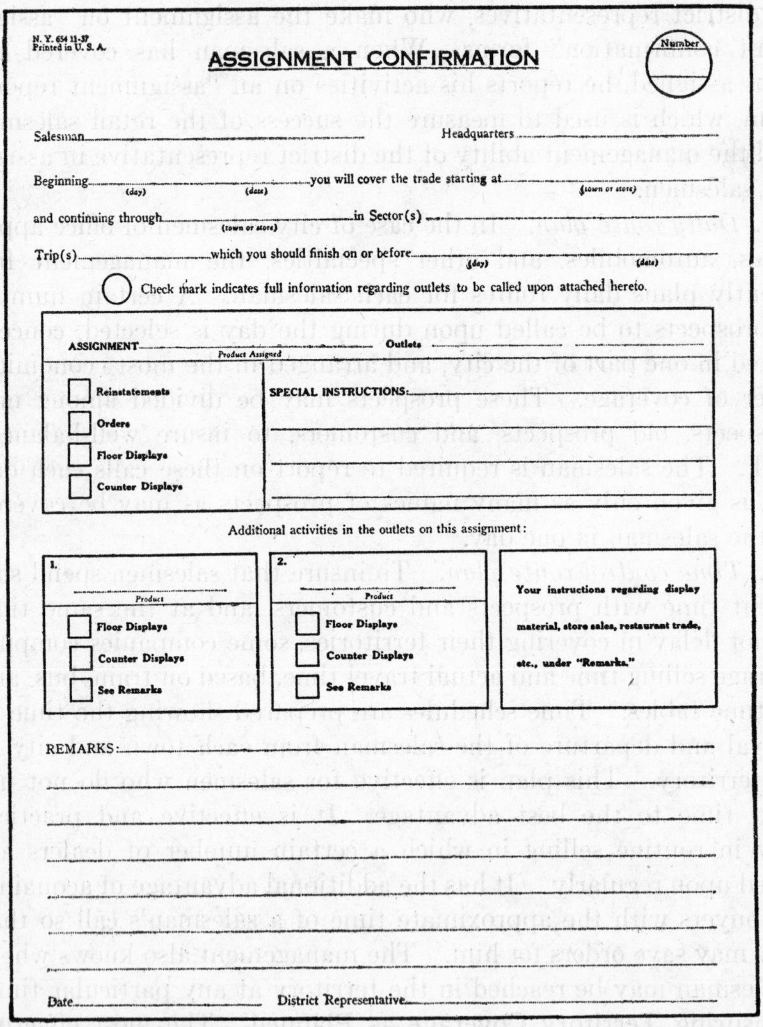

N. Y. 654 11-37
Printed in U. S. A.

Number

ASSIGNMENT CONFIRMATION

Salesman .... Headquarters ....

Beginning .... (day) .... (date) .... you will cover the trade starting at .... (town or store)

and continuing through .... (town or store) .... in Sector(s) ....

Trip(s) .... which you should finish on or before .... (day) .... (date)

Check mark indicates full information regarding outlets to be called upon attached hereto.

ASSIGNMENT .... Product Assigned .... Outlets ....

Reinstatements

Orders

Floor Displays

Counter Displays

SPECIAL INSTRUCTIONS:

Additional activities in the outlets on this assignment:

1. .... Product
Floor Displays
Counter Displays
See Remarks

2. .... Product
Floor Displays
Counter Displays
See Remarks

Your instructions regarding display material, store sales, restaurant trade, etc., under "Remarks."

REMARKS:

Date .... District Representative ....

FIGURE 59. Assignment confirmation form used by supervisors of a food manufacturer's sales organization in assigning routes to salesmen calling on retail grocers. Special instructions are given on the form for merchandising services to be performed by the salesman. An assignment may be exclusively selling, exclusively merchandising, or a combination of both interviewed, and other information to enable the management to compare the salesman's activities with the routing plan.

Mapping Salesmen's Routes. Maps showing transportation lines, trading area boundaries, towns and cities, and topographical features are indispensable in laying out salesmen's routes. These maps may be secured in national, state, county, and trading area units according to the extent of the salesmen's territories. Routes should be laid out on these maps and salesmen supplied with photostatic copies showing the territory covered.

Many companies maintain a large national master map showing boundaries of all sales territories and routes followed by salesmen. Individual maps of each territory, showing boundaries and routes, may be prepared, kept up to date, and housed in special map cabinets or swung from the wall in metal frames, like leaves in a book.

To show the boundaries of sales territories and routes of salesmen, washable surface maps are used, upon which territory and route lines may be drawn with chalk and washed off when desired. Map tacks may also be used to indicate places to be visited, and cord stretched from place to place to indicate route lines. In addition, map tacks may indicate frequency of call, number of accounts, class of dealer, and other information to facilitate routing.

N. Y. 654A 11-37
Printed in U. S. A.

ASSIGNMENT REPORT

Number ____

District Representative ____

Dear Sir. Headquarters ____

Report from your Salesman ____ Headquarters ____

on this assignment disclose that beginning ____ (day) ____ (date) he covered the trade starting at ____ (town or store)

through ____ (town or store) in Sector(s) ____ Trip(s) ____ finishing ____ (day) ____ (date)

His calls and accomplishments were as follows:

Total calls ____ Key outlets ____ Primary outlets ____ Secondary outlets ____ Chain outlets ____ Miscellaneous ____

ASSIGNMENT	1.	2.	OTHER PRODUCTS
____ Product Assigned	____ Product	____ Product	
Reinstatements ____	Reinstatements ____	Reinstatements ____	Reinstatements ____
Orders ____	Orders ____	Orders ____	Orders ____
Floor Displays ____	Floor Displays ____	Floor Displays ____	
Counter Displays ____	Counter Displays ____	Counter Displays ____	
Cases Sold ____	Cases Sold ____	Cases Sold ____	Cases Sold ____

Remarks.

Date ____ District Sales Manager ____

FIGURE 60. This assignment report form is completed by salesmen and checked by supervisors of a food manufacturer's sales organization. This report shows how well a salesman has followed his assigned route and performed his duties.

One large company has placed tacks on its territory maps at every place of sufficient size to justify a salesman's visit, and looped these places together by string to give a proper sequence of coverage, allowing sufficient time for a salesman to work his desirable accounts. By laying out routes in this way, the company saved

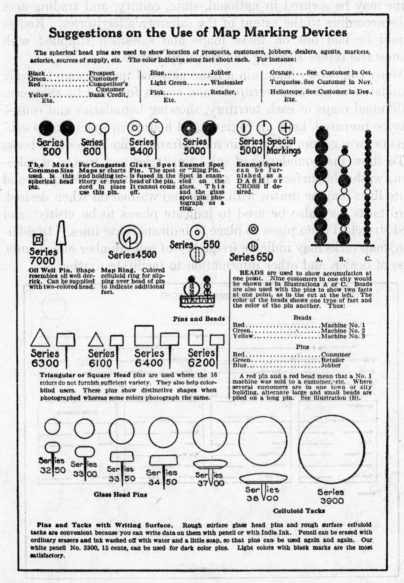

FIGURE 61. Map-marking devices including map pins and beads produced by the Educational Exhibition Company, Providence, R. I., are valuable aids in the visualization of salesmen's routes, territory boundaries, and calls.

nine thousand four hundred miles of travel in one territory in one year as against the figure for the previous year when the salesman was routing himself. A saving in travel expense of $560 was effected.

Another manufacturer outlines each sales territory in black on washable maps, with jobbing centers marked with red circles and salesmen's headquarters marked with black squares. When special sales drives are staged, the area covered is outlined with large tacks, strung with red cord. Progress is noted with black tacks bearing white numbers stuck in the map. Tacks denoting salesmen's activities are white, with black numbers. The headquarters of a section manager is noted with a tack of a special color.

A large oil company uses a map and tack system to indicate its salesmen's progress over their routes. An office girl daily takes salesmen's call reports and checks them against route lists, placing a large red thumbtack in the towns which each salesman is working that day. A white linen reinforcement ring is hung over each tack, representing a place where a salesman has worked during the current month.

Route Lists. Salesmen selling to retail dealers in foods, drugs, hardware, and tobacco are frequently provided with route lists, classifying merchants according to purchasing power, and neighborhoods by nationality and types of homes. These lists are arranged by districts, and merchants are listed in the most convenient order of coverage. Many good lists of this type are prepared by local newspapers and furnished without charge to advertisers. They are frequently used by manufacturers staging special sales campaigns among retailers in various markets.

Problem 1—Weekly Routing

Carter Container Corporation

The Carter Container Corporation of Newark, New Jersey, manufactures corrugated paper containers in seven plants located in all parts of the country. Thirty-five traveling salesmen operate out of seven district offices located at the plants. Salesmen are paid a salary and bonus.

The product is sold in carload lots to approximately 2,000 large manufacturers of case goods. There are 18,000 to 20,000 prospects for the products of the company. Selling is not routine, and calls are made largely in response to inquiries and to follow up customers.

The salesmen are allowed considerable latitude in the carrying out of their work. The salesmen usually prepare a route sheet each Saturday showing towns and places to be visited in the following week. Sometimes this route sheet is not prepared, but the district manager usually knows where salesmen are working. The route sheet does not list the specific concerns on which the salesmen expect to call.

The sales manager of the company believes that the traveling salesmen should be controlled more closely. He thinks that the route sheets should be amplified for the salesmen to include the names of concerns and individuals to be called upon a week in advance, together with the day on which each concern is to be contacted. The district managers would be required to check these weekly sheets closely to prevent the salesmen from backtracking or making unnecessary calls.

Other executives of the company do not believe that the plan would be effective, since salesmen are at times required to make emergency calls on customers with whom a new product is being developed or on other customers who require special service. They maintain that the salesmen are not order takers in the same sense as are salesmen calling regularly on wholesalers and retailers. Also, the salesmen must call on several executives in a concern, including the traffic manager, factory manager, purchasing agent, and general manager.

In spite of these objections, the sales manager thinks that such a plan would require the salesmen to plan their work and save travel expense, and that the district managers would be obliged to work more closely with the salesmen.

Questions

1. Should the company have adopted the routing plan suggested by the sales manager for the traveling salesmen only? Give reasons for your decision.

2. If the plan does not appear practical in this case, suggest another method of routing the salesmen.

3. If you think that the salesmen should largely be left to their own devices as at present, give reasons for this course.

Problem 2—Routing City Salesmen

Seward Paper Products Company

The Seward Paper Products Company, Providence, Rhode Island, was established in 1850. The company now sells an approximate annual volume of $16,000,000 of paper specialties, including tags, tissue, gummed stickers, crepe paper, and many other similar items to more than 40,000 stationery, drug, and department stores throughout the United States and foreign countries.   Three hundred salesmen travel out of forty domestic district sales offices.

Since the company was established, no attempt has been made to control the routing of the salesmen who work out of the district offices. Many of the men have been with the company for years and are very familiar with their territories. The management has always felt that the district managers were not competent to direct the salesmen, who often knew more about their individual areas than the heads of the district offices.

A change in the sales management of the company, however, led to the discovery that salesmen were spending only 15 per cent of their time with buyers. This brought about the development of a plan for routing city salesmen. Under this plan a city salesman arriving at his office in the morning would find ready for him the records of the customers and prospects to be called upon during the day. These would be arranged in geographical order, with a report form for each prospect, calling for the name of the concern, name of buyer, products discussed, products bought, products in which the buyer showed interest, and the time and length of the call.

When the salesman returned to the district office at noon, having seen as many customers and prospects as time permitted, he would make reports on calls made during the morning and find ready for him a complete new list of customers, prospects, and data for the afternoon calls.

Information reported by salesmen on daily call reports would be transferred to permanent customer and prospect record cards, which would be filed in the district sales office and given to the salesmen as previously described for repeat calls at future times.

To carry out this routing plan, the district offices would make up lists of customers and prospective buyers and arrange them by classes of trade and geographical location. While this would increase the clerical work of the district office force, it would reduce the nonproductive time of the salesmen. Instead of wasting time in unplanned traveling about their territories, the salesmen would be able to make more calls on desirable prospects and profitable customers, thereby reducing travel costs.

Objectors to the plan contended that the salesmen would resent interference and object to the preparation of reports on each call. They further believed that the salesmen were better able to control their own time than the district offices.

Questions

1. Should the new plan for routing the salesmen suggested by the new sales manager be adopted? Give reasons for your decision.

2. If you do not favor the plan suggested in the problem, what plan, if any, should be adopted to control the time of the salesmen?

Problem 3—Routing Industrial Salesmen

Nobel Bearing Corporation

The Nobel Bearing Corporation, established in Pawtucket, Rhode Island, in 1909, manufactures ball bearings sold to automobile makers, as well as manufacturers of textile machinery, machine tools, electric motors, drills, cranes, printing presses, and many other types of industrial machinery. The company employs twenty salesmen selling a line of three hundred types and sizes of bearings direct to manufacturers of industrial products.

Analysis of the activities of the company's salesmen showed that many territories offered a potential volume of sales inconsistent with the actual business produced. Salesmen operating in the same territory at different times produced very unequal results, and some territories showed a much higher ratio of sales expense to volume than other territories. The management concluded that these territorial variations were caused by failure to route and schedule salesmen's time in the field.

The advisability of taking a typical salesman's territory and setting up a test route plan by the following method was considered:

1. List all prospects and customers in the territory.

2. Classify each type of prospect according to his potential sales value to the company.

3. Establish call frequencies for each type of buyer.

4. List all the towns and places in the territory with the number of logical prospects and customers in each.

5. Determine the available methods of transportation in the territory.

6. Map towns, showing all transportation lines serving each town, indicating route numbers and mileage between places and giving the number and class of prospects and customers in each place.

7. Map out routes, by best transportation methods, for reaching each point as frequently as required.

8. Prepare route summaries showing names of towns, number and class of buyers, and call frequency.

9. Require daily call reports from the salesman indicating his progress over the routes established at the frequencies predetermined.

This plan was objected to on the grounds that it would involve considerable time to set up and supervise and that it would soon become obsolete unless revised from time to time. The plan would be too complex to be practical, and its accuracy would be questionable. Without the frequent advice of the salesman in each territory, many sales opportunities would be overlooked, and the salesman held to a too inflexible plan.

The advocates of the test plan believed that it would give the management a better knowledge of each territory so that in case a salesman left the company, a new man could become quickly acquainted with a territory. A larger percentage of time would be spent by the salesmen with customers and prospects. Customers would learn to anticipate calls of salesmen at regular times. The merits of individual salesmen could be determined readily. Travel expenses would be curtailed.

It was not proposed to schedule the time of the salesman closely, but only to enforce the call frequency established for each type of prospect and customer. The salesman in the field would be consulted and his cooperation enlisted in the preparation of the routing plan and the establishment of the frequencies.

Questions

1. Should the company have tested the routing method proposed in one territory and extended it to all sales areas if it proved satisfactory? Give reasons for your answer.

2. Should another method of routing be used in this problem? Explain in detail.

Problem 4—Routing to Retail Outlets

Wayne Chemical Company

The Wayne Chemical Company, Hollywood, California, manufactures Wayne facial cream of various types packaged in jars containing 3.6 ounces, retailing for fifty cents through drug, perfumery, and department stores. The product is nationally advertised in women's magazines to the extent of $75,000 annually and is distributed through drug jobbers as well as sold direct to retail stores.

The management is concerned over the decline in drug store sales in the state of Ohio, which is covered by one salaried salesman operating out of his home and selling an annual volume of $65,000 direct to chain and individual drug stores. There are 2,869 drug stores located in 510 of the 2,580 cities and towns in the state.

The Wayne salesman, who planned his own time, made no attempt to cover all of the drug stores in his territory, but selected by observation those which were well located and appeared to be likely prospects for Wayne cream. He sold 775 accounts. Of these accounts 556 bought once a year or less, 38 twice a year, 64 three times, and 116 four or more times.

Those druggists who bought three or four times a year constituted a little more than 23 per cent of the total number of active accounts in the state, producing 66.7 per cent of the total volume of business. Those druggists buying one or two times a year represented 76.8 per cent of the total number of customers, but accounted for only 33.3 per cent of the total volume of business.

The total direct sales to chain and individual stores by various cities in the state were: Cincinnati, 12.18 per cent; Cleveland, 21.6 per cent; Lima, 1.14 per cent; Columbus, 7.37 per cent; Dayton, 4.35 per cent; Springfield, 2.15 per cent; Toledo, 5.48 per cent; Zanesville, 1.07 per cent; Portsmouth, .92 per cent; and Akron, 6.71 per cent.

These figures indicated, in the opinion of the management, the desirability of exercising a closer control over the activities of the Ohio salesman. One sales executive suggested that route lists of druggists be secured from the newspapers in the principal cities in the state and that the salesman be provided with these lists and required to follow the published routes as laid out by the papers. He contended that such route lists would insure better coverage of the territory.

Another sales executive believed that the salesman should be required to make out a "weekly effort report," on which he would report the name and location of every dealer called upon during the past week with the result of the call, amount of sales, reasons for lost sales, and so forth. The report would be accompanied by a list of the places that the salesman expected to visit the coming week. On the basis of the information contained in these reports, the sales manager would have a closer check on the activities of the Ohio salesman and be able to advise him on more effective coverage of his territory.

A third suggestion called for the establishment of routes based on highway lines, since the salesman covered his territory by automobile. Towns with a minimum number of four drug stores would be arranged in weekly routes for economical coverage. The salesman would be assigned to cover a route each week. In this way time would be saved, travel expenses reduced, and the salesman could spend his week ends at home. The routes would be prepared in the headquarters sales office and sent to the salesman for his approval.

Questions

1. How should the Ohio salesman of the Wayne Company be routed? If you do not favor any of the methods of routing suggested in the problem, what method would you use?

2. What type of routing is indicated by the analysis of the Ohio salesman's sales?

Reading References

Selling Under Control of Management, Wilson, Chap. IX.
Scientific Sales Management Today, Hoyt, pp. 25–27.

Modern Sales Management, Frederick, p. 333.
Handbook of Sales Management, Hall, pp. 259, 630.
Sales Administration, Hayward, p. 306.
Salesmen in Marketing Strategy, Lyon, pp. 218, 226–243.

ROUTING SALESMEN

Modern Sales Management, Frederick, p. 261.
Handbook of Sales Management, Hall, pp. 299, 620.
Sales Administration, Hayward, p. 309.
Automobile Marketing Strategy, Lyon, pp. 215, 226-243.

CHAPTER SEVENTEEN

SALES TRAVEL EXPENSES

The necessity for seeking out buyers compels salesmen to travel constantly to secure orders. While salesmen who sell from house to house or call on retailers in a limited city or suburban area have little travel expense, many others must spend from 3 to 4 per cent of their net sales for transportation. Salesmen's traveling expenses have long been considered a nuisance by sales executives who are reluctant to quibble with salesmen over taxi fares or hotel meals. Salesmen have looked upon travel expenses as a legitimate source of petty larceny. While factory managers have been shaving fractions of cents from production costs, salesmen with unlimited expense accounts have been spending profits entertaining customers. However, salesmen's travel expenses are being given more serious consideration today than heretofore. Narrowing profit margins and mounting sales costs are forcing sales executives to adopt measures for controlling travel costs.

Methods of Controlling Travel Expense. There are five general methods of handling salesmen's travel expenses:

1. The honor system.
2. The flat allowance method.
3. The flexible expense method.
4. The combination flat and flexible system.
5. Miscellaneous methods.

The honor system. The honor system of handling salesmen's expenses permits salesmen to have whatever amounts they believe are necessary to cover the costs of travel, lodging, meals, and entertainment. No definite allowances are made by the management, and amounts requisitioned by salesmen will vary widely from week to week. The management trusts the salesmen to use the expense money judiciously for company purposes only.

This system has the advantages of:

1. Easy administration.
2. Improving the morale of the salesmen by showing the confidence of the management in their integrity.
3. Saving the time of the salesmen and management in accounting for expenses.
4. Avoiding petty censoring of salesmen or disagreements over expenditures.
5. Providing adequate funds for the fullest development of sales territories.

The disadvantages of the honor system are:

1. It encourages overspending by salesmen.
2. No control is exercised by the management over costs.
3. Salesmen may appropriate company funds for their own uses.
4. It does not permit the management to plan expenditures or budget.
5. It creates expense allowance inequalities between salesmen.

In practice, most companies require some form of accounting from salesmen for expense money advanced. However, the principle of the "honor system" underlies the expense account practice of many sales organizations.

The flat allowance method. The flat allowance method of expense control involves the establishment by the management of a fixed amount for certain items of expense or total expenses for a period of time. The allowance may be set for such individual expenses as lodging, breakfast, lunch, dinner, incidentals, and automobile mileage, or the allowance may be fixed to cover all expenses for a day, a week, or a month. A flat allowance may be set for individual salesmen's territories, or by types of territories, as city, rural, or suburban.

This method has these advantages:

1. Eliminates auditing by the company and figuring by salesmen.
2. It enables the company to determine costs in advance.
3. Controversies over expense accounts are eliminated.
4. Salesmen watch expenses more closely.
5. It prevents "padding" of expense accounts.
6. It restricts excessive traveling.

On the other hand, many sales managers do not favor a flat or fixed method of expense control for the following reasons:

1. It encourages salesmen to make petty economies.

2. It is difficult to change a flat allowance as a salesman considers it a part of his compensation and resents a reduction.

3. It is difficult to establish a fair allowance for every salesman.

4. It lacks flexibility and prevents the salesman from taking advantage of sales opportunities requiring expense outlays.

5. Fixed allowances demand frequent checkup and supervision to insure their correctness.

6. They do not provide for variables in travel costs from day to day or week to week.

The flat allowance method has been used effectively by companies selling staple or repeat-products. When a salesman's work is of a routine nature, involving the frequent coverage of a territory at regular intervals, a flat allowance is often practical.

A maker of hosiery and underwear used a flat allowance based on types of territories for controlling salesmen's expenses. Traveling salesmen were divided into three classes: first-class men, traveling by train to large cities throughout the country; second-class men, traveling in one state to cities of moderate size not visited by first-class men; and third-class men, traveling by automobile to small towns. The first-class men were given a flat allowance of $115 a week; the second-class men $85; and the third-class men $65. These allowances were based on an analysis of the mileage traveled, hotel rates, meals, and miscellaneous expenses.

The eastern division of a large paint company established a flat expense allowance for each individual salesman's territory, based on a three-year average of previous expenses for covering each territory. Salesmen traveling by automobile were given a separate automobile allowance based on mileage covered. Officials of the company are reported to have claimed that this method of expense control reduced selling costs $5,000 a year and reduced the cost of auditing salesmen's expense accounts.

A flour milling corporation put into effect a series of flat allowances based on various items of salesmen's expense as follows: dinner, $1.40 maximum; lunch, 85 cents maximum; breakfast, 60 cents maximum; hotel room, $2.50 per day; and automobile expenses, 3½ cents a mile.

A lubricating oil company established a daily flat allowance for salesmen of $4.50, which provided for hotel, meals, and incidental expenses. Automobile expenses, including mileage, were handled separately.

Traveling salesmen of a fountain pen company are given a flat expense allowance of $6 a day, in addition to an automobile allowance of 7 cents a mile. The automobile allowance is split, 6 cents being paid to the salesman and 1 cent being retained by the company for a depreciation fund to aid in the purchase of a new automobile. City salesmen are given a flat expense rate of $1.50 a day and an additional $1.50 for the use of their automobiles.

A large printing company controls its city salesmen's expenses on a sliding scale basis with an allowance of $12 daily in a city of two million population to $5 a day in a city of less than thirty thousand population.

In setting fixed allowances for meals and lodging, one company has established rates based on cities of various sizes as follows:

Size of City	Breakfast Allowance	Dinner Allowance	Lodging
Less than 7,500 pop.	$.50	$ .75	$2.00
7,500 to 25,000 pop.	.60	1.15	2.50
25,000 to 100,000 pop.	.75	1.50	3.00
Over 100,000	.75	1.75	3.50

A survey of the expense account practices of three hundred and twelve companies disclosed that only 10 per cent of the firms reporting granted fixed expense allowances.

Establishing flat allowances. To determine the proper amount of a daily or weekly flat allowance is one of the principal problems of using the flat allowance method. Some companies take an average of the costs of covering a territory for several years past and establish a fixed allowance figure on this basis. Since costs of travel and lodging vary from year to year as routes are shifted and new hotels are built, an average of the previous year's expenses may not be representative of the current costs of covering a territory.

Another method for arriving at the amount of a fixed allowance is to consult hotel directories for rates; write to hotels for special prices; check transportation mileage; and determine, by detailed analysis of each expense factor, the actual daily or weekly cost of traveling a specific area. One manufacturer wrote hundreds of hotels for menus and prices to determine meal costs and set fixed expense allowances for meals, which resulted in an annual reduction of $42,000 in salesmen's expenses.

A sales executive may travel a territory with a salesman, keeping accurate records of expenses, and in this way determine a fair allowance for different items of traveling expense.

After fixed allowances have been established, it is necessary to review them from time to time to insure their accuracy. A large packing house supervised expense allowances by sending an assistant sales manager to cover each territory once a year, keeping a careful account of necessary expenses.

Certain companies who pay salesmen fixed allowances for lodging, meals, or total daily expenses require reports from salesmen on these expenditures, although such reports defeat the most obvious advantage of flat allowances, which is to relieve the salesmen and management of accounting detail. The majority of companies using the flat allowance method require no such reports from salesmen. Transportation allowances made on a mileage basis are paid upon receipt of a report of the mileage traveled by the salesmen.

The flexible expense method. A large majority of companies control expenses from the standpoint of what salesmen actually spend from week to week, or on a flexible basis. Expenses are reported on printed forms provided for the purpose, itemizing the various expenses incurred by the salesman. Salesmen are not restricted to a definite expense allowance, but are expected to report expenses as incurred. The management usually has an idea what these expenses should approximate.

The principal advantages of the flexible method of controlling expenses are:

1. The expenses vary with places, territories, and conditions and should be reported and paid for accordingly.

2. Salesmen may be routed more readily.

3. Salesmen are not obliged to suffer personal loss when expenses exceed allowance.

4. Salesmen are not inclined to curtail their activities to remain within a fixed budget.

5. Salesmen do not complain about the size of allowances.

6. No expense is involved in establishing and supervising allowances.

On the other hand, the outstanding objections to the flexible expense control plan are:

1. Considerable bookkeeping on the part of the management and salesmen is involved.

2. Controversies arise between the management and salesmen over the justification of various items of expense.

3. The management is unable to determine sales expense in advance and to budget sales costs.

4. There is a temptation to "pad" expense reports by including items of unjustified expenses.

5. Salesmen are influenced to spread their efforts rather than to concentrate.

The flexible allowance method has been used very effectively by companies whose salesmen do not follow regular routes or engage in uniform activities or routine selling. Expenses of salesmen doing missionary work, opening up new territories, or rendering technical service are usually controlled by a flexible expense system.

In a study of the expense control methods of three hundred and fifteen companies, it was found that two hundred and eighty-five use a flexible method based on payment of the actual expenses of salesmen rather than by fixed allowances.

A large tire and rubber company requires its salesmen to submit weekly an itemized account of their expenses, which is criticized by the management.

An office equipment company provides all salesmen with a permanent traveling expense fund, the amount of which depends upon their average weekly expenses. Each week end itemized accounts of expenses are turned in to the company for the previous week. A check is immediately sent the salesman for the amount of his expenses, reimbursing the expense fund.

A large food product manufacturer whose salesmen report their current expenses weekly has set up at headquarters a salesmen's expense committee, whose function is to review the weekly expense reports of the salesmen and determine what items of expense are not justified and should not be allowed. This committee settles disputes between the salesmen and the management on questions of legitimate expense.

A meat packing company requires its animal feed, fertilizer, and glue salesmen to render each week an accounting of their actual expenses for hotel, meals, and incidentals, with the exception of automobile expenses, which are handled on a flat rate basis.

The home office supervisors, special agents, and traveling representatives of insurance companies usually report expenses on a weekly itemized basis.

Expense report forms. To facilitate the reporting of expenses as incurred, salesmen are provided with a variety of printed expense report forms. These forms are frequently combined with daily sales call or progress reports. By listing travel expenses opposite daily sales figures, a moral check is provided the salesman to keep costs in line with sales.

Expense report forms list the various items of allowable expenses such as meals, lodging, and transportation. Frequently these items are broken down into greater detail, as breakfast, lunch, dinner, mileage, gasoline, oil, and sundry items.

Separate forms are sometimes provided for listing each day's expenses. Small weekly expense books with a page for each day's expenses are frequently supplied to salesmen. They can be conveniently carried in a vest pocket and facilitate the recording of

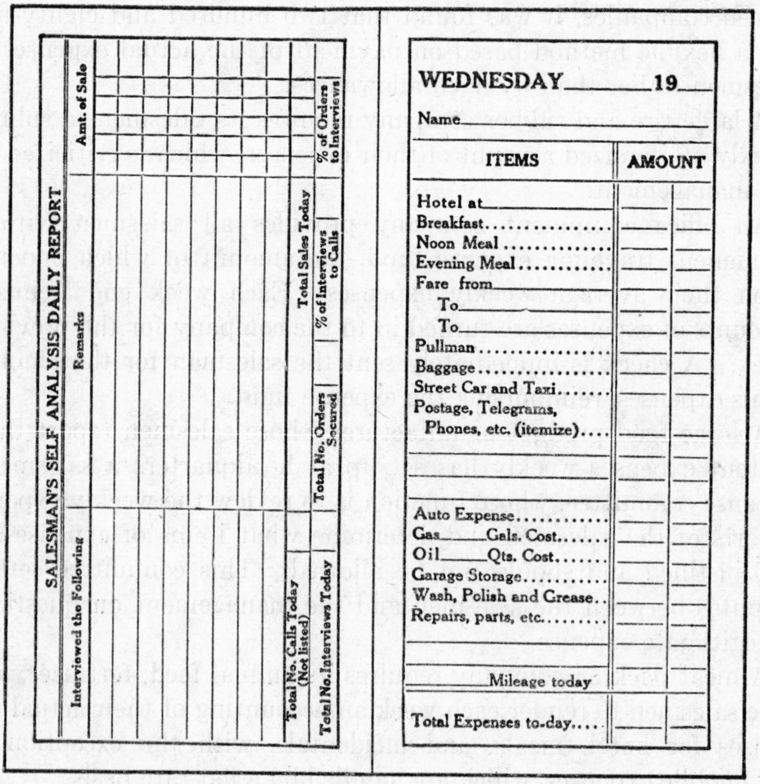
SALESMAN'S SELF ANALYSIS DAILY REPORT

Interviewed the Following | Remarks | Amt. of Sale

Total No. Calls Today (Not listed) | Total No. Interviews Today | Total No. Orders Secured | Total Sales Today | % of Interviews to Calls | % of Orders to Interviews

WEDNESDAY ______ 19__

Name ______

ITEMS	AMOUNT
Hotel at ______	
Breakfast............	
Noon Meal	
Evening Meal...........	
Fare from ______	
To ______	
To ______	
Pullman............	
Baggage............	
Street Car and Taxi........	
Postage, Telegrams, Phones, etc. (itemize)....	
Auto Expense............	
Gas____Gals. Cost.......	
Oil____Qts. Cost......	
Garage Storage........	
Wash, Polish and Grease....	
Repairs, parts, etc.........	
______Mileage today	
Total Expenses to-day....	

FIGURE 62. Two pages from a vest-pocket-size, weekly expense booklet produced by the Stevens-Davis Co., Chicago, for convenient recording of a salesman's expenses. A page is provided for a detailed account of each day's expenses.

expenses at the time they are incurred, thus relieving the salesmen of the necessity of remembering small items of expense.

The most common expense record form provides spaces for listing the daily expenses, itemized for each day of the week, for each place visited, with daily and weekly totals of expenses, the balance of cash on hand per last statement, and money received since the last statement. The reverse side of the form may provide space for listing in detail any expenses that are not self-explanatory, as entertainment costs.

To insure that expense reports will be rendered promptly and accurately, some companies return the incomplete reports to salesmen for correction and charge any loss of time or expense thereby incurred to the salesman's account. Others hold up the weekly expense check until the report is received properly filled out.

Verification of expenses is sometimes required, and salesmen must attach to expense reports receipted hotel bills, sales checks, and other evidence of expenditures.

4. *Combination flat and flexible control.* A limited number of plans for controlling salesmen's expenses are designed to restrict expenses to a definite maximum for a year and provide at the same time flexibility by variable expense allowances from week to week. A flat allowance is established for each territory on an annual basis, and salesmen are permitted to draw against this amount from week to week as required.

A large hardware manufacturer employs this method. The sales manager reviews with each salesman, at the close of each year, his expenses for the preceding year. With the suggestions of the salesman, the sales manager establishes an expense budget for the new year. The salesman knows that he must not exceed his budget for the year, but he is allowed to draw variable amounts against his budget each week, submitting itemized expense reports to the management.

The principal advantages of this combination fixed and flexible method are:

1. Salesmen know definitely their expense allowance.
2. Expenses are kept in proper ratio to sales in each territory.
3. Budgeting of expense is facilitated.
4. Variable expenses are provided for.
5. Detail control may be exercised over individual items of expense.

The disadvantages of this method are:

1. It requires frequent accounting of expenses by the salesmen and management.

2. Controversies between the management and salesmen over justified items of expense may arise.

3. An annual flat allowance figure is difficult to determine.

4. Changes in sales territories, volume, or expense factors necessitate the revision of the budget estimate.

ORIGINAL

MAIL TO DETROIT, MICH.

DAILY EXPENSE REPORT No.____ OF ____ REPRESENTING ____ OFFICE

AS ____ OF ____ DIVISION

AT ____ CITY ____ STATE. DATE ____ (DAY OF WEEK) ____ (MONTH) ____ (DATE) 193__

(1) FUND ACCOUNT

BALANCE BROUGHT FORWARD ____ $

CHECKS RECEIVED NOS. ____ $

CORRECTIONS, IF ANY ____ $

TOTAL TO ACCOUNT FOR ____ $

DISBURSEMENTS

RR FARE FROM ____ TO ____ $

RR FARE FROM ____ TO ____ $

RR FARE FROM ____ TO ____ $

RR FARE FROM ____ TO ____ $

EXTRA FARE FROM ____ TO ____ $

BUS FARE FROM ____ TO ____ $

BUS FARE FROM ____ TO ____ $

BUS FARE FROM ____ TO ____ $

BUS FARE FROM ____ TO ____ $

BUS AND CAR FARE (LOCAL) ____ $

BUS AND CAR FARE (LOCAL) ____ $

TAXI FARE AT ____ $

AUTOMOBILE MILEAGE (AUTHORIZED)

FROM ____ TO ____ MILES ____ $

FROM ____ TO ____ MILES ____ $

FROM ____ TO ____ MILES ____ $

FROM ____ TO ____ MILES ____ $

FROM ____ TO ____ MILES ____ $

TOTAL TRANSPORTATION ____ $

CHAIR / SLEEPER } FROM ____ TO ____ $

ROOM AT ____ HOTEL ____ $

MEAL A. M. AT ____ $

MEAL NOON AT ____ $

MEAL P. M. AT ____ $

TOTAL HOTEL EXPENSES ____ $

TEL. AND TELEGRAMS ____ $

OTHER EXPENSES (ITEMIZED) ____ $

____ $

____ $

EXTRA EXPENSE (IN DETAIL) ____ $

____ $

____ $

TOTAL OTHER EXPENSES ____ $

TOTAL TO ACCOUNT FOR ____ $

LESS TOTAL EXPENSES FOR THE DAY ____ $

BALANCE FUND ON HAND FORWARD ____ $

IN CASH ____ $

IN CHECK ____ $

IN MILEAGE ____ $

DEPARTMENT APPROVALS:

(2)

LIST TOWNS WITH NAMES OF CUSTOMERS CALLED ON	WHO INTERVIEWED	WAS T. R. MADE

(3) GENERAL REMARKS ____

SIGN HERE ____

FIGURE 63. Salesmen of a large paint manufacturer report their expenses daily on this daily expense report form. The principal items of expense are itemized in detail, and the names of places visited and customers and prospects called upon are recorded.

A paint manufacturer establishes an annual expense figure for each salesman based on past expenses, the type of territory, the nature of the sales job, and the expected sales volume. Weekly expense reports are rendered by each salesman to the management. Periodic checks are made by the home office to determine whether weekly expenses are exceeding the average permitted by the annual budget. If a salesman consistently exceeds his weekly average al-

_____ 19___

EXPENSE ACCOUNT of _____

DATE	AT	ITEMS	AMOUNT	DATE	AT	ITEMS	AMOUNT
SUNDAY		Hotel or Sleeper				Brought Forward	
		Meal		THURSDAY		Hotel or Sleeper	
		Meal				Meal	
		Meal				Meal	
	To	R. R. Fare				Meal	
	To	R. R. Fare			To	R. R. Fare	
		Transfer			To	R. R. Fare	
		Carfare				Transfer	
		Wires & Phone				Carfare	
						Wires & Phone	
MONDAY		Hotel or Sleeper					
		Meal		FRIDAY		Hotel or Sleeper	
		Meal				Meal	
		Meal				Meal	
	To	R. R. Fare				Meal	
	To	R. R. Fare			To	R. R. Fare	
		Transfer			To	R. R. Fare	
		Carfare				Transfer	
		Wires & Phone				Carfare	
						Wires & Phone	
TUESDAY		Hotel or Sleeper					
		Meal		SATURDAY		Hotel or Sleeper	
		Meal				Meal	
		Meal				Meal	
	To	R. R. Fare				Meal	
	To	R. R. Fare			To	R. R. Fare	
		Transfer			To	R. R. Fare	
		Carfare				Transfer	
		Wires & Phone				Carfare	
						Wires & Phone	
WEDNESDAY		Hotel or Sleeper					
		Meal				Total for Week	
		Meal		Extensions O. K.		CASH ACCOUNT	
		Meal				Balance from last report	
	To	R. R. Fare		Account Number		Cash received	
	To	R. R. Fare				Total	
		Transfer				Cash expended as above	
		Carfare				Balance	
		Wires & Phone		Division Approval			
		Carried Forward					

FIGURE 64. This weekly sales expense report form, used by salesmen of a glass manufacturer, calls for an itemized accounting of the cost of meals, lodging, transportation, and communication expenses for each day of the week.

lowance, he is warned that expenses must be reduced so that they will not exceed the annual limit.

A large flour milling company establishes expense control on a per barrel selling cost basis. Salesmen make itemized weekly expense reports, which are compared with unit sales, and expenses are expressed on a per barrel basis. If a salesman incurs expenses that are higher than the per barrel allowance, he must either reduce his expenses or increase his volume to compensate for the additional per barrel cost. Under this plan the control is flexible, since salesmen are permitted to draw variable amounts for expenses as required but at the same time must adhere to a fixed expense per unit sold.

A manufacturer of roller bearings, sold to industrial concerns, combines the flat and flexible methods of expense control by establishing at the beginning of each year individual annual expense quotas for twenty-five salesmen. Salesmen make weekly itemized expense reports, which are checked against their expense quotas, and salesmen exceeding their quotas are warned to curtail expenses.

A large converter of writing paper establishes annual salesmen's expense budgets with the aid of district managers. Monthly reports are sent to district managers comparing individual salesmen's expenses with their expense budgets. District managers inform salesmen of their expense budget position.

Miscellaneous expense control methods. An unusual method of controlling expenses of approximately four thousand traveling salesmen is used by one of the large meat packing concerns. The company issues each salesman a letter of credit, upon which a limit of $500 is placed, and which is honored by all branch houses of the company. The letter usually covers a fiscal period of four-weeks' duration, and the funds drawn on the letter must be accounted for by the salesman immediately upon return from the trip for which the letter was issued.

This form of expense control has the advantage of keeping the outstanding cash balance of the company at a minimum, since salesmen draw against their letters of credit to cover only immediate expense needs. It prevents theft or loss of sizable amounts of expense funds and gives a close control over expenses.

Salesmen pay own expenses. A large number of concerns with limited financial resources are obliged to place the burden of travel expenses on their salesmen. Other companies, able to pay salesmen's expenses, require their salesmen to assume their own travel costs for the reason that salesmen who are responsible for their own expenses are injuring themselves and not the company when expenses are excessive. Moreover, the company is relieved of the bookkeeping detail of controlling sales expenses.

Salesmen who pay their own expenses are often not subject to the close control exercised over men whose expenses are paid by their employers. Salesmen who pay their own travel costs feel free to travel when and where they wish and may be inclined to save on expenses to add to income, with a consequent reduction in sales effort. In periods of depression when sales volume falls off, salesmen paying their own expenses do little traveling.

A great number of companies using commission salesmen prefer that they pay their own expenses, and many commission salesmen would rather pay their own expenses and receive larger commissions.

The vice-president-in-charge-of-sales of a large pharmaceutical company, whose salesmen pay their own expenses, expresses the opinion of many sales executives who require salesmen to pay their own expenses, as follows:

The intelligent salesman is taught to keep a keen lookout for expenses when he faces the realization that the expense is his and not something the "house" pays for. Give any man, especially a beginner, $50 or $100 in cash for expenses. Does he feel economical? He does not. Take the same man, put him on his own to travel out of his own pocket for a week and you have a different man. He watches his outlay.

Rewarding Salesmen for Expense Economy. There are numerous plans for rewarding salesmen for cutting travel costs. The purpose of such plans is to encourage salesmen to keep their expenses low. However, rewarding salesmen for expense economies often results in serious neglect of sales opportunities by salesmen ambitious to cut costs.

A manufacturer of electrical measuring instruments at one time paid its salesmen an annual group bonus based on the amount of reduction in the annual total sales expense. The plan was abandoned for the following reasons:

1. To insure greater future sales volume, the company was obliged to increase current sales expense out of proportion to current sales.

2. Salesmen were tempted to increase their bonus by eliminating many normal sales expenditures which would not increase current

sales, but which were necessary to maintain the future sales and prestige of the company.

3. The percentage of growth of the company followed directly the percentage of sales expense; curtailment of sales expense resulted in a diminishing of the growth of the company.

4. The management wished to make its own decisions on expenditures, unhampered by the necessity for considering the effect on the salesmen's remuneration.

5. Difficulty arose between the sales and production departments, since certain service and repair work was charged to sales expense, while defects in manufacture were charged to production expense.

A manufacturer of radio receiving sets and electrical equipment bases 30 per cent of salesmen's annual salary and bonus on the ability of salesmen to restrict travel expenses to $3\frac{1}{2}$ per cent of annual sales volume. For example, a salesman selling $70,000 annually has an annual expense quota of $3\frac{1}{2}$ per cent of $70,000, or $2,450. This figure is weighted at 30 per cent in determining the salesman's value in computing his salary and bonus for the following year. In addition, the salesman's ability to sell in volume and profitable items is rated at 40 per cent and 30 per cent, respectively. If the salesman, however, spent $3,500 in selling $70,000 worth of goods, he would be penalized because he exceeded his expense quota of $2,450 by 42 per cent. His expense value would be 58 per cent of the 30 per cent par for expense, or a little over 17 per cent. If he had held his expenses down to $2,450, he would have equaled par value of 30 per cent.

A quarterly bonus payment based on reducing expenses below a predetermined maximum, combined with a deduction from commission earnings for expenses in excess of the maximum, is the plan used by a tanner and manufacturer of leather goods to encourage expense economies by salesmen. Expenses, with the exception of automobile costs, are allowed on a variable basis of from one half of 1 per cent of total net sales in a small, thickly settled territory, up to 4 per cent in a large and sparsely populated territory. If a salesman's expenses are less than his allowable expense based on a percentage of his total net sales, the difference is credited to him and paid quarterly with his earned commission. If his actual expenses are more than his allowance, however, the difference is debited against him and deducted quarterly from his commission earnings.

A manufacturer of filing equipment makes a monthly analysis

of sales expenses including salaries for each salesman's territory. If these costs do not exceed a predetermined percentage of expense fixed for each territory, the savings below the percentage figure are shared with the salesman in the territory.

In the expense economy plan of a manufacturer of a line of small hardware items, payment of an expense bonus is contingent upon the salesmen's making their volume quotas. The salesmen are paid a salary plus a bonus for volume. An expense quota is established for each territory, depending on its size and conditions. Any travel expense savings that a salesman makes during a year, below his expense quota, are paid in the form of a bonus, provided that he equals or exceeds his sales volume quota. If a salesman does not equal his sales quota, his savings in travel expenses are withheld.

Justifiable Items of Sales Expense. The determination of justifiable items of salesmen's expense is one of the most important steps in expense control. The adoption of any plan of expense control, with the exception of the fixed allowance, demands a decision as to what constitutes legitimate expenses to be paid by the company as against what must be paid by the salesmen out of their own funds.

Analysis of expense items reported by salesmen will show numerous expenses that are not clearly itemized or are simply included under the general classification of incidentals. Lack of clarity in classification accounts for much misunderstanding between the management and the men, looseness in expense control, and high costs. Each item of expense should be defined exactly and salesmen provided with lists of allowable expenses that may be printed on expense report forms.

Normally, company expense begins when a salesman leaves his established home and is required to engage additional quarters, purchase meals, and pay for transportation. Although companies sometimes pay local trolley, bus, or automobile transportation of salesmen working in their home localities, the expenses of a salesman in his home city are usually paid by the salesman. A definite understanding should be had with salesmen concerning where and when company expenses may be charged.

Seven principal items of allowable sales expense are discussed below:

1. The *cost for lodgings* outside the city in which the salesmen's headquarters are located is legitimate company expense. Some

companies indicate to salesmen the maximum amounts that they will pay for hotel rooms; others have fixed allowances for lodging. Some concerns make advance arrangements with hotels to lodge salesmen; others require salesmen to stay at certain hotels.

2. *Transportation* of salesmen is a legitimate company sales expense. Some companies, however, specify the type of transportation for which payment will be made. Senior wholesale salesmen are usually allowed Pullman chairs for day travel and lower berths for night trains, while retail specialty and junior men are often required to ride in day coaches. Extra fare trains are usually prohibited to all except company executives. Taxis are also forbidden to certain classes of salesmen, although trolley and bus fares are paid to all. Parlor cars are permitted by one company only on trips of more than one hundred miles. Air travel is sometimes limited to executives.

Automobile expenses, when cars are owned by salesmen, are usually accounted for on a mileage basis, with the allowance running from three to six cents a mile. A few concerns compensate salesmen for automobiles on a monthly flat rate ranging from $35 to $100. Some companies own the salesmen's automobiles. A detailed description of automobile expenses is included in the chapter on "Salesmen's Transportation."

Garage and storage are company expenses for which one concern makes a maximum allowance of 75 cents a night. Such expenses as tires, repairs, and washing are paid for by the company. One company, which sells oil and grease, requires its salesmen to trade with customer-garages for repairs or tires.

3. *Meals* on the road are always at company expense, unless the salesman pays his own expenses. Many companies fix allowances for meals, while others have an understanding with salesmen that meals shall not exceed an average of $2 to $2.50 a day in rural districts. Fixing allowances for meals on trains is a common practice. One company studied the menus of hotels in many cities in determining reasonable meal charges.

4. *Communication* expenses, including telephone calls, telegrams, and postage stamps, are universally accepted as company expenses. Some concerns provide salesmen with charge cards for charging telegrams, and others provide salesmen with stamped envelopes for company mail. A restriction is sometimes placed on the number of telegrams or telephone calls that a salesman may be allowed.

5. *Entertainment* is the most debatable expense item of all

Some companies make no allowance whatever for the expense of entertaining customers or prospects. Other concerns permit salesmen to charge for entertainment up to a certain amount per week. Another method of handling this item is to require salesmen to itemize entertainment costs.

A survey of expense account practices, by the Sales Manager's Bureau of the Los Angeles Chamber of Commerce, showed that allowances for entertainment have been drastically reduced; one half of the one hundred eighty-three companies questioned make no entertainment expense allowances, while the balance pay for entertainment up to various limits.

Many purchasing agents will not accept entertainment from salesmen of their suppliers, although in some lines salesmen believe that they are obliged to do considerable entertaining to secure their share of a buyer's business.

6. *Laundry and valet charges* are not assumed by many companies. They maintain that these are personal expenses which should come out of the pockets of the salesmen. A survey of three hundred companies showed that more than two thirds did not pay for these items. On the other hand, some companies believe that salesmen on the road need their clothes pressed more often than when at home where several suits are usually worn interchangeably. Laundry costs are greater, clothes must be washed more frequently and wear out more rapidly on the road, and salesmen should be compensated accordingly. The importance of having salesmen make an immaculate appearance is so great that the small cost of laundry and valet service is a minor consideration.

One company permits salesmen to charge laundry if they are away from home for longer than one week. Another company permits its men to charge for "excess laundry, above what it would cost at home."

7. *Incidentals* form the burying ground for numerous miscellaneous expenses of salesmen. Many items listed under this heading are purely personal and should not be considered authorized sales expenses. Haircuts, shaves, manicures, cigars, cigarettes, personal entertainment, and shoe shines are not company sales expense. These items bulk large in a sizable organization in a year's time, however, and should be controlled through an understanding with salesmen concerning allowances for these items. Some companies set a limit of 50 cents to $2 a week for these items; others require itemized statements of incidentals.

Factors Influencing Method of Expense Control. Several factors have a bearing on the type of sales expense control that should be adopted for an individual sales organization, as follows:

1. The *method of travel* affects the basic items of allowable expense. Salesmen who travel by their own automobiles incur various expenses not contracted by salesmen traveling exclusively by train. Automobile expense control requires a careful checking of routes, mileage, upkeep, and depreciation, which is usually provided for by a flat allowance. Train and air travel expense can be easily controlled by mileage or script books.

2. The *type of sales job* determines the nature of expense regulation. Expenses of men engaged in a routine type of selling, involving repeat calls on an established group of dealers, may be readily handled by a flat allowance. A variable type of selling entailing irregular coverage of a territory, special work, or the introduction of new items would call for a flexible type of expense control to provide for fluctuating expense needs.

3. The *method of salesmen's compensation* influences the type of expense control. A company that paid its salesmen a straight commission including expenses would be relieved of the problem of controlling expenses. The sales compensation plan may be set up to include a bonus for curtailing expenses and thus relieve the management in a measure of the necessity for expense control.

4. The *type of product sold* may dictate the method of expense control. A salesman selling a high-priced specialty or luxury product would need a more liberal expense allowance and flexible control consistent with the necessity for calling on more prospects in order to close sales. On the other hand, a salesman of staple commodities closing sales by telephone or by personal call, in a restricted area, incurs little expense and may be controlled by a simple expense plan.

5. The *individual salesman* influences expense control. Some salesmen are not economical by nature and require strict control by the management if they are to succeed in maintaining a profitable ratio of expense to sales. Other salesmen can be counted upon to travel their territories at a minimum of expense and need little travel expense control. Expense control plans may be varied to suit the requirements of individual salesmen.

6. The nature of the territory in which the salesman is traveling influences the method of expense control. Salesmen traveling in

rural areas and using automobiles extensively require a different method of expense control than city salesmen.

Expense Advances. The common practice of companies paying salesmen's expenses in the field is to advance each salesman a definite sum of expense money sufficient to defray expenses for one or two weeks. At the end of that time, or before the fund advanced has been exhausted, the company sends the salesman a check covering current expenses to restore the expense fund to its original figure. In this manner, a salesman should always have on hand the total amount of money advanced for expenses or an expense account for the difference.

Misunderstandings sometimes arise over the purpose of money advanced to salesmen for expenses. Salesmen may believe that the money was advanced to them in lieu of compensation to be earned later in the form of salary, commission, or bonus, or they may feel that the money advanced belongs to them in the event they leave the company.

Sales executives should have a clear understanding with salesmen concerning the expense advance fund. One company requires a receipt from each salesman to whom it advances money for expenses. This receipt states that the fund was loaned for the purpose of paying expenses while engaged in business for the company and must be returned by the salesmen when requested by the company. This avoids misunderstandings and is helpful in collecting expense money from salesmen when they leave the force.

Educating Salesmen in Reducing Expenses. Sales executives are obliged continually to impress salesmen with the importance of economizing on sales travel costs. Arbitrary insistence on reduction in expenses is often not so effective as securing the intelligent coöperation of the salesmen and encouraging them to economize.

Certain sales executives make it clear to their salesmen that there is a definite limit to the cost of securing business. Net profits of a business determine in the last analysis the compensation of the salesmen and the expenses of salesmen are a large factor in the determination of net profits. Until salesmen see the relationship between their costs and their compensation, expense control can be little more than a problem to the management and an annoyance to the salesmen.

Problem 1—Flat Expense Allowances

Morrison Manufacturing Company

The Morrison Manufacturing Company, Indianapolis, Indiana, manufactures electrical specialties such as switch boxes, outlet boxes and fittings, fuses, and wiring devices sold through electrical and hardware wholesalers and direct to large electrical contractors, industrial concerns, and municipalities. The company has twenty traveling salesmen and ten resident salesmen located in the principal cities of the country.

The traveling salesmen cover their territories by train and their own automobiles and report their expenses each week on itemized expense forms provided by the company. The expenses of the men are not limited to definite amounts, but are allowed on a basis of what is actually spent from week to week. However, expenses reported by the salesmen have increased gradually over a period of three years, and in the opinion of the management a closer control should be effected to curb the rising costs.

The sales manager believes that the salesmen should continue to report their itemized expenses weekly, but in addition, definite limits or allowances should be fixed on the principal items of expense, which are transportation, hotels, and meals.

Considering a survey made by two leading electrical appliance wholesalers, the company decided to set a maximum of $1.75 a day for use of the salesman's automobile, plus the exact railroad fare from place to place traveled outside of a twenty-mile radius of the salesman's home city. When traveling by train, the exact railroad fare would be allowed.

Fixed maximum allowances on hotels and meals were set by the size of cities in which the salesman was working, as follows:

	Breakfast	Lunch	Dinner	Room
Cities under 10,000 population	$ .60	$ .75	$1.00	$2.00
Cities 10,000 to 30,000	.70	.85	1.15	2.50
Cities 30,000 to 50,000	.75	1.00	1.25	3.00
Cities over 100,000	1.00	1.25	1.50	3.50

The hotel charges were established after numerous hotel rates in cities of various sizes had been checked. These amounts included tips, laundry, and incidentals. Cities of larger size were not included, since they were covered by the resident salesmen, who were not allowed expenses in their city territories.

The general manager of the company objected to the new plan of expense control on the grounds that it was unduly complicated and would be resented by the salesmen as additional labor and a reflection on their honesty in reporting.

Questions

1. Should the company have adopted the new plan of expense control? Give reasons for your answer.

2. If you do not favor the new control plan as described in the problem, what method of control would you advise?

Problem 2—Reward for Curtailing Expenses

Drew Paint Company

The Drew Paint Company, Brooklyn, New York, manufactures a complete line of paints for interior, exterior, marine, and industrial purposes. Its house paints are sold direct to fifteen hundred hardware, paint, and wallpaper retailers in the Middle Atlantic States through eight salesmen, who travel out of the headquarters of the company.

The sales manager of the company has recently made an analysis of the traveling expenses of the house paint salesmen and found an average variation of about $35 a week between the expenses of the highest and lowest man on the force. The average weekly expenditures of each of the traveling salesmen were as follows: Salesman A, $75.50; Salesman B, $75.40; Salesman C, $63.74; Salesman D, $62.08; Salesman E, $48.15; Salesman F, $46.75; Salesman G, $40.36; and Salesman H, $38.

The expenses incurred by each salesman are reported weekly on forms provided by the company for the purpose. No attempt has been made to limit the amount of each salesman's expenses beyond occasional admonitions by the sales manager to reduce travel costs.

Although it was assumed that the average expenses of some of the salesmen were not excessive, considering their volume of sales and the extent of their territories, the wide variation in expenses of the various salesmen led the management to consider closer control.

It was found that the average weekly expense of the eight men was $56.12, which amounted to 4 per cent of the total volume of their average weekly net sales. With this average in mind, it was proposed to establish an expense quota for each of the salesmen of 4 per cent of net sales. In other words, a salesman selling $1,400 worth of house paint a week at an expense quota of 4 per cent would be entitled to spend $56 a week for expenses. Salesmen selling $2,000 worth of paint weekly could spend 4 per cent of that amount, or $80, for travel, food, and lodging.

The company could sell profitably at a 4 per cent ratio for travel expenses. To reward salesmen who maintained an expense ratio of 4 per cent, the management would pay salesmen all expense savings in the form of an annual bonus. For example, a salesman selling $100,000 worth of house paint a year at 4 per cent expense ratio would be entitled to an expense allowance of $4,000. If the salesman, however, covered his territory at an expense of $3,500, he would receive a bonus of $500, representing his savings in expenses.

Some of the officials of the company were skeptical of the effect on the salesmen's efforts of paying a reward to salesmen for economizing on travel expenses. They believed that salesmen would restrict their traveling, with the result that sales volume would suffer. The sales manager maintained that salesmen were now traveling too much, increasing sales expenses, and that a more intensive coverage of territories would be beneficial.

Questions

1. Should the company have rewarded its salesmen for curtailing travel expenses by the method described in the problem? Give reasons for your decision.

2. If you do not favor the method of expense control described in the problem, what method would you use?

3. Was the management's method of determining the expense quota for each of the salesmen sound? Why?

Problem 3—Salesmen Pay Expenses

Prague & Macomb Company

The Prague & Macomb Company, Louisville, Kentucky, manufactures packaged pharmaceutical specialties including tooth paste, mouth wash, antiseptic, and a laxative. These products have been on the market since 1903 and are nationally advertised to the extent of $100,000 annually. Sixty salesmen are paid a straight commission and bonus and call upon wholesale and retail drug distributors throughout the country.

The traveling expenses of each salesman are paid weekly upon presentation of an itemized expense account. The salesmen are permitted to incur expense for gasoline, oil, hotel rooms, meals, tires, repairs, depreciation, and incidentals.

The sales manager believes the present method of handling sales expenses is not satisfactory either to the company or the salesmen because both are unintentionally likely to be unfair to one another. Some salesmen are allowed too much for expenses and others not enough. There is the temptation for salesmen to charge for items in excess of actual cost and for things not actually purchased.

The management believes that salesmen's expenses, as well as commissions and bonuses, are simply separate elements of the total direct selling expense necessary to secure distribution of the company's products.

Accordingly, these items of expense should be lumped together and salesmen paid a lump sum to cover all direct selling expenses instead of separate amounts for commission, bonus, and expenses as at present. The management feels that the sale of its products should be worth a certain fixed amount, regardless of how direct selling expense is incurred.

To make this plan effective, salesmen would be given weekly drawing accounts against their commissions, out of which amount they would pay their own expenses as well as take their compensation. In this way neither the company nor the salesmen would be concerned with expense reports and the fairness of expense allowances. Salesmen would economize on expenses because there would be a personal incentive to watch expenditures that come out of their own income rather than from the company. The company would assist salesmen in budgeting their expenses so that they could travel economically and live within their incomes.

In introducing this plan to the salesmen, the management would say, in effect:

You get the business, travel as you see fit, stop where you like, when you like, eat as you like, sleep as you like. We will pay you a larger commission to cover all your traveling expenses and give you a good income to enable you to support your family and save money.

The present commission rate of each of the salesmen would be increased sufficiently to enable each man to equal his current earnings and expenses at his present volume. For example, under the proposed plan a salesman earning a 10 per cent commission and spending 2 per cent of total net sales volume for expenses would be given a total commission of 12 per cent.

Questions

1. Should the company adopt the proposed plan whereby salesmen pay their own expenses out of their commissions? Give reasons for your decision.

2. Is the company's present method of controlling salesmen's expenses satisfactory?

3. If you do not favor either the present plan or the proposed plan, what method of expense control should be adopted by the company?

Problem 4—Allowable Items of Expense

Covington Roofing Corporation

The Covington Roofing Corporation, established in 1919 in Camden, New Jersey, manufactures asphalt roofings and sidings that are sold direct to retail lumber and building supply dealers through fifty salaried field representatives traveling by train and bus out of six district offices located in the principal cities. The products of the company are widely advertised in national magazines and local newspapers.

The expenses of the salesmen are determined by an annual analysis of each salesman's territory that takes into account his method of travel, number of accounts, frequency of calls, past sales expenses, and volume of sales. On the basis of these factors, an annual budget of expenses is established for each salesman. Salesmen are permitted to draw weekly, against their annual budgets, amounts sufficient to cover actual expenses.

Weekly itemized expense reports are made out by the salesmen, listing each item of expense as incurred. These reports are examined by branch managers, approved if satisfactory, and forwarded to the home office for payment. Weekly expense checks are mailed to salesmen from the home office.

Salesmen occasionally report items of expense that, in the opinion of the branch managers, are not justified. Branch managers are then obliged to write salesmen regarding these items, which action sometimes creates controversy between the management and men. Some managers, rather than engage in petty censoring of expense accounts, overlook many questionable items of expense. In the opinion of one of the branch managers, who has asked for a definite policy on allowable items of expenses, this situation has been brought about by failure of the general management to establish a definite policy on the question of allowable expenses.

The general sales manager has prepared a statement of policy on expense as follows:

The company expects the salary of a salesman to be net to him, and when business requires him to travel away from his established home and engage additional quarters, then the expense of the additional quarters becomes company expense.

While away from home the company will assume all necessary railroad fares and where night travel is required, one standard lower berth will be allowed. No allowance will be made for a seat in a sleeping car or parlor car where the distance traveled is less than one hundred miles. Travel upon any extra-fare train will not be allowed unless authorized in advance.

No taxicab fares between hotel and station or the reverse will be allowed where convenient trolley or bus service is available.

Charges for hotel rooms will not be allowed in excess of $4.00 a day. Charges for breakfast, lunch, and dinner will be allowed, but not in excess of $3.00 a day for weekdays and $3.50 on Sundays.

Telephone and telegraph charges will be allowed for company business only. Postage stamps for company mail only will be allowed.

The company will not assume the personal grooming expenses of its salesmen, including barber, valet service in the pressing of clothing, laundry work, tips, and shoe shines.

No allowance is made for the entertainment of customers or prospects, and if entertaining is done, it shall be at the expense of the salesman.

Questions

1. Is the company's method of controlling expenses by an annual budget for each territory and weekly itemized reports of expenses sound?   Give reasons for your decision.

2. Is the new policy on allowable sales expenses satisfactory?   Give reasons for your decision.

3. If you do not favor the new expense allowance policy, prepare a new policy describing in detail expenses that should be paid by the company.

Reading References

Directing Sales, Bonney, p. 81.
Handbook of Sales Management, Hall, Section XVI.
Management of the Sales Organization, Russell, pp. 210–217.
Modern Sales Management, Frederick, p. 336.
Policyholders' Service Bureau, Metropolitan Life Ins. Co., New York, *Methods of Checking Salesmen's Traveling Expenses.*
Principles of Personal Selling, Tosdal, pp. 605–618.
Printer's Ink Monthly:
    "Handling the Salesman's Expense Account," by E. B. Weiss, July, 1931, p. 42.
    "Plans That Cut Waste Out of the Salesmen's Expense Account," by W. B. Edwards, Dec., 1932, p. 31.
Sales Administration, Hayward, pp. 308–310.
"Study of Salesmen's Expense Account Practices," *Report No. 366*, The Dartnell Corporation, Chicago, Illinois.

CHAPTER EIGHTEEN

TRANSPORTATION FOR SALESMEN

Changes in buying habits, increasing competition, and higher selling costs have made it necessary for sales executives to give more attention to the problem of transporting salesmen. Customers are buying in smaller quantities and more frequently, making it necessary for salesmen to cover their territories more often. Buyers are demanding more service and closer contact by salesmen, and competition is compelling more intensive coverage. The development of these conditions, coincident with a marked improvement in transportation facilities in recent years, has resulted in a revision of old and the inauguration of new travel policies for salesmen by many companies.

While salesmen use train, automobile, bus, trolley, airplane, and steamer transportation in covering their territories, the most commonly used travel mediums are automobiles and railways for distant travel and busses and trolleys for local coverage.

Automobile Transportation. The majority of sales forces are now motorized. While a few years ago sales executives were asking the question, "Is the automobile practical for our salesmen?" nowadays they are seeking the answer to the question, "How can salesmen's automobiles be operated to the best advantage?" A few of the reasons why salesmen are equipped with automobiles for local and long-distance travel are as follows:

1. Automobiles enable more frequent coverage of territories, taking advantage of seasonal demand.

2. They permit more frequent contact and more calls on customers and prospects.

3. Towns not located on rail and bus lines may be reached by automobile.

4. Demonstrating equipment and samples may be carried by salesmen.

5. The prestige of the salesman is enhanced.

6. Salesmen's cars are good advertising.

7. Costs of automobile travel compare favorably with costs of other transportation.

8. Salesmen are less fatigued and more efficient when they travel by motor.

9. An automobile gives a salesman more respect for his work.

10. Automobiles permit more flexible routing.

Some of the disadvantages of traveling by automobile are as follows:

1. Parking problems in congested areas make use of automobiles expensive and slow up transportation.

2. Automobiles are slower and more expensive in traveling to cities located long distances apart.

3. Overnight travel is not practical.

4. Delays incident to accidents, maintenance, or repairs are experienced.

5. The problems of replacement, maintenance of salesmen's cars, or supervision of company-owned cars are considerable.

Ownership of Salesmen's Cars. The use of automobiles for salesmen creates numerous problems. Who shall own the cars, the company, or the salesmen?

1. *Company-owned cars versus salesmen-owned cars.* Sales executives are divided on the question of ownership of salesmen's automobiles. Numerous methods of purchasing and owning sales cars have been tried, but none has been universally adopted. Some organizations buy and maintain full control of salesmen's automobiles; while others require salesmen to buy cars from their own resources or through a financing arrangement with the employing company. Other companies rent cars for salesmen through automobile renting agencies.

The benefits derived by companies that own salesmen's cars are as follows:

a. In the experience of some manufacturers, company-owned cars cost less per mile to operate. One concern which kept an accurate record of operating cost figures for two years found that a company-owned car cost $.064 per mile for the first year, and the second year $.056; while a salesman's car cost $.079 per mile the first year, and $.075 the second year.

b. Company automobiles can be replaced more often than salesmen's cars, thus insuring better and more economical operation. Salesmen do not create a reserve out of automobile expense allowances to cover the depreciation on their own cars.

c. The use of company cars by salesmen avoids the problem of paying salesmen car expense allowances that may be excessive or, in some cases, inadequate. No two automobiles operate for the same amount, and salesmen are frequently dissatisfied with their allowances. Company ownership is fairer to all salesmen.

d. Company ownership assures better appearance of cars. Salesmen's own cars are often not washed or polished for long periods and make a poor impression on prospects and customers. A good-appearing automobile is a good advertisement.

e. Insurance protection of company-owned cars is more complete than when handled by salesmen. Salesmen sometimes seek to cut insurance costs by carrying inadequate collision, property damage, or public liability, with resulting embarrassment in case of accidents.

f. A company sales car is usually better adapted to business needs than a salesman's car, which is often purchased for family use, style, or appearance.

g. Company ownership relieves salesmen of the responsibility of operating their own cars, and at the same time induces salesmen to use company cars in all kinds of weather.

h. When salesmen resign, after obligating themselves to buy a car for use in their work, the company is often obliged to purchase the automobile from the retiring salesman and resell it to another salesman for less than the unpaid balance.

i. Company cars afford advertising opportunities through a uniform color scheme or unique body design that makes countless impressions on prospects and customers.

j. Company cars, through quantity purchase and maintenance, may be bought and operated more economically than private cars. Tires, batteries, parts, and accessories can be purchased in wholesale quantities at substantial savings.

k. Salesmen frequently spend valuable company time maintaining their own cars. This is avoided by periodic inspections and expert attention to company equipment.

l. Salesmen operating their own cars under a liberal mileage allowance may travel excessively, sacrificing economical coverage with the expectation of making extra income.

2. *Salesmen-owned cars.* There are numerous advantages to manufacturers in requiring salesmen to operate private automobiles in sales work:

a. Salesmen take better care of their own cars than of company automobiles. More careful driving with less time out for repairs is the result of individual car ownership.

b. A company does not have to make a heavy investment in automobiles, which depreciate rapidly; neither is an investment necessary in clerical services and labor to supervise the operation of a fleet of salesmen's cars.

c. Salesmen are better satisfied with their own cars, for they can buy cars of their own choice, cars in which they have the utmost confidence and know how to handle and operate at the lowest possible cost. Individual preferences for cars are strong, and individual ownership capitalizes on this preference.

d. The problem of using company cars after business hours is avoided when salesmen own their own automobiles. Some companies prohibit the use of company cars for personal purposes. Controversies between the salesmen and management sometimes arise, with resulting dissatisfaction.

e. Salesmen usually purchase better automobiles than those provided by employers, with resulting lower costs of operation and less expense to the company.

Conclusions on automobile ownership. Several factors should be considered in deciding the question of sales automobile ownership. The size of the company and the sales organization is an important consideration. Large companies with several hundred salesmen usually own salesmen's automobiles. The capital investment in equipment is no problem to these concerns. They can control a large number of company-owned vehicles more effectively and provide for maintenance, depreciation, disposal of used cars, and purchase of new equipment as needed.

Small companies, on the other hand, prefer salesmen to own their automobiles, for the use of which salesmen are paid an allowance. The company is relieved of the investment and responsibility for sales cars as well as the details of supervision. Salesmen's transportation is handled more conveniently, if not as economically and efficiently, for a small number of men by individual car ownership.

The type of product sold affects the question of car ownership. A product of general consumption, broadly distributed, can be effectively advertised through the use of company cars. A salesman of a luxury product may require a car in keeping with his commodity. Under company control, cars may be kept in good appearance. Products that must be sold by sample or by demonstration may require special cars to transport them.

The method of paying salesmen may have a bearing on the ownership of sales cars. Commission salesmen ordinarily operate their own cars on an allowance or from their compensation.

Some companies own a few salesmen's cars, while the balance is owned by the salesmen themselves. Occasionally managers and supervisors are provided with company cars, while salesmen operate their own cars. Other companies may be in the process of changing over from salesman ownership to company ownership of automobiles, or vice versa. At times, companies are obliged to assume ownership of automobiles when salesmen resign or are unable to complete car payments.

A survey of salesmen's automobile operation by the National Wholesale Druggists Association showed that a salesman should own the automobile if the mileage driven for company business is limited. If the car is driven largely for company business and only incidentally for private purposes, it should be owned by the company.

The mileage for company business should be 18,000 to 20,000 miles a year. According to the Association, if the business requires less than 18,000 to 20,000 miles annually, the car should be owned by the salesman, but if the annual mileage exceeds this amount for company business, it is usually more economical for the company to own the automobile. For many businesses this rule may mean that city salesmen should own their own cars, while country salesmen should be supplied cars by the company.

An investigation of the sales automobile practices of 234 concerns by the Dartnell Corporation showed that in 139 companies salesmen owned the cars; in 57 companies the sales cars were owned by the company; while 37 concerns operated both salesmen- and company-owned automobiles.

A survey of salesmen's car ownership in 54 companies, by Printer's Ink publications, revealed that 8,996 cars, or 75.2 per cent, were company-owned, and the remaining 2,973, or 24.8 per cent, were salesmen-owned. The average number of cars in company-owned fleets was 316, and the average number in salesmen-owned fleets was 95.

The increase in the use of automobiles by many sales organizations and the closer control being exercised over salesmen's activities indicate a trend toward company ownership of salesmen's cars by large companies. Many small organizations prefer salesmen to own their cars.

Aiding Salesmen in Financing Car Purchase. Since many salesmen are not financially able to purchase an automobile for use in business, some companies give their representatives assistance in buying personal cars.

A manufacturer of medical products aids each salesman in purchasing an automobile by advancing one third of the cost and charging this amount to the salesman's automobile account. A credit of one twelfth of the amount advanced is given to the salesman each month until by the end of the year the account is cleared. Then the salesman's automobile account continues to be credited at the rate of 25 per cent of the cost of the car for each ensuing year of its ownership. The fund accumulated in this way is available to the salesman when it becomes necessary for him to buy a new car. On the basis of disposing of a car every three years, a salesman, beginning with his third car, has a chance of realizing something on this plan. The company has set a maximum of $1,600 as the amount of its participation in car ownership. All cost of maintenance, including insurance, is paid by the company.

Personal Use of Company-owned Cars. One of the problems in the operation of company-owned salesmen's cars is the use of company cars for personal transportation. Policies of various manufacturers on the private use of company cars vary; some prohibit salesmen from using cars on any but company business; while others give definite permission to salesmen to make personal use of company automobiles.

A manufacturer with forty salesmen, traveling by automobile, charges his men five cents for each mile traveled in company cars on personal business. Personal mileage of these salesmen often exceeds one hundred miles a month, and the return thereon enables the manufacturer to meet a portion of the cost of servicing company cars.

Organizations permitting salesmen to use company cars without cost often require salesmen to assume the cost of any damage or liability sustained while the car is in private use. Salesmen are also charged with the gasoline and oil consumed while the cars are in personal service.

Operating Expenses of Salesmen's Automobiles. Salesmen who operate their own cars are compensated for the expense of operation by the following methods:

1. The fixed or flat-rate plan, whereby a salesman is given a definite amount each week for the operation and maintenance of his car.
2. The mileage plan, whereby a salesman is allowed a fixed rate for each business mile traveled.
3. The incurred-expense plan, whereby a salesman is paid for automobile expenses as reported weekly on forms provided for that purpose.

1. *The fixed or flat-rate plan.* This plan has numerous advantages, including the following:

a. The payment of a flat rate is simple to administer and economical to handle for both company and salesmen.

b. The salesmen know definitely how much they will receive for expenses.

c. The plan may be budgeted in advance by the management.

d. The plan eliminates misunderstanding between salesmen and management.

e. Salesmen will not do excess driving.

The disadvantages to this plan are as follows:

a. Salesmen may spend their car allowances, and when it comes time to make repairs or get a new car, lack the funds to make the purchase.

b. Expense requirements vary with different sections of the country, different makes of cars, and individuals, making it impossible to set a fair allowance for all men.

c. A careful estimate must be made of the costs of operating automobiles in each territory.

d. Some salesmen will make money, while others will lose on a flat allowance.

Some companies vary the amount of travel allowance with the territory. A manufacturer of automobile appliances pays salesmen covering Pennsylvania and the Pacific Coast a flat allowance of $5 a day. The Cleveland salesman, traveling in a restricted area, is allowed $3.50 a day for his car expense. Depreciation costs are included in these amounts.

The same plan is followed by a large wholesaler of electrical equipment, which allows country salesmen up to $4 a day for car expenses and city salesmen, $1.75 a day. In addition, the company allows license fees and liability insurance covering damage to others and their property. The salesmen take care of insurance for fire, theft, and damage.

2. *The mileage plan.* This method of compensating salesmen for the use of their cars is the most common form of allowance. The advantages are:

a. Convenience of application.

b. Incentive for salesmen to cover more territory.

c. Applies only to miles covered.

Sales executives who object to a mileage allowance do so for the following reasons:

a. Salesmen become dissatisfied with the amount of the allowance, particularly when they find it necessary to spend a considerable sum for overhauling.

b. It is difficult to check the actual mileage of a salesman on company business.

c. Mileage may become a salesman's objective. He may drive unnecessary distances or spend time in driving that should be spent with customers or prospects.

d. Mileage basis is unfair to a salesman working in a large city where mileage is at a minimum and maintenance at a maximum.

e. Inequalities exist in territories, automobiles, and drivers that make flat mileage figures impractical.

Some companies pay salesmen for automobile expenses at a diminishing rate; the rate per mile becomes less as the number of miles traveled increases. A manufacturer of electrical equipment with 600 salesmen has established mileage allowances for salesmen's personal cars as follows: 200 miles, $.07; 300 miles, $.068; 400 miles, $.066; 500 miles, $.064; 600 miles, $.062; 700 miles, $.06; 800 miles, $.058; 900 miles, $.056; 1,000 miles, $.054; 1,100 miles, $.052; and 1,200 miles, $.05.

A manufacturer of automotive electrical accessories, following a similar plan, allows 7 cents a mile up to two hundred and fifty miles, and 4 cents a mile beyond two hundred and fifty.

In a few companies territorial mileage allowances are made to salesmen on a basis of actual cost of travel, as determined by the management, and make of car.

3. *Incurred-expense plan.* The control of the costs of operating

salesmen's automobiles by this plan is favored by practically all companies owning their sales cars and by a few concerns whose salesmen operate private cars. The principal advantage of this plan is that it places no incentive either on excessive driving or on limited use of the car. This plan is fair to all salesmen since it covers actual costs of operation of individual cars, and some salesmen are not underpaid and others overpaid on car allowances.

The disadvantages of this plan are: some salesmen will abuse the privilege of reporting actual expenses and make unjustified claims; constant checking of expense reports is required, and disagreements arise.

Concerns using this plan require salesmen owning their cars to submit itemized reports of gasoline, oil, and repair expenses daily or weekly. These expenses are paid promptly by the company, and in addition, each salesman is allowed a fixed amount for depreciation.

Companies owning their salesmen's cars uniformly require a detailed daily or weekly report of automobile expenses, which is closely checked. One large food manufacturer operating two hundred fifty salesmen's cars requires every item of expense to be supported by a receipted voucher. Automobile expense accounts go to the district office from which each man works, where the accounts are checked and the salesman is reimbursed. They are then forwarded to the home office, where they are carefully audited.

Composition of Automobile Expense Allowances. The Committee on Sales Management of the National Association of Wholesale Druggists has made an extensive survey of salesmen's automobile expense allowances and has concluded that expenses for which the salesman should be reimbursed cover three parts:

1. A mileage allowance which covers the cost of gasoline, oil, tires, and repairs, all of which items are a function of mileage.
2. A depreciation allowance which covers the cost of depreciation and obsolescence. This should be sufficient to produce the proper reserve at the trade-in time.
3. An allowance for license plates, taxes, and insurance for public liability, property damage, theft, fire and collision.

The Association has prepared twelve graphic charts which enable a manufacturer or wholesaler who knows the mileage traveled by a salesman during a given period to compute accurately the mileage allowance that should be paid to the salesman in order that he may be fairly reimbursed for his actual expenses. These charts have been prepared for different types of territories, kinds of roads, and average gasoline cost.

AUTOMOBILE WEEKLY EXPENSE REPORT											

N. Y. 614-51655 100M-5-30.

Mail Every Saturday Night

Receipted Bills for all Expenses must accompany this Report.

Make of Car_____
Company Car No._____
Week Ending_____19___

DAY	Name of Each Town Visited	Speedometer Reading	Miles	Gasoline	Lubrication	Garage Rent	REPAIRS		Misc. Washing Etc.	Tire & Tube Expense	License
							Mechanical	Body			
Sun.											
Mon.											
Tues.											
Wed.											
Thurs.											
Fri.											
Sat.											
	TOTALS										

Time lost for repairs during working hours

Explain in detail repairs charged above_____

TOTAL ALL EXPENSE

_____, Salesman.

IMPORTANT: In case of Speedometer trouble, please insert estimated mileage; have Speedometer repaired promptly.

FIGURE 65. Automobile expenses are reported weekly on this form by salesmen of a large food specialty organization operating several hundred salesmen's cars. The principal items of automobile expense, including gasoline, oil, garage rent, repairs, tires, and tubes, are recorded on this form.

Determining Depreciation. Since depreciation is usually the largest single item in car operation, it should be determined accurately, if true costs of operation are desired. It may be calculated on a mileage basis by determining the price paid for a car, subtracting the salvage or trade-in value, and dividing by the number of miles actually operated upon company business.

The average life of a salesman's automobile from the standpoint of economical operation is usually considered from three to four years, and at this rate depreciation goes on at the rate of from 25 to 33⅓ per cent a year. This rate will vary with the size and difficulty of the territory traveled.

The weekly automobile expense allowance due a salesman may be separated into mileage and depreciation costs and the latter withheld and made available to the salesman when he purchases a new car or terminates his employment. When the salesman receives his depreciation in a lump sum, when he purchases a new car it is seldom necessary for him to arrange for financing help.

The National Wholesale Druggists Association recommends that the following amounts be set aside each week as depreciation reserves:

Miles Driven Weekly	Weekly Depreciation Allowance
300 or less	$2.88
301 to 350	3.12
351 to 400	3.36
401 to 425	3.60
426 to 475	3.84
476 to 500	4.01
501 to 550	4.03
551 or more	4.06

According to the Association, the depreciation allowance does not vary materially with the type of road, kind of territory, or typography of the area.

Controlling Operation of Company-owned Cars. In addition to keeping weekly itemized reports of automobile expenses for each salesman's car, companies operating large fleets follow a definite plan of control and education, having for its objective low transportation costs.

Company-owned cars are inspected periodically, and records are kept for comparison. Salesmen are required to take company cars to authorized service stations for periodic mechanical checkups, or branch or home office mechanics make regular inspections at company garages to detect any trouble.

Cost accounting systems are maintained at home offices to record costs of operation for each company car by months and years. The original investment and book value of each car is also recorded, as well as its cost per mile. These records are consulted when major repairs must be made or a new car purchased.

Field supervision of salesmen's cars is an important factor in the control of large fleets. Traveling inspectors check up on the driving ability of salesmen and the way they care for company cars. Supervisors sometimes travel with salesmen, advising on the proper operation of company automobiles.

Insuring Salesmen's Cars. The hazards of automobile transportation are so great that in certain states the law requires that insurance be carried on all automobiles. Company-owned fleets are usually protected with full insurance coverage, which includes the following forms:

1. Fire and theft insurance.
2. Public liability and property damage.

Other forms of insurance sometimes carried on salesmen's cars are:

1. Collision insurance.
2. Plate glass insurance.
3. Insurance on salesmen's samples and equipment, called "floater insurance."

Railway Transportation.   While many salesmen now travel exclusively by automobile, railway transportation still remains one of the principal mediums of travel for salesmen covering large cities separated by long distances.   The outstanding advantages of rail transportation are:

1. Economy for long distances.
2. Speed for long-distance travel.
3. Less fatigue to salesmen traveling distances.
4. A full business day for selling.
5. Completion of reports and detail work en route.

The principal objections to train transportation for salesmen are:

1. Long waits for trains in rural areas, thus slowing up travel time.
2. Train service to many points inadequate.
3. Train service impractical in congested territories where many calls must be made.
4. Transportation of samples or demonstrators is slow and expensive.

Rail transportation remains superior in many ways for salesmen who make long jumps or sell products with scattered distribution. A salesman calling only on large department stores in large cities can travel more rapidly and economically by train than by automobile.   On the other hand, salesmen selling many stores in one or more states can reach them more conveniently by automobile.

The type of transportation to be used by salesmen is determined largely by the nature of the distribution of the product sold and the number and frequency of calls that must be made.

Bus and Trolley Transportation.   For local transportation in cities and suburbs, busses or trolleys are often superior to other means of transportation from the standpoint of speed and economy.   Traffic congestion in large cities has made the use of automobiles impractical.   Free parking space is restricted, and parking charges for short periods of time are high. Travel in cities by automobile is slow, and operating costs increase with frequent stopping and starting. Trolley and bus schedules have been speeded up and rates reduced in many places.

Bus transportation in many suburban and rural areas has been improved to such an extent that salesmen can now travel as rapidly and more economically by bus than by automobile. More comfortable busses relieve salesmen from the fatigue of driving, and frequent schedules enable them to make as many calls in a day as would be possible by automobile.

The effectiveness of bus and trolley transportation for city salesmen depends on the density of distribution or the distance between dealers or prospects. Sales executives, by studying local transportation facilities, can frequently save considerable travel expense and reduce the travel time of their salesmen.

Air Transportation. Air travel for salesmen is increasing rapidly as air transportation costs are being reduced. Some companies operate their own salesmen's planes. These have not only speeded up coverage of sales territories but have also served as excellent advertisements. One of the large oil companies has equipped its salesman, selling aviation lubricants, with a plane to cover the principal airports.

Numerous companies with scattered distribution, whose salesmen cover a limited number of customers in large cities, travel their men by commercial airlines at rates that compare favorably with train travel, and with great economy in time. Many sales executives use airlines regularly in contacting salesmen and distributors in various parts of the country.

Problem 1—Car Ownership

Goodman Leather Company

The Goodman Leather Company, established in St. Louis, Missouri, in 1905, tans leather, and makes an annual volume of over $6,000,000 worth of leather belting and other leather products. These products are nationally distributed by fifty salaried salesmen traveling by automobile out of six branch offices located in the leading industrial centers.

The company salesmen are compensated for operating their own cars on a basis of five cents a mile. The total mileage is reported weekly on expense forms provided by the company. This five-cent mileage allowance to salesmen includes the cost of gasoline, oil, tires, garage storage, repairs, and depreciation, and was established by the company after investigation of transportation costs of various makes of cars.

The company does not specify or recommend the types of automobiles that salesmen shall buy. They own cars ranging in price from $600 up to $2,000, and in type from business coupés to five-passenger sedans. Salesmen are obliged to carry their own insurance, although the company does not specify the amount and type of coverage.

Certain of the salesmen owning higher-priced cars object to the five-cent mileage allowance as being inadequate to compensate them for operating their cars. Other salesmen owning low-priced cars are satisfied with the present allowance. Salesmen working in sections where the roads are poor and there is a great deal of mountain driving believe that their allowance should be increased.

Confronted with these problems, the company is considering the advisability of taking over the ownership of salesmen's automobiles and paying actual expenses of operation as reported by salesmen on forms provided for the purpose. In this way the actual operating costs of each sales car could be watched and expense curtailed by wholesale purchases of tires, batteries, and other equipment. Furthermore, the company cars can be inspected regularly and traded in for new equipment before operating costs and repairs become excessive.

The company would take over the present automobiles of the salesmen at their depreciated value, and in this way the initial company expense for cars would be reduced. The salesmen are agreeable to this plan.

It is contended, on the other hand, that salesmen would not be so careful of company cars as they would of their own property. Also, company cars would be used by salesmen for personal transportation, and it would be difficult to determine the exact mileage traveled for such purposes.

Questions

1. Should the company own the salesmen's cars? Give reasons for your decision.

2. Should the sales cars be salesmen-owned? Why?

3. Assuming that you approve of company ownership of these cars, is the company's plan to take over the salesmen's present automobiles satisfactory?

4. Is the mileage-allowance plan for reimbursing salesmen for company use of their cars satisfactory?

Problem 2—Automobile Expense Allowances

Bush-Gilmer Chemical Company

The Bush-Gilmer Chemical Company, established at Pittsburgh, Pennsylvania, in 1922, manufactures and sells an annual volume of $1,800,000 worth of industrial chemicals, including rosin sizes, printing inks, varnishes and compounds, dyestuffs, esters, and alcohols. Ten salaried salesmen call upon makers of paper, paints, lacquers, and other products. These men travel out of their homes located in the chief industrial centers.

The salesmen alternate the use of automobile and railway and air transportation, using personal automobiles for covering congested areas, and planes and trains for reaching distant customers and prospects.

When a salesman uses his automobile, the company pays him a flat allowance of $5 a day for each full day the car is used, and a proportionate charge when the machine is used less than a full day. If the salesman's car is used one-half day, he is allowed $2.50, and for one-quarter day he is allowed $1.25. The company trusts the salesman to report the actual length of time his car is in company use.

The flat allowance to salesmen compensates them for the cost of gasoline, oil, tires, and depreciation. The amount of the allowance was determined by keeping accurate records of the costs of operating several salesmen's cars for a period of six months and taking the average expense figure.

In two territories, where salesmen do little traveling, for the reason that customers are close together, the flat allowance is reduced to $3.50 a day. This figure meets with the approval of the salesmen concerned.

When a salesman uses a train, plane, or bus instead of an automobile he is permitted to charge the company the actual cost of the railway, plane, or bus fare for the distance traveled.

One of the principal problems arising from the use of this method of automobile allowance is the doubtful accuracy of salesmen's reports of the time their cars are used in company service. Furthermore, when the time comes for salesmen to dispose of their cars and purchase new automobiles, they have not saved enough of their daily allowances to make a sufficient initial payment to afford reasonable monthly carrying charges. The management believes that some method of extending financial assistance to its salesmen to enable them to buy new cars every three years would largely solve this difficulty.

Questions

1. Is the company's method of paying a daily flat allowance to salesmen for use of their cars in company service satisfactory? Give reasons for your answer.

2. If the present allowance plan is not sound, suggest another method of handling salesmen's automobile transportation.

3. Should the company aid its salesmen in the purchase of automobiles? How could this assistance be arranged?

Problem 3—Company-Owned Sales Cars

Blackmer Insulation Company

The Blackmer Insulation Company, Cleveland, Ohio, distributes pulpwood insulation board, and other insulation products used extensively in residential and industrial building construction through a sales organization of three hundred men. Twenty district sales offices are maintained in the principal markets of the country. Sales are made to thousands of lumber and building supply dealers as well as industrial concerns. Extensive advertising has created a wide demand for the company's products.

The company provides each of its salesmen with an automobile, identified with advertising, for use in selling the company's products. Each salesman is given a set of written instructions relative to the operation and maintenance of the company car. The company pays for all gasoline and oil, repairs, tire expense, garage rent and parking, and insurance and depreciation.

Salesmen are required to submit weekly reports showing disbursements for these items. From these reports an accurate cost record of each car is maintained so that the company can determine whether a car is operating efficiently or needs repairs and replacements.

The company makes contracts with automobile manufacturers, gasoline and oil refiners, and tire makers for automobiles and operating supplies. Tires, as well as such items of equipment as skid chains, antifreeze solution, heaters, and seat covers, are given to salesmen by the home office.

By close supervision of equipment, cost analysis, and contracts for supplies, the company operates its salesmen's cars at a cost averaging five cents a mile. This represents the purchase of supplies, garage rent, parking, washing, licenses, insurance, depreciation, and interest on investment. Property and corporation tax is not included.

Company cars operate for a total distance of approximately four million miles a year at an average cost of $200,000. The company employs an automobile supervisor, who is assisted by a full-time clerk, to keep records of operation.

The general management of the company considers that the financial burden of operating and maintaining salesmen's cars is excessive and is considering the advisability of selling company cars to salesmen and giving them an allowance for their operation.

An official of the company believes that it is not wise to require sales-men earning from $2,500 to $5,000 a year to keep one fourth of this amount tied up in equipment which will be worn out in the company's service and which is subject to such high depreciation as an automobile.

Those who favor salesmen-owned cars contend that salesmen prefer to operate cars of their own choice and will give them better care and oper-ate them more economically than they would in the case of company cars.

Questions

1. Should the company continue to own salesmen's cars? Why?
2. Is the company's method of controlling the operation of its company cars satisfactory? What might be done to secure more economical opera-tion by salesmen?

Reading References

"New Trends in Salesmen's Automobile Expense Control," *Report No. 392,* The Dartnell Corporation, Chicago, Illinois.
Printer's Ink Monthly:
    "Operating a Fleet of Salesmen's Cars," by C. L. Jones, July, 1931, p. 35.
    "The Salesman's Car," by C. B. Larrabee, Sept., 1933, p. 29.
Printer's Ink Weekly:
    "Flat Allowances for Salesmen's Cars Cause Padding," by Don Gridley, Sept. 7, 1933, p. 84.
    "Gas, Oil, and Salesmen's Cars," by editorial staff, Aug. 8, 1935, p. 89.
    "Salesmen's Cars," by editorial staff, Sept. 17, 1936, p. 69.
    "Personal Use of Firm's Cars," by editorial staff, Mar. 25, 1937, p. 71.
    "Let Salesman Own Car," by O. C. Olin, May 13, 1937, p. 88.
Sales Management Magazine, "How Twenty Companies Handle Automobile Ex-penses," by editorial staff, Aug. 10, 1929.
"Salesmen's Automobile Allowances and Expense Control," *Report No. 344,* The Dartnell Corporation, Chicago, Illinois.

CHAPTER NINETEEN

SALES QUOTAS

Why Sales Quotas? A sales quota is the estimated volume of sales that a company expects to secure within a definite period of time. A quota for salesmen may also be more broadly defined as a goal of sales accomplishment, a task, objective, or standard that a sales organization strives to attain.

Just as a good golfer tries to equal par on every hole, a good salesman should have a quota for measuring his sales performance. Salesmen, as well as marathon runners, will cover more ground when striving to equal an established record. It is impossible to win a race that has no finish.

A salesman who is told to go out and sell as much as he can rarely equals the production of the man who has a definite daily objective to see ten prospects, sell two units, or bring in $200 worth of orders. A salesman not only works harder but also works more happily when he knows what is expected of him.

In addition to providing a fixed task, sales quotas afford numerous advantages:

1. They provide convenient measuring sticks to determine the comparative value of various salesmen.
2. They facilitate the coördination of production and sales.
3. They provide a basis for salesmen's compensation plans, particularly bonus systems.
4. They serve as a basis for sales budgets.
5. They provide incentive to salesmen to increase efforts.
6. They enable the proper distribution of advertising, warehouse stocks, and manpower.
7. They increase efficiency of the distributing system.

Numerous companies have, however, established no sales quotas, largely for the following reasons:

1. It is difficult to set quotas accurately on account of the numerous variable factors affecting sales volume.

2. Salesmen are often reluctant to accept quotas established by statistical methods that they do not understand.

3. Considerable time and expense are involved in establishing quotas.

4. Quotas may be set too high, resulting in high-pressure selling methods.

5. Quotas may be set too low, resulting in no stimulation to salesmen.

6. Quotas may prove valueless on account of inadequate rewards for attainment.

7. Quotas depend too much on personal opinion.

8. Quotas require exhaustive analysis of market.

9. It is impossible to weigh fairly the many factors of demand, competition, and ability affecting the performance of an individual salesman.

Types of Sales Quotas. The most common type of sales quota is that which is set for the attainment of a volume of sales. This type of quota may be expressed in dollars and cents or in units, such as pounds and cases. Since sales volume is one of the most important as well as conveniently computed factors of sales accomplishment, volume quotas will be the type emphasized in this chapter.

Although volume is very desirable, particularly to companies with a heavy burden of overhead expense, profitable sales are also important. Accordingly, a few profit-minded concerns have established profit quotas to measure salesmen's performance from the standpoint of ability to sell profitable commodities. One manufacturer of electrical equipment gauges the work of salesmen by their ability to equal average gross profit quotas of 20 per cent by selling items carrying profit equivalent to that amount.

Another vital element in profitable sales performance is ability to sell at low expense. A few companies have established expense quotas for salesmen and reward men whose expenses are below the minimum established in the expense quota. A large leather products manufacturer has set an expense quota of 4 per cent for one class of salesmen. Men whose expenses exceed this amount are penalized, while those selling below the quota figure are given a bonus.

Activity quotas are established in some organizations. These are set for number of calls, number of interviews, number of demonstrations, number of store sales, number of prospects secured, number of customer calls, and so forth. One successful life insurance agency has established a monthly prospect quota of fifty new prospects for each agent. An outstanding insurance agent has set for himself a daily quota of six calls to maintain his volume of production.

As the value of setting definite tasks for salesmen becomes more generally recognized, sales executives will not only set up sales volume quotas, but will also establish standards of performance for each element of the sales job and measure each salesman by his ability to accomplish each quota. Success in selling may be measured by the attainment of many definite objectives, small in themselves but important in the aggregate.

Bases for Sales Volume Quotas. A sound sales volume quota takes into consideration numerous factors that indicate the volume of sales or share of the market which a company may reasonably expect to secure. Factors that should be considered to a greater or less extent in establishing a volume quota are:

1. A knowledge of the market potential, which involves an analysis of the purchasing power, number of consumers, standards of living, and distributive outlets of the area for which a quota is desired. The extent of competition, adverse conditions, or other limiting factors should also be considered.
2. Judgment of sales executives of the company on the variable market elements affecting sales volume.
3. Past sales volume performance.
4. Estimates of distributors.
5. Estimates of company salesmen.
6. Manufacturing output.
7. Cost of obtaining sales, and volume necessary to absorb the sales expense.
8. Advertising investment.
9. Product improvement.

Market analysis. This is the basis of sound quota establishment, for without a knowledge of the potential market and conditions affecting purchasing, no accurate forecast can be made to answer the question, "What sales volume should be secured?"

A market analysis of each salesman's territory is the best way to establish volume quotas, since a much more accurate estimate of market possibilities can be secured by analysis of small territory units as cities, counties, and trading areas. By totaling the quota estimates for local areas, a national sales quota may be built up that will be fair to the individual salesman and at the same time represent more accurately the potential of the organization as a whole.

Numerous *consumption factors* are an index of the potential of a market. The index factors to be considered in making a market analysis depend chiefly on the type of product, its price, whether it is a luxury or necessity or an industrial or individual consumption item, the amount of demand, and the conditions surrounding its use.

The index factor that measures the potential market for staple commodities like bread, sugar, or flour is *people*. The price of a product introduces another index factor, *buying power*. The degree of novelty or style of an article may introduce another index factor, the *desire to buy*, or *standards of living*. The number and type of *distributive outlets* serving the market are still another index factor. In analyzing markets for commodities of individual consumption, the index factors of population, buying power, standards of living, and distributive outlets should be used with varying weight, according to the type of commodity under consideration. Rarely does one of these factors alone give an adequate measure of market potential.

Other consumption factors have an important influence on sales potentials for different types of products. Climate is the principal index factor in the sale of winter sport equipment. Advertising volume, competition, local demand, and other index factors must frequently be considered.

General consumption factors in markets for industrial products include the indexes of number of industrial plants as well as buying power.

To simplify the determination of market potentials these *market indexes* are used. Consumption may be computed by applying the following specific indexes: foreign-born population, colored population, literate population, native whites, total families, rural population, urban population, adult population, dwellings, home-owning population, and number of business enterprises. Government statistics are available for each of these indexes, which may be used individually or in combination.

Buying power may be computed by applying the following indexes: income tax returns, value of farm crops, value of livestock, individual bank deposits, check transactions, per capita wholesale and retail sales, automobile ownership, number of persons per income tax return, and excise taxes.

Industrial buying power may be computed by the indexes of value added by manufacture, and value of manufactured products. These indexes may be used individually or in combination, according to the product.

The desire-to-buy or standards-of-living may be computed by the following indexes: telephones, gas-supplied homes, wired homes, radio ownership, automobile ownership, life insurance sales, magazine circulation, school enrollment, and oil burner ownership. Statistics of each of these indexes are available through trade associations and large corporations in each of the industries directly concerned.

Indexes of distributive outlets include: number of wholesalers and retailers provided by the Census of Distribution by the United States Department of Commerce; and number of grocery, drug, hardware, automotive, radio, and other types of outlets compiled by trade associations and publishers serving those fields.

Numerous *sources of statistical data* are used in measuring market potentials for the establishment of sales quotas, the principal sources of which are as follows:

DOMESTIC CONSUMPTION STATISTICS:
  Retail Shopping Areas, J. Walter Thompson Company, New York City. Hearst Magazines, Inc., New York City, Curtis Publishing Company, Philadelphia.
AGRICULTURAL STATISTICS:
  U. S. Census of Agriculture, Bureau of the Census, Washington, D. C.
STATISTICS ON MANUFACTURING:
  U. S. Census of Manufactures, Bureau of the Census, Washington, D. C.
AUTOMOTIVE STATISTICS:
  R. L. Polk & Company, Detroit, Michigan.
CONSUMER PURCHASING POWER:
  Department of Labor Statistics, U. S. Department of Labor, Washington, D. C.
CONSUMER MARKET DATA:
  Market Data Handbook of U. S., U. S. Department of Commerce, Washington, D. C.
BUSINESS CONDITIONS:
  Babson's Reports, Wellesley Hills, Massachusetts.
  Survey of Current Business, U. S. Department of Commerce.
DISTRIBUTION STATISTICS:
  Census of Distribution, Bureau of the Census, Washington, D. C.
FINANCIAL STATISTICS:

American Bankers Association, New York City.
Bureau of Internal Revenue, Washington, D. C.
Rand McNally's Bankers Directory, Chicago, Illinois.
ELECTRICAL STATISTICS:
Electrical World, New York City.
GAS STATISTICS:
American Association of Gas Companies, New York City.
TELEPHONE STATISTICS:
American Telephone & Telegraph Company, New York City.

Publishers of magazines advocate the use of magazine circulation as a reliable index of people, buying power, and desire to buy. Many companies use magazine circulation as one of several indexes in analyzing markets for the establishment of volume quotas.

Rarely does a company use one index in measuring its potential market. Several indexes are usually combined. Frequently they are given different weights. No standard set of indexes is used, as each company considers that its product and market call for indexes which are different from those used by other concerns.

A manufacturer of oil burners uses sixteen separate indexes in computing market possibilities, of which the number of wired homes, income tax returns, and automobile registrations are considered the most important.

A manufacturer of office equipment uses the combined circulation figures of a group of magazines of national circulation as an index for measuring market potential.

A food product manufacturer uses three indexes: population, food sales per capita, and circulation of the magazines in which the company advertises.

The Life Insurance Sales Research Bureau analyzes markets for life insurance on the basis of the six following indexes:

1. Insurable population, or the number of white males more than twenty years of age, excluding illiterates.
2. The number of personal income tax returns.
3. Total bank deposits.
4. The combined circulation of six national magazines.
5. The value added by manufacture.
6. Estimated yearly agricultural income.

These index factors are weighted so that the first four have a weight of one each throughout the country while the weights given to indexes five and six are determined separately for each state.

The choice of indexes may be verified on the same chart by plotting sales by territories and the index factor by territories. If the

line~
gethe~

Afte~
is to ap~
Market i~ ~es for each ~
of the total United States figure, 1~
appliances select the market index facto~
on wired homes show that salesman A's te~
homes. The United States total of wirea ~
Expressed in percentage, A's territory has .75 per~ ~nited
States total of wired homes.

The next step is to take sales figures for A's territory and translate them into a percentage of total sales in the United States. Assuming that $5,000 worth of appliances were sold by A the past year in his territory, and that total company sales for the United States, over the same period, were $1,000,000, then, expressed in percentage, A has .50 per cent of the United States total sales.

By comparing A's territory potential of .75 per cent with his sales, or .50 per cent, it is immediately clear that his sales have fallen one third below potential sales volume. This comparison indicates that A may not be exerting enough sales effort in his territory. In this example the past year's sales were used, although an average of sales for the several years preceding may be taken.

In the case cited, the company has national distribution. The same method may be used by concerns with sectional distribution, however, by combining the index factors of a group of states, counties, or trading areas.

Multiple indexes may also be used. To continue the previous example of analyzing the market potential for an electric appliance, the indexes of combined magazine circulation and department store sales may be used in addition to the single index of wired homes.

It should be remembered that market potential is only one of several factors that must be taken into consideration in establishing volume quotas. The fact that an area is accounting for only 5 per cent of sales volume, while the statistical index shows the potential to be 10 per cent of sales, is not always an indication that the salesman in the area is not performing satisfactorily. There may be factors of competition, business conditions, or the character of demand which make a 5 per cent sales volume the maximum that can profitably be secured in the area. A good sales quota should be more than a collection of statistics,

...ket potential, as indi-
... affected by other market
...rength of competition, vary-
...w inventions, changes in style,
...ributing outlets, and the extent of
... of which are readily expressed in

... executives concerning these factors as they
... is a very important factor in the evaluation
of a ... he establishment of a sales quota. These factors
cannot be ... ured quantitatively but must be arbitrarily established for each area by executives who are sufficiently familiar with
actual conditions to estimate accurately their influence on the market. Salesmen familiar with these influences in their territories
are usually consulted in the establishment of quotas.

In certain territories market conditions may be favorable to the
sale of a commodity, but all of the desirable distributing outlets may
be preëmpted at the time by competitors, with the result that the
possibilities of achieving the market potential are unlikely. Accordingly, the quota figure must be revised downward to provide for
weak distribution.

Economic conditions constitute one of the greatest variables in determining potential demand for a product in a specific area. Some
estimate of future business conditions must be made in the establishment of every volume quota. Many companies use forecasts
prepared by professional business forecasters. A few concerns forecast business trends in their own statistical departments, measuring
the influence of the business cycle, seasonal variations, and out-of-
the-ordinary changes as they affect their possible volume of sales.
Business forecasts should be made for each territorial unit, and as
frequently as possible, since long-term forecasts are of questionable
accuracy.

Judgment on these variable factors may be guided by statistics,
but in the last analysis the determination of effective quotas must
be a matter of personal opinion.

Past sales performance. A vital factor in the accurate determination of volume quotas is the volume of past sales performance.
Many companies consider past sales as the sole element in quota
setting and arbitrarily base future sales quotas entirely on past
sales performance.

Only in rare cases, however, are past sales a measure of the true

setting volume quotas. A heavy advertising investment in years
past will simplify the task of attaining a quota and make possible
the establishment of larger quotas.

Current advertising may be measured statistically by the indexes
of magazine or newspaper circulation. These indexes are often
included in a multiple index used in analyzing markets for the
establishment of quotas.

Production improvements. The improvement of an old product
or the introduction of a new one will often affect sales quotas by
stimulating sales volume. The promotion of new uses may increase consumption to a point where higher quotas may be justified. Likewise, the introduction of new competitive products may
make quotas more difficult of attainment. Careful consideration
should be given to the influence of replacement products on the
quota.

Quota Divisions. To establish standards of accomplishment and
measure sales performance for various salesmen, branches, divisions,
and products it is desirable to divide quotas into small units representing:

1. Individual products.
2. Periods of time.
3. Individual territories.
4. Individual distributors.

Organizations selling more than one product usually establish volume quotas for each product in the line to insure that it will receive its share of sales effort and that profitable items are not
ignored for easier-to-sell but less profitable commodities. Such a
division also establishes definite sales objectives for each item and
enables a salesman to distribute his effort more satisfactorily.
On account of peculiarities in local demand a certain product may
not sell in a given territory. Quotas on such products can accord-
ngly be set low in conformity with the market situation.

Quotas are normally established for annual periods, although it
s easier to forecast conditions more accurately, particularly in
periods of economic uncertainty, for a shorter time. One paint
manufacturer establishes quotas every six months. A large pharmaceutical manufacturer sets quotas on a thirty-day basis. Other
quotas are set for weekly, quarterly, and semi-annual periods. Another advantage of short quota periods is that incentive is closer to
salesmen when a reward is offered for attaining a quota. Also.

short periods enable more frequent comparison of performance with the quota standard. Seasonal variations are provided for by monthly and quarterly quotas.

The majority of quotas are divided for individual salesmen and sales territories. This division sets a task for each man and enables the comparison of performance of each member of the organization. Salesmen know what volume is expected of them. Variables in sales ability and territorial conditions can be reflected in individual quotas.

Quotas are often established by manufacturers for wholesale and retail distributors to provide a basis for comparison of their sales performances and at the same time serve as an incentive to increased sales in connection with extra allowances. Certain manufacturers set dealer quotas as an aid to salesmen calling on dealers.

Dual Volume Quotas. There are two general types of volume quotas:

1. The inspirational quota, which the management *desires* salesmen to attain.
2. The "dead-line" or "must" quota, which the house *demands* that salesmen attain.

Both types are sometimes used in a double-quota system.

The inspirational quota is the type given to salesmen to establish their tasks and stimulate them to greater effort. It is established by the methods previously described, and serves as the basis for compensation plans and the measurement of salesmen's performance. It, however, visualizes the management's optimistic conception of what *should* be accomplished, influenced by the salesman's own estimate of possible accomplishment. It is a maximum estimate.

The dead-line or must quota is a more cautious sales estimate used in establishing the company sales budget and the regulation of the production facilities, purchase of materials, and employment of labor. This is a minimum quota below which the company cannot fall if a profit is to be earned. Production is geared to the must-quota requirement. While the factory can readily accelerate production to parallel performance of salesmen exceeding their inspirational quotas, the minimum quota affords a conservative estimate of demand for the stabilization of factory costs and employment.

Securing Acceptance of Quotas by Salesmen. The finest sales

volume quota compilation is worthless unless salesmen accept it as fair and possible of attainment. Several factors aid in securing the acceptance of a quota by a sales force:

1. Simplicity insures understanding by salesmen who are usually suspicious of complex, statistical compilations. While accuracy should not be sacrificed for simplicity, there is a temptation for statisticians to strive for such a degree of mathematical precision in the setting of quotas that they are difficult for salesmen to understand.

2. Participation of salesmen in the preparation of quotas has a positive psychological effect in securing their acceptance. Every salesman feels that he knows more about his territory than the management and accordingly should be consulted when any estimate of territory potential is being made.

3. Fairness in setting quotas secures salesmen's coöperation in their operation. Arbitrary fixing of quotas on a basis of what sales executives think should be sold, without taking into consideration past sales and market conditions in each salesman's territory, usually leads to inequalities and dissatisfaction on the part of salesmen.

YEARLY SALES & QUOTA CHART															
Indicate in Black - Over Budget Indicate in Red - Under Budget								Year.............................19							
GROUP Agency · Salesman Dealers	Desc.	Jan.	Feb.	Mar.	Apr.	May	June	July	Aug.	Sept.	Oct.	Nov.	Dec.	TOTAL	
	QUOTA														
	ACTUAL														
	OVER SHORT														
	TO DATE OVER SHORT														
	QUOTA														
	ACTUAL														
	OVER SHORT														
	TO DATE OVER SHORT														
	QUOTA														
	ACTUAL														
	OVER SHORT														
	TO DATE OVER SHORT														
	QUOTA														

FIGURE 66. To compare actual sales made with monthly quotas of agents, salesmen, and dealers, a stationery manufacturer uses this annual sales and quota chart. The quota amounts are recorded by the sales department, which makes a monthly record of actual sales in the spaces provided. Salesmen, agents, and dealers are informed of their sales progress from the record shown on this chart.

After a quota has been "sold" to the sales organization, the management is confronted with the problem of getting the sales force to produce up to quota standards. One of the most common methods of inducing quota performance is by means of financial incentives, usually by bonus payments, for reaching certain percentages of quota or for exceeding quota. (Bonus plans are described in detail in the chapter on salesmen's compensation.) Other types of rewards are given for attaining quotas, including honor citations in company magazines or at sales meetings; cups, flags, medals, or other evidences of quota achievement; and trips, holidays, or special favors, all of which are effective in keeping salesmen up to quota standards.

Salesmen must also be informed of their progress in relation to quotas. Personal conferences with branch managers or home office sales executives, at least once a month, at which each salesman's activity is compared with quota standards, keep salesmen aware of their objectives.

Salesmen in the field should be posted by personal correspondence or bulletins of their relative standing in the organization and encouraged to exceed their quotas.

Wall charts or graphs illustrating the progress of each branch, division, or individual salesman in reaching established quotas are usually maintained at branch and home offices.

Who Should Establish Quotas? Many sales executives are unsuited by temperament, as well as experience, to establish quotas. Neither is a sales statistician often aware of the personality factors involved in the setting of incentive quotas for salesmen. The salesmen themselves lack perspective and facts to determine their quotas. However, a combination of the abilities of sales executives, statisticians, and salesmen should result in the production of sound volume quotas.

Sales organizations should employ a sales statistician to analyze territories and establish potentials that can be considered by sales executives and weighed with variable factors in arriving at volume quotas.

Problem 1—Establishing a Sales Volume Quota

The Geyer-Warren Company

The Geyer-Warren Company, established in 1917 in Chicago, Illinois, manufactures a line of packaged breakfast cereals sold through two hundred salesmen to wholesale and retail food and department stores throughout the country. Orders are taken by salesmen for delivery and billing by wholesalers. The distribution of the company includes nearly 90 per cent of all food outlets.

After a period of declining sales, improved business conditions convinced the management that a special sales drive should be made to secure for the company its share of increased demand. The sales manager proposed to increase the company's sales 20 per cent. To insure this gain, sales quotas would be set and the previous year's sales of each salesman would be increased 20 per cent in determining quotas for the coming year. For example, a salesman who sold $50,000 in his territory the previous year would have a quota of $60,000 for the coming year.

To stimulate salesmen to attain their quotas, special sales bonuses would be paid to each salesman whose sales equalled his quota for the year. To set the incentive closer to the salesmen, it was also proposed to pay extra bonuses for monthly progress. This plan required a division of annual quotas into monthly quotas.

Monthly quotas would be set by considering the company's total sales from all territories for the previous year and determining the percentage of sales made in each month during the year. If the total sales of the company for a single month amounted to 10 per cent of the annual total, each salesman's quota for that month would be 10 per cent of his annual quota. For example, a salesman whose annual quota was $60,000 would have a January quota of 10 per cent of $60,000, or $6,000, provided that total company sales for the preceding January were 10 per cent of annual sales of the company. If company sales for February were 20 per cent of annual volume the preceding year, each salesman's February quota would be 20 per cent of his annual quota.

The management believed that the establishment of the annual and monthly quotas would inform the salesmen definitely what the company expected of each man and give them a definite goal to strive for. Also, they would enable the company to make comparisons between the performances of various men in the organization.

Certain executives of the company were of the opinion that the salesmen would dislike having quotas assigned to them, for the reason that they would work as hard without them. Furthermore, business conditions might not improve to the extent anticipated by the sales manager, with the result that salesmen could not attain their quotas and would become discouraged.

Questions

1. Should the company have adopted the sales quota plan as proposed by the sales manager?   Give reasons for your decision.

2. If you do not favor the quota plan stated in the problem, describe in detail how you would establish a sound quota.

3. Was the division of the annual quota, as proposed, sound?

4. How should the management administer the quota, once established?

Problem 2—Bases for Sales Quotas

Barron Tool Company

The Barron Tool Company, Hartford, Connecticut, manufactures a full line of hammers, wrenches, hatchets, chisels, axes, and small tools, which are sold through wholesale, chain, and large retail hardware distributors by a force of twenty salaried salesmen located in various parts of the country.   Annual sales volume for the past five years has averaged $4,500,000.

The vice-president-in-charge-of-manufacturing and the treasurer of the company believe that an annual production of $5,000,000, expressed in gross volume of sales, is the minimum amount necessary to operate the plant profitably, and proposed to the general manager that the figure of $5,000,000 be established as the sales quota for the company for the coming year.   The estimate was submitted to the sales manager for his opinion.

Sales quotas had never been established by the company before, since the sales manager considered it impossible to estimate territorial market differences to the extent that quotas could be set fairly for all salesmen. However, at the insistence of the general manager, the sales manager took into consideration the average sales for the five years preceding, or $4,500,000, the sales for the previous year, which were $4,700,000, and the fact that business conditions showed some prospect of improvement during the coming year.   In view of these facts, the sales manager agreed to accept the annual quota of $5,000,000 for the coming year.

Next, the sales manager was obliged to break down the company quota into individual quotas for each of the twenty salesmen.   A division of the company quota in equal proportions among the salesmen meant that each man would have to sell $250,000 worth of tools the coming year. However, as some territories were more desirable than others and some salesmen were more competent, the sales manager decided that the total company quota should be divided according to the percentage contributed by each salesman to total company sales volume the preceding year. For example, a salesman who sold $94,000, or 2 per cent of company volume the previous year, would be given a quota of $100,000, or 2 per cent, the coming year.

The salesmen would be required to subdivide their own territory quotas according to their individual customers. Since each salesman kept a record of annual sales by customers, it would be easy for him to establish customer quotas on the basis of the increased volume.

Questions

1. Was the proposed method of establishing a sales volume quota for the company sound? Why?

2. If you object to the plan described in the problem, what method of setting quotas should be used? Describe in detail.

Problem 3—Territorial Quotas

Helms Equipment Company

The Helms Equipment Company, Detroit, Michigan, capitalized at $1,500,000, makes cylinder printing presses sold to publishers, job printing offices, and large business concerns throughout the world. Domestic sales are administered through five branch offices, the country being divided into five territories, each under a branch manager and located as follows: northeastern territory, headquarters Boston; eastern territory, headquarters New York City; midwestern territory, headquarters Detroit; southern territory, headquarters Memphis; and western territory, headquarters Los Angeles. Twenty salaried salesmen are employed.

Heretofore, the company has set no sales quotas for its salesmen. However, the management believes that an accurate forecast of sales will enable the establishment of a sales budget that will also help the production and financial departments to determine more precisely their requirements for materials and funds. Such a quota may also serve as the basis for an incentive quota for salesmen.

The sales manager proposes first to request branch managers to require each salesman to submit to his branch manager an estimate of the number of presses he can sell during the coming year. These estimates would be submitted in individual conference with branch managers, at which time complete information on the individual salesman's territory would be presented.

Each branch office keeps a record of every prospect in its territory, stating the equipment in use, prospects of expansion, and possibility of replacing obsolete equipment of other makes by modern presses. In addition, a market analysis has been made classifying each county in each salesman's territory as "excellent," "good," "fair," or "poor," according to the number of daily papers, other papers, and population. This information would be used by the branch manager in judging the individual salesman's estimate. Past sales in each territory would be considered, as would also the outlook for better business conditions in each area.

After getting each salesman's estimate, considering past sales, economic conditions, and the record of each prospect, the branch manager would be expected to set an annual quota figure for each salesman operating out of his branch. These individual quotas would be consolidated to form the branch volume quota. After review by the home office sales executives, the consolidation of branch quotas would give the company quota.

In order to make monthly comparisons, the branch, individual, and company quotas would be broken down into twelve quota periods and performance reviewed every thirty days, to insure that salesmen produced at quota speed.

Questions

1. Should the company have adopted the method of establishing a quota described in the problem? Give reasons for your answer.

2. What types of dual volume quotas may be established for this company?

3. Is the breakdown of the company quota satisfactory?

Problem 4—Sales Quota Indexes

Bishop-Barnes Company

The Bishop-Barnes Company, established in Louisville, Kentucky, in 1910, manufactures cash registers, adding machines, and calculators, which are sold direct to manufacturers, banks, government offices, public utilities, and other types of business concerns through an organization of five hundred commission salesmen operating out of one hundred branch offices located in the principal cities of the country.

The vice-president-in-charge-of-sales favors the establishment of a sales volume quota as a standard for bonus payments to salesmen. He proposes to base the sales quota on two factors: past sales and the number of business enterprises that are logical prospects for the company's products. The company has compiled annual sales figures for the past ten years, covering good and bad times, for each of its branches and salesmen. These annual figures would be expressed in percentages of the national total.

To prepare the index of business enterprises, the two and one-half million enterprises in the country would be classified according to size and potential value as prospects for the company's products. The number of enterprises qualifying as prospects in each salesman's territory and branch office would be expressed in percentage of the national total. For example, the quota standing of one salesman would be established as follows:

| | Ten-Year Annual Average | | |
	Company Total	Salesman's Total	Percentage
Annual sales volume basis	$20,000,000	$20,000	.001%
Total business enterprises	500,000	1,000	.002
	(national count)	(territorial count)	

In this example the salesman's actual sales are equal to only half of his territory potential as expressed by the index of business enterprises. Accordingly, the sales manager would advocate the establishment of a quota for this salesman of $40,000, or two times his past annual sales average of $20,000.

Individual salesmen's quotas as set in the above example would be accumulated to form branch totals, which, when added together, would form the total quota figure for the company.

The quota would be distributed in quarterly amounts so that sales executives and salesmen would be able to compare their performance every ninety days, at which time the home office would publish the standing of each man in the organization, using symbols instead of surnames.

Each salesman's quota would be further divided according to the various products in the company's line; a certain percentage of quota would be allotted for cash registers, another percentage for adding machines, and a third for calculators. In the opinion of the management, this would insure that salesmen gave proper emphasis to each product in the line. The product quotas would be set by the various branch managers, since there would be considerable variation in demand for various products in the territories of each of the salesmen.

Questions

1. Was the method of establishing the sales quota as described in the problem sound? Give reasons for your answer.

2. If you do not approve of the quota method suggested in the problem, describe in detail what changes you would make in the method, or how you would establish a quota for this company.

3. Was the index used in measuring market potential adequate?

4. Was the division of the quota satisfactory?

Reading References

Budgetary Control of Distribution, Grisell, Chap. IV.
Developing and Managing Salesmen, Giles, Chap. XXI.

Directing Sales, Bonney, pp. 77–79.

Handbook of Sales Management, Hall, Section XII.

Intensive Sales Management, Aspley, Chap. IX.

Modern Sales Management, Frederick, p. 241.

Printer's Ink Monthly, "Scientific Determination of Sales Quotas," by L. D. H. Weld, May 30, 1929.

Printer's Ink Weekly, "Sales Quotas Pro and Con," by F. H. Meeks, Nov. 15, 1934, p. 94.

Sales Administration, Hayward, pp. 299–304.

Sales Management Fundamentals, Hay, pp. 104–118.

Sales Management Today, Doubman, Chap. XII.

Sales Quotas, White, Chaps. I, II.

Scientific Marketing Management, White, pp. 121–125.

Scientific Sales Management Today, Hoyt, Chap. XI.

CHAPTER TWENTY

SALES COSTS AND BUDGETS

Why Compute Sales Costs? The two basic reasons why a manufacturer should know his costs of distribution are: to determine profitable distribution and to determine efficient distribution. Contributing to these are many other reasons for costing sales, chief among which are:

1. To determine profitable prices.
2. To employ efficient methods of selling and distribution.
3. To compare abilities of salesmen.
4. To discover where and to whom to sell.
5. To control transportation expenses.
6. To determine the most economical channels of distribution.
7. To determine the justification for branch warehouses.
8. To control the routing of salesmen.
9. To allocate sales territories.
10. To determine discount policies.
11. To distribute advertising pressure.
12. To set salesmen's compensation.
13. To control billing, accounting, packing, and shipping expenses.
14. To determine the profitable size of orders.
15. To determine profitable products.

Many other uses for distribution cost figures might be listed, but for the present these are the principal applications.

A knowledge of distribution costs is the only scientific basis for the management of salesmen and the establishment of sales policies. Competent sales executives, in operating and controlling salesmen, are making similar analyses of distributing methods and policies through the medium of sales cost accounting.

It is not difficult to inject temporary measures of relief into ailing sales policies and methods. Such remedies, usually based on guess, serve to intensify and not to correct the sales difficulty. Consequently no permanent improvement results. It is impossible for a sales manager to operate his organization with full effectiveness unless facts about sales operations are available. With the development of sales costing, sales executives will no longer be uncertain as to the cause and remedy for declining sales volume and expenses.

Many of the important questions of sales policy and method confronting sales executives today can be quickly solved with the aid of a knowledge of sales costs. A few of the vital questions which sales managers could readily solve by the use of sales cost figures are:

1. Which product or products in a line should be pushed?

2. Which of two salesmen selling an approximately equal volume is the most profitable?

3. Should salesmen travel by train or automobile?

4. Should salesmen spend the same amount of time or make the same number of calls on all customers?

5. What is a profitable price for a product?

6. What discounts should be given to various types of customers?

7. What is the minimum size of order which is profitable to handle?

8. Should a territory be covered by a salesman or circularized by mail?

9. Should a branch or warehouse be established in a certain territory?

10. Should the size of a salesman's territory be reduced or increased?

The pressure of price competition is forcing many manufacturers to resort to computing sales costs for a more accurate determination of total costs as they affect the fixing of prices. The Robinson-Patman Act, prohibiting price discrimination, makes it necessary for manufacturers to prove differences in cost of sale or delivery as well as cost of manufacture. To prove such differences, sales cost figures are necessary.

Hand-to-mouth buying has brought a great increase in the number of small orders. Manufacturers are approaching the solution of this problem by determining the costs of selling and handling orders of various sizes. The increased volume of returned goods has greatly increased selling costs, and progressive manufacturers are making cost analyses of returns in an effort to secure facts leading to a solution of this problem.

The difficulty of allocating sales costs to individual products is one of the reasons why sales costing has not kept pace with factory cost accounting, as shown by the following examples:

1. The equitable distribution of salesmen's salaries and travel expenses to individual items is very difficult, even impractical, in companies making numerous products.

2. The allocation of advertising expense to individual products featured in joint advertisements must be arbitrary.

3. The prorating of sales and general management expense to individual products must be arbitrary.

4. The accurate allocation of financial expenses, including billing, credit extension, and collection, to individual items is a difficult problem.

Other difficulties in the control of sales costs arise from the facts that:

1. Distribution costs are dependent on many factors that cannot be forecasted accurately.

2. The expense of accounting for distribution costs is very great.

3. Changing market conditions demand departure from established budgets.

One of the most progressive of manufacturers has said of sales costing:

We have just barely begun on sales costs. We just have a few tentative classifications and don't know yet what units to use or what classifications. There were difficulties to conquer in order to keep factory costs, sometimes they were very severe, but they are nowhere like the difficulties that will have to be overcome in sales costing.

This point of view has been confirmed by the president of a large firm of management engineers, who recently stated:

The costing of selling expense is still darkest Africa in most businesses. Many concerns still figure their entire selling expense divided by their entire sales as giving a fixed percentage of selling expense.

What Constitutes Selling and Distributing Costs? There is considerable difference of opinion concerning the cost items that should be considered as distribution expenses. Formerly accounting practice classified numerous expense items, such as officers' salaries, clerical expenses, billing, credit extension, and maintenance and depreciation of office equipment, under the heading of "administrative" costs. Today these items are classified by many sales cost accountants as distributing expenses. Likewise, financial expenses, such as financial management and accounting, as applied to sales, are now often classified as distributing costs instead of being given a separate classification.

The number and character of various items of distribution expense will vary with the size of the company, the channels of distribution, the scope of distribution, and the nature of the product sold. Typical classifications of marketing expenses are given in the following paragraphs.

William B. Castenholz, in his book *The Control of Distribution Costs and Sales,* classifies all costs of a manufacturing business engaged in distribution as either production or distribution expenses, with financing functions auxiliary to either manufacturing or marketing. He classifies the following expenses by functions as distribution costs.

1. General management.
2. Direct sales management.
3. Branch supervision.
4. Advertising and sales promotion.
5. Selling, including salaries and traveling expenses.
6. Shipping activities.
7. Outbound freight, including traffic department functions and record keeping.

Expenses of the auxiliary functions of financing included in distribution costs are:

1. General management.
2. Direct financial management.
3. Corporate financial duties, including secretaryship.
4. Credits and collections.
5. Allowances and discounts.
6. Accounting (including invoicing).

A similar classification of distribution expenses by functions is made by a shoe manufacturer selling to retailers by traveling salesmen and direct mail advertising.   The various classifications follow:

1. Advertising, including space, direct mail, dealer helps, supervision.
2. Selling, including sales force compensation, traveling expenses, sampling, and supervision.
3. Handling and delivery, including filling orders, packing and loading, delivery to station, preparation of invoice and shipping documents, pricing, extending and footing inventory, freight, express and parcel post, traffic department, and claims.
4. Credit and collection, including posting invoices, posting cash, statements, trial balances, credit investment, and collection expense.
5. Administration, including officers' salaries, maintenance and depreciation of office equipment, general expense, analysis, and reports.

The United States Department of Commerce, in distribution cost studies of wholesale electrical goods distribution, divided marketing costs into three expense groups: maintenance, movement, and contact.   Maintenance expense included all costs of maintaining capacity for distribution, such as rent, light, heat, cleaning and repairs, depreciation, interest on inventory, insurance and taxes on merchandise, and stock and plant.   Movement expenses included those arising from the flow of merchandise through the establishment, for example, office salaries, purchasing, telephone, telegraph, handling, packing, and cartage.   The contact expense represented costs of securing compensation from customers.   This was divided into two groups: promotion costs, including sales salaries, traveling and entertainment, advertising and catalogs; and reimbursement costs, including bad debt losses, salaries of credit personnel, collection, accounts receivable ledgers, cashier, interest on receivable investment, and cash discounts given.

The Association of National Advertisers made an analysis of the distribution costs of three hundred and twelve manufacturers and classified them into eight groups as follows:

1. Direct selling costs, including salesmen's salaries, traveling expenses, sales office expenses.
2. Advertising and sales promotion expenses, including space costs, salaries and office expenses of sales promotion departments, and samples.
3. Transportation.
4. Warehousing and storage.

5. Credit and collection expenses, including losses from bad debts.
6. Financial expenses and cash discounts on sales.
7. General administrative expenses.
8. Other distribution costs.

Allocating Distributing Expenses. One of the principal problems of sales costing is the allocation of various items of selling expense to:

1. Individual products.
2. Individual sales territories or salesmen.
3. Individual customers.
4. Individual orders.
5. Marketing factors for which a cost analysis may be desired by the management.

Many items of expense may be charged directly to products, territories, salesmen, customers, and so on. For example, in a cost analysis of salesmen's territories, a salesman's salary and traveling expense may be charged directly to his territory expense. Local advertising is ordinarily a direct territorial expense, as is also freight on sales in a territory. Storage cost may be distributed on a basis of square foot valuation. The allocation of these items of direct expense is not difficult.

The distribution of indirect sales expenses, however, presents a difficult problem, one that many sales executives believe cannot be practically solved. The prorating of such indirect expenses as general management, direct sales management, financial costs, and office overhead to individual sales territories, accounts, or products must be done arbitrarily, with consequent inequalities.

The most common method of allocation of various items of distribution expense follows:

Expense Factor	*Method of Allocation*
1. General management.	1. Time-spent basis. In proportion to the number of accounts.
2. Direct sales management.	2. Time-spent basis. In proportion to the number of accounts.
3. Branch supervision.	3. Time-spent basis. In proportion to the number of accounts. Ratio of supervision costs to salesmen's costs.
4. Advertising (local).	4. Direct charge to sales territory. Percentage of gross margin.
5. Advertising (national).	5. Relative circulation of media used, weighted by relative purchasing power of subscribers. Percentage of gross margin.

Expense Factor	*Method of Allocation*
6. Salesmen's compensation.	6. Direct charge to sales territory. Percentage of gross margin. Per-call basis. Percentage gross sales.
7. Salesmen's expenses.	7. Direct charge to sales territory. Percentage gross margin. Per-call basis. Percentage gross sales.
8. Shipping.	8. Number of units handled. Time study. Time spent estimated.
9. Warehousing.	9. Square-feet-occupied basis. Percentage gross sales.
10. Billing, accounting, credit.	10. Number of accounts.
11. Freight.	11. Direct charge on account and territory.

Five major conclusions on cost allocation, of a committee on costs of distribution of the American Marketing Association, are:

1. Division of cost as fixed or variable is of no practical value in allocating costs to customers or commodities and should be replaced by a functional grouping of costs.

2. No difference should be made in the basis of allocating a cost item because of difference in the way the expense is paid.

3. Interest on investment should be included as a cost since it is the only means of providing equitable cost comparisons.

4. Labor costs in retail marketing should be standardized only so far as the amount of time required for each commodity is concerned. Each establishment requires a different rate per hour to compensate for differences in wage scale and in decrease of utilization of labor.

5. No distinctions should be made in cost rates between customers according to whether their major volume comes at a peak period or a low period.

Sales Cost Applications. Various applications of sales costing illustrate the value of a knowledge of distribution costs as they apply to the solution of such sales problems as:

1. The relative profit from orders of various sizes.
2. The relative value of various accounts from a profit stand-point.
3. The profit value of different sales branches.
4. The relative profit performance of individual salesmen.
5. The comparative cost of selling and distributing individual commodities.
6. The relative profit from various methods of distribution.

Cost of distributing individual orders. The general increase in hand-to-mouth buying by distributors and ultimate consumers has greatly multiplied the frequency and reduced the size of individual orders, causing additional costs of selling and handling. This problem has caused many manufacturers to analyze the relative profit from orders of various sizes, with the result that more sales costing has probably been done on this problem than on any other phase of distribution.

The Western Electric Company made an analysis, under the direction of O. D. Street, of several hundred thousand orders to determine the profit from various units of shipment and unit value of orders. According to the Business Analyses Committee of the National Wholesalers' Conference, this analysis disclosed that 60 per cent of all the orders handled, during the period of the investigation, resulted in a loss of $754,820. The record of this cost investigation showed the following relative profit from orders:

Number of orders	309,000	162,000	108,000	193,000
Value of orders	$42,577,800.00	$2,783,160.00	$783,000.00	$463,200.00
Gross profits	$7,630,200.00	$725,760.00	$223,560.00	$137,030.00
Handling expense	$4,505,700.00	$810,000.00	$403,920.00	$627,250.00
Net profits	$3,124,500.00	$84,240.00	$180,360.00	$490,220.00
Unit value	$137.80	$17.18	$7.25	$2.40
Unit gross profit	$24.70	$4.48	$2.07	$ .71
Unit handling cost	$14.58	$5.00	$3.74	$3.25
Unit net profit	$10.12	$.52	$1.67	$2.54

RELATION OF UNPROFITABLE ORDERS TO NET PROFIT*

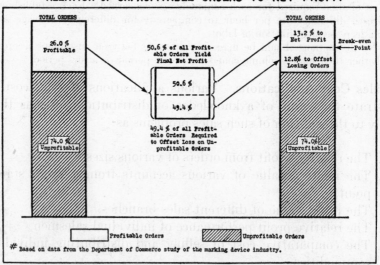

Based on data from the Department of Commerce study of the marking device industry.

FIGURE 67. The large volume of unprofitable orders executed by manufacturers is illustrated by this chart showing that only twenty-six per cent of all orders, costed by the U. S. Department of Commerce in a study of sales costs of the marking device industry, were profitable to sellers. Only half of all profitable orders contributed to the final net profit of the sellers.

The Graybar Electric Company is reported to have made a similar distribution cost analysis and found that 60 per cent of its orders were under $25 and that the average gross profit on such orders was $3.98. The average cost of these orders was $5.61, resulting in a loss of $1.63 on each order, and an annual loss of nearly three quarters of a million dollars on small-order business.

By analysis of the cost of filling orders, the Champion Manufacturing Company found that its base cost of filling any order, regardless of size, was $2.98.

Numerous other companies have made similar cost surveys and obtained facts upon which to base policies dealing with the short-order problem.

Cost of selling individual customers. A critical analysis of the expense of selling individual customers is of great assistance in solving the problem of selling the small customer who does not buy enough, over a period of a year, to warrant a salesman's visit. A classification of accounts, by volume and profit yield, caused the Champion Manufacturing Company to drop 57½ per cent of the company's customers from active sales solicitation. The company found that the 2.7 per cent of its sales volume, secured from 57½ per cent of its total number of accounts, was obtained at a loss. Ninety per cent of the salesmen's efforts was spent on accounts that yielded less than 10 per cent of the total sales volume.

According to Carle M. Bigelow, industrial engineer, a manufacturer of a metal product who was spending 19.2 per cent of sales for salesmen and receiving profit of 6.8 per cent wondered why his sales expenses were so high. An analysis of sales expenses by customers showed the following:

Annual Sales Per Customer	No. of Accts.	Sales	Selling Expense	Per Cent	Profit	Per Cent
$50,000 and up	9	$ 639,822.11	$ 71,020.26	11.1%	$ 95,333.49	14.9%
$10,000 to $50,000	26	936,021.62	131,933.96	13.7	118,451.66	12.3
$1,000 to $10,000	186	1,119,637.34	261,995.14	23.4	29,110.57	2.6
$1.00 to $1,000	811	321,461.19	119,583.56	37.2	36,003.65	11.2
Total	1,032	$3,043,942.26	$584,532.92	19.2% (av.)	$206,892.07	6.8% (av.)

While the thirty-five customers buying $10,000 and up annually, and providing a little more than half of the total volume, showed a profit in excess of 12 per cent, the selling expense on the 997 remaining accounts was so high that 811 of them showed a loss in excess of 11 per cent.

As a result of this cost analysis, the company concentrated on

322 customers, cutting selling expense from 19.2 per cent to 14.1 per cent, while net profits increased from 6.8 per cent to 9.7 per cent.

The Bronson & Townsend Company, wholesalers of hardware, made a cost analysis of the profit from 1,464 individual accounts, and found that a customer's purchases must equal $540 annually to be profitable, according to the Business Analyses Committee of the National Wholesalers' Conference. On this basis, 730 accounts were found to be unprofitable. As a result of the cost analysis, the company dropped 60 per cent of the accounts, and the average operating profit for the four years following the change increased 10 per cent over the preceding period. The Western Grocer Mills made a similar study and dropped more than 2,000 of its 4,500 accounts without a loss in volume.

Cost of operating sales branches. Sales branches are one of the principal profit problems of many manufacturing concerns. In many companies branches have been established to meet competition and give service to customers, while profit has often been a secondary consideration. However, sales cost accounting is providing facts about branch expenses that enable sales executives to make sound decisions concerning the operation of branch houses.

According to C. M. Bigelow, a manufacturer believed, without sound sales cost figures, that his five sales branches were approximately equally profitable. However, proper sales costing showed that the profit varied from 1.4 to 10.7 per cent of sales, as follows:

Branch	Net Sales	Mfg. Cost	Gross Profit	Salesman A Selling Cost	Salesman B Profit Amount	Sales Dollar
A	$ 780,891	$ 530,225	$250,666	$166,959	$ 83,707	10.7%
B	636,480	432,170	204,310	140,705	63,605	10.0
C	540,205	366,799	173,406	137,453	35,953	6.7
D	377,074	256,033	121,041	111,282	9,759	2.6
E	339,634	230,612	109,022	104,149	4,873	1.4
Total	$2,674,284	$1,815,839	$858,445	$660,458	$197,897	7.4%

By this analysis the manufacturer discovered that two of the supposedly equally profitable branches were showing almost no profit because of high selling costs.

Cost of individual salesmen. One of the most important sales cost analyses to be made is of the operations of individual salesmen. Although such a study is often complicated by the difficulty of allocating various indirect items of sales expense, a cost analysis of a salesman's performance is the only sound basis for judging his ability, determining his compensation, controlling his travel, and directing his efforts effectively.

Volume of sales is too often the only standard of measuring a salesman's performance. Neither gross profit nor volume of sales reveals a salesman's ability.

A manufacturing concern employing sixty salesmen analyzed the distribution costs in each man's territory and discovered that the second man, in point of sales volume, stood fortieth in the organization as a profit maker. His net profit was smaller than that of another salesman who sold half as much volume.

Frequently salesmen selling practically the same volume will show great variation in net profit. William B. Castenholz [1] gives an example of two salesmen having identical sales volume. One showed a net profit of $4,500 as compared with a net of $800 for the other. This difference is revealed in an analysis of their respective costs of distribution, as follows:

	Salesman A	Salesman B
Sales	$27,000	$27,000
Cost of sales	16,000	18,000
Gross Profit	$11,000	$ 9,000
Distribution costs:		
Freight	$ 1,500	$ 200
Salesman's salary	3,000	2,500
Salesman's traveling	2,500	300
Advertising:		
Local	$ 1,000	$ 200
National, prorated	500	300
Sales management, prorated	500	500
Total	$ 9,000	$ 4,000
Financial costs, prorated	1,200	500
Grand Total	$10,200	$ 4,500
Net Profit	$ 800	$ 4,500

Such an analysis of the operations of salesmen gives a sales executive an opportunity to discover weaknesses and apply correctives. In the preceding example, it is readily seen that the freight cost allocated to Salesman *A*'s territory is very much out of line with that of Salesman *B*. Perhaps this difference is justified on a prepaid freight policy if *A*'s territory is further removed from the shipping point than *B*'s territory. On the other hand, if the policy

---

[1] *The Control of Distribution Costs and Sales.*

of the shipper is f.o.b. shipping point, the freight charges are probably unwarranted freight allowances, made by Salesman *A* as a concession to get business. The freight item may also indicate an extraordinary amount of l.c.l. shipments—that the salesman is taking too many small orders.

The high traveling expense of Salesman *A* may indicate that he is not only covering too much territory, but also not routing effectively. Is the $3,000 annual salary paid Salesman *A* justified when compared with the profit showing of Salesman *B*, who is paid $500 a year less than *A*?

These are but a few of many questions raised by a comparison of the cost of distribution of individual salesmen. The answers to these questions make possible more effective operation of salesmen, based on a knowledge of actual conditions in a territory, as expressed in terms of sales costs.

5. *Cost of distributing individual products.* When there are many products in a line and the unit of sale is small, it is practically impossible, on account of difficulties of allocation, to determine accurately distribution costs of individual products. It is quite possible and desirable, however, to distribute costs fairly on a limited number of commodities and thereby determine which items are worthy of salesmen's efforts and which should be dropped as unprofitable. A knowledge of sales costs by products will also indicate where and to whom various products can be most profitably sold. A salesman's profit performance is largely determined by the type of commodity he is selling—whether profitable or unprofitable. A salesman who concentrates his efforts on selling a product with a high cost of manufacture, yielding a low gross profit, is handicapped at the start. A salesman who for the most part sells a heavy product, on a prepaid freight basis, is assuming the burden of large transportation costs. While it may not be possible to divert a salesman's efforts from low-profit goods, on account of strong demand, a knowledge of the costs of distributing individual commodities will enable the management to divert salesmen's efforts from the low-profit to the high-profit merchandise.

One of the most scientific analyses of wholesale distribution costs by individual commodities was undertaken by the National Electrical Wholesalers Association to induce manufacturers to set equitable wholesale discounts on various electrical products. While the average percentage of distributing costs to total sales of all products studied was 18 per cent, the costs of distributing individual products ranged from 9.98 per cent for underfloor ducts to 29.5 per cent for signaling apparatus.

The wholesaler's cost of distributing a radio set, as expressed in percentage of sales, was: investment in merchandise, 5.87 per cent; warehousing and storage, 2.10 per cent; handling, .83 per cent; office, including sales clerical, .79 per cent; customer contact, including selling and advertising, 7.37 per cent; and reimbursement, including credit and collection expenses, 3.75 per cent, making a total distributing cost of 20.71 per cent.

It was found that the cost of distributing electric ranges and water heaters was much less, as expressed in percentage of sales, as follows: investment in merchandise, 7.42 per cent; warehousing and storage, 2.10 per cent; handling, .83 per cent; office, including sales clerical, .79 per cent; customer contact, including sales salaries and advertising, 4.02 per cent; and reimbursement, including credit and collection expenses, .80 per cent, making a total distributing cost of 15.96 per cent.

A total of twenty-two separate items were costed in the analyses based on a sales cost study previously made of an electrical goods wholesaler by the United States Bureau of Foreign and Domestic Commerce, which has made numerous distribution cost studies.

An analysis of the cost of wholesale distribution of various grocery products, made by the United States Bureau of Foreign and Domestic Commerce, showed a wide variation in distribution costs between articles of a staple nature, as expressed in percentage of sales value, as follows:

	Tobacco	Sugar	Canned Fruits	Canned Vegetables
Warehousing and handling	.63%	2.31%	8.20%	7.41%
Delivery	.06	1.39	.87	1.33
Office	.93	.77	2.33	2.33
Selling	2.50	2.50	2.50	2.50
Administrative	2.00	2.00	2.00	2.00
Total	6.12%	8.97%	15.9%	15.57%

Cost of various methods of distribution. In their search for lower costs of distribution, manufacturers are studying the relative cost of different methods of distribution. An analysis of the sales of one packing house, for the purpose of determining the most economical distributing method, was made by Howard C. Greer and published by the Institute of American Meat Packers. It showed a wide variation in profit in six types of meat distribution as follows:

Class of Sales	Per Cent Total Sales	Margin	Selling Expense per Cwt.	Profit per Cwt.
Bulk	8.4%	$3.97	$3.74	$ .23
City	42.0	2.80	2.47	.33
Country motor	16.8	2.45	2.00	.45
Country freight	15.3	2.88	3.83	(loss) .95
Country agents	4.3	2.46	3.47	(loss) 1.01
House and misc.	13.2	1.60	.72	.88
Total	100.0%	$2.64	$2.46	$0.18

The comparative costs of distribution through four different types of jobbers was studied by T. M. McNiece for the National Carbon Company. The relative costs of distribution ranged from 14.55 per cent of sales value to 20.76 per cent, as shown in the following table.

	CLASSES OF JOBBERS			
	Electrical	Hardware	Automotive	Drug
Total selling	5.05%	5.83%	7.70%	4.34%
Total warehousing	2.16	3.04	3.16	3.65
Total administrative	6.00	4.73	6.46	3.93
Total fixed	1.93	2.17	2.66	1.98
Total miscellaneous	.75	.91	.78	.65
Total	15.89%	16.68%	20.76%	14.55%

The National Carbon Company also analyzed the costs of distribution, for various products, by types of distributors, and found a wide variation in the average profit per item earned by the manufacturer when distributed by different types of jobbers, as follows:

Type of Jobber	Product No. 1 Average Profit per Item	Product No. 2 Average Profit per Item	Product No. 3 Average Profit per Item	Product No. 4 Average Profit per Item
Electrical	(loss) $.109	(loss) $.391	$1.330	$ .912
Hardware	.779	.136	1.844	1.473
Automotive	.022	(loss) .207	1.569	1.174
Drug	.710	.370	.616	1.155

An analysis of the relative profit to be gained from retail department and chain store customers as distributing channels for rubber footwear was made for a large manufacturer of rubber footwear by J. F. Cullen for the purpose of establishing equitable trade discounts. The method used in computing costs, of distributing costs to a department store and a chain store system, is illustrated in the following example, selected at random from the many ana-lyzed:

	Department Store	Chain Store System
List sales	$21,422.68	$68,472.69
Seconds and job discount	1,454.06	45.27
Allowances	7.27	14.76
Discounts	2,927.91	13,447.26
Net sales	17,033.44	54,965.40
Cost merchandise	15,669.95	53,134.81
Balance	$ 1,363.49	$ 1,830.59
Direct charges:		
Freight	$104.00	$530.73
Cash discount	136.71	701.92
Stock shortage loss	1.22	......
Total	241.93	1,232.65
Balance	$1,121.56	$597.94
Salesmen's cost	405.28	......
Other selling and supervision cost	77.82	760.04
Total selling	482.10	760.04
Packing and shipping	273.31	663.64
Bill, acct. credit	374.46	693.01
Warehousing	370.61	1,184.58
Branch operation and admin.		
Total selling and operating	1,501.48	3,304.27
Balance or net profit	377.92	2,703.33

Standard or Unit Costs of Distribution. For years, factory pro-duction costs have been determined on a per-unit basis with a standard cost for performing each operation in the process. Little attempt, however, has been made to establish standard distribu-tion costs based on units of functional service.

In the past, analyses of distribution costs have been confined largely to determining average costs of various operations for se-lected groups of manufacturers or wholesalers; or individual manu-facturers have simply added all salesmen's salaries and traveling expenses, divided the total by dollars of total sales, and secured an average percentage of selling expense ranging from 5 to 20 per cent. This percentage is a meaningless average.

Instead of meaningless averages, standard or unit costs enable the costing of such specific distributing functions as salesmen's calls, advertising, order handling, and shipping by establishing the nor-mal or standard expense of performing each function. By com-paring actual costs of each operation with the standard unit costs, a sales executive can readily see, by the variation between actual and standard costs, weaknesses in the distributing mechanism and apply corrective measures accordingly.

The establishment of reliable standard sales costs is a difficult problem, since many expense factors vary greatly with changes in volume. Standards should not be merely an average of past costs of performing an operation, but a reasonable figure based on normal conditions. Standard costs should be modified from time to time as conditions warrant.

H. C. Greer [2] has outlined the steps that must be taken to arrive at standard unit distribution costs as follows:

1. All distribution expenses of the business must be allocated to specific distribution activities as advertising, selling, handling and delivery, credit and collection, and administrative functions. This distribution may be made according to individual salesmen, specific products, or specific types of customers.

2. A certain unit of measurement for each functional distribution activity must be selected as a basis for measuring the amount of service required and the unit cost of such service. The units are chosen to represent the factors in relation to which individual costs tend to vary. A shoe company employing traveling salesmen and direct mail advertising, given as an example by Greer, selected nine units of measurement as follows:

a. *Number of mail solicitations.* This factor was selected for the measurement of advertising costs for the reason that the cost of direct mail advertising is proportionate to the number of solicitations by mail; that is, if more or fewer pieces of mail advertising are sent out, this cost will be proportionately increased or reduced.

Using this unit, the company may plan for a certain number of mail solicitations at a definite unit cost per solicitation.

b. *Number of salesmen's calls.* This factor was selected as a unit of salesmen's compensation because the cost of salesmen's calls is not influenced by the amount of business done or the amount of profit obtained, but by the number of sales calls made and the cost of each call.

c. *Number of days of travel.* This factor was selected as a unit of measurement of traveling expenses because the expense of salesmen is related more closely to the number of days spent on the road than to the number of calls made.

d. *Number of accounts sold.* This factor was selected as a unit

[2] *N.A.C.A. Bulletin,* Vol. XIII, No. 14.

of measurement of credit, collection, billing, and dealer help expenses.

e. *Number of orders taken.* This factor was selected as a unit for costing the preparation and posting of invoices and traffic claims.

f. *Number of items on the orders.* This factor was taken as a unit of measurement of the cost of filling orders, pricing, and sales analysis.

g. *Number of units of the product sold.* This factor was taken as a unit for costs of packing, loading, and delivery to carrier.

h. *Weight and shipping mileage.* These factors were used as a unit to measure freight, parcel post, and express costs.

i. *Number of cash collections.* This was used as a unit measurement of the expense of posting.

These units are merely a few of many that may be used in a standard cost system, depending on the degree of refinement which the company wishes to introduce in its calculations. Other unit cost bases may be: cost per salesman's hour, cost per salesman's mile, cost per letter of sales correspondence, and so on.

3. Next, the unit cost figure is obtained by dividing the total function or sales activity cost by the number of units of functional service represented. For example, the shoe company previously mentioned spent a total of $16,422 for direct mail advertising in one year—the total advertising activity cost. During the year 12,320 units of direct mail were mailed. Dividing the total cost by the number of units used gives a direct mail advertising unit cost of $1.33.

Another example will illustrate how the unit cost of salesmen's compensation is computed. The salesmen were paid $66,590 during the year. Using the "Number of Salesmen's Calls" factor, a total of 6,036 calls were made. Dividing the total amount of salesmen's compensation, or $66,590, by the number of salesmen's calls, or 6,036, gives $11.03 per call.

The total cost, number of units, and unit cost of the balance of the nine units of the shoe manufacturing company follow:

	Total Cost	Number Units	Unit Cost
Number days travel:			
Sales force travel	$42,303	4,451	$9.50
Number accounts sold:			
Dealer helps	10,117	2,428	4.17
Statements	5,774	2,428	2.38
Credit and collections	8,533	2,428	3.51

	Total Cost	Number Units	Unit Cost
Number orders taken:			
Preparation of invoices	7,914	18,662	.43
Posting of invoices	2,923	18,662	.16
Traffic claims	5,009	18,662	.27
Number items (lines):			
Filling orders	5,787	70,931	.08
Pricing	4,676	70,931	.07
Sales analyses	2,904	70,931	.03
Number Units Product:			
Packing and loading	18,813	545,355	.03
Delivery to station	5,795	545,355	.01
Wtd. Shipt. Mileage:			
Freight, express, parcel post	63,214	283,526*	.22
Number cash collections:			
Posting cash	2,086	12,720	.16

* Thousand wt. miles.

The Western Electric Company established unit costs for handling orders of various sizes as follows: Orders over $25, unit handling cost, $14.58; orders from $10 to $25, unit handling cost, $5; orders from $5 to $10, unit handling cost, $3.74; and orders under $5, unit handling cost, $3.25.

The establishment of unit costs for various distributing operations enables:

1. The analysis of various distributing operations for profit comparison.
2. The establishment of a sales budget.
3. The measurement of individual salesmen's performance.
4. The determination of sales policies.
5. Many other fundamental functions of sales administration.

Sales Budgeting. Closely related to the establishment of standard distributing costs is the preparation of a sales budget that is a coördinated series of distributing expense standards. Budgets for distribution have been variously defined as "systematizing of foresight," "an architect's plans or blueprints for sales," and "an analysis of the financial aspects of sales effort and policy."

"Budgeting is buying according to sales" says J. H. Barber. "That is, budgeting is buying materials and the services of men, machines, and money so that sales will be profitable."

Why budget sales? A sales budget is indispensable in controlling sales expenses and stopping leaks. It forces careful planning of sales programs. A budget tells how much to sell, when to sell, where to sell, and regulates selling costs. A sales executive without a budget, like a mariner without a compass, does not know where he is going. Budgeting eliminates much guesswork and substitutes a plan for the future, based on past experience.

Who budgets sales? A few companies operate all phases of their businesses under a system of budgetary control. Budgets are established for the principal departments of the business: a production and inventory budget, for which the production department is responsible; a financial budget, for which the treasurer's department is responsible; a maintenance budget, a matter of joint responsibility; and a sales budget, for which the sales manager is responsible. All of these budgets are compiled into a master budget for the company by a director of budgets, or comptroller, working with the accounting department.

The sales budget is usually prepared jointly. Branch managers may be responsible for the budgets for their individual branches; the advertising manager is responsible for the advertising and promotion section of the budget; and the general sales manager, with the assistance of the market research manager, sales cost accountant, statistician, and accounting department, determines the final sales budget figures.

Steps in Preparing a Sales Budget. There are two principal phases in the preparation of a sales budget:

1. Determining the quantity of goods to be sold is the most difficult budgeting problem. When a sales volume quota has been established, by the methods discussed in the preceding chapter, this quota, if sufficiently accurate, may be accepted for budget purposes.

The usual methods of determining quotas are employed in setting up budget quotas, including estimates by salesmen, estimates of distributors, past sales performance, analysis of the market, judgment of sales executives on competition, business conditions, and the like.

When carefully prepared, budget estimates of sales and actual orders received show a remarkably small variation. Budget estimates of the General Electric Company have been within 3 per cent of actual orders. Estimates made by the Walworth Company have shown as little as one half of one per cent variation from orders received.

Estimates of sales volume must be broken down by territories, branches, months, product lines, or whatever divisions of the budget are planned.

2. Determining the cost of selling the volume budgeted is the

next step. In determining the cost of securing the desired volume, the sales executive must decide upon the amount of each functional sales service required as expressed in dollars and cents. The amount of salesmen's services required must be set, the volume of advertising necessary must be determined, and the expense of handling and shipping and the cost of all other distribution functions must be considered. In determining the amounts that must be spent for each of these activities, a sales executive is forced to plan in detail his selling operations, which is one of the most desirable features incident to budgetary control of sales.

In setting the amounts to be spent for each sales activity, past costs are examined to provide a basis for future estimates. If unit costs have been figured for each operation, the number of operations to be performed will simply be multiplied by the cost of each operation to give the budget expense total for each operation.

In listing expense items in the budget, fixed and unavoidable expenses, such as rent, light, and insurance, are usually listed separately from the variable or controllable expense items, such as salaries and travel costs. This separation is useful in providing a fixed amount in dollars, regardless of the volume of business, and a further allowance of expense is made depending upon the volume of orders expected.

Budget Periods. By consolidating all department budget estimates, an annual budget is established. This is, in effect, a forecast of an annual profit and loss statement. In the opinion of W. B. Castenholz,[3] in establishing an annual company sales budget the investment in the business and the return thereon are the primary considerations. Mr. Castenholz cites an example of a manufacturing corporation with a net worth of $500,000, composed of $400,000 capital stock and $100,000 surplus, and an annual sales volume of $2,000,000. It is necessary for the business to earn 15 per cent on its net worth, or $75,000. With the net profit, or $75,000, made the goal, the budget would appear as follows:

As this budget is planned, $2,000,000 of sales must be secured and a net profit of $75,000 must be made, with an allowed expense of $610,000 for distribution. The plans of sales executives must be made to accomplish this goal. The general sales budget will probably be broken down into branch budgets, individual salesmen's budgets, product budgets, and so on.

---

[3] *The Control of Distribution Costs and Sales.*

ANNUAL SALES BUDGET

	Total
Sales	$2,000,000
Cost of sales	1,315,000
Gross profit	$ 685,000
Deduct expected net profit of 15% of $500,000	75,000
Amount available for administrative and financial expenses and distribution costs	$ 610,000
Deduct fixed charges:	
Executive and administrative salaries	60,000
Financial salaries	70,000
Sales management salaries	50,000
Salesmen's salaries	125,000
Depreciation, insurance, taxes	10,000
Advertising	100,000
Estimated freight on sales	15,000
	$430,000
Available for variable expenses as:	
Traveling, general office, interest on money, discounts on sales, etc.	180,000
Total fixed and variable costs	$610,000

On account of variable business conditions, it is impossible to establish an inflexible sales budget that would not be subject to revision for a year. Accordingly, companies using budgets break them down into thirty-day periods and quarterly intervals, which are of more value for comparison than monthly budgets. Budget reports are prepared monthly and quarterly, showing current performance compared with budget estimates and with actual sales and estimates for the preceding year. These are used for controlling current expenses and operations and planning future budgets.

Sales budgets serve to make sales executives profit-minded and provide facts for the intelligent direction of sales operations by indicating the profit performance of salesmen and branches and the necessity for changes in methods and policies.

Problem 1—Industrial Sales Budget

Carrier Electric Company

The Carrier Electric Company, with headquarters in St. Louis, Missouri, manufactures and distributes a wide line of several thousand items of electrical equipment, ranging from turbine generators to flashlight bulbs. These items sell in annual volume of more than $200,000,000 through nine hundred salesmen operating out of fourteen district offices.

Salesmen selling to industrial concerns carry eight major lines of products. In preparing sales budgets for each line, each industrial salesman is asked to submit an estimate of the orders that he expects to secure from each of his principal customers. In addition, each salesman makes up an estimate of sales to smaller customers.

These estimates are reviewed by each salesman's district manager and forwarded to the regional sales manager, who also reviews the estimates and forwards them, in turn, to the home office. The home office sales executives review the district office estimates and determine the final sales quota. In determining the final quota, estimates are checked against past sales performances, existing conditions in plants and industry, forecasts of business conditions, and the character of competition.

After the estimates of orders for industrial lines as well as other product lines have been prepared, these are translated into terms of sales billed, for the budget period. The reason for expressing the budget figures in terms of sales billed is that there is frequently a long interval elapsing between the receipt of an order and its completion and billing to the customer. Orders received for any period will not correspond with the record of sales billed.

Next, the cost of sales billed is figured, from which the gross profit is determined. From the gross profit are deducted the various distribution expenses for the period, such as salesmen's salaries, advertising, freight, administration, and the like. Finally, a net profit or return on investment figure is determined.

In addition to a sales budget, the company budget director also supervises the preparation of budgets of factory operations and financial requirements. From all of these budgets, the company obtains a profit and loss statement indicating the expected profit at the end of the budget year.

Certain executives of the company believe that the method of estimating the budget quota is not accurate, since the actual volume of sales billed often varies as much as 10 and 15 per cent from the estimate. For semiannual periods on some products, the variation is as great as 20 per cent.

Questions

1. Is the general method of preparing the company's sales budget sound? Give reasons for your decision.

2. Is the quota or estimate of possible sales volume established correctly?

3. Should the budget be based on orders received or sales billed?

Problem 2—Salesmen's Costs

Vince Packing Company

The Vince Packing Company, Kansas City, packs and distributes a complete line of dressed pork and beef products through sixty salesmen calling on retail meat dealers and institutions in the Southwest.

The accounting department of the company has established average gross profit, selling expense, and net profit figures on a hundredweight basis, as follows: gross profit, 10 per cent of sales volume; selling expense, 9 per cent; and net profit, 1 per cent.

To determine the profit performance of a salesman, a sales executive applies these average cost percentage figures. For example, a salesman with $10,000 sales should show a gross profit of $1,000, a selling expense of $900, and a net profit of $100. Another salesman, selling $8,000, would show a gross of $800, a selling expense of $720, and a net profit of $80.

In the opinion of a sales executive of the company, this method of determining the relative value of a salesman is not correct. He believes that average costs are meaningless because some salesmen largely sell products carrying a high gross profit, while others may have travel costs that are less than the average sales travel expense. To secure an accurate picture of the profit performance of each salesman, a cost analysis should be made of the work of each salesman in the organization.

The viewpoint of another sales executive is that such an analysis would be very costly and would be no more accurate than an average cost figure. To obtain a reliable accounting of the selling expense of each salesman, numerous indirect distribution cost elements, such as the costs of billing, accounting and credits, shipping expenses, and the expense of sales supervision and sales management would have to be allocated to each man. This executive considers that it would be impossible to distribute these indirect costs fairly to individual salesmen.

He cites the difficulty of determining the shipping expenses on orders of an individual salesman. There is a certain amount of expense incident to all orders regardless of size, as well as additional expense, which varies with the size of the individual order. It may cost more to fill a small order than a large one. On the other hand, a small order might be filled economically at a time when the shipping department was idle. A time study of the operation of filling an order presupposes that the shipping department is always working at 100 per cent capacity, whereas there are often no orders being shipped, and each order has to bear its share of such idle time.

The opinion of the sales executive who opposes the analysis of individual salesmen's costs is that the only method of distributing the expense of order handling, on account of the many variable factors previously mentioned, is on an arbitrary basis, which is no more accurate than the use of an average percentage figure in determining salesmen's costs.

Questions

1. Is the present method of determining salesmen's profit value, by using an average percentage of total sales, satisfactory? Why?

2. Should a detailed analysis be made of the actual sales and distributing costs of each salesman to determine his profit value, taking into consideration shipping, billing, accounting, credit, warehousing, branch operating, and administrative costs? Give reasons for your answer.

3. Assuming that a cost analysis should be made of each salesman's territory, on what basis should the various distribution costs be distributed?

4. How would standard costs of distribution be established for the company?

Problem 3—Customer Evaluation

Hackley Wholesale Grocery Company

The Hackley Wholesale Grocery Company, Buffalo, New York, selis an annual volume of $500,000 worth of food products, of which 75 per cent is private brand coffee, and the remaining 25 per cent represents five hundred items of canned fruits, vegetables, spices, and packaged specialties.

The increase in the number of small rural customers whose annual purchases amount to only a few dollars has focused attention on the expense of selling such small accounts and the desirability of eliminating customers whose annual purchases do not equal a minimum volume.

To determine the annual volume of the company's country sales, classified by size of account, the accountant made the following analysis:

Customer Groups by Annual Purchases	Annual Purchases	Volume by Per Cent	Number of Customers	Customer by Per Cent	Number of Orders	Av. No. Orders Per Customer	Av. Size Order
Under $25	$ 5,717	2.0%	349	17.4%	460	1.3%	$12.45
$25 to $50	16,433	5.8	459	22.8	791	1.7	20.78
$50 to $100	29,607	10.5	420	20.9	1,337	3.2	22.14
$100 to $250	80,051	28.3	502	25.0	2,768	5.5	28.92
$250 to $500	66,074	23.3	195	9.7	1,801	9.2	36.67
$500 to $1,000 ...	42,006	14.8	63	3.1	818	13.0	51.35
$1,000 or over ...	43,409	15.3	21	1.1	546	26.0	79.50

The company further analyzed the costs of handling individual orders and found that the handling cost on a mail order, irrespective of value, was 96 cents, and if taken by an outside salesman, was $1.96 minimum. A one-item order, costing $1.96 to handle, required that the item sell for at least $15 to enable the company to break even; with more items on an order, the value must increase to show the company a profit. On orders valued at less than $15, the loss increased as the value decreased.

The company found that orders between $15 and $25 were in the twilight zone, profitable or unprofitable depending on the number of items making up the order.

An account that did not give an average of $25 volume a month in one order, or $300 a year total, was unprofitable to sell. If two orders a month were received, they must average $20; if three orders a month, they must average $15; and the annual volume must exceed $540 to be profitable to handle.

With these figures in hand, the officials of the company were uncertain as to whether they should accept them as valid, and what action to take, if any, concerning the elimination of unprofitable accounts.

Questions

1. What conclusions should the sales manager draw from the statistics classifying annual volume into customer groups on the basis of size of purchase?

2. What further conclusions should be drawn from the cost analysis of handling orders and the relative profit from accounts of various size?

3. Can the company's figures, on costs of handling and selling accounts of various sizes, be accepted as valid? How were these cost estimates probably computed?

4. What action should the company take concerning the operation of its country salesmen, in the light of the facts stated in the problem?

Problem 4—Unit Sales Costs

Dale Machinery Company

The Dale Machinery Company, San Francisco, California, manufactures equipment for dry cleaning plants, laundries, hospitals, and hotels, advertised in business papers and by direct mail. This equipment is sold direct through seventy salesmen, who travel out of five branch offices located in the principal cities of the country. The salesmen are paid by salary and bonus.

The company has analyzed its administrative, producing, and distributing costs and found that gross profit must not be less than 20 per cent of sales. Fixed sales expense, including salesmen's salaries, bonus and travel costs, and advertising, must not exceed 10 per cent. The balance, of 10 per cent, includes general administrative, sales management, sales overhead, and dividends to stockholders.

Further analysis of the operations of the company's salesmen has resulted in the establishment of a standard unit sales cost of $8 for each salesman's call. A standard unit cost of thirteen cents each has also been established by the company for direct mail solicitations. The unit cost setup for business magazine solicitations is five cents.

The company uses these unit costs in setting up its sales budget. For example, in determining its expenditure for direct mail advertising, the company makes plans for circularizing 3,500 hotels, which constitute 80 per cent of the purchasing power in the hotel field. At a cost of thirteen cents a unit, the cost of direct mail for reaching the hotels will be 3,500 units multiplied by 13, or $455.

At the end of the year, the management checks the actual expenditure against the estimated cost to determine whether there has been any variation from the anticipated total, and if so, whether it is due to a difference in the number of solicitations actually made, a difference in the cost of each solicitation, or both. If, for example, the total actual expenditure at the end of the year for direct mail to hotels was found to be $520, the management would look into the reason for the increase of $65 over the budgeted estimate of $455. First, the number of units would be checked. Assuming that a total of 4,000 units were used at thirteen cents each, the total expenditure would be $520, which shows that the difference between the budget estimate and actual expenditure was brought about by an increase in the number of solicitations, rather than by an increase in the unit cost.

The result of using standard unit costs in establishing the sales budget is that the total amount of the budget is fixed; but it is flexible in the sense that each of its divisions can be readily analyzed and judged independently of other factors, and control can be exercised over individual functions.

One of the executives of the company has criticized the use of standard or unit costs for the reason that the cost of each unit may vary with the volume of units employed.

Questions

1. Should the company have established a sales budget? Give reasons for your decision.

2. Should standard unit sales costs be established for each sales operation? Give reasons for fixing unit costs.

3. What method should be used in arriving at standard unit costs? For salesmen's calls? For direct mail solicitations? For business magazine solicitations?

Reading References

Accountants' Handbook, Paton, pp. 1207–8, Section 25.
American Management Association, Sales Executive Series, No. 21—"Budgeting

Sales Expense and Sales Quotas," by J. H. Barber; No. 22—"Sales Budget Practices and Principles," by G. C. Willings.

Budgetary Control of Distribution, Grisell.

Class and Industrial Marketing, "What Do We Know about Selling Costs?" by C. M. Bigelow, July, 1931, p. 40.

Control of Distribution Costs and Sales, Castenholz, Chaps. IV–VI.

Cost Accounting for Sales, Hilgert.

Distribution Costs, Bureau of Business Research, Harvard Graduate School of Business Administration, Boston, Massachusetts.

Handbook of Sales Management, Hall, Section IV.

Modern Salesmanship, Frederick, Chap. XXIII.

National Association of Cost Accountants:

Bulletin I. "Administrative and Selling Costs," Jan. 2, 1925; "Analysis and Distribution of Sales Distribution Costs," Feb. 15, 1928; "New Technique in Selling and Administrative Cost Accounting," Oct. 1, 1928; "Sales Cost Accounting," Nov. 1, 1928; "Allocation of Selling and Administrating Expenses to Units Sold," Jan. 15, 1929; "Distribution Cost Analysis—Methods and Examples," June 1, 1930.

Bulletin II. "Treatment of Distribution Costs," Jan. 15, 1928; "Budgetary Control of Administrative and Sales Expenses," Aug. 15, 1929, pp. 1465–1471.

Bulletin XIV. "An Approach to the Problem of Cost Finding in the Marketing of Rubber Footwear," and "Development of Standards for the Control of Selling Activities," Mar. 15, 1932.

Printer's Ink Weekly:

"Sales Costing—the Next Big Step in Distribution," by H. S. Dennison, May 23, 1929, p. 84.

"Is It Profitable to Drop Unprofitable Dealers?" by Roland Cole, Sept. 5, 1929, p. 121.

"Examine Costs Carefully before Dropping Unprofitable Dealers," by H. C. Ludeke, Sept. 26, 1929, p. 175.

Sales Management, June 25, 1927, p. 1211.

Sales Management Today, Doubman, Chap. XIV.

Sales Quotas, White, p. 134.

Scientific Marketing Management, Hall, Section IV.

PART FOUR

SALES PROMOTION

CHAPTER TWENTY-ONE

SALES PROMOTION

What Is Sales Promotion? The term sales promotion has been applied to almost every activity connected with the selling and distribution of goods and services. The Committee on Definitions of the National Association of Teachers of Marketing and Advertising defined sales promotion as "the coördination of publicity and personal salesmanship" and describes it as follows:

1. A sort of dumping ground for all forms of sales activity not included in advertising and sales management.
2. All those sales activities which do not involve direct physical contact between the buyer and the seller or their agents. Such usage includes all forms of sales effort except the activities of salesmen.
3. A coördination activity superior to such general divisions as advertising, management of salesmen, direct mail, etc.

The sales promotion manager of one of the largest industrial organizations in the country defines sales promotion as including those functions in the marketing process which the management wants emphasized, or which the advertising department and the sales department either do not want to perform or are not qualified to perform. It includes advertising; the use to which advertising is put; and the education of the salesman, either wholesale or retail, in the method of selling a particular product.

The rapid expansion of various specialized marketing functions, such as sales research, product development, dealer education, and stimulation and development of salesmen, has made consolidation of these numerous activities imperative. From such consolidation developed what is now known as sales promotion.

The pressure of competition to render more service to distributors and consumers, the more intensive cultivation of markets, changes in buying habits, more selective selling methods—all have helped to emphasize the need for sales promotion to cope with these problems.

Functions of Sales Promotion. The nature of sales promotion is more clearly understood when the operations performed in the name of sales promotion are described. The fact that no two companies carry out the same promotion functions or give equal emphasis to various promotion activities makes it impossible to designate any function as standard. In the majority of cases, however, promotion activities are used for the following purposes:

1. To assist salesmen.
2. To assist dealers.
3. To coördinate sales and advertising.
4. To plan sales programs.
5. To conduct product and market investigations.
6. To develop customers.

Assisting Salesmen with Sales Promotion. The most common use of sales promotion is to assist salesmen by:

1. Securing inquiries to be followed up by salesmen.
2. Preceding salesmen's calls.
3. Following up salesmen's calls.
4. Contacting customers between salesmen's calls.
5. Stimulating salesmen.
6. Training salesmen.
7. Relieving salesmen of unprofitable contacts.

1. *Securing inquiries to be followed up by salesmen* is one of the chief functions of many sales promotions departments. Names of prospects are secured from salesmen, distributors, and mailing list houses. Series of sales letters and enclosures are prepared, and sent out to these lists. Inquiries are turned over to salesmen for follow-up work.

The sales promotion department of a large manufacturer of printed forms developed an inquiry-producing campaign consisting of a series of sales letters sent to prospects whose names were furnished by salesmen. Return cards enclosed were turned over to salesmen for follow-up work.

Using large lists of investors, a financial service makes monthly mailings of form letters and enclosures to secure inquiries, which are then given to salesmen for closing.

Many life insurance companies use inquiry-producing letters to select lists of prospects provided by agents. Inducements to inquire, in the form of memorandum books or novelties, increase the number of inquiries to be turned over to agents. Twenty-eight per cent of the applications of one large life insurance company originate from this type of promotion.

2. *Preceding salesmen's calls with advertising* is another valuable aid given salesmen by sales promotion departments. No attempt is made to secure inquiries, but an announcement of the salesman's forthcoming call is made.

A large automobile manufacturer developed a foot-in-the-door campaign, consisting of a series of mailing cards to be sent to owners of old automobiles. Owners' names were furnished by salesmen in lots of twenty-five. Salesmen followed up each mailing with personal calls. A manufacturer of addressing equipment requires salesmen to send in to its sales promotion department the names of prospects to be called upon. These names are circularized in advance of salesmen's calls. The largest manufacturer of dental equipment precedes salesmen's calls with a four-page personalized letter, followed by a four-page folder. Salesmen are supplied with booklets to deliver to prospects at the time calls are made.

3. *Following up salesmen's calls* is a profitable sales promotion function. Salesmen's call report forms are designed so that salesmen can check objections of each prospect contacted. Follow-up letters are written to answer each of the principal objections received by salesmen.

The salesmen of a manufacturer of lift trucks and factory conveying equipment are aided by a series of seven form follow-up letters, each answering an objection to the products made by the company. One or more of the letters are sent to prospects called upon by salesmen, who indicate the outstanding objections of prospects. The salesmen then follow up the letters with personal calls.

When salesmen of a manufacturer of disinfectants are unable to secure interviews with desirable prospects, the sales promotion department writes each prospect a registered letter requesting an interview for a salesman on a definite day and hour. Salesmen then call on these prospects and are usually successful in securing interviews.

Following each call, a personal letter is sent out by the sales promotion staff of a large shoe manufacturer. The letter opens as follows: "Thank you, Mr. Jones, for looking at our Mr. A. B. Doe's samples of Blank Brand shoes, even though you did not buy."

The way is paved in the balance of the letter for a future interview.

4. *Contacting customers between salesmen's calls* can be done by a sales promotion department to create good will and get fill-in orders that might otherwise go to competitors. Salesmen of a manufacturer of glass-lined steel containers give the sales promotion department of the company information which enables it to write personal letters to prospects and customers in the interval between salesmen's calls. The follow-up letters may quote prices or provide additional information to prospects for salesmen, who are schooled to inform the sales promotion department when and what help may be needed.

Letter Mailed____ Mailing list checked____ Man Credited____

REPORT BLANK

PRINT ALL NAMES

Name____

Street & No.____

City____ State____

Person Interviewed____

Title____ Nature of Business____

Remarks____

CHECK ITEMS PROSPECT COULD USE
DOUBLE CHECK IF LITERATURE IS TO BE SENT

Lift Trucks ☐☐ Steelegs ☐☐ Elevator ☐☐
Multiple Truck ☐☐ Barrel Truck ☐☐ Racks ☐☐

Send Letter____ Cut off Mailing List____

Representative____ Date____

Write additional remarks on other side.

FIGURE 68. Requests for advertising assistance are made to the sales promotion department by salesmen of a lift truck organization on this report blank. The name of the prospect to be circularized by the sales promotion department and the products in which the prospect is interested are shown on the form.

A company manufacturing calculating equipment operates a school for training operators of its products to insure customer satisfaction. The sales promotion department helps to keep customers satisfied between salesmen's calls by sending out special letters intended to keep the school in the minds of customers.

5. *Stimulating salesmen* is one of the functions of many sales promotion departments. The development of salesmen's contests, the arrangement of conventions, and the preparation of promotional material to arouse and maintain interest in sales competitions are often undertaken in this division. The preparation of salesmen's

bulletins, magazines, and portfolios of advertising is usually a sales promotion activity.

A manufacturer of industrial heating equipment, through its promotion department, publishes every ten days a mimeographed bulletin for all salesmen to give information on recent orders, performance reports, tips on the activities of competitors, and descriptions of advertising campaigns.

The sales promotion department of a large vacuum cleaner company organizes and supervises national sales conventions held in various parts of the country. Promotion material, programs, and exhibits are prepared and distributed. A manufacturer of notions uses a sales promotion section for the same purpose.

6. *Training salesmen* is one of the chief activities of some sales promotion departments whose functions are identical with sales training departments in other organizations.

The major purpose of the sales promotion department of a large automobile manufacturer is sales education. Sales instruction manuals are prepared, equipment manuals produced, and semimonthly salesmen's publications edited in this department, which is also responsible for motion picture films used in sales training. A sales training course is also conducted at the factory.

The sales promotion division of a large producer of building materials is responsible for salesmen and dealer training programs, the conduct of training meetings, instruction in the product, and methods of selling it.

Sales training is not conducted in many organizations on such a scale as to warrant the establishment of a separate department. Accordingly, when undertaken, it is usually delegated to the sales promotion department.

7. *Relieving salesmen of unprofitable accounts* by giving them to the sales promotion department to develop is a practice in many concerns. One firm analyzed its 29,000 accounts and found that about 17,000 were buying less than $100 worth of goods a year. Salesmen's calls were discontinued to these small buyers, and the sales promotion department sent out monthly mailings, with the result that many small orders were converted into profitable accounts.

Assisting Dealers with Sales Promotion. Many manufacturers recognize that they cannot profit unless their dealers also make money. Accordingly, large sums are being spent for dealer help or resale work through sales promotion departments. This assistance includes such activities as: dealer advertising, dealer sales assistance, and dealer management aid.

1. *Dealer advertising.* Assistance in the form of advertising is given to wholesale distributors and retail dealers by manufacturers. Wise manufacturers have made special efforts to determine in advance of production the advertising needs of dealers and have prepared advertising of such character that dealers request it and use it. The distribution of dealer advertising is another important problem often given little consideration by manufacturers.

The principal mediums of advertising prepared for distributors are:

1. Local newspaper advertising.
2. Direct mail advertising.
3. Store and window display advertising.
4. Outdoor advertising.
5. Premiums and novelties.

1. *Newspaper advertising.* Many manufacturers' sales promotion departments provide retailers with electrotypes or paper mats of complete newspaper advertisements for insertion in local papers over the name of the dealer. These tie up with national advertising programs and identify local points of sale.

Other concerns furnish dealers with newspaper illustrations in mat form, copy suggestions, and layouts so that a merchant can prepare his own advertisement to his liking, using the materials furnished by the manufacturer.

Some manufacturers share the cost of the space in which dealer newspaper advertising is run on a fifty-fifty basis; while others require dealers to pay the entire cost of the space. In certain instances manufacturers seek to select the papers in which dealer advertising is run; others make no restrictions on the medium used.

2. *Direct mail advertising.* Because direct mail advertising is more selective than newspaper advertising and can be used economically to reach a small segment of a market, many small dealers can use this medium to best advantage. Accordingly, manufacturers' sales promotion programs usually include dealer letterheads, blotters, envelope inserts, package inserts, mailing cards, billheads, calendars, folders, booklets, catalogs, and other minor forms of direct advertising.

A large manufacturer of sheeting, through its sales promotion division, provides department and dry goods stores, free of charge, with a series of twenty-four-page envelope inserts in colors imprinted with the dealer's name. Each folder contains a swatch of the sheeting described therein.

A large drug manufacturer's sales promotion department provides over four thousand merchants with personalized direct mail advertising in the form of a sales letter series, a sixteen-page monthly magazine, an annual calendar, and a family almanac, all for a small charge.

A large manufacturer of electrical refrigeration provides dealers with specialized mail campaigns consisting of imprinted booklets, folders and letters on each of the principal products in the line—domestic refrigerators, water coolers, and commercial refrigerators.

Direct advertising is supplied to distributors free of charge by many companies; others require dealers to pay the cost of production. On account of the opportunities for waste in the distribution of direct advertising, it is usually distributed on order.

3. *Store and window display advertising.* Sales promotion departments are responsible, in many companies, for the development of exterior signs, window and counter displays, wall hangers, floor displays, installation signs, and banners for retail dealers. Manufacturers recognize the importance of identifying their products at the point of sale, on the outside of stores, in display windows and on counters. The liberal adoption by retailers of the open display, and the discovery that goods moved from shelf to counter sell much faster, have caused many manufacturers to produce store and counter displays for dealers.

A few large manufacturers supply dealers with monthly window and counter display service. The sales promotion department of a large electric lamp bulb manufacturer supplies dealers with pre-tested window displays. Each display is accompanied by price cards, display baskets, lamp holders, and counter cards. The cost to the dealer is less than a cent a day. Wire display bins, metal demonstrators, and stands for interior display are furnished at cost. In addition, more than forty different sales promotion pieces, including newspaper advertisements, matches, blotters, folders, and calendars, are provided dealers.

The sales promotion division of a large electric refrigerator manufacturer develops illuminated, motion window displays for dealers, featuring product appeals.

4. *Outdoor advertising.* Many manufacturers supply dealers with exterior hanging and wall signs, both illuminated and unil-

luminated, as a sales promotion service. Such signs sometimes carry the name of the dealer as well as the name or trade-mark of the manufacturer's product. Porcelain enamel and metal lithographed signs in colors are the most common types, while a few

FIGURE 69. Eye-catching lithographed enlargement of the product for window or counter display created by The Forbes Lithograph Mfg. Co.

manufacturers supply dealers at cost with illuminated letter or neon signs. One concern sells illuminated signs to dealers for $150 each.

A few companies supply dealers with outdoor posters in three-sheet and twenty-four-sheet sizes, carrying the name and address of the local dealer.

5. *Premiums and novelties.* To build good will for dealers, the sales promotion departments of numerous companies prepare pre-

FIGURE 70. Lithographed counter display basket illustrating uses of the product in natural colors. This jumble display is an inexpensive, effective example of sales promotion produced by The Forbes Lithograph Mfg. Co. for a manufacturer of mayonnaise.

miums or novelties bearing the trade-mark or name of the manufacturer's product. These are supplied to dealers at cost for distribution by salesmen in prospecting; or to give away to old customers or to new customers during special selling events. The sales promotion department of an electric equipment manufacturer offers

FIGURE 71. A well-known food product manufacturer provides food retailers with this floor display stand, an example of sales promotion produced by The Forbes Lithograph Mfg. Co.

dealers imprinted golf balls, paper matches, key containers, mechanical pencils, and playing cards. An electric refrigerator manufacturer provides dealers with refrigerator water bottles for free distribution to prospects.

The sales promotion division of a large drug manufacturer supplies dealers with premiums including silverware, china, electric casseroles, and glass baking dishes for sale to customers on purchase card sales plans.

Dealer Sales Assistance. Sales plans and programs for dealers, education of retail sales persons, and factory schools for retail salesmen are a few of the many ways in which manufacturers' sales promotion departments are assisting dealers with their selling problems. Manufacturers' salesmen or special sales promotion department representatives conduct this educational resale work.

Sales plans. Manufacturers are stimulating sales of their products by providing retailers with special sales plans. A well-known manufacturer of towels has prepared a special promotion for department stores, the featuring of store-wide towel sales. In holding a store-wide towel sale, every selling, as well as nonselling employee is made a promoter of the manufacturer's brand of towels. Displays of the towels are shown in every department of the store as well as in show windows. Samples are distributed to each employee, and sales meetings are held. Employees are paid extra commissions. Newspaper advertising is run, and for thirty days an intensive drive is made by all employees. Leading department stores have reported record sales from this special sales plan.

A maker of rubber aprons, hot-water bottles, syringes, and other rubber sundries, has produced a forty-four-page book, *Retail Selling and the Drug Store,* describing special sales plans.

Education of retail sales people. The sales promotion activities of some manufacturers embrace the training of retail sales people. The influence of sales people at the point of sale is an important

FIGURE 72. Counter or window display lithographed in five colors with a special die-cut shelf arrangement which provides display space for actual cans of the product. Created and produced by The Forbes Lithograph Mfg. Co.

factor in the sale of much convenience-type consumer merchandise. Large sums are being spent by progressive concerns to improve the quality of retail selling and to increase the turnover of manufacturers' products.

FIGURE 73. Counter display card lithographed in four colors. The die-cut openings permit easy insertion of inhalers and the tabs hold them firmly in place while presenting them to shoppers. Produced by The Forbes Lithograph Mfg. Co.

A large linoleum manufacturer has produced a talking motion picture for sales people in linoleum departments, in addition to a one hundred and twenty-six-page manual for retail salesmen describing a practical technique for making linoleum sales.

The sales promotion department of a large refrigerator manufacturer has prepared numerous talking-slide training films for the development of dealer salesmen, and has published a one-hundred-page retail, household, salesman's guide.

A manufacturer of electrical appliances has prepared six manuals, for training retail sales persons of electrical appliances. The titles of three of these are: Understanding the Customer's Viewpoint, Fitting the Customer's Needs, and Overcoming Sales Difficulties.

The Westinghouse Electric Corporation lamp division has prepared for utility lighting salesmen eighteen sound slide films and recordings on the subject "Illumination—Fundamentals and Application."

Factory schools for retail salesmen. A few manufacturers train retail salesmen at the factories. Factory training is usually given in connection with technical products. The dealer salesmen of a large tractor company go to the headquarters of the company for instruction during the late fall, winter, and early spring months. One- and two-week's courses are given.

A large domestic oil burner producer gives one-week courses at the home office of the company for retail dealers and their salesmen. A typical program includes the theory of selling, the sales talk, the approach, how to create confidence, how to answer objections and questions, and why good salesmen sometimes fail to make money.

Dealer Management Aid. Manufacturers are taking greater interest in their dealers' management methods, and sales promotion is functioning to aid merchants with stock control methods, accounting, buying policies, store arrangement and lighting, and credit and collection policies. While many of these management problems seem far removed from manufacturers' immediate objectives of increasing sales, they directly affect retailers' profits. Unless retailers operate profitably, they cannot be effective outlets for manufactured commodities. Those retailers which stock the products of one or a few manufacturers are the principal recipients of management aid from manufacturers.

The Goodyear Tire and Rubber Company has established at its home office at Akron a Visual Merchandising Laboratory for the

benefit of the company's independent tire dealers.   The purpose of
the laboratory is to experiment and advise dealers in seven fundamental phases of merchandising:

Figure 74. The sales promotion activities of many manufacturers aid retail distributors in improving store management through better store arrangement, stock
control, advertising, salesmanship, accounting, credit and collections, and other
retail functions. Illustrated are resale manuals prepared by manufacturers for
gratis distribution to retail merchants.

1. Product and package design.
2. Store design and color.
3. Fixture and equipment layout.
4. Store layout.
5. Interior display arrangements.
6. Window display installations.
7. Display material and methods of pricing.

A series of exhibits is used to show tire dealers:

1. How to select a business address.
2. Store identification.
3. Store planning and display.
4. Hiring and training sales people.
5. Selling the product.
6. Exhibiting the product; sales promotion.
7. Advertising and keeping records.

Three complete stores are on display showing how selling space may be utilized to the fullest.

Soda fountain management for drug and confectionery stores was studied by a large soft drink manufacturer in a national survey that supplied valuable information on fountain labor costs, overhead, material costs, and sales by items to fountain operators.

An extensive accounting program for retail dealers was perfected by a large motor car manufacturer for its twenty-six thousand dealers. The program gave each dealer a specific analysis of his financial position showing where and how he was falling short of profitable operation.

Coördinating Sales and Advertising. Sales promotion also performs an important function in coördinating the two fundamental selling forces of general advertising and personal salesmanship.

The usual objective of general advertising, such as radio broadcasting, and newspaper, outdoor, and magazine advertising, is to secure the attention of prospects and arouse their interest in a product or service. Rarely does it seek to close sales, but rather to produce inquiries or send prospects to dealers.

The objective of salesmen, on the other hand, is to *close* sales. They cannot secure the attention of prospects and arouse their interest as economically as general advertising.

Between these two objectives, one extensive, the other intensive, lies an important step in the sales transaction—the arousing of a prospect's desire. This vital step in the sale is usually neglected by general advertising and slighted by salesmen.

Sales promotion serves to bridge the gap between mass advertising and the efforts of the individual salesman by arousing the desire of the specific prospects with printed evidence of performance, proof of satisfactory service, and concrete descriptions of values. In this way the time spent by salesmen with prospects is reduced, sales expense is curtailed, and the morale of the salesmen is strengthened. Salesmen are not obliged to do as much nonproductive canvassing or development work.

While in practice neither sales promotion nor mass advertising can wholly relieve salesmen of the necessity for prospecting and developing prospects into customers, much of the slow, expensive cultivation of markets can be done more effectively by printed promotion pieces.

Coördinating advertising response and personal selling. Much general advertising is designed to secure evidence of interest from readers in the form of coupons and letters of inquiry. The function of many sales promotion departments is to coördinate these advertising responses with the efforts of individual salesmen:

1. By following up inquiries direct by correspondence.
2. By referring the inquiries to factory salesmen or dealers for personal follow-up.

The volume of advertising inquiries received by large advertisers is enormous. One large food advertiser has received in one year more than 3,217,000 inquiries from magazine, radio, and newspaper advertising. On some days 35,000 letters were received. A force of more than one hundred men and women is necessary to handle the seven hundred tons of parcel-post matter dispatched in a year.

When an inquiry is received in a sales promotion department in response to national advertising, it is usually classified according to:

1. Type of territory, open or closed, from which it originated.
2. Type of product.
3. Type of inquirer—consumer or dealer.
4. Type of distribution—direct to retailer or through wholesaler.

After classification, inquiries are either answered by the home office sales promotion department or forwarded for answer to branch offices in the territories from which the inquiries originated.

Inquiries are immediately answered in various ways:

1. Individually dictated letter answering specific questions of the inquirer.
2. A form letter naming the local dealer.

REQUEST for MERCHANTS' SERVICE LETTER to a P.P.

Don't confuse this with request for Sales Letters

Date_____

Address letter to_____

Firm name_____

Street address_____

City and State (or Province)_____

Kind of business_____

Total sales last year $_____ Amount of credit business_____ % of total

Average Inventory $_____ At cost_____ At retail_____

Location of store: Downtown ☐   Residential ☐   Suburban ☐   Rural ☐

Type of trade: High ☐   Medium ☐   Low ☐   Price appeal ☐   Service store ☐

Number of salespeople_____ Departments_____ (List on other side)

Present   System, if any _____

PP for_____

Is this merchant now receiving Sales Letters?

Write a letter on the subject checked below:

☐ How to collect past-due accounts.   ☐ How to train salespeople.

☐ How to increase sales.   ☐ How to make and analyze a Financial Statement.

☐ How to get employees to take greater interest in the business.   ☐ How to know what to buy, how much, and when.

☐ Advantages of departmentizing, and how to go about it.   ☐ Proper way to figure selling prices.

☐ Better window display.

☐ How to pay salespeople according to their selling ability.   ☐ Good ways to advertise.

☐ How to increase stock-turn.

☐ How to move slow stock.   ☐ Whether to change from credit to strictly cash.

☐ How to reduce expenses.

Other subject_____

My chief difficulty with this merchant is_____

_____

NOTE: Use other side of this sheet to give more details about this store and its problems.   (Over)

Salesman_____

Agency_____

Form 2095—Printed in U.S.A.

FIGURE 75. A request form used by salesmen of an office specialty organization in securing retail management aid, for prospects and customers, from the sales promotion department of the company. The promotion department sends information to prospects on the subjects checked by the salesmen.

3. A form letter and enclosure of booklet, folder, or card of introduction to local dealer.

Simultaneously with a reply to the inquirer, the inquiry is referred to the dealer or factory salesman in the inquirer's territory.

To transmit the details of each inquiry to the dealer or factory salesman, several sales promotion departments have devised "tip sheets," or inquiry report forms. These forms provide for a report by the salesman on the interview with the inquirer and indicate objections of the prospect for follow-up by the sales promotion department. A copy of the inquiry report form is preserved by the sales promotion department for future follow-up.

When dealers or factory representatives report on interviews with prospects, sales promotion departments again write inquirers, in an attempt to remove the objections that prevented the factory or dealer's salesman from closing a sale. Sometimes a series of letters is used. If factory men or dealers fail to report on inquiries, sales promotion departments follow them up for reports on inquiries.

The amount of sales promotion effort spent on advertising inquiries depends to a large extent on the size of the sale involved.

Securing coöperation of salesmen and dealers in advertising campaigns. To secure maximum results from advertising campaigns, factory salesmen and distributors must be informed by the sales promotion department of advertising plans, appeals, schedules, copy, and objectives. Advertising is one of the principal inducements to a dealer to stock and push a consumer product, and salesmen selling to dealers must be fully informed and enthusiastic about their advertising programs. Dealers' advertising should be coördinated with manufacturers' advertising. Accordingly, dealers should be informed of advertising schedules and appeals for use in preparing local advertising campaigns.

Personal contact with salesmen and dealers is the most effective method of merchandising an advertising program. The personal methods used by sales promotion departments with successful sales organizations are:

1. Conferences with salesmen and dealers on the subject of advertising.
2. Personal conferences with salesmen for discussion of the advertising program.

FACTORY SALESMAN REPORT

DATE

☐ WE HAVE SECURED ORDER FOR QUIET MAYS

☐ PROSPECT NOT INTERESTED

☐ PROSPECT INTERESTED BUT HAS OBJECTIONS CHECKED BELOW:

☐ THINKS OIL BURNERS NOISY

☐ THINKS OPERATING COST EXCESSIVE

☐ THINKS SERVICE EXCESSIVE

☐ THINKS BURNER IS NOT PERFECTED

☐ THINKS BURNER WILL CAUSE SOOT

☐ THINKS PRICE TOO HIGH

☐ CANNOT AFFORD AT PRESENT

OTHER OBJECTIONS:

OFFICE COPY

NATIONAL ADVERTISING INQUIRY

DATE

OWNER

ADDRESS

CITY-STATE

INQUIRY RESULTED FROM ADVERTISEMENT IN

TYPE OF BUILDING: ☐ WOOD ☐ STUCCO ☐ STONE OR BRICK

TYPE HEATING PLANT: ☐ HOT AIR ☐ STEAM ☐ HOT WATER ☐ VAPOR

TYPE BOILER: ☐ SQUARE ☐ ROUND

HOUSE WIRED: ☐ YES ☐ NO

DEALER

ADDRESS

CITY-STATE

☐ INQUIRY REPORTED BY DEALER

☐ PROSPECT SOLD

DEALER SALESMAN REPORT

DATE

☐ WE HAVE SECURED ORDER FOR QUIET MAYS

☐ PROSPECT NOT INTERESTED

☐ PROSPECT INTERESTED BUT HAS OBJECTIONS CHECKED BELOW:

☐ THINKS OIL BURNERS NOISY

☐ THINKS OPERATING COST EXCESSIVE

☐ THINKS SERVICE EXCESSIVE

☐ THINKS BURNER IS NOT PERFECTED

☐ THINKS BURNER WILL CAUSE SOOT

☐ THINKS PRICE TOO HIGH

☐ CANNOT AFFORD AT PRESENT

OTHER OBJECTIONS:

To Dealer Salesman: It is absolutely necessary for you to check ✓ the objections offered by prospect. We require this information for follow-up letters.

FORM 414 DEALER COPY

NATIONAL ADVERTISING INQUIRY

DATE

OWNER

ADDRESS

CITY-STATE

INQUIRY RESULTED FROM ADVERTISEMENT IN

TYPE OF BUILDING: ☐ WOOD ☐ STUCCO ☐ STONE OR BRICK

TYPE HEATING PLANT: ☐ HOT AIR ☐ STEAM ☐ HOT WATER ☐ VAPOR

TYPE BOILER: ☐ SQUARE ☐ ROUND

HOUSE WIRED: ☐ YES ☐ NO

DEALER

ADDRESS

CITY-STATE

REPORT RESULTS ON REVERSE SIDE

To the Sales Manager:

This tip is valuable! Give one copy to your salesman. Insist upon immediate report. Return this sheet to us, for our Sales and Advertising records. We have mailed literature to prospect and advised him you will call. Be sure that your salesman checks ✓ the objections, if any, as we require this information for future assistance to you, if you are unable to close this sale at the present time.

FIGURE 76. A "tip sheet," or inquiry report form, typical of those used by sales promotion departments in informing dealers, dealer salesmen, and factory salesmen of national advertising inquiries. One section is kept by the home office promotion department; one is sent to dealers; and one is sent to the factory salesmen in whose territory the inquiry originated. Dealer salesmen are asked to report a prospect's objections to the sales promotion department for follow-up.

3. Visits by the advertising manager with distributors.
4. Sales promotion specialists to accompany salesmen and help dealers use advertising.
5. A traveling section of the sales promotion department visits wholesalers and demonstrates presentation of advertising plan to retailers.
6. Visits by advertising manager to branches to outline plans.
7. Distributors hold monthly meetings of dealers to discuss advertising plans.

Printed promotion material, to sell an advertising program to a sales organization, is widely used. The printed matter includes:

1. Annual advertising portfolios for factory and distributors' salesmen, containing proofs of advertisements, dates of insertions, media used, and circulation coverage.
2. Special portfolios for seasonal advertising drives or specific campaigns on a single product.
3. Reprints of single advertisements with memoranda attached emphasizing features.
4. Letters and bulletins to salesmen and dealers describing advertising plans and response.
5. Talking slide films illustrating advertisements and describing the features of the advertising program.
6. Copies of media in which advertising appears.

Some sales promotion departments secure coöperation of salesmen by asking for their suggestions or criticisms on advertising programs. Others urge salesmen to write advertising copy and offer prizes for the best advertisement submitted, although the value of this practice lies not so much in the character of advertising submitted as in its psychological benefits.

Planning Sales Programs. In some organizations sales promotion is largely a sales planning activity. The sales planning function includes coördination of sales and advertising operations, sales policies, changes in product, market analysis, and methods of distribution.

The sales promotion department of a large manufacturer of plumbing and heating equipment is largely concerned with planning and the performance of the following functions:

1. Finding new markets for existing products.

2. Intensifying present market.
3. Suggesting new products.
4. Advising upon the salability of a product.
5. Finding new ways to present products.
6. Creating and executing sales campaigns.
7. Establishing quotas for sales force.
8. Creating and distributing sales aids.
9. Market analysis.
10. Testing new ideas in the field.
11. Keeping records of campaigns, sales, and channels of distribution.

The functions of some sales promotion departments are very broad. A national distributor of sixty thousand items of electrical supplies maintains a separate merchandising division engaged in marketing private and manufacturer branded electrical specialties, such as radios, washers, and vacuum cleaners for resale through electrical dealers. The sales promotion manager of the company is responsible for the entire merchandising division, including the engineering department, the manufacturing department, the advertising department, and the merchandising sales department. Involved in his functions are product development, production, advertising, and field selling.

Product and Market Development. In a few companies sales promotion is largely devoted to product development. A large camera manufacturer has a business development department, whose main duties are to investigate the possibilities of sale of a suggested product, or the possibilities of promoting a particular application of photography, and to work out ways and means of promotion.

The sales promotion department of a transparent wrapping material manufacturer largely functions as a package development service to give suggestions to customers concerning the use of the manufacturer's material—a technical service where the performance of the product is tested in advance. In addition, market surveys are made of the possible uses of the product.

Developing Customers. One of the important functions of sales promotion in many companies is the development of customers by reviving inactive accounts, regaining lost customers, and increasing sales to present customers. While salesmen are largely concerned with opening new accounts or covering their territories as rapidly as possible, sales promotion can cultivate a market more intensively. An old customer retained is worth more than a new customer gained. In their anxiety to sell new accounts, salesmen lose many desirable customers through oversight, disagreements, or misunderstandings.

The first step in customer development is the listing of inactive accounts or those which are not buying up to their potential. An automatic call-up plan for bringing inactive accounts to the attention of the sales promotion department is necessary. In one company a copy of every invoice goes to the sales promotion follow-up file for attention sixty days after date of the invoice.

Next, an investigation of the causes of inactivity of customers is undertaken by tactful correspondence, call of a salesman, or by personal investigation by a company executive or sales promotion representative. An analysis of the reasons for inactive retail accounts showed that 5 per cent were influenced to buy elsewhere by friends; 10 per cent were influenced to buy elsewhere by price; 15 per cent stopped buying because of grievances; and 70 per cent discontinued for no particular reason. Usually an investigation will result in adjustments that tend to restore confidence.

Using the facts disclosed in the investigation, sales promotion departments may employ several methods of reviving or stimulating accounts, as follows:

1. A series of letters to the customer.
2. A personal adjustment by a salesman or sales promotion representative.
3. A special deal to revive inactive accounts.
4. A premium to old customers who send in new orders.
5. Distribution of a company magazine to customers.
6. Holiday greetings sent by the president.
7. Monthly statement enclosures.
8. Letters to customers at end of installment period.
9. Letters following up adjustments or complaints.
10. Letters of appreciation to customers who have increased purchases.

Functions of Typical Sales Promotion Departments. The sales promotion functions of large sales organizations indicate the diversity of duties and responsibilities that are assigned to this phase of sales operation. The sales promotion department of the domestic appliance division of a large electrical equipment manufacturer performs the following duties:

1. Production of the departmental sales manuals and supplements.
2. Production of two house organs.
3. Liaison between the advertising agency and product selling sections.
4. Planning of specific campaign activities for and with customers.
5. Coördination of advertising between sales sections.
6. Assistance given in connection with exhibits.
7. Sales educational work with student salesmen and among customer's salesmen.

A large maker of printed forms maintains a sales promotion department for:

1. Conducting direct mail campaigns to assist salesmen in presenting the product.
2. Sending letters and samples on request of salesmen.
3. Using direct mail to recover lost accounts.
4. Holding the interest of new customers with regular mailings.
5. Preparing advertising matter for the use of salesmen.

Position of Sales Promotion in an Organization. The need for promotion developed after other marketing functions had been established. It occupies no recognized position in relation to other sales operations. In certain companies sales promotion functions as a section of the advertising department; in others, it is a division of the sales department. Still other companies have created separate sales promotion departments and placed them on a par with the sales and advertising departments, responsible to a vice-president-in-charge-of-distribution. This form of organization is normally the most effective.

The sales promotion section manager of the domestic appliance department of a large electrical equipment manufacturer is on a par with five product section managers and a sales service manager, all of whom are responsible to the sales manager.

The general sales manager of a large printing company is responsible for the sales promotion department, which is headed by a sales promotion manager. Formerly the sales promotion department operated separately from the sales department, directly under the general manager.

Qualifications of Sales Promotion Executives. Sales promotion executives require both sales and advertising experience to coördinate these two marketing functions. They should have the following qualifications:

1. Creative imagination.
2. Analytical mind.
3. Executive ability.
4. Knowledge of retail problems, if selling to retailers.
5. Ability to visualize the promotional possibilities of a product.
6. Determination.
7. General business experience.

Before engaging in sales promotion, many sales promotion managers were salesmen, others were connected with advertising agencies, and some served as assistants in advertising departments.

Size of Sales Promotion Departments. The sales promotion department of a manufacturer of electrical equipment employs forty persons engaged in producing direct mail advertising, window displays, sales plans, sales education, publicity, store decoration, house organ, exhibits, and sales manuals.

Another manufacturer in the same industry has a sales promotion department with a staff of five men and three girls engaged in editing a house organ, conducting a correspondence course for salesmen, producing sales manuals, and coördinating sales and advertising.

Problem 1—Assisting Salesmen

Dahlberg Oil Company

The Dahlberg Oil Company, Columbus, Ohio, processes and distributes a line of industrial lubricating oils direct to large industrial concerns throughout the country through a sales organization of twenty salesmen. The salesmen, traveling out of their homes located in the principal industrial centers, are paid a straight salary and expenses.

An analysis of the industrial oil market showed that the company was selling only a small portion of the available buyers of industrial oils, and the general manager believed that a definite effort should be made to cultivate potential prospects. Accordingly, he favored the creation of a sales promotion department to assist the company's salesmen in securing new business.

The objectives of the department would be:

1. To provide salesmen with a list of all industrial lubricating oil prospects in their territories.

2. To pave the way for salesmen's calls with direct mail advertising.

3. To follow up salesmen's calls with direct advertising.

The first step in the promotion program would be the preparation of a mailing list of prospects from commercial directories. The list would be separated according to salesmen's territories and typed on prospect cards. Each salesman would be sent prospect cards for his territory and asked to arrange them in lots of from ten to twenty cards each. Each lot would represent one week's work by a salesman, in addition to calls on regular customers and prospects requiring attention during the same period. After the salesmen separated their prospect cards into weekly lots, all cards would be returned to the sales promotion department at the home office.

Upon receipt of the prospect cards from salesmen, arranged in order of coverage, the sales promotion department would begin mailings, featuring company products, to prospects so that this literature would reach them shortly in advance of salesmen's calls. Mailings would be made in weekly lots of from fifteen to twenty prospects. Otherwise, too long a period would elapse between the time a mailing was received and a salesman made the follow-up call.

Salesmen would be required to make daily call reports on prospects interviewed for future follow-up with additional mailings by the sales promotion department. A series of ten mailing pieces would be used to follow up worth-while prospects over a period of as many weeks.

The general manager of the company believed that the sales promotion department could in this way lessen the sales resistance encountered by salesmen. A systematic, thorough coverage of each territory would be accomplished. Advertising and personal selling would be coördinated most effectively.

On the other hand, several objections were raised to the proposed plan. The expense of the promotion would be considerable. Salesmen would not follow up the mailings as planned since the program was too inflexible. Buyers receive so much mail advertising that they would pay little attention to the mailings.

Questions

1. Should the general manager's proposal to organize a sales promotion department be adopted? Give reasons for your answer.

2. Should the promotion plan as outlined in the problem be adopted? Why?

3. If you do not favor the use of sales promotion, how would you solve the company's problem?

Problem 2—Coördinating Sales and Advertising Inquiries

Martin Heating Corporation

The Martin Heating Corporation, incorporated in 1924 in Buffalo, New York, manufactures industrial and domestic oil burners and domestic electric refrigerators. The annual capacity of the company is 180,000 burners and 65,000 refrigerators.

Both oil burners and refrigerators are distributed through plumbers, heating contractors, and household appliance retailers in the principal cities of the country. An organization of factory salesmen secures and assists retail distributors.

The corporation assists distributors by national magazine advertising. Inquiries produced by this advertising have not been coördinated with the personal sales efforts of distributors.

The sales manager proposes to coördinate national advertising inquiries with dealers' sales efforts by establishing a sales promotion department, which would adopt the following procedure in handling inquiries:

1. When national advertising inquiries are received at Buffalo, the sales promotion department answers them promptly with a multigraphed filled-in form letter, a fourteen-page booklet entitled "Oil Heating Is Best," and an introduction card to the inquirer's nearest dealer.

2. The prospect's inquiry is then reported by the sales promotion department to the dealer in whose locality the inquirer is located by means of a "red-hot prospect" form. This form is filled in in triplicate; one copy goes to the distributor; the second to the factory salesman in whose territory the dealer is located; and the third copy is retained in the sales promotion department's prospect file.

3. Accompanying the "red-hot prospect" form to the distributor is a form letter urging the dealer to coöperate by interviewing the prospect promptly and reporting the interview to the sales promotion department on the reverse side of the "red-hot prospect" report form.

4. If the distributor does not report an interview with the prospect within thirty days, a follow-up letter is sent to the dealer by the sales promotion department, requesting him to report on the inquiry.

5. If the distributor does not respond to the first follow-up letter asking for a report on the inquiry, a second letter is sent two weeks later.

6. While the distributor is being followed up for an interview report on the prospect, the sales promotion department also sends the factory salesman in whose territory the dealer is located his copy of the "red-hot prospect" form and writes the salesman to see to it that the dealer interviews the prospect.

7. If no report on the prospect is received from the factory salesman by the sales promotion department within thirty days, a form follow-up letter is sent to the factory salesman.

8. If both distributor and factory representative fail to report on an inquiry from a prospect, the sales promotion department sends a form letter to the factory sectional sales manager in whose territory the distributor is located, to get a report on the inquiry.

9. When a distributor reports on his interview with a prospect, the sales promotion department follows up the prospect with a form letter to overcome the objections of the prospect.

The general manager of the company does not favor the creation of a sales promotion department, believing that it would be expensive and that dealers would not coöperate under the plan advocated by the sales manager.

Questions

1. Should the sales manager's plan of coördinating sales and advertising be adopted? Give reasons for your decision.

2. Assuming that a sales promotion department would be established, what would be its position in the company organization?

3. Name five common functions of sales promotion in addition to coördinating sales and advertising.

Problem 3—Resale

The Mackintosh Motor Company

The Mackintosh Motor Company, Detroit, Michigan, established in 1908, sold annually a million six- and eight-cylinder passenger automobiles through ten thousand automobile distributors in the principal cities of the country.

A force of two hundred factory salesmen covered the country regularly in an attempt to obtain additional dealers and aid present dealers in securing greater sales.

The Mackintosh Company advertised nationally in magazines, by radio, and through outdoor media to the extent of $1,500,000 annually, and spent $50,000 every year in promotion material in trade magazines.

Faced with declining sales and the imminent bankruptcy of a considerable number of its distributors, the company was confronted with the problem of securing and retaining competent dealers to insure a flow of its cars into the hands of consumers.

A survey of the sales and management methods of the company's dealers disclosed great weaknesses in selling, accounting, service credits, and advertising methods by many distributors.

The company executives decided to consider improving the business methods of distributors, and the following program of resale work with dealers was considered:

1. Analysis of the operating problems of five hundred representative distributors by a competent organization of retail management engineers.

2. The production of bulletins written by retail experts on the basis of studies made of dealers who had successfully solved these problems. These bulletins were to cover such subjects as: "sales methods," "credits and collections," "profits from service sales," "effective automobile advertising," and others.

3. The establishment of a standard accounting system for distributors and a staff of traveling auditors to instruct distributors' bookkeepers how to install and operate the standard system. Periodic audits would be made by the company.

4. Factory salesmen would be instructed in retail management problems to assist dealers in carrying out the successful methods described in the bulletins.

Some officials objected to these resale plans on account of the indifference on the part of distributors and the antagonism and resentment to interference by the manufacturer. They doubt that the benefits derived from this assistance would be commensurate with the benefits to be obtained from consumer advertising.

Questions

1. Should the Mackintosh Company adopt the contemplated resale program? Why?

2. If you do not favor the resale plan, what should the company have done in this case?

3. Should distributors be charged for the proposed aid?

4. Name six other methods of aiding the distributors.

Problem 4—Trade Deals

Hall Cosmetic Company

The Hall Cosmetic Company, established in 1931, in Cincinnati, Ohio, manufacturers of shaving preparations, distributed, through its own sales force of thirty salesmen and ten brokers, direct to retail drug chain stores, department stores, and drug jobbers throughout the country. The company is planning to place on the market a new product, "Soft as Silk" hand lotion.

"Soft as Silk" is made and sold in two varieties: No. 1, concentrated; and No. 2, regular. The former is for severe cases and the regular for normal cases. The manufacturer considered introducing the product on an introductory consumer deal of one five-ounce package, 25 cents, second package, 1 cent. The retail merchant's profit on this deal (minimum quantity, three dozen at $1 per dozen) is more than 35 per cent, if all the packages are sold at two for 26 cents. If two thirds are sold at two for 26 cents, and the other third at 25 cents, the merchant more than doubles his investment. The jobber's discount is 16⅔ per cent.

This deal would be supported with advertising in Sunday newspapers in large cities, the combined circulation of which is more than 30,000,000. The advertisements would carry coupons, redeemable at drug stores, offering two full-sized bottles for 26 cents. In addition, a counter display and window strips would be used.

To secure retail clerk coöperation, a sales contest for cash prizes would be offered. With the purchase of each gross of "Soft as Silk" lotion, merchants would receive one dollar prize money for their clerks. Clerks selling the greatest quantity of lotion would be awarded the prize money.

Another consumer deal considered was a free deal, giving away a new 25-cent, two-and-one-half-oz. bottle of "Soft as Silk" lotion. The consumer would pay 15 cents for the 25-cent bottle and receive her 15 cents back when she returned this bottle and purchased the 40-cent, five-ounce size.

The retail merchant would buy one gross of the 15-cent size at $14.40 and sell them at 15 cents each for $21.60. He would also buy one-half gross of the 40-cent size at $18 and sell them for 25 cents each, or $18 a half-gross. The manufacturer would give one-half gross of the 40-cent size free to the merchant, who would sell them for $18. The total cost would be $32.40 and selling price $57.60, or 56 per cent, if every customer brought back the 15-cent size for credit on a 40-cent package.

The manufacturer would support this deal with quarter-page space in *Ladies' Home Journal, Good Housekeeping,* and a counter display card. A dealer coöperative advertising allowance of 5 cents a bottle would be offered, payable on proof of publication.

Questions

1. Are such deals as those considered by the Hall Company sound merchandising? Give reasons for your answer.

2. Which of the two deals should be used? Give your reasons.

3. Would the deals be effective without consumer advertising?

Reading References

Class and Industrial Marketing, "Making Advertising Work Harder by Training Salesmen to Use It," by G. H. Starbuck, June, 1930, p. 48.

Executives Service Bulletin, "Manufacturer-Dealer Alliance Reduces Selling Costs," by J. A. Bush, Policyholder's Service Bureau, Metropolitan Life Ins. Co., New York, Sept., 1932, Vol. X, No. 9.

Handbook of Business Administration, Donald, Chap. VIII.

Handbook of Sales Management, Hall, Sections XVIII–XX.

How to Sell to and Through Department Stores, Weiss, Chap. XII.

Modern Sales Management, Frederick, Chap. XXIX.

Principles of Personal Selling, Tosdal, p. 373.

Printer's Ink Weekly:

"Why Sales Promotion Is Esential as a Selling Aid," by C. H. Lang, Mar. 23, 1933, p. 72.

"Sales Promotion," by editorial staff, Oct. 24, 1935, p. 41.

"How the Westinghouse Sales Promotion Department Functions," by George Maertz, Nov. 1, 1928, p. 33.

Sales Administration, Hayward, Chaps. XXIV–XXV.

Sales Management Fundamentals, Hay, Chaps. VII, IX.

Sales Management Today, Doubman, Chap. XI.

Salesmen in Marketing Strategy, Lyon, Chap. XII.

Scientific Sales Management Today, Hoyt, Chap. X.

Selling Policies, Converse, Chap. XXVI.

PART FIVE

SALES POLICIES

CHAPTER TWENTY-TWO

SALES POLICIES

Profitable sales depend not only on the proper control and operation of salesmen but also on sound sales policies. A sales policy is a settled or definite long-term course of procedure adopted by a company for dealing with the fundamental problems affecting sales. Some of the basic sales problems concerning which policies should be formulated involve prices, credits, guarantees, returns and adjustments, and freight payments.

Many sales managers have adopted no long-term, fixed policies concerning these problems. Definite policies enable sales executives to act promptly along well-considered lines of action. Policies provide for uniformity of action by all executives. Good policies anticipate changing conditions and provide sound methods to insure future sales and profits.

Major sales policies are formulated by either executive committees, presidents, general managers, or sales managers. Frequently policies are created jointly by all of these officials. Policies are carried out by line executives; section, division, or branch managers; and salesmen.

Sales policies are based on the experiences of the company; facts obtained from records; or product, market, or distribution investigations.

Price Policies. One of the basic problems to be considered in sales administration is the establishment of selling prices. The close relationship of price to profits, the adjustment of price to supply and demand, the effect of price on volume, and the influence of competing prices—all contribute to make the determination of price policies an important marketing function.

There are three prevailing types of basic price policy:

1. Selling at the market price.

2. Selling above the market price.
3. Selling below the market price.

Selling at the Market Price. The policy of pricing a product at the prevailing market price for similar commodities is universally followed by sellers of raw materials or products of standard quality, when the grades among competing manufacturers differ only slightly. Small manufacturers, or those selling limited quantities, usually follow this policy. Companies with limited competition often sell at the market price. A small group of competitors dominating an industry follows the policy of selling at the market price. High-cost producers may be obliged to follow this policy, since their overhead will not permit them to sell for less than the price offered by competitors.

The principal advantages of selling at market price are:

1. Price cutting by competitors is not encouraged.
2. More money is available for advertising.
3. Distributors' margins are protected.
4. Customers are not driven away by high prices.
5. Better service and delivery are possible.
6. The reputation of the seller for comparable quality is maintained.
7. Superior salesmanship is effective.

On the other hand, a policy of following competitors' prices has the following disadvantages:

1. The seller has no price individuality.
2. Demand is not stimulated.
3. Superior quality is not indicated.
4. The available market is simply shared with competitors.
5. Consumers do not receive the benefits of lower prices.
6. Distribution through aggressive, low-price-policy retail outlets is sacrificed.

Selling Above the Prevailing Market Price. A policy of selling at the market plus is usually pursued by manufacturers of high-quality goods or specialties having peculiar characteristics not possessed by other products of similar type. Manufacturers with monopoly or patent rights and others with unique methods of manufacture or unusual market reputations often adopt this policy.

The major advantages of this price policy are:

1. Quality is emphasized.
2. Better service is possible.
3. More money may be spent for advertising.
4. A wider margin is available for distributors.
5. Higher prices may be secured for cheaper lines on the strength of quality reputation.
6. Price distinctiveness is attained.

The chief disadvantages of selling at prices above the market are:

1. Volume is reduced and overhead increased.
2. The demand and size of the market are restricted.
3. Selling effort must be increased, with greater sales costs.
4. Turnover is slackened.
5. Substitutes are encouraged.
6. Good will is lost when patents expire.
7. Certain classes of buyers are lost.

Selling Below the Market Price. In periods of business depression particularly, many sellers adopt a policy of selling at the market minus. Few companies consistently maintain this price policy. Only those with a large volume of sales and low production costs have been successful with this policy. The R. H. Macy Company has consistently followed this policy on many items.

The benefits of such a low-price policy are:

1. Competition is discouraged.
2. The size of the market is increased.
3. Sales volume is increased.
4. Sales resistance is reduced.
5. Consumers are benefited.
6. The policy is consistent with the prevailing downward trend of manufactured commodity prices.
7. The advertising value of a low-price policy is great.

On the other hand, there are several disadvantages of selling at the market minus:

1. Competitors are antagonized.
2. Margins of the manufacturer and distributors are curtailed.
3. Increased sales may not produce permanently greater demand.
4. Competitors follow price reductions and nullify advantages.
5. Little service is rendered to buyers.
6. Reputation for quality is threatened.

Factors Affecting Choice of Basic Price Policy. Several of the numerous factors influencing the type of basic price policy that should be adopted for a specific commodity, are:

1. *The nature of the market* affects the price policy. Since the demand for industrial or capital goods depends upon the demand for consumer goods, price is not a vital factor in the sale of industrial products. If there is no demand for consumer goods, no decrease in the price of industrial machinery will either create a consumer demand or induce manufacturers to buy new equipment.

The income of the potential buyers of a commodity affects the size of the market and influences the price policy. The number of likely buyers of steam yachts, for example, is so small that a high price is necessary to provide for the small turnover and high selling expense of this product. On the other hand, the market for coffee is so large, since the number of people who can afford to purchase it is great, that the volume and quick turnover make a low price possible.

2. *The type of product* affects the price policy. Sales of staple commodities of low price are rarely permanently increased by price reductions. A price reduction on sugar would not permanently increase the sales of that commodity. Furthermore, the ready sale and high turnover of staple products create low production and selling costs, making possible low prices. Luxury products of slow turnover and high selling cost must be sold at high prices. Other product factors, including style and seasonableness, have a bearing on price policy. The presence of distinguishable quality in a product often justifies a higher price.

3. *The method of distribution* may have an influence on the price policy. Commodities sold direct from maker to consumer are frequently distributed at a high cost that must be reflected in the price. Chain stores are able to price numerous items lower than individual stores, by reason of economies in distribution.

4. *Competition* often directly affects a manufacturer's choice of a price policy. The prices of many staple products are established largely by the price policies of leading producers, particularly in the sale of gasoline and steel. Manufacturers adopting a policy of pricing at the market are chiefly following competitors. If a seller has little competition, higher prices may be justified; but if competition is severe, a price policy of the market minus may be advisable.

5. *The general business outlook* has a direct relation to price

policies of many commodities. With a falling price level and depressed economic conditions, price reductions often fail to stimulate demand, since buyers are waiting in anticipation of further price reductions to make purchases. It is much easier to increase prices on a rising market.

6. *Profit margins of distributors* sometimes influence price policies of manufacturers. Resale prices are often established to afford wholesalers and retailers sufficient margin to cover their costs of doing business and permit a net profit. Merchants prefer to stock and push those items carrying adequate discounts.

7. *Custom* is also an important factor in price determination. Buyers accustomed to paying a certain price for a commodity are reluctant to pay an unusual price. Chewing gum, for example, has long sold for five cents a package. It is questionable whether a six-cent package of gum, even though it was of superior quality, would sell readily. Variety stores sell at established price levels of ten, twenty-five, fifty cents, and one dollar. Price policies that violate customary price levels are often unsuccessful.

8. *Price maintenance contracts*, legalized by state and federal legislation, determine the minimum resale prices for numerous consumer commodities. The sale of certain products below the price set by manufacturers is illegal in many states.

Determining Prices. While price policies are influenced by the several factors previously discussed, the fundamental bases for commodity price determination are:

1. Cost of production.
2. Cost of distribution.
3. Desired profit.

Cost of production. This includes labor, materials, and factory overhead. While products are often sold for less than the actual cost of production, over extended periods prices usually include manufacturing costs. Although production costs may serve only as a guide to market price for short periods, no other cost basis is so practical or in the long run so satisfactory.

Production costs are more or less scientifically established and definitely known in efficiently operated manufacturing organizations and are consequently a convenient base for determining prices.

Cost of distribution. Direct sales costs are included in this factor, as:

1. Salesmen's compensation.
2. Expenses.
3. Sales management.
4. Advertising.
5. Branch supervision.
6. Indirect distributing costs such as credit, billing, accounting, outfreight, and financial management.

The difficulty in using distribution costs as a base for prices lies in their accurate determination. So many variable factors affect distribution costs that few executives will agree on the elements of marketing costs. Distribution costs will vary widely with different types of commodities, sold in different quantities and in different territories. It is impossible to calculate the cost of style depreciation.

Margin of profit desired by a seller. This is the most important factor in price determination. Invested capital and labor must be profitably employed to insure the continuation of a business. Theoretically, the amount of profit earned by a business should be in proportion to the service rendered. A normal profit should include a reasonable rate of interest on the investment and compensation for risks incurred in operating the business. A sound price should be based on these two elements of profit. The rate of profit should also be varied with the type of product since the investment and risk differ with different types of commodities. A flat percentage of sales should not be designated as a profit figure and applied identically in the determination of prices of all products in a line.

Consideration of these three basic price factors in the determination of price policies insures the return of all outlays in the manufacture and marketing of a commodity and also provides an adequate profit. In addition, other factors previously mentioned, as the market, type of product, method of distribution, competition, business conditions, distributors' profit margins, price maintenance, and custom, must be considered in setting prices. The influence of any or all of these factors may be reflected in a selling price.

Computing Selling Prices. In figuring selling prices, certain words and phrases are commonly used. A knowledge of the definitions of these terms is necessary to avoid mistakes in computing prices.

List prices are often quoted by manufacturers and wholesalers and suggest the prices at which distributors are expected to resell commodities. Wholesale and retail discounts are taken from list prices. They are usually the advertised prices printed in catalogs and price lists. The advantages of using list prices are:

1. They promote resale price uniformity among distributors.
2. Distributors are saved the labor of figuring resale prices.
3. Price changes may be readily made by altering discounts, without changing the published list price.

Net prices are final prices after all discounts or allowances have been granted to wholesalers or retailers.

Net profit is the amount of money a company earns after all costs of production and distribution have been paid; or in the case of a retail or wholesale business, that which remains over and above all costs of merchandise and expenses of operation.

Zone prices are uniform prices quoted to buyers within certain geographical areas or zones. They are usually based on the distance of a buyer from the point of shipment and include freight costs.

Margin, defined by distributors, is the difference between the cost and the selling price of a product.

Sliding scale prices are used in quoting prices of commodities for future delivery when costs of manufacture or raw materials are uncertain.

Price lining is the establishment, by retail distributors, of certain price levels or ranges at which particular items of merchandise sell most readily. Unwanted price levels are eliminated.

Markup is the percentage by which the cost of a product is multiplied to get an amount, which, when added to the cost of the product, gives the selling price. Markup is equivalent to margin expressed in dollars and cents but is greater than margin when expressed in percentage.

Resale price maintenance is the practice of manufacturers of making contracts or agreements with distributors to sell manufacturers' products at prices established by manufacturers.

Fixed price differentials are sometimes established by manufacturers to give one type of distributing organization a price advantage over another. One price is quoted to wholesalers, and another to retailers, based on their functions.

Price guarantees protect buyers against price changes for a definite period of time. If prices rise, buyers are given the benefit of the original price.

Markdowns are reductions from the original selling price taken by wholesalers and retailers.

Selling price is a price established by a manufacturer that includes the costs of production and distribution and yields a desired net profit. In the case of distributors, it is the price that pays for merchandise and all operating expenses and yields a net profit.

The retail and wholesale method of figuring prices. The method universally used by retailers in determining selling prices is by markup on the cost price. The successive steps in this method are:

1. Determining the margin necessary to yield a desired net profit.
2. Determining the markup that will give the margin desired.
3. Applying the markup to individual items.

Margin is expressed in percentage by adding the operating expenses of a business, including compensation of sales people, rent, light, heat, advertising, accounting, delivery, and storage, to the desired net profit and dividing by the total sales. For example, the total sales are $100,000; operating expenses are $15,000; desired net profit is $5,000. First, add the operating expenses, $15,000, to the desired net profit, $5,000, to get the margin, or $20,000. Next, divide the margin, $20,000, by the total sales, or $100,000 which gives 20 per cent margin.

This example shows that, in order to cover operating expenses and secure a 5 per cent net profit, the company must secure a margin of 20 per cent.

When the margin, expressed in percentage, has been determined, it must next be converted into markup percentage. While margin and markup are the same in dollars and cents, they differ when expressed in percentage, because margin is figured as a percentage of sales while markup is usually expressed as a percentage of cost. For example, a piece of merchandise costs $2.50, and the merchant must price it to secure a margin of 20 per cent, which includes operating expenses and net profit.

One simple way to determine the markup is to consider the unknown selling price as 100 per cent. The margin assumed is 20 per cent. Therefore, the cost of the goods must be the difference between margin and selling price, or 80 per cent of the selling price. For example, the cost of the merchandise is $2.50, which is 80 per cent of the selling price. To find the selling price, or 100 per cent, divide the cost, $2.50, by 80 per cent, which equals .0312, or 1 per cent of the selling price. One hundred per cent, or the selling price, equals one hundred times .0312, or \$3.12. Test the correctness of

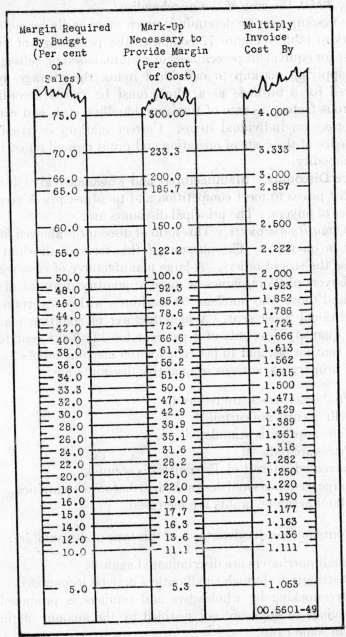

Margin Required By Budget (Per cent of Sales)	Mark-Up Necessary to Provide Margin (Per cent of Cost)	Multiply Invoice Cost By
75.0	300.00	4.000
70.0	233.3	3.333
66.0	200.0	3.000
65.0	185.7	2.857
60.0	150.0	2.500
55.0	122.2	2.222
50.0	100.0	2.000
48.0	92.3	1.923
46.0	85.2	1.852
44.0	78.6	1.786
42.0	72.4	1.724
40.0	66.6	1.666
38.0	61.3	1.613
36.0	56.2	1.562
34.0	51.5	1.515
33.3	50.0	1.500
32.0	47.1	1.471
30.0	42.9	1.429
28.0	38.9	1.389
26.0	35.1	1.351
24.0	31.6	1.316
22.0	28.2	1.282
20.0	25.0	1.250
18.0	22.0	1.220
16.0	19.0	1.190
15.0	17.7	1.177
14.0	16.3	1.163
12.0	13.6	1.136
10.0	11.1	1.111
5.0	5.3	1.053
		00.5601-49

FIGURE 77. This margin and markup table saves the time of salesmen and dealers in calculating markup. It was published in "Hardware Distribution in the Gulf Southwest" by the U. S. Department of Commerce.

this price by subtracting the desired margin of 20 per cent from the selling price of the goods, or \$3.12, and the cost price is approximately \$2.50, the cost of the merchandise.

The markup may be determined much more easily by consulting a markup table. Figure 77 computes the percentage of markup on cost for equivalent percentages of margin, based on selling price.

In applying markup to individual items, the average markup required for a business as a whole must be varied according to numerous factors, as rate of turnover, handling cost, and competitive prices on individual items. Correct markup is based on a knowledge of the costs of operation and profit desired on each class of commodity.

Price Discounts. Manufacturers and wholesalers give discounts from list prices to meet competition and to adjust prices according to types of buyers. The principal discounts are:

A. *Quantity discounts.* This form of discount is allowed for purchases in quantity. The purpose of this form of discount is to increase the size of orders. A large manufacturer of cash registers gives buyers of 25 machines or more a quantity discount of 5 per cent; and those who purchase 50 machines, within a certain time, an additional 2 per cent. A manufacturer of counting machines allows quantity discounts of 3 per cent for 12; 5 per cent for 25; 10 per cent for 50; and 15 per cent for 100 machine orders.

The primary advantages of quantity discounts are:

1. Production costs are reduced.
2. Selling costs are curtailed.
3. Consumption is stimulated.
4. Prices are reduced.
5. Increased interest of distributors is secured.
6. Large customers and desirable distributors are obtained.
7. Manufacturers' profits are increased.

The outstanding disadvantages of this type of discount are:

1. Small purchasers are discriminated against.
2. Distribution through small outlets may be jeopardized.
3. Overstocking by wholesalers and retailers is promoted.
4. Savings to seller are not justified by the amount of the discount, in some cases.
5. Turnover of distributors is reduced.
6. Heavy inventories of perishables may deteriorate.

To avoid conflict with the Robinson-Patman Act, manufacturers who give quantity discounts as well as other types of price concessions that may serve to discriminate between purchasers must justify such discounts from the standpoint of manufacturing or distributing economies.

The two principal types of quantity discounts are: single order discounts, which are the most common; and deferred or term quantity discounts, which are allowed on the total amount purchased over a period of one month or a year. The advantages of term discounts, from the standpoint of the seller, are:

1. Perishable merchandise, ordered in small quantities, may be kept fresher.
2. Continuous buying is encouraged.
3. Stock turnover of dealers is promoted.
4. Distributors take increased interest in pushing and displaying merchandise.

On the other hand, disadvantages of this policy are:

1. Quantity production and distributing economies are in a measure sacrificed.
2. Price cutting by distributors is encouraged.
3. The amount of administrative detail of the seller is increased.

B. *Trade discounts*. Many manufacturers establish discounts based on functional types of distributors. That is, certain discounts are given to wholesalers, other discounts allowed to chain stores, and still others to coöperative purchasers and other types of distributing organizations. Trade discounts are deducted from wholesale or retail resale list prices established by manufacturers.

Distinction in trade discount rates is made by manufacturers in selling to various types of distributors:

1. To insure distributors adequate margins.
2. To compensate distributors in proportion to services rendered to manufacturers.
3. To protect one type of distributor against another and secure his coöperation.

The establishment of trade discounts presents numerous difficulties, chief among which is an equitable classification of buyers. To establish discount rates for the numerous types of functional wholesalers, including cash and carry, wagon, mail order, service, and coöperatives, on the basis of distributing services rendered to a manufacturer, is a very difficult task. Classifying distributors as wholesalers or retailers presents another problem, since many wholesalers are also retailers. Chain stores, which perform the functions of wholesalers, believe that they are entitled to wholesale discounts. Mail order houses likewise claim wholesale discounts. Department stores, which buy direct from manufacturers in wholesale quantities, consider that they are entitled to wholesale discounts.

Trade discounts are frequently so discriminatory that retailers can go to chain stores and mail order houses and buy at consumer prices that are lower than the prices at which the same merchandise can be bought from wholesalers. Through such discrimination a manufacturer soon loses the good will of wholesalers and individual retailers.

To solve the problem of classifying distributors by function, some manufacturers have abolished all trade discounts and have established distributor quantity discounts. Sometimes a combination of quantity and trade discounts is established.

C. *Introductory discounts.* To facilitate the introduction of new items, manufacturers sometimes offer "introductory discounts" on initial orders. The purpose of this type of discount is to break down sales resistance and secure the coöperation of distributors in stocking and pushing new items. Frequently introductory discounts are given in the form of free goods. This form of discount, unless offered to all purchasers on proportionately equal terms, is illegal under the Robinson-Patman Act.

Other similar types of discounts are "free deals," advertising allowances, bonuses, prizes, and premiums to distributors to induce sales coöperation. These must also be made available on proportionately equal terms to all customers competing in the distribution of the product.

D. *Territorial discounts.* To provide for uniform delivered prices in all parts of the country, some manufacturers establish discounts by geographical areas or zones. The amount of these discounts covers the cost of transportation from the seller's factory and enables buyers to maintain the same price list in each territory.

E. *Forward datings.* Some manufacturers request payment thirty and sometimes sixty days after merchandise has been shipped. This practice, known as "forward dating," or "deferred dating," is, in effect, an additional discount since it gives the purchaser longer use of his money. This policy is often followed in the sale of seasonable goods. It enables a manufacturer to keep his factory busy for longer periods, to reduce excess inventories, and to get stocks into the hands of distributors in advance of seasonal demand. The practice often results in price cutting. In the oil stove industry it is customary to invoice goods shipped after November 1 as of April 1 the following year. Sometimes forward datings are allowed only to meet exceptional conditions.

F. *Miscellaneous types of discounts.* There are numerous types of special discounts given to customers. An advance order discount is occasionally given distributors as an inducement to place orders in advance of immediate needs. Manufacturers of seasonal goods, such as holiday lines, sometimes use this form of discount.

Price Protection. Some manufacturers have adopted a policy of protecting customers against loss from price declines in order to stimulate sales in periods when prices are declining. This practice is largely used in the sale of seasonal products, the prices of which fluctuate widely. Prices are usually protected for a definite period ranging from thirty days to one year. Sometimes protection is afforded only on the unshipped portion of orders. Another form of price guarantee is to give buyers advance notice of price declines so that they may dispose of existing stocks and reorder at new prices.

The principal advantages of price protection to manufacturers are:

1. Buying is stimulated.
2. Good will of customers is secured.
3. Larger orders are secured.
4. Production is stabilized.
5. Inventories are reduced.

Certain disadvantages of price guarantees are:

1. The seller may suffer severe losses in periods of falling prices.
2. Distributors may be overstocked.
3. Merchandise may deteriorate or become shopworn.
4. The seller assumes undue risks.

Price Quotations. To facilitate price quotations, manufacturers have adopted various methods of quoting prices. A uniform price policy is followed by some manufacturers and retailers. All sizes and styles of a product are sold at a fixed price. A shoe manufacturer, distributing through company-owned stores, adopted a uniform price of $6.60 a pair on nearly a hundred styles and a wide variety of sizes of shoes. This policy is also used by manufacturers of men's clothing who distribute through their own retail stores. The practice affords good advertising, but it is difficult to maintain in periods of rising costs.

The basing-point system of price quotation is used in quoting prices on iron and steel products. Under this method of pricing, producers quote prices as of various producing centers or basing points. There are four basing points—Buffalo, Cleveland, Gary, and Pittsburgh—each with a specific price for cold finished steel. The basing points for galvanized sheets are Pittsburgh, Gary, and Birmingham; while for pig iron, there are twenty basing points. Buyers are charged the base rate from a particular basing point to their own plants. The base rate used is the one that, when added to the freight charge, gives the lowest price to the purchaser. Shippers who are located elsewhere than at the basing point do not quote delivered prices in accordance with freight costs from their own plants, but are governed by the freight rates from the basing point.

According to Donald E. Montgomery:

The effect of a basing-point price policy is that every nonbasing-point seller discriminates between his customers in the prices which he charges them for his product. A second significant characteristic of the basing-point system is the sharing of territories which it promotes as between shippers located at different points. The price relationships of the basing-point system make it possible and probable that a sharing of territories becomes general over a wide area. Basing-point sellers are able to sell without sacrifice to any point in that territory. The nonbasing-point seller, on the other hand, receives low net returns on sales toward the basing-point and beyond, but makes up the deficit through the high returns received in the area near its plant where it has an advantage in freight rates over the basing-point.

A third consequence of basing-point prices is the levying of larger total freight costs upon consumers because of the cross-hauling. Under a system of mill-base prices the amount of such excess freight incurred would probably be insignificant as compared with the very extreme amount of cross-hauling which appears to be normal in the basing-point industries.

As to remedies, one substitute suggested is the mill-base system in which each mill at any given time charges uniformly to all customers its one current price at the mill regardless of destination. Some compelling force would be required to install and retain this system, as it is no more natural or self-sustaining than the other.

Increase in the number of basing-points employed in a multiple basing-point system appears as a step in the direction of striking a balance between the two extremes, but this would reduce neither cross-hauling nor discrimination in prices.

A more promising substitute would be to place a limit on price discrimination, to stimulate price competition. Under such a rule each mill would sell at its maximum mill price in the territory surrounding its location, and would expand that territory outward until it reached a point where the delivered prices of another mill would prevent it from getting its maximum return. Beyond that point it would continue into the territory of other mills, receiving less than its maximum net return in doing so. Instead of reciprocity in the matter of sales there would be mutual exclusion. Reduction in the limit of permissible discrimination would confine each mill more strictly to the area carved out for it by the relation of its base price to the base price of other mills. The incentive to price competition would be called into play, but could be controlled by the extent of discrimination permitted, and it need not be pushed so far as to lead producers to eliminate themselves from the competitive picture through consolidations or secret price agreements.

An automatic price reduction policy is sometimes followed by retailers. Under this policy prices of unsold merchandise are automatically reduced at the expiration of certain time periods. This results in compulsory moving of slow-turning stock. At the expiration of a definite time, one large store gives away all unsold stock.

An "odd-price" policy is employed by many retailers. One large drug chain store system uses "odd prices" on higher-priced items, but "even" prices on all articles selling at small prices. Odd prices are most effective when they succeed in taking an article out of a higher price level into a lower level, as from $2 to $1.98. The constant use of odd prices by a seller may destroy the impression of saving with buyers. Other merchants believe that odd prices have little value, as buyers are chiefly concerned with quality and a convenient source of supply.

An analysis of the most common prices in retail drug stores made by the United States Department of Commerce, showed that the most frequent combination of prices for a product made in three sizes is 25 cents, 50 cents, and $1. In seven commodity groups, the investigators found the following to be the most common prices: candy bars, 5 cents; toilet soaps, 25 cents; headache remedies, 25 cents; laxatives, 25 cents; deodorants, 50 cents; toothbrushes, 50 cents; and tooth paste and powders, 50 cents.

Price Maintenance. Resale price maintenance is one of the fundamental price problems concerning manufacturers of branded merchandise. Price maintenance has been defined as a system of distribution by which a manufacturer of trade-marked goods names the prices at which his products shall be sold and distributed by wholesalers and retailers. The margins of distributors, as well as prices paid by consumers, are controlled by the manufacturer.

Manufacturers have attempted for many years, by means of notices, patents, licenses, copyrights, and contracts, to fix the prices at which their products are to be sold by wholesalers and retailers.

However, in 1911, the Supreme Court of the United States decided the case of Dr. Miles Medical Company vs. John D. Park & Sons Company. This decision established that a manufacturer cannot consistently, within the Sherman Anti-Trust Act, sell his product to distributors and by contract with them fix its resale price. Numerous bills have since been introduced in Congress to validate resale price maintenance contracts.

However, no effective resale legislation was enacted until the passage of the California Fair Trade Act on May 8, 1931. This act, which went into effect on August 14, 1931, states in part:

No contract relating to the sale or resale of a commodity which bears the trade-mark, brand, or name of the producer or owner of such commodity and which is in fair and open competition with commodities of the same general class produced by others shall be deemed in violation of any law of the state of California by reason of any of the following provisions which may be contained in such contract:

1. That the buyer will not resell such commodity except at the price stipulated by the vendor.

2. That the vendee or producer require in delivery to whom he may resell such commodity to agree that he will not, in turn, resell except at the price stipulated by such vendor or by such vendee.

Contested in several suits, the constitutionality of this act was upheld on December 7, 1936, by the United States Supreme Court, which declared that under this law, a manufacturer of trade-marked goods has the right to enter into contracts, with distributors in intrastate trade, prescribing a resale price.

As a result of this ruling, similar price maintenance laws were enacted in forty-two states. However, manufacturers wishing to take advantage of these laws were faced with the necessity of domesticating contracts with distributors in each state in which they desired to make resale price maintenance contracts. The expense of contracting with retailers in several states and the likelihood of violating the Sherman Act prevented many manufacturers from making direct contracts with retailers, located in other states, under the state fair trade acts.

The passage of the Tydings-Miller Act on August 17, 1937, however, amended the anti-trust laws so as to enable manufacturers to make direct contracts with retailers and wholesalers in all states having fair trade acts. This legislation practically cleared the way for national resale price maintenance by enabling manufacturers of trade-marked merchandise to establish minimum resale prices.

Some of the benefits to manufacturers of resale price maintenance are:

1. Price cutting is eliminated.
2. Unfair competition is outlawed.
3. Prices are standardized.
4. Dealer coöperation is secured.
5. Profits are increased.
6. Substitution is lessened.
7. Distribution is expedited.

Among the numerous disadvantages to manufacturers in establishing resale prices are:

1. Private brand competition is encouraged.
2. Large, aggressive distributors may be lost.
3. The good will of consumers may be jeopardized.
4. Increased prices may reduce volume.
5. Policing of violations may be expensive and difficult.
6. Dealers may resent interference with their pricing privilege.
7. A premium is placed on dealer inefficiency.
8. Retailers may have difficulty in moving surplus stocks.

Manufacturers of nationally advertised, branded drug specialties, commonly used as loss leaders, were among the first to take advantage of the opportunity to establish minimum resale prices.

Delivered vs. Shipping Point Price Quotations. The question of whether the buyer or the seller will pay transportation costs confronts manufacturers in many lines. Certain manufacturers, desiring uniform selling prices in all parts of the country, pay transportation charges. Others, making small items on which freight costs are relatively small, follow the same policy. Producers of heavy, bulky commodities attempt to shift the payment of transportation charges to their distributors.

Narrowing margins make it difficult for distributors to assume the expense of merchandise transportation. Manufacturers with rising distributing costs likewise find freight charges burdensome. Manufacturers seeking increased volume, however, often hope to break down sales resistance by assuming freight charges on shipments of their products. Increased competition also causes many producers to make freight allowances.

A survey by the Federal Trade Commission of the price-basing methods of three thousand five hundred firms, including manufacturers in practically all industries, showed that 44 per cent use an f.o.b. basis; 18 per cent use a prepaid or delivered price basis; and 38 per cent use both bases.

The four common policies for the payment of transportation charges are:

1. F.o.b., or shipping-point basis.
2. Prepaid or delivered basis.
3. Freight allowance basis.
4. Averaged freight charge.

F.o.b., or free on board at point of shipment, is the most common freight payment policy. The advantages of this basis from the standpoint of manufacturers are:

1. The seller is relieved of the expense of transportation.
2. Buyers are treated impartially.
3. No risks of damage in transit are assumed by the seller.

The disadvantages of this price policy are:

1. Sales are often restricted to the vicinity of the shipping point.
2. Sales volume may suffer.
3. Prices in various parts of the country may not be uniform.
4. Buyers are put to the trouble of ascertaining transportation charges.

This policy is usually adopted by manufacturers whose products are heavily advertised or in strong demand. Those whose factories are located close to consumers or distributors can readily adopt this policy. In industries where producers are concentrated in a single area, an f.o.b. factory policy is effective. An example is the automobile industry concentrated in the state of Michigan.

Prepaid or delivered prices make possible a uniform price throughout the country; sale volume is increased; buyers are relieved of the cost and trouble of paying freight; and competition is met more effectively.

On the other hand, when a seller pays transportation charges:

1. Local buyers are penalized in favor of more distant customers.
2. The cost of freight is a heavy distributing expense that must be paid by the seller.
3. More capital is required.
4. Cash discounts are allowed on freight costs as well as merchandise costs.
5. Credit losses include freight as well as cost of merchandise.

This policy is often used by sellers whose products are little known or who are suffering from keen competition. A small manufacturer must often prepay transportation charges to meet competition.

A freight allowance is sometimes made by manufacturers to buyers. This allowance usually covers a portion of the cost of transportation and is established on a hundredweight basis. A confectionery manufacturer allows jobber-customers 75 cents a hundred pounds for transportation charges. If freight costs exceed this allowance, jobbers pay the difference.

A freight allowance enables a seller to extend his market and at least partially meet competition in areas distant from his shipping point. Sales volume is stimulated. The disadvantages of this policy are:

1. A customer near the point of shipment is favored over a distant buyer.
2. Inequalities in delivered prices prevail.
3. Price competition in distant markets is not equaled.
4. Accounting is increased.

A freight allowance policy is usually adopted by manufacturers whose products are not in sufficient demand to warrant an f.o.b. policy. Unbranded staples of equal quality are often distributed on a freight allowance basis.

An average freight charge that is uniform for all buyers, irrespective of their location, is sometimes made by manufacturers. This charge is determined by averaging the shipping costs on all outgoing freight and applying the average cost to every shipment. Under this policy, a Chicago customer of a New York manufacturer pays the same amount for freight as a buyer in Philadelphia. This policy favors buyers located at a distance from the shipper, but works to the disadvantage of those customers located close to the point of shipment.

Factors Influencing Freight Payment Policy. The seven principal factors affecting the freight payment policy of a manufacturer are as follows:

1. *Consumer demand.* When a product is in strong demand, a manufacturer is not obliged to assume transportation charges to distributors. Wholesalers and retailers are compelled to stock demanded commodities. The manufacturer of a popular 5-cent chocolate bar employs an f.o.b. factory policy without making any

freight allowances. Wholesalers buying this candy maker's products figure their freight costs into the cost of the candy and establish wholesale prices accordingly. Certain items of this manufacturer are priced at 65 cents, f.o.b. factory, and wholesalers in the same state in which the factory is located price them as low as 70 cents to the retail trade. The same items sold by wholesalers at greater distances are sold to the retail trade for 85 cents, owing to higher freight cost. However, the consumer price of these items is uniform throughout the country, the wholesalers and retailers absorbing the freight costs in their margins.

2. *Advertising.* The ability to advertise a product and create a demand for it makes it possible for a manufacturer to place the burden of transportation costs on wholesalers and retailers. The freight on branded specialties is often paid by distributors. On staple commodities of identical quality to competing products, producers often assume shipping costs.

3. *Factory location.* If a manufacturer is located at a long distance from his principal market, he is often compelled to assume all or part of the transportation charges on his products. Manufacturers established in New England, seeking a national market, are under a severe freight handicap compared with their competitors in the Middle West. Branch plants are sometimes located in various parts of the country to effect transportation savings to customers. A large manufacturer of marshmallows has one factory in the East, one in the Middle West, and another on the Pacific Coast.

4. *Profit margins.* If a product affords ample profit margin, many manufacturers prefer to absorb transportation costs. On many highly competitive commodities, manufacturers cannot pay transportation costs and secure profits. The size of distributors' margins also indicates the ability or willingness of wholesalers and retailers to pay freight on purchases.

5. *Distributing warehouses.* Manufacturers with warehouse stocks located in various parts of the country are able to reduce transportation costs by shipping from stocks to near-by customers. The expense of warehouse facilities, particularly for perishable products, makes it unprofitable for some manufacturers to maintain spot stocks in various markets. The profit margins on many products will not permit the establishment of regional warehouses from which shipments may be made to customers.

6. *The character of competition.* Competition may force a manufacturer to adopt a prepaid or delivered price policy. Par-

ticularly if competition is localized in numerous markets throughout the country, it is often necessary for a producer to prepay freight
to meet local competition.

7. *The type of product.* A quality product may often be sold
under an f.o.b. factory policy as buyers will be willing to pay the
cost of transportation to obtain quality. Producers of specialty
products with unique characteristics may enjoy freedom from
freight costs. Makers of a staple commodity with no distinguish-
ing features may be obliged to prepay transportation to secure distribution.

Credit Policies. Reliable estimates have established that more
than 90 per cent of the annual wholesale and retail business of the
country is transacted on a credit basis. Credit is defined as the
ability to obtain goods or services immediately by promising to pay
for them at a definite time in the future. Credit is an important
function in sales management because:

1. Sales transactions are not completed until the goods sold
have been paid for.

2. Salesmen's performance is judged by net profits earned, and
bad debts destroy profits.

3. Manufacturers and distributors operate on narrow profit margins, and credit losses make substantial inroads on profits.

4. Commission salesmen do not receive their full compensation
until final payment has been made.

5. Salesmen may waste valuable selling time soliciting prospects
with questionable credit.

6. Liberal credit policies reduce sales resistance and aid salesmen
in closing sales.

7. A better class of trade may be secured.

8. Customers concentrate purchases with sellers who extend
credit.

9. Credit customers usually buy in larger quantities.

10. Adjustments may be made more readily.

Bases of Credit. In establishing a basis for extending credit,
three principal factors universally considered are: character, capacity, and capital.

Character is undoubtedly the most important basis of credit.
Although a borrower may have capacity and capital, if he lacks
character, it is unlikely that he has the moral responsibility to pay

his obligations. Accordingly, sales executives must direct salesmen to seek buyers of character. Character of a debtor may be revealed by such factors as temperate habits, domestic relations, religious inclination, associations, standing in community, ethical standards, social standing, and court record.

Capacity represents the ability of a debtor so to conduct his business that he can pay his debts when they fall due. Capacity comes from business experience and knowledge of financial, merchandising, or producing principles. A merchant of capacity knows how to buy, speed up stock turn, departmentalize, arrange stock and fixtures, make profitable deliveries, make prompt collections, and keep accurate financial records.

Capital is the most tangible but least important basis of credit. Capital includes: quick assets, such as cash in hand, cash in bank, accounts receivable, and stock on hand; and fixed assets, such as store furniture and fixtures, real estate, and other items. Questions that may be asked a borrower in order to evaluate his capital are:

1. What are his current liabilities?
2. Total liabilities?
3. Net worth?
4. Total debt?
5. What is the relation of current assets to liabilities?
6. The rate of turnover?

The balance sheet of a company shows its financial condition, while its operating statement shows sales activity.

Sources of Credit Information. The principal sources from which sellers can secure information concerning the character, capacity, and capital of buyers are:

1. Mercantile agencies, such as Dun and Bradstreet's, secure and publish credit information on all classes of business concerns. This information is contained in books revised quarterly, or in special reports giving greater detail on the financial standing of individual buyers.

2. Competitors frequently exchange information on the credit standing of customers. Much valuable information on the promptness of buyers in meeting their obligations, the amount of their obligations to sellers, and their volume of purchases can be obtained directly from other companies selling the same buyers.

3. Observation by salesmen of a buyer's inventory, size of establishment, business methods, location, store arrangement, fixtures,

as well as local conditions prevailing in a buyer's community, is invaluable in judging a buyer's credit standing.

4. Local banks, attorneys, trade associations, and newspapers are all logical sources of credit information frequently consulted by sellers. Salesmen often visit these sources and report information received therefrom to their credit departments.

5. Credit exchange bureaus are established in some industries to facilitate the exchange of credit data between selling concerns in the same industry. These organizations employ systematic methods of collection and distribution of credit data that insure current, reliable information at a much lower cost than if sought by individual companies.

6. References furnished by buyers are another source of credit information. Frequently buyers will give references of questionable value, since it is unlikely that a buyer would give the names of concerns that would report unfavorably. Observation of merchandise on a buyer's shelves indicates sources of supply that may be consulted for credit experience.

7. Financial statements furnished by a buyer give evidence of capital and ability to pay. Many sellers require financial statements from all new customers and occasional statements from old customers. Careful analyses are made to determine the financial soundness of a buyer.

Types of Mercantile Credit. The four principal types of mercantile credit used are:

1. The most common type of mercantile credit is book credit or open-account credit, which is extended by a manufacturer to a wholesaler or retailer, or by a wholesaler to a retailer.

Book credit is simple and easy to administer. It relieves buyers of the detail of making and handling credit papers, and stimulates sales by facilitating credit arrangements. On the other hand, a seller has no evidence of a buyer's indebtedness; no security is afforded a seller; and payment of indebtedness may be readily delayed.

2. Written promises or orders to pay are frequently required of buyers of large amounts, or buyers who are poor credit risks.

The most common credit instrument involving a promise to pay is a promissory note. It is a written promise to pay a certain sum of money at a definite future time. A promissory note has the advantages of being a positive evidence of indebtedness; it may be discounted by a seller in need of immediate cash; it affords a seller a psychological advantage by presentation at a debtor's bank; and renders a debtor liable to court action.

There are several "orders-to-pay" credit instruments. The most commonly used instruments in this class are: (1) checks, which are convenient to use and considered the equivalent of cash; (2) trade and bank acceptances, which may be discounted by sellers desiring ready cash.

A trade acceptance represents a particular sale of goods and an absolute acknowledgment of the correctness of the seller's claims by the buyer, as well as a definite promise by the buyer to pay on a certain day. Trade acceptances have the advantages of making for close collections; providing cash, if discounted by sellers; and securing cash discounts and better credit standing for buyers. A bank acceptance is a written agreement executed by a bank agreeing to pay at a certain time and place a definite amount to a seller of merchandise, on behalf of the buyer of the merchandise.

3. Bank drafts are orders issued by the seller's bank on the buyer's bank, ordering the buyer's bank to pay money to the seller named on the face of the draft. Sight drafts are commonly used in selling merchandise on a C.O.D. basis. The bill of lading for the merchandise shipped is attached to the sight draft sent to the buyer's bank, which secures acceptance of the draft by the buyer and releases the bill of lading to the buyer. A commercial draft is often used to collect past-due accounts. It is drawn on the buyer by the seller through a bank in the buyer's community.

4. Letters of credit are used largely by foreign buyers who arrange with banks in their countries to make funds available in banks in this country.

Credit Terms. The terms on which credit is extended are frequently dictated by the customs of the industry in which a buyer and seller are engaged. However, sellers frequently liberalize credit terms and secure a decided sales advantage over competitors.

The length of the term for which credit is extended frequently depends on the rate of turnover of the merchandise purchased, the credit standing of a buyer, or the time when buyers have funds to settle obligations.

The usual length of credit terms is thirty, sixty, and ninety days. The credit period begins ordinarily when shipment is made by a seller. When buyers are located at long distances from sellers, the credit period is usually extended and begins from the date of receipt of goods by the buyer.

Cash discounts are given for prompt payment of bills. The principal advantages of giving cash discounts from the standpoint of sellers are:

1. Credit risks are reduced.
2. Losses by bad debts are curtailed.

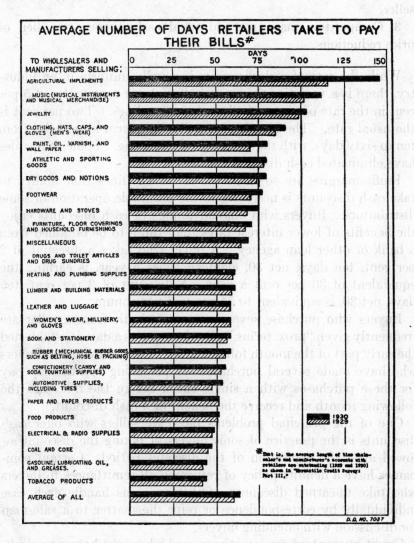

FIGURE 78. The Mercantile Credit Survey of the U. S. Department of Commerce found that retailers of agricultural implements took approximately 145 days to pay for their purchases, while tobacco retailers paid in less than 50 days. The credit terms of manufacturers are usually based on payment practices in their industry, as well as on the rate of turnover of the merchandise.

3. The liquid position of a seller is strengthened.

4. The credit standing of buyers is revealed.

The chief disadvantages of giving cash discounts are:

1. Buyers often take unearned discounts.

2. The amount of the discount outweighs the benefits to the seller.

3. Competitors may give additional cash discounts in lieu of price reductions.

While the rate of cash discounts is usually uniform in an industry, there is a variation from one half of 1 per cent to 4 and 5 per cent in the rate of discount allowed in some lines. Two per cent is the usual rate. The length of the discount term also varies from ten to sixty days, with the former predominating. Some companies have eliminated cash discounts entirely.

Profit margins are so restricted in certain lines that ability to take cash discounts is necessary to the profitable operation of some distributors. Buyers who take advantage of cash discounts enjoy the benefits of lower interest rates than those to be obtained from a bank or other loan agency. A buyer who takes a discount of 2 per cent, ten days, net 30, eighteen times a year, is earning the equivalent of 36 per cent a year. A discount of 3 per cent, ten days, net 30, is equivalent to 54 per cent per annum.

Buyers who purchase several times a month from a seller are frequently given "prox. terms." By these terms a date is established the early part of the month following the time of purchase. Buyers who have made several purchases the preceding month may pay for these purchases with a single check before the due date the following month and receive the benefit of a cash discount.

One of the principal problems faced by sellers who offer cash discounts is the practice of some buyers of taking the discount allowed after the expiration of the discount period. Certain companies have a definite policy of returning all remittances to buyers who take unearned discounts. Other concerns handle each case individually by correspondence or refer the matter to a salesman for discussion with offending buyers.

Credit guarantees are sometimes used when purchasers are lacking in character, capacity, and capital to such an extent that sellers do not feel warranted in extending credit on open account. A credit guarantee is signed by a financially responsible guarantor who has been investigated by the seller and has been found reliable.

Installment credit has become one of the most important factors in the distribution of many manufactured commodities. Buyers using this form of credit are loaned the full purchase price of a product and are given the opportunity of liquidating the loan in successive fractions in the future under a plan agreed upon at the time the loan is made.

Manufacturers extend both wholesale installment credit to retailers and retail installment credit to ultimate consumers. Both types of financing are handled by either a manufacturer through a subsidiary finance company or by a finance company specializing in installment sales.

While installment credit is offered by many manufacturers of consumer specialties, such as oil burners, refrigerators, and radios, the principal users of this form of credit are automobile manufacturers. Wholesale purchases of motorcars are financed by dealers depositing a portion of the purchase price to the credit of the finance company, which pays the invoice price to the manufacturer. The finance company takes title to the cars purchased by dealers and releases them to dealers under trust receipts. Dealers pay for cars by ninety-day time drafts covering the full purchase price less initial deposit.

Retail installments are usually financed by the same companies that finance wholesale purchases. The finance company purchases a retailer's interest in the conditional sales contract with the purchaser, thereby giving the dealer cash. The finance company assumes responsibility for making the monthly installment collections; and upon payment in full, the contract is returned to the dealer, who delivers it to the purchaser. Fire and theft insurance coverage is usually included in the installment plan.

Some of the advantages of installment credit are:

1. Sales volume is increased.
2. Dealers are relieved of the burden of financing.
3. Sales resistance is reduced.

The principal disadvantages of installment selling are:

1. Buyers are sold more than they can afford.
2. Repossession is costly.
3. Current sales are made at the expense of future business.
4. Sales prices are increased.
5. The reputation of a seller is cheapened.

The advisability of having a manufacturer sell with installment credit depends largely on the type of product sold. Installment credit is most effective in the sale of luxuries or novelties with high value, durable in character, and reclaimable. Products that depreciate rapidly or cannot be repossessed readily are not suitable for sale on installment credit.

Some companies require salesmen to make collections for the reasons that:

1. Salesmen are usually well acquainted with customers.
2. Salesmen are on the ground.
3. Collections by salesmen may be made more economically than by collectors.
4. Salesmen are thereby taught the importance of credits in selling.

On the other hand, many concerns refuse to permit salesmen to make collections for the following reasons:

1. Customers are so well acquainted with salesmen that it is difficult for the latter to become effective collectors.
2. Salesmen can spend their time more profitably selling than collecting.
3. Salesmen cannot sell and collect without losing the good will of buyers.

Return and Adjustment Policy. One of the outstanding sales problems with which retailers, wholesalers, and manufacturers are confronted is the return of purchases for credit. While this problem is more pronounced in the case of retailers, much of the $1,600,-000,000 worth of merchandise returned to retail stores annually finds its way back to wholesalers and producers. The National Retail Dry Goods Association has estimated that 14 per cent of all merchandise sold at retail is returned by buyers.

The consequences of this excessive return of merchandise are increased selling costs, higher prices to buyers, depleted stocks, and dissatisfied customers.

The cost of handling and reselling this huge volume of returned goods has been estimated at 20 per cent. On this basis, the sales expense alone would approximate $320,000,000 annually.

Causes of Returns. The causes of this huge annual waste in returned goods may be charged to both buyers and sellers. The chief causes for returns, traceable to the practices and policies of sellers or manufacturers, wholesalers, or retailers, are:

1. Poor salesmanship.
2. Wrong handling of orders, including wrong addresses, poor packing, late delivery, and poor order filling.
3. Poor merchandise—faulty quality.
4. Weak credit policies—too liberal terms.
5. Misleading advertising.
6. Incomplete stocks.
7. Lax return and adjustment policies.

Buyers are often responsible for unjustified returns of merchandise because of:

1. Careless buying.
2. Overbuying.
3. Abuse of return privilege of seller.
4. Speculative buying.
5. Unbalanced stocks.

Solutions to Returned-goods Problem. Various solutions to the returned-goods problem have been tried by manufacturers and middlemen, the most practical of which are:

1. *Coöperation between competitors.* Particularly in the retail department store trade, competitors have coöperated to educate consumers in curtailing returns, to adopt uniform return policies, and to train sales personnel.

2. *Instruction of salesmen.* Education of salesmen is undertaken:

a. To give customers assistance in selecting the right type of merchandise.
b. To avoid making promises difficult to fulfill.
c. To avoid overselling customers.
d. To book orders properly.
e. To understand thoroughly and explain clearly the company's claim and adjustment policy.

3. *Establishment of a system for handling returns.* The adoption of a routine for disposing of each case of returned merchandise often brings about a reduction in the volume of returns. Some of the methods adopted by sellers are:

a. Requiring buyers to receive authorization before making returns.

   b. Requiring customers to fill out a returned-goods form.
   c. Requiring that a replacement order must accompany merchandise returned for exchange.
   d. Limiting the time in which goods will be accepted for credit.
   e. Charging customers a handling fee for returned goods.
   f. Establishing a returned-goods committee to pass on all claims and adjustments.
   g. Requiring customers to pay transportation on returned goods.
   h. Limiting the volume of returned goods.

4. *Education of customers.* In some cases sellers have sought to educate buyers, by mail and display advertising, regarding the effect of unjust claims on their credit standing.

5. *Analysis of returned merchandise.* Analysis of returns of merchandise sold by individual salesmen, by items and individual customers, indicates sources of and reasons for excessive returns.

6. *Strict sales policies.* More stringent policies in regard to conditional sales, guaranteed sales, and sales on approval or with privilege of examination serve to discourage returns of merchandise.

7. *Instructing customers in use of product.* Returns from consumers are often reduced by detailed instructions for operation or care of products of a mechanical nature.

8. *A strict return policy* is an important factor in reducing the volume of returns. When buyers know definitely the return policy of a seller, there is no misunderstanding regarding the conditions under which merchandise may be returned for credit. The following policy, adopted by a trade association of manufacturers, is a typical example of return policies:

Rules on Return of Merchandise

1. No merchandise is returnable except with the consent of the house from which it was bought.

2. We hold ourselves responsible for all damage to our merchandise due to defect in our manufacture. We are not responsible for damage caused after merchandise leaves our possession or while it is in the hands of the carrier company.

3. Merchandise returned to us improperly or carelessly packed cannot be credited, nor can any merchandise be returned for credit or exchange on account of damage occurring due to mishandling or faulty handling in stock.

4. Goods held over a year are not returnable for credit or exchange under any circumstances.

Guarantees. The subject of guarantees has a definite bearing on the problem of returns and adjustments. A guarantee is a written promise by a seller obligating himself for the satisfactory performance of his product for a certain period of time. A guarantee serves:

1. To establish confidence in an unknown product or service.
2. To overcome sales resistance.
3. To create desire for a product.
4. To protect a product against competition.
5. To assure laymen of technical value.
6. To satisfy mail order buyers.

Guarantees also serve the following purposes:

1. To protect buyers against defects in construction.
2. To assure quality or source of materials.
3. To assure freedom from operating failure.
4. To certify that a buyer will receive benefits promised.
5. To promise return of purchase price in event of dissatisfaction.

Guarantees are usually extended for a definite time period. In the case of automobiles, ninety days or four thousand miles, whichever shall occur first, is the time covering defects in materials and workmanship.

Distributors are often compensated by manufacturers for their services in fulfilling guarantees. Some manufacturers, however, prefer to deal direct with consumers in fulfilling guarantees. A razor manufacturer requires every purchaser to file a register card as a record of puchase. The product is not guaranteed unless registered by a purchaser. Mechanical service is rendered by the factory free of charge for one year from date of purchase.

Guarantees are subject to the disadvantages of abuse by consumers and distributors, who frequently make unwarranted claims under a guarantee. Long-term guarantees are often difficult to adjust fairly and frequently create ill will on the part of buyers, who feel that they have been unfairly treated. Furthermore, changes in the terms of a guarantee frequently lead to discrimination against present owners, and consequent dissatisfaction.

Problem 1—Resale Price Policy

Robson Manufacturing Company

The Robson Manufacturing Company, established in Boston, Massachusetts, in 1909, manufactures toothbrushes and tooth powder sold direct to retail druggists in all parts of the country by a sales organization of sixty salesmen. The products of the company are nationally advertised, under the brand names of "Hygo Tooth Powder," and "Hygo Toothbrush," to the extent of $80,000 annually.

For several years the Robson Company's products have been used as loss leaders by numerous large cut-rate drug store chains in various parts of the country. This practice of price cutting has made it difficult for the majority of individual drug stores to sell Robson products at a profit. Accordingly, many retailers refused to stock or push Robson tooth powder and toothbrushes. Sales to individual stores declined sharply in areas where price cutting flourished.

The company considered the advisability of making contracts with retailers to maintain minimum resale prices in the various states where such contracts were legal.

Should it make resale price contracts with retailers, the Robson Company proposed to establish list prices, suggested resale prices, and fair trade minimum prices to afford retailers adequate margins of profit. These prices would be no higher than current prices in a majority of individual drug stores.

The resale price list under consideration was the following:

HYGO TOOTHBRUSHES

Type	List Price per Dozen	Suggested Resale Price	Fair Trade Minimum Price
No. 1	$4.00	$.50	$.43
No. 2	4.00	.50	.43
No. 3	2.80	.35	.33
No. 4	2.00	.25	.23

HYGO TOOTH POWDER

No. 1 tin	$3.20	$.40	$.39
No. 2 tin	2.00	.25	.23

The Commonwealth of Massachusetts had a fair trade act legalizing the making of resale price maintenance contracts between manufacturers and retailers. A form of fair trade contract which is legal in Massachusetts follows:

THIS AGREEMENT, made in the City of . . . ., Commonwealth of Massachusetts, on this . . . . day of . . . ., 194. ., by and between Robson Manufacturing Company of Boston, Mass., a Mass. Corp., hereinafter called the "Manufacturer," and . . . ., druggist of Boston, hereinafter called the "Retailer,"

WITNESSETH:

WHEREAS, the Manufacturer is engaged in the manufacture, production and distribution of various commodities, hereinafter specified and hereinafter sometimes referred to as the "Products of the Manufacturer," which bear, or the label or container of which bears, and which are advertised, distributed and sold under the trade-marks, brands or names of the Manufacturer or owner thereof and which are in fair and open competition with commodities of the same general class produced by others; and

WHEREAS, the Commonwealth of Massachusetts has enacted a Fair Trade Act

(Chapter 398, Acts of 1937), and the Manufacturer and Retailer desire to avail themselves of the benefits of said Act and in order to prevent the making of the said products the subject of injurious and uneconomic practices and to avoid the depreciation of and damage to said trade-marks, brands or names through such practices; and

WHEREAS, the Retailer is engaged in the sale at retail in the Commonwealth of Massachusetts of goods, wares and merchandise, and sells, handles and deals in commodities dealt in by others which are in the same general class as the products of the Manufacturer and which are also in fair, open and active competition with the products of the Manufacturer;

NOW, THEREFORE, in consideration of the premises and of the agreements herein made and the benefits contemplated thereby, and also in consideration of such sales of the products of the Manufacturer as the said Manufacturer may make to the Retailer from time to time while this agreement shall be in effect and the purchase thereof by the Retailer, the parties hereto agree as follows:

1. The Retailer will not, either directly or indirectly, advertise, offer for sale or sell to any person, firm or corporation, any of such products manufactured or sold by the Manufacturer at less than the minimum resale prices then in effect for such products as established hereunder from time to time by the Manufacturer. The minimum resale prices now in effect and hereby established by the Manufacturer are set forth in the schedule hereto annexed and made a part hereof.

2. The Manufacturer may at any time, and from time to time, by notice given as hereinafter provided, add to the products specified in this agreement other products manufactured by the Manufacturer and which products bear, or the label or container of which bears, the trademark, brand or name of the Manufacturer and which are in fair and open competition with products of the same general class produced by others.

3. The Manufacturer may at any time, and from time to time, in its sole discretion, revise the minimum resale prices at the time in effect under this agreement and each such addition and each such revision shall be deemed to be effective at such time as shall be specified by the Manufacturer, which shall be at least ten (10) days after the Manufacturer shall have given written notice thereof to the Retailer, which notice shall be given either by mailing the same in a postage prepaid envelope addressed to the Retailer, or delivering the same in person to the Retailer.

4. It is agreed between the parties hereto that the giving by the Retailer of any article of value in connection with the sale of any of the products, or the making of any concession whether by the giving of coupons or otherwise, in connection with the sale of any of the products of the Manufacturer shall constitute a sale by the Retailer of said products at prices less than the prices at the time in effect under this agreement. It is further agreed by the parties hereto that the sale by the Retailer of any of the products of the Manufacturer in combination with any other commodity or product at a price for the combination which shall be less than the minimum resale price at the time in effect hereunder of the products so sold, plus the minimum resale price of such other commodity or product, or if no such price shall be in force in respect of such other commodity or product, then plus the cost of such other commodity or product and a reasonable profit thereon, shall constitute a sale by the Retailer of the Manufacturer's products at a price less than the price at the time in effect under this agreement.

5. It is agreed that this contract may be cancelled by either party hereto on ten (10) days written notice to the other.

6. The Retailer agrees that in the case of any sale by the Retailer of any of the products of the Manufacturer, otherwise than at retail, he will enter into and make a written agreement with the vendee that such products will not be resold by such vendee at retail except at prices not less than the minimum resale price at the time in effect under this agreement.

7. It is agreed between the parties hereto that it is impossible to determine the actual damage which will result to the Manufacturer from sales made by the Retailer in violation of the terms of this agreement and it is therefore agreed between the parties hereto that the Retailer shall pay to the Manufacturer as liquidated damages, the sum of Fifty Dollars ($50.00) for each sale made by the Retailer in violation of any of the provisions of this agreement, and if, and as often as, the Manufacturer shall institute any proceedings or action in any court against the Retailer for any breach of this agreement, the Retailer agrees, in addition to all court costs, to pay the Manufacturer a reasonable attorney's fee. It is further agreed between the parties hereto that in addition to other legal rights and remedies and in addition to the provisions of this paragraph, the Manufacturer shall be entitled to injunctive relief against any and all actual or threatened breaches of this agreement by the Retailer.

8. It is agreed that the products of the Manufacturer may be resold by the Retailer without reference to this agreement in the following cases:

(a) In closing out the products of the Manufacturer purchased by the Retailer in such cases where the Retailer is desirous of discontinuing the sale and delivery of any of such of the Manufacturer's products; provided that such products are first offered to the Manufacturer at the original invoice stock price, at least ten (10) days before such products shall be offered for sale to the public;

(b) When the products purchased from the Manufacturer have become damaged or deteriorated in quality and notice is given to the public thereof;

(c) When any of the products of the Manufacturer in the possession of the Retailer are sold by any officer acting under the orders of any court.

9. It is the agreement and the intention of the parties hereto that if any provision or part of this agreement shall be held invalid, the remainder of this agreement shall nevertheless be deemed valid and binding upon the parties hereto, and that no oral changes in this printed form of contract shall be binding.

IN WITNESS WHEREOF, the parties hereto have caused this agreement to be duly executed the day and year first above written.

> ....
> Manufacturer
> By: ....
> Druggist
> ....
> Retailer
> By: ....

The Robson officials considered signing this contract with a Boston retail druggist, thereby establishing prices binding on all other retailers in the Commonwealth of Massachusetts.

Questions

1. Should the Robson Company have contracted with a Boston retailer to maintain resale prices in Massachusetts? Give reasons for your decision.

2. Should the Robson Company have made similar contracts with retailers in states legalizing price maintenance? Why?

3. Under what act of Congress is price maintenance legalized in interstate commerce?

Problem 2—Freight Payment Policy

The Connery Confectionery Company

The Connery Confectionery Company, with a factory located in Boston, Massachusetts, makes and distributes direct from its factory a general line of candies to selected jobbers located in all parts of the country.

The company manufactures three distinct lines of candy:

1. General line candies, sold unbranded. These are bulk items and staples resold in penny lots to children and are made practically identical in quality by all manufacturers of this type of candy. The maker's and distributors' profits on this type of candy are restricted. An average case of candy contains forty boxes and will weigh from 125 to 180 pounds, depending on the kind of candy and type of case used. The maker's cost per box will run between 55 cents and 65 cents, and the wholesale sales price from 60 cents to 70 cents. This line can be readily substituted by dealers.

2. Fancy packages, often advertised, sold on demand and carrying a higher profit than general line candies. A competing manufacturer of this type is S. F. Whitman & Son, Inc.

3. Specialties, advertised and carrying less profit than fancy packages, but more profit than general line candies. Typical of this group are products of The Cracker Jack Company, and Chocolate Sales Corporation, distributors of Hershey Products.

The Connery Company does not consider it practical or profitable to advertise its general line candies, which constitute 75 per cent of its production. Limited advertising is run on the fancy packages and specialties.

Since the company maintains no branch warehouses and makes shipments from Boston, it experiences keen competition from local candy manufacturers in various parts of the country, who are able to give candy jobbers in their territories lower prices than the Connery organization on account of the freight disadvantage imposed by shipments from Boston, Massachusetts.

To overcome this price handicap imposed by freight rates, the Connery Company follows the policy of allowing its jobber-customers 75 cents maximum per hundred pounds on all shipments. Accordingly, jobbers located within the hundred-pound-freight-allowance zone are not obliged to pay freight, while those jobbers beyond the 75-cent-allowance zone must pay freight in excess of the allowance, and their delivered price is accordingly higher. The freight charges on one hundred pounds of candy shipped from Boston to Albany, New York, is 65 cents.

The Connery Confectionery Company believes that the ideal solution to the problem would be to bill every shipment f.o.b. factory at Boston allowing each jobber-customer to pay his own freight, but it hesitates to adopt such a policy since it feels that it would confine distribution to localities within a short radius of the factory.

The company has considered the adoption of an average freight charge on all shipments, but doubts the fairness to nearby customers in making an average charge so that uniform delivered selling prices might be maintained throughout the country.

Believing that its present freight policy is not satisfactory, the Connery Confectionery Company is anxious to extend its market and is seeking a more constructive freight policy.

Questions

1. Name four freight payment policies.

2. What is the influence of each of the following factors on a manufacturer's freight payment policy? (a) location of factory; (b) demand for the product; (c) quality of product; (d) advertising on product; (e) competition; and (f) profit margin.

3. What freight policy must a manufacturer pursue who wishes to stabilize and equalize the price of his product in all parts of the country?

4. Name three advantages to the Connery Company in an f.o.b. factory policy. Two disadvantages.

5. Does the fact that the confectionery industry is largely decentralized affect the freight policies of candy manufacturers? How?

6. What freight policy should the Connery Confectionery Company adopt? Give three reasons for your choice.

Problem 3—Return and Adjustment Policy

Allen & Son

Allen & Son, established in Baltimore, Maryland, in 1915, manufactures a full line of men's haberdashery, including shirts, neckties, hosiery, pajamas, and underwear under the brand name, "Wearite." The line is

distributed direct to retail haberdashers and department stores throughout the country. Much of the merchandise sold by the company is seasonable and subject to a high rate of depreciation.

Confronted with a growing volume of returned goods, approximating
8 per cent of net sales, the company officials considered ways of reducing
returns. Heretofore the company had maintained a liberal return policy,
accepting without question practically all returns except large and obvious abuses of this liberal policy.

As the first step in arriving at a new return policy, the company listed
the following as legitimate reasons for returns: defective merchandise,
substitutions, late delivery, salesman's mistakes, poor wrapping and
packing, wrong sizes and colors, and financial difficulties of buyer. The
company considered accepting without question the above mistakes made
and admitted by the seller.

In addition, the following six requirements incident to the return of
goods, for all other reasons, were considered for adoption:

1. No merchandise is to be returned without the permission of the seller.

2. Transportation charges on returned goods must be prepaid by the
buyer.

3. When merchandise is returned for exchange, a replacement order
should accompany it.

4. Buyers are limited to the volume of returned goods, based on a
stipulated percentage of purchases.

5. A 10 per cent handling charge based on the cost of the goods is
made on all returned goods.

6. No merchandise is accepted for return longer than ninety days from
the date of invoice.

One official of the company believed that a distinction in policy should
be made between style and staple merchandise. A more liberal policy
should be adopted in the case of staple lines such as underwear and
hosiery, which are not subject to style depreciation; while a strict return policy should be adopted for style goods that depreciate rapidly.
In the opinion of other executives, such a distinction in types of merchandise would unduly complicate the return policy and result in enforce-
ment difficulties.

The general manager of the company believed that the new six-point
return policy suggested would create ill will among the trade and lose
the company many valuable customers, who would object to complying
with the strict requirements. He advocated the education of the company's salesmen to avoid extravagant promises to customers, to aid
customers in making careful selections, to fill out orders correctly, and
to inform customers of the extremely high cost of returned goods. To
make this policy effective, salesmen would be charged a 10 per cent
handling charge on all unjustified returns made by their customers. A

review committee made up of home office sales executives would consider each claim.

Questions

1. Should the company adopt the six-point return goods policy described in the problem? Give reasons for your answer.

2. Should the company make a distinction in return policy between staple and style merchandise? Give reasons for your decision.

3. Should the general manager's plan for educating the company salesmen and penalizing them for returns be adopted? Why?

Problem 4—Leasing Policy

The Vocagraph Corporation

The Vocagraph Corporation was organized in Boston in 1945 to make and distribute an entirely new type of electronic recorder for use in business offices to record dictation and to make automatic recordings of telephone conversations, records of important meetings, verbal understandings, interviews, and reports.

The recorder consists of a microphone wired to a cased recording device which embosses grooves on an unbreakable, wafer-thin plastic disk. The disks are played back through a speaker built in the same case with the recorder. The sound volume is regulated by a radio-type control. An accessory transcribing unit is made for typing transcriptions. It is equipped with various types of listening devices and a foot control for starting and stopping. Various types of microphones are also made for dictation, speakers, and conference use.

The product can be made to sell in single units for $325, with accessories extra. It is expected that several units can be sold to an interested concern when it is used for correspondence dictation, as each dictator would require a unit and an accessory transcribing unit would be needed for each transcriber. These units are made to sell for $250 each. A sale to a company employing twenty dictators and four transcribers would amount to $7,500.

In determining its sales policy, the company is considering the advisability of selling its equipment outright at the prices stated above or leasing the Vocagraph so that it may be used without being purchased. The lease policy offers advantages to both the company and its customers.

From the company's point of view leasing provides an opportunity to secure a higher margin of profit. The sales can be maintained in depressions as the buyer does not have to make a large investment in the equipment. This feature also stimulates sales under normal conditions. As title is retained in the seller, credit risk is reduced. Sales of supplies to lessees may be controlled by the contract. The seller has control of the second-hand market. Lower prices may be possible and the vendor's patent position would be protected.

From the buyer's standpoint there are a number of advantages in leasing this equipment. It is unnecessary for him to invest his working capital or become involved in installment financing. He does not have to postpone procuring the equipment for lack of funds. If the product is unsatisfactory the buyer is not overloaded with excessive or unsuitable equipment. Adequate servicing is assured on account of the lessor's continued interest in the equipment. Improvements become available to the buyer much sooner than if he purchased outright. Lower prices are possible because of lower selling costs.

The lease policy, on the other hand, presents certain serious objections from the standpoint of the company. Leasing is considered monopolistic and has acquired an unfavorable name because of the controls inherent in leasing contracts. Because the maker is responsible for proper servicing a fundamental defect in the product would be costly to service. Unless the product is constantly improved, competitors can capture the market with new devices making obsolete all of the company's equipment. A reliable service organization can be maintained only at great expense and with constant supervision. The company must finance all of its customers, which may result in overextending its financial position.

The company is also considering a combination of lease and outright purchase policies to run concurrently to give customers their choice of buying outright or leasing. An alternate plan would involve initial leasing and the application of rental payments toward the ultimate purchase of the equipment.

Questions

1. Should the Vocagraph Corporation adopt a leasing policy in distributing its product? Give additional reasons or analyze more fully the reasons stated in the problem for this policy.

2. Should the company adopt an outright sale policy? Give reasons for this choice of policy.

3. Should the company adopt a combination of outright sale and lease or a variation of such a policy?

Problem 5—Price Policy

Jergens, Jackson Company

The Jergens, Jackson Company, mill supply distributors, located in a large mid-West industrial city, handles such products as nuts, bolts and other industrial hardware; belting and similar rubber and leather items; bearings, valves and fittings, cutting tools, hand and portable power tools and metal rods, bars, pipes, and tubing. A total of from fifteen thousand to twenty thousand items of this character are stocked.

Pricing of these items is usually a routine procedure of following the discount sheets, published by manufacturers, showing list prices and wholesale discounts and making the proper extension for quantities purchased.

Some of the company's larger customers have objected to this pricing method on certain items which they claim does not take into account the amount of service given by the distributor or the differences in cost of filling specific orders. The objections of these customers are based on the fact that they anticipate their requirement on these items, carry their own stock, purchase in large quantities, and receive shipments direct from the factory. In their case, *none* of the services customarily rendered by the mill supply distributor are performed. These services are convenient stocks, collections, packing, delivery, selling, and credit.

In view of these objections, the Jergens, Jackson Company is considering adopting a price policy which will reflect the difference in cost of handling orders of different sizes. A special study will be made of the cost of handling orders of various sizes and discount schedules established on this basis.

On the other hand, higher prices would have to be established on orders which involve greater than normal handling expense. If higher prices are charged it might result in the loss of substantial business to the company.

Furthermore, the expense of determining handling costs, transportation, selling expense and other factors in adjusting prices to service rendered would be considerable and their accuracy might be questionable.

Questions

1. Should the company establish prices with reference to services rendered?

2. Is the present method of pricing sound? What are its advantages and disadvantages?

Problem 6—Net Price vs Multiple Discount Policy

MacJohnson Manufacturing Company

The MacJohnson Manufacturing Company, Chicago, makes a line of industrial tools and accessories, including shop tools, twist drills, gaskets, lock washers and fasteners, and machine tool accessories, which are distributed through mill supply, automotive, and machinery wholesalers in all parts of the country.

The pricing policy of the company is based on multiple discounts to distributors. Those carrying the complete line of an item are allowed one set of discounts; distributors selling certain parts of the line receive another set of discounts; while large direct buyers receive another set. For example, discounts on lock washers and fasteners are 75 and 10 per cent of list to distributors who stock the full line of washers and fasteners; distributors selling fewer items of the line receive 75 and 5 per cent; while large direct buyers receive 75 per cent of list on all purchases. The discounts on shop tools are 10 and 27 per cent to mill supply and machinery houses who stock these tools; nonstocking distributors receive 10 and 10 per cent; and direct buyers, 10 per cent. The discounts on twist drills, also distributed through mill supply and machinery wholesalers, are 50, 5, and 20 per cent to distributors who stock this item; nonstocking distributors receive 40 and 20 per cent; and large direct buyers, 40 per cent.

This complicated system of multiple discounts under which the list price is merely used as a basis for applying discount percentages has been criticized by the sales manager, who would like to establish uniform resale prices which could be featured in the company's advertising. He prefers to have all distributors operating on an even price basis in order to afford equal opportunity for volume and profit and provide equally satisfactory sources of supply to industrial buyers. The multiple discounts now in effect are responsible for variations in prices quoted by distributors to customers who are often unable to buy from a favorite distributor who may have a less favorable discount than a competitor in the same territory.

The sales manager feels that the multiple discount policy is awkward to handle and that it increases clerical work and errors. He also believes that the company should establish a net price schedule to all distributors and eliminate the multiple discounts. He favors a net price schedule on each line to replace the present method.

In the opinion of the management, the keen competition prevailing in the market for many of the company's products, however, makes it necessary to adopt a price policy with sufficient flexibility to meet competitive prices. The most flexible way to adjust the price of various products to competitive conditions is by means of multiple discounts.

Furthermore, the necessity for compensating distributors according to the amount of service that they render to the company by maintaining stocks, servicing items, extending credit, and performing other marketing functions, justifies a differential in the net prices.

Questions

1. Should the MacJohnson Manufacturing Company adopt a net price policy as favored by the sales manager? Give reasons for favoring or opposing this policy.

2. Should the company continue its present multiple discount policy? Give reasons for your choice of this policy.

3. If you favor neither the net nor present multiple discount policy, describe the policy which should be adopted and give reasons for your choice.

Reading References

INSTALLMENT SALES POLICIES

Economics of Installment Selling, Seligman, Chaps. I–III.
Introduction to Sales Management, Tosdal, pp. 171–172.
Principles of Merchandising, Copeland, pp. 346–348.
Sales Administration, Hayward, pp. 482–486.
Selling Policies, Converse, Chap. XXVI.

PRICING POLICIES

Elements of Marketing, Converse and Huegy, Second Revised Edition, Chap. 34.
Marketing Principles, Pyle, pp. 350–362.
Modern Sales Management, Frederick, Chap. V.
Pricing for Profit, Churchill, Chaps. III–V, VIII.
Principles of Marketing, Clark, Chap. XXII.
Sales Administration, Hayward, Chap. XXIX, pp. 455–466.
Selling Policies, Converse, Chap. XII.

PART SIX

SALES ABROAD

CHAPTER TWENTY-THREE

EXPORT SALES MANAGEMENT

What Is Export Sales Management? Export sales management is the planning, administration, and promotion of sales in foreign markets. It involves the analysis of markets, the development of products and policies, the selection of methods of distribution, as well as the choice of distributors. Management of foreign sales may include the selection, training, direction, and compensation of export salesmen; the establishment of branches; and packing, transportation, and financing of export shipments. The handling of foreign advertising, which entails the selection of an export agency, the approval of plans, and the coördination with sales operations, is the responsibility of the export sales executive.

Why Export? A few of the reasons why American manufacturers should engage in exporting are:

1. Foreign sales are insurance against domestic depressions.

2. Distribution in many foreign countries serves to overcome seasonal fluctuation in domestic sales.

3. Declining sales volume in saturated domestic markets may be augmented by sales in unexploited markets abroad.

4. Surplus domestic production may be disposed of in foreign markets.

5. American sales methods are more intensive and efficient than those of other countries.

6. Foreign demand already exists in many lines for domestic merchandise.

7. Export selling costs are not increasing as rapidly as domestic sales costs.

Objections commonly raised against foreign distribution are:

1. High tariffs of foreign countries build up artificial walls against trade.

2. Little is known about many overseas markets.

3. Exporting is hampered by legal technicalities.

4. Foreign credit is often questionable.

5. Foreigners do not demand quality merchandise.

6. Products must often be changed to satisfy foreign buyers.

7. Language presents an obstacle to trade.

8. Purchasing power in many foreign countries is too low to justify sales effort.

9. Heavy commodities must shoulder prohibitive duties in markets where duty is based on weight.

10. Trade quotas of foreign nations restrict trade.

11. Exchange restrictions are sometimes a serious obstacle to foreign sales.

12. Slow transportation makes the investment in merchandise in transit substantial.

Export Sales Organizations. Export departments vary widely in size and complexity from one-man organizations to those employing hundreds of people. There are various types of foreign sales organizations, including

1. The integrated export department.
2. The separate export department.
3. The export sales company separately incorporated in the United States.
4. The foreign subsidiary sales corporation, incorporated in a foreign country.
5. The combination export association.
6. The combination export manager.

1. *The integrated export department.* The most common type of export department, this form of organization utilizes the administrative personnel already engaged in domestic selling— that is, the domestic advertising and sales promotion manager, credit manager, research and statistical manager, treasurer, and traffic manager—who devote a portion of their time to foreign sales in addition to their domestic duties. The planning, operating, and control of foreign sales may be administered by a domestic sales manager in this form of organization, sometimes referred to as a "built-in" export department. Or, an export sales manager may be employed with exclusive responsibility for foreign sales.

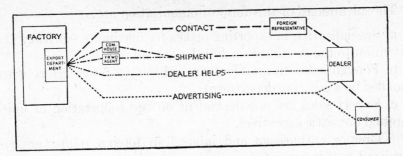

FIGURE 79. Chart showing the flow of export sales, shipments, and advertising of a United States manufacturer of small hand tools and machine tools. Here an integrated export department is used in conjunction with export commission houses, forwarding agents, and foreign representatives. This company exports to more than one hundred countries. Advertising and dealer helps include export catalogs, dealer letterheads, direct mail folders, consumer booklets, signs, technical charts, and manuals.

The merits of this integrated form of organization are:

a. It is economical, since no additional personnel is necessary for handling advertising, credits, shipping, and accounting.

b. It utilizes the experience, ability, and support of the personnel of the domestic organization.

c. It is flexible in operation and readily adaptable to the available personnel.

d. This type of organization is simple.

e. It insures coördination of administrative functions.

Objections to the integrated department organization are:

a. Personnel trained in domestic selling are inexperienced in foreign selling.

b. Coöperation of domestic executives in export sales is sometimes difficult to secure.

c. Export managers sometimes lack authority to secure efficient operation.

d. This type of department lacks foreign trade consciousness.

2. *The separate export department.* This type of department handles all of the functions of export selling independently of the domestic sales department. An export credit manager, traffic department, advertising department, billing and shipping department, accounting department, sales statistical or research, and correspondence section are organized to handle foreign sales exclusively.

The advantages of this form of organization are:

a. Specialization in exporting makes for maximum efficiency and attention to the development of sales abroad.

b. Foreign sales transactions are subject to fewer errors when handled by a separate department.

c. Export sales are not dependent on the coöperation of uninterested domestic executives.

d. Greater enthusiasm and interest in foreign selling are engendered in this type of organization.

On the other hand, the expense of establishing and operating a separate department is considerable for all companies except those doing an extensive foreign business. Outside of large corporations, few concerns operate separate export departments.

The location of the separate export department at the seaboard or the factory is an important consideration in the successful operation of this type of organization. This question also concerns the location of the separately incorporated export sales company. Many export departments, chiefly those of the larger corporations, are located in New York City, while others are located at inland cities where their factories are situated.

The advantages of locating an export department on the seaboard are:

a. Closer contact with export commission houses.
b. Sales to visiting buyers.
c. Personal contact with leading export managers.
d. Close-at-hand sources of export information.
e. Better opportunities to secure ocean freight space.
f. Active participation in many export organizations.
g. More frequent voluntary suggestions for agents and customers.
h. Better trained export personnel.
i. Conferences with experienced exporters on abnormal conditions.
j. Greater certainty of "Documents on same steamer as goods."
k. Last-minute corrections of errors in shipments.
l. Time saving in correspondence and translations.
m. Social entertainment of customers.
n. Fullest use of service of export publications and organizations.

o. Hearing and questioning the widest range of export authorities.

The principal advantages of locating the export department at the factory are as follows:

a. Daily conferences with the highest executives of the enterprise.
b. Personal and constant participation in the formation of the general policies of the enterprise.
c. Decidedly lower overhead cost of the operation of the export department.
d. Incentive to think individually.
e. Better opportunity to supervise interior and exterior packing of export shipments.
f. Daily conferences with advertising, credit, finance, and traffic managers and factory superintendent.
g. The immeditae securing of proper preferences for export production and shipment.
h. Wiser coördination of export and domestic selling.
i. Greater elasticity of clerical force.
j. The correct application of the "built-in" export department plan.
k. The correct viewpoint from which to see the enterprise as a whole.
l. The certainty of a correct mutual understanding of export, instructions, policies, and plans.
m. The position to present the full export argument to executives at the most favorable moment.
n. The correct business entertainment of visiting customers.
o. The protection of personal interest.

3. *The separately incorporated foreign sales company in the United States.* This type of export organization is used by a limited number of large corporations to divorce export sales from the parent manufacturing organization. The export sales company simply serves as a customer of the parent producing concern. Typical of separate foreign sales companies are: General Motors Export Corporation, Goodyear Tire and Rubber Export Company, and Tobacco Products Export Corporation.

The advantages of this type of foreign sales organization, as outlined by the American Manufacturers' Export Association, are:

a. Executive control is concentrated with responsibility in officials who possess experience on export problems.

b. Conflicts are eliminated between those in charge of domestic business and those in charge of exports.

c. A separate corporation brings more rapid development of foreign business because of the two previous reasons.

d. A separate company will show larger profits by elimination of overhead expense that cannot be directly attributed to export business.

e. The export executive is given greater power and responsibility.

The disadvantages of a separately incorporated export sales company are chiefly the costs of incorporation and the time and trouble involved in the organization.

4. *The foreign subsidiary sales corporation.* Incorporated in foreign countries, this is a form of export organization used largely by exporters with established factories or sales branches in foreign countries. Typical of such foreign incorporated subsidiaries of American companies are: Walworth, Ltd., English subsidiary of the Walworth Company; Black & Decker (Australasia), Ltd., Sydney, Australia, subsidiary of Black & Decker Manufacturing Company; Belting & Leather Products Association, Inc., Bombay, India, subsidiary of Graton & Knight Company.

The advantages of separate incorporation abroad are:

a. Full judicial protection is given in the foreign country where the corporation is licensed. In some countries abroad an American corporation is denied the right to sue or is subjected to serious restrictions.

b. Many foreign countries tax firms doing business within their boundaries on the basis of total capitalization or profits. The lower capitalization of a separate foreign sales company makes possible lower taxes in many countries.

c. National prejudice against foreign products is broken down by a local corporation.

d. If foreign capital is required, foreign incorporation is desirable.

If, in addition to a sales branch, partial or full manufacture or assembly is undertaken, foreign incorporation affords:

a. Circumvention of high foreign tariffs.

b. Reduction in transportation costs of bulky commodities.

c. Lower wages abroad, thus effecting economies in production or assembly costs.

d. Better service and distribution.

e. Protection of patents, as in many countries patent rights are invalidated unless manufacture is undertaken, within a certain time, in the country granting the patent.

f. Raw materials and climatic advantages that facilitate manufacturing in some foreign countries.

On the other hand, there are numerous objections to foreign branches and incorporation:

a. Many foreign obstacles or stimulants to sales, such as tariffs and quotas, are often of a temporary nature, and favorable duties may be abolished, leaving a foreign corporation without commercial advantages. An American automobile manufacturer is said to have established a costly branch plant in a large European city, after having governmental assurance of favorable rates on the chassis and other car parts to be imported. Soon the motorcar manufacturer was involved in a discussion as to the definition of a "chassis," with the result that the favorable rates, on which the factory had been established, disappeared.

b. Political conditions abroad are often unstable, leaving the foreign company at the mercy of ruthless politicians.

c. Laws may be enacted in foreign countries with unfavorable results to industry.

d. Interstate tariff agreements between nations may handicap a manufacturer who has concentrated in one country.

e. Home control is weakened.

f. Personnel problems arise—some countries require native managers or a certain percentage of the personnel must be native to the country.

In spite of these disadvantages, it is estimated that $1,250,000,000 has been invested by American concerns in subsidiary branch plants abroad.

Coöperation with existing establishments abroad, by contracting with foreign manufacturers to produce merchandise according to specifications and formulas of American companies, is frequently resorted to in lieu of establishing foreign branch factories.

5. *The combination export association.* This is a coöperative arrangement by a group of domestic producers of raw materials or manufactured products, under the Webb-Pomerene Act passed in 1918, authorizing coöperation among competitors to save expense

in distribution, combat foreign buying organizations, stabilize and fix export prices, standardize sales terms, and divide sales territories abroad. The act frees exporters who are members of a registered Webb-Pomerene association from prosecution under the Federal antitrust laws when engaged in export trade from the United States or any territory to any foreign nation.

Less than one hundred associations have been organized, typical of which is the Electrical Apparatus Export Association formed by the subsidiary organizations of the two largest electrical manufacturing organizations, Westinghouse Electric International Company and the International General Electric Company.

The export of branded goods by a Webb-Pomerene association is sometimes complicated by competitive antagonisms of members and the difficulty in marketing coöperatively competing brands.

6. *The combination export manager.* Employed on a salary or commission basis by several small exporters, for whom he handles all details of export sales, the combination export manager maintains an independent office and gives part-time service to each of his clients in the development of foreign distribution, the procurement of export orders, and the placing of advertising abroad. Through contacts with agents in foreign countries and by correspondence, the combination export manager is often successful in developing a profitable volume of foreign business at little expense to the individual concern.

The principal limitations of a combination export manager are:

1. His division of effort over several lines of products may result in poor service on slow-moving, high-priced lines.

2. Limited capital restricts his activities.

3. His knowledge of foreign markets for many products is questionable.

Methods of Foreign Distribution. The two principal methods of foreign distribution are indirect and direct exporting. By indirect exporting is meant the sale of American goods through middlemen, located in this country, who specialize in foreign trade. Direct export is selling direct to foreign distributors or consumers through the medium of the seller's own export department, a separate export corporation, an export association, or a combination export manager.

1. *Indirect exporting.* A domestic manufacturer doing indirect exporting is not actually selling abroad, since he is relieved of for-

eign credit risk, foreign selling, forwarding, and advertising by the middleman located at the seaboard in this country.

There are four common types of middlemen in the United States engaged in indirect exporting:

a. The export commission house.
b. The export merchant.
c. The export manufacturer's agent.
d. The export broker.

The principal export middleman is the export commission house, many of which are located in New York City, whose functions are:

(1) To place orders with American manufacturers for the account of foreign buyers.
(2) To assemble merchandise.
(3) To ship to foreign buyer.
(4) To pay supplier.
(5) To finance the operation by draft on the foreign buyer.

Commission houses effect transportation economies and assume the responsibility as to the character of goods shipped, proper packing, and protection. For their services they receive a commission from the buyer ranging from 2½ to 5 per cent.

Export commission houses benefit American manufacturers desiring foreign distribution by relieving them of the problems of foreign exchange, foreign credits, packing and shipping, and discovering and developing customers abroad. Commission houses have been criticized for competing with manufacturers for foreign sales; and for collecting commissions from both buyer and seller and adding to the cost of goods. In practice, many commission houses buy for their own account and sell abroad as export merchants.

The export merchant is similar to a domestic wholesaler buying merchandise from domestic manufacturers, but with the distinction that sales are made in foreign markets. The export merchant may stock goods here or abroad and sell by mail or through salesmen overseas. American manufacturers selling to export merchants are relieved of the problems of securing and selling distributors or consumers abroad, foreign credits, advertising, and packing and shipping for export. Export merchants are not paid a commission by either buyer or seller but earn their profit by buying here for a lower price and selling abroad for a higher price.

The export manufacturer's agent is similar to a domestic manufacturer's agent in that he contracts with a domestic manufacturer to represent him as a sales agent in foreign markets. He resembles a commission house in that he receives a commission for his services, but this is paid by the seller rather than the buyer, as in the case of the commission house. The export agent performs the same functions as a foreign agent, with the difference that his headquarters are in the United States rather than in a foreign country.

The usual services of an export manufacturer's agent to a domestic manufacturer are:

a. Secure orders abroad.
b. Take delivery from manufacturer of the merchandise ordered.
c. Insure, pay freight, invoice buyer, assume credit risk.
d. Reimburse the manufacturer in United States currency.

The export broker functions largely in the sale of staples and raw materials, as coffee, cotton, wool, sugar, and the like, by bringing domestic producers in contact with foreign buyers.

2. *Direct exporting.* Direct sales to foreign buyers by American manufacturers are made by the following types of distributors located in foreign markets:

a. The indent or foreign resident sales agent.
b. Foreign wholesaler, jobber, or factor.
c. Foreign commission house.
d. Foreign brokers.

In addition to these foreign agents and middlemen, direct sales are made by:

e. Export salesmen traveling out of American headquarters or resident abroad.
f. Foreign branches of American companies.

Indent or foreign resident sales agents are individuals or organizations located in foreign countries and canvassing for orders from foreign dealers in a prescribed territory. Orders received are placed with the agent's principals, American manufacturers, for shipment direct to the foreign buyers for the account of the suppliers. These agents are sometimes called "commission agents," since their compensation is a commission ranging from 1 per cent to 20 per cent, based on the net invoice value of the merchandise shipped into their territories. Contracts are signed by manufacturer and agent prescribing the extent of the sales territory, compensation, terms of sale, and other details.

Foreign agents may be given exclusive or partial exclusive sales rights in their territories. Some agents, called "del credere" agents, guarantee payments by the buyers, whose orders they submit to manufacturers. This type of agent usually demands a higher commission for this service. Agencies are sometimes given to merchant distributors.

Direct foreign distribution through resident sales agents benefits American manufacturers in numerous ways:

a. Resident agents are in the best position to judge the credit standing of buyers.

b. They are best able to extend service, make adjustments, and settle claims.

c. The cost of foreign representation is not excessive.

d. Knowledge of local markets enables foreign agents to sell more effectively.

e. More constant and intensive sales effort is possible through foreign agents.

f. Local identity of a foreign agent facilitates the procurement of export orders.

Some of the disadvantages of distributing through foreign agents are:

a. Agents may handle competing lines or too many lines to be able to give proper attention to a manufacturer's merchandise.

b. Some agents do not have sufficient capital to render good service.

c. An agent may take on a line to forestall competition, offer rebates to foreign buyers, or seek commissions from both buyer and seller.

d. A foreign agent may be lacking in sales ability.

Foreign wholesalers, jobbers, or factors are direct importers buying for their own account and selling to other foreign wholesalers, retailers, or both, fixing their resale prices on a basis of landed costs and desired profit. They usually do not handle competing lines, but seek exclusive sales rights in their territories.

These merchant-agents, sometimes called "customer-agents," have an owner's interest in the lines that they distribute. They place sizeable orders and have established trade in their territories and good reputations.

The disadvantages of selling abroad through this type of agent are:

a. Exclusive sale to one agent in a territory limits distribution.

b. Competing foreign wholesalers are reluctant to buy from merchant agents.

c. Merchant-agents may not push aggressively products for which they have exclusive sales rights.

d. They may stock competing lines.

Foreign commission houses operate similarly to commission houses located in this country. They serve as purchasers for concerns in countries other than those in which they are located and in addition they import for their own account. Many such concerns stock merchandise of American manufacture for resale to foreign wholesalers, retailers, and consumers. Some of them are branches of American commission houses. Serving as foreign agents of American manufacturers, they perform the same functions and are subject to the same limitations as merchant-agents.

Foreign brokers are sometimes classified as general agents. Their main function is to bring American sellers and foreign buyers in contact with one another. Foreign brokers frequently receive consigned merchandise from American manufacturers or producers of raw materials and sell for the supplier's account, remitting proceeds of sales, less commission, to the supplier. Foreign brokers often receive shipments and arrange for handling, storage, and delivery to buyers. They are most active in the foreign sale of cotton, grain, and copper, and frequently operate on exchanges.

Export salesmen, traveling from American headquarters, are employed by many exporters in this country to call on foreign buyers. The functions of an export salesman are:

a. To secure, assist, and train foreign agents.

b. To sell foreign distributors and consumers.

c. To report on credits.

d. To make market surveys.

e. To conduct advertising campaigns.

f. To make adjustments.

g. To handle shipments.

In other words, they perform the same duties as a domestic sales representative.

The principal reasons for direct factory representation abroad are:

a. Buyers often prefer to deal with direct factory representatives.

b. Salesmen with special technical knowledge are necessary in the sale of many mechanical products.

c. More adequate supervision of foreign distribution is secured by personal contact.

d. Accurate knowledge of markets, habits, and customers can often be obtained only by direct contact.

e. Distribution for certain lines can be secured only by personal contacts.

In addition to salesmen traveling from the United States to foreign countries, there are salesmen resident abroad operating from foreign branches of domestic companies, or directly from headquarters in this country. Another type of export salesman is the combination representative who carries the products of several domestic manufacturers, thus effecting economies in expense to those concerns represented. The disadvantages in employing a combination salesman lie chiefly in his divided interest in several lines and the conflicts in authority as to the direction of his efforts.

The use of export salesmen depends largely on the type of men available, the diversity and technical aspects of the line, the distance of the foreign market from headquarters, the potential volume of sales, the seasonable nature of the goods, and the character of the product.

Foreign branches of American companies are a direct channel of distribution for large exporters. Through American or native salesmen, distribution is secured, advertising campaigns are conducted, and warehouse stocks maintained.

Bases for Selecting Methods of Foreign Distribution. The choice of direct or indirect methods of export distribution depends on numerous factors, including the size of the export organization, the types of products sold, and the markets to be exploited. The average small exporter usually initiates sales abroad through indirect channels or by correspondence in response to inquiries originating abroad. In some cases a domestic representative is sent abroad to establish agencies, or a combination export salesman is employed. Larger concerns and those making technical products often employ direct methods of foreign distribution by the incorporation of export sales companies or the establishment of foreign branches.

1. *Analyzing foreign markets.* The determination of the method of export distribution and type of foreign agent selected should be preceded by a thorough analysis of foreign markets under consideration. The Commercial Intelligence Division of the United States Department of Commerce advises prospective exporters to determine:

a. That a market exists for the product, as certain products will sell in some areas and not in others.

b. That the goods can be placed in the hands of the ultimate foreign consumer at prices within reach of the average consumer. This means that the price at which the product will be sold abroad must include a calculation of the net selling price, plus all transportation charges, freight, insurance and cartage, documentation, draft interest, and customs duties.

c. What competition must be expected, and from what sources, and what sales resistance must be overcome to enable continuous selling of the product in the market under consideration.

As in the analysis of domestic markets, exporters must determine:

a. The character of demand abroad, involving a study of the characteristics of individuals composing the foreign market— their age, sex, race, religion, and class—as well as the characteristics of the market, including climate, standards of living, habits, customs, and traditions.

b. The size of the foreign market or the number of potential purchasers, replacement, or repeat possibilities.

c. The trend of the market abroad as indicated by changes in styles, new inventions, and competitive products.

In selling abroad, specific information is necessary on foreign tariffs, commercial laws, transportation and communication, and financing foreign sales, including banking connections, customary terms, foreign exchange, credits, acceptances, collections, marine insurance, documentation, marking shipping containers, and trade methods and practices.

Sources of information on foreign markets and trade practices are numerous, the principal source being the Bureau of Foreign and Domestic Commerce, United States Department of Commerce, which collects and furnishes exporters with:

a. Foreign trade statistics, showing monthly exports and imports of the most important commodities.

b. Foreign tariff information as to duties, internal taxes, and official regulations to which export shipments are subjected by foreign countries.

c. Commercial legal information on foreign tax laws, bills of exchange, bankruptcy proceedings, sales contracts, agency laws, and other legal phases of foreign trade.

d. Financial information on foreign exchange and foreign trade financing.

e. Transportation information on the facilities, regulations, and charges in foreign-ports.

f. Statistical research on the trade and other statistics of foreign countries.

In addition, assistance and market information is available to exporters from:

a. Commercial attachés in many foreign countries render assistance to exporters by securing distributors and agencies, supplying reports on markets, adjusting trade disputes, and keeping exporters informed of business conditions.

b. A directory of about four hundred thousand foreign buyers is available for use by exporters.

c. Foreign trade opportunities are published in *Commerce Reports*.

d. *Exporters' Index* lists the names of American manufacturers interested in receiving confidential information on foreign trade opportunities.

Other nongovernmental sources of export information are:

a. The Foreign Trade Bureau of the National Association of Manufacturers.

b. The Philadelphia Commercial Museum Foreign Trade Bureau.

c. The National Foreign Trade Council.

d. The National Council of American Importers and Traders.

e. The American Exporters and Importers Association.

f. Export Managers Club of New York City.

In addition to the Foreign Commerce Department of the Chamber of Commerce of the United States, there are numerous foreign chambers of commerce located in this country and American chambers of commerce located abroad. These organizations publish information and collect statistics of value to exporters.

The foreign departments of leading banks and financial institutions, such as the National City Bank of New York and the First National Bank of Boston, which maintain branches in foreign countries, are a source of financial information on many foreign countries.

Experienced exporters are usually willing to exchange information on foreign markets or advise beginner exporters on the market conditions in numerous countries.

Export publications, as the *American Exporter,* collect valuable data on foreign trade opportunities and market conditions, which information is available to exporters.

Export Packing and Shipping. American manufacturers engaged in direct exporting are confronted with the problem of special packing for export shipments to insure proper protection against severe climatic conditions in foreign countries, to avoid the hazards of transportation, to satisfy the requirements of customers abroad, and to reduce import duties and transportation charges. These considerations demand special packing for export shipments.

Proper marking, including the gross and net weight, package numbers, consignee's mark, port mark designating destination, as well as other information based on legal requirements of the customs of the consignee's country, is important in the proper dispatch of foreign orders.

Shipments may be made by the export traffic department of the exporter or by professional ocean freight forwarders, whose functions are:

1. To combine small shipments with other goods for the same destination.
2. To prepare and execute proper shipping documents.
3. To transfer goods from land to ocean carriers at ports of shipment.
4. To pay freight and marine insurance premiums and clear shipments through customs.

They are reimbursed by the exporters on a flat-fee and special-charge basis.

In making foreign shipments, there is required, not only the usual steamship bill of lading, but also a shipper's export declaration, made out to the United States Customs, as well as a consular invoice, in many cases, describing the merchandise in the language of the country of destination. All ocean shipments are insured by exporters or their insurance brokers for the benefit of foreign buyers, who usually pay the cost of the insurance.

Export Price Quotations. Merchandise sold abroad is usually priced in the currency of the exporting country, and the place of delivery is specified as "f.o.b. vessel," meaning free on board vessel, or "f.a.s. vessel," meaning, free alongside vessel.

Price quotations are usually made "c.i.f.," meaning cost, insurance, freight, or the cost of goods to the buyer, including freight to the seaboard and drayage, plus cost of marine insurance and the ocean freight to port of destination. Foreign buyers are usually obliged to pay the cost of unloading, customs duties, warehouse charges, and transportation from the port of receipt. Prices are usually quoted net. Terms may be cash before shipment or on a sight draft or C.O.D. basis. A greater part of the foreign sales transactions are conducted with bills of exchange, or documentary drafts of the sight, arrival, or date types. Exporters frequently discount foreign drafts. Commercial letters of credit are sometimes used because they afford an exporter greater security of payment, since drafts are drawn upon banks and not upon foreign buyers.

Foreign credit may be extended by means of time drafts, letters of credit, or open account.

Export Advertising. The need for foreign advertising arises from the same necessity for creating desires, establishing buying habits, overcoming prejudices, and creating good will of foreign buyers as in the development of consumer preference in this country. The backwardness of much foreign advertising offers American manufacturers an unusual opportunity to use superior advertising methods abroad.

1. *Organization for foreign advertising.* Export advertising may be planned, produced, and placed by either the domestic advertising department of the exporter, in the case of the integrated export department, or a specialized export advertising department, in the case of a separate export department or a separately incorporated foreign sales company. In small organizations advertising is handled ordinarily as a function of the export sales department. In a few companies export advertising is planned and produced entirely within the organization, while in the majority of concerns outside counsel is given the responsibility for planning and creating foreign advertising.

There are three types of advertising agencies that act in advising American manufacturers in export advertising:

a. The foreign advertising agencies located abroad are largely space brokers, and few of these attempt to give any constructive advertising service. While these agencies may be in touch with local conditions, their value to American advertisers is questionable.

b. The export advertising agency, located in the United States, is in a position to give a unified service, write foreign language copy, prepare illustrations, and handle production and place advertising with foreign publications, from which they receive a commission. They are handicapped by a lack of knowledge of local conditions abroad and of ability to execute local campaigns.

c. The domestic advertising agency, with branches in foreign countries, combines the benefits of the first two types, with the added advantage of high-grade domestic service. One such American agency has 17 main offices employing 350 people and serving more than 60 clients in the leading trading countries of the world.

2. *Foreign advertising media.* The available media of advertising abroad are the same as in the United States, but the problems entailed in their use are much more complex than is the case with domestic media. The foreign media most commonly used are:

a. Publications.
b. Outdoor.
c. Radio.
d. Direct mail.
e. News publicity.
f. Fairs and exhibits.
g. Dealer helps, including window and store displays.
h. Moving pictures.
i. Sampling.

Publications used in foreign advertising are of two types: domestic publications circulating abroad and foreign publications.

Of the domestic publications, there are the specialized export trade magazines, for example, *American Exporter,* which are circulated to foreign importers and dealers, and the technical publications published in the United States for foreign engineers. In addition to the trade and technical publications are the general magazines, for example, The *Saturday Evening Post,* and others, which enjoy a wide circulation abroad. While not selected for export advertising, these general magazines frequently give the first impetus to foreign sales for domestic manufacturers.

ΟΤΑΝ ΧΡΗΣΙΜΟΠΟΙΗΤΕ ΛΕ
ΠΙΔΑΣ ΖΙΛΛΕΤΤ ΗΜΠΟΡΕΙΤΕ
ΝΑ ΗΣΘΕ ΒΕΒΑΙΟΣ ΟΤΙ ΘΑ
ΚΑΛΟΞΥΡΙΣΘΗΤΕ. ΠΑΝΤΟΤΕ,
ΧΩΡΙΣ ΚΑΝ ΝΑ ΤΟ ΑΙΣΘΑΝ
ΘΗΤΕ.

Αἱ λεπίδες αὗται εἶναι κατασκευασμέ
ναι ἐξ εἰδικοῦ καὶ ἀρίστου μετάλλου καὶ
ἐφαρμόζουν τελείως ἐντὸς τῶν μηχανῶν
Ζιλλέττ. Κατὰ τὸ ταξείδιόν σας μὴ λη
σμονεῖτε νὰ πέρνητε μαζύ σας ἕνα πα
χι λεπίδας Ζιλλέττ.

FIGURE 80. An example of Greek newspaper advertising of an American manufacturer of safety razors. This advertisement was produced in the United States for insertion in Greek newspapers.

The principal foreign publications are newspapers that are national in circulation and occupy the same position as national magazines in this country. With the exception of a few outstanding newspapers, it is difficult to secure definite and accurate information on the circulation, distribution, and character of readers of foreign publications. There is an absolute lack of uniformity in rates and commissions and a wide variation in mechanical requirements of various publications.

Outdoor advertising abroad offers many opportunities for American concerns. In countries where there is a high percentage of illiteracy, pictures are the only practical medium of advertising. In China it is estimated that only 10 per cent of the population can read. Structures are not standardized as in this country, but posters are used on vans, kiosks, walls, and street-light standards. There is little uniformity in rates.

FIGURE 81. In the native city of Shanghai, China, an American breakfast food exporter uses four outdoor poster bulletins, similar to the one illustrated here, to reach Chinese consumers.

Direct mail advertising is used extensively by American exporters to reach foreign distributors as a source of mail order business. Catalogs and house organs in foreign languages are one of the principal forms of direct mail used. They are supplemented by sales letters. This medium is also used to aid foreign distributors in reaching consumers.

Advertising in the guise of editorial material is a common medium of publicity in many foreign countries where publishers provide advertisers with a liberal amount of "free publicity." No foreign advertising campaign is functioning to the fullest that does not take advantage of the opportunities for press propaganda.

Foreign fairs and exhibitions have long been an outstanding advertising medium for American exporters. Fairs at Leipzig, Prague, Paris, London, and other trading centers have afforded American concerns excellent opportunities not only to seek consumer preference but to make foreign agency connections. Samples are often shown at these fairs by local distributors, who share the expenses with their principals.

Exporters usually help foreign distributors with advertising, including sales letters, direct mail campaigns, counter cards, local newspaper advertisements, and window displays. Lack of good local mailing lists or methods of preparing them limits the use of consumer direct mail abroad. Since many dealers do not have adequate windows, displays are not a practical medium in many countries.

FIGURE 82. Painted outdoor advertising of Quaker Oats in English and native languages appears in Bombay, India.

Motion pictures are used for public advertising exhibitions more frequently abroad than in this country. Trucks equipped with projectors, screens, and public address systems may be effectively used in reaching groups of consumers, making showings to dealers, and for educational publicity in schools.

Sampling is a common method of advertising abroad, and exporters of food and drug products use this medium extensively. A "dash" or article that is distributed gratis is a successful medium of advertising on the Gold Coast of Africa, where the agent of an American soap exporter once hired twenty native mammies with small babies. He gave each of them a small wash tub, a bar of the American soap, took them to the market place, and set them to work. Each mammy lathered her baby until the twenty pickaninnies were white, soapy balls of lather. Then sample bars of the soap were distributed to the milling crowd of blacks, with the result that the sales increased enormously.

An enterprising American safety razor manufacturer employed a "Miss São Paulo" to distribute twenty thousand free safety razors to Brazilian soldiers.

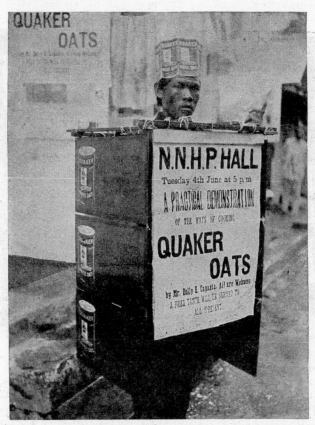

FIGURE 83. Sandwich boards are a popular medium of advertising in India. An American cereal manufacturer is using this sandwich board to advertise a public demonstration of the product to English-reading consumers in Bombay, India.

3. *Creating export advertising.* Market research, as a basis for the preparation of export advertising, is more vital to the success of advertising abroad than in this country, where many of the customs and habits of consumers are already known. Accurate information on the characteristics of consumers, racial habits, religious prejudices, and language is fundamental to sound foreign advertising. Much of this information may be obtained from foreign agents, other advertisers, government agents, or actual field observation abroad. Foreign media of advertising should also be studied.

Only through a knowledge of foreign markets and media can a

sound advertising plan be prepared. Foreign advertising copy is a serious problem because of the many idioms and dialects. An advertiser in India encounters six languages and more than two hundred dialects; while in Europe twenty-eight languages are spoken. The problem is best solved by writing advertising copy locally in the country where the advertising is to be done, rather than by translation. American advertisers often prepare copy in English for translation by agents or branches abroad, or copy is written by foreign branches of American advertising agencies using American copy treatment and standards.

Foreign illustrations present a similar but not so complex a problem as copy. Illustrations must, of course, be correct in every detail if they are to be typical of the country in which they will be used. When products are sold abroad from catalog illustrations, the reproductions must be true in every feature. Illustrations of a product and trade mark present no problem of local adaptation. Foreign artists, working in the United States, solve the problem for some export advertisers; others generalize foreign illustrations.

Many export advertisers use "pattern campaigns," that is, copy and illustrations prepared in this country and sent abroad for translation and adaptation to the country where the advertising will be used.

Problem 1—Foreign Distributor Agreements

Barber Footwear Company

The Barber Footwear Company, Akron, Ohio, makes rubber boots and canvas rubber-soled footwear in two hundred styles. Annual domestic and foreign sales are approximately $7,000,000, of which amount 15 per cent is export volume. European sales average $700,000.

Foreign distribution of the company is through foreign wholesalers or factors, who buy from the Barber Company for their own account and sell to other foreign wholesalers and retailers, fixing their resale prices on landed costs and desired profits. To circumvent the payment of foreign taxes by the company, these distributors are not deemed agents of the Barber Company.

The foreign distributors pay for their purchases by a sixty-day draft and occasionally in ninety days. No consignment sales are made, and credit losses are a fraction of 1 per cent. Distributors are quoted prices that enable them to meet price competition in their territories.

The Barber Company signs a uniform agreement with all of its foreign distributors as follows:

BARBER FOOTWEAR COMPANY

Export Distributor Agreement

Agreement, made this .... day of ...., 19.., between Barber Footwear Company, an Ohio corporation with its principal office at Akron, Ohio, hereinafter called the "Company," and ...., of the City of ...., hereinafter called the "Distributor," Witnesseth:

1. The Company hereby grants to the Distributor, upon terms and conditions hereinafter mentioned, the exclusive right to sell Barber Footwear Company Canvas and Rubber Footwear, or other articles of its manufacture in the following territories—namely:

....

In consideration whereof, the Distributor agrees to buy, indent, and distribute exclusively, and to keep on hand at all times during the period of this contract, sufficient stocks of said goods to meet the demand of the trade, using his best efforts to promote the sale and distribution of said Company's goods within said territories.

2. Prices: All purchases within this Agreement shall be at prices stated in Barber Footwear Company's latest published Rubber Footwear and Canvas Footwear Price List.

Prices quoted for special merchandise not regularly listed shall be considered as part of the published price lists.

It is understood and agreed that all prices are subject to change without notice at any time hereafter and before the expiration of this Agreement, but the Distributor shall be entitled, on each order placed, to the Distributor's prices in force for the Distributor's territory at the time such orders are accepted by said Company.

3. Deliveries: The Company will make deliveries f.a.s. vessel, Boston or New York, without extra charge for usual export packing, reserving the privilege of supplying standard packing wherever in its judgment advisable. The Company reserves the right to route all shipments when other than f.a.s. shipments are made. Delivery to carrier shall constitute delivery to Distributor.

4. Terms: The terms of the Company shall be:

....

The Company reserves the right to change or withdraw its terms when, in its judgment, such action shall be advisable.

5. Discounts: The discounts of the Company shall be:

....

6. Orders: Distributor's orders, detailed as to quantities and styles of merchandise desired, shall be subject to the Company's written acceptance. Company, however, shall not be bound to furnish the exact quantities of the styles specified, but shall furnish such quantities as it can supply in the economical administration of its business, it being understood that Company shall not be liable for delays in delivery occasioned by war, fire, the elements, labor troubles, interruption or shortage of transportation facilities, or for any other cause beyond Company's control.

Cancellation of orders by Distributor, or changes in the quantities ordered will be accepted by the Company provided the manufacture of the merchandise ordered has not begun.

7. Adjustments: Distributor agrees to make fair and equitable adjustments on the Company's products when occasion arises, and to report in detail such adjustments, and with sufficient evidence, that Company may in its judg-

ment reimburse Distributor. No claims for adjustment will be considered by Company unless accompanied by full report of defects claimed, conditions of service, samples of the merchandise, or when requested, the return to Company of adjusted merchandise.

8. REPORTS: Distributor will make such reports as may be required by Company from time to time as to general conditions in his territory regarding any competitive product which may be offered from time to time, supplying full detail as to price, duties, deliveries, etc.

9. It is understood and agreed that this Agreement is not to be construed as constituting the Distributor an Agent of the Company for any purpose whatever.

10. The contract between the parties hereto is fully set forth in this Agreement and has been entered into under the inducements herein expressed and no others, and shall become effective only when executed by the duly authorized representative of the Company at Akron, Ohio, in the United States of America. It is agreed that the terms of this Agreement cannot be altered, waived or modified, except by a written endorsement thereon executed on behalf of the Company at Akron, Ohio, and that no separate verbal or written agreements which may be made between the Distributor and the Company's salesmen or other employees, and no letters or correspondence of any kind shall in any way modify or affect this Agreement.

11. This Agreement may be cancelled at any time by either party hereto, provided .... months' written notice shall have been previously given, except that in the event of a breach of any of the covenants herein contained, this Agreement may be terminated by either party upon written or cable notice to last known address, otherwise this Agreement shall remain in full force and effect until the .... and continue from year to year thereafter until cancelled by notice as hereinbefore provided.

WITNESS: BARBER FOOTWEAR COMPANY

The current export sales of the Barber Company have declined 20 per cent from the figure for the preceding year on account of high tariffs, growing foreign competition, and the failure of foreign distributors to push Barber products aggressively. The export sales manager believes that the failure of distributors abroad to meet competition is due largely to the exclusive feature in its distributor agreements.

Given exclusive territory, foreign distributors are not stimulated to push the sale of the company's products, in the opinion of the export manager. Furthermore, many wholesalers and retailers abroad prefer to deal directly with the Barber Company rather than through a foreign wholesaler. The number of foreign outlets is limited by the granting of exclusive distributorships.

The export sales manager is considering the appointment of indent or foreign resident sales agents to represent the Barber Company in the principal foreign markets. He believes that they will give the company more constant and intensive sales effort than foreign wholesalers.

A foreign resident sales agent once represented the Company in Rome, with Italy as an exclusive territory. He failed to secure satisfactory sales volume for the reason that he divided his efforts over too many lines to give proper attention to Barber products.

Questions

1. Should the Barber Company continue to distribute abroad through foreign wholesale distributors? Why?

2. Assuming that foreign distribution should be continued through wholesalers, should the distributor agreement of the Barber Company be amended in any way? Examine the agreement and describe desirable changes, if any are needed.

3. Is the appointment of indent or resident sales agents a desirable solution of the Barber problem? Give reasons for your decision.

4. Would another type of foreign distribution be more desirable than either foreign wholesalers or resident agents? Describe.

Problem 2—Channels of Foreign Distribution

Production Instrument Corporation

The Production Instrument Corporation, established in New York City in 1912, manufactures a complete line of indicating, recording, and controlling instruments for temperature, humidity, flow regulation in the production of oil, refined petroleum products, electricity, sugar, paper, rayon, and so forth. Annual domestic sales are approximately $5,000,000.

The products of the company are largely custom-made to specifications of purchasers for special applications. Stock parts are assembled when orders are received, and the completed product is adapted to the requirements of the buyer. The company's research department is constantly engaged in discovering new applications to widen the market for the instruments.

In 1922 domestic salesmen began calling upon export commission houses located in New York City, as well as resident purchasing agents of foreign concerns. As a result of these contacts, an annual volume of $75,000 is secured from middlemen located in New York, who take delivery in New York and pay in United States currency.

Encouraged by this indirect export activity, the company has established an "integrated" export department at the factory, utilizing the domestic sales and office organization to handle export sales. Foreign credits will be handled by the domestic credit manager, formerly in business in Mexico. Foreign advertising will be handled by the domestic advertising manager. A full-time export manager has been appointed to take charge of all foreign business.

The first problem of the new export manager is to secure foreign distribution. He is considering the appointment of indent or resident sales agents, several of whom have applied to the company for territories abroad. They would receive a commission of from 20 to 30 per cent on sales.

The vice-president and general sales manager of the company, to whom the export manager is responsible, doubts that foreign agents will have sufficient engineering or technical knowledge to represent the company effectively. The fact that foreign agents handle allied lines of products may cause them to take little interest in the company's instruments, he believes. The vice-president advocates the employment of full-time resident salesmen abroad or traveling salesmen operating out of the headquarters in New York.

The employment of a combination traveling export salesman has been suggested by another executive of the company. A combination salesman, traveling out of New York City, has sought to represent the Production Instrument Corporation abroad. He claims that his knowledge of export technique and his acquaintance with established foreign manufacturers will enable him to secure a desirable volume of business. He now represents manufacturers of leather belting, lubricants, ball bearings, and machine tools. The company would pay this man a commission and expenses in accordance with the practice of the other manufacturers whose lines he is carrying. Objection to the employment of a combination salesman has been made on the ground that he lacks the technical knowledge to sell instruments.

The export manager plans to bill all foreign customers direct on sight draft or sixty- or ninety-day open accounts. Quotations will be made c.i.f. and f.o.b. vessel. An instrument selling in the United States for $100 costs a buyer in England about $140.

Foreign freight forwarding agents will be employed to handle the detail of export shipments and shipping documents at an average cost of $3.50 per shipment.

Questions

1. What channels of direct foreign distribution should the Production Instrument Corporation use? Give reasons for your choice.

2. What are your reasons for rejecting some of the distributing channels mentioned in the problem?

3. What methods should be used in selecting foreign distributors, and what factors should be considered in making a selection?

4. What services may be expected from the foreign distributors whom you believe should be used by the Production Instrument Corporation?

Problem 3—Export Sales Organization

Wallgate Tool Company

The Wallgate Tool Company, established in Pittsburgh, Pennsylvania, in 1912, manufactures a line of small tools sold throughout the United

States by automotive, mill supply, electrical, hardware, machinery, and plumbing supply wholesalers to garages, machine shops, and manufacturers. Annual sales in this country average approximately $4,000,000. Branches are maintained in ten leading industrial centers.

In 1922 the company began to advertise its products in trade magazines, among which were a few with international circulation, bringing inquiries from foreign distributors and manufacturers. By 1938 export sales resulting from this limited foreign advertising amounted to less than $100,000. However, executives of the Wallgate Company believed that a profitable export business could be developed from this small beginning and considered the problem of creating an organization to secure export sales.

It was proposed by the executive committee that an outstanding domestic salesman who was manager of the Wallgate branch at Cleveland, Ohio, be selected to take charge of export sales. This man knew nothing about exporting but was familiar with the products made by the company as well as its policies and merchandising methods.

Should export business be handled by the domestic sales, credit, and advertising departments as at present, or should a separate export department be organized with specialists engaged exclusively in dealing with foreign sales? These were the questions that confronted the executives of the company. If a separate export department were created, should it be located at the factory in Pittsburgh or at the seaboard in New York City? This question was raised by the domestic sales manager of the company, who believed that the export activities should be housed in the New York City domestic branch office.

The attorney of the company advocates the incorporation of subsidiary companies in the principal foreign countries where the company plans to do business. Since the bulk of foreign sales originated in the British Isles, he advises the establishment of an office and the incorporation of a company in London to serve the British Isles and continental Europe. This company would import parts, assemble, and sell.

In countries where the volume of potential sales would not warrant the incorporation of a separate company, the executive committee is confronted with the problem of resorting to foreign distributors or export salesmen traveling from the export department in the United States.

The company has received numerous small orders from various out-of-the-way places where limited volume would not justify visits by traveling export salesmen or the appointment of foreign distributors. Typical of these small countries from which orders have been received are: Mozambique, Belgian Congo, Martinique, Iceland, and Trinidad. The company desires to maintain these contacts and believes that a considerable volume of export sales can be secured from these sources.

Questions

1. Should the domestic branch manager be placed in charge of export sales, or should an export manager be secured from some other source? Give reasons for your answer.

2. What type of export department should be created—an integrated department, a separate department within the company, or a separately incorporated export sales company? Give reasons for your decision in either case.

3. Should separately incorporated foreign sales companies be organized in the principal foreign markets? Why?

4. Should the company establish foreign branches of the American organization? State your reasons.

5. Would you advise the appointment of foreign distributors or the use of export salesmen in countries with limited sales potential?

6. How can the company develop export sales in out-of-the-way countries?

Problem 4—Export Advertising

Noble Tire Export Corporation

The Noble Tire Export Corporation, New York City, incorporated in Delaware in 1919, is a subsidiary of the Noble Tire and Rubber Corporation, with headquarters in Akron, Ohio, and manufactures automobile tires, tubes, and rubber sundries. The parent company netted approximately $10,000,000 profit in 1945.

The Noble Tire Export Corporation has foreign distribution in twenty countries through one hundred and forty foreign distributors. Sales branches are located in ten principal foreign markets. Each branch is manned by a branch manager, branch sales manager, accountant, and salesmen. Foreign distribution was initiated in Great Britain in 1906.

The export tire advertising of the Noble Export Corporation is prepared by the export advertising department of the company in New York. The principal medium used for advertising tires abroad is newspaper advertising, which is placed by branch managers in the various countries where Noble branches are located. Each branch is allotted an annual advertising budget based on a percentage of anticipated sales.

The export advertising department in New York creates an annual series of newspaper advertisements, writes the copy in English, and then proceeds to make suitable illustrations. The entire series is sent to each foreign branch manager in semi-finished form. Actual photographic reproductions of the original art work are included, from which foreign engravers may produce line cuts in any size or quantity according to the mechanical requirements of foreign newspapers, thus saving delay, expense, and duties on shipments of plates.

This method of preparation enables foreign branch managers to adapt the company's advertising copy to the idiom of the foreign country by local translation and employ American standards of illustration and arrangement in the reproduction of foreign advertising. The same procedure is used for the foreign production of a series of direct mail folders.

However, in spite of these precautions, much of the company's export advertising is indifferent in appearance, and foreign branch managers have criticized the character of the copy and illustrations sent out from the export advertising department. Although a suggested schedule of insertions is provided for foreign branch managers, this schedule is frequently not observed. The newspapers selected by the branch managers for foreign advertising are not always the best.

Confronted with this problem, the vice-president in charge of sales of the Noble Tire Export Corporation is considering the advisability of using the services of a specialized export advertising agency in New York City, experienced in the planning, creating, and placing of advertising in many foreign countries. The use of advertising agencies located in foreign countries is also being considered. Under the direct supervision of branch managers, it is believed that these agencies can render efficient service.

Advertising of the domestic company, the Noble Tire and Rubber Corporation, is handled by a large domestic advertising agency, which also maintains branches in numerous foreign countries. These branches are equipped to make market investigations and to plan and execute advertising campaigns in the countries where they are located. The international department of this agency desires to handle the foreign advertising of the Noble Export Corporation.

The company has made no attempt heretofore to create display advertising for its foreign dealers for the reason that the display requirements of dealers in various countries differed so widely that the management considered such advertising impractical. However, branch managers have requested display advertising.

Questions

1. Should the export advertising department of the company continue to prepare export advertising in New York as described in the problem? Give reasons for your answer.

2. Should an advertising agency handle the Noble export advertising? What type of agency should be used? Why?

3. Should dealer display advertising be used by the company? What forms of display should be used? Who should prepare them?

4. What other media of export advertising should be used by the Noble Export Corporation? Give reasons for your choice.

Reading References

Advertising and Selling Abroad, Eldridge, Chaps. IV–VI, VIII, X, XI.

Essentials of International Trade, Simon Litman, John Wiley & Sons, Inc., New York, 1923, Chaps. XIV, XVI–XXI.

Export Advertising, Brown, Chaps. VIII, XI, XII, XIV.

Export Advertising Practice, Propson, Chaps. III, IV, IX, XIII, XIX, XX.

Export Merchandising, Wyman, Chaps. IV–IX, XIV, XVII, XVIII, XXVIII.

Financing Export Shipments, Eldridge, Chaps. I–III, V–VIII.

Foreign Trade, Principles and Practices, Huebner and Kramer, Part III, Chaps. XII–XIX, XXII, XXVI.

Foreign Trade Organization, De Haas, Chap. XIII.

Practical Exporting, Hough, Chaps. IV, VI–X.

U. S. Bureau of Foreign and Domestic Commerce, Trade Promotion Series.

BIBLIOGRAPHY

BIBLIOGRAPHY

Agnew, H. E., Jenkins, R. B., and Drury, J. C., *Outlines of Marketing*, McGraw-Hill Book Company, New York, 1936.

American Management Association, *Marketing Executive Series*, New York.

American Marketing Society, *Technique of Marketing Research*, McGraw-Hill Book Company, New York, 1937.

Aspley, John C., editor, *Sales Manager's Handbook*, The Dartnell Corporation, Chicago, 1934.

Association of National Advertisers, Inc., *An Analysis of the Distribution Costs of 312 Manufacturers*, New York, 1933.

Baker, John C., *The Compensation of Executive Officers of Retail Companies, 1928–1935*, Business Research Studies No. 17, Bureau of Business Research, Harvard Business School, Boston, 1936.

Balderston, C. C., Karabasz, V. S., and Brecht, R. P., *Management of an Enterprise*, Prentice-Hall, Inc., New York, 1935.

Beckman, Theodore N., *Wholesaling Principles and Practice*, The Ronald Press Company, New York, 1937.

Blankenship, A. B., *Consumer and Opinion Research*, Harper & Bros., New York, 1943.

Boston Conference on Distribution (Seventeenth Report, 1945), D. Bloomfield, Editor, Boston Retail Trade Board, Boston.

Brisco, N. A., *Retailing*, Prentice-Hall, Inc., New York, 1947.

Brown, L. O., *Market Research and Analysis*, Ronald Press Co., New York, 1937.

Brown, Theodore H., *The Use of Statistical Techniques in Certain Problems of Market Research*, Business Research Studies No. 12, Bureau of Business Research, Harvard Business School, Boston, 1935.

Castenholz, W. B., *The Control of Distribution Costs and Sales*, Harper & Brothers, New York, 1930.

Churchill, W. L., *Pricing for Profit*, The Macmillan Company, New York, 1932.

Clark, Fred E., *Principles of Marketing*, rev. ed., The Macmillan Company, New York, 1932.

Converse, Paul D., *Essentials of Distribution*, Prentice-Hall, Inc., New York, 1936.

————, and Huegy, Harvey W., *Elements of Marketing*, 2d rev. ed., Prentice-Hall, Inc., New York, 1945.

Coutant, Frank R., and Doubman, J. R., *Simplified Market Research*, Walther Printing House, Philadelphia, 1935.

Dartnell Corporation, *Sales Executives Library*, Chicago, Illinois.

Donald, W. J., editor-in-chief, *Handbook of Business Administration*, McGraw-Hill Book Company, New York, 1931.

Doubman, *Sales Management Today*, Sears Publishing Company, New York, 1933.

Duncan, D. J. and Phillips, C. F., *Retailing Principles and Methods*, Richard D. Irwin, Chicago, 1946.

Dynner, E., *Successful Sales Training*, Advertising Publications, Chicago, 1945.

Editors of "Printer's Ink," *Tested Sales Compensation Plans*, McGraw-Hill Book Co., New York.

Elder, Robert F., *Fundamentals of Industrial Marketing*, McGraw-Hill Book Company, New York, 1935.

Ettinger, R. P., and Golieb, D. E., *Credits and Collections*, rev. ed., Prentice-Hall, Inc., New York, 1926.

Fernald, Chas. H., *Salesmanship*, third ed., Prentice-Hall, Inc., New York, 1935.

Fox, W. M., *Profitable Control of Salesmen's Activities*, McGraw-Hill Book Co., New York, 1937.

Frederick, John H., *Industrial Marketing*, Prentice-Hall, Inc., New York, 1935.

——————, *Public Warehousing 1940*, Ronald Press Co., New York.

Frey, A. W., *Manufacturers' Product, Package and Price Policies*, Ronald Press Co., New York, 1940.

Heckert, J. B., *The Analysis and Control of Distribution Costs*, Ronald Press Co., New York, 1940.

Hegarty, E. J., *Building a Sales Training Plan*, McGraw-Hill Book Co., New York, 1945.

——————, *How to Run a Sales Meeting*, McGraw-Hill Book Co., New York, 1944.

Holtzclaw, Henry F., *Principles of Marketing*, Thomas Y. Crowell Company, New York, 1935.

Horn, P. V., *International Trade Principles and Practices*, Revised, Prentice-Hall, New York, 1945.

Howard, W. H., and Edwards, C. M., Jr., *Retail Advertising and Sales Promotion*, Prentice-Hall, Inc., New York, 1936.

Ivey, Paul W., *Successful Salesmanship*, Prentice-Hall, Inc., New York, 1937.

James, Alden, *Careers in Advertising*, The Macmillan Company, New York, 1932.

Johnson, R. W., and Lynch, R. W., *The Sales Strategy of John H. Patterson, Founder of The National Cash Register Company*, The Dartnell Corporation, Chicago, 1932.

Kaufman, M. Zenn, *How to Run Better Sales Contests*, Harper & Brothers, New York, 1935.

Laird, Donald A., *The Psychology of Selecting Employees*, 3rd ed., McGraw-Hill Book Company, New York, 1927.

——————, *What Makes People Buy*, McGraw-Hill Book Company, New York, 1935.

Larrabee, Carroll B., and Marks, Henry W., editors, *Tested Selling Ideas*, McGraw-Hill Book Company, New York, 1936.

Lester, Bernard, *Marketing Industrial Equipment*, McGraw-Hill Book Company, New York, 1935.

Link, Henry C., *The New Psychology of Selling and Advertising*, The Macmillan Company, New York, 1932.

McNair, M. P., *Expenses and Profits of Limited Price Variety Chains in 1936*, Bulletin No. 105, Harvard Business School, Boston, 1937.

Maynard, H. H., Weidler, W. C., and Beckman, T. N., *Principles of Marketing*, third ed., The Ronald Press Company, New York, 1939.

Nash, B., *Developing Marketing Products and their Packages*, McGraw-Hill Book Co., New York, 1945.

Nolan, H. C. and Maynard, H. H., *Sales Management 1940*, Ronald Press Co., New York.

Nystrom, Paul H., *Retail Institutions and Trends*, rev., Ronald Press Co., New York, 1932.

———, *Retail Store Operation*, fourth ed., Ronald Press Co., New York, 1937.

Osborne, D., *Salesmen for Tomorrow*, Harper & Bro., New York, 1945.

Patman, Wright, *The Robinson-Patman Act*, Ronald Press Co., New York, 1938.

Paton, W. A., *Accountants Handbook*, 3rd ed., The Ronald Press Company, New York, 1943.

Phillips, C. F., editor, *Marketing by Manufacturers*, Richard D. Irwin, Chicago, 1946.

Pyle, John F., *Marketing Principles, Organization and Policies*, 2nd ed., McGraw-Hill Book Company, New York, 1936.

Rados, William, *How to Select Better Salesmen*, Prentice-Hall, Inc., New York, 1946.

Rothenstein, J. L., *Scientific Selection of Salesmen*, McGraw-Hill Book Co., New York, 1945.

Sandberg, Lars J., *Truck Selling: Simultaneous Selling and Delivery in Wholesale Food Distribution*, Business Research Studies No. 7, Harvard Business School, Boston, 1934.

Schmalz, Carl N., *Expenses and Profits of Food Chains in 1934*, Bulletin No. 99, Harvard Business School, Boston, 1935.

———, *Operating Results of Department and Specialty Stores in 1936*, Bulletin No. 104, Harvard Business School, Boston, 1937.

Sheldon, Roy, and Arens, Egmont, *Consumer Engineering*, Harper & Brothers, New York, 1932.

Simmons, H., *Practical Sales Management*, Prentice-Hall, New York, 1946.

Tosdal, Harry R., *Introduction to Sales Management*, McGraw-Hill Book Company, second edition.

———, *Principles of Personal Salesmanship*, McGraw-Hill Book Company, New York, abridged edition.

Tosdal, Harry R., *Problems in Sales Management*, fourth ed., McGraw-Hill Book Company, New York.

Wheeler, Elmer, *Tested Sentences That Sell*, Prentice-Hall, Inc., New York, 1937.

Wingate, J. W. and Brisco, N. A., *Elements of Retail Merchandising*, Prentice-Hall, New York, 1938.

Zorn, B. A., and Feldman, G. J., *Business under the New Price Laws*, Prentice-Hall, Inc., New York, 1937.

INDEX

INDEX

Date Due